A Greek–En

The Ne

Revised and Enlarged
by

Thomas Sheldon Green

with a preface by
H. L. Hastings

Editor of the Christian, Boston, U.S.A.
and

A Supplement

Prepared by Wallace N. Stearns Under The Supervision of

J. H. Thayer, D.D., Litt.D.

PREFACE

The hidden depths both of the wisdom and knowledge of God were manifest, not only in the revelation of his will contained in the Scriptures of truth, but in the manner of giving that revelation, and in the language in which is was given.

Egypt had wisdom, but it was enshrined in hieroglyphics so obscure that their meaning faded centuries ago from the memory of mankind, and for many successive ages no man on earth could penetrate their mysteries. Assyria and Babylon had literature, art, and science; but with a language written in seven or eight hundred cuneiform signs, some of them having fifty different meanings, what wonder is it that for more than two thousand years the language and literature of these nations was lost, buried, and forgotten? The vast literature of China has survived the changes of centuries, but the list of different characters, which in a dictionary of the second century numbered 9353, and in the latest imperial Chinese Dictionary numbers 43,960,—some of them requiring fifty strokes of the pencil to produce them, —shows how unfit such a language must be for a channel to convey the glad tidings of God's salvation to the poor, the weak, the sorrowful, and to people who cannot spend ten or twenty years in learning to comprehend the mysteries of the Chinese tongue.

Who can imagine what would have been the fate of a divine revelation if the words of eternal life had been enswathed in such cerements as these?

In the wisdom of God, the revelation of his will was given in the Hebrew tongue, with an alphabet of twenty-two letters, some of which, as inscribed on the Moabite stone, b.c. 900, are identical in form and sound with those now used in English books.

This Hebrew alphabet, so simple that a child might learn it in a day, has never been lost or forgotten. The Hebrew language in which the Oracles of God were given to man, has never become a dead language. Since the day when the Law was given to Moses on Mount Sinai, there never has been a day or hour when the language in which it was written was not known to living men, who were able to read, write, and expound it. And the Hebrew is the only language of those ages that has lived to the present time, preserving the record of a divine revelation, and being conserved by it through the vicissitudes of conflict, conquest, captivity, and dispersion; while the surrounding idolatrous nations perished in their own corruption, and their languages and literature were buried in oblivion.

In later ages, when the gospel of the Son of God was to be proclaimed to all mankind, another language was used as a vehicle for its communication. The bulk of the Israelitish race, through their captivities and eternal associations, had lost the knowledge of the holy tongue, and had learned the languages of the Gentiles among whom they dwelt; and now as their corporate national existence was to be interrupted, and they were to be dispersed among the peoples of the earth, the Hebrew language was not a fit channel for conveying this revelation to the Gentile world. Hence the same wise Providence which chose the undying Hebrew tongue for the utterances of the prophets, selected the Greek, which was at that time, more nearly than any other, a universal language, as the medium through which the teachings of the Saviour and the messages of the apostles should be sent forth to mankind.

This language, like the Hebrew, has maintained its existence,—though it has been somewhat changed by the flight of years,—and the modern Greek spoken in Athens to-day is substantially the Greek of 1800 years ago.

The gospel of Christ was to go forth to every nation; and the miracle of Pentecost indicated that it was the Divine purpose that each nation should hear in their own tongue wherein they were born, the wonderful works of God. Hence the Scriptures have been translated into hundreds of languages, and to-day six hundred millions of people, comprising all the leading races and nations of the earth, may have access to the Word of God in their native tongues. Nevertheless, no translation can perfectly express the delicate shades of thought which are uttered in another language, and it often becomes necessary and desirable to recur to the original Scriptures, and by searching them to find out the precise meaning of those words which were given by the Holy Ghost, and which are "more to be desired than gold, yea, than much fine gold." For while, speaking in a general way, we have faithful translations, which give us with great accuracy the sense of the Scriptures as a whole, yet there are times when we desire fuller and more accurate information concerning particular words uttered by those men to whom the Holy Ghost was given to bring all things to their remembrance, to guide them into all truth, and to show them things to come. Frequently there are depths of meaning which the casual reader does not fathom, and the study of the Greek and Hebrew becomes as needful as it is agreeable to those who love God's law, who delight in his gospel, and who have time and opportunity to prosecute such studies.

There are few lovers of the Bible who do not at times wish that they might clearly know the precise sense of some one original word which may sometimes be obscurely translated; or who would not be delighted to inquire of some competent scholar as to the meaning of certain expressions contained in that Book of God. Such persons are glad to study the original Scriptures, that they may learn, as far as possible, exactly what God has said to man.

The learning of a living language from those who seek it is no trifling task; but a language which must be learned from books, presents much greater difficulties; and to many persons the mastery of the Greek tongue looks like the labor of a lifetime. It is; and yet it is possible for studious Bible readers to learn the things they specially need to know, with an amount of labor which need not appall or dishearten any diligent student.

There are contained in the Greek New Testament about 5594 words; but in the whole Greek literature the words are a great multitude, which perhaps no man has ever numbered. The student of the Scriptures is not anxious to master or explore this vast wealth of Greek literature, but his ambition is to know something of those 5594 New Testament words in which the message of God's mercy is conveyed to fallen man. Hence he may pass by the bulk of Greek literature, and confine his investigations to those few Greek words which are used in the New Testament to convey to man the treasures of Divine truth.

A lexicon of the entire Greek language might extend through thousands of pages. There stands on the shelves of the writer a copy of Stephen's *"Thesaures Græcæ Linguæ,"* in eight folio volumes, (London, 1816-1825,) which contains more than thirteen thousand large, closely printed pages. A later edition of the same work is still larger; and there are critics and students who would find use for a lexicon as elaborate as this; but for the great mass of Biblical students most of this material would be entirely useless, and a very small volume would contain all they would find necessary in their study of the Scriptures of truth. Thus a portable volume, confining itself to the definition of the words included in the New

Testament, could give them fuller treatment than a very large volume which, covering the entire language would be obliged to condense and abridge at every point, omitting perhaps the very matter most desired by a student of the Sacred Word.

There is another consideration; the Greek of the New Testament differs materially in its character from the classical Green, or from the Greek language as a whole. About b.c. 288, the law of Moses was translated from Hebrew into Greek, by request of Ptolemy Philadelphus, who sought everywhere for books to enrich his great library at Alexandria. Subsequently other portions were translated, and hence, we have what is known as the Septuagint version of the Old Testament. This was largely used among the Jewish people in Egypt and elsewhere in the time of our Saviour. It was a Greek version of a Hebrew book, and it was through this book, as well as by intercourse with Grecian people and foreigners of the Jewish stock, that the Jewish people became acquainted with the Greek tongue. But the Greek of the Septuagint was full of Hebrew ideas and idioms, and hence the Greek of the Jews in Palestine, and of the New Testament which is also saturated with Old Testament ideas, differed from the ordinary language of the Greeks, new meanings having been imparted to various words, in order that they might represent Hebrew words and Hebrew ideas. For example, when the Greek word *hades* is used, we are not thereby committed to a belief in all the fabulous ideas of the Greeks concerning the abode of the dead, for the word was but the representative of the Hebrew word *sheol*, which is almost always translated *hades* in the Greek Testament. Hence in studying this Greek word in the New Testament we are not to go to the Greek classics to find out what they mean by the word *hades*, but rather to the Hebrew prophets to learn in what sense they use the Hebrew word *sheol*, of which it is the Greek equivalent. So the word *diatheke* in classic Greek signifies a will, testament, covenant, and so the term in the common English version is translated in both these ways. But in the Septuagint the word *diatheke* is used to translate the Hebrew word *berith*, which signifies a covenant, but does *not* signify a will or testament.[1*] Hence, instead of speaking of "The New Testament" we should more correctly call it the "The New Covenant." A variety of instances might be adduced where New Testament Greek words have meaning widely different from the same words in classic Greek.

It must also be remembered, that there are words in the New Testament which are not found at all in the classical writers. When new ideas are to be conveyed, new words must be found to convey them. In the language of the Hindus there is no word for *home*, simply because the Hindu has no *home*. The idea of a home as understood by Christians, is utterly foreign to the Hindu nation and religion. There are heathen nations that have no word for gratitude, because gratitude is unknown to them; so the word *agape* or charity, which describes unselfish love, a love which reaches to enemies, and which seeks no personal gratification or reward,—that love which is of God, and concerning which it is said, "God is Love," refers to something unknown to the heathen world. They had no word to express it, because they had not the thing itself to express.

These illustrations indicate some of the peculiarities of the New Testament Greek, and serve to show use why the student of the Bible needs an especial apparatus for studying the Greek New Testament. For this purpose, he has been most generously furnished with New Testament lexicons, in different languages, Latin, German, and English, by the labor of devout and learned students. Among the most noteworthy may be mentioned Robinson's Greek Lexicon of the New Testament, and Prof. J. H. Thayer's later and more elaborate Greek-English Lexicon of the New Testament, based upon Prof. Grimm's get Lexicon; which is well adapted to meet the needs of the critical student.

The meaning of words is determined finally by their usage by those who employ them, and the only way to settle the sense of disputed and difficult words is carefully to examine each word in its connection, in all the passages where it is used, and in the light of that examination decide as to its meaning or meanings. In some of the more elaborate lexicons a large number of passages are thus cited, illustrating the use of the words under consideration, and it some cases authors have endeavored to give nearly every passage where a word occurs in the New Testament. This however, cumbers the lexicon with a large amount of material which in most instances is of little use. This examination and comparison of passages, the careful student should make for himself, and his interests in this direction are better served by the use of a concordance; and for those who wish to investigate carefully the meaning of Greek words in the New Testament, ample provision has been made in the *Critical Greek and English Concordance*, prepared by Prof. C. F. Hudson, under the direction of H. L. Hastings, and revised and completed by the late Ezra Abbot, D.D., LL.D., Profession of New Testament Criticism and Interpretation in the Divinity School of Harvard University.

This book contains (1) the more than five thousand words in the Greek Testament, in alphabetical order. (2) Reference to every passage where those words occur. (3) Every English word which is used to translate the given Greek word. (4) The passages in which the Greek word is translated by each English word, classified and set by themselves, so that the more usual translations are also exhibited. (5) The various readings of the leading critical editions and manuscripts of the Greek Testament. (6) An English index, so that with this book a person who does not know a letter of the Greek alphabet is enabled to find the original for any English word in the New Testament, learn in how many places it occurs, and in how many ways it is translated, so that by examining every passage, he may have the data before him for making up and independent judgment from the facts in the case.

This Greek Concordance obviates the necessity for an exhaustive citation of the passages containing any particular Greek word, and brings us back to the proper sphere of a Lexicon, as a book defining the words contained in the language, with occasional references to passages which illustrate the different meanings; and when equipped with Hudson's Concordance, a manual lexicon of New Testament Greek serves the purpose of the ordinary student.

It is for the accommodation of such students, who know little of the Greek language, but who desire to "search the Scriptures," and of others more scholarly, who yet find it needful to refresh their memories as to the sense of Greek words, that this Lexicon is offered. It was originally prepared by William Greenfield, who was born in London, in 1799, and died there November 5, 1831. He edited Bagster's *Comprehensive Bible*, a Syriac New Testament, a Hebrew New Testament, and prepared an abridgement of Schmidt's Greek Concordance. In 1830 he was appointed editor of the Foreign Versions of the British and Foreign Bible Society; and though he died at an early age, he had a high reputation as an accomplished linguist.

In preparing his Lexicon of the New Testament, he drew materials from every accessible source; the Lexicons of Parkhurst, Schleusner, Wahl, and Robinson being especially examined and laid under contribution. This Lexicon, issued by Bagster & Sons as a companion for a portable edition of the Greek Testament, served an excellent purpose. At a later date it was carefully revised with numerous additions and improvements, by Rev. Thomas Sheldon Green, M.A. and it has received the hearty approval of competent Greek scholars, like the late Professor Ezra Abbot of Cambridge.

Though the body of this Lexicon includes all the words contained in the Received Text of the Greek New Testament, yet in the texts now more or less current, in particular those of Lachmann, Tischendorf, Tregelles, Westcott and Hort, and the Westminster Revised, certain *new words and forms* are introduced, not found in the Received Text.

With a desire to give completeness to this Lexicon, a list of these words is presented, with definitions and a record of the places where they occur, at the end of the Lexicon. This list has been prepared by Mr. Wallace N. Stearns, under the supervision of Prof. J. Henry Thayer, of Harvard Divinity School, the successor of the lamented Dr. Ezra Abbot, and one of the revisers of the New Testament, whose arduous labors in the department of sacred lexicography are too well-known to need further mention.

With these statements as to the object and character of this Lexicon, we commit this new edition to the kind of providence of Him whose words of truth are therein expounded, and without whose blessings all labor and effort is but in vain.   H.L. Hastings

Scriptural Tract Repository,
   Boston, Mass., June, 1896.

EXPLANATIONS

Allusion has been made in the preface to certain peculiarities of New Testament Greek, which distinguish it from the classic Greek of the heathen world.

This Lexicon indicates some of these peculiarities, by distinguishing *three classes* of words:

I. Later Greek words, marked L. G., the occurrence of which may be regarded as commencing within the Later Greek period, which is here reckoned from and includes the writing of the historian Polybius, B.C. 204-123.

II. New Testament words, marked N. T., which only occur in the New Testament, or if found elsewhere are only in certain peculiar quarters.

III. Septuagint words, marked S., which besides their occurrence in the New Testament are found only in the Septuagint Version of the Old Testament, the Greek Apocryphal books, and kindred writings; and the meaning of which is to be studied, not in the usage of classical Greek writings, but rather in the light of the Hebrew Old Testament, and the writings of Jewish authors who were familiar with Hebrew ideas and Hebrew literature.

ABBREVIATIONS,

ETC.

Used In The Following Lexicon

a.	Aorist.	meton.	by metonymy
absol	absolutely, without case or adjunct.	metath.	metathesis, the transportation of letter.
accus	accusative case	mid.	middle voice.
		N.T.	New Testament
adj.	adjective.	opt.	optative mood.
adv.	adverb.	O.T.	Old Testament
al.	*alibi*, in other texts.	part.	participle.
		pass.	passive voice.
al. freq.	*alibi frequenter.* in many other texts	r. per.	perfect tense.
		plu. p.	pluperfect tense.
Aram	Aramaena.	pl.	plural.
At.	Attic dialect	pr.	properly.
bis.	twice.	preced.	preceding.
cf.	*confer,* compare.	prep.	preposition.
		pron.	pronoun.
coll.	*collato,* being compared.	quater	four times.
comp.	comparative.	sc.	*scilicet,* that is to say, that is.
conj.	conjunction.		*sequente,* as, seq. gen. *sequente genitivo,* with a genitive following.
contr.	contraction, or contracted.	seq.	
dat.	dative case.		
dimin.	diminutive.		
enclit.	enclitic, throwing the accent on the preceding syllable.	sing.	signular–the figure, placed before sign. or pl. denote the person.
& et.	and.	spe.	specially, i.e. in a special and local meaning.
e.g.	*exempli gratia,* for example.		
f.	future tense.	subj.	subjunctive mood.
fr.	from.		
gen.	genitive case.	subs.	substantive.
		superl.	superlative.

genr.	generally, in a general sense, not affected by adjuncts.	ter.	thrice.
		trans.	transitively.
Heb.	Hebrew, or the Hebrew idiom.	trop.	tropically, i.e. turned aside from its strick literal meaning.
i.e.	*id est,* that is.	v.	*vel,* or.
idem.	the same.		a various
imperat.	imperative mood	v.r.	reading to the commond text.
imperf.	imperfect tense.	vix.	*videlicet,* that is, namely
impers.	impersonal.	voc.	vocative case
impl.	implication.		ὁ attached to a word
i.q.	same as.		show it to be masculine; ἡ, to be
inf.	infinitive mood.		feminine; ὁ ἡ to be common, i.e. masculine
int. interj.	interjection.		or feminine; and τό, to be neuter.
intrans.	intransitive.		
lit.	litterally		
met.	metaphorically		

GREEK AND ENGLISH LEXICON

To The

NEW TESTAMENT

A, α, Ἄλφα

A, α, *Alpha,*
    1the first letter in the Greek Alphabet, and used for the *first*, Re. 1.8, 11; 21.6; 22.13.
    In composition, it denotes privation; sometimes augmentation, and union.
Ἀβᾰρής, έος, οὖς, ὁ, ἡ, τὸ, -ές, (ἀ & βάρος)
    not burdensome, not chargeable, 2 Co. 11.9.
Ἀββᾶ

ind. ch. or Sy. אבא, father, Mar. 14.36. Ro.8.15 Ga. 4.6.

Ἄβυσσος, ου, ἡ,
  pr. bottomless; place of the dead, hell.

Ἀγαθοεργέω, ῶ, Ἀγαθουργῶ, (ἀγαθός & ἔργον)
  f. ήσω,
  to do good, confer benefits, 1 Ti.6.18 N.T.

Αγαθοποιέω, ῶ, (ἀγαθός & ποιέω)
  f. ήσω,
  to do good, benefit, do well: (S.) *whence*

Ἀγαθοποιΐα, ας, ἡ,
  well-doing, probity, 1 Pe. 4.19 L.G.

Ἀγαθοποιός, οῦ, ὁ, ἡ,
  a well-doer, 1 Pe. 2.14 L.G.

Ἀγᾰθός, ή, όν,
  good, profitable, generous, beneficent, upright, virtuous: *whence*

Ἀγαθωσύνη, ης, ἡ,
  goodness, virtue, beneficence. S.

Αγαλλίᾱσις, εως, ἡ,
  exultation, extreme joy: (S.) *from*

Ἀγαλλιάω, ῶ,
  f. άσω,
  to celebrate, praise; *also equivalent to* Αγαλλιάομαι, ῶμαι, to exult, rejoice
  exceedingly; to desire ardently, Jno. 8.56. S.

Ἀγᾰμος, ου, ὁ, ἡ (ἀ & γάμος)
  unmarried. 1 Co. 7.8, 11, 32, 34.

Ἀγανακτέω, ῶ,
  f. ήσω,
  to be pained; to be angry, vexed, indignant; to manifest indignation: *whence*

Ἀγανάκτησις, εως, ἡ,
  indignation, 2 Co. 7.11.

Ἀγαπάω, ῶ,
  f. ήσω, p. ἠγάπηκα,
  to love, value, esteem, feel or manifest generous concern for, be faithful towards; to
  delight in; to set store upon, Re. 12.11: *whence*

Ἀγάπη, ης, ἡ,
  to love, generosity, kindly concern, devotedness; *pl.* love-feasts, Ju. 12. S.

Ἀγαπητός, ή, όν,
  beloved, dear; worthy of love.

Ἀγγαρεύω, (ἄγγαρος, a Persian courier, or messenger, who had authority to press into his
  service men, horses, &c.)
  f. εύσω,
  to press or compel another to go somewhere, or carry some burden.

Ἀγγεῖον, ου, τό,(ἄγγος, the same)
  a vessel, utensil, Mat. 13.48; 25.4

Ἀγγελία, ας, ἡ,
  a message, doctrine, or precept, delivered in the name of any one, 1 Jno. 3.11: *from*

Ἄγγελος, ου, ὁ, ἡ,
  one sent, a messenger, angel.

Ἄγε,
  a particle of exhortation, (pr. imperat. of ἄγω)

come, come now, Ja 4.13; 5.1.

Ἀγέλη, ης, ἡ (ἄγω)
    a drove, flock, herd.

Ἀγενεαλόγητος, ου, ὁ, ἡ (ἀ & γενεαλογέω)
    not included in a pedigree, independent of pedigree, He. 7.3 N.T.

Ἀγενής, έος, ὁ, ἡ, τό -ός. (ἀ & γένος)
    ignoble, base, 1 Co 1.20.

Ἁγιάζω, (ἅγιος)
    f. άσω, p. pass. ἡγίασμαι,
    to separate, consecrate: 2cleanse, purify, sanctify; regard or reverence as holy: (S.)
    whence

Ἁγιασμός, οῦ, ὁ
    sanctification, moral purity, sanctity. S.

Ἅγιος, ία, ιον,
    separate from common condition and use; dedicated, Lu. 2.23; hallowed; used of
    things τά ἅγια, the sanctuary; and of persons, saints, e.g. members of the first
    Christian communities; pure, righteous, ceremonially or morally; holy: whence

Ἁγιότης, ητος, ἡ,
    holiness, sanctity, He. 12.10 S.

Ἁγιωσύνη, ης, ἡ,
    sanctification, sanctity, holiness. S.

Ἀγκάλη, ης, ἡ (ἀγκή, the same)
    the arm, Lu. 2.28 (ᾱ)

Ἄγκιστρον, ου, τό,
    a hook, fish-hook, Mat. 17.27.

Ἄγκῡρα, ας, ἡ,
    an anchor, Ac. 27.29, 30, 40.

Ἄγνᾰφος, ου, ὁ, ἡ, (ἀ & γνάπτω, to full, dress)
    unfulled, undressed; new Mat. 9.16. Mar. 2.21. N.T.

Ἁγνεία, ας, ἡ, (ἁγνός)
    purity, chastity, 1 Ti. 4.12; 5.2.

Ἁγνίζω,
    f. ίσω,
    to purify; to purify morally, reform. Ἁγνίζομαι, p. ἥγνισμαι, a. 1. ἡγνίσθην, to live
    like one under a vow of abstience, as the Nazarites: whence

Ἁγνισμός, οῦ, ὁ,
    purification, abstinence, Ac 21.26. L.G.

Ἀγνοέω, ῶ,
    f. ήσω,
    to be ignorant; not to understand; sin through ignorance: whence

Ἀγνόημα, ατος, τό,
    error, sin of ignorance, He. 9.7.

Ἄγνοια, ας, ἡ,
    ignorance.

Ἁγνός, ή, όν,
    pure, chaste, modest, innocent, blameless: whence

Ἁγνότης, τητος, ἡ,
    purity, life of purity, 2 Co. 6.6.

Ἁγνῶς,
    adv. purely, sincerely, Phi. 1.16.

Ἀγνωσια, ας, ὁ, ἡ, (ἀ & γνῶσις)
    ignorance, 1 Co. 15.34. 1 Pe. 2.15.
Ἄγνωστος, ου, ὁ, ἡ, (ἀ & γνωστός)
    unknown, Ac. 17.23.
Ἀγορά, ᾶς, ἡ, ἀγείρω,
    to gather together) a place of public concourse, forum, market-place; things sold in
    the market, provisions: *whence*
Ἀγοράζω,
    f. άσω, p. pass. ἠγόρασμαι, a. 1. pass. ἠγοράσθην,
    to buy; redeem, acquire *by a ransom or price paid.*
Ἀγοραῖος, ου, ὁ, ἡ,
    one who visits the forum; a lounger, one who idles away his time in public places a
    low fellow, Ac. 17.5.
Ἀγόραιος, ου, ὁ, ἡ,
    pertaining to the forum, judicial; ἀγόραιοι, court days, Ac. 19.38.
Ἄγρα, ας, ἡ,
    a catching, thing taken, draught *of fishes*, Lu 5.4, 9.
Ἀγράμμᾰτος, ου, ὁ, ἡ, (ἀ & γράμμα)
    illiterate, unlearned, Ac. 4.13.
Ἀγραυλέω, ῶ, (ἀγρός & αὐλή)
    f. ήσω,
    to remain in the open air, *especially* by night, Lu. 2.8.
Ἀγρεύω, (ἄγρα)
    f. εύσω,
    to take in hunting, catch, Mar 12.13.
Ἀγριέλαιος, ου, ἡ, (ἄγριος & ἐλαία)
    a wild olive-tree, oleaster, Ro. 11.17, 24
Ἄγριος, ία, ιον,
    belonging to the field, wild; fierce, raging: *from*
Ἀγρός, ου, ὁ,
    a field, especially a cultivated field; *pl* the country; lands, farms, villages.
Ἀγρυπνέω, ῶ,
    f. ησω,
    to be awake, watch; to be watchful, vigilant: *whence*
Ἀγρυπνία, ας, ἡ,
    want of sleep, watching, 2 Co. 6.5; 11.27.
Ἄγω,
    f. ἄξω, p. ἦχα, ἀγήοχα, a.2. ἤγαγον, f.1. pass. ἀχθήσομαι, a.1. pass. ἤχθην p. pass.
    ἦγμαι,
    to lead, bring; lead away, drive off *as a booty of cattle;* conduct, accompany; lead out,
    produce; conduct with force, drag, hurry away; guide, in cite, entice; convey oneself,
    go, go away; pass or spend *as time;* celebrate: *whence*
Ἀγωγή, ῆς, ἡ,
    guidance, mode of instruction, discipline, course of life, 2 Ti. 3.10.
Ἀγών, ῶνος, ὁ,
    place of contest, race-course, stadium; a contest, strife contention; peril, toil: *whence*
Ἀγωνία, ας, ἡ,
    contest, violent struggle; agony, anguish, Lu. 22.44.
Ἀγωνίζομαι,
    3f. ἰσομαι, p. pass. ἠγώνισμαι,

to be a combatant in public games; to contend, fight, strive earnestly.

Ἀδάπᾰνος, ου, ὁ, ἡ (ἀ & δαπάνη)
    without expence, gratuitous, 1 Co. 9.18.

Ἀδελφή, ῆς, ἡ,
    a sister; near kins-woman or female relative; a female member of the Christian
    community: *from*

Ἀδελφός, οῦ, ὁ (ἀ & δελφύς, the womb)
    a brother; near kinsman or relative; one of the same nation or nature; one of equal
    rank and dignity; an associate, a member of the Christian community: *whence*

Ἀδελφότης, τητος, ἡ,
    brotherhood, the body of the Christian brotherhood, 1 Pe. 2.17; 5.9 S.

Ἄδηλος, ου, ὁ, ἡ, τό, ον, (ἀ & δῆλος)
    not apparent or obvious; uncertain, not distinct, Lu. 11.44. 1 Co. 14.8: *whence*

Ἀδηλότης, τητος, ἡ,
    uncertainty, inconstancy, 1 Ti. 6.17. L.G.

Ἀδήλως,
    adv. not manifestly, uncertainly, dubiously, 1 Co. 9.26.

Ἀδημονέω, ῶ,
    f. ήσω,
    to be depressed or dejected, full of anguish or sorrow.

Ἅιδης, ου, ὁ,
    the invisible abode or mansion of the dead; the place of punishment, hell; the lowest
    place or condition, Mat. 11.23. Lu. 10.15.

Ἀδιάκρῐτος, ου, ὁ, ἡ (ἀ & διακρίνω)
    undistinguishing, impartial, Ja. 3.17.

Ἀδιάλειπτος, ου, ὁ, ἡ (ἀ & διαλείπω)
    unceasing, constant, settled, Ro. 9.2. 2 Ti. 1.3: *whence*

Ἀδιαλείπτως,
    adv. unceasingly, by an unvarying practice.

Ἀδιαφθορία, ας, ἡ, (ἀ & διαφθορά)
    incorruptness, genuineness, pureness, Tit. 2.7.

Ἀδικέω, ῶ
    f. ήσω, p. ηκα, (ἀ & δίκη)
    to act unjustly; wrong; injure; violate a law: *whence*

Ἀδίκημα, ατος, τό,
    an act of injustice, crime.

Ἀδικία, ας, ἡ
    injustice, wrong; iniquity, falsehood, deceitfulness.

Ἄδῐκος, ου, ὁ, ἡ, τό, -ον,
    unjust, unrighteous, iniquitous, vicious; deceitful, fallacious.

Ἀδίκως,
    adv. unjustly, undeservedly, 1 Pe. 2.19.

Ἀδόκιμος, ου, ὁ, ἡ, (ἀ & δόκιμος)
    unable to stand test, rejected refuse, worthless.

Ἄδολος, ου, ὁ, ἡ, (ἀ & δόλος)
    without deceit, sincere, 1 Pe. 2.2

Ἁδρότης, τητος, ἡ (ἁδρός, mature, full)
    abundance, 2 Co. 8.20.

Ἀδυνατέω, ῶ,
    f. ήσω,

not to be able; to be impossible: *from*

Ἀδύνᾰτος, ου, ὁ, ἡ, τό, -ον, (ἀ & <u>δύναμαι</u>)
    impotent, weak; impossible.

Ἄιδω (contr. fr. ἀείδω)
    f. ᾄσω, ᾄσομαι,
    to sing.

Ἀεί,
    alway, for ever, aye.

Ἀετός, οῦ, ὁ,
    an eagle.

Ἄζῡμος, ου, ὁ, ἡ, (ἀ & <u>ζύμη</u>)
    unleavened; τὰ ἄζυμα, the feast of unleavened bread; *metaph.* pure from foreign matter, unadulterated, genuine; τὸ ἄζθμον, genuineness, 1 Co. 5.7, 8.

Ἀήρ, ἀέρος, ὁ,
    air, atmosphere.

Ἀθανασία, ας, ἡ, (ἀ & <u>θάνατος</u>)
    immortality, 1 Co. 15.53, 54. 1 Ti. 6.16.

Ἀθέμῐτος, ου, ὁ, ἡ, τό, -ον, (ἀ & θεμιτός, lawful)
    unlawful, criminal, wicked, Ac. 10.28. 1 Pe. 4.3.

Ἄθεος, ου, ὁ, ἡ (ἀ & <u>Θεός</u>)
    an Atheist; godless, estranged from the knowledge and worship of the true God, Ep. 2.12.

Ἄθεσμος, ου, ὁ, ἡ, (ἀ & θεσμός, law)
    lawless, unrestrained, licentious, 2 Pe. 2.7; 3.17. L.G.

Ἀθετέω, ῶ, (ἀ & <u>τίθημι</u>)
    f. ήσω,
    pr. to displace, set aside; to abrogate, annul, violate, swerve from; reject, contemn: (L.G.) *whence*

Ἀθέτησις, εως, ἡ,
    abrogation, annulling, He. 7.18; 9.26.

Ἀθλέω, ῶ, (ἄεθλος, strife, contest)
    f. ήσω, p. ἤθληκα,
    to strive, contend, be a champion in the public games, 2 Ti. 2.5: *whence*

Ἄθλησις, εως, ἡ
    contest, combat, struggle, conflict, He. 10.32. L.G.

Ἀθυμέω, ῶ, (ἀ & <u>θυμός</u>)
    4f. ήσω,
    to despond, be disheartened, Col 3.21.

Ἄθῷος, ου, ὁ, ἡ (ἀ & θῴή, a penalty)
    unpunished; *metaph.* innocent, Mat. 27.4, 24.

Αἴγειος, εία, ειον, (αἴξ, γός, a goat)
    belonging to a goat, He. 11.37.

Αἰγιᾰλός, οῦ, ὁ,
    sea-shore.

Ἀΐδιος, ου, ὁ, ἡ, (ἀεί)
    always existing, eternal, Ro. 1.20. Jude 6.

Αἰδώς, οῦς, ἡ,
    modesty, reverence, 1 Ti. 2.9. He. 12.28.

Αἷμα, ατος, τό,
    blood; of the colour of blood; bloodshed; blood-guiltiness; natural descent.

Αἱματεκχυσία, ας, ἡ (αἷμα & ἔκχυσις, fr. ἐκχέω)
    an effusion or shedding of blood, He. 9.22. N.T.

Αἱμορρόέω, ῶ, (αἷμα & ῥόος, fr. ῥέω)
    f. ήσω,
    to have a flux of blood, Mat. 9.20.

Αἴνεσις, εως, ἡ,
    praise, He. 13.15: (S>) *from*

Αἰνέω, ῶ, (αἶνος)
    f. έσω,
    to praise, celebrate.

Αἴνιγμα, ατος, τό, (αἰνίσσω, to intimate obscurely)
    an enigma, any thing obscurely expressed or intimated, 1 Co. 13.12.

Αἶνος, ου, ὁ,
    praise, Mat. 21.16. Lu. 18.43.

Αἵρεσις, εως, ἡ (αἱρέομαι)
    strictly, a choice or option; *hence,* a sect, faction; *by impl.* discord, contention.

Αἱρετίζω,
    f. ίσω, a.1. ἡρέτισα, (fr. same)
    to choose, choose with delight or love, Mat. 12.18.

Αἱρετικός, οῦ, ὁ, (fr. same)
    one who creates or fosters factions, Tit 3.10.

Αἱρέω, ῶ,
    f. ήσω, p. ᾕρηκα, p. pass. ᾕρημαι, mid. αἱρέομαι, οῦμαι, a.2 εἱλόμην,
    to take; *mid* to choose.

Αἴρω,
    f. ἀρῶ, a.1. ᾖρα,
    to take up, lift, raise; bear, carry; take away, remove; destroy, kill.

Αἰσθάνομαι,
    f. αἰσθήσομαι, a.2. ᾐσθόμην,
    to perceive, understand, Lu. 9.45: *whence*

Αἴσθησις, εως, ἡ,
    perception, understanding, Phi. 1.9

Αἰσθητήριον, ου, τό,
    an organ of perception; internal sense, He. 5.14.

Αἰσχροκερδής, έος, οῦς, ὁ, ἡ (αἰσχρός & κέρδος)
    eager for dishonourable gain, sordid, 1 Ti. 3.3, 8. Tit 1.7: *whence*

Αἰσχροκερδῶς,
    adv. for the sake of base gain, sordidly, 1 Pe. 5.2. N.T.

Αἰσχρολογία, ας, ἡ, (αἰσχρός & λόγος)
    vile or obscene language, foul talk, Col. 3.8.

Αἰσχρός, ά, όν,
    strictly, deformed, opp. to καλός; *metaph.* indecorous, indecent, dishonourable, vile:
    whence

Αἰσχρότης, τητος, ἡ,
    indecorum, indecency, Ep. 5.4.

Αἰσχύνη, ης, ἡ,
    shame, disgrace; cause of shame, dishonourable conduct: (ῡ) *whence*

Αἰσχύνομαι,
    f.υνοῦμαι, & υνθήσομαι,
    to be ashamed, confounded.

Αἰτέω, ῶ,
    f. ἤσω, a.1. ἤτησα,
    to ask, request; demand; desire, Ac. 7.46: *whence*
Αἴτημα, ατος, τό,
    a thing asked or sought for; petition, request, Lu. 23.24. 1 Jno. 5.15.
Αἰτία, ας, ἡ,
    cause, motive, incitement; accusation, crime; case.
Αἰτίᾱμα, ατος, τό,
    charge, accusation, Ac. 27.7: *form*
Αἰτιάομαι, ῶμαι, (αἰτία)
    v.r. Ro. 3.9, to charge, accuse.
Αἴτιος, ου, ὁ, ἡ,
    causative; αἴτιος, an author or causer, He. 5.9; τὸ αἴτιον, *equivalent to* αἰτία.
Αἰτίωμα, ατος, τό,
    v.r. Ac. 25.7, *equivalent to* αἰτίαμα. N.T.
Αἰφνίδιος, ου, ὁ, ἡ,
    unforeseen, unexpected, sudden, Lu. 21.32. 1 Thes. 5.3.
Αἰχμαλωσία, ας, ἡ (αἰχμάλωτος)
    captivity, state of captivity; captive multitude, Ep. 4.8. Re. 13.10. L.G.
Αἰχμαλωτεύω,
    f. εύσω,
    to lead captive; *met.* to captivate, Ep. 4.8. 2 Ti. 3.6
Αἰχμαλωτίζω,
    f. ίσω,
    to lead captive, *by impl.* to subject, Lu. 21.24. Ro. 7.23. 2 Co. 10.5. L.G.
Αἰχμάλωτος, ου, ὁ (αἰχμή, a spear & ἱλίσκομαι, to capture)
    a captive, Lu. 4.18.
Αἰών, ῶνος, ὁ,
    5pr. a period of time of significant character; life; an era; an age; *hence,* a state of
    things making an age or era; the present order of nature; the natural condition of man,
    the world; ὁ αἰών, illimitable duration, eternity; *as also,* οἱ αἰῶες, ὁ αἰὼν τῶν αἰώνων,
    οἱ αἰῶνες τῶν αἰώνων; *by an Aramaism* οἱ αἰῶνες, the material universe. He. 1.2.
    whence
Αἰώνιος, ίου, ὁ, ἡ, & αἰώνιος, ια, ον,
    indeterminate as to duration, eternal, everlasting.
Ἀκαθαρσία, ας, ἡ, (ἀ & καθαίρω)
    uncleanness; lewdness; impurity of motive, 1 Thes. 2.3.
Ἀκαθάρτης, τητος, ἡ,
    impurity, Re. 17.4. N.T.
Ἀκάθαρτος, ου, ὁ, ἡ,
    impure, unclean; lewd; foul.
Ἀκαιρέομαι, οῦμαι, (ἀ & καιρός)
    f. ήσομαι,
    to be without opportunity, or occasion, Phi. 4.10. N.T.
Ἀκαίρως,
    adv. unseasonably, 2 Ti. 4.2.
Ἄκᾰκος, ου, ὁ, ἡ, (ἀ & κακός)
    free from evil, innocent, blameless; artless, simple, Ro. 16.18. He. 7.26.
Ἄκανθα, ης, ἡ,
    a thorn, thorn-bush, Mat. 7.16: *whence*

Ἀκάνθινος, ου, ὁ, ἡ,
>   throny, made of thorns, Mar. 15.17. Jno. 19.5.
Ἄκαρπος, ου, ὁ, ἡ, τό, -ον, (ἀ & καρπός)
>   without fruit, unfruitful, barren; by impl. noxious.
Ἀκατάγνωστος, ου, ὁ, ἡ, τό, -ον, (ἀ & καταγινώσκω)
>   pr. not worthy of condemnation by a judge; hence, irreprehensible, Tit. 2.8. S.
Ἀκατακάλυπτος, ου, ὁ, ἡ, (ἀ & κατακαλύπτω)
>   uncovered, unveiled, 1 Co. 11.5, 13. L.G.
Ἀκατάκρῐτος, ου, ὁ, ἡ (ἀ & κατακρίνω)
>   uncondemned in a public trial, Ac. 16.37; 22.25. N.T.
Ἀκατάλῠτος, ου, ὁ, ἡ, (ἀ & καταλύω)
>   incapable of dissolution, indissoluble; hence, enduring, everlasting, He. 7.16. L.G.
Ἀκατάπαυστος, ου, ὁ, ἡ (ἀ & καταπαύω)
>   which cannot be restrained from a thing, unceasing, 2 Pe. 2.14. L.G.
Ἀκαταστασία, ας, ἡ, (ἀ & καθίσταμαι, to be in a fixed and tranquil state)
>   pr. instability; hence an unsettled state; disorder, commotion, tumult, sedition, Lu. 21.9. 1 Co. 14.33. 2 Co. 6.5; 12.20. Ja. 3.16. L.G.
Ἀκατάστᾰτος, ου, ὁ, ἡ,
>   unstable, inconstant, Ja. 1.8.
Ἀκατάσχετος, ου, ὁ, ἡ, (ἀ & κατέχω)
>   not coercible, irrestainable, untameable, unruly, Ja. 3.8. L.G.
Ἀκέραιος, ου, ὁ, ἡ, (ἀ & κεράννυμι, to mix)
>   pr. unmixed; hence, without mixture of vice or deceit, sincere, artless, blameless, Mat. 10.16.. Ro. 16.19. Phi. 2.15.
Ἀκλῐνής, εος, ὁ, ἡ (ἀ & κλίνω)
>   not declining, unwavering, steady, He. 10.23.
Ἀκμάζω,
>   f. άσω,
>   to flourish, ripen, be in one's prime, Re. 14.18: from
Ἀκμή, ῆς, ἡ, (ἀκή, idem)
>   pr. the point of a weapon; point of time; ἀκμήν for κατ' ἀκμήν, adv. yet, still, even now, Mat. 15.16.
Ἀκοή, ῆς, ἡ (ἀκούω)
>   hearing, the act or sense of hearing; the instrument of hearing, the ear; a thing heard, instruction, doctrine, report.
Ἀκολουθέω, ῶ,
>   f. ήσω, p. ἠκολούθηκα,
>   to follow; follow as a disciple; imitate.
Ἀκούω,
>   f. ουσω, ούσομαι, p. ἄκηκοα, p. pass. ἤκουσμαι, a.1. pass. ἠκούσθην,
>   to hear; hearken, listen to; heed, obey; understand.
Ἀκρασία, ας, ἡ, (ἀκρατής)
>   intemperance, incontinence, Mat. 23.25. 1 Co. 7.5.
Ἀκρᾰτής, ίος, οῦς, ὁ, ἡ, τό, -ές, (ἀ & κράτος)
>   not master of one's self, intemperate, 2 Ti. 3.3.
Ἄκρᾱτος, ου, ὁ, ἡ, τό, -ον, (ἀ & κεράννυμι)
>   unmixed, unmingled, wine, Re. 14.10.
Ἀκρίβεια, ας, ἡ,
>   accuracy, exactness; or rigour, severe discipline, Ac. 22.3: from
Ἀκρῑβής, έος, ὁ, ἡ, τό, -ές,

accurate, exact; severe, rigorous, Ac. 18.26; 23.15, 20; 24.22; 26.5: *whence*

Ἀκριβόω, ῶ,
f. ώσω, p. ἠκρίβωκα,
to inquire accurately, or assiduously, Mat. 2.7, 16: *comp.* ver. 8.

Ἀκριβῶς,
6*adv.* diligently, accurately, Mat. 2.8. Lu. 1.3. Ac. 18.25. Ep. 5.15. 1 Thes. 5.2.

Ἀκρίς, ίδος, ἡ,
a locust, Mat. 3.4. Mar. 1.6. Re. 9.3, 7.

Ἀκροατήριον, ου, τό, (ἀκροάομαι, to hear)
a place of audience, auditorium, Ac. 25.23. L.G.

Ἀκροατής, οῦ, ὁ,
a hearing, Ro. 2.13. Ja. 1.22, 23, 25.

Ἀκροβυστία, ας, ἡ, (ἄκρον & βύω, to cover)
the prepuce, foreskin; uncircumcision, the state of being uncircumcised; *the abstract being put for the concrete,* uncircumcised men. i.e. Gentiles. S.

Ἀκρογωνιαῖος, α, ον, (ἄκρος & γωνία)
corner-foundation *stone* Ep. 2.20. 1 Pe. 2.6. S.

Ἀκροθίνιον, ου, τό, (ἄκρος & θίν, a heap)
the first-fruits of the produce of the ground, which were taken from the top of the heap and offered to the gods; the best and choicest of the spoils of war, usually collected in a heap, He. 7.4.

Ἄκρον, ου, τό,
the top, tip,end, extremity, Mat. 24.31. Mar. 13.27. Lu. 16.24. He. 11.21: *from*

Ἄκρος, α, ον, (ἀκή)
pointed; *hence,* extreme, uppermost.

Ἀκῡρόω, ῶ (ἀ & κυρόω)
f. ώσω,
to deprive of authority, annul, abrogate, Mat. 15.6. Mar. 7.13. Gal. 3.17. L.G.

Ἀκωλύτως, (ἀ & κωλύω)
without hindrance, freely, Ac. 28.31. (ῡ).

Ἄκων, ουσα, ον, (for ἀέκων, fr. ἀ & ἑκών)
unwilling, 1 Co. 9.17.

Ἀλάβαστρον, ου, τό,
alabaster; a vase to hold perfumed ointment, *properly made of alabaster, but also of other materials,* Mat. 26.7. Mar. 14.3. Lu. 7.37.

Ἀλαζονεία, ας, ἡ,
ostentation; boasting; haughtiness, 1 Jno. 2.16: *from*

Ἀλαζών, όνος, ὁ, ἡ,
ostentatious, vain-glorious, arrogant, boasting, Ro. 1.30. 2 Ti. 3.2.

Ἀλαλάζω,
f. άξω, άξομαι,
pr. to raise the war-cry, ἀλαλά; *hence,* to utter other loud sounds; to wail, Mar. 5.38; to tinkle, ring, 1 Co. 13.1.

Ἀλάλητος, ου, ὁ, ἡ τό, -ον, (ἀ & λαλέω)
unutterable, *or* unexpressed, Ro. 8.26. L.G.

Ἄλαλος, ου, ὁ, ἡ, (fr. same)
unable to speak, dumb, Mar. 7.37.

Ἅλας, ατος, τό, (ἅλς)
salt; *met.* wisdom and prudence. L.G.

Ἀλείφω,

f. ψω,

 to anoint *with oil or ointment.*

Ἀλεκτοροφωνία, ας, ἡ, (ἀλέκτωρ & φωνή)

 the cock-crowing, the third watch of night, *intermediate to midnight and daybreak, and termed* cock-crow, Mar. 13.35. L.G.

Ἀλέκτωρ, ορος, ὁ,

 a cock, *gallus,* Mat. 26.34. Mar. 14.30. Lu. 22.34. Jno. 13.38..

Ἄλευρον, ου, τό, (ἀλέω, to grind)

 meal, flour, Mat. 13.33. Lu. 13.21.

Ἀλήθεια, ας, ἡ, (ἀληθής)

 truth, verity; love of truth, veracity, sincerity; divine truth revealed to man; practice in accordance with Gospel truth.

Ἀληθεύω,

 f. εύσω,

 to speak or maintain the truth; act truly or sincerely, Ga. 4.16. Ep. 4.15: *from*

Ἀληθής, έος, ὁ, ἡ, τό, -ές,

 true; worthy of credit; studious of truth, veracious: *whence*

Ἀληθινός, ή, όν,

 sterling; real; unfeigned, trustworthy, true.

Ἀλήθω,

 f. ἀλήσω, (ἀλέω, idem)

 to grind, Mat. 24.41. Lu. 17.35.

Ἀληθῶς, (ἀληθής)

 adv. truly, really; certainly, of a truth; truly, veraciously.

Ἁλιεύς, έος, έως, ὁ (ἅλς, the sea)

 a fisherman, Mat. 4.18, 19. Mar. 1.16, 17. Lu. 5.2: *whence*

Ἁλιεύω,

 f. εύσω,

 to fish, Jno. 21.3.

Ἁλίζω, (ἅλς)

 f. ίσω,

 to salt, season with salt, perserve by salting, Mat. 5.13. Mar. 9.49.

Ἀλίσγημα, ατος, τό, (ἀλισγέω, to pollute, *in the Sept.*)

 pollution, defilement, Ac. 15.20. N.T.

Ἀλλά,

 conj. but; however; but still more; ἀλλάγε, at all events; ἀλλ' ἤ, unless, except. Ἀλλά *also serves to introduce a sentence with keenness and emphasis,* Ro. 6.5; 7.7. Phil. 3.8. Jno. 16.2.

Ἀλλάσσω,

 f. ἀξω, a.1.pass ἠλάχθην, a.2. ἠλλάγην, f. ἀλλαγήσομαι, (fr. ἄλλος)

 7to change, alter, transform, Ac. 6.14. Ro. 1.23. 1 Co. 15.51, 52. Ga. 4.20. He. 1.12.

Ἀλλαχόθεν, (ἄλλος & -θεν, denoting *from* a place)

 from another place or elsewhere, Jno. 10.1. L.G.

Ἀλληγορέω, ῶ, (ἄλλος & ἀγορεύω, to speak)

 to say what is either designed or fitted to convey a meaning other than the leteral one, to allegorize, Ga. 4.24. L.G.

Ἀλληλούϊα, Heb. הי־וללה

 Praise ye Jehovah, Re. 19.1, 3, 4, 6.

Ἀλλήλων,

 gen. pl., ἀλλήλοις, αις, οις, dat. ἀλλήλους, ας, α, acc. (fr. ἄλλος) one another, each other.

Ἀλλογενής, έος, ὁ, ἡ, (ἄλλος & γένος)
of another race or nation *i.e. not a Jew;* a stranger, foreigner, Lu. 17.18. S.

Ἅλλομαι,
f. ἁλοῦμαι, a.1. ἡλάμην,
to leap, jump, leap up, Ac. 3.8; 14.10; to spring, *as water,* Jno. 4.14.

Ἄλλος, η, ο,
another, some other; ὁ ἄλλος, the other; οἱ ἄλλοι, the others, the rest.

Ἀλλοτριοέπισκοπος, ου, ὁ, ἡ,
pr. one who meddles with the affairs of others, a busy-body in other men's matters; factious, 1 Pe. 4.15 (N.T.) fr ἐπίσκοπος *and*

Ἀλλότριος, ία, ιον, (ἄλλος)
belonging to another, alienus, foreign; a foreigner, alien.

Ἀλλόφῡλος, ου, ὁ, ἡ, (ἄλλος & φυλή)
of another race or natio, i.e. not a Jew, a foreigner, Ac. 10.28.

Ἄλλως,
adv. (ἄλλος) otherwise, 1 Ti. 2.25.

Ἀλοάω, ῶ,
f. ήσω, & άσω,
to thresh; to tread, or thresh out, 1 Co. 9.9, 10. 1 Ti. 5.18.

Ἄλογος, ου, ὁ, ἡ, τό, -ον, (ἀ & λόγος)
without speech or reason, irrational, brute; unreasonable, absurd, Ac. 25.27. 2 Pe. 2.12. Jude 10.

Ἀλόη, ης, ἡ,
also termed ξυλαλόη, ἀγάλλογον, aloe, lign-aleo, *excoecaria agallochon* Linn., a tree which grows in India and Cochin-China, the wood of which is soft and bitter though highly aromatic. It is used by the Orientals as a perfume; and employed for the purposes of embalming, Jno. 19.39. L.G.

Ἅλς, ἁλός, ὁ,
salt, Mar. 9.49.

Ἁλῠκός, ή, όν, (ἅλς)
brackish, bitter, salt, Ja. 3.12.

Ἄλῡπος, ου, ὁ, ἡ, (ἀ & λύπη)
free from grief or sorrow, Phi. 2.28.

Ἅλῠσις, εως, ἡ,
a chain, Mar. 5.3, 4.

Ἀλυσιτελής, έος, ὁ, ἡ, (ἀ & λυσιτελής, i.e. λύων τὰ τέλη)
pr. bringing in no revenue or profit; *hence,* unprofitable, useless; *and by impl.* destructive, fatal, He. 13.17.

Ἅλων, ωνος, ἡ
(a later form of ἅλως, ω, ἡ)
a threshing-floor, a place where corn is trodden out; *meton.* the corn which is trodden out, Mat. 3.12. Lu. 3.17.

Ἀλώπηξ, εκος, ἡ,
a fox; *met.* a crafty man, Mat. 8.20. Lu. 9.58; 13.32.

Ἅλωσις, εως, ἡ, (ἁλίσκομαι)
a taking, catching, capture.

Ἅμα,
adv. with, together with; at the same time.

Ἀμᾰθής, έος, ὁ, ἡ, (ἀ & μανθάνω)

unlearned, uninstructed, rude, 2 Pe. 3.16.

Ἀμαράντινος, ου, ὁ, ἡ,
&
Ἀμάραντος, ου, ὁ, ἡ, (ἀ & μαραίνομαι)
unfading; *hence,* enduring, 1 Pe. 1.4; 5.4. L.G.

Ἁμαρτάνω,
f. ἁμαρτήσομαι & ἁμαρτήσω, a.1. ἡμάρτησα, a.2, ἥμαρτον,
pr. to miss a mark; to be in error; to sin; to wrong: *whence*

Ἁμάρτημα, ατος, τό,
an error, sin; offence, Mar. 3.28; 4.12. Ro. 3.25. 1 Co. 6.18.

Ἁμαρτία, ας, ἡ,
error; offence, sin; a principle or cause of sin; proneness to sin, sinful propensity; guilt or imputation of sin; a guilty subject, sin-offering, expiatory victim.

Ἀμάρτυρος, ου, ὁ, ἡ, (ἀ & μάρτυς)
without testimony or witness, without proof, Ac. 14.17.

Ἁμαρτωλός, οῦ, ὁ, ἡ, (ἁμαρτάνω)
one who deviates from the path of virtue, a sinner; depraved, sinful, detestable. L.G.

Ἄμᾰχος, ου, ὁ, ἡ, (ἀ & μάχομαι)
8not disposed to fight; not quarrelsome or contentious, 1 Ti. 3.3. Tit. 3.2.

Ἀμάω, ῶ
f. ήσω,
to collect; to reap, mow, or cut down, Ja. 5.4.

Ἀμέθυστος, ου, ὁ, (ἀ & μεθύω)
an amethyst, a gem of a deep purple or violet colour, *so called from its supposed efficacy in keeping off drunkenness,* Re. 21.20.

Ἀμελέω, ῶ, (ἀ & μέλει)
f. ήσω, p. ἠμέληκα, ἀμελής,
not to care for, to neglect, disregard, Mat. 22.5. 1 Ti. 4.14. He. 2.3; 8.9. 2 Pe. 1.12.

Ἄμεμπτος, ου, ὁ, ἡ, (ἀ & μεμπτός, fr. μέμφομαι)
blameless, irreprehensible, without defect, Lu. 1.6. Phi. 2.15; 3.6. 1 Thes. 3.13. He. 8.7.

Ἀμέμπτως,
adv. blamelessly, unblameably, unexceptionably, 1 Thes. 2.10; 5.23.

Ἀμέριμνος, ου, ὁ, ἡ, (ἀ & μέριμνα)
free from care of solicitude, Mat. 28.14. 1 Co. 7.32.

Ἀμετάθετος, ου, ὁ, ἡ, (ἀ & μετατίθημι)
unchangeable, He. 6.17, 18. L.G.

Ἀμετακίνητος, ου, ὁ, ἡ, (ἀ & μετακινέω)
immoveable, firm, 1 Co. 15.58.

Ἀμεταμέλητος, ου, ὁ, ἡ, (ἀ & μεταμέλομαι)
not to be repented of; *by impl.* irrevocable, enduring, Ro. 11.29. 2 Co. 7.10.

Ἀμετανόητος, ου, ὁ, ἡ, (ἀ & μετανοέω)
impenitent, obdurate. Ro. 2.5. L.G.

Ἄμετρος, ου, ὁ, ἡ, τό, -ον, (ἀ & μέτρον)
without or beyond measure, immoderate, 2 Co. 10.13, 15.

Ἀμήν (Heb. אמן firm, faithful, true)
used as a particle both of affirmation and assent, in truth, verily, most certainly; so be it; ὁ ἀμήν, the faithful and true One, Re. 3.14.

Ἀμήτωρ, ορος, ὁ, ἡ, (ἀ & μήτηρ)
without mother; independent of maternal descent, He. 7.3.

Ἀμίαντος, ου, ὁ, ἡ, (ἀ & μιαίνω)

    pr. unstained, unsoiled; *met.* undefiled, chaste, He. 13.4; pure, sincere, Ja. 1.27; inviolate, unimpaired, 1 Pe. 1.4.

Ἄμμος, ου, ἡ,

    sand.

Ἀμνός, οῦ, ὁ,

    a lamb, Jno. 1.29, 36. Ac. 8.32. 1 Pe. 1.19.

Ἀμοιβή, ῆς, ἡ, (ἀμείβω, ἀμείβομαι, to requite)

    requital; *of kind offices,* recompence, 1 Ti. 5.4.

Ἄμπελος, ου, ἡ

    a vine, grape-vine.

Ἀμπελουργός, οῦ, ὁ, ἡ, (ἄμπελος & ἔργον)

    a vine-dresser, Lu. 13.7.

Ἀμπελών, ῶνος, ὁ,

    a vineyard.

Ἀμύνω,

    f. υνῶ, a.1. ἤμυνα,

    to ward off, help, assist; *mid.* ἀμύνομαι, to repel from one's self, resist, make a defence, assume the office of protector and avenger, Ac. 7.24.

Ἀμφιβάλλω, (ἀμφὶ, about, & βάλλω)

    f. Βαλῶ,

    v.r. Mar. 1.16, to throw around; to cast *a net: whence*

Ἀμφίβληστρον, ου, τό,

    pr. what is thrown around, e.g. *a garment,* a large kind of fish-net, drag, Mat. 4.18. Mar. 1.16.

Ἀμφιέννυμι, (ἀμφί & ἕννυμι, to put on)

    f. ἀμφιέσω p. pass. ἠμφίεσμαι,

    to clothe, invest, Mat. 6.30; 11.8. Lu. 7.25; 12.28.

Ἄμφοδον, ου, τό, (equivalent to ἄμφοδος, ου, ἡ fr. ἀμφί & ὁδός)

    a road leading round a town or village; the street of a village, Mar. 11.4.

Ἀμφότεροι, αι, α, (ἄμφω, both)

    both.

Ἀμώμητος, ου, ὁ, ἡ, (ἀ & μῶμος)

    blameless, irreprehensible, Phi. 2.15. 2 Pe. 3.14.

Ἄμωμον, ου, τό,

    v.r. Re. 18.13, amomum, an odoriferous shrub, from which a precious ointment was prepared.

Ἄμωμος, ου, ὁ, ἡ, (ἀ & μῶμος)

    blameless.

Ἄν

    The various constructions of this particle, and their significations, must be learnt from the grammars. Standing at the commencement of a clause, it is another form of ἐάν, *if Jno. 20.23.*

Ἀνά,

    prep. used in the N.T. only in certain forms.

    Ἀνὰ μέρος, in turn; ἀνὰ μέσον, in turn; ἀνὰ μέσον, through the midst, between; ἀνὰ δηνάριον, at the rate of a denarius; *with numeral,* ἀνὰ ἑκατόν, 9in parties of a hundred. *In composition,* step by step, up, back, again.

Ἀναβαθμός, οῦ, ὁ, (ἀνά & βαθμός)

    the act of ascending; means of ascent, steps, stairs, Ac. 21.35, 40: *from*

Ἀναβαίνω, (ἀνά & βαίνω)
    f. βήσομαι, p. βέβηκα, a.2 ἀνέβηω,
    to go up, ascend; climb; embark; to rise, mount upwards, *as smoke;* to grow or spring up, *as plants;* to spring up, arise, *as thoughts.*
Ἀναβάλλω, (ἀνά & βάλλω)
    f. βαλῶ, p. βέβληκα,
    to throw back; *mid.* to put off, defer, adjourn, Ac. 24.22.
Ἀναβιβάζω, (ἀνά & βιβάζω)
    f. άσω, a.1. ἀνεβιβασα,
    to cause to come up or ascend, draw or bring up, Mat. 13.48.
Ἀναβλέπω, (ἀνά & Βλέπω)
    f. ψω,
    to look upwards; to see again, recover sight: *whence*
Ἀνάβλεψις, εως, ἡ,
    recovery of sight, Lu. 4.18.
Ἀναβοάω, ῶ, (ἀνά & βοάω)
    f. ήσομαι, a.1. ησα,
    to cry out or aloud, exclaim, Mat. 27.46. Mar. 15.8. Lu. 9.38.
Ἀναβολή, ῆς, ἡ, (ἀναβάλλω)
    delay, Ac. 25.17.
Ἀνάγαιον, ου, τό
    v.r. for ἀνώγεον, *which see.*
Ἀναγγέλλω, (ἀνά & ἀγγέλλω)
    f. γελῶ, a.1. ἀνήγγειλα, a.2. pass. ἀνηγγέλην,
    to bring back word, announce, report; to declare, set forth, teach.
Ἀναγεννάω, ῶ, (ἀνά & γεννάω)
    f. ήσά, p. pass. ἀναγεγέννημαι,
    to beget or bring forth again; regenerate, 1 Pe. 1.3, 23. N.T.
Ἀναγινώσκω, (ἀνά & γινώσκω)
    f. γνώσομαι, a.2. ἀνέγνων, a.1. pass. ἀνεγνώσθην,
    to gather exact knowledge of, recognise, discern; *especially,* to read.
Ἀναγκάζω, (ἀνάγκη)
    f. άσω,
    to force, compel; constrain, urge.
Ἀναγκαῖος, α, ον, (ἀνάγκη)
    necessary, indispensable, 1 Co. 12.22; necessary, needful, right, proper, Ac. 13.46. 2 Co. 9.5. Phi. 1.24; 2.25. He. 8.3; near, initimate, closely connected, *necessarius, as friends,* Ac. 10.24.
Ἀναγκαστῶς,
    adv. by contraint or compulsion, unwillingly, *opp. to* ἑκουσίως, 1 Pe. 5.2: *from*
Ἀνάγκη, ης, ἡ, (ἄγχω, to compress)
    necessity, constraint, compulsion; obligation of duty, moral or spiritual necessity; distress, calamity, affliction.
Ἀηαγνωρίζω, (ἀνά & γνωρίζω)
    f. ισω, a.1. pass. ἀηεγνωρίσθην,
    to recognise; *pass.* to be made known, or to cause one's self to be recognised, Ac. 7.13.
Ἀνάγνωσις, εως, ἡ, (ἀναγινώσκω)
    reading, Ac. 13.15. 2 Co. 3.14. 1 Ti. 4.13.
Ἀνάγω, (ἀνά & ἄγω)

f. ἄξω, a.2. ἀνήγαγον, a.1. pass. ἀνήχθην,

to conduct; to lead or convey from a lower place to a higher; to offer up, *as a sacrifice;* to lead out, produce; ἀνάγομαι, *as a nautical term,* to set sail, put to sea.

Ἀναδείκνυμι, (ἀνά & δείκνυμι)

v. νύω, f. ξω,

pr. to show anything by raising it aloft, *as a torch;* to display, manifest, show plainly or openly, Ac. 1.14; to mark out, constitute, appoint *by some outward sign,* Lu. 10.1:*whence*

Ἀνάδειξις, εως, ἡ,

a showing forth, manifestation; entrance upon the duty or office to which one is consecrated, Lu. 1.80. L.G.

Ἀναδέχομαι, (ἀνά & δέχομαι)

f. ξομαι,

to receive, *as opposed to shunning or refusing;* to receive *with hospitality,* Ac. 28.7; to embrace *a proffer or promise,* He. 11.17.

Ἀναδίδωμι, ἀνά & δίδωμι

f. δώσω, a.2. ἀνέδων,

to give forth, up, or back; deliver, present, Ac. 23.33.

Ἀναζάω, ῶ, (ἀνά & ζάω)

f. ήσω,

to live again, recover life, Ro. 14.9. Re. 20.5; to revive, recover activity, Ro. 7.9; *met.* to live a new and reformed life, Lu. 15.24, 32. L.G.

Ἀναζητέω, ῶ, (ἀνά & ζητέω)

f. ήσω,

to track; seek diligently, inquire after, search for, Lu. 2.44. Ac. 11.25.

Ἀναζώννυμι, (ἀνά & ζώννυμι)

f. ζώσω,

to gird *with a belt or girdle;* mid. ἀναζώννυμαι, to gird one's self, 1 Pe. 1.13. S.

Ἀναζωπῠρέω, ῶ, (ἀνά & ζωπυρέω, to revive a fire, fr. ζωός & πῦρ)

10f. ήσω,

pr. to kindle up a dormant fire; *met.* to revive, excite; stir up, cultivate one's power, 2 Ti. 1.6.

Ἀναθάλλω, (ἀνά & θάλλω, to thrive, flourish)

f. θαλῶ, a.2. ἀνέθαλον,

pr. to recover verdure, flourish again; *met.* to recover activity, Phi. 4.10.

Ἀνάθεμα, ατος, τό, (*a later equivalent to* ἀνάθημα, fr. ἀνατίθημι)

a devoted thing, *but ordinarily in a bad sense,* a person or thing accursed, Ro. 9.3. 1 Co. 12.3; 16.22. Ga. 1.8, 9; a curse, execration, anathema, Ac. 23.14: *whence*

Ἀναθεματίζω,

f. ίσω,

to declare any one to be ἀνάθεμα, to curse, bind by a curse, Mar. 14.71. Ac. 23.12, 14, 21. S.

Ἀναθεωρέω, ῶ, (ἀνά & θεωρέω)

f. ήσω,

to view, behold attentively, comtemplate, Ac. 17.23. He. 13.7.

Ἀνάθημα, ατος, τό, (ἀνατίθημι)

a gift or offering consecrated to God, Lu. 21.5.

Ἀναίδεια, ας, ἡ, (ἀ & αἰδώς)

pr. impudence; *hence,* importunate solicitation, or pertinacious importunity, *without regard to time, place, or person,* Lu. 11.8.

Ἀναίρεσις, εως, ἡ,

    pr. a taking up or away; death, a putting to death, murder, Ac. 8.1; 22.20: *from*

Ἀναιρέω, ῶ (ἀνά & αἱρέω)

    f. ήσω, a.2. ἀνεῖλον, a.1. pass. ἀνῃρέθην,

    pr. to take up, lift, *as from the ground;* to take away or off, put to death, kill, murder; to take away, abolish, abrogate, He. 10.9; *mid.* to take up *infants in order to bring them up,* Ac. 7.21.

Ἀναίτιος, ίου, ὁ, ἡ, (ἀ & αἰτία)

    guiltless, innocent, Mat. 12.5, 7.

Ἀνακαθίζω, (ἀνά & καθίζω)

    f. ίσω,

    to set up; *intrans.* to sit up, Lu. 7.15. Ac. 9.40.

Ἀνακαινίζω, (ἀνά & καινίζω)

    f. ίσω,

    to renovate, renew, He. 6.6.

Ἀνακαινόω, ῶ, (ἀνά & καινός)

    f. ώσω

    to renovate, invigorate, renew, 2 Co. 4.16. Col. 3.10: (N.T.) *whence*

Ἀνακαίνωσις, εως, ἡ,

    renovation, reformation, Ro. 12.2. Tit. 3.5.

Ἀνακαλύπτω, (ἀνά & καλύπτω)

    f. ψω,

    to unveil, uncover; *pass. met.* to be freed from obscurity or impediments to knowledge, 2 Co. 3.14, 18.

Ἀνακάμπτω, (ἀνά & κάμπτω)

    f. ψω,

    pr. to reflect, bend back; *hence,* to bend back one's course, return, Mat. 2.12. Lu. 10.6. Ac. 18.21. He. 11.15.

Ἀνάκειμαι, (ἀνά & κεῖμαι)

    f. είσομαι,

    to be laid up, *as offerings; later,* to lie, be in a recumbent posture, recline *at table.*

Ἀνακεφαλαιόω, ῶ, (ἀνά & κεφάλαιον)

    f. ώσω,

    to bring together several things under one, reduce under one head, Ep. 1.10; to comprise, Ro. 13.9. L.G.

Ἀνακλίνω, (ἀνά & κλίνω)

    f. ἴνῶ,

    to lay down; to cause to recline *at table,* &c.: *mid.* ἀνακλίνομαι, to recline at table.

Ἀνακόπτω, (ἀνά & κόπτω)

    f. ψω,

    pr. to beat back; *hence,* to check, impede, hinder, restrain, Ga. 5.7.

Ἀνακράζω, (ἀνά & κράζω)

    f. ξω,

    to cry aloud, exclaim, shout, Mar. 1.23; 6.49. Lu. 4.33; 8.28; 23.18.

Ἀνακρίνω, (ἀνά & κρίνω)

    f. ἴνῶ,

    to sift, examine, question; to try; to judge, give judement upon: *hence*

Ἀνάκρῖσις, εως, ἡ,

    investigation, judicial examination, hearing of a cause, Ac. 25.26.

Ἀνακύπτω, (ἀνά & κύπτω)

f. ψω,

pr. to raise up one's self, look up, Lu. 13.11. Jno. 8.7, 10; *met.* to recover from dejection, be cheered. Lu. 21.28.

Ἀναλαμβάνω,

f. λήψομαι, a.2. ἀνέλαβον, a.1. pass ἀνελήφθην,

to take up, receive up; bear, carry; take *as a companion,* take to one's self, assume: *hence*

Ἀνάληψις, εως, ἡ,

a taking up, receiving up, Lu. 9.51.

Ἀνᾱλίσκω, (ἀνά & ἁλίσκω)

f. λώσω, a.1. ἀνήλωσα, & ἀνάλωσα, a.1. pass. ἀνηλώθην & ἀναλώθην,

to consume, destroy, Lu. 9.54, Ga. 5.15. 2 Thes. 2.8.

Ἀναλογία, ας, ἡ, (ἀνά & λόγος)

analogy, ratio, proportion, Ro. 12.6.

Ἀναλογίζομαι, (ἀνά & λογίζομαι)

f. ίσομαι,

to consider attentively, He. 12.3.

Ἀνᾰλος, ου, ὁ, ἡ, τό, -ον, (ἀ & ἅλς)

11without saltness, or the taste and pungency of salt, insipid, Mat. 9.50.

Ἀνάλῡσις, εως, ἡ,

pr. dissolution; *met.* departure, death, 2 Ti. 4.6: *from*

Ἀναλύω, (ἀνά & λύω)

f. ύσω,

pr. to loose, dissolve; *intrans.* to loose *in order to departure,* depart, Lu. 12.36; *from life,* Phi. 1.23.

Ἀναμάρτητος, ου, ὁ, ἡ, (ἀ & ἁμαρτάνω)

without sin, guiltless, Jno. 8.7.

Ἀναμένω, (ἀνά & μένω)

f. ενῶ,

to await, wait for, expect, 1 Thes. 1.10.

Ἀναμιμνήσκω, (ἀνά & μιμνήσκω)

f. μνήσω, a.1. pass. ἀνεμνήσθην,

to remind, cause to remember, 1 Co. 4.17; to exhort, 2 Ti. 1.6; *mid.* to call to mind, recollect, remember, Mar. 14.72. 2 Co. 7.15. He. 10.32: *hence*

Ἀνάμνησις, εως, ἡ,

rememberance; a commemoration, memorial, Lu. 22.19. 1 Co. 11.24, 25. He. 10.3.

Ἀνανεόω, ῶ,

f. ώσω,

to renew; *mid.* to reform, become a new person, Ep. 4.23.

Ἀνανήφω, (ἀνά & νήφω)

f. ψω,

to become sober; *met.* to recover sobriety of mind, 2 Ti. 2.26. L.G.

Ἀναντίῤῥητος, ου, ὁ, ἡ, (ἀ & ἀντερῶ)

not to be contradicted, indisputable, Ac. 19.36: (L.G.) *hence*

Ἀναντιῤῥήτως,

adv. pr. without contradiction or gainsaying; without hesitation, promptly, Ac. 10.29.

Ἀνάξιος, ίου, ὁ, ἡ, (ἀ & ἄξιος)

unworthy, inadequate, 1 Co. 6.2: *hence*

Ἀναξίως,

adv. unworthily, in an improper manner, 1 Co. 11.27, 29.

Ἀνάπαυσις, εως, ἡ,
> rest, intermission, Mat. 11.29. Re. 4.8; 14.11; *meton.* place of rest, fixed habitation, Mat. 12.43. Lu. 11.24: *from*

Ἀναπαύω, (ἀνά & παύω)
> f. αύσω,
> to cause to rest, give rest or quiet; *mid.* to take rest, repose, refreshment; to have a fixed place of rest, abide, dwell, 1 Pe. 4.14.

Ἀναπείθω, (ἀνά & πείθω)
> f. είσω,
> to persuade *to a different opinion;* to seduce, Ac. 18.13.

Ἀναπέμπω, (ἀνά & πέμπω)
> f. ψω,
> to send back, or again, Phile. 11, to send up, remit *to a tribunal,* Lu. 23.7, 11, 15.

Ἀνάπηρος, ου, ὁ, ἡ, (ἀνά & πηρός, maimed)
> maimed, deprived of some member of the body, or at least of its use, Lu. 14.13, 21.

Ἀναπίπτω, (ἀνά & πίπτω)
> f. πεσοῦμαι, a.2. ἀνέπεσον,
> to fall or recline backwards; recline *at table,* &c.

Ἀναπληρόω, ῶ, (ἀνά & πληρόω)
> f. ώσω,
> to fill up, complete; fulfil, confirm, *as a prophecy by the event;* full *the place of any one;* to supply, make good; to observe fully, keep, *the law.*

Ἀναπολόγητος, ου, ὁ, ἡ, (ἀ & ἀπολογέομαι)
> inexcusable, Ro. 1.20; 2.1. L.G.

Ἀναπτύσσω, (ἀνά & πτύσσω)
> f. ξω,
> to roll back, unroll, unfold, Lu. 4.17.

Ἀνάπτω, (ἀνά & ἅπτω)
> f. ψω,
> to light, kindle, set on fire, Lu. 12.49. Ac. 28.2. Ja. 3.5.

Ἀναρίθμητος, ου, ὁ, ἡ, (ἀ & ἀριθμός)
> innumerable, He. 11.12.

Ἀνασείω, (ἀνά & σείω)
> f. είσω,
> *pr.* to shake up; *met.* to stir up, instigate, Mar. 15.11. Lu. 23.5.

Ἀνασκευάζω, (ἀνά & σκευάζω, fr. σκεῦος)
> f. άσω,
> *pr.* to collect one's effects or baggage (σκεύη) *in order to remove;* to lay waste by carrying off or destroying every thing, destroy; *met.* to unsettle, pervert, subvert, Ac. 15.24.

Ἀνασπάω, ῶ, (ἀνά & σπάω)
> f. άσω,
> to draw up, or out, Lu. 14.5. Ac. 11.10. (ἄ)

Ἀνάστᾰσις, εως, ἡ, (ἀνίστημι)
> a raising or rising up; resurrection; *meton.* the author of resurrection, Jno. 11.25; *met.* & *meton.* the author and cause of felicity, Lu. 2.34.

Ἀναστατόω, ῶ (fr. same)
> f. ώσω,

i.e. ἀνάστατον ποιεῖν, to lay waste, destroy; to disturb the public tranquillity, excite to sedition and tumult, Ac. 17.6; 21.38; to disturb the mind of any one *by doubts,* &c., to subvert, unsettle, Gal. 5.12. L.G.

Ἀνασταυρόω, ῶ, (ἀνά & σταυρόω)

12*pr.* to crucify; *met.* to treat with the greatest indignity, He. 6.6.

Ἀναστενάζω, (ἀνά & στενάζω)

f. ξω,

to sigh, groan deeply, Mar. 8.12.

Ἀναστρέφω, (ἀνά & στρέφω)

f. ψω,

to overturn, throw down; to turn back, return; *mid.* versari, to be employed, occupied, engaged; to have intercourse or be conversant with; to live, pass one's life, follow any mode of life: *hence*

Ἀναστροφή, ῆς, ἡ,

conversation, mode of life, conduct, deportment.

Ἀνατάσσομαι, (ἀνά & τάσσω)

f. τάξομαι,

pr. to arrange; *hence,* to compose, Lu. 1.1. L.G.

Ἀνατέλλω, (ἀνά & τέλλω, to make to rise)

f. τελῶ, a.1. ἀνέτειλα,

to cause to rise; *intrans.* to rise, spring up, *as the sun, stars,* &c.

Ἀνατίθεμαι, (ἀνά & τίθημι)

a.2. ἀνεθέμην,

to submit to a person's consideration a statement or report of *matters,* Ac. 25.14. Gal. 2.2.

Ἀνατολή, ῆς, ἡ, (ἀνατέλλω)

pr. a rising *of the sun,* &c.; the place of rising, the east; *met.* the dawn or day-spring, Lu. 1.78.

Ἀνατρέπω, (ἀνά & τρέπω)

f. ψω,

pr. to overturn, overthrow; *met.* to subvert, corrupt, 2 Ti. 2.18. Tit. 1.11.

Ἀνατρέφω, (ἀνά & τρέφω)

f. θρέψω, p. pass. ἀνατέθραμμαι, a.2. pass. ἀνετράφην,

to nurse, *as an infant,* Ac. 7.20; to bring up, educate, Ac. 7.21; 22.3.

Ἀναφαίνω, (ἀνά & φαίνω)

f. φανῶ,

to bring to light, display; *mid.* to appear, Lu. 19.11; *a nautical term,* to come in sight of. Ac. 21.3.

Ἀναφέρω, (ἀνά & φέρω)

f. οἴσω, a.1. ἤνεγκα, a.2. ἀνήνεγκον,

to bear or carry upwards, lead up; to offer *sacrifices;* to bear aloft or sustain a burden, *as sins,* 1 Pe. 2.24. He. 9.28.

Ἀναφωνέω, ῶ, (ἀνά & φωνέω)

f. ήσω,

to exclaim, cry out, Lu. 1.42.

Ἀνάχῠσις, εως, ἡ, (ἀναχέω, to pour out)

a pouring out; *met.* excess, 1 Pe. 4.4. L.G.

Ἀναχωρέω, ῶ, (ἀνά & χωρέω)

f. ήσω,

to go backward; depart, go away; withdraw, retire.

Ἀνάψυξις, εως, ἡ,
  pr. a refreshing coolness after heat; *met.* refreshing, recreation, rest, Ac. 3.19. L.G.
  from
Ἀναψύχω, (ἀνά & ψύχω)
  f. ξω,
  to recreate by fresh air; to refresh, cheer, 2 Ti. 1.16. (ῡ).
Ἀνδραποδιστής, οῦ, ὁ, (ἀνδράποδον, a slave)
  a man-stealer, kidnapper, 1 Ti. 1.10.
Ἀνδρίζω, (ἀνήρ)
  f. ίσω,
  to render brave or manly; *mid.* to show or behave one's self like a man, 1 Co. 16.13.
Ἀνδροφόνος, ου, ὁ, (ἀνήρ & φόνος)
  a homicide, man-slayer, murderer, 1 Ti. 1.9.
Ἀνέγκλητος, ου, ὁ, ἡ, (ἀ & ἐγκαλέω)
  not arraigned; unblameable, irreproachable, 1 Co. 1.8. Col. 1.22. 1 Ti. 3.10. Tit. 1.6, 7.
Ἀνεκδιήγητος, ου, ὁ, ἡ, (ἀ & ἐκδιηγέομαι)
  which cannot be related, inexpressable,unutterable, 2 Co. 9.15. L.G.
Ἀνεκλάλητος, ου, ὁ, ἡ, (ἀ & ἐκλαλέω)
  unspeakable, ineffable, 1 Pe. 1.8. L.G.
Ἀνέκλειπτος, ου, ὁ, ἡ, (ἀ & ἐκλείπω)
  unfailing, exhaustless, Lu. 12.33. L.G.
Ἀνεκτός, ή, όν, (ἀνέχω)
  tolerable, supportable, Mat. 10.15; 11.22, 24. Mar. 6.11. Lu. 10.12, 14.
Ἀνελεήμων, ονος, ὁ, ἡ, (ἀ & ἐλεήμων)
  unmerciful, uncompassionate, cruel, Ro. 1.31.
Ἀνεμίζω,
  f. ίσω,
  to agitate with the wind; *pass.* to be agitated or driven by the wind, Ja. 1.6. (L.G.)
  from
Ἄνεμος, ου, ὁ,
  the wind; *met.* levity, emptiness, Ep. 4.14.
Ἀνένδεκτος, ου, ὁ, ἡ, τό, -ον, (ἀ & ἐνδέχεται)
  impossible, what cannot be, Lu. 17.1 N.T.
Ἀνεξερεύνητος, ου, ὁ, ἡ, τό, -ον, (ἀ & ἐξερευνάω)
  unsearchable, inscrutable, Ro. 11.33.
Ἀνεξίκᾰκος, ου, ὁ, ἡ, (ἀνέχομαι & κακός)
  enduring or patient under evils and injuries, 2 Ti. 2.24. L.G.
Ἀνεξιχνίαστος, ου, ὁ, ἡ, (ἀ & ἐξιχνιάζω, to explore)
  which cannot be explored, inscrutable, incomprehensible, Ro. 11.33. Ep. 3.8. S.
Ἀνεπαίσχυντος, ου, ὁ, ἡ, (ἀ & ἐπαισχύνομαι)
  13without cause of shame, irreproachable, 2 Ti. 2.15. N.T.
Ἀνεπίληπτος, ου, ὁ, ἡ, (ἀ & ἐπιλαμβάνω)
  pr. not to be laid hold of, *met.* irreprehensible, unblameable, 1 Ti. 3.2; 5.7; 6.14.
Ἀνέρχομαι, (ἀνά & ἔρχομαι)
  f. ελεύσομαι, a.2. ἀνῆλθον,
  to ascend, go up, Jno. 6.3. Gal. 1.17, 18.
Ἄνεσις, εως, ἡ, (ἀνίημι)
  pr. the relaxing of any state of constraint; relaxation *of rigour of confinement,* Ac. 24.23; *met.* ease, rest, peace, tranquillity, 2 Co. 2.12; 7.5; 8.13. 2 Thes. 1.7.

Ἀνετάζω,
    f. άσω,
    to examine throughly; to examine *by torture,* Ac. 22.24, 29. S.
Ἄνευ,
    without, Mat. 10.29. 1 Pe. 3.1; 4.9.
Ἀνεύθετος, ου, ὁ, ἡ, (ἀ & εὔθετος)
    not commodious, inconvenient, Ac. 27.12. N.T.
Ἀνευρίσκω, (ἀνά & εὑρίσκω)
    f. ρήσω,
    to find by diligent search, Lu. 2.16. Ac. 21.4.
Ἀνέχομαι, (ἀνά & ἔχω)
    f. ἕξομαι, imperf. ἀνειχόμην, ἠνειχόμην, ἠνεσχόμην,
    to endure, bear with; to suffer, admit, permit.
Ἀνεψιός, οῦ, ὁ,
    a nephew, Col. 4.10.
Ἄνηθον, ου, τό,
    anethum, dill, an aromatic plant, Mat. 23.23.
Ἀνήκω, (ἀνά & ἥκω)
    to come up to, to pertain to; ἀνήκει, *impers.* it is fit, proper, becoming, Col. 3.18. Ep. 5.4. Phile. 8.
Ἀνήμερος, ου, ὁ, ἡ, (ἀ & ἥμερος, gentle, mild,)
    ungentile, fierce, ferocious, 2 Ti. 3.3.
Ἀνήρ, ἀνδρός, ὁ,
    a male person of full age and stature, as opposed to a child or female; a husband; a man, homo, human being; a certain man; some one; that man, he, ille; *used also pleonastically with other nouns and adjectives.*
Ἀνθίστημι, (ἀντί & ἵστημι)
    f. ἀντιστήσω, a.2. ἀντέστην, perf. ἀνθέστηκα,
    to oppose, resist, stand out against.
Ἀνθομολογέομαι, οῦμαι, (ἀντί & ὁμολογέω)
    pr. to come to an agreement; *hence,* to confess openly what is due; to confess, give thanks, praise, celebrate, extol, Lu. 2.38.
Ἄνθος, εος, ους, τό,
    a flower, Ja. 1.10, 11. 1 Pe. 1.24. *bis.*
Ἀνθρακιά, ᾶς, ἡ
    a mass or heap of live coals, Jno. 18.18; 21.9: *from*
Ἄνθραξ, ἄκος, ὁ
    a coal, burning coal, Ro. 12.20.
Ἀνθρωπάρεσκος, ου, ὁ, ἡ, (ἄνθρωπος & ἀρέσκω)
    desirous of pleasing men, Ep. 6.6. Col. 3.22. S.
Ἀνθρώπινος, η, ον, (ἄνθρωπος)
    human, belonging to man, 1 Co. 2.4, 13; 4.3; 10.13. Ja. 3.7. 1 Pe 2.13; suited to man, Ro. 6.19.
Ἀνθρωποκτόνος, ου, ὁ, ἡ, (ἄνθρωπος & κτείνω)
    a homicide, murderer, Jno. 8.44. 1 Jno. 3.15.
Ἄνθρωπος, ου, ὁ, ἡ,
    a human being; an individual; *used also pleonastically with other words; met.*a spiritual frame or character, 1 Pe. 3.4.
Ἀνθυπατεύω,
    f. εύσω,

to be proconsul, Ac. 18.12: *from*

Ἀνθύπᾰτος, ου, ὁ, (ἀντί & ὕπατος, a consul)
    a proconsul, Ac. 13.7, 8, 12; 19.38. L.G.

Ἀνίημι, (ἀνά & ἵημι)
    f. ἀνήσω, a.2. ἀνῆν, s. ἀνῶ, a.1. pass. ἀνέθην,
    to loose, slacken, Ac. 27.40; to unbind, unfasten, Ac. 16.26; to omit or lessen, Ep. 6.9;
    to leave or neglect, He. 13.5.

Ἀνίλεως, ω, ὁ, ἡ, (ἀ & ἵλεως)
    uncompassionate, unmerciful, stern, Ja. 2.13. N.T.

Ἄνιπτος, ου, ὁ, ἡ, (ἀ & νίπτω)
    unwashed, Mat. 15.20. Mar. 7.2, 5.

Ἀνίστημι,
    f. ἀναστήσω, a.1. ἀνέστησα,
    trans. to cause to stand up or rise; to raise up, *as the dead;* to cause to appear or exist;
    intrans a.2. ἀνέστην, imperat. ἀνάστηθι, ἀνάστα, and *mid.,* to rise up; to come into
    existence.

Ἀνόητος, ου, ὁ, ἡ, (ἀ & νοέω)
    inconsiderate, unintelligent, unwise; Lu. 24.25. Ro. 1.14. Gal. 3.1, 3. Tit. 3.3; brutish,
    1 Ti. 6.9.

Ἄνοια, ας, ἡ, (ἀ & νοῦς)
    want of understanding, folly, rashness, madness, Lu. 6.11. 2 Ti. 3.9

Ἀνοίγω, (ἀνά & οἴγω)
    f. ἀνοίζω, a.1. ἀνέῳξα, ἤνοιξα, p. ἀνέῳχα,
    14*trans.* to open;
    intrans. p.2 ἀνέῳγα, p. pass. ἀνέῳγμαι, ἠνέῳγμαι, a.1. pass. ἀνεῴχθην, ἠνεῴχθην,
    ἠνοίχθην,
    to be opened, to be open.

Ἀνοικοδομέω, ῶ, (ἀνά & οἰκοδομέω)
    f. ήσω,
    to rebuild, Ac. 15.16. *bis.*

Ἄνοιξις, εως, ἡ, (ἀνοίγω)
    an opening, act of opening, Ep. 6.19.

Ἀνομία, ας, ἡ,
    lawlessness, violation of law, iniquity, sin: *from*

Ἄνομος, ου, ὁ, ἡ (ἀ & νόμος)
    lawless, without law, not subject to law; violating the law, wicked, impious, a
    transgressor: *whence*

Ἀνόμως,
    adv. without law, Ro. 2.12. *bis.*

Ἀνορθόω, ῶ, (ἀνά & ὀρθόω)
    f. ώσω,
    to restore to straightness or erectness, Lu. 13.13; to reinvigorate, He. 12.12; to rerect,
    Ac. 15.16.

Ἀνόσιος, ὁ, ἡ, (ἀ & ὅσιος, pious)
    impious, unholy, 1 Ti. 1.9. 2 Ti. 3.2.

Ἀνοχή, ῆς, ἡ, (ἀνέχομαι)
    forbearance, patience, Ro. 2.4; 3.26.

Ἀνταγωνίζομαι, (ἀντί & ἀγωνίζομαι)
    f. ίσομαι,
    to contend, strive against, He. 12.4.

Ἀντάλλαγμα, ατος, τό, (ἀνταλλάσσω, to exchange)
a price paid in exchange for a thing, compensation, ransom, Mat. 16.26. Mar. 8.37.
Ἀνταναπληρόω, ῶ, (ἀντί & ἀναπληρόω)
f. ώσω,
to fill up, complete, supply, Col. 1.24.
Ἀνταποδίδωμι, (ἀντί & ἀποδίδωμι)
f. δώσω, a.2. ἀνταπέδων, a.1. pass. ἀνταπεδόθην,
to repay, requite, recompense, Lu. 14.14. bis. Ro. 11.35; 12.19. 1 Thes. 3.9. 2 Thes. 1.6. He. 10.30: whence
Ἀνταπόδομα, ατος, τό,
requital, recompence, retribution, retaliation, Lu. 14.12. Ro. 11.9. S.
Ἀνταπόδοσις, εως, ἡ,
recompence, reward, Col. 3.24.
Ἀνταποκρίνομαι, (ἀντί & ἀποκρίνομαι)
a.1. ἀνταπεκρίθην,
to answer, speak in answer, Lu. 14.6; to reply against, contradict, dispute, Ro. 9.20. S.
Ἀντεῖπον, inf. ἀντειπεῖν,
see ἀντιλέγω.
Ἀντέχομαι, (ἀντί & ἔχω)
f. ἀνθέξομαι,
to hold firmly, cling or adhere to; to be devoted to any one, Lu. 16.13. Tit. 1.9; to exercise a zealous care for any one, 1 Thes. 5.14.
Ἀντί,
pr. over against; hence, in correspondence to; in place of; in retribution or return for; in consideration of; on account of.
Ἀντιβάλλω, (ἀντί & βάλλω),
pr. to throw or toss from one to another; met. to agitate, converse or discourse about, Lu. 24.17.
Ἀνταδιατίθημι, (ἀντί & διατίθημι)
to oppose; mid. to be of an opposite opinion, to be adverse or averse to, 2 Ti. 2.25. L.G.
Ἀντίδῐκος, ου, ὁ, ἡ, (ἀντί & δίκη)
pr. an opponent in a lawsuit, Mat. 5.25. bis. Lu. 12.58; 18.3; an adversary, 1 Pe. 5.8.
Ἀντίθεσις, εως, ἡ, (ἀντί & τίθημι)
pr. opposition; hence, a question proposed for dispute, disputation, 1 Ti. 6.20.
Ἀντικαθίστημι, (ἀντί & καθίστημι)
f. ήσω,
trans. to set in opposition;
intrans. a.2. ἀντικατέστην, to withstand, resist, He. 12.4.
Ἀντικαλέω, (ἀντί & καλέω)
to invite in return, Lu. 14.12.
Ἀντίκειμαι, (ἀντί & κεῖμαι)
f. είσομαι,
pr. to occupy an opposite position; met. to oppose, be adverse to.
Ἀντικρύ,
adv., opposite to, over against, Ac. 20.15.
Ἀντιλαμβάνομαι, (ἀντιλαμβάνω, to take in turn)
f. λύψομαι,
to aid, assist, help, Lu. 1.54. Ac. 20.35; to be a receipient, 1 Ti. 6.2.
Ἀντιλέγω, (ἀντί & λέγω)

f. λέξω, a.2. ἀντεῖπον,
  to speak against, contradict; gainsay, deny; to oppose, be adverse to, Lu. 2.34; 20.27. Jno. 19.12. Ac. 13.45; 28.19, 22. Ro. 10.21. Tit. 1.9; 2.9.
Ἀντίληψις, εως, ἡ (ἀντιλαμβάνω)
  aid, assistance; *met.* one who aids or assists, a help, 1 Co. 12.28.
Ἀντιλογία, ας, ἡ, (ἀντιλέγω)
  contradiction, question, He. 6.16; 7.7; opposition, rebellion, Jude 11; contumely, He. 12.3.
Ἀντιλοιδορέω, ῶ, (ἀντί & λοιδορέω)
  f. ήσω,
  15to reproach or revile again or in return, 1 Pe. 2.23. L.G.
Ἀντίλυτρον, ου, τὸ, (ἀντί & λύτρον)
  a ransom, 1 Ti. 2.6. N.T.
Ἀντιμετρέω, ῶ, (ἀντί & μετρέω)
  f. ήσω,
  to measure again or in return, Lu. 6.38. Mat. 7.2. N.T.
Ἀντιμισθία, ας, ἡ, (ἀντί & μισθός)
  a retribution, recompence, Ro. 1.27. 2 Co. 6.13. L.G.
Ἀντιπαρέρχομαι, (ἀντί & παρέρχομαι)
  f. ελεύσομαι, a.2. ἦλθον,
  to pass over against, to pass by unnoticed, Lu. 10.31, 32. L.G.
Ἀντιπέραν,
  adv. over against, on the opposite side, Lu. 8.26.
Ἀντιπίπτω, (ἀντί & πίπτω)
  f. πεσοῦμαι,
  pr. to fall upon, rush upon *any one; hence,* to resist by force, oppose, strive against, Ac. 7.51.
Ἀντιστρατεύομαι, (ἀντί & στρατεύω)
  to war against; to contravene, oppose, Ro. 7.23.
Ἀντιτάσσω, (ἀντί & τάσσω)
  f. τάξω,
  to post in adverse array, *as in army; mid.* to set one's self in opposition, resist, Ac. 18.6. Ro. 13.2. Ja. 5.6; to be averse, Ja. 4.6. 1 Pe. 5.5.
Ἀντίτυπος, ου, ὁ, ἡ, (ἀντί & τύπος)
  of correspondent stamp or form, corresponding, similar, 1 Pe. 3.21; τὸ ἀντίτυπον, a copy, He. 9.24.
Ἀντίχριστος, ου, ὁ, (ἀντί & χριστός)
  antichrist, an opposer of Christ, 1 Jno. 2.18, 22; 4.3. 2 Jno. 7.
Ἀντλέω, ῶ (ἄντλος, a sink)
  f. ήσω,
  to draw, e.g. *wine, water,* &c. Jno. 2.8, 9; 4.7, 15: *whence*
Ἄντλημα;, ατος, τό,
  pr. that which is drawn; a bucket, vessel for drawing water, Jno. 4.11. L.G.
Ἀντοφθαλμέω, ῶ, (ἀντί & ὀφθαλμός)
  f. ήσω,
  pr. to look in the face, i.e. *rectis oculis; met. a nautical term,* to bear up against *the wind,* Ac. 27.15. L.G.
Ἄνυδρος, ου, ὁ, ἡ, (ἀ & ὕδωρ)
  without water, dry, 2 Pe. 2.17. Jude 12. τόποι ἄνυδροι, dry places, *and therefore, in the East,* barren, desert, Mat. 12.43. Lu. 11.24.

Ἀνυπόκρῐτος, ου, ὁ, ἡ (ἀ & ὑποκρίνομαι)
    unfeigned, real, sincere, Ro. 12.9, et al. L.G.
Ἀνυπότακτος, ου, ὁ, ἡ, (ἀ & ὑποτάσσω)
    not subjected, not made subordinate, He. 2.8; insubordinate, refractory, disorderly,
    contumacious, lawless, 1 Ti. 1.9. Tit. 1.6, 10. L.G.
Ἄνω,
    adv. above; up, upwards; ὁ, ἡ, τό, ἄνω, that which is above, higher.
Ἀνώγεον, v. ἀνώγαιον, v. ἀνώγεων, v. ἀνάγειον, ου, τό, (ἄνω & γῆ)
    an upper room, or chamber, cœnaculum, Mar. 14.15. Lu. 22.12.
Ἄνωθεν,
    adv. of place, from above, from a higher place; *of time,* from the first or beginning;
    again, anew; *with a preporition,* the top or upper part, Mat. 27.51.
Ἀνωτερικός, ή, όν,
    upper, higher; inland, Ac. 19.1. N.T.
Ἀνώτερος, α, ον, (comp. of ἄνω)
    higher, superior; to a higher place, Lu. 14.10; above, before, He. 10.8. L.G.
Ἄνωφελής, έως, ὁ, ἡ, τό, -ες, (ἀ & ὠφελέω)
    useless, unprofitable, mischievous, Tit. 3.9. He. 7.18.
Ἀξίνη, ης, ἡ,
    an axe, Mat. 3.10. Lu. 3.9. (ῑ)
Ἄξιος, ία, ιον,
    of equal value; worthy, estimable; worthy of, deserving, *either good or evil;*
    correspondent to; comparable to; suitable, due: *whence*
Ἀξιόω, ῶ,
    f. ώσω, p. pass. ἠξίωμαι,
    to judge or esteem worthy or deserving; to deem fitting, to require, Ac. 15.38; 28.22.
Ἀξίως,
    adv. worthily, suitably, properly, in a becoming manner.
Ἀόρᾱτος, ου, ὁ, ἡ, τό, -ον, (ἀ & ὁράω)
    invisible, Ro. 1.20. Co. 1.15, 16, 1 Ti. 1.17. He. 11.27.
Ἀπαγγέλλω, (ἀπό & ἀγγέλλω)
    f. γελῶ, a.1. ἀπήγγειλα, a.2. pass ἀπηγγέλην,
    to enounce that with which a person is charged, or which is called for by
    circumstances; to carry back word; to report; to declare plainly; to announce formally.
Ἀπάγχω, (ἀπό & ἄγχω, to compress)
    f. ἄγξω,
    to strangle; *mid.* to choke or strangle one's self, hang one's self, Mat. 27.5.
Ἀπάγω, (ἀπό & ἄγω)
    16f. ξω, a.2. ἀπήγαγον, a. 2. pass. ἀπήχθην,
    to lead away, conduct; *met.* to seduce.
Ἀπαίδευτος, ου, ὁ, ἡ, (ἀ & παιδεύω)
    uninstructed, ignorant; silly, unprofitable, 2 Ti. 2.23.
Ἀπαίρω, (ἀπό & αἴρω)
    f. αρῶ, a.1. pass. ἀπήρθην, subj. ἀπαρθῶ,
    to take away; *pass.* to be taken away; *in the sense of* departing, Mat. 9.15. Mar. 2.20.
    Lu. 5.35.
Ἀπαιτέω, ῶ, (ἀπό & αἰτέω)
    f. ήσω,
    to demand, require, demand back, Lu. 6.30; 12.20.
Ἀπαλγέω, ῶ, (ἀπό & ἀλγέω, to be in pain, grieve)

f. ήσω, p. ἀπήλγηκα,

    pr. to desist from grief; *hence,* to become insensible or callous, Ep. 4.19.

Ἀπαλλάσσω, (ἀπό & ἀλλάσσω)

    f. ξω, a.1. pass. ἀπηλλάχθην,

    to set free, deliver, set at liberty, He. 2.15; to rid *judicially,* Lu. 12.58; *mid.* to leave, depart, remove from, Ac. 19.12.

Ἀπαλλοτριόω, ῶ, (ἀπό & ἀλλοτριόω, to alienate)

    f. ώσω, p. pass. ἀπηλλοτρίωμαι,

    to alienate; *pass.* to be alienated from, be a stranger to, Ep. 2.12; 4.18. Col. 1.21.

Ἀπαλός, ή, όν,

    soft, tender, Mat. 24.32. Mar. 13.28.

Ἀπαντάω, ῶ, (ἀπό & ἀντάω, to meet)

    f. ήσω,

    to meet, encounter: *whence*

Ἀπάντησις, εως, ἡ,

    a meeting, encounter: εἰς ἀπάντησιν, i.q. ἀπαντᾶν, to meet, Mar. 25.1, 6. Ac. 28.15. 1 Th. 4.17. L.G.

Ἅπαξ,

    adv. once; once for all; actually, in fact, Jude 3, 5.

Ἀπαράβᾰτος, ου, ὁ, ἡ, (ἀ & παραβαίνω)

    not transient; not to be superseded, unchangeable, He. 7.24. L.G.

Ἀπαρασκεύαστος, ου, ὁ, ἡ, (ἀ & παρασκευάζω)

    unprepared, 2 Co. 9.4.

Ἀπαρνέομαι, οῦμαι, (ἀπό & ἀρνέομαι)

    f. ήσομαι, & pass. ἀπαρνηθήσομαι,

    to deny, disown; to renounce, disregard.

Ἀπαρτί, (ἀπό & ἄρτι)

    adv. from this time, henceforth, Jno. 1.52. Re. 14.13; forthwith.

Ἀπαρτισμός, ου, ὁ, (ἀπαρτίζω, to perfect, fr. ἀπό & ἄρτιος)

    completion, perfection, Lu. 14.28. L.G.

Ἀπαρχή, ῆς, ἡ, (ἀπό & ἀρχή)

    pr. the first act of a sacrifice; *hence,* the first-fruits, first portion, firstling. Ro. 8.23, et al.

Ἅπας, ασα, αν, (a strengthened form of πᾶς)

    all, the whole.

Ἀπατάω, ῶ,

    f. ήσω, a.1. pass. ἠπατήθη,

    to deceive, seduce into error, Ep. 5.6. 1 Ti. 2.14. Ja. 1.26: *whence*

Ἀπάτη, ης, ἡ,

    deceit, deception, defusion.

Ἀπάτωρ, ορος, ὁ, ἡ, (ἀ & πατήρ)

    pr. without a father, fatherless; *hence,* independent of paternal descent, He. 7.3. (ἄ)

Ἀπαύγασμα, ατος, τό, (ἀπό & αὐγάζω)

    an effulgence, He. 1.3. L.G.

Ἀπεῖδον,

    subj. ἀπίδω, see ἀφοράω.

Ἀπείθεια, ας, ἡ, (ἀπειθής)

    that disposition of mind which will not be persuaded, which refuses belief and obedience, obstinacy, contumacy, disobedience, unbelief, Ro. 11.30, 32. Ep. 2.2; 5.6. He. 4.6, 11. Col. 3.6.

Ἀπειθέω, ῶ,
  f. ήσω,
  not to suffer one's self to be persuaded; to refuse belief, disbelieve, be incredulous; to refuse obedience through unbelief, disobey; refuse belief and obedience, be contumacious: *from*
Ἀπειθής, έος, οῦς, ὁ, ἡ, (ἀ & πείθω)
  who will not be persuaded, who refuses belief and obedience, unbelieving, disobedient, contumacious.
Ἀπειλέω, ῶ,
  f. ήσω, a.1. ἠπείλησα,
  to threaten, menace, rebuke, Ac. 4.17. 1 Pe. 2.23: *whence*
Ἀπειλή, ῆς, ἡ,
  threat, commination, Ac. 4.17, 29; 9.1; harshness of language, Ep. 6.9.
Ἄπειμι, (ἀπό & εἰμί)
  f. ἔσομαι,
  to be absent.
Ἄπειμι, (ἀπό & εἶμι, to go)
  imperfect, ἀπῆειν,
  to go away, depart, A. 17.10.
Ἀπεῖπον,
  a.2. *act.* to tell out; to refuse, forbid; *mid.* a.1. ἀπειπάμην, to renounce, disclaim, 2. Co. 4.2.
Ἀπείραστος, ου, ὁ, ἡ, (ἀ & πειράζω)
  not having tried, inexperienced, *or,* untried *or,* incapable of being tried, Ja. 1.13. L.G.
Ἄπειρος, ου, ὁ, ἡ, (ἀ & πεῖρα)
  17unexperienced, unskilful, ignorant, He. 5.13.
Ἀπεκδέχομαι, (ἀπό & ἐκδέχομαι)
  f. ἔξομαι,
  to expect, wait or look for, Ro. 8.19, 23, 25. 1 Co. 1.7. Gal. 5.5. Phi. 3.20. He. 9.28. L.G.
Ἀπεκδύομαι, (ἀπό & ἐκδύω)
  f. ύσομαι,
  to put off, strip, divest, renounce, Col. 2.15; 3.9. (L.G.) *whence*
Ἀπέκδυσις, εως, ἡ,
  a putting or stripping off, renunciation, Col. 2.11. N.T.
Ἀπελαύνω, (ἀπό & ἐλαύνω)
  f. ελάσω, a.1. ἀπήλᾶσα,
  to drive away, Ac. 18.16.
Ἀπελεγμός, οῦ, ὁ, (ἀπελέγχω, to refute, fr. ἀπό & ἐλέγχω)
  pr. refutation; *by impl.* disesteem, contempt, disgrace, Ac. 19.27. N.T.
Ἀπελεύθερος, ου, ὁ, ἡ, (ἀπό & ἐλεύθερος)
  a freed-man, 1 Co. 7.22.
Ἀπελπίζω, (ἀπό & ἐλπίζω)
  f. ίσω,
  to lay aside hope, despond, despair; *also,* to hope for something in return, Lu. 6.35. L.G.
Ἀπέναντι, (ἀπό & ἔναντι)
  adv. opposite to, over against, Mat. 21.2; 27.61; contrary to, in opposition to, against, Ac. 17.7; before, in the presence of, Mat. 27.24. Ac. 3.16. L.G.
Ἀπέραντος, ου, ὁ, ἡ, (ἀ & πέρας)

unlimited, interminable, endless, 1 Ti. 1.4.

Ἀπερισπάστως, (ἀ & περισπάω)
    adv. without distraction, without care or solicitude, 1 Co. 7.35. L.G.

Ἀπερίτμητος, ου, ὁ, ἡ, τό, -ον, (ἀ & περιτέμνω)
    pr. uncircumcised; *met.* obdurate, pertinacious, Ac. 7.51. L.G.

Ἀπέρχομαι, (ἀπό & ἔρχομαι)
    f. ελεύσομαι, a.2. ἦλθον,
    to go away, depart; to go forth, pervade, *as a rumour;* to arrive at *a destination;* to pass away, disappear; *in N.T.,* ἀπέρχομαι ὀπίσω, to follow.

Ἀπέχω, (ἀπό & ἔχω)
    f. ἀφέξω,
    trans. to have in full *what is due or is sought; hence, impers.* ἀπέχει, it is enough; *intrans.* to be distant, to be estranged; *mid.* to abstain from.

Ἀπιστέω, ῶ, (ἀ & πίστις)
    f. ήσω,
    to refuse belief, be incredulous, disbelieve; Mar. 16.11, 16. Lu. 24.11, 41. Ac. 28.24; to prove false, violate one's faith, be unfaithful, 2 Ti. 2.13. Ro. 3.3.

Ἀπιστία, ας, ἡ, (fr. same)
    unbelief, want of trust and confidence; a state of unbelief, 1 Ti. 1.13; violation of faith, perfidy, Ro. 3.3. He. 3.12, 19.

Ἄπιστος, ου, ὁ, ἡ, τό, -ον, (ἀ & πιστός)
    unbelieving, incredulous, without confidence *in any one;* violating one's faith, unfaithful, false, treacherous; one who has not embraced the Christian faith, an unbeliever, infidel, pagan; *pass.* incredible, Ac. 26.8.

Ἁπλόος, όη, όον, contr. οὖς, ῆ, οῦν,
    pr. single; *hence,* simple, uncompounded; sound, perfect, Mat. 6.22. Lu. 11.34: *whence*

Ἁπλότης, ητος, ἡ,
    simplicity, sincerity, purity or probity of mind, Ro. 12.8. 2 Co. 1.12; 11.3. Ep. 6.5. Col. 3.22; liberality, *as arising from simplicity and frankness of character,* 2 Co. 8.2; 9.11, 13.

Ἁπλῶς,
    adv. in simplicity; sincerely, really; *or,* liberally, bountifully, Ja. 1.5.

Ἀπὸ,
    prep. *pr.* forth from, away from; *hence it variously signifies* departure; distance of time or place; avoidance; riddance; derivation from a quarter, source, or material; origination from agency or instrumentality.

Ἀποβαίνω, (ἀπό & βαίνω)
    f. βήσομαι, a.2. ἀπέβην,
    to descend *from a ship,* disembark, Lu. 5.2. Jno. 21.9; to become, result, happen, Lu. 21.13. Phi. 1.19.

Ἀποβάλλω, (ἀπό & βάλλω)
    f. βαλῶ, a.2. ἀπέβαλον,
    to cast or throw off, cast aside, Mar. 10.50.

Ἀποβλέπω, (ἀπό & βλέπω)
    f. ψω,
    pr. to look off from all other objects and at a single one; *hence,* to turn a steady gaze, to look with fixed and earnest attention, He. 11.26.

Ἀπόβλητος, ου, ὁ, ἡ, τό, -ον, (ἀποβάλλω)
    pr. to be cast away; *met.* to be contemned, regarded as vile, 1 Ti. 4.4.

Ἀποβολή, ῆς, ἡ, (fr. same)

18a casting off; rejection, reprobation, Ro. 11.15; loss, deprivation, *of life,* &c. Ac. 27.22.

Ἀπογίνομαι, (ἀπό & γίνομαι)

a.2. ἀπεγενόμην,

to be away from, unconnected with; to die; *met.* to die to, or renounce, *any thing,* 1 Pe. 2.24.

Ἀπογρᾰφή, ῆς, ἡ,

a register, inventory; registration, enrolment, Lu. 2.2. Ac. 5.37: *from*

Ἀπογράφω, (ἀπό & γράφω)

f. ψω,

pr. to copy; *hence,* to register, enrol; *mid.* to procure the registration of one's name, to give in one's name for registration, Lu. 2.1, 3, 5.

Ἀποδείκνῡμι,

f. δείξω,

to point out, display; prove, evince, demonstrate, Ac. 25.7; to designate, proclaim, hold forth, 2 Thes. 2.4; to constitute, appoint, Ac. 2.22; 1 Co. 4.9. 2 Thes. 2.4: *whence*

Ἀπόδειξις, εως, ἡ,

manifestation, demonstration, indubitable proof, 1 Co. 2.4.

Ἀποδεκατόω, ῶ (ἀπό & δεκατόω)

to pay or give tithes of, Mat. 23.23. Lu. 11.42; 18.12; to tithe, levy tithes upon, He. 7.5. S.

Ἀπόδεκτος, ου, ὁ, ἡ, τό, -ον,

acceptable, 1 Ti. 2.3; 5.4. (L.G.): *from*

Ἀποδέχομαι, (ἀπό & δέχομαι)

f. δέξομαι,

to receive *kindly* or *heartily,* welcome, Lu. 8.40. Ac. 15.4; 18.27; 28.30; to receive with approbation, assent to approve, Ac. 2.41; to accept with satisfaction, applaud, Ac. 24.3.

Ἀποδημέω, ῶ,

f. ήσω,

to be absent from one's home or country; to travel into foreign countries, Mat. 21.33; 25.14, 15. Mar. 12.1. Lu. 15.13; 20.9: *from*

Ἀπόδημος, ου, ὁ, ἡ, (ἀπό & δῆμος)

absent in foreign countries, Mar. 13.34.

Ἀποδίδωμι, (ἀπό & δίδωμι)

f. δώσω,

to render that on which there is a claim, or which is looked for; to render in full; to give back, restore, refund; render back, requite, retaliate; pay a debt; discharge an obligation, perform whatever is to be performed; *mid.* to sell.

Ἀποδιορίζω, (ἀπό & διορίζω, to set bounds)

f. ίσω,

pr. to separate by intervening boundaries; to separate, Jude 19. N.T.

Ἀποδοκιμάζω, (ἀπό & δοκιμάζω)

f. άσω,

to reject upon trial, to reject, Mat. 21.42. Mar. 12.10. Lu. 20.17. 1 Pe. 2.4, 7; to repulse, refuse credence or admittance, disallow, Lu. 9.22; 17.25. He. 12.17.

Ἀποδοχή, ῆς, ἡ (ἀποδέχομαι)

pr. reception, welcome; *met.* cordial assent, 1 Ti. 1.15; 4.9.

Ἀπόθεσις, εως, ἡ (ἀποτίθημι)

a putting off or away, laying aside, 1 Pe. 3.21. 2 Pe. 1.14.

Ἀποθήκη, ης, ἡ, (fr. same)
a place where any thing is laid up for preservation, repository, granary, storehouse, barn, Mat. 3.12; 6.26; 13.30. Lu. 3.17; 12.18, 24.

Ἀποθησαυρίζω, (ἀπό & θησαυρίζω)
f. ίσω,
pr. to lay up in store, hoard; met. to collect abundantly, treasure up, 1 Ti. 6.19. L.G.

Ἀποθλίβω, (ἀπό & θλίβω)
f. ψω,
pr. to press out; to press close, press upon, crowd, Lu. 8.45. (ῑ).

Ἀποθνήσκω, (ἀπό & θνήσκω)
f. θανοῦμαι, a.2. ἔθανον,
to die; to become putrescent, rot, as seeds, Jno. 12.24. 1 Co. 15.36; to wither, become dry, as a tree, Jude 12; met. to be obnoxious to condemnation and punishment, be exposed to misery or the second death, Jno. 6.50; 8.21, 24; to die to any thing, i.e. to renounce, refuse submission to, be completely severed from, Ro. 6.2. Gal. 2.19. Col. 3.3.

Ἀποκαθίστημι, v. ἀποκαθιστάνω, (ἀπό & καθίστημι)
f. στήσω, a.1. pass. ἀποκατεστάθη,
to restore any thing to its former place or state, Mat. 12.13; 17.11. Mar. 3.5; 8.25, et al.

Ἀποκαλύπτω, (ἀπό & καλύπτω)
f. ψω,
pr. to uncover, bring to light what was hidden; to reveal; to set in clear light; to display; pass. to be manifested, appear: whence

Ἀποκάλυψις, εως, ἡ,
a disclosure, revelation; met. illumination, instruction; manifestation, appearance. L.G.

Ἀποκαρᾱδοκία, ας, ἡ, (ἀπό & καραδοκέω, to watch with the head stretched out, to keep an eager lookout; fr. κάρα, the head, and δοκεύω to watch)
earnest expectation, hope, Ro. 8.19. Phi. 1.20. N.T.

Ἀποκαταλλάσσω, (ἀπό & καταλλάσσω)
19f. ξω,
to transfer from a certain state to another which is quite different; hence, to reconsile, restore to favour, Ep. 2.16. Col. 1.20, 21. N.T.

Ἀποκατάστᾰσις, εως, ἡ, (ἀποκαθίστημι)
pr. a restitution or restoration of any thing to its former state; hence, change from worse to better, melioration, introduction of a new and better era, Ac. 3.21.

Ἀπόκειμαι, (ἀπό & κεῖμαι)
f. είσομαι,
to be laid up, preserved, Lu. 19.20; to be in store for, be reserved, await any one, Col. 1.5. 2 Ti. 4.8. He. 9.27.

Ἀποκεφαλίζω, (ἀπό & κεφαλή)
f. ίσω,
to behead, Mat. 14.10. Mar. 6.16, 28. Lu. 9.9.

Ἀποκλείω, (ἀπό & κλείω)
to close, shut up, Lu. 13.25.

Ἀποκόπτω, (ἀπό & κόπτω)
f. ψω,
to cut off, amputate, Mar. 9.43, 45. Jno. 18.10, 26. Ac. 27.32. Gal. 5.12.

Ἀπόκρῐμα, ατος, τό,
    a judicial sentence, 2 Co. 1.9: (L.G.) *from*
Ἀποκρίνομαι, (ἀποκρίνω, to separate, fr. ἀπό & κρίνω)
    a.1. ἀπεκρινάμην & ἀπεκρίθην, f. ἀποκριθήσομαι,
    to answer; *in N.T.,* to speak with reference to certain present circumstances, Mat.
    11.23, et al.: *whence*
Ἀπόκρῐσις, εως, ἡ,
    an answer, reply, Lu. 2.47; 20.26. Jno. 1.22; 19.9.
Ἀποκρύπτω, (ἀπό & κρύπτω)
    f. ψω,
    to hide away; to conceal, withhold from sight or knowledge, Mat. 11.25; 25.18, et
    al.:*whence*
Ἀπόκρῠφος, ου, ὁ, ἡ, τό, -ον,
    hidden away; concealed, Mar. 4.22. Lu. 8.17; stored up, Col. 2.3.
Ἀποκτείνω, (ἀπό & κτείνω)
    f. κτενῶ, a.1. pass. ἀπεκτόηθην,
    to kill, put to death, murder, destroy, annihilate.
Ἀποκυέω, ῶ, (ἀπό & κυέω)
    f. ήσω,
    pr. to bring forth, *as women; met.* to be the cause of, produce, Ja. 1.15; to be the
    author of spiritual generation, Ja. 1.18. L.G.
Ἀποκυλίω, (ἀπό & κυλίω)
    f. ίσω,
    to roll away, Mat. 28.2. Mar. 16.3, 4. Lu. 24.2. (ῑ) L.G.
Ἀπολαμβάνω, (ἀπό & λαμβάνω)
    f. λήψομαι, a.2. ἔλαβον,
    to receive in full, Lu 16.25; to receive what is due, sought, or needed; to receive back,
    recover; to receive in hospitality, welcome, 3 Jno. 8; to take aside, lead away, Mar.
    7.33.
Ἀπόλαυσις, εως, ἡ, (ἀπολαύω, to obtain a portion *of a thing,* enjoy)
    beneficial participation, 1 Ti. 6.17; enjoyment, pleasure, He. 11.25.
Ἀπολείπω, (ἀπό & λείπω)
    to leave, leave behind; *pass.* to be left, remain, 2 Ti. 4.13, 20. He. 4.6, 9; 10.26; to
    relinquish, forsake, desert, Jude 6.
Ἀπολείχω, (ἀπό & λείχω, to lick)
    f. ξω,
    pr. to lick off; to cleanse by licking, lick clean, Lu. 16.21. L.G.
Ἀπόλλῡμι, (ἀπό & ὄλλυμι)
    f. ολέσω, & ολῶ, a.1. ἀπώλεσα, p. ἀπολώλεκα,
    to destroy utterly; to kill; to bring to nought, render vain, 1 Co. 1.19; to lose, be
    deprived of; *mid.* ἀπόλλῡμαι, f. ολοῦμαι, a.2. ἀπωλόμην, p. ἀπόλωλα, to be destroyed,
    perish; to be put to death, die; to be lost, wander, Mat. 10.6; 15.24.
Ἀπολλύων, οντος, ὁ,
    Apollyon, the destroyer, i.q. Ἀβαδδών, Re. 9.11. N.T.
Ἀπολογέομαι, οῦμαι, (ἀπό & λόγος)
    f. ήσομαι, a.1. ἀπελογησάμην & ἀπελογήθην
    to defend one's self against a charge, to make a defence, Lu. 12.11; 21.14, et al.:
    whence
Ἀπολογια, ας, ἡ,
    a verbal defence, Ac. 22.1; 25.16, et al.

Ἀπολούω, (ἀπό & λούω)
f. ούσω,
to cleanse by bathing; *mid.* to cleanse one's self; to procure one's self to be cleansed; *met. of sin,* Ac. 22.16. 1 Co. 6.11.

Ἀπολύτρωσις, εως, ἡ, (ἀπολυτρόω, to dismiss any one for a ransom paid, fr. ἀπό & λυτρόω) redemption, a deliverance procured by the payment of a ransom; *meton.* a redeemer, the author of redemption, 1 Co. 1.30; deliverance, *simply, the idea of a ransom being excluded,* Lu. 21.28. He. 11.35. N.T.

Ἀπολύω, (ἀπό & λύω)
f. ύσω,
pr. to loose; to release from any tie or burden; *hence,* to give liberty, riddance, forgiveness; to divorce; 20to allow to depart; to permit, *or,* signal a departure from life, Lu. 2.29; *mid.* to depart. (ῡ).

Ἀπομάσσω, (ἀπό & μάσσω, to wipe)
f. ξω,
to wipe off; *mid.* to wipe off one's self, Lu. 10.11.

Ἀπονέμω, (ἀπό & νέμω, to allot)
f. νεμῶ,
to portion off; to assign, bestow, 1 Pe. 3.7.

Ἀπονίπτω, (ἀπό & νίπτω)
f. ψω,
to cleanse *a part of the body* by washing; *mid. of one's self,* Mat. 27.24.

Ἀποπίπτω, (ἀπό & πίπτω)
f. πεσοῦμαι, a.2. ἀπέπεσον,
to fall off, or from, Ac. 9.18.

Ἀποπλανάω, ῶ, (ἀπό & πλανάω)
f. ήσω,
to cause to wander; *met.* to deceive, pervert, seduce, seduce, Mar. 13.22; *pass.* to wander; *met.* to swerve from, apostatise, 1 Ti. 6.10.

Ἀποπλέω, (ἀπό & πλέω)
f. πλεύσομαι, a.1. ἀπέπλευσα,
to depart by ship, sail away, Ac. 13.4; 14.26; 20.15; 27.1.

Ἀποπλύνω, (ἀπό & πλύνω)
f. υνῶ,
to wash, rinse, Lu. 5.2. (ῡ).

Ἀποπνίγω, (ἀπό & πνίγω)
f. ξω, a.2. pass. ἀπεπνίγην,
to choke, suffocate, Mat. 13.7. Lu. 8.33; to drown, Lu. 8.7. (ῑ).

Ἀπορέω, ῶ, (ἀ & πόρος, a way)
f. ήσω, & ἀπορέομαι,
pr. to be without means; *met.* to hesitate, be at a stand, be in doubt and perplexity, Jno. 13.22. Ac. 25.20. 2 Co. 4.8. Gal. 4.20: *whence*

Ἀπορία, ας, ἡ
doubt, uncertainty, perplexity, Lu. 21.25.

Ἀπορρίπτω, (ἀπό & ῥίπτω)
f. ψω,
to throw off, Ac. 27.43.

Ἀπορφανίζω, (ἀπό & ὄρφανος)
f. ίσω,
to deprive, dereave, 1 Thes. 2.17.

Ἀποσκευάζομαι, (ἀπό & σκευάζω to pack up articles, σκεύη, for removal)
f. άσομαι,
to prepare for a journey, take one's departure, Ac. 21.15.
Ἀποσκίασμα, ατος, τό, (ἀπό & σκίαζο, to throw a shadow, fr. σκιά)
a shadow cast; *met.* the slightest trace, Ja. 1.17. L.G.
Ἀποσπάω, ῶ, (ἀπό & σπάω)
f. άσω,
to draw away from, to draw out or forth, Mat. 26.51; to draw away, seduce, Ac. 20.30.
mid. a.1. ἀπεσπάσθην, to separate one's self, to retire, part, Lu. 22.41. Ac. 21.1. (ἄ)
Ἀποστασία, ας, ἡ (ἀφίστημι)
a defection, apostasy; Ac. 21.21. 2 Thes. 2.3. L.G.
Ἀποστάσιον, ίου, τό, (fr. same)
defection, desertion, *as of a freedman from a patron; in N.T.,* the act of putting away a wife, repudiation, divorce, Mat. 19.7. Mar. 10.4, *meton.* a bill of repudiation, deed of divorce, Mat. 5.31.
Ἀποστεγάζω, (ἀπό & στέγη)
f. άσω,
to remove or break through a covering or roof of a place, Mar. 2.4.
Ἀποστέλλω, (ἀπό & στέλλω)
f. στελλῶ, a.1. ἀπέστειλα, p. ἀπέσταλκα, p. pass. ἀπέσταλμαι, a.2. pass. ἀπεστάλην,
to send forth *a messenger, agent, message, or command;* to issue, publish; put forth into action, Mar. 4.29; to despatch; to liberate, dismiss, send away.
Ἀποστερέω, ῶ, (ἀπό & στερέω, to deprive)
f. ήσω, p. pass. ἀπεστέρημαι,
to deprive, detach; to debar, 1 Co. 7.5; to deprive *in a bod sense,* defraud, Mar. 10.19.
1 Co. 6.7. *mid.* to suffer one's self to be deprived or defrauded, 1 Co. 6.8; *pass.* to be destitute or devoid of, 1 Ti. 6.5; to be unjustly withheld, Ja. 5.4.
Ἀποστολή, ῆς, ἡ, (ἀποστέλλω)
a sending, expedition; office or duty of one sent as a messenger or agent; office of an apostle, apostleship, Ac. 1.25. Ro. 1.5. 1 Co. 9.2. Gal. 2.8.
Ἀπόστολος, ου, ὁ, (fr. same)
one sent as a messenger or agent, the bearer of a commission, messenger; an apostle.
Ἀποστοματίζω, (ἀπό & στόμα)
f. ίσω,
pr. to speak or repeat off hand; *also,* to require or lead others to speak without premeditation, *as by questions calculated to elicit unpremeditated answer,* to endeavour to entrap into unguarded language, Lu. 11.53.
Ἀποστρέφω, (ἀπό & στρέφω)
f. ψω,
to turn away; to remove, Ac. 3.26. Ro. 11.26. 2 Ti. 4.4; to turn *a people from their allegiance to their sovereign,* pervert, incite to revolt, Lu. 23.14; to replace, restore, Mat. 26.52; 27.3; *mid.* a.2. ἀπεστράφην, 21to turn away from any one, to slight, reject, repulse, Mat. 5.42. Tit. 1.14. Heb. 12.25; to desert, 2 Ti. 1.15.
Ἀποστὕγέω, ῶ, (ἀπό & στυγέω, to hate)
f. ήσω,
to shrink from with abhorrence, detest, Ro. 12.9.
Ἀποσυνάγωγος, ου, ὁ, ἡ, (ἀπό & συναγωγή)
expelled or excluded from the synagogue, excommunicated, cut off from the rights and privileges of a Jew, and excluded from society, Jno. 9.22; 12.42; 16.2. N.T.
Ἀποτάσσομαι, (ἀποτάσσω, to set apart, fr. ἀπό & τάσσω)

f. ξομαι,
to take leave of, bid farewell to, Lu. 9.61. Ac. 18.18, 21. 2 Co. 2.13; to dismiss, send away, Mar. 6.46; to renounce, forsake, Lu. 14.33.

Ἀποτελέω, ῶ, (ἀπό & τελέω)
f. έσω, a.1. pass ἀπετελέσθην,
to complete; *pass.* to be perfected, to arrive at full stature or measure, Ja. 1.15.

Ἀποτίθημι, (ἀπό & τίθημι)
f. θήσω, & mid. ἀποτίθεμαι, a.2. ἀπεθέμην,
to lay off, lay down or aside, *as garments,* Ac. 7.58; *met.* to lay aside, put off, renounce, Ro. 13.12. Ep. 4.22, 25. Col. 3.8, et al.

Ἀποτινάσσω, (ἀπό & τινάσσω, to shake)
f. ξω,
to shake off, Lu. 9.5. Ac. 28.5.

Ἀποτίνω, (ἀπό & τίνω)
f. ίσω,
to pay off *what is claimed or due;* to repay, refund, make good, Phile. 19.

Ἀποτολμάω, ῶ, (ἀπό & τολμάω)
f. ήσω,
to dare or risk outright; to speak without reserve or restraint, Ro. 10.20.

Ἀποτομία, ας, ἡ, (ἀπότομος, cut off, shear, fr. ἀποτέμνω, to cut off, fr. ἀπό & τέμνω)
pr. abruptness; *met.* unmitigated severity, rigour, Ro. 11.22. L.G.

Ἀποτόμως,
adv. sharply, severely, 2 Co. 13.10. Tit. 1.13.

Ἀποτρέπω, (ἀπό & τρέπω)
f. ψω,
to turn *any one* away *from a thing; mid.* to turn one's self away *from any one;* to avoid, shun, 2 Ti. 3.5.

Ἀπουσία, ας, ἡ, (ἄπειμι)
absence, Phi. 2.12.

Ἀποφέρω, (ἀπό & φέρω)
f. ἀποίσω, a.1. ήνεγκα, a.2. ήνεγκον, a.1. pass. ηνέχθην,
to bear or carry away, conduct away, Mar. 15.1. Lu. 16.22. 1 Co. 16.3. Re. 17.3; 21.10.

Ἀποφεύγω, (ἀπό & φεύγω)
f. ξομαι, a.2. ἀπέφυγον,
to flee from, escape; *met.* to renounce, be free from. 2 Pe. 1.4; 2.18, 20.

Ἀποφθέγγομαι, (ἀπό & φθέγγομαι)
f. έγξομαι,
to speak out, declare, *particularly solemn, weighty, or pithy sayings,* Ac. 2.4, 14; 26.25. L.G.

Ἀποφορτίζομαι, (ἀπό & φόρτος)
f. ίσομαι,
to unlade, Ac. 21.3. L.G.

Ἀπόχρησις, εως, ἡ, (ἀποχράομαι, to use up, consume by use)
a using, *or* a discharge of an intended use, Col. 2.22. L.G.

Ἀποχωρέω, ῳ (ἀπό & χωρέω)
f. ήσω,
to go from or away, depart, Mat. 7.23. Lu. 9.39. Ac. 13.13.

Ἀποχωρίζω, (ἀπό & χωρίζω)
f. ίσω, a.1. pass. ἀπεχωρίσθην,

to separate; *pass.* to be swept aside, Re. 6.14; to part, Ac. 15.39.

Ἀποψύχω, (ἀπό & ψύχω)

f. ξω,

pr. to breathe out, faint away, die; *met.* to faint at heart, be dismayed, Lu. 21.26. (ῡ).

Ἀπρόσῐτος, ου, ὁ, ἡ, τό, -ον, (ἀ & προσιτός, accessible, fr. πρόσειμι, to approach) unapproached, unapproachable, 1 Ti. 6.16. L.G.

Ἀπρόσκοπος, ου, ὁ, ἡ, (ἀ & προσκοπή)

act. not causing to stumble; *met.* not causing others to stumble in the path of duty, 1 Co. 10.32; *pass.* not stumbling, advancing without stumbling; *met.* not obnoxious to moral exception, unblameble, clear, Ac. 24.16. Phi. 1.10. N.T.

Ἀπροσωπολήπτως, (ἀ & προσωποληπτέω)

adv. without respect of persons, impartially, 1 Pe. 1.17. N.T.

Ἄπταιστος, ου, ὁ, ἡ, (ἀ & πταίω)

free from stumbling; *met.* free from offence and sin; irreprehensible, Jude 24.

Ἅπτω,

f. ψω,

pr. to bring in contact, fit, fasten; to light, kindle; *mid.* ἅπτομαι, f. ψομαι, a.1. ἡψάμην, to touch; to partake, Col. 2.21; to have intercourse with; to know carnally, 1 Co. 7.1; *by impl.* to harm, 1 Jno. 5.18.

Ἀπωθέω, ῶ, (ἀπό & ὠθέω, to thrust)

f. ωθήσω & ώσω, & mid. ἀπωθέομαι, οῦμαι, a.1. ἀπωσάμην, 22to thrust away, repel from one's self, repulse, Ac. 7.27; to refuse, reject, cast off, Ac. 7.39; 13.46. Ro. 11.1, 2. 1 Ti. 1.19.

Ἀπώλεια, ας, ἡ, (ἀπόλλυμι)

consumption, destruction; waste, profusion, Mat. 26.8. Mar. 14.4; destruction, state of being destroyed, Ac. 25.16; perdition, misery, eternal ruin, Mat. 7.13. Ac. 8.20, et al.

Ἄρα

This particle denotes, first, transition from one thing to another by natural sequence; secondly, logical inference; in which case the premises are either expressed, Mat. 12.28, *or to be variously supplied.* Therefore, then, consequently; should it so result. Ac. 17.27.

Ἆρα,

a stronger form of the preceding, used in interrogations.

Ἀρά, ᾶς, ἡ,

pr. a prayer; *more commonly* a prayer for evil; curse, cursing, imprecation, Ro. 3.14.

Ἀργέω, ῶ

f. ήσω,

pr. to be unemployed; to be inoperative, linger, 2 Pe. 2.3: *from*

Ἀργός, ή, όν, (ἀ & ἔργον) *contr. fr.* ἀεργός,

pr. inactive, unemployed, Mat. 20.3, 6; idle, averse from labour, 1 Ti. 5.13. Tit. 1.12; *met.* 2 Pe. 1.8; unprofitable, hollow, *or by impl.* injurious, Mat. 12.36.

Ἀργύρεος, έα, εον, contr. οῦς, ᾶ, οῦν, (ἄργυρος)

made of silver, Ac. 19.24. 2 Ti. 2.20. Re. 9.20.

Ἀργύριον, ίου, τό, (fr. same)

silver; *meton.* money; *spc.* a piece of silver money, a shekel.

Ἀργυροκόπος, ου, ὁ, (same & κόπτω)

a forger of silver, silversmith, Ac. 19.24. L.G.

Ἄργῠρος, ου, ὁ,

silver; *meton.* any thing made of silver; money.

Ἀρειοπαγίτης,

a judge of the court of Areopagus. (ῑ).

Ἄρειος, ου, ὁ, ἡ, (Ἄρης, Mars)
 of or belonging to Mars, Ac. 17.19, 22.

Ἀρεσκεία, ας, ἡ
 a pleasing, desire of pleasing, Col. 1.10: *from*

Ἀρέσκω,
 f. ἀρέσω, imperf. ἤρεσκον, a.1. ἤρεσα,
 to please; to be pleasing, acceptable; to consult the pleasure of: *whence*

Ἀρεστός, ή, όν,
 pleasing, acceptable, 1 Jno. 3.22; Jno. 8.29; Ac. 12.3; deemed proper, Ac. 6.2.

Ἀρετή, ῆς, ἡ,
 goodness, good quality *of any kind;* gracious dealing *of God,* 1 Pe. 2.9; 2 Pe. 1.3; virtue, uprightness, Phi. 4.8. 2 Pe. 1.5.

Ἀριθμέω, ῶ,
 f. ήσω, a.1. ἠρίθμησα, p. pass. ἠρίθμημαι,
 to number, Mat. 10.30. Lu. 12.7. Re. 7.9: *from*

Ἀριθμός, οῦ, ὁ,
 a number, Lu. 22.3. Jno. 6.10. Ac. 4.4. Re. 20.8; 13.18.

Ἀριστάω, ῶ (ἄριστον)
 f. ήσω, a.1. ἠρίστησα,
 to take the first meal, breakfast, Jno. 21.12, 15; *also,* to take a midday meal, Lu. 11.37.

Ἀριστερός, ά, όν,
 the left; ἀριστερά, sc. χείρ, the left hand, Mat. 6.3; *so* ἐξ ἀριστερῶν sc. μερῶν, Lu. 23.33. 2 Co. 6.7.

Ἄριστον, ου, τό,
 pr. the first meal, breakfast; *afterwards extended to signify also* a slight midday meal, luncheon, Mat. 22.4.

Ἀρκετός, ή, όν,
 sufficient, enough, Mat. 6.34; 10.25; 1 Pe. 4.3: *from*

Ἀρκέω, ῶ,
 f. ήσω, a.1. ἤρκεσα,
 pr. to ward off; *thence,* to be of service, avail; to suffice, be enough; *pass.* to be contented, satisfied, Lu. 3.14. 1 Ti. 6.8. He. 13.5. 3 Jno. 10.

Ἄρκος,
 v.r. for the following.

Ἄρκτος, ου, ὁ, ἡ,
 a bear, Re. 13.2.

Ἅρμα, ατος, τό,
 a chariot, vehicle, Ac. 8.28, 29, 38.

Ἁρμόζω,
 f. όσω,
 to fit together; *mid.* ἁρμόζομαι, a.1. ἡρμοσάμην, to join, unite, *in marriage,* espouse, betroth, 2 Co. 11.2.

Ἁρμός, οῦ, ὁ,
 a joint or articulation *of the bones,* He. 4.12.

Ἀρνέομαι, οῦμαι,
 f. ήσομαι, p. ἤρνημαι, a.1. ἠρνησάμην,
 to deny, contradict, affirm not to be; *by impl.* to reject, renounce, disown; to be unwilling, refuse, He. 11.24.

Ἀρνίον, ου, τό,

    a young lamb, lambkin, lamb, Jno. 21.15. Re. 5.6, 8.

Ἀρνός,

    a gen. without a nom. in use, its place being supplied by ἀμνός, *a lamb.*

Ἀροτριάω, ῶ,

    f. άσω,

    to plough, Lu. 17.7. 1 Co. 9.10: *from*

Ἄροτρον, ου, τό (ἀρόω, to plough)

    23a plaugh, Lu. 9.62.

Ἁρπᾰγν, ῆς, ἡ (ἁρπάζω)

    plunder, pillage, rapine; the act of plundering, He. 10.34; prey, spoil, *or,* rapacity, Mat. 23.25. Lu. 11.39.

Ἁρπαγμός, οῦ, ὁ

    rapine, robbery, thing plundered; *met. & meton.* what is retained with an eager grasp, or eagerly claimed and conspicuously exercised, Phi. 2.6: *from*

Ἁρπάζω,

    f. άσω & ξω, a.1. ἥρπασα, a.1. pass. ἡρπάσθην, a.2. pass. ἡρπάγην,

    to seize, *as a wild beast,* Jno. 10.12; take away by force, snatch away, Mat. 13.19. Jno. 10.28, 29. Ac. 23.10. Jude 23; *met.* to seize on with avidity, claim, vindicate one's right, Mat. 11.12; to convey away suddenly, transport hastily, Jno. 6.15, et al.

Ἅρπαξ, ᾰγος, ὁ, ἡ, τό,

    pr. ravenous, ravening, *as a wild beast,* Mat. 7.15; *met.* rapacious, given to extortion and robbery, an extortioner, Lu. 18.11. 1 Co. 5.10, 11; 6.10.

Ἀῤῥᾰβών, ῶνος, ὁ, (Hebrew, זוברן)

    a pledge, earnest, 2 Co. 1.22; 5.5. Ep. 1.14.

Ἄῤῥᾰφος, ου, ὁ, ἡ, (ἀ & ῥάπτω, to sew)

    not sewed, without seam, Jno. 19.23. N.T.

Ἄῤῥην, ἄῤῥεν, ενος, ὁ, τό,

    male, of the male sex, Ro. 1.27. Re. 12.5, 13.

Ἄῤῥητος, ου, ὁ, ἡ, τό, -ον, (ἀ & ῥητός)

    pr. not spoken; what ought not to be spoken, secret; which cannot be spoken or uttered, ineffable, 2 Co. 12.4.

Ἄῤῥωστος, ου, ὁ, ἡ, (ἀ & ῥώννυμι)

    infirm, sick, an invalid, Mat. 14.14. Mar. 6.5, 13; 16.18. 1 Co. 11.30.

Ἀρσενοκοίτης, ου, ὁ, (ἄρσην & κοίτη)

    one who lies with a male, a sodomite, 1 Co. 6.9. 1 Ti. 1.10. L.G.

Ἄρσην, ἄρσεν, ενος, ὁ, τό,

    male, of the male sex, Mat. 19.4. Mar. 10.6. Lu. 2.23. Ro. 1.27. Gal. 3.28.

Ἄρτεμις, ιδος, ἡ,

    Artemis or Diana, Ac. 19.24, 27, 28, 34.

Ἀρτέμων, ονος, ὁ, (ἀρτάω, to suspend)

    a topsail, artemon, supparum; *or, according to others,* the dolon of Pliny and Pollux, a small sail near the prow of the ship, which was hoisted when the wind was too strong to use larger sails, Ac. 27.40. N.T.

Ἄρτι

    adv. of time, pr. at the present moment, close upon at *either before or after;* now, at the present juncture, Mat. 3.15; forthwith, presently, just now, recently, already, 1 Thes. 3.6; ἕως ἄρτι, until now, hitherto, Mat. 11.12. Jno. 2.10, et al.; ἀπ' ἄρτι, v. ἀπάρτι, from this time, henceforth, Mat. 23.39. et al.

Ἀρτιγέννητος, ου, ὁ, ἡ, (ἄρτι & γεννάω)

just born, new-born, 1 Pe. 2.2. L.G.

Ἄρτιος, ου, ὁ, ἡ, (ἄρω, to fit, adapt)
    complete, perfect, 2 Ti. 3.17.

Ἄρτος, ου, ὁ,
    bread; a loaf or thin cake of bread, Mat. 26.26, et al.; food, Mat. 15.2. Mar. 3.20, et al.; support, maintenance, living, necessaries of life, Mat. 6.11. Lu. 11.3. 2 Thes. 3.8.

Ἀρτύω, v. ἀρτύνω, (ἄρω, to fit)
    f. ύσω, f. pass. ἀρτυθήσομαι, p. pass. ἤρτυμαι,
    pr. to fit, prepare; to season, make savoury, Mar. 9.50. Lu. 14.34. Col. 4.6.

Ἀρχάγγελος, ου, ὁ, (ἀρχι- & ἄγγελος)
    an archangel, chief angel, 1 Thes. 4.16. Jude 9. N.T.

Ἀρχαῖος, αία, αῖον,
    old, ancient, of a former age, Mat. 5.21, 27, 33, et al.: from

Ἀρχή, ῆς, ἡ,
    a beginning; in respect of time, beginning of things; commencement of the gospel dispensation; of place, first place or precedence in rank or power, sovereignty; one invested with authority, a magistrate, potentate, prince; an extremity, corner, Ac. 10.11. Τὴν ἀρχήν, used adverbially, wholly, altogether, Jno. 8.25.

Ἀρχηγός, ου, ὁ, (ἀρχή & ἄγω)
    a chief, leader, prince, sovereign, Ac. 5.31; author, efficient cause, Ac. 3.15. He. 2.10; 12.2.

Ἀρχιερατικός, ή, όν,
    pontifical, belonging to, or connected with the high priest or his office, Ac. 4.6: (N.T.) from

Ἀρχιερεύς, έως, ὁ, (ἀρχι- & ἱερεύς)
    a high priest, chief priest.

Ἀρχιποίμην, ενος, ὁ, (ἀρχι- & ποιμήν)
    chief shepherd, 1 Pe. 5.4 N.T.

Ἀρχισυναγώγος, ου, ὁ, (ἀρχι- & συναγωγή)
    24a president or moderating elder of a synagogue, Mar. 5.22, 35, 36, 38. Lu. 8.49, et al. N.T.

Ἀρχιτέκτων, ονος, ὁ, (ἀρχι- & τέκτων)
    architech, head or masterbuilder, 1 Co. 3.10

Ἀρχιτελώνης, ου, ὁ, (ἀρχι- & τελώνης)
    a chief publican, chief collector of the customs or taxes, Lu. 19.2. N.T.

Ἀρχιτρίκλῑνος, ου, ὁ, (ἀρχι- & τρίκλινος, triclinium, a dining-room in which three couches were placed round the table, &c.)
    director of a feast, Jno. 2.8, 9. N.T.

Ἄρχω,
    f. ξω,
    pr. to be first; to reign, govern; mid. to begin; to attempt; to take commencement.

Ἄρχων, οντος, ὁ,
    one invested with power and dignity, chief, ruler, prince, magistrate, Mat. 9.23; 20.25, et al. freq.

Ἄρωμα, ατος, τό,
    any aromatic substance, spice, &c. Mar. 16.1. Lu. 23.56; 24.1. Jno. 19.40.

Ἀσάλευτος, ου, ὁ, ἡ, τό, -ον, (ἀ & σαλεύω)
    unshaken, immoveable, Ac. 27.41; met. firm, stable, enduring, He. 12.28.

Ἄσβεστος, ου, ὁ, ἡ, τό, -ον, (ἀ & σβέννυμι)
    unquenched; inextinguishable; unquenchable, Mat. 3.12. Mar. 9.43, 45. Lu. 3.17.

Ἀσέβεια, ας, ἡ, (ἀσεβής)

    impiety, ungodliness; improbity, wickedness, Ro. 1.18; 11.26. 2 Ti. 2.16. Tit. 2.12. Jude 15, 18.

Ἀσεβέω, ῶ,

    f. ήσω, p. ἠσέβηκα, a.1. ἠσέβησα,

    to be impious, to act impiously or wickedly, live an impious life, 2 Pe. 2.6. Jude 15: *from*

Ἀσεβής, έος, οὖς, ὁ, ἡ, τό, -ές, (ἀ & σέβομαι)

    impious, ungodly; wicked, sinful, Ro. 4.5; 5.6, et al.

Ἀσέλγεια, ας, ἡ, (ἀσέλγης, outrageous)

    intemperance, licentiousness, lasciviousness, Ro. 13.13, et al.; insolence, outrageous behaviour, Mar. 7.22.

Ἀσήμος, ου, ὁ, ἡ, (ἀ & σῆμα)

    pr. not marked; *met.* not noted, not remarkable, unknown to fame, ignoble, mean, inconsiderable, Ac. 21.39.

Ἀσθένεια, ας, ἡ, (ἀσθενής)

    want of strength, weakness, feebleness, 1 Co. 15.43; bodily infirmity, state of ill health, sickness, Mat. 8.17. Lu. 5.15, et al.; *met.* infirmity, frailty, imperfection, *intellectual or moral,* Ro. 6.19. 1 Co. 2.3. He. 5.2; 7.28; *by impl.* suffering, affliction, distress, calamity, Ro. 8.26, et al.

Ἀσθενέω, ῶ, (fr. same)

    f. ήσω, a.1. ἠσθένησα,

    to be weak, infirm, deficient in strength; to be inefficient, Ro. 8.3. 2 Co. 13.3; to be sick, Mat. 25.36, et al.; *met.* to be weak *in faith,* to doubt, hesitate, be unsettled, timid, Ro. 14.1. 1 Co. 8.9, 11, 12. 2 Co. 11.29; to be deficient in authrity, dignity, or power, be comtemptible, 2 Co. 11.21; 13.3, 9; *by impl.* to be afflicted, distressed, needy, Ac. 20.35. 2 Co. 12.10; 13.4, 9: *whence*

Ἀσθένημα, ατος, τό,

    pr. weakness, infirmity; *met.* doubt, scruple, hesitation, Ro. 15.1. N.T.

Ἀσθενής, έος, οὖς, ὁ, ἡ, τό, -ές, (ἀ & σθένος, strength)

    without strength, weak, infirm, Mat. 26.41. Mar. 14.38. 1 Pe. 3.7; helpless, Ro. 5.6; imperfect, inefficient, Gal. 4.9; feeble, without energy, 2 Co. 10.10; infirm in body, sick, sickly, Mat. 25.39, 43, 44, et al.; weak, *mentally or spiritually,* dubious, hesitating, 1 Co. 8.7, 10; 9.22. 1 Thes. 5.14; *by impl.* afflicted, distressed, oppressed with calamities, 1 Co. 4.10.

Ἀσιανός, οῦ, ὁ, ἡ, (Ἀσία)

    belonging to the Roman province of Asia, Ac. 20.4.

Ἀσιάρχης, ου, ὁ, (Ἀσία & ἀρχή)

    an Asiarch, an officer in the province of Asia, as in other eastern provinces of the Roman empire, selected, with others, from the more opulent citizens, to preside over the things pertaining to religious worship, and to exhibit annual public games at their own expense in honour of the gods, in the manner of the ædiles at Rome, Ac. 19.31. L.G.

Ἀσιτία, ας, ἡ,

    abstinence from food, fasting, Ac. 27.21: *from*

Ἄσῑτος, ου, ὁ, ἡ, (ἀ & σῖτος)

    abstaining from food, fasting, Ac. 27.33.

Ἀσκέω, ῶ,

    f. ήσω,

    to exercise or exert one's self, endeavour, Ac. 24.16.

Ἀσκός, οῦ, ὁ,
25a leathern bag or bottle, bottle of skin, Mat. 9.17. Mar. 2.22. Lu. 5.37, 38.

Ἀσμένως,
adv. gladly, joyfully, Ac. 2.41; 21.17.

Ἄσοφος, ου, ὁ, ἡ, (ἀ & σοφός)
unwise; destitute of Christian wisdom, Ep. 5.15.

Ἀσπάζομαι,
f. σομαι, a.1. ἠσπασάμην, p. ἤσπασμαι,
to salute, greet, welcome, express one's good wishes, pay one's respects, Mat. 10.12. Mar. 9.15, et al. freq.; to bid farewell, Ac. 20.1; 21.6; to treat with affection, Mat. 5.47; met. to embrace mentally, welcome to the heart or understanding, He. 11.13: whence

Ἀσπασμός, οῦ, ὁ,
salutation, greeting, Mat. 23.7. Mar. 12.38, et al.

Ἄσπῑλος, ου, ὁ, ἡ, (ἀ & σπίλος)
spotless, unblemished, pure, 1 Ti. 6.14. Ja. 1.27. 1 Pe. 1.19. 2 Pe. 3.14. L.G.

Ἀσπίς, ίδος, ἡ,
an asp, a species of serpent of the most deadly venom, Ro. 3.13.

Ἄσπονδος, ου, ὁ, ἡ, (ἀ & σπονδή, a libation usually conjoined with the making of a treaty)
pr. unwilling to make a tready; hence, implacable, irreconcilable, Ro. 1.31. 2 Ti. 3.3.

Ἀσσάριον, ίου, τό,
dimin. of the Latin as a Roman brass coin of the value of one-tenth of a denarious or δραχμή, and equal to 3 and one-tenth farthings of our money, used to convey the idea of a very trifling sum, Mat. 10.29. Lu. 12.6. N.T.

Ἆσσον,
adv. nearer; very nigh, close, Ac. 27.13; used as the comp. of ἄγχι.

Ἀστατέω, ῶ, (ἄστατος, unfixed, unstable, fr. ἀ & ἵστημι)
to be unsettled, have no fixed residence, wander about without a home, 1 Co. 4.11. L.G.

Ἀστεῖος, ου, ὁ, ἡ, (ἄστυ, a city)
pr. belonging to a city; well-bred, polite, polished; hence, elegant, fair, comely, beautiful, Ac. 7.20. He. 11.23.

Ἀστήρ, έρος, ὁ,
a star, liminous body like a star, liminary, Mat. 2.3, 7, 9, 10. Re. 1.16, et al.

Ἀστήρικτος, ου, ὁ, ἡ, (ἀ & στηρίζω)
not made firm; unsettled, unstable, unsteady, 2 Pe. 2.14; 3.16. L.G.

Ἄστοργος, ου, ὁ, ἡ, (ἀ & στοργή, natural or instinctive affection)
devoid of natural or instinctive affection, without affection to kindred, Ro. 1.31. 2 Ti. 3.3.

Ἀστοχέω, ῶ, (ἀ & στόχος, a mark)
f. ήσω, a.1. ἠστόχησα,
pr. to miss the mark; met. to err, deviate, swerve from, 1 Ti. 1.6, 21. 2 Ti. 2.18. L.G.

Ἀστρᾰπή, ῆς, ἡ,
lightning, Mat. 24.27; by impl. light, brightness, lustre, Lu. 11.36: whence

Ἀστράπτω,
f. ψω,
to lighten, flash as lightning, Lu. 17.24; to be bright, shining, Lu. 24.4.

Ἄστρον, ου, τό,
a constellation; a star, Lu. 21.25. Ac. 7.43; 27.20. He. 11.12.

Ἀσύμφωνος, ου, ὁ, ἡ, (ἀ & σύμφωνος)

discordant in sound; disagreeing, of a different opinion, Ac. 28.25.

Ἀσύνετος, ου, ὁ, ἡ, (ἀ & συνετός, fr. συνίημι)
>   without understanding, dull of apprehension, stupid, Mat. 15.16. Mar. 7.18. Ro. 1.21;
>   foolish, wicked, ungodly, corrupt, Ro. 1.31; 10.19.

Ἀσυνθετος, ου, ὁ, ἡ, (ἀ & συντίθεμαι, to make a covenant)
>   a violator of covenants, covenant breaker, perfidious, Ro. 1.31.

Ἀσφάλεια, ας, ἡ,
>   *pr.* state of one who is secure from falling, firmness; safety, security, 1 Thes. 5.3;
>   certainty, truth, Lu. 1.4; diligence, carefulness, vigilance, Ac. 5.23: *from*

Ἀσφᾰλής, έος, οῦς, ὁ, ἡ, τό, -ές, (ἀ & σφάλλομαι, to stumble, fall)
>   *pr.* firm, secure from falling; firm, sure, steady, immoveable, He. 6.19; *met.* certain,
>   sure, Ac. 21.34; 22.30; 25.26; affording means of security, making secure, Phi. 3.1:
>   *whence*

Ἀσφαλίζω,
>   f. ίσω,
>   to make fast, safe, or secure, Mat. 27.64--66. Ac. 16.24. L.G.

Ἀσφαλῶς,
>   *adv.* securely, safely; with care and diligence, Mar. 14.44. Ac. 16.23; certainly,
>   assuredly, Ac. 2.36.

Ἀσχημονέω, ῶ,
>   f. ήσω,
>   26to be ἀσχήμων, indecorous, to behave in an unbecoming manner, or indecorously, 1
>   Co. 13.5; to behave in a manner open to censure, 1 Co. 7.36.

Ἀσχημοσύνη, ης, ἡ
>   *pr.* external indecorum; nakedness, shame, pudenda, Re. 16.15; indecency, infamous
>   lust or lewdness, Ro. 1.27: *from*

Ἀσχήμων, ονος, ὁ, ἡ, τό, -ον, (ἀ & σχῆμα)
>   indecorous, uncomely, indecent, 1 Co. 12.23.

Ἀσωτία, ας, ἡ, (*pr.* the disposition and life of one who is ἄσωτος, abandoned, recklessly debauched)
>   profligacy, dissoluteness, debauchery, Ep. 5.18. Tit. 1.6. 1 Pe. 4.4.

Ἀσώτως,
>   *adv.* dissolutely, profligately, Lu. 15.13.

Ἀτακτέω, ῶ,
>   f. ήσω,
>   *pr.* to desert one's ranks; *met.* to neglect one's duties, behave disorderly, 2 Thes. 3.7:
>   *from*

Ἄτακτος, ου, ὁ, ἡ, (ἀ & τάσσω)
>   *pr. spoken of soldiers* who desert their ranks; *met.* neglectful of duties, disorderly, 1
>   Thes. 5.14.

Ἀτάκτως,
>   *adv.* disorderly, 2 Thes. 3.6, 11.

Ἄτεκνος, ου, ὁ, ἡ, (ἀ & τέκνον)
>   childless, Lu. 20.28, 29, 30.

Ἀτενίζω, (ἀτενής, intent)
>   f. ίσω, a.1. ἠτένισα,
>   to fix one's eyes upon, to look steadily, gaze intently, Lu. 4.20, et al.

Ἄτερ,
>   without, Lu. 22.6, 35.

Ἀτῑμάζω, (ἄτιμος)

f. άσω, a.1. ἠτίμασα, a.1. pass. ἠτιμάσθην,
> to dishonour, treat with contumely or indignity, Lu. 20.11. Jno. 8.49, et al.

Ἀτιμία, ας, ἡ
> dishonour, infamy, Ro. 1.26; indecorum, 1 Co. 11.14; inaneness, vileness, Ro. 9.21. 1
> Co. 15.43. 2 Ti. 2.20: *from*

Ἄτιμος, ου, ὁ, ἡ, (ἀ & τιμή)
> unhonoured, without honour, exposed to contumelious treatment, Mat. 13.57. Mar.
> 6.4. 1 Co. 4.10; 12.23.

Ἀτιμόω, ῶ,
> p. pass. ἠτίμωμαι,
> to dishonour, treat with contumely, Mar. 12.4.

Ἀτμίς, ίδος, ἡ,
> an exhalation, vapour, smoke, Ac. 2.19. Ja. 4.14.

Ἄτομος, ου, ὁ, ἡ, (ἀ & τέμνω)
> indivisible, *and by impl.* exceedingly minute: ἐν ἀτόμῳ sc. χρόνῳ, in an indivisible
> point of time, in an instant or moment, 1 Co. 15.52.

Ἄτοπος, ου, ὁ, ἡ, (ἀ & τόπος)
> *pr.* out of place; inopportune, unsuitable, absurd; new, unusual, strange, *in N.T.,*
> improper, amiss, wicked. Lu. 23.41. 2 Thes. 3.2; noxious, harmful, Ac. 28.6.

Αὐγάζω,
> f. άσω,
> to shine upon, illuminate, irradiate, 2 Co. 4.4: *from*

Αὐγή, ῆς, ἡ,
> radiance; day-break, Ac. 20.11.

Αὐθάδης, εος, οῦς, ὁ, ἡ, (αὐτός & ἥδομαι)
> one who pleases himself, wilful, obstinate; arrogant, imperious, Ti. 1.7. 2 Pe. 2.10.
> (ᾰ).

Αὐθαίρετος, ου, ὁ, ἡ, (αὐτός & αἱρέομαι)
> *pr.* one who chooses his own course of action; acting spontaneously, of one's own
> accord, 2 Co. 8.3, 17.

Αὐθεντέω, ῶ, (to be αἰθέντης, one acting by his own authority or power, *contr. fr.* αὐτοέντης,
one who executes with his own hand)
> f. ήσω,
> to have authority over, domineer, 1 Ti. 2.12. N.T.

Αὐλέω, ῶ, (αὐλός)
> f. ήσω, a.1. ηὔλησα,
> to play on a pipe or flute pipe, Mat. 11.17. Lu. 7.32. 1 Co. 14.7.

Αὐλή, ῆς, ἡ,
> *pr.* an unroofed enclosure; court-yard; sheepfold, Jno. 10.1, 16; an exterior court, i.q.
> προαύλιον, i.e. *an enclosed place between the door and the street,* Re. 11.2; an
> interior court, quadrangle, i.e. *the open court in the middle of oriental houses, which
> are commonly built in the form of a square enclosing this court,* Mat. 26.58, 69, et al.;
> *by synecd.* a house, mansion, palace, Mat. 26.3. Lu. 11.21.

Αὐλητής, οῦ, ὁ, (αὐλέω)
> a player on a pipe or flute, Mat. 9.23. Re. 18.22.

Αὐλίζομαι, (αὐλή)
> f. ίσομαι, a.1. ηὐλίσθην,
> *pr.* to pass the time in a court-yard; to lodge, bivouac; *hence,* to pass the night in any
> place, to lodge at night, pass or remain through the night, Mat. 21.17. Lu. 21.37.

Αὐλός, οῦ, ὁ,

27a pipe or flute, 1 Co. 14.7.

Αὐξάνω, υ, αὔξω,

f. ήσω, a.1. ηὔξησα, a.1. pass. ηὐξήθην,

trans. to cause to grow or increase; *pass.* to be increased, enlarged, Mat. 13.32. 1 Co. 3.6, 7, et al.; *intrans.* to increase, grow, Mat. 6.28. Mar. 4.8, et al.: *whence*

Αὔξησις, εως, ἡ,

increase, growth, Ep. 4.16. Col. 2.19.

Αὔριον,

adv. to-morrow, Mat. 6.30, et al.; ἡ αὔριον sc. ἡμέρα, the morrow, the next day, Mat. 6.34, et al.

Αὐστηρός, ά, όν

pr. harsh, sour in flavour; *met.* harsh, rigid, ungenerous, Lu. 19.21, 22.

Αὐτάρκεια, ας, ἡ,

a competence of the necesssaries of life, 2 Co. 9.8; a frame of mind viewing one's lot as sufficient, contentedness, 1 Ti. 6.6: *from*

Αὐτάρκης, εος, ους, ὁ, ἡ, (αὐτός & ἀρκέω)

pr. sufficient or adequate in one's self; contented with one's lot, Phi. 4.11.

Αὐτοκατάκρῐτος, ου, ὁ, ἡ, (αὐτός & κατακρίνω)

self-condemned, Tit. 3.11. N.T.

Αὐτόμᾰτος, ου, ὁ, ἡ, (αὐτός & μέμαα, to be excited)

self-excited, acting spontaneously, spontaneous, of his own accord, Mar. 4.8. Ac. 12.10.

Αὐτόπτης, ου, ὁ, ἡ, (αὐτός & ὄψομαι)

an eye-witness, Lu. 1.2.

Αὐτός, ή, ό,

a reflexive pron., self, very; alone, Mar. 6.31. 2 Co. 12.13; of one's self, of one's own motion, Jno. 16.27; *used also in the oblique cases independently as a personal pron. of the third person;* ὁ αὐτός, the same; unchangeable, He. 1.12; κατὰ τὸ αὐτό, at the same time, together, Ac. 14.1; ἐπὶ τὸ αὐτό, in one and the same place, Mat. 22.34; at the same time, together, Ac. 3.1. *But for a full account of the uses of* αὐτός, *see the Grammars.*

Αὐτοῦ, ῆς, οῦ,

recip. pron. contr. fr. ἑαυτοῦ, ῆς, οῦ, himself, herself, itself, Mat. 1.21, et al. freq.; for σεαυτοῦ, ῆς, οῦ, thyself, Mat. 23.37.

Αὐτοῦ,

adv. of place. pr. in the very place; here, there, in this, or that place, Mat. 26.36. Ac. 15.34; 18.19; 21.4.

Αὐτόχειρ, ρος, ὁ, ἡ, (αὐτός & χείρ)

acting or doing any thing with one's own hands, Ac. 27.19.

Αὐχμηρός, ά, όν, (αὐχμέω, to be dry, squalid, filthy)

squalid, filthy; *by impl.* dark, obscure, murky, 2 Pe. 1.19.

Ἀφαιρέω, ῶ, (ἀπό & αἱρέω)

f. ήσω, a.2. ἀφεῖλον, a.1. pass. ἀφαιρεθήσομαι,

to take away, remove, Lu. 1.25; 10.42, et al.; to take off, cut off, remove by cutting off, Mat. 26.51. Mar. 14.47. Lu. 22.50.

Ἀφᾰνής, έος, οῦς, ὁ, ἡ, τό, -ές, (ἀ & φαίνω)

out of sight; not manifest, hidden, concealed, He. 4.13: *whence*

Ἀφανίζω,

f. ίσω,

to remove out of sight, cause to disappear; *pass.* to disappear, vanish, Ja. 4.14; *by impl.* to destroy, consume, *so that nothing shall be left visible,* Mat. 6.19, 20; *met.* to spoil, deform, disfigure, Mat. 6.16: *whence*

Ἀφανισμός, οῦ, ὁ,
a disappearing, vanishing away; *met.* destruction, abolition, abrogation, He. 8.13. L.G.

Ἄφαντος, ου, ὁ, ἡ, (ἀ & φαίνω)
not appearing, not seen, invisible; *hence,* ἄφαντος γενέσθαι, to disappear, vanish, Lu. 24.31.

Ἀφεδρών, ῶνος, ὁ, (ἀπό & ἕδρα, a seat)
a privy, Mat. 15.17. Mar. 7.19. L.G.

Ἀφειδία, ας, ἡ, (ἀ & φείδομαι)
pr. the disposition of one who is ἀφειδής, unsparing; *hence, in N.T.,* unsparingness *in the sense of* rigour, severity, austerity, Col. 2.23.

Ἀφελότης, τητος, ἡ, (ἀφελής, not rough, plain, *met.* simple, sincere, fr. ἀ & φελλεύς, a rough, stony region)
sincerity, simplicity, Ac. 2.46. N.T.

Ἄφεσις, εως, ἡ, (ἀφίημι)
dismission, deliverance *from captivity,* Lu. 4.18, *bis;* remission, forgiveness, pardon, Mat. 26.28, et al.

Ἀφή, ῆς, ἡ, (ἅπτω)
a fastening; a ligature, *by which the different members are connected,* commissure, joint, Ep. 4.16. Col. 2.19.

Ἀφθαρσία, ας, ἡ, (ἀ & φθείρω)
incorruptibility, incorruptness; *by impl.* immortality, 1 Co 15.42, 53, 54. 28*with the accessory idea of* felicity, Ro. 2.7, et al.; ἐν ἀφθαρσίᾳ, purely, sincerely, constantly, Ep. 6.24. L.G.

Ἄφθαρτος, ου, ὁ, ἡ, (fr. same)
incorruptible, immortal, imperishable, undying, enduring, Ro. 1.23. 1 Co. 9.25; 15.52, et al.

Ἀφθορία, ας, ἡ, (fr. same)
v.r. Tit. 2.7, *pr.* incapability of decay; *met.* incorruptness, integrity, genuineness, purity. N.T.

Ἀφίημι, (ἀπό & ἵημι)
f. ἀφήσω, a.1. ἀφῆκα, a.1. pass. ἀφειθην & ἀφέθην, f. pass. ἀφεθήσομαι, imperf. 3 per. s. ἤφει, Mar. 1.34; 11.16, p. pass. 3 per. pl. ἀφέωνται, pres. 2 pers. s. ἀφεῖς, v.r. Re. 2.20.
to send away, dismiss, suffer to depart; to emit, send forth; τὴν φωνήω, the voice, to cry out, utter an exclamation, Mar. 15.37; τὸ πνεῦμα, the spirit, to expire, Mat. 27.50; to omit, pass over or by, neglect, care not, Mat. 15.14; 23.23. He. 6.1; to permit suffer, let, forbid not; to give up, yield, resign, Mat. 5.40; to remit, forgive, pardon; to relax, suffer to become less intense, Re. 2.4; to leave, depart from; to desert, forsake; to leave, remaining or alone; to leave behind, *sc. at one's death,* Mar. 12.19, 20, 21, 22. Jno. 14.27.

Ἀφικνέομαι, οῦμαι, (ἀπό & ἱκνέομαι, to come, arrive)
f. ἵξομαι, a.2 ἀφικόμην,
to come, arrive at; to reach *as a report,* Ro. 16.19.

Ἀφιλάγαθος, οῦ, ὁ, ἡ, (ἀ & φίλος & ἀγαθός)
not a lover of, inimical to, good and good men, 2 Ti. 3.3. N.T.

Ἀφιλάργῠρος, ου, ὁ, ἡ, (ἀ & φίλος & ἄργυρος)
not fond of money, not covetous, liberal, generous, 1 Ti. 3.3. He. 13.5. N.T.

Ἄφιξις, εως, ἡ, (ἀφικνέομαι)
arrival; departure, Ac. 20.29.
Ἀφίστημι, (ἀπό & ἵστημι)
f. ἀποστήσω, a.1. ἀπέστησα,
trans. to put away, separate; to draw off or away, withdraw, induce to revolt, Ac. 5.37; *intrans.*, p. ἀφέστηκα, a.2. ἀπέστην, *and mid.* to depart, go away from, Lu. 2.27. et al.; *met.* to desist or refrain from, let alone, Ac. 5.38; 22.29. 2 Co. 12.8; to make defection, fall away, apostatise, Lu. 8.13. 1 Ti. 4.1. He. 3.12; to withdraw from, have no intercourse with, 1 Ti. 6.5; to abstain from, 2 Ti. 2.19.
Ἄφων,
adv. suddenly, unexpectedly, Ac. 2.2; 16.26; 28.6.
Ἀφόβως, (ἄφοβος, fearless, fr. ἀ & φόβος)
fearlessly, boldly, in trepidly, Phi. 1.14; securely, peacefully, tranquilly, Lu. 1.74. 1 Co. 16.10; impudently, shamefully, Jude 12.
Ἀφομαιόω, ῶ, (ἀπό & ὁμοιόω)
f. ώσω,
to assimilate, cause to resemble, He. 7.3.
Ἀφοράω, ῶ, (ἀπό & ὁράω)
f. ἀπόψομαι, a.2. ἀπεῖδον,
to view with undivided attention *by looking away from every other object;* to regard fixedly and earnestly, He. 12.2; to see distinctly, Phi. 2.23.
Ἀφορίζω, (ἀπό & ὁρίζω)
f. ίσω, & ἀφοριῶ, p. pass. ἀφώρισμαι,
to limit off; to separate, sever from the rest, Mat. 13.49, et al.; to separate from society, cut off from all intercourse, excommunicate, Lu. 6.22; to set apart, select, Ac. 13.2. Ro. 1.1. Gal. 1.15.
Ἀφορμή, ῆς, ἡ, (ἀπό & ὁρμή)
pr. a starting point; means to accomplish an object; occasion, opportunity, Ro. 7.8, 11, et al.
Ἀφρίζω,
f. ίσω,
to froth, foam, Mar. 9.18, 20: *from*
Ἀφρός, οῦ, ὁ,
froth, foam, Lu. 9.39.
Ἀφροσύνη, ης, ἡ,
inconsiderateness, folly; folly, *in the sense of* ostentation, boasting, 2 Co. 11.1, 17, 21; foolishness, levity, wickedness, impiety, Mar. 7.22: *from*
Ἄφρων, ονος, ὁ, ἡ, (ἀ & φρήν)
unwise, inconsiderate, simple, foolish, Lu. 11.40; 12.20.. 1 Co. 15.36; ignorant, destitute of the knowledge of the true religion, Ro. 2.20. Ep. 5.17. 1 Pe. 2.15; vain, ostentatious, 2 Co. 11.16, 19; 12.6, 11.
Ἀφυπνόω, ῶ, (ἀπό & ὕπνος)
f. ώσω,
to awake from sleep; *in N.T.,* to go off into sleep, fall asleep, Lu. 8.23.
Ἄφωνος, ου, ὁ, ἡ, (ἀ & φωνή)
dumb, destitute of the power of speech, 1 Co. 12.2. 2 Pe. 2.16; silent, mute, uttering no voice, Ac. 8.32; inarticulate, consisting of inarticulate sounds, unmeaning 1 Co. 14.10.
Ἀχάριστος, ου, ὁ, ἡ, (ἀ & χάρις)
29unthankful, ungrateful, Lu. 6.35. 2 Ti. 3.2.

Ἀχειροποίητος, ου, ὁ, ἡ, (ἀ & χειροποίητος)
    not made with hands, Mar. 14.58. 2 Co. 5.1. Col. 2.11. N.T.
Ἀχλύς, ύος, ἡ,
    a mist; darkening of the sight, Ac. 13.11.
Ἀχρεῖος, α, ον, (ἀ & χρεία)
    useless, unprofitable, worthless, Mat. 25.30; unmeritorious, Lu. 17.10: *whence*
Ἀχρειόω, ῶ,
    f. ώσω, a.1. pass. ἠχρειώθην,
    to render useless; *met. pass.* to become corrupt, depraved, Ro. 3.12. L.G.
Ἄχρηστος, ου, ὁ, ἡ, (ἀ & χρηστός)
    unuseful, useless, unprofitable, *and by impl.* detrimental, causing loss, Phile. 11.
Ἄχρι, v. ἄχρις,
    originally an adv. of place; used as a prep., with respect to place, as far as; *to time,*
    until, during; *as a conj.,* until.
Ἄχυρον, ου, τό,
    chaff, straw broken up *by treading out the grain,* Mat. 3.12. Lu. 3.17.
Ἀψευδής, έος, οῦς, ὁ, ἡ, (ἀ & ψευδής)
    free from falsehood; incapable of falsehood, Tit. 1.2.
Ἄψινθος, ου, ἡ,
    wormwood, Re. 8.11, *where, as a proper name, it is masculine, according to the v.r.*
Ἄψῡχος, ου, ὁ, ἡ, τό, -ον, (ἀ & ψυχή)
    void of life or sense, inanimate, 1 Co. 14.7.

B, β, *Βῆτα*

Βαθμός, οῦ, ὁ, (βαίνω)
    pr. a step, stair; *met.* grade of dignity, degree, rank standing, 1 Ti 3.13.
Βάθος, εος, ους, τό,
    depth; τὸ βάθος, deep water, Lu. 5.4. Mat. 13.5, et al.; *met.* fullness, abundance,
    immensity, Ro. 11.33. 2 Co. 8.2; an extreme degree, 2 Co. 8.2; *pl.* deep laid plans,
    profound, secret things, 1 Co. 2.10. Re. 2.24.
Βαθύνω,
    f. ὕνῶ,
    to deepen, excavate, Lu. 6.48 *from*
Βαθύς, εῖα, ύ,
    deep. Jno. 4.11; *met.* deep, profound, Ac. 20.9; ὄρθρου βαθέος, *lit.* at deep morning
    twilight *i.e.* at the earliest dawn, Lu. 24.1.
Βάϊον, v. Βαΐον, ου, τό,
    a palm branch, Jno. 12.13. S.
Βαλάντιον, ου, τό,
    a bag, purse, Lu. 10.4; 12.33; 22.35, 36.
Βάλλω,
    f. βαλῶ, a.2 ἔβαλον, p. βέβληκα, p. pass. βέβλημαι, a.1. pass. ἐβλήθην, f. pass.
    βληθήσομαι,
    to throw, cast; to lay, Re. 2.22 Mat. 8.6, 14, et. al.; to put, place, Ja. 3.3; to place,
    deposit, Mat. 27.6 Mar. 2.41-44. Lu. 21.1-4; Jno 12.6; to pour, Jno. 13.5; to thrust,
    Jno. 18.11; 20.27. Mar. 7.33. Re. 14.19; to send forth, Mat. 10.34; to assault, strike,
    Mar. 14.65; *met.* to suggest, Mat. 10.34. Jno. 13.2; *intrans.* to rush, beat, *as the wind,*
    Ac 27.14.
Βαπτίζω, (βάπτω)

f. ίσω, a.1. ἐβάπτισα, p. pass. βεβάπτισμαι, a.1. pass. ἐβαπτίσθην,

pr. to dip, immerse; to cleanse or purify by washing; to administer the rite of baptism, to baptize; *met. with various reference to the ideas associated with Christian baptism as an act of dedication, e.g. marked designation, devotion, trial, &c.; mid.* to procure baptism for one's self, to undergo baptism, Ac. 22.16.

Βάπτισμα, ατος, τό,

pr. immersion; baptism, ordinance of baptism, Mat. 3.7. Ro. 6.4, et al.; *met.* baptism *in the trial of suffering,* Mat. 20.22, 23. Mar. 10.38, 39. N.T.

Βαπτισμός, οῦ, ὁ,

pr. an act of dipping or immersion; a baptism, He. 6.2; an ablution, Mar. 7.4, 8. He. 9.10. N.T.

Βαπτιστής, οῦ, ὁ,

one who baptises, Mat. 3.1; 11.11, 12, et al. N.T.

Βάπτω,

f. ψω, a.1. ἔβαψα, p. pass. βέβαμμαι,

to dip, Jno, 13.26. Lu. 16.24; to dye, Re. 19.13.

Βάρ, indec. ὁ, (בַּר, Chald, or Syr.)

a son, Mat. 16.17.

Βάρβᾰρος, ου, ὁ,

a barbarian, *pr.* one to whom a pure Greek dialect is not native; one who is not a proper Greek, Ro. 1.14. Col 3.11. Ac. 28.2, 4; a foreigner speaking a strange language, 1 Co. 14.11.

Βαρέω, ῶ, (βάρος)

f. ήσω, p. pass. βεβάρημαι,

to be heavy upon, weigh down, burden, oppress, *as sleep,* Mat. 26.43. 30Mar. 14.40. Lu. 9.32; *surfeiting,* v.r. Lu. 21.34; *calamities,* 2 Co. 1.8; 5.4; *or trouble, care, expense,* &c. 1 Ti. 5.16.

Βαρέως,

adv. heavily; *met.* with difficulty, dully, stupidly, Mat. 13.15. Ac. 28.27.

Βάρος, εος, τό,

weight, heaviness; a burden, any thing grievous and hard to be borne, Mat. 20.12. Ac. 15.28. Re. 2.24; burden, charge, *or,* weight, influence, dignity, honour, 1 Thes. 2.6; *with another noun in government,* fullness, abundance, excellence, 2 Co. 4.17.

Βαρύνω,

f. υνῶ, a.1. pass. ἐβαρύνθην,

(see βαρέω), Lu. 21.34. (ῠ):*from*

Βαρύς, εῖα, ύ,

heavy; *met.* burdensome, oppressive, or difficult of observance, *as precepts,* Mat. 23.4. 1 Jno. 5.3; weighty, important, momentous, Mat. 23.23. Ac. 25.7; grievous, oppressive, afflictive, violent, rapacious, Ac. 20.29; authoritative, strick, stern, severe, 2 Co. 10.10.

Βαρύτῑμος, ου, ὁ, ἡ, (βαρύς & τιμή)

of great price, precious, Mat. 26.7.

Βασανίζω, (βάσανος)

f. ίσω, a.1. pass. ἐβασανίσθην,

pr. to apply the lapis Lydius or touchstone; *met.* to examine, scrutinise, try *either by words or torture; in N.T.* to afflict, torment; *pass.* to be afflicted, tormented, pained, *by diseases,* Mat. 8.6, 29, et al.; to be tossed, agitated, *as by the waves,* Mat. 14.24: *whence*

Βασανισμός, οῦ, ὁ,

pr. examination *by the lapis Lydius or by torture;* torment, torture, Re. 9.5; 14.11; 18.7, 10, 15.

Βασανιστής, οῦ, ὁ,

pr. an inquisitor, tormentor; *in N.T.* a keeper of a prison, gaoler, Mat. 18.34.

Βάσᾰνος, ου, ἡ,

pr. lapis Lydius, *a species of stone from Lydia, which being applied to metals was thought to indicate any alloy which might be mixed with them, and therefore used in the trial of metals; hence,* examination *of a person, especially by torture; in N.T.* torture, torment, severe pain, Mat. 4.24. Lu. 16.23, 28.

Βασιλεία, ας, ἡ (βασιλεύς)

a kingdom, realm, *the region or country governed by a king;* kingly power, authority, dominion, reign; royal dignity, the title and honour of king; ἡ βασιλεία, Mat. 9.35, ἡ βασιλεία τοῦ Θεοῦ,—τοῦ Χριστοῦ,—τοῦ οὐρανοῦ,—τῶν οὐρανῶν, the reign or kingdom of the Messiah, *both in a false and true conception of it; used also, with various limitation, of its* administration and coming history *as in the parables;* its distinctive nature, Ro. 14.17, requirements, privileges, rewards, consummation.

Βασίλειος, ου, ὁ, ἡ,

royal, regal; *met.* possessed of high prerogatives and distinction, 1 Pe. 2.9; τὰ βασίλεια sc. δώματα, regal mansions, palaces, Lu. 7.25: *from*

Βασιλεύς, έως, ὁ,

a king, monarch, one possessing regal authority: *whence*

Βασιλεύω,

f. εύσω,

to possess regal authority, be a king, reign; to rule, govern, Mat. 2.22; *met.* to be in force, predominate, prevail, Ro. 5.14, 17, 21; 6.12; to be in a state of prosperity and happiness, 1 Co. 4.8.

Βασιλικός, ή, όν,

royal, regal, Ac. 12. 20, 21; βασιλικός, *used as a subst* a person attached to the king, courtier; *by impl.* of the highest excellence, Ja. 2.8.

Βασίλισσα, ης, ἡ, (a later from of βασιλίς)

a queen, Mat. 12.42. Lu. 11.31. Ac. 8.27. Re. 18.7.

Βάσις, εως, ἡ, (βαίνω)

pr. a step; the foot, Ac. 3.7.

Βασκαίνω,

f. ανῶ, a.1. ἐβάσκηνα & ἐβάσκᾱνα,

pr. to slander; *thence,* to bewitch *by spells, or by any other means;* to delude, Gal. 3.1.

Βαστάζω,

f. άσω, a.1. ἐβάστασα,

pr. to lift, raise, bear aloft; to bear, carry, *in the hands or about the person;* carry *as a message,* Ac. 9.15; to take away, remove, Mat. 8.17. Jno. 20.15; to take up, Jno. 10.31. Lu. 14.27; to bear *as a burden,* endure, suffer; to sustain, Ro. 11.18; to bear with, tolerate; to sustain *mentally,* comprehend, Jno. 16.12.

Βάτος, ου, ὁ & ἡ,

a bush, bramble, Mar. 12.36, et al.

Βάτος, ου, ὁ (Heb בת)

a bath, a measure for liquids, which is stated by Josephus (Ant. 1. viii. c. 9.9) to 31contain 72 sextarii, or about 13 and a half gallons. Others make it about 9 gallons; and others, 7 and a half gallons.

Βάτραχος, ου, ὁ,

a frog, Re. 16.13.

Βαττολογέω, ῶ, (βάττος, stammerer),
f. ήσω,
pr. to stammer; *hence,* to babble; to use vain repetitions, Mat. 6.7. L.G.
Βδέλυγμα, ατος, τό, (βδελύσσομαι)
an abomination, an abominable thing, Mat. 24.15. Mar. 13.14, et al.; idolatry with all its pollutions, Re. 17.4, 5; 21.27. S.
Βδελυκτός, ή, όν,
abominable, detestable, Tit. 1.16: (S.) *from*
Βδελύσσομαι,
f. ξομαι, p ἐβδέλυγμαι,
to abominate, loathe, detest, abhor, Ro. 2.22; *pass.* to be abominable, detestable, Re. 21.8.
Βέβαιος, αία, ον, (βέβαα, p. of βαίνω)
firm, stable, stedfast, He. 3.6, 14; 6.19; sure, certain, established, Ro. 4.16, et al.; *whence*
Βεβαιόω, ῶ,
f. ώσω, a.1. ἐβεβαίωσα,
to confirm, establish; to render constant and unwavering, 1 Co. 1.8, et al.; to strengthen or establish *by arguments or proofs,* ratify, Mar. 16.20; verify, *as promises,* Ro. 15.8.
Βεβαίσις, εως, ή,
confirmation, firm establishment, Phi. 1.7. He. 6.16.
Βέβηλος, ου, ὁ, ή, (βαίνω, to tread, and βηλός, a threshold)
pr. what is open and accessible to all; *hence,* profane, not religious, not connected with religion; unholy; a despiser, scorner, 1 Ti. 1.9; 4.7, et al.; *whence*
Βεβηλόω, ῶ,
f. ώσω, a.1. ἐβεβήλωσα,
to profane, pollute, violate, Mat. 12.5. Ac. 24.6. L.G.
Βελόνη, ης, ή,
v.r. Lu. 18.25, *pr.* the point of a spear; needle.
Βέλος, εος, τό,
a missile weapon, dart, arrow, Ep. 6.16.
Βελτίων, ονος, ὁ, ή, τό, -ον, (comp. of ἀγαθός)
better; βέλτιον, *as an adv.* very well, too well to need informing, 2 Ti. 1.18.
Βῆμα, ατος, τό, (βαίνω)
a step, foot-step, foot-breadth, space to set the foot on, Ac. 7.5; an elevated place ascended by steps, tribunal, throne, Mat. 27.19. Ac. 12.21. et al.
Βήρυλλος, ου, ὁ, ή,
a beryl, a precious stone of a sea-green colour, found chiefly in India, Re. 21.20. L.G.
Βία, ας, ή,
force, impetus, violence, Ac. 5.26; 21.35, et al.: *hence*
Βιάζω,
f. άσω, and mid. βιάζομαι,
to urge, constrain, overpower by force; to press earnestly forward, to rush, Lu. 16.16; *pass.* to be an object of an impetuous movement, Mat. 11.12.
Βίαιος, α, ον,
violent, vehement, Ac. 2.2.
Βιαστής, οῦ, ὁ, (βιάζω)
one who uses violence, or is impetuous; one who feels an eager, vehement desire for anything, Mat. 11.12. L.G.

Βιβλαρίδιον, ου, τό, (*dimin. of* βιβλάριον, a roll, fr. βίβλος)
a small volume or scroll, a little book, Re. 10.2, 8, 9, 10. L.G.

Βιβλίον, ου, τό, (*pr. dmin. of* βίβλος)
a written volume or roll, book, Lu. 4.17, 20, et al.; a scroll, bill, billet, Mat. 19.7. Mar. 10.4.

Βίβλος, ου, ἡ,
pr. the inner bark or rind of papyrus, *which was anciently used instead of paper; hence,* a written volume, or roll, book, catalogue, account, Mat. 1.1. Mar. 12.26, et al.

Βιβρώσκω,
f. βρώσομαι, p. βέβρωκα,
to eat.

Βίος, ου, ὁ,
life; means of living; sustenance, maintenance, substance, goods, Mar. 12.44, et al.; *whence*

Βιόω, ῶ,
f. ώσω, a.1. ἐβίωσα,
to live, 1 Pe. 4.2.

Βίωσις, εως, ἡ,
manner of life, Ac. 26.4. S.

Βιωτικός, ή, όν,
pertaining to this life, or the things of this life, Lu. 21.34. 1 Co. 6.3, 4.

Βλαβερός, ά, όν,
hurtful, 1 Ti. 6.9: *from*

Βλάπτω,
f. ψω, a.1. ἔβλαψα,
pr. to weaken, hinder, disable; hurt, harm, injure, Mar. 16.18. Lu. 4.35.

Βλαστάνω,
f. ήσω, a.1. ἐβλάστησα, a.2. ἔβλαστον,
intrans. to germinate, bud, sprout, spring up, Mat. 13.26. Mar. 4.27. He. 9.4; *trans ans. causat.* 32to cause to shoot, produce, yield, Ja. 5.18.

Βλασφημέω, ῶ,
f. έσω, p. βεβλασφήμηκα, a.1. ἐβλασφήμησα,
to calumniate, revile, treat with calumny and contumely, Mat. 27.39, et al.; to speak of God or divine things in terms of impious irreverence, to blaspheme, Mat. 9.3; 26.65, et al.: *whence*

Βλασφημία, ας, ἡ,
calumny, railing, reproach, Mat. 15.19. Mar. 7.22, et al.; blasphemy, Mat. 12.31; 26.65, et al.

Βλάσφημος, ου, ὁ, ἡ,
calumnious, railing, reproachful, 2 Ti. 3.2. 2 Pe. 2.11; blasphemous, Ac. 6.11, 13. 1 Ti. 1.13.

Βλέμμα, ατος, τό,
a look; the act of seeing, sight, 2 Pe. 2.8: *from*

Βλέπω,
f. ψω, a.1. ἔβλεψα,
to possess and use the faculty of sight; to direct the eyes towards; to behold; to face, Ac. 27.12; to descry, observe; *met.* to direct the thoughts towards, consider; to discern mentally, perceive; to have regard to; to mind; to take heed; *in N.T.* βλέπειν ἀπό, to beware of, shun. Mat. 8.15.

Βλητέος, α ον, (*verbal adj.* fr. βάλλω)

requiring to be cast or put, Mar. 2.22. Lu. 5.38. N.T.

Βοάω, ῶ,
    f. ήσω, a.1. ἐβόησα,
    to cry out; to exclaim, proclaim, Mat. 3.3; 15.34. Ac. 8.7, et al.; πρός τινα, to invoke, implore the aid of any one, Lu. 18.7: *from*

Βοή, ῆς, ἡ,
    a cry, outcry, exclamation, Ja. 5.4.

Βοήθεια, ας, ἡ,
    help, succour, He. 4.16; *meton. pl.* helps, contrivances for relief and safety, Ac. 27.17: *from*

Βοηθέω, ῶ, (βοή & θέω, to run)
    f. ήσω, a.1. ἐβοήθησα,
    pr. to run to the aid of those who cry for help; to advance to the assistance of any one, help, aid, succour, Mat. 15.25. Mar. 9.22, 24, et al.: *from*

Βοηθός, οῦ, ὁ,
    a helper, He. 13.6.

Βόθῡνος, ου, ὁ,
    a pit, well, or cistern, Mat. 12.11; 15.14. Lu. 6.39.

Βολή, ῆς, ἡ, (βάλλω)
    a cast, a throw; the distance to which any thing can be throw, Lu. 22.41.

Βολίζω,
    f. ίσω, a.1. ἐβόλισα,
    to heave the lead, sound, Ac. 27.28: (L.G.) *from*

Βολίς, ίδος, ἡ, (βάλλω)
    a missile weapon, dart, javelin, He. 12.20; *also* a plummet, lead for sounding. L.G.

Βόρβορος, ου, ο,
    mud, mire, dung, filth, 2 Pe. 2.22.

Βορρᾶς, ᾶ, ὁ, i.q. Βορέας,
    pr. the north, or N.N.E. wind; *meton.* the north, Lu. 13.29. Re.21.13.

Βόσκω,
    f. βοσκήσω, a.1. ἐβόσκησα,
    to feed, pasture, tend while grazing; βόσκομαι, to feed, be feeding, Mat. 8.30, 33. Lu. 8.32, 34, et al.

Βοτάνη, ης, ἡ, (βόσκω)
    herb, herbage, produce *of the earth,* He. 6.7.

Βότρυς, υος, ὁ,
    a bunch or cluster of grapes, Re. 14.18.

Βουλευτής, οῦ, ὁ,
    a counsellor, senator; member of the Sanhedrim, Mar. 15.43. Lu. 23.50: *from*

Βουλεύω,
    f. εύσω,
    to give counsel, to deliberate; *mid.* βουλεύομαι, to deliberate, Lu. 14.31. Jno. 12.10. Ac. 5.33; to purpose, determine, Ac. 15.37; 27.39. 2 Co. 1.17: *from*

Βουλή, ῆς, ἡ (βούλομαι)
    counsel, purpose, design, determination, decree, Lu. 7.30; 23:51, et al. freq.; *by impl.* secret thoughts, congitation *of mind,* 1 Co. 4.5.

Βούλημα, ατος, τό,
    to purpose, will, determination, Ac. 27.43. Ro. 9.19.

Βούλομαι,

f. βουλήσομαι, *imperf.* ἐβουλόμην & At. ἠβουλόμην, a.1. pass. ἐβουλήθην & ἠβουλήθην, p. βεβούλημαι,
    to be willing, disposed, Mar. 15.15. Ac. 25.20; 28.18, et al.; to intend, Mat. 1.19. Ac. 5.28; 12.4. 2 Co. 1.15; to desire, 1 Ti. 6.9; to choose, be pleased, Jno. 18.39. Ac. 18.15. Ja. 3.4; to will, decree, appoint, Lu. 22.42. Ja. 1.18. 1 Co. 12.11. 1 Ti. 2.8; 5.14, et al.; ἐβουλόμην, I could wish, Ac. 25.22.

βουνός, οῦ, ὁ,
    a hill, hillock, rising ground, Lu. 3.5; 23.30.

Βοῦς, βοός, ὁ, ἡ,
    an ox, a bull or cow, *an animal of the ox kind,* Lu. 13.15, et al.

Βραβεῖον, ου, τό, (βραβεύς, a judge or arbiter in the public games)
    33a prize *bestowed on victors in the public games, such as a crown, wreath, chaplet, garland, &c.* 1 Co. 9.24. Phi. 3.14. L.G.

Βραβεύω, (fr. same)
    f. εύσω,
    pr. to be a director, or arbiter in the public games; *in N.T.* to preside, direct, rule, govern, be predominant, Col. 3.15.

Βραδύνω, (βραδύς)
    f. υνῶ,
    to be slow, to delay, be behindhand, 1 Ti. 3.15. 2 Pe. 3.9.

Βραδυπλοέω, ῶ,
    f. ήσω,
    to sail slowly, Ac. 27.7: (L.G.) fr. πλέω &

Βραδύς, εῖα, ύ,
    slow; not hasty, Ja. 1.19; slow of understanding, heavy, stupid, Lu. 24.25: *whence*

Βραδῠτής, τῆτος, ἡ,
    slowness, tardiness, delay, 2 Pe. 3.9.

Βραχίων, ονος, ὁ,
    the arm; *meton.* strength, might, power, Lu. 1.51. Jno. 12.38. Ac. 13.17. (ῑ).

Βραχύς, εῖα, ύ,
    short, brief; few, small, Lu. 22.58. Jno. 6.7, et al.

Βρέφος, εος, τό,
    a child; *whether unborn,* an embryo, fœtus, Lu. 1.41, 44; *or just born,* an infant, Lu. 2.12, 16. Ac. 7.19; *or partly grown,* Lu. 18.15. 2 Ti. 3.15; *met.* one who has just embraced the Christian faith, 1 Pe. 2.2.

Βρέχω,
    f. ξω, a.1. ἔβρεξα,
    to wet, moisten, Lu. 7.38; to rain, cause or send rain, Mat. 5.45. Lu. 17.29, et al.

Βροντή, ῆς, ἡ,
    thunder, Mar. 3.17. Jno. 12.29, et al.

Βροχή, ῆς, ἡ (βρέχω)
    rain, Mat. 7.25, 27. L.G.

Βρόχος, ου, ὁ,
    a cord, noose, 1 Co. 7.35.

Βρυγμός, οῦ, ὁ,
    a grating or gnashing of the teeth, Mat. 8.12; 13.42, 50, et al.: *from*

Βρύχω,
    f. ξω,
    to grate or gnash *the teeth,* Ac. 7.54 (ῠ).

Βρύω,

pr. to be full, to well *with any thing;* to emit, send forth, Ja. 3.11.

Βρῶμα, ατος, τό, (βιβρώσκω)
food, Mat. 14.15. Mar. 7.19, et al.; solid food, 1 Co. 3.2.

Βρώσιμος, ον, ὁ, ἡ (fr. same)
eatable, that may be eaten, Lu. 24.41.

Βρῶσις, εως, ἡ,
eating, the act of eating, Ro. 14.17. 1 Co. 8.4, et al.; meat, food, Jno. 6.27 He. 12.16; a canker or rust, æruge Mat. 6.19, 20.

Βυθίζω,
f. ίσω, a.1. ἐβύθισα,
to immerse, submerge, cause to sink, Lu. 5.17; to plunge deep, drown, 1 Ti. 6.9: *from*

Βυθός, ου, ὁ,
the bottom, lowest part; the deep, sea, 2 Co. 11.25.

Βυρσεύς, έως, ὁ (βύρσα, a hide)
a tanner, leather-dresser, Ac. 9.43; 10.6, 32. L.G.

Βύσσῖνος, η, ον,
made of byssus or fine cotton, Re. 18.16 *from*

Βύσσος, ου, ἡ,
byssus, *a species of fine cotton highly prized by the ancients,* Lu. 16.19. v.r. Re. 18.13.

Βωμός, οῦ, ὁ,
pr. a slightly elevated spot, base, pedestal; *hence,* an altar. Ac. 17.23.

Γ, γ, *Γάμμα*

Γάγγραινα, ης, ἡ, (γράω, γραίνω, to eat, gnaw)
gangrene, mortification, 2 Ti. 2.17.

Γάζα, ης, ἡ,
a treasure, treasury, Ac. 8.27.

Γαζοφυλάκιον, ου, τό, (γάζα & φυλακή)
a treasury; the sacred treasury, Mar. 12.41, 43. Lu. 21.1 Jno. 8.20. L.G.

Γάλα, γάλακτος, τό,
milk, 1 Co. 9.7; *met. spiritual* milk, the elementary parts of Christian instruction, 1 Co. 3.2. He. 5.12, 13; *spiritual* nutriment, 1 Pe. 2.2

Γαλήνη, ης, ἡ,
tranquillity of the sea, a calm, Mat. 8.26. Mar. 4.39. Lu. 8.24.

Γαμέω, ῶ,
f. ῶ, &, later, ήσω, p. γεγάμηκα, a.1. ἔγημα & ἐγάμησα, a.1. pass. ἐγαμήθην,
to marry, take a wife; to marry, enter the marriage state; *mid.* to marry, be married, Mar. 10.12. 1 Co. 7.9, 10, 28, 39, et al.; *whence*

Γαμίζω,
ίσω,
to give in marriage, permit to marry, v.r. 1 Co. 7.38. N.T.

Γαμίσκομαι,
to be given in marriage, Mar. 12.25. L.G.

Γάμος, ου, ὁ,
34a wedding, nuptials, *the nuptial ceremonies;* the attendant festivities, Mat. 25.10. Jno. 2.1, 2. Re. 19.7, 9; any feast or banquet, Lu. 12.36; 14.8; *meton.* the room in which a banquet is held, Mat. 22.10; the marriage state, He. 13.4.

Γάρ,

a causal particle or conjunction, for; *it is, however, frequently used with an ellipsis of the clause to which it has reference, and its force must then be variously expressed:* Mat. 15.27; 27.23, et al.: *it is also sometimes epexegetic, or introductory of an intimated detail of circumstances,* now, then, to wit, Mat. 1.18.

Γαστήρ, τέρος, τρός, ἡ,

the belly, stomach; the womb, Lu. 1.13; ἐν γαστρὶ ἔχειν, to be with child, Mat. 1.18, 23; 24.19, et al.; γαστέρες, paunches, gluttons, Tit. 1.12.

Γε,

an enclitic particle imparting emphasis; indicating that a particular regard is to be had to the term to which it is attached. Its force is to be conveyed, when this is possible, by various expression: at least, indeed, even, &c.

Γέεννα, ης, ἡ, (Heb. סon אינ)

Gehenna, *pr.* the valley of Hinnom *south of Jerusalem, once celebrated for the horrid worship of Moloch, & afterwards polluted with every species of filth, as well as the carcases of animals, and dead bodies of malefactors; to consume which, in order to avert the pestilence which such a mass of corruption would occasion, constant fires were kept burning; hence,* hell, the fires of Tartarus, the place of punishment in Hades, Mat. 5.22, 29, 30; 10.28; 18.9, et al. N.T.

Γείτων, ονος, ὁ, ἡ

a neighbour, Lu. 14.12; 15.6, 9. Jno. 9.8

Γελάω, ῶ,

f. ἁσομαι, &, later, ασω, a.1. ἐγέλασα,

to laugh, smile; *by impl.* to be merry, happy, to rejoice, Lu. 6.21, 25. (ᾰ).

Γέλως, ωτος, ὁ,

laughter; *by impl.* mirth, joy, rejoicing, Ja. 4.9.

Γεμίζω,

f. ίσω, a.1. ἐγέμισα, a.1 pass. ἐγεμίσθην,

to fill, Mar. 4.37; 15.26, et al: *from*

Γέμω,

to be full, Mat. 23.27. Lu. 11.39, et al.

Γενεά, ᾶς, ἡ,

pr. birth; *hence,* progeny; a generation *of mankind,* Mat. 11.16; 23.36, et al.; a generation, *a step in a genealogy,* Mat. 1.17; a generation, *an interval of time,* age; *in N.T.* course of life, *in respect of its events, interests, or character,* Lu. 16.8. Ac. 13.36.

Γενεαλογέω, ῶ, (γενεά & λέγω)

f. ήσω,

to reckon one's descent, derive one's origin, He. 7.6: *whence*

Γενεαλογία, ας, ἡ,

genealogy, catalogue of ancestors, history of descent, 1 Ti. 1.4. Tit. 3.9.

Γενέσια, ων, τά,

pr. a day observed in memory of the dead; *in N.T.* equivalent to γενέθλια, celebration of one's birth-day, birth-day festival. Mat. 14.6. Mar. 6.21.

Γένεσις, εως, ἡ,

birth, nativity, Mat. 1.18. Lu. 1.14. Ja. 1.23; successive generation, descent, lineage, Mat. 1.1; *meton.* life, Ja. 3.6.

Γενετή, ῆς, ἡ,

birth, Jno, 9.1.

Γένημα, τό,

v.r. Lu. 12.18. 2 Co. 9.10, natural produce, fruit, increase. N.T.

Γεννάω, ω,

f. ἥσω, p. γεγέννηκα, a.1. ἐγέννησα, p. pass. γεγέννημαι, a.1. pass. ἐγεννήθην, *spoken of men,* to beget, generate, Mat. 1.2...16, et al.; *of women,* to bring forth, bear, give birth to, Lu. 1.13, 57, et al.; *pass.* to be born, produced, Mat. 2.1, 4, et al.; *met.* to produce, excite, give occasion to, effect, 2 Ti. 2.23; *from the Heb.* to constitute as son, to constitute as king, or as the representative or vicegerent of God, Ac. 13.33. He. 1.5; 5.5; *by impl.* to be a parent to *any one; pass.* to be a son or child *to any one,* Jno. 1.13. 1 Co. 4.15, et al.: *whence*

Γέννημα, ατος, τό,
 what is born or produced, offspring, progeny, brood, Mat. 3.7; 12.34, et al.; fruit, produce, Mat. 26.29. Mar. 14.25, et al.; fruit, increase, Lu. 12.18; 2 Co. 9.10.

Γέννησις, εως, ἡ,
 birth, nativity, Mat. 1.18. Lu. 1.14.

Γεννητός, ή, όν,
 born, or produced of, Mat. 1.18. Lu. 7.28.

Γένος, εος, τό, (γίνομαι)
 offspring, progeny, Ac. 17.28, 29; family, kindred, lineage, Ac. 7.13, et al.; race, nation, people, Mar. 7.26. Ac. 4.36. et al.; 35kind, sort, species, Mat. 13.47, et al.

Γερουσία, ας, ἡ,
 a senate, assembly of elders; the elders *of Israel collectively,* Ac. 5.21: *from*

Γέρων, οντος, ὁ,
 an old man, Jno. 3.4.

Γεύομαι, (mid of γεύω, to cause to taste)
 f. γεύσομαι, a.1 ἐγευσάμην,
 to taste, Mat. 24.34. Jno. 2.9; *absol.* to take food, Ac. 10.10, et al.; *met.* to have perception of, experience, He. 6.4, 5. 1 Pe. 2.3; θανάτου γεύεσθαι, to experience death, to die Mat. 16.28, et al.

Γεωργέω, ῶ, (γεωργός)
 f. ἥσω,
 to cultivate, till the earth, He. 6.7.

Γεώργιον, οὗ, τό,
 cultivated field, or ground, a farm, 1 Co. 3.9: *from*

Γεωργός, οὗ, ὁ, (γῆ & ἔργον)
 a husbandman, one who tills the earth, 2 Ti. 2.6. Ja. 5.7; *in N.T. spc.* a vine-dresser, keeper of a vineyard, i.q. ἀμπελουργός, Mat. 21.33, 34, et al.

Γῆ, γῆς, ἡ, (contr. fr. γέα)
 earth, soil, Mat. 13.5. Mar. 4.8, et al.; the ground, surface of the earth, Mat. 10.29. Lu. 6.49, et al.; the land, *as opposed to the sea or a lake,* Lu. 5.11. Jno. 21.8, 9, 11; the earth, world, Mat. 5.18, 35, et al.; a land, region, tract, country, territory, Mat. 2.20; 14.34; *by way of eminence,* Canaan or Palestine, Mat. 5.5; 24.30; 27.45. Ep. 6.3; the inhabitants of any region or country, Mat. 10.15; 11.24, et al.

Γῆρας, αος, ως, τό, *dat.* γήραϊ, γήρᾳ, also γήρει,
 old age, Lu. 1.36: *whence*

Γηράσκω, v. γηράω, ω,
 f. άσομαι, a.1. ἐγήρᾱσα, & ἐγήρᾱνα,
 to be or become old, Jno. 21.18. He. 8.13.

Γίνομαι, (a later form of γίγνομαι)
 f. γενήσομαι, p, γέγονα & γεγένημαι, a.1. ἐγενήθην, a.2. ἐγενόμην,
 to come into existence; to be created, exist by creation, Jno. 1.3, 10. He. 11.3. Ja. 3.9; to be born, produced, grow, Mat. 21.19. Jno. 8.58, et al.; to arise, come on, occur, *as the phenomena of nature,* &c.; Mat. 8.24, 26; 9.16, et al.; to come, approach, *as*

morning or evening, Mat. 8.16, 14.15, 23; to be appointed, constituted, established, Mar. 2.27. Ga. 3.17, et al.; to take place, come to pass, happen, occur, Mat. 1.22; 24.6, 20, 21, 34, et al. freq.; to be done, performed, effected, Mat. 21.42, et al.; to be fulfilled, satisfied, Mat. 6.10; 26.42, et al.; to come into a particular state or condition; to become, assume the character and appearance *of any thing,* Mat. 5.45; 12.45, et al.; to become or be made *any thing,* be changed or converted, Mat. 4.3; 21.42. Mar. 1.17, et al.; to be, esse, Mat. 11.26; 19.8; γίνεσθαι ὑπό τινα, to be subject to, Ga. 4.4; γίνεσθαι ἐν ἑαυτῷ, to come to one's self, to recover from a trance or surprise, Ac. 12.11; μὴ γένοιτο, let it not be, far be it from, God forbid, Lu. 20.16. Ro. 3.4, 31, et al.; to be kept, celebrated, solemnised, *as festivals,* Mat. 26.2, et al.; to be finished, completed, He. 4.3.

Γῑνώσκω, (a later form of γιγνώσκω)

    f. γνώσομαι, p. ἔγνωκα, a.2. ἔγνων, p. pass. ἔγνωσμαι, a.1. pass. ἐγνώσθην, to know, *whether the action be inceptive or complete and settled;* to preceive, Mat. 22.18. Mar. 5.29; 8.17; 12.12. Lu. 8.46; to mark, discern, Mat. 25.24. Lu. 19.44; to ascertain by examination, Mar. 6.38. Jno. 7.51. Ac. 23.28; to understand, Mar. 4.13. Lu. 18.34. Jno. 12.16; 13.7. Ac. 8.30, 1 Co. 14.7, 9; to acknowledge, Mat. 7.23. 2 Co. 3.2; to be resolve, conclude, Lu. 16.4. Jno. 7.26; 17.8; to be assured, Lu. 21.20. Jno. 6.69; 8.52. 2 Pe. 1.20; to be skilled, to be master of *a thing,* Mat. 16.3. Ac. 21.37; to know *carnally,* Mat. 1.25. Lu. 1.34; *fr. the Heb.* to view with favour, 1 Co. 8.3. Gal. 4.9.

Γλεῦκος, εος, τό,

    pr. the unfermented juice of grapes, must; *hence,* sweet new wine. Ac. 2.13: *from*

Γλῠκύς, εῖα, ύ,

    sweet, Ja. 3.11, 12. Re. 10.9, 10.

Γλῶσσα, ης, ἡ,

    the tongue, Mar. 7.33, 35, et al.; *meton.* speech, talk, 1 Jno. 3.18; a tongue, language, Ac. 2.11. 1 Co. 13.1, et al.; *meton.* a language not proper to a speaker, a gift or faculty of such language, Mar. 16.17. 1 Co. 14.13, 14, 26, et al.: *fr. Heb.* a nation *as defined by its language,*36 Re. 5.9, et al.; *met.* a tongue-shaped flame, Ac. 2.3.

Γλωσσόκομον, ου, τό, (γλῶσσα & κομέω, to keep, perserve)

    pr. a box for keeping tongues, mouthpieces, or reeds, of musical instruments; *hence, genr.* any box or receptacle; *in N.T.* a purse, money bag. Jno. 12.6; 13.29. L.G.

Γναφεύς, έως, ὁ, (γνάφος, a teasel, or thistle)

    a fuller, *part of whose business was to raise a nap by meanss of teasels,* &c., Mar. 9.3.

Γνήσιος, ου, ὁ, ἡ, (γένος)

    lawful, legitimate, *as children;* genuine, *in faith,* &c. 1 Ti. 1.2. Tit. 1.4; true, sincere, 2 Co. 8.8. Phi. 4.3: *whence*

Γνησίως,

    adv. genuinely, sincerely, Phi. 2.20.

Γνόφος, ου, ὁ,

    a thick cloud, darness, He. 12.18.

Γνώμη, ης, ἡ, (γινώσκω)

    the mind, *as the means of knowing and judging; various operations of the mind, as* inclination, 1 Co. 1.10; accordance, consent, Phile. 14; purpose, resolution, Ac. 20.3; opinion, judgement, 1 Co. 7.25, 40. 2 Co. 8.10.

Γνωρίζω,

    f. ίσω, At. ιῶ, a.1. ἐγνώρισα, a.1. pass. ἐγνωρίσθην, to make known, reveal, declare, Jno. 15.15; 17.26, et al.; to know, Phi. 1.22.

Γνῶσις, εως, ἡ, (γινώσκω)

knowledge, Lu. 1.77; knowledge *of an especial kind and relatively high character,* Lu. 11.52. Ro. 2.20. 1 Ti. 6.20, *more particularly in respect of Christian enlightenment,* Ro. 15.14. 1 Co. 8.10; 12.8. 2 Co. 11.6, et al.

Γνώστης, ου, ὁ, (fr. same)

one acquainted with *a thing,* knowing, skilful, Ac. 26.3. L.G.

Γνωστός, ή, όν, (fr. same)

known, Jno. 18.15, 16, et al.; certain, incontrovertible, Ac. 4.16; τὸ γνωστόν, that which is known or is cognisable, the unquestionable attributes, Ro. 1.19; *subst.* an acquaintance, Lu. 2.44; 23.49.

Γογγύζω,

f. ύσω, a.1. ἐγόγγυσα,

to speak privately and in a low voice, mutter, Jno. 7.32; to utter secret and sullen discontent, express indignant complaint, murmer, grumble, Mat. 20.11. Lu. 5.30. Jno. 6.4, 43, 61: (L.G.) *whence*

Γογγυσμός, οῦ, ὁ,

a muttering, murmuring, low and suppressed discourse, Jno. 7.12; the expression of secret and sullen discontent, murmuring, complaint, Ac. 6.1. Phi. 2.14. 1 Pe. 4.9. L.G.

Γογγυστής, οῦ, ὁ,

a murmurer, Jude 16. L.G.

Γόης, ητος, ὁ,

a juggler, diviner; *hence, by impl.* an imposter, cheat, 2 Ti. 3.13.

Γόμος, ου, ὁ (γέμω)

the lading of a ship, Ac. 21.3; *by impl.* mechandise, Re. 18.11, 12.

Γονεύς, έως, ὁ, (γίνομαι)

a father; *pl.* parents, Mat. 10.21. Lu. 2.27, 41. 2 Co. 12.14.

Γόνυ, ἄτος, τό,

the knee, Lu. 22.41. He. 12.12, et al.

Γονυπετέω, ῶ, (γόνυ & πίπτω)

f. ήσω, a.1. ἐγανυπέτησα,

to fall upon one's knees, to kneel before, Mat. 17.14; 27.29. Mar. 1.40; 10.17.

Γράμμα, ἄτος, τό, (γράφω)

pr. that which is written or drawn; a letter, character of the alphabet, Lu. 23.38; a writing, book, Jno. 5.47; an acknowledgement of debt, an account, a bill, note, Lu. 16.6, 7; an epistle, letter, Ac. 28.21. Ga. 6.11; ἱερὰ γράμματα, Holy writ, the sacred books of the Old Testament, the Jewish Scriptures, 2 Ti. 3.15; *spc.* the letter of the law of Moses, *i.e.* the bare literal sense, Ro. 2.27, 29. 2 Co. 3.6, 7; *pl.* letters, learning, Jno. 7.15. Ac. 26.24: *whence*

Γραμμἄτεύς, εως, ὁ,

a scribe, a clerk, town-clerk, register, recorder, Ac. 19.35; one skilled in the Jewish law, a teacher or interpreter of the law, Mat. 2.4; 5.20, et al. freq.; *genr.* a religious teacher, Mat. 13.52; *by synecd.* any one distinguished for learning or wisdom, 1 Co. 1.20.

Γραπτός, ή, όν, (γράφω)

written, Ro. 2.15.

Γραφή, ῆς, ἡ,

a writing; *in N.T.* the Holy Scriptures, the Jewish Scriptures or books of the Old Testament, Mat. 21.42. Jno. 5.39, et al.; *by synecd.* doctrines, declarations, oracles, or promises *contained in the sacred books,* Mat. 22.29. Mar. 12.24, et al.; *spc.* a prophecy, 37Mat. 36.54. Mar. 14.49. Lu. 4.21; 24.27, 32; *with the addition of* προφητική, Ro. 16.26, *of* τῶν προφητῶν, Mat. 26.56: *from*

Γράφω,

f. ψω, p. γέγρᾰφα, a.1. ἔγραψα,

to engrave, write, *according to the ancient method of writing on plates of metal, waxed tables,* &c. Jno. 8.6, 8; to write *on parchment, paper,* &c. *generally,* Mat. 27.37, et al.; to write *lettrs to another,* Ac. 23.25. 2 Co. 2.9; 13.10, et al.; to describe in writing, Jno. 1.46. Ro. 10.5; to inscribe *in a catalogue,* &c. Lu. 10.20. Re. 13.8; 17.8, et al.; to write or impose a law, command or enact in writing, Mar. 10.5; 12.19. Lu. 2.23, et al.

Γραώδης, εος, ὁ, ἡ, τό, -ες, (γραῦς, an old woman)

old-womanish; *by impl.* silly, absurd, 1 Ti. 4.7. L.G.

Γρηγορέω, ῶ, (a later form from the *perf.* ἐγρήγορα)

f. ήσω, a.1. ἐγρηγόρησα,

to be awake, to watch, Mat. 26.38, 40, 41. Mar. 14.34, 37, 38; to be alive, 1 Thes. 5.10; *met.* to be watchful, attentive, vigilant, circumspect, Mat. 25.13. Mar. 13.35, et al.

Γυμνάζω, (γυμνός)

f. άσω, p. pass. γεγύμνασμαι,

pr. to train in gymnastic discipline; *hence,* to exercise *in any thing,* train to use, discipline, 1 Ti. 4.7. He. 5.14; 12.11. 2 Pe. 2.14: *whence*

Γυμνασία, ας, ἡ,

pr. gymnastic exercise; *hence,* bodily discipline *of any kind,* 1 Ti. 4.8.

Γυμνητεύω,

f. εύσω,

to be naked; *by synecd.* to be poorly clad, or destitute of proper and sufficient clothing, 1 Co. 4.11: (L.G.) *from*

Γυμνός, ή, όν,

naked, without clothing, Mar. 14.51, 52; without the upper garment, and clad only with an inner garment or tunic, Jno. 21.7; poorly or meanly clad, destitute of proper and sufficient clothing, Mat. 25.36, 38, 43, 44. Ac. 19.16. Ja. 2.15; *met.* without a body, 2 Co. 5.3; not covered, uncovered, open, manifest, He. 4.13; bare, mere, 1 Co. 15.37; naked of spiritual clothing, Re. 3.17; 16.15; 17.16: *whence*

Γυμνότης, τητος, ἡ,

nakedness; want of proper and sufficient clothing, Ro. 8.35. 2 Co. 11.27; *spiritual* nakedness, being destitute of spiritual clothing, Re. 3.18. S.

Γυναικάριον, (dimin. of γυνή)

a little woman, muliercula; a trifling, weak, silly woman, 2 Ti. 3.6. L.G.

Γυναικεῖος, εία, εῖον,

pertaining to women, female, 1 Pe. 3.7: *from*

Γυνή, γυναικός, ἡ,

a woman, Mat. 5.28, et al.; a married woman, wife, Mat. 5.31, 32; 14.3, et al.; *in the voc.* ὦ γύναι, O woman, *an ordinary mode of addressing females under every circumstance; met. used of the church, as united to Christ,* Re. 19.7; 21.9.

Γωνία, ας, ἡ,

an exterior angle, projecting corner, Mat. 6.5; 21.42, et al.; an interior angle; *by impl.* a dark corner, obscure place, Ac. 26.26; corner, extremity, or quarter *of the earth,* Re. 7.1; 20.8.

Δ, δ, *Δέλτα*

Δαιμονίζομαι,

f. ἴσομαι, a.1. ἐδαιμονίσθην,

in N.T. to be possessed, afflicted, vexed, by a demon, or evil spirit; i.q. δαιμόνιον ἔχειν, Mat. 4.24; 8.16, 28, 33, et al.: *from*

Δαιμίνιον, ίου, τό, (δαίμων)

a *heathen* god, deity, Ac. 17.18. 1 Co. 10.20, 21. Re. 9.20; *in N.T.,* a demon, evil spirit, Mat. 7.22; 9.33, 34; 10.8; 12.24, et al.: *whence*

Δαιμονιώδης, εος, ό, ή;

pertaining to or proceeding from demons; demoniacal, devilish, Ja. 3.15. L.G.

Δαίμων, ονος, ό, ή,

a god, a superior power; *in N.T.* a malignant demon, evil angel, Mat. 8.31. Mar. 5.12. Lu. 8.29. Re. 16.14; 18.2.

Δάκνω,

f. δήξομαι, a.2. ἔδακον, p. δέδηχα,

to bite, string; *met.* to molest, vex, injure, Gal. 5.15.

Δάκρυ, υος, τό, & δάκρυον, ύου, τό,

a tear.

Δακρύω,

f. ὑσω, a.1. ἐδάκρυσο,

to shed tears, weep, Jno. 11.35 (ῡ)

Δακτύλιος, ου, ό,

a ring for the finger, Lu. 15.22: *from*

Δάκτῠλος, ου, ό,

a finger, Mat. 28.4. Mar. 7.33, et al.; *fr. Heb.* power, Lu. 11.20.

Δαμάζω, (δαμάω, the same)

f. άσω, a.1. ἐδάμασο, p. pass. δεδάμασμαι,

38to subdue, tame, Mar. 5.4. Ja. 3.7; *met.* to restrain within proper limits, govern, Ja. 3.8. (μᾰ).

Δάμᾰλις, εως, ή,

a heifer, He. 9.13.

Δανείζω,

f. είσω, a.1. ἐδάνεισα,

to lend money, Lu. 6.34, 35; *mid.* to borrow money, Mat. 5.42: *from*

Δάνειον, ου, τό, (δάνος, a gift, loan)

a loan, debt. Mat. 18.27.

Δανειστής, οῦ, ό, (δαωείζω)

a lender, creditor, Lu. 7.41. L.G.

Δαπανάω, ῶ,

f. ήσω, a.1. ἐδαπάνησα,

to expend, be at expense, Mar. 5.26. Ac. 21.24. 2 Co. 12.15; to spend, waste, conosume by extravagance, Lu. 15.14. Ja. 4.3: *from*

Δαπάνη, ης, ή,

expense, cost, Lu. 14.28. (πᾰ).

Δέ,

a conjunctive particle, marking the superaddition of a clause, whether in opposition or in continuation, to what has preceded, and it may be variously rendered but, on the other hand, and, also, now, &c; καὶ δέ, *when there is a special superaddition in continuation,* too, yea, &c. *It sometimes is found at the commencement of the apodosis of a sentence, Ac. 11.17. It serves also to mark the resumption of an interrupted discourse, 2 Co. 2.10. Gal. 2.6*

Δέησις, εως, ή, (δέομαι)

want, entreaty; prayer, supplication, Lu. 1.13; 2.37; 5.33, et al.

Δεῖ,

    imperson. fr. δέω, f. δεήσει, a.1. ἐδέησε, *imperf.* ἔδει, *subj.* δέη, *inf.* δεῖν, *part.* δέον, it is binding, it is necessary, it behoveth, it is proper; it is inevitable, Ac. 21.22.

Δεῖγμα, ἄτος, τό, (δείκνυμι)

    pr. that which is shown, a speciment, sample; *met.* an example *by way of warning,* Jude 7: *whence*

Δειγματίζω,

    f. ίσω, a.1. ἐδειγμάτισα,

    to make a public show or spectacle of, Col. 2.15. *N.T.*

Δεικνύω, (ῠ) v. δείκνῡμι,

    f. δείξω, a.1. ἔδειξα, a.1. pass. ἐδείχθην,

    to show, point out, present to the sight, Mat. 4.8; 8.4, et al.; to exhibit, permit to see, cause to be seen, Jno. 2.18; 10.32. 1 Ti. 6.15; to demonstrate, prove, Ja. 2.18; 3.13; met. to teach, make known, declare, announce, Mat. 16.21. Jno. 5.20. Ac. 10.28, et al.

Δειλία, ας, ἡ (δειλός)

    timidity. 2 Ti. 1.7.

Δειλιάω, ῶ,

    f. άσω,

    to be timid, be in fear, Jno. 14.27: (L.G.) *from*

Δειλός, ή, όν,

    timid, fearful, pusillanimous, cowardly, Mat. 8.26, Mar. 4.40. Re. 21.8.

Δεῖνα, ὁ, ἡ, τό,

    gen. δεῖνος, acc. δεῖνα,

    such a one, a certain one, Mat. 26.18.

Δεινῶς, (δεινος, terrible, vehement)

    adv. dreadfully, grievously, greatly, vehemently, Mat. 8.6. Lu. 11.53.

Δειπνέω, ῶ,

    f. ήσω & ήσομαι, a.1. ἐδείπνησα,

    to sup, Lu. 17.8; 22.20. 1 Co. 11.25. Re. 3.20: *from*

Δεῖπνον, ου, τό,

    pr. a meal; supper, the principal meal taken in the evening, Lu. 14.12. Jno. 13.2, 4, et. al.; *meton.* food, 1 Co. 11.21; a feast, banquet, Mat. 23.6. Mar. 6.24, 12.39, et al.

Δεισιδαιμονία, ας, ἡ,

    fear of the gods; *in a bad sense,* superstition; a form of religious belief, Ac. 25.19: (L.G.) *from*

Δεισιδαίμων, ονος, ὁ, ἡ, (δείδω, to fear, & δαίμων)

    reverencing the gods and divine things, religious; *in a bad sense,* superstitious; *in N.T.* careful and precise in the discharge of religious services, Ac. 17.22.

Δέκα, οἱ, αἱ, τά,

    ten, Mat. 20, 24; 25.1, et al.; ἡμερῶν δέκα, ten days, a few days, a short time, Re. 2.10.

Δεκαδύο, οἱ, αἱ, τά, (δέκα & δύο)

    i.q. δώδεκα, twelve, Ac. 19.7; 24.11.

Δεκαπέντε, οἱ, αἱ, τά, (δέκα & πέωτε)

    fifteen, Jno. 11.18. Ac. 27.28. Gal. 1.18.

Δεκατέσσαρες, ων, οἱ, αἱ, & τὰ δεκατέσσαρα, (δέκα & τέσσαρες)

    fourteen, Mat. 1.17. 2 Co. 12.2. Gal. 2.1

Δέκᾰτος, η, ον, (δέκα)

tenth, Jno. 1.40. Re. 11.13; 21.20; δεκάτη, sc. μερίς, a tenth part, tithe, He. 7.2, 4, 8, 9: *whence*

Δεκατόω, ῶ,
    f. ώςω, p. δεδεκάτωκα,
    to cause to pay tithes; *pass* to be tithed, pay tithes, He. 7.6, 9. N.T.

Δεκτός, ή, όη, (δέχομαι)
    accepted, acceptable, agreeable, approved, Lu. 4.24. Ac. 10.35. Phi. 4.18; 39*by impl. when used for a certain time,* marked by a favourable manifestation of the devine pleasure, propitious, Lu. 4.19. 2 Co. 6.2. S.

Δελεάζω, (δέλεαρ, a bait,)
    f. άσω,
    pr. to entrap, take or catch *with a bait; met.* allure, entice, delude, Ja. 1.14. 2 Pe. 14, 18.

Δένδρον, ου, τό,
    a tree, Mat. 3.10; 7.17; 13.32.

Δεξιολάβος, ου, ό, (δεξιός & λαμβάνω)
    one posted on the right hand; a flank guard; a light armed spearman, Ac. 23.23. (ᾰ). N.T.

Δεξιός, ά, όν,
    right, *as opposed to left,* dexter, Mat. 5.29, 30. Lu. 6.6, et al.; ή δεξιά, sc. χείρ, the right hand, Mat. 6.3; 27.39, et al.; τὰ δεξιά, sc. νέρη, the parts towards the right hand, the right hand side; καθίζειν, v. καθῆσθαι, v. ἑστάναι, ἐκ δεξιῶν (μερῶν) τινος, to sit or stand at the right hand of any one, to enjoy with any one the highest honour and dignity which he can bestow, Mat. 20.21; 26.64, et al.; εἶναι ἐκ δεξιῶν (μερῶν) τινος, to be at one's right hand, to be one's helper, to afford aid to any one, Ac. 2.25; δεξιὰς (χεῖρας) διδόναι, to give the right hand *to any one, as a pledge of sincerity in one's promises,* Gal. 2.9.

Δέομαι,
    see δέω.

Δίον, οντος, τό, (*part. of* δεῖ)
    necessary, 1 Pe. 1.6; proper,right, Ac. 19.36. 1 Ti. 5.13.

Δέος, δέους, τό, (δείδω, to fear)
    fear, v.r. He. 12.28.

Δέρμα, ἄτος, τό, (δέρω)
    the skin *of an animal,* He. 11.37: *whence*

Δερμάτῐνος, η, ον,
    made of skin, leathern, Mat. 3.4. Mar. 1.6.

Δέρω,
    f. δερῶ, a.1. ἔδειρα, 2. f. pass. δαρήσομια,
    to skin, flay; *hence,* to beat, scourge, Mat. 21.35. Mar. 12.3, 5; 13.9, et al.

Δεσμεύω, (δεσμός)
    f. εύσω,
    to bind, bind up, *as a bundle,* Mat. 23.4; to bind, confine, Ac. 22.4.

Δεσμέω, ῶ, (fr. same)
    f. ήσω,
    to bind, confine, i.q. δεσμεύω, Lu. 8.29. L.G.

Δεσμή, ῆς, ή (δέω)
    a bundle *as of tares,* Mat. 13.20.

Δέσμιος, ίου, ό, (fr. same)
    one bound, a prisoner, Mat. 27.15, 16. Mar. 15.6, et al,

Δεσμός, οῦ, ὁ, *pl.* τά δεσμά, & οἱ δεσμοί, (fr. same)
a bond, any thing by which one is bound, a cord, chain, fetters, &c.; *and by meton.* imprisonment, Lu. 8.29. Ac. 16.26; 20.23, et al.; a string or ligament, *as of the tongue,* Mar. 7.35; *met.* an impediment, infirmity, Lu. 13.16.

Δεσμοφύλαξ, ἄκος, ὁ, (δεσμός & φυλάσσω)
a keeper of a prison, jailer, Ac. 16.23, 27, 36. (ῠ). L.G.

Δεσμωτήριον, ίου, τό, (δεσμόω)
a prison, Mat. 11.2. Ac. 5.21, 23; 16.26.

Δεσμώτης, ου, ὁ, (fr. same)
a prisoner, i.q. δέσμιος, Ac. 27.1, 42.

Δεσπότης, ου, ὁ,
a lord, master, *especially of salves,* 1 Ti. 6.1, 2. 2 Ti. 2.21. Tit. 2.9. 1 Pe. 2.18; *by impl. as denoting the possession of supreme authority,* Lord, sovereign, *used of God,* Lu. 2.29. Ac. 4.24. Re. 6.10, *and of Christ,* 2 Pe. 2.1. Jude 4.

Δεῦρο,
adv. hither, here; *used also as a sort of imperative,* come, come hither! Mat. 19.21. Mar. 10.21, et al.; *used of time,* ἄχρι τοῦ δεῦρο, sc. χρόνου, to the present time, Ro. 1.13.

Δεῦτε, i.e. δεῦρ' ἴτε,
an exclamation in the plural, of which the singular form is δεῦρο, come, Mat. 4.19; 11.28, et al.; *as a particle of exhortation, incitement, &c., and followed by an imperative,* come now, &c. Mat. 21.38; 28.6, et al.

Δευτεραῖος, αία, αῖον, (δεύτερος)
on the second day *of a certain state or process, and used as an epithet of the subject or agent,* Ac. 28.13.

Δεύτερον, *neut. of* δεύτερος,
used as an *adv.* the second time, again, Jno. 3.4; 21.16, et al.

Δευτερόπρωτος, ου, ὁ, ἡ, δεύτερος & πρῶτος)
second-first, *an epithet of uncertain meaning, but probably appropriated to the Sabbath following the first day of unleavened bread,* Lu. 6.1. N.T.

Δεύτερος, α, ον, (δύο)
second, Mat. 22.26, et al.; τὸ δεύτερον, again, 40the second time, another time, Jude 5; *so* ἐκ δευτέρου, Mat. 26.42, et al.; & ἐν τῷ δευτέρῳ, Ac. 7.13.

Δέχομαι,
f. ξομαι, p. δέδεγμαι, a.1. ἐδεξάμην,
to take *into one's hands,* &c. Lu. 2.28; 16.6, 7, et al.; to receive, Ac. 22.5; 28.21. Phi. 4.18; to receive into and retain, contain, Ac. 3.21; *met.* to receive *by the hearing,* learn, acquire a knowledge of, 2 Co. 11.4. Ja. 1.21; to receive, admit, grant access to, to receive kindly, welcome, Mat. 10.40, 41; 18.5, et al.; to receive in hospitality, entertain, Lu. 9.53. He. 11.31; to bear with, bear patiently, 2 Co. 11.16; *met.* to receive, approve, assent to, Mat. 11.14. Lu. 8.13. Ac. 8.14; 11.1, et al.; to admin, *and by impl.* to embrace, follow, 1 Co. 2.14. 2 Co. 8.17, et al.

Δέω,
f. δήσω, p. δέδεκα, a.1. ἔδησα, p. pass. δέδεμαι, a.1. pass. ἐδέθην,
to bind, tie, Mat. 13.30; 21.2, et al.; to bind, confine, Mat. 27.2; 14.3, et al.; to impede, hinder, 2 Ti. 2.9; to affect with disease, Lu. 13.16; to bind *by a legal or moral tie, as marriage,* Ro. 7.2. 1 Co. 7.27, 39; *by impl.* to impel, compel, Ac. 20.22; *in N.T.,* to pronounce or declare any thing to be binding or obligatory; *or,* to declare any thing prohibited and unlawful, Mat. 16.19; 18.18.

Δέω,

f. δεήσω, a.1. ἐδέησα,
to lack, fall short of;
mid. δέομαι, f. δεήσομαι, a.1. ἐδεήθην,
to be in want, to need; to ask, request, Mat. 9.38. Lu. 5.12; 8.23, 38, et al.; *in N.T. absol.* to pray, offer prayer, beseech, supplicate, Lu. 21.36; 22.32. Ac. 4.31; 8.22, 24, et al.

Δή,
a particle serving to add an intensity of expression to a term or clause. Its simplest and most ordinary uses are when it gives impressiveness to an affirmation, indeed, really, doubtless, Mat. 13.23. 2 Co. 12.1, *or earnestness to a call, injunction or entreaty,* Lu. 2.15. Ac. 13.2; 15.36. 1 Co. 6.20.

Δῆλος, η, ον,
pr. clearly visible; plain, manifest, evident, Mat. 26.73. 1 Co. 15.27. Gal. 3.11. 1 Ti. 6.7: *whence*

Δηλόω, ῶ
f. ώσω, a.1. ἐδήλωσα,
to render manifest or evident; to make known, to tell, relate, declare, 1 Co. 1.11. Col. 1.8; to show, point out, bring to light, 1 Co. 3.13, to intimate, signify, He. 9.8; 12.27; 1 Pe. 1.11.

Δημηγορέω, ῶ, (δῆμος, & ἀγορεύω)
f. ήσω,
to address a public assembly, to deliver an harangue or public oration, Ac. 12.21.

Δημιουργός, οῦ, ὁ, (δῆμος, & ἔργον)
pr. one who labours for the public, or, exercises some public calling; an architect, *especially* the Divine Architect of the universe, He. 11.10.

Δῆμος, ου, ὁ,
the people, Ac. 12.22; 17.5; 19.30, 33: *whence*

Δημόσιος, ία, ον,
public, belonging to the public, Ac. 5.18; δημοσίᾳ, publicly, Ac. 16.37; 18.28; 20.20.

Δηνάριον, ίου, τό,
Lat. denarius, *a Roman silver coin. The silver denarius was at first equivalent to about 8 ½d. of English money, declining, under the empire, to about 7 ½d., and was therefore somewhat less than the Greek* δραχμή. *The name originally imported* ten ases.

Δήποτε,
an intensive combination of the particle δή *with* πότε; *which see; as an intensive,* Jno. 5.4.

Δήπου,
see που.

Διά,
prep., with a genitive, through, *used of place or medium,* Mat. 7.13. Lu. 6.1. 2 Co. 11.33. et al.; through, *of time,* during, in the course of, He. 2.15. Ac. 5.19, et al.; through, *of immediate agency, causation, instrumentality,* by means of, by, Jno. 1.3. Ac. 3.18, et al.; *of means or manner,* throught, by, with Lu. 8.4. 2 Co. 5.7; 8.8, et al.; *of state or condition,* in a state of, Ro. 4.11, et al.;
with an accusative, used of causation which is not direct and immediate in the production of a result, on account of, because of, for the sake of, with a view to, Mar. 2.27. Jno. 1.31, et al.; *rearely,* through, while subjected to *a state of untoward circumstances,* Gal. 4.13.

Διαβαίνω, (διά & βαίνω)

f. βήσομαι, a.2 διέβην,
to pass through or over, Lu. 16.26. Ac. 16.9. He. 11.29.
Διαβάλλω, (διά & βάλλω)
f. βαλῶ,
to throw or convey through or over to thrust through; 41to defame, to inform against,
Lu. 16.1.
Διαβεβαιόομαι, (διά & βεβαιόω)
to assert strongly, asseverate, 1 Ti. 1.7. Tit. 3.8.
Διαβλέπω, (διά & βλέπω)
f. ψω,
to look through; to view steadily; to see clearly or steadily, Mat. 7.5. Lu. 6.42.
Διάβολος, ου, ὁ, ἡ, (διαβάλλω)
to calumniator, slanderer, 1 Ti. 3.11. 2 Ti. 3.3. Tit. 2.3; a treacherous informer, traitor,
Jno. 6.70; ὁ διάβολος, the devil.
Διαγγέλλω, (διά & ἀγγέλλω)
f. γελῶ, a.1. διήγγειλα, a.2. pass διηγγέλην,
to publish abroad, Lu. 9.60. Ro. 9.17; to certify *to the public,* Ac. 21.26; to tell,
announce, give notice of, divulge, publish abroad, Ac. 21.26; to declare, promulgate,
teach, Lu. 9.60; *fr. the Heb.* to celebrate, priase, Ro. 9.17.
Διαγίηομαι, (διά & γίνομαι)
f. γενήσομαι, a.2. διεγενόμην,
to continue through; to intervene, elapse, Mar. 16.1. Ac. 25.13; 27.9.
Διαγινώσκω, (διά & γινώσκω)
f. γνώσομαι,
pr. to distinguish; to resolve determinately; to examine, inquire into, *judicially,* Ac.
23.15; 24.22.
Διαγνωρίζω, (διά & γνωρίζω
f. ίσω,
to tell abroad, publish, Lu. 2.17. N.T.
Διάγνωσις, εως, ἡ (διαγινώσκω)
pr. an act of distingishing or discernment; a determination; examination *judicially,*
hearing, trial, Ac. 25.21.
Διαγογγύζω, (διά & γογγύζω)
f. ύσω,
to murmur, mutter, Lu. 15.2; 19.7. L.G.
Διαγρηγορέω, ῶ (διά & γρηγορέω)
to remain awake; to wake thoroughly, Lu. 9.32. L.G.
Διάγω, (διά & ἄγω)
f. ξω,
to conduct or carry through or over; to pass or spend *time,* live, 1 Ti. 2.2. Tit. 3.3.
Διαδέχομαι, (διά & δέχομαι)
f. δέξομαι,
to receive by transmission; to receive by succession, Ac. 7.45.
Διάδημα, ατος, τό, (διαδέω, διά & δέω)
pr. a band or fillet; a diadem, *the badge of a sovereign,* Re. 12.3; 13.1; 19.12
Διαδίδωμι, (διά & δίδωμι)
f. δώσω, a.1. διέδωκα,
to deliver from hand to hand; to distribute, divide, Lu. 11.22; 18.22. Jno. 6.11. Ac.
4.35.
Διάδοχος, ου, ὁ, ἡ, (διαδέχομαι)

a successor, Ac. 24.27.

Διαζώννῦμι, v. ζωννύω, (διά & ζώννυμι)
 f. ζώσω, p. pass. διέζωσμαι,
 to gird firmly round, Jno. 13.4, 5; *mid.* to gird round one's self, Jno. 21.7.

Διαθήκη, ης, ἡ, (διατίθημι)
 a testamentary disposition, will; a covenant, He. 9.16, 17. Gal. 3.15; *in N.T.,* a
 covenant *of God with men,* Gal. 3.17; 4.24. He. 9.4. Mat. 26.28, et al.; the writings of
 the old conenant, 2 Co. 3.14.

Διαίρεσις, εως, ἡ,
 a division; a distinction, differenc, diversity, 1 Co. 12.4, 5, 6: *from*

Διαιρέω, ῶ, (διά & αἱρέω)
 f. ήσω, a.2. διεῖλον,
 to divide, to divide out, distribute, Lu. 15.12. 1 Co. 12.11.

Διακαθαρίζω, (διά & καθαρίζω)
 f. ιῶ,
 to cleanse thoroughly, Mat. 3.12. Lu. 3.17. N.T.

Διακατελέγχομαι, (διά, κατά, & ἐλέγχομαι)
 f. έγξομαι,
 to confute strenuously or thoroughly, Ac. 18.28. N.T.

Διᾱκονέω, ῶ, (διάκονος)
 f. ήσω, imperf. ἐδιακόνουν, a.1. ἐδιακόνησα, p. δεδιακόνηκα, but later, διηκόνουν,
 διηκόνησας, δεδιηκόνηκα,
 to wait, attend upon, serve, Mat. 8.15. Mar. 1.31. Lu. 4.39, et al.; to be an attendant or
 assistant, Ac. 19.22; to perform a service by commission, 2 Co. 3.3. 1 Pe. 1.12; to
 minister to another's necessities, relieve, assist, or supply with the necessaries of life,
 provide the means of living, Mat. 4.11; 27.55. Mar. 1.13; 15.41. Lu. 8.3; to fill the
 office of διάκονος, deacon, perform the duties of that office, 1 Ti. 3.10, 13. 1 Pe. 4.11;
 to collect and make distribution of alms, Ro. 15.25. 2 Co. 8.19, 20. He. 6.10.

Διακονία, ας, ἡ,
 serving, service, waiting, attendance, the act of rendering friendly offices, Lu. 10.40. 2
 Ti. 4.11. He. 1.14; relief, aid, Ac. 6.1; 11.29. 2 Co. 8.4; 9.1, 12, 13; a commission, Ac.
 12.25. Ro. 15.31; a commission or ministry *in the service of the Gospel,* 42Ac. 1.17,
 25; 20.24. Ro. 11.13. 2 Co. 4.1; 5.18. 1 Ti. 1.12; service *in the Gospel,* Ac. 6.4; 21.19.
 1 Co. 16.15. 2 Co. 6.3; 11.8. Ep. 4.12. Re. 2.19; a function, ministry, or office *in the
 church,* Ro. 12.7. 1 Co. 12.5. Col. 4.17. 2 Ti. 4.5; a ministering *in the conveyance of a
 revelation from God,* 2 Co. 3.7, 8, 9.

Διάκονος, ου, ὁ, ἡ,
 one who renders service to another, an attendant, servant, Mat. 20.26; 22.13. Jno. 2.5,
 9, et al.; one who executes a commission, a deputy, Ro. 13.4; 15.8. Χριστοῦ, Θεοῦ, ἐν
 κυριω, &c. a religious instructor, preacher of the gospel, 1 Co. 3.5. 2 Co. 3.6; 6.4, et
 al.; a follower, disciple, Jno. 12.26; a deacon or deaconess, *whose official duty was to
 superintend the alms of the church, with other kindred services,* Ro. 16.1. Phi. 1.1. 1
 Ti. 3.8, 12. (ᾱ).

Διᾱκόσιοι, αι, α,
 two hundred, Mar. 6.37. Jno. 6.7, et al.

Διακούω, (διά & ἀκούω)
 f. ούσομαι,
 to hear a thing through; to hear *judicially,* Ac. 23.35.

Διακρίνω, (διά & κρίνω)
 f. ῑνῶ,

to separate, sever; to make a distinction or difference, Ac. 15.9. 1 Co. 11.29; to make to differ, distinguish, prefer, confer a superiority, 1 Co. 4.7; to exame, scrutinise, estimate, 1 Co. 11.31; 14.29; to discern, discriminate, Mat. 16.3; to judge, hear and decide a cause, 1 Co. 6.5; *mid.* διακρίνομαι, a.1. διεκρίθην, to dispute, contend, Ac. 11.2. Jude 9; to make a distinction mentally, Ja. 2.4. Jude 22; *in N.T.,* to hesitate, be in doubt, doubt, Mat. 21.21. Mar. 11.23, et al.: *whence*

Διάκρῐσις, εως, ἡ,
  a separation; a distinction, *or,* doubt, Ro. 14.1; a discerning, the act of discerning or distinguishing, He. 5.14; the faculty of distinguishing and estimating, 1 Co. 12.10.

Διακωλύω, (διά & κωλύω)
  f. ύσω,
  to hinder, restrain, prohibit, Mat. 3.14. (ῡ).

Διαλαλέω, ῶ, (διά & λαλέω)
  f. ήσω,
  to talk with; *by impl.* to consult, deliberate, Lu. 6.11; to divulge, publish, spread by rumour, Lu. 1.65

Διαλέγομαι, (διά & λέγω)
  f. λέξομαι, a.1. διελέχθην,
  to discourse, reason, argue, Ac. 17.2, 17; 24.12, et al.; to address, speak to, He. 12.5; to contend, dispute, Mar. 9.34. Jude 9.

Διαλείπω, (διά & λείπω)
  f. ψω, a.2. διέλιπον,
  to leave an interval; to intermit, cease, Lu. 7.45.

Διάλεκτος, ου, ἡ,
  speech; manner of speaking; peculiar language of a nation, dialect, vernacular idiom, Ac. 1.19; 2.6, 8; 21.40; 22.2; 26.14.

Διαλλάσσω, (διά & ἀλλάσσω)
  to change, exchange; *pass.* διαλλάσσομαι, a.2. διηλλάγην, to be reconciled *to another,* Mat. 5.24.

Διαλογίζομαι, (διά & λογίζομαι)
  f. ίσομαι,
  pr. to make a settlement of accounts; to reason, deliberate, ponder, consider, Mat. 16.7, 8. Mar. 2.6, 8. Jno. 11.50, et al.; to dispute, contend, Mar. 9.33: *whence*

Διαλογισμός, οῦ, ὁ,
  reasoning, ratiocination, thought, cogitation, purpose, Mat. 15.19. Mar. 7.21, et al.; discourse, dispute, disputation, contention, Lu. 9.46, et al.; doubt, hesitation, scruple, Lu. 24.38.

Διαλύω, (διά & λύω)
  f. ύσω,
  to dissolve, dissipate, disperse, Ac. 5.36.

Διαμαρτύρομαι, (διά & μαρτύρομαι)
  f. ροῦμαι, a.1. διεμαρτυράμην,
  to make solemn affirmation, protest; to charge, exhort with entreaty, admonish solemnly, Lu. 16.28. Ac. 2.40, et al.; to testify or teach earnestly, enforce publicly, Ac. 8.25; 18.5, et al. (ῡ).

Διαμάχομαι, (διά & μάχομαι)
  f. χέσομαι, οῦμαι,
  to fight out, to fight resolutely; *met.* to contend vehemently, insist, Ac. 23.9.

Διαμένω, (διά & μένω)
  f. ενῶ, a.1. διέμεινα, p. διαμενένηκα,

to continue throughout; to continue, be permanent or unchanged, Lu. 1.22. Gal. 2.5. He. 1.11. 2 Pe. 3.4; to continue, remain constant, Lu. 22.28.

Διαμερίζω, (διά & μερίζω)
    f. ίσω,
    to divide into parts and distribute, Mat. 27.35. Mar. 15.24. Ac. 2.3, et al.; *pass. in N.T.,* to be in a state of dissension, Lu. 11.17, 18; 12.52, 53: *whence*

Διαμερισμός, οῦ, ὁ,
    43division; *met. in N.T.,* disunion, dissension, Lu. 12.51. L.G.

Διανέμω, (διά & νέμω)
    f. εμῶ, a.1. pass. διενεμήθην,
    to distribute; to divulge, spread abroad, Ac. 4.17.

Διανεύω, (διά & νεύω)
    f. εύσω,
    to signify by a nod, beckon, make signs, Lu. 1.22. L.G.

Διανόημα, ατος, τό, (διανοέμαι, to turn over in the mind, think, fr. διά & νοέω)
    thought, Lu. 11.17.

Διάνοια, ας, ἡ, (fr. same)
    pr. thought, intention; the mind, intellect, understanding, Mat. 22.37. Mar. 12.30. Lu. 10.17, et al.; an operation of the understanding, thought, imagination, Lu. 1.51; insight, comprehension, 1 Jno. 5.20; mode of thinking and feeling, disposition of mind and heart, the affections, Ep. 2.3. Col. 1.21.

Διανοίγω, (διά & ἀνοίγω)
    f. οίξω,
    to open, Mar. 7.34, 35. Lu. 2.23; 24.31; *met.* to open the sense *of a thing,* explain, expound, Lu. 24.32. Ac. 17.3; διανοίγειν τὸν νοῦν, τὴν καρδίαν, to open the mind, the heart, *so as to understand and receive,* Lu. 24.45. Ac. 16.14.

Διανυκτερεύω, (διά & νύξ)
    f. εύσω,
    to pass the night, spend the whole night, Lu. 6.12.

Διανύω, (διά & ἀνύω, to accomplish)
    f. ύσω,
    to complete, finish, Ac. 21.7. (ῠ)

Διαπαντός, (i.e. διὰ παντός)
    through all time, throughout; always, Mar. 5.5, et al.; continually *by stated routine,* Lu. 24.53. He. 9.6.

Διαπαρατρῐβή, ῆς, ἡ, (διά & παρατριβὴ, collision, altercation, fr. παρατρίβω, to rub against, παρά & τρίβω)
    pertinacious disputation, v.r. 1 Ti. 6.5. N.T.

Διαπεράω, ῶ (διά & περάω)
    f. άσω,
    to pass through or over, Mat. 9.1; 14.34. Mar. 5.21, et al. (ᾱ)

Διαπλέω, (διά & πλέω)
    f. εύσομαι, a.1. διάπλευσα,
    to sail through or over, Ac. 27.5.

Διαπονέομαι, οῦμαι, (διαπονέω, to elaborate, fr. διά & πονέω)
    f. ήσομαι, a.1. διεπονήθην,
    pr. to be thoroughly exercised with labour; to be wearied; to be vexed, Ac. 4.2; 16.18.

Διαπορεύομαι, (διά & πορεύομαι)
    f. εύσομαι,

to go or pass through, Lu. 6.1; 13.22. Ac. 16.4; to pass by, Lu. 18.36, i.q. παρέρχομαι, v. 37.

Διαπορέω, ῶ, (διά & ἀπορέω)
 f. ήσω,
 to be utterly at a loss; to be in doubt and perplexity, Lu. 9.7; 24.4, et al.

Διαπραγματεύομαι, (διά & πραγματεύομαι)
 f. εύσομαι,
 to dispatch a matter thoroughly; to make profit in business, gain in trade, Lu. 19.15.

Διαπρίω, (διά & πρίω)
 f. ίσω,
 to divide with a saw, saw asunder; to grate *the teeth in a rage; pass. met.* to be cut *to the heart,* to be enraged, Ac. 5.33; 7.54. (ῑ)

Διαρθρόω, ῶ, (διά & ἄρθρον, a joint)
 f. ώσω, & διαρθροῦμαι, a.1. διηρθρώθην,
 to articulate, speak distinctly, v.r. Lu. 1.64.

Διαρπάζω, (διά & ἁρπάζω)
 f. άσω,
 to plunder, spoil, pillage, Mat. 12.29, *bis.* Mar. 3.27, *bis.*

Διαρρήγνῡμι & διαρρήσσω, (διά & ῥήγνυμι)
 f. ήξω,
 to break asunder, rend, tear, burst, Mat. 26.65, et al.

Διασαφέω, ῶ, (διά & σαφής, manifest)
 f. ήσω, a.1. διεσάφησα,
 to make known, declare, tell plainly, or fully. Mat. 18.31.

Διασείω, (διά & σείω)
 f. σω,
 pr. to shake thoroughly or violently; to harass, intimidate, extort from, Lu. 3.14.

Διασκορπίζω, (διά & σκορπίζω)
 f. ίσω,
 to disperse, scatter, Mat. 26.31. Mar. 14.27, et al.; to dissipate, waste, Lu. 15.13; 16.1; to winnow, *or,* to strew, Mat. 25.24, 26. L.G.

Διασπάω, ῶ, (διά & σπάω)
 f. άσομαι, p. pass. διέσπασμαι, a.1. pass. διεσπάσθην,
 to pull or tear asunder or in pieces, burst, Mar. 5.4. Ac. 23.10. (ᾰ).

Διασπείρω, (διά & σπείρω)
 f. ερῶ, a.2. p. pass διεσπάρην,
 to scatter abroad or in every direction, *as seed;* to disperse, Ac. 8.1, 4; 11.19: *whence*

Διασπορά, ᾶς, ἡ,
 pr. a scattering *as of seed;* dispersion; *in N.T., meton.* the dispersed portion of the Jews, *specially termed* the dispersion, Jno. 7.35. Ja. 1.1. 1 Pe. 1.1. L.G.

Διαστέλλω, (διά & στέλλω)
 44to separate, distinguish; *mid.* διαστέλλομαι, a.1. διεστειλάμην, to determine, issue a decision; to state or explain distinctly and accurately; *hence,* to admonish, direct, charge, command, Ac. 15.24. He. 12.20; *when followed by a negative clause,* to interdict, prohibit, Mat. 16.20. Mar. 5.43, et al.

Διάστημα, ατος, τό, (διΐστημι)
 interval, space, distance, Ac. 5.7.

Διαστολή, ῆς, ἡ (διαστέλλω)
 distinction, difference, Ro. 3.22; 10.12. 1 Co. 14.7. L.G.

Διαστρέφω, (διά & στρέφω)

f. ψω, p. pass. διέστραμμαι,

to distort, turn awry; *met.* to pervert, corrupt, Mat. 17.17. Lu. 9.41, et al.; to turn out of the way, cause to make defection, Lu. 23.2. Ac. 13.8; διεστραμμένος, perverse, corrupt, erroneous.

Διασώζω, (διά & σώζω)

f. σῶσω, a.1. pass. διασώθην,

to bring safe through; to convey in safety, Ac. 23.24; *pass.* to reach a place or state of safety, Ac. 27.44; 28.1, 4. 1 Pe. 3.20; to heal, to restore to health, Mat. 14.36. Lu. 7.3.

Διατᾰγή, ῆς, ἡ, (διατάσσω)

an injunction, institute, ordiance, Ro. 13.2. Ac. 7.53. L.G.

Διάταγμα, ατος, τό, (fr. same)

a mandate, commandment, ordinance, He. 11.23. L.G.

Διαταράσσω, (διά & ταράσσω)

f. ξω,

to throw into a state of perturbation, to move or trouble greatly, Lu. 1.29.

Διατάσσω, (διά & τάσσω)

f. ξω, & mid. διατάσσομαι,

pr. to arrange, make a precise arrangement; to prescribe, 1 Co. 11.34; 16.1. Tit. 1.5; to direct, Lu. 8.55. Ac. 20.13; to charge, Mat. 11.1; to command, Ac. 18.2, et al.; to ordain, Gal. 3.19.

Διατελέω, ῶ, (διά & τελέω)

f. έσω,

to complete, finish; *intrans.* to continue, persevere, *in a certain state or course of action,* Ac. 27.33.

Διατηρέω, ῶ, (διά & τηρέω)

f. ήσω,

to watch carefully, guard with vigilance; to treasure up, Lu. 2.51; εαυτὸν ἐκ, to keep one's self from, to abstain wholly from, Ac. 15.29.

Διατί, i.e. διὰ τί,

interrog. for what? why? wherefore? Mat. 9.14; 13.16. Lu. 19.23, 31.

Διατίθημι, (διά & τίθημι)

to arrange; *mid.* διατίθεμαι, f. θήσομαι, a.2. διεθέμην, to arrange according to one's own mind; to make a disposition, to make a will; to settle the terms of a convenant, to ratify, Ac. 3.25. He. 8.10; 10.16; to assign, Lu. 22.29.

Διατρίβω, (διά & τρίβω)

f. ψω,

pr. to rub, wear away by friction; *met.* to pass or spend *time,* to remain, stay, tarry, continue, Jno. 3.22; 11:54. Ac. 12.19; 14.3, 28, et al. (ῑ).

Διατροφή, ῆς, ἡ, (διατρέφω, to nourish)

food, sustenance, 1 Ti. 6.8.

Διαυγάζω, (διά & αὐγάζω)

f. άσω,

to shine through, shine out, dawn, 2 Pe. 1.19. L.G.

Διαυγής, έος, οῦς, ὁ, ἡ, (διά & αὐγή)

translucent, transparent, pellucid, v.r. Re. 21.21.

Διαφᾰνής, έος, οῦς, ὁ, ἡ (διαφαίνω, to show through)

transparent, pellucid, Re. 21.21.

Διαφέρω, (διά & φέρω)

f. οίσω, a.1. ήνεγκα, a.2. ήνεγκον,

to convey through, across, Mar. 11.16; to carry different ways or into different parts, separate; *pass.* to be borne, driven, or tossed hither and thither, Ac. 27.27; to be promulated, proclaimed, published, Ac. 13.49; *intrans. Met.* to differ, 1 Co. 15.41; to excel, be better or of greater value, be superior, Mat. 6.26; 10.31, et al.; *impers.* διαφέρει, it makes a difference, it is of consequence; *with* οὐδέν, it makes no difference, it is nothing, Gal. 2.6.

Διαφεύγω, (διά & φεύγω)
    f. ξομαι, a.2. διέφυγον,
    to flee through, escape by flight, Ac. 27.42.

Διαφημίζω, (διά & φημή)
    f. ίσω, a.1. διεφήμισα,
    to report, proclaim, pulblish, spread abroad, Mat. 9.31; 28.15. Mar. 1.45.

Διαφθείρω, (διά & φθείρω)
    f. φθερῶ, a.1. διέφθειρα, p. διέφθαρκα, a.2. pass. διεφθάρην, p. pass. διέφθαρμαι,
    to corrupt or destroy utterly; to waste, bring to decay, Lu. 12.33. 2 Co. 4.16; to destroy, Re. 8.9; 11.18; *met.* to corrupt, pervert utterly, 1 Ti. 6.5: *whence*

Διαφθορά, ᾶς, ἡ
    45corruption, dissolution, Ac. 2.27, 31; 13.34, 35, 36, 37.

Διάφορος, ου, ὁ, ἡ, (διαφέρω)
    different, diverse, of different kinds, Ro. 12.6. He. 9.10; excellent, superior, He. 1.4; 8.6.

Διαφυλάσσω, (διά & φυλάσσω)
    f. ξω,
    to keep or guard carefully or with vigilance; to gard, protect, Lu. 4.10.

Διαχειρίζω & διαχειρίζομαι, (διά & χείρ)
    pr. to have in the hands, to manage; *mid., later,* to kill, Ac. 5.30; 26.21.

Διαχλευάζω, (διά & χλευάζω)
    f. άσω,
    to jeer outright, deride, v.r. Ac. 2.13.

Διαχωρίζομαι, (mid. of διαχωρίζω, to separate, fr. διά & χωρίζω)
    to depart, go away, Lu. 9.33.

Διδακτικός, ή, όν, (διδάσκω)
    apt or qualified to teach, 1 Ti. 3.2. 2 Ti. 2.24. N.T.

Διδακτός, ή, όν, (fr. same)
    pr. taught, teachable, *of things; in N.T.,* taught, *of persons,* Jno. 6.45. 1 Co. 2.13.

Διδασκαλία, ας, ἡ,
    the act or occupation of teaching, Ro. 12..7. 1 Ti. 4.13, et al.; information, instruction, Ro. 15.4. 2 Ti. 3.16; matter taught, precepts, doctrine, Mat. 15.9. 1 Ti. 1.10, et al.: *from*

Διδάσκᾰλος, ου, ὁ,
    a teacher, master, Ro. 2.20, et al.; *in N.T. as an equivalent to* ῥαββί, Jno. 1.39, et al.

Διδάσκω,
    f. διδάξω, p. δεδίδαχα, a.1. ἐδίδαξα, a.1. pass. ἐδιδάχθην,
    to teach, Mat. 4.23; 22.16, et al.; to teach or speak in a public assembly, 1 Ti. 2.12; to direct, admonish, Mat. 28.15. Ro. 2.21, et al.: *whence*

Διδαχή, ῆς, ἡ,
    instruction, the giving of instruction, teaching, Mar. 4.2; 12.38, et al.; instruction, what is taught, doctrine, Mat. 16.12. Jno. 7.16, 17, et al.; *meton.* mode of teaching and kind of doctrine taught, Mat. 7.28. Mar. 1.27.

Δίδραχμον, ου, τό, (δίς & δραχμή)

a didrachmon, or double drachm, *a silver coin equal to the drachm of Alexandria, to two Attic drachms, to two Roman denarii, and to the half-shekel of the Jews, in value about 15d. halfpenny of our money,* Mat. 7.24. *bis.*

Διδῦμος, ου, ὁ, ἡ, (δύο)
    twofold, a twin; *the Greek equivalent to the name Thomas,* Jno. 11.16; 20.24; 21.2.

Δίδωμι,
    f. δώσω, p. δέδωκα, a.1. ἔδωκα, a.2. ἔδων, p. pass. δέδομαι, a.1. pass. ἐδόθην,
    to give, bestow, present, Mat. 4.9; 6.11. Jno. 3.16; 17.2, et al. freq.; to give, cast, throw, Mat. 7.6; to supply, suggest, Mat. 10.19. Mar. 13.11; to distribute *alms,* Mat. 19.21. Lu. 11.41, et al.; to pay *tribute, &c.* Mat. 22.17. Mar. 12.14. Lu. 20.22; to be the author or source *of a thing,* Lu. 12.51. Ro. 11.8, et al.; to grant, permit, allow, Ac. 2.27; 13.35. Mat. 13.11; 19.11, et al.; to deliver to, intrust, commit to the charge *of any one,* Mat. 25.15. Mar. 12.9, et al.; to give or deliver up, Lu. 22.19. Jno. 6.51, et al.; to reveal, teach, Ac. 7.38; to appoint, constitute, Ep. 1.22; 4.11; to consecrate, devote, offer in sacrifice, 2 Co. 8.5. Gal. 1.4. Re. 8.3, et al.; to present, expose *one's self in a place,* Ac. 19.31; to recompense, Re. 2.23; to attribute, ascribe, Jno. 9.24. Re. 11.13; *fr. the Heb.* to place, put, infix, inscribe, He. 8.10; 10.16, et al.; to infix, impress, 2 Co. 12.7. Re. 13.16; to inflict, Jno. 18.22; 19.3. 2 Thes. 1.8; to give in charge, assign, Jno. 5.36; 17.4. Re. 9.5; to exhibit, put forth, Mat. 24.24. Ac. 2.19; to yield, bear *fruit,* Mat. 13.8; διδόναι ἐργασίαν, operam dare, to endeavour, strive, Lu. 12.58; διδόναι ἀπόκρισιν, responsum dare, to answer, reply, Jno. 1.22; διδόναι τόπον, locum dare, to give place, yield, Lu. 14.9. Ro. 12.19.

Διεγείρω, (διά & ἐγείρω)
    f. δειγερῶ, a.1. pass. διηγέρθην,
    to arouse or awake thoroughly, Mat. 1.24. Mar. 4.38, 39. Lu. 8.24; *pass.* to be raised, excited, agitated, *as a sea,* Jno. 6.18; *met.* to stir up, arouse, animate, 2 Pe. 1.13; 3.1.

Διενθυμέομαι, οῦμαι, (διά & ἐνθυμέομαι)
    to revolve thoroughly in the mind, consider carefully, v.r. Ac. 10.19. L.G.

Διέξοδος, ου, ἡ, (διά & ἔξοδος)
    a passage throughout; a line of road, a thoroughfare, Mat. 22.9.

Διερμηνευτής, οῦ, ὁ,
    46an interpreter, 1 Co. 14.28: (L.G.) *from*

Διερμηνεύω, *a late compound used as an equivlent to the simple* ἑρμηνεύω,
    f. εύσω,
    to explain, interpret, translate, Lu. 24.27. Ac. 9.36. 1 Co. 14.5, 13, 27; to be able to interpret, 1 Co. 12.30.

Διέρχομαι, (διά & ἔρχομαι)
    f. ἐλεύσομαι, a.2. διῆλθον,
    to pass through, Mar. 10.25. Lu. 4.30, et al.; to pass over, cross, Mar. 4.35. Lu. 8.22; to pass along, Lu. 19.4; to proceed, Lu. 2.15. Ac. 9.38, et al.; to travel through or over *a country,* wander about, Mat. 12.43. Lu. 9.6, et al.; to transfix, pierce, Lu. 2.35; to spread abroad, be prevalent, *as a rumour,* Lu. 5.15; *met.* to extend to, Ro. 5.12.

Διερωτάω, ῶ, (διά & ἐρωτάω)
    f. ήσω,
    to sift by questionings, *of persons; in N.T., of things,* to ascertain by inquiry, Ac. 10.17.

Διετής, έος, οῦς, ὁ, ἡ, τό, -ές, (δίς & ἔτος)
    of two years; of the age of two years, Mat. 2.16: *whence*

Διετία, ας, ἡ,
    the space of two years, biennium, Ac. 24.27; 28.30. N.T.

Διηγέομαι, οῦμαι, (διά & ἡγέομαι)
f.ήσομαι,
pr. to lead throughout; to declare thoroughly, detail, recount, relate, tell, Mar. 5.16; 9.9. Lu. 8.39. Ac. 8.33. He. 11.32, et al.: *whence*

Διήγησις, εως, ἡ,
a narration, relation, history, Lu. 1.1

Διηνεκής, έος, οῦς, ὁ, ἡ, τό, -ές, (διά & ἡνεκής, extended, prolonged)
continuous, uninterrupted; εἰς τὸ διηνεκές, perpetually, He. 7.3; 10.1, 12, 14.

Διθάλασσος, ου, ὁ, ἡ, (δίς & θάλασσα)
bimaris, washed on both sides by the sea; τόπος διθάλασσος, a shoal or sand bank formed by the confluence of opposite currents, Ac. 27.41. L.G.

Διϊκνέομαι, οῦμαι, (διά & ἱκνέομαι)
f. ίξομαι,
to go or pass through; to penetrate, He. 4.12.

Διΐστημι, (διά & ἵστημι)
f. διαστήσω,
to set at an interval, apart; to station at an interval *from a former position,* Ac. 27.28; *intrans.* a.2. διέστην, to stand apart; to depart, be parted, Lu. 24.51; *of time,* to intervene, be interposed, Lu. 22.59.

Διϊσχυρίζομαι, (διά & ἰσχυρίζομαι, fr. ἰσχυρός)
f. ίσομαι,
to feel or express reliance; to affirm confidently, asseverate, Lu. 22.59. Ac. 12.15.

Δικαιοκρισία, ας, ἡ, (δίκαιος & κρίσις)
just or righteous judgment, Ro. 2.5. S.

Δίκαιος, αία, αιον,
used of things, just equitable, fair, Mat. 20.4. Lu. 12.57. Jno. 5.30. Col. 4.1, et al.; *of persons,* just, righteous, *absolutely,* Jno. 17.25. Ro. 3.10, 26. 2 Ti. 4.8. 1 Pe. 3.18. 1 Jno. 1.9; 2.1, 29. Re. 16.5; righteous *by account and acceptance,* Ro. 2.13; 5.19, et al.; *in ordinary usage,* just, upright, innocent, pious, Mat. 5.45; 9.13, et al. freq.; ὁ δίκαιος, the Just One, *one of the distinctive titles of the Messiah,* Ac. 3.14; 7.52; 22.14: *whence*

Δικαιοσύνη, ης, ἡ,
fair and equitable dealing, justice, Ac. 17.31. He. 11.33. Ro. 9.28; rectitude, virtue, Lu. 1.75. Ep. 5.9; *in N.T.,* generosity, alms, 2 Co. 9.10. v.r. Mat. 6.1; piety, godliness, Ro. 6.13, et al.; investiture with the attribute of righteousness, acceptance as righteous, justification, Ro. 4.11; 10.4, et al. freq.; a provision or means for justification, Ro. 1.17. 2 Co. 3.9, et al.; an instance of justification. 2 Co. 5.21.

Δικαιόω, ῶ,
f. ώσομαι, & ώσω, a.1. ἐδικαίωσα, p. pass. δεδικαίωμαι, a.1. pass. ἐδικαιώθην,
pr. to make or render right or just; *mid.* to act with justice, R. 22.11; to avouch to be a good and true, to vindicate, Mat. 11.19. Lu. 7.29, et al.; to set forth as good and just, Lu. 10.29; 16.15; *in N.T.,* to hold as guiltless, to accept as righteous, to justify, Ro. 3.26, 30, 4.5; 8.30, 33, et al.; *pass.*to be held acquit, to be cleared, Ac. 13.39. Ro. 3.24; 6.7; to be approved, to stand approved, to stand accepted, Ro. 2.13; 3.20, 28, et al.: *whence*

Δικαίωμα, ατος, τό,
pr. a rightful act, act of justice, equity; a sentence, *of condemnation,* Re. 15.4; *in N.T., of acquittal,* justification, Ro. 5.16; a decree, law, ordinance, Lu. 1.6. Ro. 1.32; 2.26; 8.4. He. 9.1, 10; 47a meritorious act, perfect righteousness, Ro. 5.18; state of righteousness, Re. 19.8.

Δικαίως,
    adv. justly, with strict justice, 1 Pe. 2.23; desevedly, Lu. 23.41; as it is right, fit or proper, 1 Co. 15.34; uprightly, honestly, piously, religiously, 1 Thes. 2.10. Tit. 2.12.

Δικαίωσις, εως, ἡ,
    pr. a making right or just; a declaration of right or justice; a judicial sentence; *in N.T.,* acquittal, acceptance, justification, Ro. 4.25; 5.18.

Δικαστής, οῦ, ὁ, (δικάζω, to judge, fr. δίκη)
    a judge, Lu. 12.14. Ac. 7.27, 35.

Δίκη, ης, ἡ,
    right, justice; *in N.T.,* judicial punishment, vengeance, 2 Thes. 1.9. Jude 7; sentence of punishment, judgment, Ac. 25.15; *personified,* the goddess of justice or vengeance, Nemesis, Pœna, Ac. 28.4.

Δίκτῦον, ου, τό,
    a net, fishing-net, Mat. 4.20, 21. et al.

Δίλογος, ου, ὁ, ἡ, (δίς & λόγος)
    pr. saying the same thing twice; *in N.T.,* double-tongued, speaking one thing and meaning another, deceitful in words, 1 Ti. 3.8. N.T.

Διό, (i.e. δι' ὅ)
    on which account, wherefore, therefore, Mat. 27.8. 1 Co. 12.3, et al.

Διοδεύω, (διά & ὁδεύω)
    f. εύσω,
    to travel through *a place,* traverse, Lu. 8.1. Ac. 17.1. L.G.

Διόπερ, *strengthened from* διό,
    conj. on this very account, for this very reason, wherefore, 1 Co. 8.13; 10.14; 14.13.

Διοπετής, έος, οῦς, ὁ, ἡ, τό -ές, (Ζεύς, Διός, & πίπτω)
    which fell from Jupiter, or heaven; τοῦ διαπετοῦς, sc. ἀγάλματος, Ac. 19.35.

Διόρθωμα, ατος, τό, (διορθόω, to correct, fr. διά & ὀρθόω, to make straight, fr. ὀρθός)
    correction, emendation, reformation, v.r. Ac. 24.3.

Διόρθωσις, εως, ἡ, (fr. same)
    a complete rectification, reformation, He. 9.10.

Διαρύσσω, (διά & ὀρύσσω)
    f. ξω,
    to dig or break through, Mat. 6.19, 20; 24.43. Lu. 12.39.

Διόσκουροι, v. διόσκοροι, ων, οἱ, (Ζεύς, Διός, & κοῦρος, a youth)
    the Dioscuri, Castor & Pollux, *sons of Jupiter by Leda, and patrons of sailors,* Ac. 28.11.

Διότι, (διά, ὅτι)
    conj. on the account that, because, Lu. 2.7; 21.28; in as much as, Lu. 1.13. Ac. 18.10, et al.

Διπλόος, οῦς, όη, ῆ, όον, οῦν,
    double, Mat. 23.15. 1 Ti. 5.17. Re. 18.6: *whence*

Διπλόω, ῶ,
    f. ώσω, a.1. ἐδίπλωσα,
    to double; to render back double, Re. 18.6.

Δίς, (δύο)
    adv. twice, Mar. 14.30, 72, et al.; *in the sense of* entirely, utterly, Jude 12; ἅπαξ καὶ δίς, once and again, repeatedly, Phi. 4.16.

Διστάζω, (δίς)
    f. άσω, a.1. ἐδίστασα,
    to doubt, waver, hesitate, Mat. 14.31; 28.17.

Δίσταομος, ου, ὁ, ἡ, (δίς & στόμα)
    pr. having two mouths; two-edged, He. 4.12. Re. 1.16; 2.12.
Δισχίλιοι, αι, α, (δίς & χίλιοι)
    two thousand, Mar. 5.13. (ῑ)
Διϋλίζω, (διά & ὑλίζω, to strain, filter)
    f. ίσω,
    to strain, filter thoroughly; to strain out or off, Mat. 23.24.
Διχάζω, (δίχα, apart)
    f. άσω,
    to cut asunder, disunite; *met.* to cause to disagree, set at variance, Mat. 10.35.
Διχοστασία, ας, ἡ, (δίχα & στάσις)
    a standing apart; a division, dissension, Ro. 16.17. 1 Co. 3.3. Gal. 5.20.
Διχοτομέω, ῶ, (δίχα & τέμνω)
    f. ήσω,
    pr. to cut into two parts, cut asunder; *in N.T.,* to inflict a punishment of extreme severity, Mat. 24.51. Lu. 12.46.
Διψάω, ῶ, (δίψα, thirst)
    f. ήσω,
    to thirst, be thirsty, Mat. 25.35, 37, 42, 44, et al.; *met.* to desire or long for ardently, Mat. 5.6. Jno. 4.14; 6.35, et al.
Δίψος, εος, τό,
    thirst, 2 Co. 11.27.
Δίψῡχος, ου, ὁ, ἡ, (δίς & ψυχή)
    double-minded, inconstant, fickle, Ja. 1.8; 4.8. L.G.
Διωγμός, ου, ὁ, (διώκω)
    pr. chase, pursuit; persecution, Mat. 13.21. Mar. 4.17; 10.30, et al.
Διώκτης, ου, ὁ,
    a persecutor, 1 Ti. 1.13: (L.G.) *from*
Διώκω,
    48f. ώξω, a.1. ἐδίωξα, p. pass. δεδίωγμαι, a.1. pass. ἐδιώχθην,
    to put in rapid motion; to pursue; to follow, pursue the direction of, Lu. 17.23; to follow eagerly, endeavour earnestly to acquire, Ro. 9.30, 31; 12.13, et al.; to press forwards, Phi. 3.12, 14; to pursue *with malignity,* pursecute, Mat. 5.10, 11, 12, 44, et al.
Δόγμα, ατος, τό, (δοκέω)
    a decree, statute, ordinance, Lu. 2.1. Ac. 16.4; 17.7. Ep. 2.15. Col. 2.14; *whence*
Δογματίζω,
    f. ίσω,
    to decree, prescribe an ordinance; *mid.* to suffer laws to be imposed on one's self, to submit to, bind one's self by, ordinances, Col. 2.20. L.G.
Δοκέω, ῶ,
    f. δόξω, a.1. ἔδοφα,
    to think, imagine, suppose, presume, Mat. 3.9; 6.7, et al.; to seem, appear, Lu. 10.36. Ac. 17.18, et al.; *impers.* δοκεῖ, it seems; it seems good, best or right, it pleases, Lu. 1.3. Ac. 15.22, 25, et al.
Δοκιμάζω, (δόκιμος)
    f. άσω, a.1. ἐδοκίμασα, p. pass. δεδοκίμασμαι,
    to prove *by trial;* to test, assay *metals,* 1 Pe. 1.7; to prove, try, examine, scrutinise, Lu. 14.19. Ro. 12.2, et al.; to put to the proof, tempt, He. 3.9; to approve *after trail,* judge

worthy, choose, Ro. 14.22. 1 Co. 16.3. 2 Co. 8.22, et al.; to decide upon *after examination,* judge of, distinguish, discern, Lu. 12.56. Ro. 2.18. Phi. 1.10.

Δοκιμασία, ας, ἡ
proof, probation, v.r. He. 3.9.

Δοκιμή, ῆς, ἡ,
trial, proof by trial, 2 Co. 8.2; the state or disposition of that which has been tried and approved, approved character or temper, Ro. 5.4. 2 Co. 2.9, et al.; proof, document, evidence, 2 Co. 13.3. L.G.

Δοκίμιον, ου, τό,
that by means of which any thing is tried, proof, criterion, test; trial, the act of trying or putting to proof, Ja. 1.3; approved character, 1 Pe. 1.7: *from*

Δόκιμος, ου, ὁ, ἡ,
proved, tried; approved *after examination and trial,* Ro. 16.10. Ja. 1.12, et al.; *by impl.* acceptable, Ro. 14.18.

Δοκός, οῦ, ἡ & ὁ,
a beam or spar *of timber;* Mat. 7.3, 4, 5. Lu. 6.41, 42.

Δίλιος, ία, ιον, & ος, ον, (δόλος)
fraudulent, deceitful, 2 Co. 11.13: *whence*

Δολιόω, ῶ,
f. ώσω,
to deceive, use fraud or deceit, Ro. 3.13. S.

Δόλος, ου, ὁ,
pr. a bait or contrivance for entrapping; fraud, deceit, insidious artifice, guile, Mat. 26.4. Mar. 7.22; 14.1, et al.: *whence*

Δολόω, ῶ,
f. ώσω,
pr. to entrap, beguile; to adulterate, corrupt, falsify, 2 Co. 4.2.

Δόμα, ατος, τό, (δίδωμι)
a gift, present, Mat. 7.11, et al. L.G.

Δόξα, ης, ἡ, (δοκέω)
pr. a seeming; appearance; a notion, imagination, opinion; the opinion which obtains respecting one; reputation, credit, honour, glory; *in N.T.,* honourable consideration, Lu. 14.10; praise, glorification, honour, Jno. 5.41, 44. Ro. 4.20; 15.7, et al.; dignity, majesty, Ro. 1.23. 2 Co. 3.7, et al.; a manifestation of some glorious attribute, Jno. 11.40. 2 Pe. 1.3, et al.; *pl.* dignitaries, 2 Pe. 2.10. Jude 8; glorification *in a future state of bliss,* 2 Co. 4.17. 2 Ti. 2.10, et al.; pride, ornament, 1 Co. 11.15. 1 Thes. 2.20; splendid array, pomp, magnificence, Mat. 6.29; 19.28, et al.; radiance, dazzling lustre, Lu. 2.9. Ac. 22.11. et al.

Δοξάζω,
f. άσω, a.1. ἐδόξασα, p. pass. δεδόξασμαι, a.l. pass. ἐδοξάσθην,
according to the various significations of δόξα, to think, suppose, judge; to extol, magnify, Mat. 6.2. Lu. 4.15, et al.; *in N.T.,* to adore, worship, Ro. 1.21, et al.; to invest with dignity, or majesty, 2 Co. 3.10. He. 5.5, et al.; to cause a manifestation of dignity, excellence, or majesty, Jno. 12.28; 13.32, et al.; to glorify *by admission to a state of bliss,* to beatify, Ro. 8.30, et al.

Δορκάς, άδος, ἡ
a gazelle or antelope, Ac. 9.36, 39.

Δόσις, εως, ἡ, (δίδωμι)
pr. a giving; outlay, Phi. 4.15; a donation, gift, Ja. 1.17.

Δότης, ου, ὁ, (fr. same)

a giver, 2 Co. 9.7. S.

Δουλαγωγέω, ῶ, (δοῦλος & ἄγω)
    f. ήσω,
    49*pr.* to bring into slavery; to treat as a slave; to discipline into subjection, 1 Co. 9.27.
    L.G.

Δουλεία, ας, ή, (δοῦλος)
    slavery, bondage, servile condition; *in N.T., met. with reference to degradation and unhappiness,* thraldom *spiritual or moral,* Ro. 8.15, 21. Gal. 4.24; 5.1. He. 2.15.

Δουλεύω, (fr. same)
    f. εύσω, p. δεδούλευκα, a.1. ἐδούλευσα,
    to be a slave or servant; to be in slavery or subjection, Jno. 8.33. Ac. 7.7. Ro. 9.12; to discharge the duties of a slave or servant, Ep. 6.7. 1 Ti. 6.2; to serve, be occupied in the service of, be devoted, subservient, Mat. 6.24. Lu. 15.29. Ac. 20.19. Ro. 14.18; 16.18, et al.; *met.* to be enthralled, involved in a slavish service, *spiritually or morally,* Gal. 4.9, 25. Tit. 3.3.

Δοῦλος, η ον
    adj. enslaved, enthralled, subservient, Ro. 6.19; *as a subst.* δοῦλος, a male slave, or servant, *of various degrees,* Mat. 8.9, et al. freq.; a person of mean condition, Phi. 2.7; *fem.* δούλη, a female slave; a handmaiden, Lu. 1.38, 48. Ac. 2.18; δοῦλος, *used figuratively, in a bad sense,* one involved in *moral or spiritual* thraldom, Jno. 8.34. Ro. 6.17, 20. 1 Co. 7.23. 2 Pe. 2.19; *in a good sense,* a devoted servant, follower or minister, Ac. 16.17. Ro. 1.1, et al.; one pledged or bound to serve, 1 Co. 7.22. 2 Co. 4.5: *whence*

Δουλόω, ῶ
    f. ώσω, a.1. ἐδούλωσα, p. pass. δεδούλωμαι, a.1. pass. ἐδουλώθην,
    to reduce to servitude, enslave, oppress by retaining in servitude, Ac. 7.6. 2 Pe. 2.19; *met.* to render subservient, 1 Co. 9.19; *pass.* to be under restraint, 1 Co. 7.15; to be in bondage, *spiritually or morally,* Gal. 4.3. Tit. 2.3; to become devoted to the service of, Ro. 6.18, 22.

Δοχή, ῆς, ή, (δέχομαι)
    pr. reception *of guests; in N.T.,* a banquet, feast, Lu. 5.29; 14.13.

Δράκων, οντος, ό,
    a dragon or large serpent; *met.* the devil or Satan, Re. 12.3, 4, 7, 9, 13, 16, 17; 13.2, 4, 11; 16.13; 20.2.

Δράσσομαι, (δράξ, the fist)
    pr. to grasp with the hand, clutch; to lay hold of, seize, take, catch, 1 Co. 3.19.

Δραχμή, ῆς, ή,
    a drachm, *an Attic silver coin of nearly the same value as the Roman* denarius, *about 7¾d. of our money,* Lu. 15.8, 9.

Δρέπανον, ου, τό, (δρέπω, to crop, cut off)
    an instrument with a curved blade, *as* a sickle, Mar. 4.29. Re. 14.14, 15, 16, 17, 18, 19.

Δρόμος, ου, ό, (δέδρομα)
    a course, race, race-course; *met.* course *of life or ministry,* career, Ac. 13.25; 20.24. 2 Ti. 4.7.

Δύναμαι,
    f. δυνήσομαι, imperf. ἐδθνάμην, & ἠδυνάμν, a.1. ἐδυνησάμην, & ἐδυνάσθην, ἐδυνήθην, ἠδυνήθην,
    to be able, *either intrinsically and absolutely, which is the ordinary signification; or, for specific reasons,* Mat. 9.15. Lu. 16.2.

Δύναμις, εως, ἡ

power; strength, ability, Mat. 25.15. He. 11.11; efficacy, 1 Co. 4.19, 20. Phi. 3.10. 1 Thes. 1.5. 2 Ti. 3.5; energy, Col. 1.29. 2 Ti. 1.7; meaning, purport *of language*, 1 Co. 14.11; authority, Lu. 4.36; 9.1; might, power, majesty, Mat. 22.29; 24.30. Ac. 3.12. Ro. 9.17. 2 Thes. 1.7. 2 Pe. 1.16; *in N.T.,* a manifestation or instance of power, mighty means, Ac. 8.10. Ro. 1.16. 1 Co. 1.18, 24; ἡ δύναμις, omnipotence, Mat. 26.64. Lu. 22.69. Mar. 14.62; *pl.* authorities, Ro. 8.38. Ep. 1.21. 1 Pe. 3.22; miraculous power, Mar. 5.30. Lu. 1.35; 5.17; 6.19; 8.46; 24.49. 1 Co. 2.4; a miracle, Mat. 11.20, 21, et al. freq.; a worker of miracles, 1 Co. 12.28, 29; *fr. the Heb.* αἱ δυνάμεις τῶν οὐρανῶν, the heavenly luminaries, Mat. 24.29. Mar. 13.25. Lu. 21.26; αἱ δυνάμεις, the spiritual powers, Mat. 14.2. Mar. 6.14: *whence*

Δυναμόω, ῶ,

f. ώσω,

to strengthen, confirm, Col. 1.11. L.G.

Δυνάστης, ου, ὁ,

a potentate, sovereign, prince, Lu. 1.52. 1 Ti. 6.15; a person of rank and authority, a grandee, Ac. 8.27.

Δυνατέω, ῶ,

f. ήσω,

to be powerful, mighty, to show one's self powerful, 2 Co. 13.3. v.r. Ro. 14.4. (N.T.): *from*

Δυνατός, ή, όν, (δύναμαι)

able, having power, powerful, mighty, δυνατὸς εἶναι, to be able, i.q. δύνασθας, Lu. 14.31. Ac. 11.17, et al.; 50ὁ δυνατός, the Mighty One, God, Lu. 1.49; τὸ δυνατόν, power, i.q. δύναμις, Ro. 9.22; valid, powerful, efficacious, 2 Co. 10.4; distinguished for rank, authority or influence, Ac. 25.5. 1 Co. 1.26; distinguished for skill or excellence, Lu. 24.19. Ac. 7.22. Ro. 15.1; δυνατόν & δυνατά, possible, capable of being done, Mat. 19.26; 24.24, et al.

Δύνω,

a.2. ἔδυν,

to sink, go down, set *as the sun,* Mar. 1.32. Lu. 4.40.

Δύο,

both indecl. & also gen. and dat. δυοῖν, v. gen. δυῶν, dat. δυσί; *in N.T.,* both indecl. and also with dat. δυσί, two, Mat. 6.24; 21.28, 31, et al. freq.; οἱ δύο, both, Jno. 20.4; δύο ἢ τρεῖς, two or three, some, a few, Mat. 18.20; *from the Heb.* δύο δύο, two and two, Mar. 6.7, i.q. ἀνὰ δύο, Lu. 10.1, and κατὰ δύο, 1 Co. 14.27.

Δυς—,

an inseparable particle, conveying the notion of untowardness, as hard, ill, unlucky, dangerous, *like the English* un–, mis– *opp. to* εὖ.

Δυσβάστακτος, ου, ὁ, ἡ, (δυς & βαστάζω)

difficult or grievous to be borne, oppressive, Mat. 23.4. Lu. 11.46. L.G.

Δυσεντερία, ας, ἡ, (δυς & ἔντερον, an intestine)

a dysentery, Ac. 28.8.

Δυσερμήνευτος, ου, ὁ, ἡ, (δυς & ἑρμηνεύω)

difficult to be explained, hard to be understood, He. 5.11. L.G.

Δύσκολος, ου, ὁ, ἡ, (δυς & κόλον, food)

pr. peevish about food; hard to please; disagreeable; *in N.T.,* difficult, Mar. 10.24: *whence*

Δυσκόλως,

adv. with difficulty, hardly, Mat. 19.23. Mar. 10.23, et al.

Δυσμή, ῆς, ἡ, (δύω)
a sinking or settling; *pl.* δυσμαί, αἱ, the setting of the sun; *hence,* the west, Mat. 8.11; 24.27, et al.

Δυσνόητος, ου, ὁ, ἡ, (δυς & νοητός, fr. νοέω)
hard to be understood, 2 Pe. 3.16. L.G.

Δυσφημέω, ῶ,
f. ἡσω,
pr. to use ill words; to reproach, revile, v.r. 1 Co. 4.13.

Δυσφημία, ας, ἡ, (δυς & φήμη)
ill words; words of ill omen; reproach contumely, 2 Co. 6.8.

Δώδεκα, οἱ, αἱ, τά, (δύο & δέκα)
twelve, Mat. 9.20; 10,1, et al.; οἱ δώδεκα, the twelve *apostles,* Mat. 26.14, 20, et al.: *whence*

Δωδέκατος, η, ον,
the twelfth, Re. 21.20.

Δωδεκάφῦλον, ου, τό, (δώδεκα & φυλή)
twelve tribes, Ac. 26.7. N.T.

Δῶμα, ατος, τό,
pr. a house; *synecd.* a root, Mat. 10.27; 24.17, et al.

Δωρεά, ας, ἡ,
a gift, free gift, benefit, Jno. 4.10. Ac. 2.38, et al.

Δωρεάν, accus. of δωρεά,
adv. gratis, gratuitously, freely, Mat. 10.8. Ro. 3.24, et al.; *in N.T.,* undeservedly, without cause, Jno. 15.25; in vain, Gal. 2.21.

Δωρέομαι, οῦμαι, (δῶρον)
f. ἡσομαι, a.1. ἐδωρήσατο, p. δεδώρημαι,
to give freely, grant, Mar. 15.45. 2 Pe. 1.3, 4: *whence*

Δώρημα, ατος, το,
a gift, free gift, Ro. 5.16. Ja. 1.17.

Δῶρον, ου, τό, (δίδωμι)
a gift, present, Mat. 2.11. Ep. 2.8. Re. 11.10; an offering, sacrifice, Mat. 5.23, 24; 8.4. et al.; δῶρον, sc. ἐστι, it is consecrated to God, Mat. 15.5. Mar. 7.11; contribution *to the temple,* Lu. 21.1, 4.

Ε, ε, Ἔ ψῖλόν

Ἔᾱ,
interj. ha! *an expression of surprise or displeasure,* Mar. 1.24. Lu. 4.34.

Ἐάν,
conj. if. *The particulars of the use of* ἐάν *must be learnt from the grammars.* Ἐάν μή, except, unless; *also equivalent to* ἀλλά, Gal. 2.16. Ἐάν, *in N.T., as in the later Greek, is substitued for* ἄν *after relative words,* Mat. 5.19, et al. freq.

Ἐάνπερ,
a strengthing of ἐάν by the enclitic particle περ, if it be that, if at all events, He. 3.6, 14; 6.3.

Ἑαυτοῦ, ῆς, οῦ, contr. αὑτοῦ, ῆς, οῦ, pl. ἑαυτῶν,
a reflective pronoun of the third person, himself, herself, itself, Mat. 8.22; 12.26; 9.21, et al.; *also used for the first and second persons,* Ro. 8.23. Mat. 23.31; *also equivalent to* ἀλλήλων, Mar. 10.26. Jno. 12.19; ἀφ' ἑαυτοῦ, ἀφ' ἑαυτῶν, of himself, themselves, voluntarily 51spontaneously, Lu. 12.47; 21.30, et al.; of one's own will

merely, Jno. 5.19; δι' ἑαυτοῦ, per se, of itself, in its own nature, Ro. 14.14; ἐξ ἑαυτῶν, of one's self merely, 2 Co. 3.5; καθ' ἑαυτόν, by one's self, alone, Ac. 28.16. Ja. 2.17; παρ' ἑαθτῷ, with one's self, at home, 1 Co. 16.2; πρὸς ἑαυτόν, to one's self, to one's home, Lu. 24.12. Jno. 20.10; *or,* with one's self, Lu. 18.11.

Ἐάω, ῶ,
    f. άσω, imperf. εἴων, a.1. εἴασα,
    to let, allow, permit, suffer to be done, Mat. 24.43. Lu. 4.14, et al.; to let be, let alone, desist from, Lu. 22.51. Ac. 5.38; to commit *a ship to the sea,* let *her* drive, Ac. 27.40.

Ἐβδομήκοντα, οἱ, αἱ, τά, (ἕβδομος)
    seventy, Ac. 7.14, et al.; οἱ ἑβδομ. the seventy *disciples,* Lu. 10.1, 17.

Ἐβδομηκοντάκις,
    adv. seventy times, Mat. 18.22.

Ἕβδομος, η, ον, (ἑπτά)
    seventh, Jno. 4.52. He. 4.4. et al.

Ἑβραϊκός, ή, όν,
    Hebrew, Lu. 23.38: *from*

Ἑβραῖος, αία, αῖον, v. ου, ὁ
    a Hebrew, one descended from Abraham the Hebrew, 2 Co. 11.22. Phil. 3.5; *in N.T.,* a Jew of Palestine, *opp. to* Ἑλληνιστής, Ac. 6.1: *whence*

Ἑβραΐς, ΐδος, ἡ, sc. διάλεκτος,
    the Hebrew *dialect,* i.e. *the Hebræo-Aramæan dialect of Palestine,* Ac. 21.40, et al.

Ἑβραϊστί,
    in Hebrew, Jno. 5.2; 19.13, et al.

Ἔδραμον,
    part. δραμών, see τρέχω.

Ἐγγίζω,
    f. ίσω, At. ιῶ, p. ἤγγικα, a.1. ἤγγισα, (fr. ἐγγύς)
    pr. to cause to approach; *in N.T. intrans.* to approach, draw near, Mat. 21.1. Lu. 18.35, et al.; *met.* to be at hand, impend, Mat. 3.2; 4.17, et al.; μέχρι θανάτου ἐγγίζειν, to be at the point of death, Phi. 2.30; *fr. Heb.* to draw near *to God,* to offer *him* reverence and worship, Mat. 15.8. He. 7.19. Ja. 4.8; *used of God,* to draw near *to men,* assist *them,* bestow favours *on them,* Ja. 4.8. L.G.

Ἐγγράφω,
    f. ψω, p. pass. ἐγγέγραμμαι, (ἐν & γράφω)
    to engrave, inscribe; *met.* to infix or impress deeply, 2 Co. 3.2, 3.

Ἔγγυος, ου, ὁ, ἡ, (fr. ἐγγύη, a pledge)
    a surety, sponsor, He. 7.22.

Ἐγγύς,
    adv. near, *as to place,* Lu. 19.11, et al.; close at hand, Ro. 10.8; near, *in respect of ready interposition,* Phi. 4.5; near, *as to time,* Mat. 24.32, 33, et al.; near *to God, as being in covenant with him,* Ep. 2.13; οἱ ἐγγύς, the people near *to God,* the Jews, Ep. 2.17.

Ἐγγύτερον,
    adv. (pr. neut. of ἐγγύτερος, comp. of ἐγγύς) nearer, Ro. 13.11.

Ἐγείρω,
    f. ἐγερῶ, p. ἐγήγερκα, a.1. ἤγειρα, p. pass. ἐγήγερμαι, a.1. pass. ἠγέρθην,
    to excite, arouse, awaken, Mat. 8.25, et al.; *mid.* to awake, Mat. 2.13, 20, 21, et al.; *met. mid.* to rouse one's self to a better course of conduct, Ro. 13.11. Ep. 5.14; to raise from the dead, restore to life, Jno. 12.1, et al., *and mid.* to rise from the dead, Mat. 27.52. Jno. 5.21, et al.; *met.* to raise as it were from the dead, 2 Co. 4.14; to raise up,

cause to rise up *from a recumbent posture,* Ac. 3.7, *and mid.* to rise up, Mat. 17.7, et al.; to restore to health, Ja. 5.15; *met. et seq.* ἐπί, to excite *to war, mid.* to rise up against, Mat. 24.7, et al; to raise up again, rebuild, Jno. 2.19, 20; to raise up from a lower place, to draw up or out of *a ditch,* Mat. 12.11; *fr. Heb.* to raise up, to cause to arise or exist, Ac. 13.22, 23; *mid.* to arise, exist, appear, Mat. 3.9; 11.11, et al.: *whence*

Ἔγερσις, εως, ἡ,
 pr. the act of waking or rising up; resurrection, resuscitation, Mat. 27.53.

Ἐγκάθετος, ου, ὁ, ἡ, (ἐν & καθίημι)
 suborned, Lu. 20.20.

Ἐγκαίνια, ίων, τά, (ἐν & καινός)
 initiation, consecration; *in N.T.,* the feast of dedication, *an annual festival of eight days in the month Kisleu,* Jno. 10.22.

Ἐγκαινίζω,
 f. ίσω, a.1. ἐνεκαίνισα, p. pass. ἐγκεκαίνισμαι,
 to handsel, initiate, consecrate, dedicate, renovate; to institute, He. 9.18; 10.20. S.

Ἐγκαλέω, ῶ, (ἐν & καλέω)
 f. έσω,
 to bring a charge against, accuse; to institute judicial proceedings, Ac. 19.38, 40; 23.28, 29; 26.2, 7. Ro. 8.33.

Ἐγκαταλείπω, (ἐν & καταλείπω)
 f. ψω, a.2. ἐγκατέλιπον,52
 to leave *in a place or situation,* Ac. 2.27; to leave behind; to forsake, abandon, Mat. 27.46, et al.; to leave, as a remnant from destruction, Ro. 9.29.

Ἐγκατοικέω, ῶ, (ἐν & κατοικέω)
 f. ήσω,
 to dwell in or among, 2 Pe. 2.8.

Ἐγκεντρίζω, (ἐν & κεντρίζω, to prick)
 f. ίσω,
 to ingraft; *met.* Ro. 11.17, 19, 23, 24.

Ἔγκλημα, ατος, τό, (ἐγκαλέω)
 an accusation, charge, crimination, Ac. 23.29; 25.16.

Ἐγκομβόομαι, οῦμαι,(κόμβος, a string, band; *whence* ἐγκόμβωμα, a garment which is fastened by tying)
 f. ώσομαι,
 pr. to put on a garment which is to be tied; *in N.T.,* to put on, clothe; *met.* 1 Pe. 5.5.

Ἐγκοπή, ῆς, ἡ,
 pr. an incision, *e.g. a trench, &c. cut in the way of an enemy;* an impediment, hindrance, 1 Co. 9.12: (L.G.) *from*

Ἐγκόπτω, (ἐν & κόπτω)
 f. ψω,
 pr. to cut or strike in; *hence,* to impede, interrupt, hinder, Ro. 15.22. 1 Thes. 2.18. 1 Pe. 3.7. Gal. 5.7.

Ἐγκράτεια, ας, ἡ, (ἐγκρατής)
 self-control, continence, temperance, Ac. 24.25, et al.

Ἐγκρατεύομαι,
 f. εύσομαι,
 to possess the power of self-control or continence, 1 Co. 7.9; to practise abstinence, 1 Co. 9.25.

Ἐγκρᾰτής, έος, ὁ, ἡ, (κράτος)

strong, stout; possessed of mastery; master of self, Tit. 1.8.

Ἐγκρίνω, (ἐν & κρίνω)

f. ινῶ,

to judge or reckon among, consider as belonging to, adjudge to the number of, class with, place in the same rank, 2 Co. 10.12 (ῑ)

Ἐγκρύπτω, (ἐν & κρύπτω)

f. ψω,

to conceal in *any thing;* to mix, intermix, Mat. 13.33. Lu. 13.21.

Ἔγκυος, ου, ἡ, (ἐν & κύω)

with child, pregnant, Lu. 2.5.

Ἐγχρίω, (ἐν & χρίω)

f. ίσω,

to rub in, anoint, Re. 3.18. (ῑ)

Ἐγώ,

gen. ἐμοῦ & μου, I.

Ἐδαφίζω,

f. ίσω, At. ιῶ,

pr. to form a level and firm surface; to level with the ground, overthrow, raze, destroy, Lu. 19.44: *from*

Ἔδαφος, εος, τό,

pr. a bottom, base, *hence,* the ground, Ac. 22.7.

Ἑδραῖος, αία, αῖον, (ἕδρα, a seat)

sedentary; *met.* settled, steady, firm, stedfast, constant, 1 Co. 7.37; 15.58. Col. 1.23.

Ἑδραίωμα, ατος, τό, (ἑδραιόω, to settle, fr. preceding)

a basis, foundation, 1 Ti. 3.15. N.T.

Ἐθελοθρησκεία, ας, ἡ, (ἐθέλω & θρησκεία)

self-devised worship, supererogatory worship, will-worship, Col. 2.23.

Ἐθέλω & θέλω, *the latter being the form in the present in N.T.,*

f. ἐθελήσω & θελήσω, imperf. ἤθελον, a.1. ἠθέλησα,

to exercise the will, *properly by an unimpassioned operation;* to be willing, Mat. 17.4, et al.; to be inclined, disposed, Ro. 13.3, et al.; to choose, Lu. 1.62; to intend, design, Lu. 14.28, et al.; to will, Jno. 5.21; 21.22, et al.; ἤθελον, I could wish, Gal. 4.20.

Ἐθίζω, (ἔθος)

f. ίσω, p. pass. εἴθισμαι,

to accustom; *pass.* to be customary, Lu. 2.27.

Ἐθνάρχης, ου, ὁ, (ἔθνος & ἄρχω)

a governor, chief, or head of any tribe or nation, prefect, 2 Co. 11.32. L.G.

Ἐθνικός, ή, όν, (ἔθνος)

national; *in N.T.,* gentile, heathen, not Israelitish, Mat. 6.7; 18.17: (L.G.) *whence*

Ἐθνικῶς,

adv. after the manner of the gentiles, heathenishly, Gal. 2.14. N.T.

Ἔθνος, εος, τό,

a multitude, company, Ac. 17.26. 1 Pe. 2.9. Re. 21.24; a nation, people, Mat. 20.25; 21.43, et al.; *pl.* ἔθνη, *fr. the Heb.,* nations or people, *as distinguished from the Jews,* the heathen, gentiles, Mat. 4.15; 10.5. Lu. 2.32, et al.

Ἔθος, εος, τό,

a custom, usage, Lu. 2.42; 22.39, et al.; an institute, rite, Lu. 1.9. Ac. 6.14; 15.1, et al.

Εἰ,

conj. if, Mat. 4.3, 6; 12.7. Ac. 27.39, et al. freq.; since, Ac. 4.9, et al.; whether, Mar. 9.23. Ac. 17.11, et al.; that, *in certain expressions,* Ac. 26.8, 23. He. 7.15; *by a suppression of the apodosis of a sentence* εἰ 53*serves to express a wish;* O if! O that! Lu. 19.42; 22.42; *also a strong negation,* Mar. 8.12. He. 3.11; 4.3; εἰ καί, if even, though, although, Lu. 18.4, et al.; εἰ μή, unless, except, Mat. 11.27, et al.; *also equivalent to* ἀλλά, but, Mat. 12.4. Mar. 13.32. Lu. 4.26, 27; εἰ μήτι, unless perhaps, unless it be, Lu. 9.13, et al.; εἴ τις, εἴ τι, *pr.* if any one: whosoever, whatsoever, Mat. 18.28, et al. *The syntax of this particle must be learnt from the grammars. As an interrogative particle,* whether, Ac. 17.11, et al.; *in N.T. as a mere note of interrogation,* Lu. 22.49, et al.

Εἶδον,
    imperat. ἰδέ & ἴδε, optat. ἴδοιμι, subj. ἴδω, inf. ἰδεῖν, part. ἰδών, *see* ὁράω.

Εἶδος, εος, τό,
    form, external appearance, Lu. 3.22; 9.29. Jno. 5.37; kind, species, 1 Thes. 5.22; sight, perception, 2 Co. 5.7.

Εἰδῶ, εἰδέναι, εἰδώς,
    see οἶδα.

Εἰδωλεῖον, ου, τό, (εἴδωλον)
    a heathen temple, 1 Co. 8.10. N.T.

Εἰδωλόθῠτος, ον, (εἴδωλον & θύω)
    pr. sacrificed to an idol; *meton.* the remains of victims sacrificed to idols, *reserved for eating,* Ac. 15.29; 21.25, et al. N.T.

Εἰδωλολατρεία, ας, ἡ, (εἴδωλον & λατρεία)
    idolatry, worship of idols, 1 Co. 10.14. Gal. 2.20, et al. N.T.

Εἰδωλολάτρης, ου, ὁ, (εἴδωλον & λάτρις, a servant, worshipper)
    an idolater, worshipper of idols, 1 Co. 5.10, 11; 6.9; 10.7, et al. N.T. (ᾰ)

Εἴδωλον, ου, τό, (εἶδος)
    pr. a form, shape, figure; image or statue; *hence,* an idol, image of a god, Ac. 7.41, et al.; *meton.* a heathen god, 1 Co. 8.4, 7, et al.; *for* εἰδωλόθυτον, the flesh of victims sacrificed to idols, Ac. 15.20.

Εἰκῆ,
    adv. without plan or system; without cause, lightly, rashly, Mat. 5.22. Co. 2.18; to no purpose, in vain, Ro. 13.4. 1 Co. 15.2. Gal. 3.4; 4.11.

Εἴκοσι, οἱ, αἱ, τά,
    twenty, Lu. 14.31, et al.

Εἰκοσιπέντε (εἴκοσι & πέντε)
    twenty-five, Jno. 6.19.

Εἰκοσιτέσσαρες, (εἴκοσι & τέσσαρες)
    twenty-four, Re. 5.8, 14.

Εἰκοσιτρεῖς, (εἴκοσι & τρεῖς)
    twenty-three, 1 Co. 10.8.

Εἴκω,
    f. ξω,
    to yield, give place, submit, Gal. 2.5.

Εἰκών, ονος, ἡ,
    a material image, likeness, effigy, Mat. 22.20. Mar. 12.16, et al.; a similitude, representation, exact image, 1 Co. 11.7, et al.; resemblance, Ro. 8.29, et al.

Εἰλικρίνεια, ας, ἡ,
    clearness, purity, *met.* sincerity, integrity, ingenuousness, 1 Co. 5.8, et al.: *from*

Εἰλικρῐνής, έος, ὁ, ἡ, (εἵλη, sun shine & κρίνω)
    pr. that which being viewed in the sunshine is found clear and pure; *met.* spotless, sincere, ingenuous, Phi. 1.10. 2 Pe. 3.1.

Εἰλίσσω, (εἰλέω, to roll)
f. ξω,
properly Tonic for ἑλίσσω, to roll up, Re. 6.14.
Εἰμί,
imperf. ἦν & ἤμην, f. ἔσομαι, imperat. ἴσθι, ἔστω & ἤτω, subj. ὦ, inf. εἶναι, part. ὤν,
a verb of existence, to be, to exist, Jno. 1.1; 17.5. Mar. 6.30. Lu. 4.25, et al. freq.; ἐστί,
it is possible, proper, He. 9.5; *a simple copula to the subject and predicate, and
therefore in itself affecting the force of the sentence only by its tense, mood, &c.,* Jno.
1.1; 15.1, et al. freq.; *it also forms a frequent circumlocution with the participles of
the present and perfect of other verbs, Mat. 19.22. Mar. 2.6, et al.*
Εἶμι,
to go, come, *but generally with a future signification,* v.r. Jno. 7.34, 36.
Εἵηεκεν, *equivalent to* ἕνεκα,
on account of, 2 Co. 7.12, ter.
Εἶπα,
Mat. 26.25, et al., imperat. εἶπον or εἰπόν, v.r. Ac. 28.26, *see* λέγω.
Εἴπερ,
a strengthening of εἰ *by the enclitic particle* περ, if indeed, if it be so that, Ro. 8.9. 1
Co. 15.15; since indeed, since, 2 Thes. 1.6. 1 Pe. 2.3; although indeed, 1 Co. 8.5.
Εἶπον,
imperat. εἰπέ, subj. εἴπω, opt. εἴποιμι, inf. εἰπεῖν, part. εἰπών, *see* λέγω.
Εἴπως, (εἰ & πως)
if by any means, if possible, Ac. 27.12, et al.
Εἰρηνεύω,
f. εύσω,
to be at peace; to cultivate peace, concord, or 54harmony, Mar. 9.50. Ro. 12.18, et al.:
from
Εἰρήνη, ης, ἡ,
peace, Lu. 14.32. Ac. 12.20, et al.; tranquillity, Lu. 11.21. Jno. 16.33. 1 Thes. 5.3;
concord, unity, love of peace, Mat. 10.34. Lu. 12.51, et al.; *meton.* the author of peace
or concord, Ep. 2.14; *fr. the Heb.* felicity, every kind of blessing and good, Lu. 1.79;
2.14, 29, et al.; *meton.* a salutation expressive of good wishes, a benediction, blessing,
Mat. 10.13, et al.: *whence*
Εἰρηνικός, ή, όν,
pertaining to peace; peaceable, disposed to peace and concord, Ja. 3.17; *fr. the Heb.*
profitable, blissful, He. 12.11.
Εἰρηνοποιέω, ῶ, (εἰρήνη & ποιέω)
f. ήσω,
to make peace, restore concord, Col. 1.20. L.G.
Εἰρηνοποιός, οῦ, ὁ, ἡ,
a peacemaker, one who cultivates peace and concord, Mat. 5.9.
Εἰς,
into, Mat. 2.11, et al.; to, as far as, to the extent of, Mat. 2.23; 4.24, et al.; until, Jno.
13.1, et al.; against, Mat. 18.15. Lu. 12.10; before, in the presence of, Ac. 22.30, et al.;
in order to, for, with a view to, Mar. 1.38, et al.; for the use or service of, Jno. 6.9. Lu.
9.13. 1 Co. 16.1; in accordance with, Mat. 12.41. Lu. 11.32. 2 Ti. 2.26; *also
equivalent to* ἐν, Jno. 1.18, et al.; by, *in forms of swearing,* Mat. 5.35, et al.; *fr. the
Heb.* εἶναι, γίνεσθαι εἰς—, to become, result in, amount to, Mat. 19.5. 1 Co. 4.3, et al.;
εἰς τί, why, wherefore, Mat. 26.8.
Εἷς, μία, ἕν, gen. ἑνός, μιᾶς, ἑνός,

one, Mat. 10.29, et al. freq.; only, unicus, Mar. 12.6; one, united *as as to be, in a manner, one,* Mat. 19.5, 6. Jno. 10.30; one and the same, Lu. 12.52. Ro. 3.30, et al.; of one and the same standing or value, 1 Co. 3.8; *equivalent to* τις, a certain one, Mat. 8.19; 16.14, et al.; a, an, Mat. 21.19. Ja. 4.13, et al.; εἷς ἕκαστος, each one, every one, Lu. 4.40. Ac. 2.3, et al.; εἷς τὸν ἕνα, one another, 1 Thes. 5.11; εἷς—καὶ εἷς, the one— and the other, Mat. 20.21, et al.; εἷς καθ' εἷς & ὁδὲ καθ' εἷς, one by one, one after another, in succession, Mar. 14.19. Jno. 8.9, et al.; *fr. the Heb, as an ordinal,* first, Mat. 28.1, et al.

Εἰσάγω, (εἰς & ἄγω)
to lead or bring in, introduce, conduct or usher in or to *a place or person,* Lu. 2.27; 14.21; 22.54, et al. (ἄ).

Εἰσακούω, (εἰς & ἀκούω)
f. ούσομαι,
to hear or hearken to, *i.e.,* obey, 1 Co. 14.21; to listen to *the prayers of any one,* accept one's petition, Mat. 6.7. Lu. 1.13. Ac. 10.31. He. 5.7.

Εἰσδέχομαι, (εἰς & δέχομαι)
f. δέξομαι,
to admit; to receive into *favour,* receive kindly, accept with favour, 2 Co. 6.17.

Εἴσειμι, (εἰς & εἶμι)
imperf. εἰσῄειν,
to go in, enter, Ac. 3.3; 21.18, 26. He. 9.6.

Εἰσέρχομαι, (εἰς & ἔρχομαι)
f. ελεύσομαι, a.2. εἰσῆλθον,
to go or come in, enter, Mat. 7.13; 8.5, 8, et al.; *spc.* to enter by force, break in, Mar. 3.27. Ac. 20.29; *met. with* εἰς κόσμον, to begin to exist, come into existence, Ro. 5.12. 2 Jno. 7; *or* to make one's appearance on earth, He. 10.5; to enter into or take possession of, Lu. 22.3. Jno. 13.27; to enter into, enjoy, partake of, Mat. 19.23, 24, et al.; to enter into *any one's labour,* be *his* successor, Jno. 4.38; to fall into, be placed in *certain circumstances,* Mat. 26.41, et al.; to be put into, Mat. 15.11. Ac. 11.8; to present one's self before, Ac. 19.30; *met.* to arise, spring up, Lu. 9.46; *fr. the Heb.* εἰσέρχεσθαι καὶ ἐξέρχεσθαι, to go in and out, to live, discharge the ordinary functions of lie, versari, Ac. 1.21.

Εἰσκαλέω, ῶ, (εἰς & καλέω)
f. έσω, & mid. εἰσκαλέομαι, οῦμαι,
to call in; to invite in, Ac. 10.23.

Εἴσοδος, ου, ἡ, (εἰς & ὁδός)
a place of entrance; the act of bringing in or introducing; admission, reception, 1 Thes. 1.9. He. 10.19. 2 Pe. 1.11; a coming, approach, access, 1 Thes. 2.1; entrance upon office, commencement of official duties, Ac. 13.24.

Εἰσπηδάω, ῶ, (εἰς & πηδάω, to leap)
f. ήσω,
to leap or spring in, rush in eagerly, Ac. 14.14; 16.29.

Εἰσπορεύομαι, (εἰς & πορεύομαι)
f. εύσομαι,
to go or come in, enter, Mar. 1.21; 5.40, et al.; to come to, visit, Ac. 28.30; to be put in, Mat. 15.17. Mar. 7.15, 18, 19; to 55intervene, Mar. 4.19; *fr. the Heb.* εἰσπορεύεσθαι καὶ ἐκπορεύεσθαι, *equivalent to* εἰσέρχεσθαι καὶ ἐξέρχεσθαι, *above,* Ac. 9.28.

Εἰστρέχω, (εἰς & τρέχω)
a.2. εἰσέδραμον,

to run in, Ac. 12.14.

Εἰσφέρω, (εἰς & φέρω)

f. οἴσω, a.1. ἤνεγκα, a.2. ἤνεγκον,

to bring in, to, or into, Lu. 5.18, 19. 1 Ti. 6.7. He. 13.11; to bring to *the ears of any one,* to announce, Ac. 17.20; to lead into, Mat. 6.13. Lu.11.4.

Εἶτα,

adv. then, afterwards, thereupon, Mar. 4.17, 28. Lu. 8.12, et al.; in the next place, 1 Co. 12.28; besides, He. 12.9.

Εἴωθα,

2. p. *from an old pr.* ἔθω *with a present signification,* plup. εἰώθειν, part. εἰωθώς, to be accustomed, to be usual, Mat. 27.15, et al.

Ἐκ, *before a consonant,* ἐξ *before a vowel,*

prep. from, out of, *a place,* Mat. 2.15; 3.17; of, from, out of, *denoting origin or source,* Mat. 1.3; 21.19; of, from *some material,* Mat. 3.9. Ro. 9.21; of, from, among, *partitively,* Mat. 6.27; 21.31. Mar. 9.17; from, *denoting cause,* Re. 8.11; 17.6; *means or instrument,* Mat. 12.33, 27; by, through, *denoting the author or efficient cause,* Mat. 1.18. Jno. 10.32; of, *denoting the distinguishing mark of a class,* Ro. 2.8. Gal. 3.7, et al.; *of time,* after, 2 Co. 4.6. Re. 17.11; from, after, since, Mat. 19.12. Lu. 8.27; for, with, *denoting a rate of payment, price,* Mat. 20.2; 27.7; at, *denoting position,* Mat. 20.21, 23; *after passive verbs,* by, of, from, *marking the agent,* Mat. 15.5. Mar. 7.11; *forming with certain words a periphrasis for an adverb,* Mat. 26.42, 44. Mar. 6.51. Lu. 23.8; *put after verbs of freeing,* Ro. 7.24. 2 Co. 1.10; *used partitively after verbs of eating, drinking, &c.* Jno. 6.26. 1 Co. 9.7.

Ἕκαστος, η, ον,

each one, every one separately, Mat. 16.27. Lu. 13.15, et al.: *whence*

Ἑκάστοτε,

adv. always, 2 Pe. 1.15.

Ἑκᾰτόν, οἱ, αἱ, τά,

one hundred, Mat. 13.8. Mar. 4.8, et al.

Ἑκατονταετής, έος, ὁ, ἡ, (ἑκατόν & ἔτος)

a hundred years old, Ro. 4.19.

Ἑκατονταπλασίων, ονος, ὁ, ἡ,

a hundredfold, centuple, Mat. 19.29, et al.

Ἑκατοντάρχης, ου, ὁ, *and*

Ἑκατόνταρχος, ου, ὁ, (ἑκατόν & ἄρχος)

commander of 100 men, a centurion, Mat. 8.5, 8, 13. Lu. 7.2, 6, et al.

Ἐκβάλλω, (ἐκ & βάλλω)

f. βαλῶ, a.2. ἐξέβαλον,

to cast out, eject by force, Mat. 15.17. Ac. 27.38; to expel, force away, Lu. 4.29. Ac. 7.58; to refuse, Jno. 6.37; to extract, Mat. 7.4; to reject with contempt, despise, contemn, Lu. 6.22; *in N.T.,* to send forth, send out, Mat. 9.38. Lu 10.2; to send away, dismiss, Mat. 9.25. Mar. 1.12; *met.* to spread abroad, Mat. 12.20; to bring out, produce, Mat. 12.35; 13.52, et al.

Ἔκβᾰσις, εως, ἡ, (ἐκβαίνω)

way out, egress; *hence,* result, issue, He. 13.7; means of clearance or successful endurance, 1 Co. 10.13.

Ἐκβολή, ῆς, ἡ, (ἐκβάλλω)

a casting out; *especially,* a throwing overboard *of cargo,* Ac. 27.18.

Ἐκγαμίζω, (ἐκ & γαμίζω)

f. ίσω,

to give in marriage, Mat. 22.30; 24.38. Lu. 17.27. v.r. 1 Co. 7.38. L.G.

Ἐκγαμίσκω, (ἐκ & γαμίσκω)
i.q. ἐκγαμίζω, Lu. 20.34, 35. L.G.

Ἔκγονος, ου, ὁ, ἡ (ἐκγίνομαι, to be born)
born of, descended from, ἔκγονα, descendants, grandchildren, 1 Ti. 5.4.

Ἐκδαπανάω, ῶ, (ἐκ & δαπανάω)
f. ήσω,
to expend, consume, exhaust, 2 Co. 12.15. L.G.

Ἐκδέχομαι, (ἐκ & δέχομαι)
f. ξομαι,
pr. to receive from another; to expect, look for, Ac. 17.16, et al.; to wait for, to wait, 1 Co. 11.33. 1 Pe. 3.20, et al.

Ἔκδηλος, ου, ὁ, ἡ, (ἐκ & δῆλος)
clearly manifest, evident, 2 Ti. 3.9.

Ἐκδημέω, ῶ, (ἐκ & δῆμος)
f. ήσω,
pr. to be absent from home, go abroad, travel; hence, to be absent from any place or person, 2 Co. 5.6, 8, 9.

Ἐκδίδωμι, (ἐκ & δίδωμι)
f. ἐκδώσω, a.2. mid ἐξεδόμην,
to give ouot, to give up; to put out at interest; in N.T., to let out to tenants, Mat.21.33, 41, et al.

Ἐκδιηγέομαι, οῦμαι, (ἐκ & διηγέομαι)
f. ήσομαι,
56to narrate fully, detail, Ac. 13.14; 15.3. L.G.

Ἐκδικέω, ῶ, (ἐκ & δίκη)
pr. to execute right and justice; to punish, 2 Co. 10.6; in N.T., to right, avenge a person, Lu. 18.3, 5, et al.: (L.G.) whence

Ἐκδίκησις, εως, ἡ,
satisfaction; vengeance, punishment, retributive justice, Lu. 21.22. Ro. 12.19, et al.; ἐκδίκησιν ποῖειν, to vindicate, avenge, Lu. 18.7, 8, et al.; διδόναι ἐκδ. to inflict vengeance, 2 Thes. 1.8.

Ἔκδῐκος, ου, ὁ, ἡ,
maintaining right; an avenger, one who inflicts punishment, Ro. 13.4. 1 Thes. 4.6.

Ἐκδιώκω, (ἐκ & διώκω)
f. ώξω,
pr. to chase away, drive out; in N.T., to persecute, vex, harass, Lu. 11.49. 1 Thes. 2.15.

Ἔκδοτος, ου, ὁ, ἡ, (ἐκδίδωμι)
delivered up, Ac. 2.23.

Ἐκδοχή, ῆς, ἡ, (ἐκδέχομαι)
in N.T., a looking for, expectation, He. 10.27.

Ἐκδύω, v. δύνω, (ἐκ & δύνω)
f. ύσω,
pr. to go out from; to take off, strip, unclothe, Mat. 27.31; 27.28, et al.; mid. to lay aside, to put off, 2 Co. 5.4. (ὔω, ὔνω, ὗσω)

Ἐκεῖ,
adv. there, in that place, Mat. 2.13, 15, et al.; thither, Mat. 2.22; 17.20, et al.: whence

Ἐκεῖθεν,
adv. from there, thence, Mat. 4.21; 5. 26, et al.

Ἐκεῖνος, η, ο, (ἐκεῖ)

    a demonstrative pronoun, used with reference to a thing previously mentioned or implied, or already familiar; that, this, he, &c., Mat. 17.27; 10.14. 2 Ti. 4.8, et al.; *in contrast with* οὗτος, *referring to the former to two things previously mentioned,* Lu. 18.14, et al.

Ἐκεῖσε,

    adv. thither, there, Ac. 21.3; 22.5.

Ἐκζητέω, ῶ, (ἐκ & ζητέω)

    to seek out, investigate diligently, scrutinise, 1 Pe. 1.10; to ask for, beseech earnestly, He. 12.17; to seek diligently or earnestly after, Ac. 15.17. Ro. 3.11. He. 11.6; *fr. the Heb.* to require, exact, demand, Lu. 11.50, 51. L.G.

Ἐκθαμβέομαι, οῦμαι,

    to be amazed, astonished, awe-struck, Mar. 9.15; 14.33; 16.5, 6: *from*

Ἔκθαμβος, ου, ὁ, ἡ, (ἐκ & θάμβος)

    amazed, awe-struck, Ac. 3.11. L.G.

Ἔκθετος, ου, ὁ, ἡ, τό, ον, (ἐκτίθημι)

    exposed, cast out, abandoned, Ac. 7.19.

Ἐκκαθαίρω, (ἐκ & καθαίρω)

    f. αρῶ, a.1. ηρα, & later, ᾶρα,

    to cleanse thoroughly, purify, 2 Ti. 2.21; to purge out, eliminate, 1 Co. 5.7.

Ἐκκαίομαι, (ἐκκαίω, to kindle up, ἐκ & καίω)

    a.1. pass. ἐξεκαύθην,

    to blaze out; to be inflamed, Ro. 1.27.

Ἐκκακέω, ῶ, (ἐκ & κακός)

    f. ήσω,

    to lose spirits, to be faint-hearted, despond, Ep. 3.13; to faint, to flag, be remiss, indolent, slothful, Lu. 18.1. Gal. 6.9. 2 Co. 4.1, 16. 2 Thes. 3.13. L.G.

Ἐκκεντέω, ῶ, (ἐκ & κεντέω)

    f. ήσω,

    to stab, pierce deeply, transfix, Jno. 19.37. Re. 1.7. L.G.

Ἐκκλάω, (ἐκ & κλάω)

    f. άσω, a.1. pass. ἐξεκλάσθην,

    to break off, Ro. 11.17, 19, 20.

Ἐκκλείω, (ἐκ & κλείω)

    f. είσω,

    to shut out, exclude; to shut off, separate, insulate, Gal. 4.17; to leave no place for, eliminate, Ro. 3.27.

Ἐκκλησία, ας, ἡ, (ἐκκαλέω, to summon forth)

    a popular assembly, Ac. 19.32, 39, 41; *in N.T.,* the congregation *of the children of Israel,* Ac. 7.38; *transferred to the Christian body, of which the congregation of Israel was a figure,* the church, 1 Co. 12.28. Col 1.18, et al.; *a local portion of the church, a local* church, Ro. 16.1, et al.; a *Christian* congregation, 1 Co. 14.4, et al.

Ἐκκλίνω, (ἐκ & κλίνω)

    f. ινῶ,

    to deflect, deviate, Ro. 3.12; to decline or turn away from, avoid, Ro. 16.17. 1 Pe. 3.11.

Ἐκκολυμβάω, ῶ, (ἐκ & κολυμβάω)

    f. ήσω,

    to swin out *to land,* Ac. 27.42.

Ἐκκομίζω, (ἐκ & κομίζω)

f. ίσω,

to carry, bring out; *especially,* to carry out *a corpse for burial,* Lu. 7.12.

Ἐκκόπτω, (ἐκ & κόπτω)

f. ψω,

to cut out; to cut off, Mat. 3.10; 5.30, et al.; *met.* to cut off *occasion,* 57remove, prevent, 2 Co. 11.12; to render ineffectual, 1 Pe. 3.7.

Ἐκκρέμαμαι, (ἐκ & κρέμαμαι)

to hang upon *a speaker,* fondly listen to, be earnestly attentive, Lu. 19.48.

Ἐκλαλέω, ῶ (ἐκ & λαλέω)

f. ήσω,

to speak out; to tell, utter, divulge, Ac. 23.22.

Ἐκλάμπω, (ἐκ & λάμπω)

f. ψω,

to shine out or forth, be resplendent, Mat. 13.43.

Ἐκλανθάνω, (ἐκ & λανθάνω)

to make to forget, quite; *mid.* ἐκλανθάνομαι, p. ἐκλέλησμαι, to forget entirely, He. 12.5.

Ἐκλέγω,

f. ξε,

to pick out; *in N.T., mid.* ἐκλέγομαι, a.1. ἐξελεξάμην, to choose, select, Lu. 6.13; 10.42, et al.; *in N.T.,* to choose out *as the receipients of special favour and privilege,* Ac. 13.17. 1 Co. 1.27, et al.

Ἐκλείπω, (ἐκ & λείπω)

f. ψω,

intrans., to fail, Lu. 22.32; to come to an end, He. 1.12; to be defunct, die, Lu. 16.9.

Ἐκλεκτός, ή, όν, (ἐκλέγομαι)

chosen out, selected; *in N.T.,* chosen *as a recipient of special privilege,* elect, Col. 3.12, et al.; specially beloved, Lu. 23.35; possessed of prime excellence, exalted, 1 Ti. 5.21; choice, precious, 1 Pe. 2.4, 6.

Ἐκλογή, ῆς, ἡ, (same)

the act of choosing out, election; *in N.T.,* election *to privilege by divine grace,* Ro. 11.5, et al.; ἡ ἐκλογή, the aggregate of those who are chosen, the elect, Ro. 11.7; ἐκλογῆς, *equivalent to* ἐκλεκτόν, *by Hebraism,* Ac. 9.15.

Ἐκλύομαι, (ἐκλύω, to loosen, debilitate, ἐκ & λύω)

to be weary, exhausted, faint, Mat. 9.36; 15.32. Mar. 8.3. Gal. 6.9; to faint, despond, He. 12.3, 5.

Ἐκμάσσω, (ἐκ & μάσσω)

f. ξω,

to wipe off; to wipe dry, Lu. 7.38, 44. Jno. 11.2; 12.3; 13.5.

Ἐκμυκτηρίζω, (ἐκ & μυκτηρίζω, fr. μυκτήρ, the nose)

f. ίσω,

to mock, deride, scoff at, Lu. 16.14; 23.35.

Ἐκνέω,

f. ἐκνεύσομαι, a.1. ἐξένευσα,

pr. to swim out, to escape by swimming; *hence, generally,* to escape, get clear of *a place,* Jno. 5.18; *though* ἐκνεύσας, *in this place, may be referred to* ἐκνεύω, to deviate, withdraw.

Ἐκνήφω, (ἐκ & νήφω)

f. ψω,

pr. to awake sober after intoxication; *met.* to shake off mental bewilderment, to return to a right mode of thinking, feeling, acting, &c. 1 Co. 15.34.

Ἑκούσιος, α, ον, & ου, ὁ, ἡ, (ἑκών)
  voluntary, spontaneous, Phile. 14. *whence*
Ἑκουσίως,
  adv. voluntarily, spontaneously, He. 10.26. 1 Pe. 5.2.
Ἔκπᾰλαι, (ἐκ & πάλαι)
  adv. of old, long since, 2 Pe. 2.3; 3.5. L.G.
Ἐκπειράζω, (ἐκ & πειράζω)
  f. άσω,
  to tempt, put to the proof, Mat. 4.7. Lu. 4.12. 1 Co. 10.9; to try, sound, Lu. 10.25. L.G.
Ἐκπέμπω, (ἐκ & πέμπω)
  f. ψω,
  to send out, or away, Ac. 13.4; 17.10.
Ἐκπερισσῶς, (strengthened fr. περισσῶς)
  adv. exceedingly, vehemently, v.r. Mar. 14.31.
Ἐκπετάννῦμι, (ἐκ & πετάννυμι)
  f. άσω,
  to stretch forth, expand, extend, Ro. 10.21. (ᾱ)
Ἐκπηδάω, ῶ, (ἐκ & πηδάω, to leap, spring)
  f. ήσω,
  to leap forth, rush out, v.r. Ac. 14.14.
Ἐκπίπτω,
  f. πεσοῦμαι, p. πέπτωκα, a.1. εξέπεσα, a.2. ἐξέπεσον,
  to fall off or from, Mar. 13.25. Ac. 12.7; 27.32, et al.; *met.* to fall from, forfeit, lose, Gal. 5.4. 2 Pe. 3.17. Re. 2.5; to be cast ashore, Ac. 27.17, 26, 29; to fall to the ground, be fruitless, ineffectual, Ro. 9.6; to cease, come to an end, 1 Co. 13.8.
Ἐκπλέω, (ἐκ & πλέω)
  f. εύσομαι, a.1. ἐξέπλευσα,
  to sail out or from *a place,* Ac. 15.39; 18.18; 20.6.
Ἐκπληρόω, ῶ (ἐκ & πληρόω)
  f. ώσω,
  to fill out, complete, fill up; *met.* to fulfil, perform, accomplish, Ac. 13.32: *whence*
Ἐκπλήρωσις, εως, ἡ,
  pr. a filling up, completion; *hence,* a fulfilling, accomplishment, Ac. 21.26. L.G.
Ἐκπλήσσω, v. ττω, (ἐκ & πλήσσω)
  f. ξω, a.2. pass. ἐξεπλάγην,
  pr. to strike out of; *hence,* to strike out of *one's wits,* to astound, amaze; *pass.* Mat. 7.28; 13.54, et al.
Ἐκπνέω, ῶ, (ἐκ & πνέω)
  58f. ευσω & εύσομαι,
  to breathe out; to expire, die, Mar. 15.37, 39. Lu. 23.46.
Ἐκπορεύομαι, (ἐκ & πορεύομαι)
  f. εύσομαι,
  to go from or out of *a place,* depart from, Mar. 11.19; 13.1, et al.; to be voided, Mar. 7.19; to be cast out, Mat. 17.21; to proceed from, be spoken, Mat. 4.4; 15.11, et al.; to burst forth, Re. 4.5; to be spread abroad, Lu. 4.37; to flow out, Re. 22.1; *fr. the Heb.* ἐκπορ. καὶ εἰσπορ. *see* εἰσέρχομαι, Ac. 9.28.
Ἐκπορνεύω, (ἐκ & πορνεύω)

f. εύσω,
to be given to fornication, Jude 7. L.G.

Ἐκπτύω, (ἐκ & πτύω)
f. ύσω & ύσομαι,
to spit out; *met.* to reject, Gal. 4.14. (ῠ).

Ἐκριζόω, ῶ, (ἐκ & ῥιζόω)
f. ώσε,
to root up, eradicate, Mat. 13.29; 15.13. Lu. 17.6. Jude 12. L.G.

Ἔκστᾰσις, εως, ἡ, (ἐξίστημι)
pr. a displacement; *hence,* a displacement of the mind from its ordinary state and self-possession; amazement, astonishment, Mar. 5.42; excess of fear; fear, terror, Mar. 16.8. Lu. 5.26. Ac. 3.10; *in N.T.,* an ecstasy, a trance, Ac. 10.10; 11.5; 22.17.

Ἐκστρέφω, (ἐκ & στρέφω)
f. ψω, p. pass. ἐξέστραμμαι,
pr. to turn out of, to turn inside out; *hence,* to change entirely; *in N.T., pass.* to be perverted, Tit. 3.11.

Ἐκταράσσω, (ἐκ & ταράσσω)
f. ξω,
to disturb, disquiet, throw into confusion, Ac. 16.20.

Ἐκτείνω, (ἐκ & τείνω, to stretch)
f. τενῶ,
to stretch out, Mat. 8.3; 12.13, et al.; to lay *hands on any one,* Lu. 22.53; to exert *power and energy,* Ac. 4.30; to cast out, let down *an anchor,* Ac. 27.30.

Ἐκτελέω, ῶ, (ἐκ & τελέω)
f. έσω,
to bring quite to an end, to finish, complete, Lu. 14.29, 30.

Ἐκτένεια, ας, ἡ, (ἐκτενής)
pr. extension; *in N.T.,* intenseness, intentness; ἐν ἐκτενείᾳ, intently, assiduously, Ac. 26.7. L.G.

Ἐκτενέστερον,
adv. very earnestly, Lu. 22.44; *pr. neut. comp. of*

Ἐκτενής, έος, ὁ, ἡ, τό, -ές, (ἐκτείνω)
pr. extended; *met.* intense, earnest, fervent, Ac. 12.5. 1 Pe. 4.8: *whence*

Ἐκτενῶς,
adv. intensely, fervently, earnestly, 1 Pe. 1.22.

Ἐκτίθημι, (ἐκ & τίθημι)
f. ἐκθήσω,
pr. to place outside, put forth; to expose *an infant,* Ac. 7.21; *met.* to set forth, declare, explain, Ac. 11.4; 18.26; 28.23.

Ἐκτινάσσω, (ἐκ & τινάσσω, to shake)
f. ξω,
to shake out, shake off, Mat. 10.14. Mar. 6.11, et al.

Ἕκτος, ην, ον, (ἕξ)
sixth, Mat. 20.5; 27.45, et al.

Ἐκτός, (ἐκ)
adv. without, on the outside; τὸ ἐκτός, the exterior, outside, Mat. 23.26; *met.* besides, Ac. 26.22. 1 Co. 15.27; ἐκτὸς εἰ μή, unless, except, 1 Co. 14.5, et al.

Ἐκτρέπω, (ἐκ & τρέπω)
f. ψω, a.2. pass. ἐξετράπην,

to turn out or aside, He. 12.13; *mid.* to turn away or aside, swerve, 1 Ti. 1.6; 5.15. 2
Ti. 4.4; to turn from, avoid, 1 Ti. 6.20.

Ἐκτρέφω, (ἐκ & τρέφω)
    f. ἐκθρέψω,
    to nourish, promote health and strength, Ep. 5.29; to bring up, educate, Ep. 6.4.

Ἔκτρωμα, ατος, τό, (ἐκτιτρώσκω, to cause abortion)
    an abortion, fœtus prematurely born, 1 Co. 15.8.

Ἐκφέρω, (ἐκ & φέρω)
    f. ἐξοίσω, a.1. ἐξήνεγκα, a.2 ἐξήνεγκον,
    to bring forth, carry out, Lu. 15.22. Ac. 5.15. 1 Ti. 6.7; to carry out *for burial,* Ac. 5.6,
    9, 10; to produce, yield, He. 6.8.

Ἐκφεύγω, (ἐκ & φεύγω)
    f. ξομαι, a.2. ἐξέφυγον, p. ἐκπέφευγα,
    intrans., to flee out, to make an escape, Ac. 16.27; 19.16; *trans.,* to escape, avoid, Lu.
    21.36. Ro. 2.3, et al.

Ἐκφοβέω, ῶ, (ἐκ & φοβέω)
    f. ήσω,
    to terrify, 2 Co. 10.9

Ἔκφοβος, ου, ὁ, ἡ, (ἐκ & φόβος)
    affrighted, Mar. 9.6. He. 12.21.

Ἐκφύω, (ἐκ & φύω)
    f. ὑσω,
    to generate; to put forth, shoot, Mat. 24.32. Mar. 13.28. (ŭ, ῡσ–)

Ἐκχέω,
    f. ἐκχέω, or ἐκχεῶ, a.1. ἐξέχεα, p. ἐκκέχυκα, pass. p. ἐκκέχῡμαι, a.1. ἐξεχύθην,
    59to pour out, Re. 16.1, 2.3, et al.; to shed *blood,* Mat. 26.28. Mar. 14.24, et al.; *pass.*
    to gush out, Ac. 1.18; to spill, scatter, Mat. 9.17. Jno. 2.15; *met.* to give largely,
    bestow liberally, Ac. 2.17, 18, 33; 10.45, et al.; *pass.* to rush headlong *into any thing,*
    be abandoned to, Jude 11.

Ἐκχύνω,
    a later form equivalent to ἐκχέω. Mat. 23.35, et al.

Ἐκχωρέω, ῶ, (ἐκ & χωρέω)
    f. ήσω,
    to go out, depart from, flee, Lu. 21.21.

Ἐκψύχω,
    f. ξω,
    to expire, give up the ghost, Ac. 5.5, 10; 12.23. (ῡ)

Ἑκών, οῦσα, όν,
    willing, voluntary, Ro. 8.20. 1 Co. 9.17.

Ἐλαία, ας, ἡ,
    an olive tree, Mat. 21.1; 24.3, et al.; an olive, fruit of the olive tree, Ja. 3.12: *whence*

Ἔλαιον, ου, τό,
    olive oil, oil, Mat. 25.3, 4, 8. Mar. 6.13, et al.

Ἐλαιών, ῶνος, ὁ,
    an olive garden; *in N.T., the mount* Olivet, Ac. 1.12.

Ἐλάσσων, v. ττως, ονος, ὁ, ἡ, τό, -ον, (comp. of old word ἐλαχύς)
    less; less *in age,* younger, Ro. 9.12; less *in dignity,* inferior, He. 7.7; less *in quality,*
    inferior, worse, Jno. 2.10: *whence*

Ἔλαττον, (pr. neut. of preced.)
    adv. less, 1 Ti. 5.9.

Ἐλαττονέω, ῶ,
    f. ήσω, a.1. ήλαττόνησα,
    trans. to make less; *intrans.* to be less, inferior; to have too little, want, lack, 2 Co. 8.15. L.G.
Ἐλαττόω, ῶ,
    f. ώσω, p. pass. ήλάττωμαι,
    to make less or inferior, He. 2.7; *pass.* to be made less or inferior, He. 2.9; to decline *in importance,* Jno. 3.30.
Ἐλαύνω,
    f. ἐλάσω, p. ἐλήλακα,
    to drive, urge forward, spur on, Lu. 8.29. Ja. 3.4. 2 Pe. 2.17; to impel *a vessel by oars,* to row, Mar. 6.48. Jno. 6.19.
Ἐλαφρία, ας, ή,
    lightness *in weight; hence,* lightness of mind, thoughtlessness, levity, 2 Co. 1.17: (L.G.) *from*
Ἐλαφρός, ά, όν,
    light, not heavy, Mat. 11.30. 2 Co. 4.17.
Ἐλάχιστος, η, ον, (sup. of μικρός, fr. ἐλαχύς)
    smallest, least, Mat. 2.6; 5.19, et al.
Ἐλαχιστότερος, α, ον, (comp. of preced.)
    far less, far inferior, Ep. 3.8. L.G.
Ἐλεγμός, οῦ, ὁ,
    a later equivalent to ἔλεγχος. v.r. 2 Ti. 3.16.
Ἔλεγξις, εως, ή, (a later form for ἔλεγχος)
    reproof, confutation, 2 Pe. 2.16.
Ἔλεγχος, ου, ὁ, (ἐλέγχω)
    pr. a trial in order to proof, a proof; *meton.* a certain persuasion, He. 11.1; reproof, refutation, 2 Ti. 3.16: *from*
Ἐλέγχω,
    f. ξχ, a.1. ήλεγξα, a.1. pass. ήλέγχθην,
    to convict, Jno. 8.9, 46; to refute, confute, 1 Co. 14.24. Tit. 1.9; to detect, lay bare, expose, Jno. 3.20. Ep 5.11, 13; to put to shame; to reprove, reprehend, rebuke, Mat. 18.15. Lu. 3.19. 1 Ti. 5.20; to discipline, correct by chastisement, chastise, He. 12.5. Re. 3.19.
Ἐλεεινός, ή, όν, (ἔλεος)
    pitiable, wretched, miserable, 1 Co. 15.19. Re. 3.17.
Ἐλεέω, ῶ, (fr. same)
    f. ήσω, a.1. ήλέησα, p. pass. ήλέημαι, a.1. pass. ήλεήθην,
    to pity, commiserate, have compassion on; *pass.* to receive pity, experience compassion, Mat. 5.7; 9.27; 15.22, et al.; to be gracious to *any one,* show gracious favour and saving mercy towards; *pass.* to be an object of gracious favour and saving mercy, Ro. 9.15, 16, 18; 11.30, 31, 32, et al.; *spc.* to obtain pardon and forgiveness, 1 Ti. 1.13, 16.
Ἐλεημοσύνη, ης, ή,
    pity, compassion, *in N.T.,* alms, almsgiving, Mat. 6.2, 3, 4. Lu. 11.41, et al.: *from*
Ἐλεήμων, ονος, ὁ, ή, (ἐλεέω)
    merciful, pitiful, compassionate, Mat. 5.7. He. 2.17.
Ἔλεος, ου, ὁ, & in N.T. έους, τό,

pity, mercy, compassion, Mat. 9.13; 12.7. Lu. 1.50, 78; et al.; *meton.* benefit *which results from compassion,* kindness, mercies, blessings, Lu. *1.54, 58, 72;* 10.37. Ro. 9.23, et al.

Ἐλευθερία, ας, ἡ,
    liberty, freedom, 1 Co. 10.29. Gal. 2.4, et al.: *from*

Ἐλεύθερος, α, ον,
    free, in a state of freedom *as opposed to slavery,* 1 Co. 12.13. Gal. 3.28, et al.; free, exempt, Mat. 17.26. 1 Co. 7.39, et al.; 60unrestricted, unfettered, 1 Co. 9.1; free *from the dominion of sin,* &c. Jno. 8.36. Ro. 6.20; free *in the possession of Gospel privileges,* 1 Pe. 2.16: *whence*

Ἐλευθερόω, ῶ,
    f. ώσω,
    to free, set free, Jno. 32.36. Ro. 6.18, 22, et al.

Ἔλευσις, εως, ἡ, (obs. ἐλεύθω)
    a coming, advent, Ac. 7.52. L.G.

Ἐλεφάντῐνος, η, ον, (ἐλέφας, ivory)
    ivory, made of ivory, Re. 18.12.

Ἑλίσσω,
    f. ξω,
    to roll, fold up, *as garments,* He. 1.12.

Ἕλκος, εος, τό,
    pr. a wound; *hence,* an ulcer, sore, Lu. 16.21. Re. 16.2, 11: *hence,*

Ἑλκόω, ῶ,
    f. ώσω,
    to ulcerate, exulcerate; *pass.* to be afflicted with ulcers, Lu. 16.20.

Ἕλκω, & L.G. ἑλκύω,
    imp. εἶλκον, f. ύσω, a.1. εἵλκῠσα,
    to draw, drag, Jno. 21.6, 11. Ac. 16.19; 21.30. Ja. 2.6; to draw *a sword,* unsheath, Jno. 18.10; *met.* to draw *mentally and morally,* Jno. 6.44; 12.32.

Ἑλλάς, άδος, ἡ,
    Hellas, Greece; *in N.T.,* the southern portion of Greece *as distinguished from Macedonia,* Ac. 20.2.

Ἕλλην, ηνος, ὁ,
    a Greek, Ac. 18.17. Ro. 1.14; one not a Jew, a gentile, Ac. 14.1; 16.1, 3, et al.

Ἑλληνικός, ή, όν,
    Greek, Grecian, Lu. 23.28. Re. 9.11.

Ἑλληνίς, ίδος, ἡ,
    a female Greek, Mar. 7.26. Ac. 17.12.

Ἑλληνιστής, οῦ, ὁ, (ἑλληνίζω, to imitate the Greeks)
    pr. one who uses the language and follows the customs of the Greeks; *in N.T.,* a Jew by blood but a native of a Greek-speaking country, Ac. 6.1; 9.29.

Ἑλληνιστί,
    adv. in the Greek language, Jno. 19.20. Ac. 21.37.

Ἐλλογέω, ῶ, (ἐν & λόγος)
    f. ήσω,
    to enter in an account, to put to one's account, Phile. 18; *in N.T.,* to impute, Ro. 5.13.

Ἐλπίζω,
    f. ίσω, At. ιῶ, p. ἤλπικα, a.1. ἤλπισα,
    to hope, expect, Lu. 23.8; 24.21, et al.; to repose hope and confidence in, trust, confide, Mat. 12.21. Jno. 5.45, et al.: *from*

Ἐλπις, ίδος, ή,
>   *pr.* expectation; hope, Ac. 24.15. Ro. 5.4, et al.; *meton.* the object of hope, thing
>   hoped for, Ro. 8.24. Gal. 5.5, et al.; the author or source of hope, Col. 1.27. 1 Ti. 1.1,
>   et al.; trust, confidence, 1 Pe. 1.21; ἐπ' ἐλπίδι, in security, with a guarantee, Ac. 2.26.
>   Ro. 8.20.

Ἐλωΐ, (Aram. יהלא)
>   my God, Mar. 15.34.

Ἐμαυτοῦ, ῆς, οῦ, (ἐμοῦ & αὐτοῦ)
>   *reflective pron.* myself, mei, ipsius, Lu. 7.7. Jno. 5.31, et al.

Ἐμβαίνω, (ἐν & βαίνω)
>   f. ἐμβήσομαι, a.2. ἐνέβην,
>   to step in; to go on board *a ship,* embark, Mat. 8.23; 9.1; 13.2. et al.

Ἐμβάλλω, (ἐν & βάλλω)
>   f. βαλῶ, a.2. ἐνέβαλον,
>   to cast into, Lu. 12.5.

Ἐμβάπτω, (ἐν & βάπτω)
>   f. ψω,
>   to dip in, Mat. 26.23. Jno. 13.26; *mid.* ἐμβάπτομαι, to dip *for food in a dish,* Mar.
>   14.20.

Ἐμβατεύω, (ἐν & βαίνω)
>   f. εύσω,
>   *pr.* to step into or upon; *met.* to search into, investigate; to pry into intrusively, Co.
>   2.18.

Ἐμβιβάζω, (ἐν & βιβάζω)
>   f. άσω,
>   to cause to step into or upon; to set in or upon; *especially,* to put on board, Ac. 27.6.

Ἐμβλέπω, (ἐν & βλέπω)
>   f. ψω,
>   to look attentively, gaze earnestly *at an object, followed by* εἰς, Mar. 6.26. Ac. 1.11; to
>   direct a glance, to look searchingly or significantly, *at a person, followed by the dat.,*
>   Mar. 10.21; 14.67. Lu. 22.16, et al.; *absol.* to see clearly, Mar. 8.25. Ac. 22.11.

Ἐμβριμάομαι, ῶμαι, (ἐν & βριμάομαι, to snort)
>   f. ήσομαι,
>   to be greatly fretted or agitated, Jno. 11.33; to charge or forbid sternly or vehemently,
>   Mat. 9.30. Mar. 1.43; to express indignation, to censure, Mar. 14.5.

Ἐμέω, ῶ,
>   f. έσω,
>   to vomit, Re. 3.16.

Ἐμμαίνομαι, (ἐν & μαίνομαι)
>   f. ανοῦμαι,
>   to be mad against, be furious towards, Ac. 26.11. L.G.

Ἐμμένω, (ἐν & μένω)
>   f. ενῶ,
>   *pr.* to remain in *a place; met.* to abide by, to continue firm in, perservere in, Ac.
>   14.22. Gal. 3.10. He. 8.9.

Ἐμός, ή, όν,
>   61*possessive adj. of the first pers.,* my, mine, Jno. 7.16; 8.37, et al.

Ἐμπαιγμονή, ῆς, ή, (ἐμπαίζω)
>   mocking, scoffing, derision, v.r. 2 Pe. 3.3. N.T.

Ἐμπαιγμός, οῦ, ὁ,

mocking, scoffing, scorn, He. 11.36: (L.G.) *from*

Ἐμπαίζω, (ἐν & παίζω)

f. αίξω,

to play upon, deride, mock, treat with scorn and contumely, Mat. 20.19; 27.29, et al.; *by impl.* to illude, delude, deceive, Mat. 2.16: *whence*

Ἐμπαίκτης, ου, ὁ,

a mocker, derider, scoffer, 2 Pe. 3.3. Jude 18. L.G.

Ἐμπεριπατέω, ῶ, (ἐν & περιπατέω)

f. ήσω,

pr. to walk about in *a place; met. in N.T.,* to live among, be conversant with, 2 Co. 6.16.

Ἐμπίπλημι, & ἐμπιπλάω, ῶ, (ἐν & πίμπλημι)

f. ἐμπλήσω, a.1. pass ἐνεπλήσθην,

to fill, Ac. 14.17; *pass.* to be satisfied, satiated, full, Lu. 1.53; 6.25. Jno. 6.12; *met.* to have full enjoyment of, Ro. 15.24.

Ἐμπίπρημι,

f. πρήσω,

to set on fire, to burn, Mat. 22.7.

Ἐμπίπτω, (ἐν & πίπτω)

f. πεσοῦμαι, a.2. ἐνέπεσον,

to fall into, Mat. 12.11. Lu. 14.5; to encounter, Lu. 10.36; to be involved in, 1 Ti. 3.6, 7; 6.9; εἰς χεῖρας, to fall under the chastisement of, He. 10.31.

Ἐμπλέκω, (ἐν & πλέκω)

f. ξω,

pr. to intertwine; *met.* to implicate, entangle, involve; *pass.* to be implicated, involved, or to entangle one's self in, 2 Ti. 2.4. 2 Pe. 2.20.

Ἐμπλοκή, ῆς, ἡ, (ἐμπλέκω)

braiding or plaiting *of hair,* 1 Pe. 3.3. L.G.

Ἐμπνέω, (ἐν & πνέω)

f. εύσω,

to breathe into or upon; to respire, breathe; *met.* to breathe of, be animated with the spirit of, Ac. 9.1.

Ἐμπορεύομαι, (ἐν & πορεύομαι)

f. εύσομαι,

to travel; to travel for business' sake; to trade, traffic, Ja. 4.13; *by impl.* to make a gain of, deceive for one's own advantage, 2 Pe. 2.3: *whence*

Ἐμπορία, ας, ἡ,

traffic, trade, Mat. 22.5.

Ἐμπόριον,

a mart, market-place, emporium; *meton.* traffic, Jno. 2.16.

Ἔμπορος, ου, ὁ,

a passenger by sea; a traveller; one who travels about for traffic, a merchant, Mat. 13.45. Re. 18.3, 11, 15, 23.

Ἔμπροσθεν,

adv., used also as a prep., before, in front of, Lu. 19.4. Phi. 3.14; before, in the presence of, in the face of, Mat. 5.24; 23.14; before, previous to, Jno. 1.15, 27, 30; *fr. the Heb.* in the sight or estimation of, Mat. 11.26; 18.14, et al.

Ἐμπτύω, (ἐν & πτύω)

f. ύσω,

to spit upon, Mat. 26.67; 27.30, et al. (ῠω, ῠσω) L.G.

Ἐμφανής, έος, οῦς, ὁ, ἡ, τό, -ές, (ἐν & φαίνω)
    apparent, conspicuous, obvious to the sight, Ac. 10.40; *met.* manifest, known, comprehended, Ro. 10.20: *whence*
Ἐμφανίζω,
    f. ίσω, a.1. ἐνεφάνισα,
    to cause to appear clearly; to communicate, report, Ac. 23.15, 22; to lay an information, Ac. 24.1; 25.2, 15; to manifest, intimate plainly, He. 11.14; to reveal, make known, Jno. 14.21, 22; *pass.* to appear, be visible, Mat. 27.53; to present one's self, He. 9.24.
Ἔμφοβος, ου, ὁ, ἡ, (ἐν & φόβος)
    terrible; *in N.T.,* terrified, affrighted, Lu. 24.5, 37. Ac. 10.4; 22.9, et al.
Ἐμφυσάω, ῶ, (ἐν & φυσάω, to breathe)
    f. ήσω,
    to blow or breath into, inflate; *in N.T.,* to breathe upon, Jno. 20.22.
Ἔμφυτος, ου, ὁ, ἡ, (ἐν & φύω)
    implanted, ingrafted, infixed, Ja. 1.21.
Ἐν,
    prep. pr. referring to place, in, Mat. 8.6. Mar. 12.26. Re. 6.6, et al. freq.; upon, Lu. 8.32, et al.; among, Mat. 11.11, et al.; before, in the presence of, Mar. 8.38, et al.; in the sight, estimation of, 1 Co. 14.11, et al.; before, *judicially,* 1 Co. 6.2; in, *of state, occupation, habit,* Mat. 21.22. Lu. 7.25. Ro. 4.10, et al.; in the case of, Mat. 17.12, et al.; in respect of, Lu. 1.7. 1 Co. 1.7, et al.; on occasion of, on the ground of, Mat. 6.7. Lu. 1.21, et al.; *used of the thing by which an oath is made,* Mat. 5.34, et al.; *of the instrument, means, efficient cause,* Ro. 12.21. Ac. 4.12, et al.; equipped with, furnished with, 1 Co. 4.21. He. 9.25, et al.; arrayed with, accompanied by, Lu. 14.31. Ju. 14, et al.; 62*of time,* during, in the course of, Mat. 2.1, et al.; *in N.T., of demoniacal possession,* possessed by, Mar. 5.2, et al.
Ἐναγκαλίζομαι, (ἐν & ἀγκάλη)
    f. ισομαι,
    to take into or embrace in one's arms, Mar. 9.36; 10.16. L.G.
Ἐνάλιος, ία, ιον, & ου, ὁ, ἡ, (ἐν & ἅλς)
    marine, living in the sea, Ja. 3.7.
Ἔναντι, (ἐν & ἀντί)
    adv. over against, in the presence of, Lu. 1.8. L.G.
Ἐναντίον, (pr. neut. of ἐναντίος)
    before, in the presence of, Mar. 2.12. Lu. 20.26. Ac. 8.32; *fr. the Heb.* in the sight or estimation of, Ac. 7.10; *with* τοῦ Θεοῦ, *an intensive expression,* Lu. 24.19.
Ἐναντίος, α, ον, (ἐν & ἀντί)
    opposite to, over against, Mar. 15.39; contrary, *as the wind,* Mat. 14.24. Ac. 26.9; 28.17. 1 Thes. 2.15; ὁ ἐξ ἐναντίας, an adverse party, enemy, Tit. 2.8; adverse, hostile, counter, 1 Thes. 2.15.
Ἐνάρχομαι, (ἐν & ἄρχομαι)
    f. ξομαι,
    to begin, commence, Gal. 3.3. Phi. 1.6.
Ἔνατος,
    see ἔννατος
Ἐνδεής, έος, οῦς, ὁ, ἡ, (ἐνδέω)
    indigent, poor, needy, Ac. 4.34.
Ἔνδειγμα, ατος, τό,
    a token, evidence, proof, 2 Thes. 1.5: *from*

Ἐνδείκνῦμαι, (mid. of ἐνδείκνῦμι, to point out)
f. δείξομαι,
to manifest, display, Ro. 9.17, 22. He. 6.10, et al.; to give outward proof of, Ro. 2.15; to display *a certain bearing towards a person; hence,* to perpetrate openly, 2 Ti. 4.14: *whence*

Ἔνδειξις, εως, ἡ,
a pointing out; *met.* manifestation, public declaration, Ro. 3.25, 26; a token, sign, proof, i.q. ἔνδειγμα, 2 Co. 8.24. Phi. 1.28.

Ἕνδεκα, οἱ, αἱ, τά, (εἷς, ἕν & δέκα)
eleven, Mat. 28.16. Mar. 16.14, et al.: *whence*

Ἑνδέκατος, άτη, ατον,
eleventh, Mat. 20.6, 9. Re. 21.20.

Ἐνδέχεται, *impers.* (ἐνδέχομαι, to admit)
it is possible, Lu. 13.33.

Ἐνδημέω, ῶ, (ἐν & δῆμος)
f. ήσω,
to dwell in *a place,* to be at home, 2 Co. 5.6, 8, 9.

Ἐνδιδύσκα,
a later form, equivalent to ἐνδύω, Lu. 8.27; 16.19; & v.r. Mar. 15.17.

Ἔνδῐκος, ου, ὁ, ἡ, (ἐν & δίκη)
fair, just, Ro. 3.8. He. 2.2.

Ἐνδόμησις, εως, ἡ, (ἐνδομέω)
pr. a thing built in; *in N.T.,* a building, structure, Re. 21.18. L.G.

Ἐνδοξάζω, (ἐν & δοξάζω)
f. άσω,
to invest with glory; *pass.* to be glorified, to be made a subject of glorification, 2 Thes. 1.10, 12. S.

Ἔνδοξος, ου, ὁ, ἡ, (ἐν & δόξα)
honoured, 1 Co. 4.10; notable, memorable, Lu. 13.17; splendid, gorgeous, Lu. 7.25; in unsullied array, Ep. 5.27.

Ἔνδῠμα, ατος, τό, (ἐνδύω)
clothing, a garment, Mat. 6.25, 28; 22.11, 12, et al.; *in particular,* an outer garment, cloak, mantle, Mat. 3.4. L.G.

Ἐνδυναμόω, ῶ, (ἐν & δύναμις)
f. ώσω,
to empower, invigorate, Phi. 4.13. 1 Ti. 1.12. 2 Ti. 4.17; *mid.* to summon up vigour, put forth energy, Ep. 6.10. 2 Ti. 2.1; *pass.* to acquire strength, be invigorated, be strong, Ac. 9.22. Ep. 6.20. He. 11.34. N.T.

Ἐνδύω & ἐνδύνω, (ἐν & δύω)
f. ύσω,
to enter, 2 Ti. 3.6; to put on, clothe, invest, array, Mat. 27.31. Mar. 15.17, 20; *mid.* clothe one's self, be clothed or invested, Mat. 22.11; 27.31, et al.; *trop.* to be invested *with spiritual gifts, graces, or character,* Lu. 24.49. Ro. 13.14, et al. (ὔω, ὔνω, ὔσω): *whence*

Ἔνδῠσις, εως, ἡ,
a putting on, or wearing *of clothes,* 1 Pe. 3.3.

Ἐνέδρα, ας, ἡ, (ἐν & ἕδρα)
pr. a sitting in or on *a spot;* an ambush, ambuscade or lying in wait, Ac. 23.16; 25.3: *whence*

Ἐνεδρεύω,

f. εύσω,
to lie in wait or ambush for, Ac. 23.21; to endeavour to entrap, Lu. 11.54.

Ἔνεδρον, ου, τό,
i.q. ἐνέδρα Ac. 23.16. N.T.

Ἐνειλέω, ῶ (ἐν & εἴλεω)
f. ήσω,
to inwrap, envelope, Mar. 15.46.

Ἔνειμι, (ἐν & εἰμί)
to be in or within; τὰ ἐνόντα, those things which are within, Lu. 11.41.

Ἕνεκα, v. ἕνεκεν, v. εἵνεκεν,
63adv. on account of, for the sake of, by reason of, Mat. 5.10, 11; 10.18, 39, et al.

Ἐνέργεια, ας, ἡ, (ἐνεργής)
energy, efficacy, power, Phi. 3.21. Col. 2.12; active energy, operation, Ep. 4.16. Col. 1.29, et al.

Ἐνεργέω, (fr. same)
f. ήσω, a.1. ἐνήργνσα,
to effect, 1 Co. 12.6, 11. Gal. 3.5. Ep. 1.11, 20. Phi. 2.13; absol. to be active, Mat. 14.2. Mar. 6.14. Ep 2.2; in N.T., to communicate energy and efficiency, Gal. 2.8; pass. to be called into activity, be actively developed, take effect, Ro. 7.5. 2 Co. 1.6, et al.; ἐνεργουμίνη, Ja. 5.16, full of energy, fervent: whence

Ἐνέργημα, ατος, τό,
an effect, thing effected, 1 Co. 12.6; operation, working, 1 Co. 12.10. L.G.

Ἐνεργής, έος, οῦς, ὁ, ἡ, (ἐν & ἔργον)
active, Phile. 6; efficient, energetic, He. 4.12; adapted to accomplish a thing, effectual, 1 Co. 16.9

Ἐνευλογέω, ῶ, (ἐν & εὐλογέω)
f. ήσω,
to bless in respect of, or by means of, Ac. 3.25. Gal. 3.8. S.

Ἐνέχω, (ἐν & ἔχω)
f. ξω, imperf. ἐνεῖχον,
to hold within; to fix upon; in N.T., intrans. (scil. χόλον) to entertain a grudge against, Mar. 6.19; to be exasperated against, Lu. 11.53; pass. to be entangled, held fast in, Gal. 5.1.

Ἐνθάδε, (ἔνθα, here, & δε, an enclitic particle)
adv. pr. hither, to this place, Jno. 4.15, 16, et al.; also, here, in this place, Lu. 24.41, et al.

Ἔνθεν, (ἐν)
adv. hence, from this place, v.r. Lu. 16.26.

Ἐνθῦμέομαι, οῦμαι, (ἐν & θυμός)
f. ήσομαι, a.1. ἐνεθυμήθην,
to ponder in one's mind, think of, meditate on, Mat. 1.20; 9.4 Ac. 10.19: whence

Ἐνθύμησις, εως, ἡ,
the act of thought, cogitation, reflection, Mat. 9.4; 12.25. He. 4.12; the result of thought, invention, device, Ac. 17.29.

Ἔνι, (for ἔνεστι, fr. ἔνειμι)
there is in, there is contained, there exits, Gal. 3.28, ter. Col. 3.11. Ja. 1.17.

Ἐνιαυτός, οῦ, ὁ, (ἔνος)
a year, more particularly as being a cycle of seasons, and in respect of its revolution, Jno. 11.49, 51; 18.13, et al.; in N.T., an era, Lu. 4.19.

Ἐνίστημι, (ἐν & ἵστημι)

f. ἐνστήσω,

to place in or upon; *intrans.* p. ἐνέστηκα, part. ἐνεστηκώς & ἐνεστώς, f. ἐνστήσομαι, to stand close upon; to be at hand, impend, to be present, Ro. 8.38. 2 Thes. 2.2, et al.

Ἐνισχύω, (ἐν & ἰσχύω)

f. ύσω,

to strengthen, impart strength and vigour, Lu. 22.43; *intrans.* to gain, acquire, or recover strength and vigour, be strengthened, Ac. 9.19 (ῦσ).

Ἔννᾰτος, v. ἔνᾰτος, άτη, ον,

ninth, Mat. 20.5. Re. 21.20, et al.: *from*

Ἐννέα, οἱ, αἱ, τά,

nine, Lu. 17.17.

Ἐννενήκοντα, οἱ, αἱ, τά,

ninety.

Ἐννενηκονταεννέα, οἱ, αἱ, τά, (fr. two preced.)

ninety-nine, Mat. 18.12, 13. Lu. 15.4, 7.

Ἐννεός, οῦ, ὁ, & ἐνεός,

stupid; dumb; struck dumb with amazement, bewildered, stupified, Ac. 9.7.

Ἐννεύω, (ἐν & νεύω)

f. εύσω,

to nod at, signify by a nod; to make signs; to intimate by signs, Lu. 1.62.

Ἔννοια, ας, ἡ, (ἐν & νοέω, νοῦς)

notion, idea; thought, purpose, intention, He. 4.12. 1 Pe. 4.1.

Ἔννομος, ου, ὁ, ἡ, (ἐν & νόμος)

within law, lawful, legal, Ac. 19.39; *in N.T.,* subject or under a law, obedient to a law, 1 Co. 9.21.

Ἔννῠχος, ου, ὁ, ἡ, (ἐν & νύξ)

nocturnal; *neut.* ἔννυχον, *as an adv.,* by night, Mar. 1.35.

Ἐνοικέω, ῶ, (ἐν & οἰκέω)

to dwell in, inhabit; *in N.T., met.* to be indwelling *spiritually,* Ro.8.11. Col. 3.16. 2 Ti. 1.14; to be infixed *mentally,* 2 Ti. 1.5; *of the Deity,* to be specially present, 2 Co. 6.16.

Ἑνότης, τητος, ἡ, (εἷς, ἑνός)

oneness, unity, Ep. 4.3, 13.

Ἐνοχλέω, ῶ, (ἐν & ὀχλέω)

f. ήσω,

to trouble, annoy; to be a trouble, He. 12.15.

Ἔνοχος, ου, ὁ, ἡ, (ἐνέχω)

held in or by; subjected to, He. 2.15; obnoxious, liable to, Mat. 5.21, 22; 26.66. Mar. 3.29; 14.64; an offender against, 1 Co. 11.27. Ja. 2.10.

Ἔνταλμα, ατος, τό, (ἐντέλλομαι)

64*equivalent to* ἐντολύ, a precept, commandment, ordinance, Mat. 15.9. Mar. 7.7. Col. 2.22. S.

Ἐνταφιάζω, (ἐντάφιος, θάπτω)

f. άσω,

to prepare *a body* for burial, Mat. 26.12; *absol.* to make the ordinary preprations for burial, Jno. 19.40: (L.G.) *whence*

Ἐνταφιασμός, οῦ, ὁ,

the preparation of a corpse for burial, Mar. 14.8. Jno. 12.7. N.T.

Ἐντέλλομαι,

f. τελοῦμαι, a.1. ἐνετειλάμην, p. ἐντέταλμαι,

to enjoin, charge, command, Mat. 4.6; 15.4; 17.9, et al.; to direct, Mat. 19.7. Mar. 10.3.

Ἐντεῦθεν,
    adv. hence, from this place, Mat. 17.20. Lu. 4.9, et al.; ἐντεῦθεω καὶ ἐντεῦθεν, hence and hence, on each side, Re. 22.2; hence from this cause, Ja. 4.1.

Ἔντευξις, εως, ἡ, (ἐντυγχάνω)
    pr. a meeting with; *hence,* converse, address; prayer, supplication, intercession, 1 Ti. 2.1; 4.5.

Ἔντῑμος, ου, ὁ, ἡ, (ἐν & τιμή)
    honoured, estimable, dear, Lu. 7.2; 14.8. Phi. 2.29; highly valued, precious, costly, 1 Pe. 2.4, 6.

Ἐντολή, ῆς, ἡ, (ἐντέλλομαι)
    an injunction; a precept, commandment, Mat. 5.19; 15.3, 6; instruction in one's duties, 1 Ti. 6.14. 2 Pe. 2.21; a command, direction, Jno. 10.18. Ac. 17.15; an edict, Jno. 11.57; a direction, Mar. 10.5; a commission, instructions committed to any one to be proclaimed, a charge, Jno. 12.49, 50, et al.

Ἐντόπιος, ου, ὁ, ἡ, (ἐν & τόπος)
    i.q. ἔντοπος, in or of a place; an inhabitant, citizen, Ac. 21.12.

Ἐντός, (ἐν)
    adv. inside, within, Lu. 17.21; τὸ ἐντός, the interior, inside, Mat. 23.26.

Ἐντρέπω, (ἐν & τρέπω)
    f. ψω,
    pr. to turn one back upon himself; *hence,* to put to shame, make ashamed; *mid.* ἐντρέπομαι, f. ἐντραπήσομαι, a.2. ἐνετραπόμην, to revere, revenence, regard, Mat. 21.37. Mar. 12.6, et al.; *absol.* to feel shame, be put to shame, 2 Thes. 3.14. Tit. 2.8.

Ἐντρέφω, (ἐν & τρέφω)
    f. ἐνθρέψω,
    to nourish in, bring up or educate in; *pass.* to be imbued, 1 Ti. 4.6.

Ἔντρομος, ου, ὁ, ἡ, (ἐν & τρόμος)
    trembling, terrifed, Ac. 7.32; 16.29. He. 12.21. L.G.

Ἐντροπή, ῆς, ἡ, (ἐντρέπω)
    reverence; *in N.T.,* shame, 1 Co. 6.5; 15.34.

Ἐντρυφάω, ῶ, (ἐν & τρυφάω)
    f. ήσω,
    to live luxuriously, riot, revel, 2 Pe. 2.13.

Ἐντυγχάνω, (ἐν & συγγάνω)
    f. τεύξομαι, a.2. ἐνετύχον,
    to fall in with, meet; to have converse with, address; to address or apply to *any one,* Ac. 25.24; ὑμέρ τινος, to intercede for any one, plead the cause of, Ro. 8.27, 34. He. 7.25; κατά τινος, to address a representative or suit against any one, to accuse, complain of, Ro. 11.2.

Ἐντυλίσσω, (ἐν & τυλίσσω)
    f. ξω, p. pass. ἐντετύλιγμαι,
    to wrap up in, inwrap, envelope, Mat. 27.59. Lu. 23.53; to wrap up, roll or fold together, Jno. 20.7.

Ἐντυπόω, ῶ, (ἐν & τυπόω, fr. τύπος, an impress)
    f. ώσω,
    to impress a figure, instamp, engrave, 2 Co. 3.7.

Ἐνυβρίζω, (ἐν & ὕβρις)
    f. ίσω,

to insult, outrage, contemn, He. 10.29.

Ἐνυπνιάζω,

    f. άσω, & ἐνυπνιάζομαι, f. ἐνυπνιασθήσομαι,

    to dream; *in N.T.,* to receive some supernatural impression or information in a dream, Ac. 2.17; to cherish vain opinions, Jude 8: *from*

Ἐνύπνιον, ου, τό, (pr. neut. of ἐνύπνιος, presented during sleep, fr. ἐν & ὕπνος)

    a dream; *in N.T.,* a supernatural suggestion or impression receive during sleep, a vision, Ac. 2.17.

Ἐνώπιον, (pr. neut. of ἐνώπιος, in sight or front)

    adv. before, in the presence of, Lu. 5.25; 8.47; in front of, Re. 4.5, 6; immediately preceding *as a forerunner,* Lu. 1.17. Re. 16.19; *fr. the Heb.* in the presence of, *metaphysically, i.e. in the sphere of sensation or thought,* Lu. 12.9; 15.10. Ac. 10.31; in the eyes of, in the judgment of, Lu. 16.15; 24.11. Ac. 4.19, et al. L.G.

Ἐνωτίζομαιν, (ἐν & οὖς)

    f. ίσομαι, a.1. ἐνωτισάμην,

    to give ear, listen, hearken to, Ac. 2.14. L.G.

Ἐξ,

    see ἐκ.

Ἔξ, οἱ, αἱ, τά,

    65six, Mat. 17.1. Mar. 9.2, et al.

Ἐξαγγέλλω, (ἐξ & ἀγγέλλω)

    f. γελῶ

    to tell forth, divulge, publish; to declare abroad, celebrate, 1 Pe. 2.9.

Ἐξαγοράζω, (ἐξ & ἀγοράζω)

    f. άσω,

    to buy out *of the hands of a person;* to redeem, set free, Gal. 3.13; *mid.* to redeem, buy off, to secure for one's self or one's own use; to rescue from loss or misapplication, Ep. 5.16. Col. 4.5. L.G.

Ἐξάγω, (ἐξ & ἄγω)

    f. ξω, a.2. ἐξήγαγον,

    to bring or lead forth, conduct out of, Mar. 8.23; 15.20. Lu. 24.50, et al.

Ἐξαιρέω, ῶ, (ἐξ & αἱρέω)

    f. ήσω, a.2. ἐξεῖλον,

    to take out of; to pluck out, tear out, Mat. 5.29; 18.9; *mid.* to take out of, select, choose, Ac. 26.17; to rescue, deliver, Ac. 7.10, 34; 12.11; 23.27. Gal. 1.4.

Ἐξαίρω, (ἐξ & αἴρω)

    f. αρῶ,

    pr. to lift up out of; *in N.T.,* to remove, eject, 1 Co. 5.2, 13.

Ἐξαιτέω, ῶ, (ἐξ & αἰτέω)

    f. ήσω,

    to ask for from; to demand; *mid.* to demand for one's self, Lu. 22.31; *also,* to obtain by asking.

Ἐξαίφνης, (ἐξ & αἴφνης)

    suddenly, unexpectedly, Mar. 13.36, et al.

Ἐξακολουθέω, ῶ, (ἐξ & ἀκολουθέω)

    f. ήσω,

    to follow out; to imitate, 2 Pe. 2.2, 15; to observe as a guide, 2 Pe. 1.16. L.G.

Ἐξακόσιοι, αι, α, (ἐξ & ἑκατόν)

    six hundred, Re. 13.18; 14.20.

Ἐξαλείφω, (ἐξ & ἀλείφω)

f. ψω,

pr. to anoint or smear over; to wipe off or away, Re. 7.17; 21.4; to blot out, obliterate, expunge, Col. 2.14. Re. 3.5; *met.* to wipe out *guilt,* Ac. 3.19.

Ἐξάλλομαι, (ἐξ & ἅλλομαι)

f. αλοῦμαι,

to leap or spring up or forth, Ac. 3.8.

Ἐξανάστᾰσις, εως, ἡ, (ἐξ & ἀνάστασις)

a raising up; a dislodgment; a rising up; a resurrection from *the dead,* Phi. 3.11.

Ἐξανατέλλω, (ἐξ & ἀνατέλλω)

f. τελῶ,

to raise up, make to spring up; *intrans.* to rise up, sprout, spring up or forth, Mat. 13.5. Mar. 4.5.

Ἐξανίστημι, (ἐξ & ἀνίστημι)

f. ἐξαναστήσω,

to cause to rise up, raise up; *fr. the Heb.* to cause to exist, Mar. 12.19. Lu. 20.28; *intrans.* a.2. ἀνέστην, to rise up from, stand forth, Ac. 15.5.

Ἐξαπατάω, ῶ, (ἐξ & ἀπατάω)

f. ήσω,

pr. to deceive thoroughly; to deceive, delude, beguile, Ro. 7.11; 16.18. 1 Co. 3.18, et al.

Ἐξάπῐνα

adv., a later form for ἐξαπίνης, suddenly, immediately, unexpectedly, Mar. 9.8.

Ἐξαπορέω, ῶ, & ἐξαπορέομαι, οῦμαι, (ἐξ & ἀπορέω)

f. ήσομαι,

to be in the utmost perplexity or despair, 2 Co. 1.8; 4.8. L.G.

Ἐξαποστέλλω, (ἐξ & ἀποστέλλω)

f. στελῶ,

to send out or forth; to send away, dismiss, Lu. 1.53, et al.; to dispatch *on a service or agency,* Ac. 7.12, et al.; to send forth *as a pervading influence,* Gal. 4.6.

Ἐξαρτίζω, (ἐξ & ἄρτιος)

f. ίσω, p. pass. ἐξήρτισμαι,

to equip or furnish completely, 2 Ti. 3.17; to complete *time,* Ac. 21.5. L.G.

Ἐξαστράπτω, (ἐξ & ἀστράπτω)

f. ψω,

pr. to flash forth; *hence,* to glisten, Lu. 9.29.

Ἐξαυτῆς, (ἐξ & αὐτῆς, sc. τῆς ὥρας)

adv. lit. at the very time; presently, instantly, immediately, Mar. 6.25. Ac. 10.33; 11.11, et al.

Ἐξεγείρω, (ἐξ & ἐγείρω)

f. γερῶ,

to excite, arouse *from sleep;* to raise up *from the dead,* 1 Co. 6.14; to raise up into existence, *or,* into a certain condition, Ro. 9.17.

Ἔξειμι, (ἐξ & εἶμι)

imperf. ἐξῇειν, inf. ἐξιέναι, part. ἐξιών,

to go out or forth, Ac. 13.42; to depart, Ac. 17.15; 20.7; ἐπὶ τὴν γῆν, to get to land, *from the water,* Ac. 27.43.

Ἐξελέγχω, (ἐξ & ἐλέγχω)

f. ξω,

to search thoroughly, to test; to convict; *by impl.* to punish, Jude 15.

Ἐξέλκω, (ἐξ & ἕλκω)

f. ξω,

to draw or drag out; *met.* to withdraw, allure, hurry away, Ja. 1.14.

Ἐξέραμα, ατος, τό, (ἐξεράω, to vomit)

vomit, 2 Pe. 2.22. L.G.

Ἐξερευνάω, ῶ, (ἐξ & ἐρευνάω)

f. ήσω,

to search out, to examine closely, 1 Pe. 1.10.

Ἐξέρχομαι, (ἐξ & ἔρχομαι)

66f. ἐξελεύσομαι, a.2. ἐξῆλθον, p. ἐξελήλυθα,

to go or come out of; to come out, Mat. 5.26; 8.34, et al.; to proceed, emanate, take rise from, Mat. 2.6; 15.18. 1 Co. 14.36, et al.; to come abroad, 1 Jno. 4.1, et al.; to go forth, go away, depart, Mat. 9.31. Lu. 5.8, et al.; to escape, Jno. 10.39; to pass away, come to an end, Ac. 16.19.

Ἔξεστι

impers., part. ἐξόν, it is possible; it is permitted, it is lawful, Mat. 12.2, 4, et al.

Ἐξετάζω, (ἐξ & ἐτάζω, to inquire, examine)

f. άσω,

to search out; to inquire by interrogation, examine strictly, Mat. 2.8; 10.11; to interrogate, Jno. 21.12.

Ἐξηγέομαι, οῦμαι, (ἐξ & ἡγέομαι)

f. ήσομαι,

to be a leader; to detail, to set forth in language; to tell, narrate, recount, Lu. 24.35. Ac. 10.8, et al.; to make known, reveal, Jno. 1.18.

Ἐξήκοντα, οἱ, αἱ, τά, (ἓξ)

sixty, Mat. 13.8, 23, et al.

Ἑξῆς,

adv. successively, in order; *in N.T., with the art.,* ὁ, ἡ, τό ἑξῆς, next, Lu. 7.11; 9.37, et al.

Ἐξηχέω, ῶ, (ἐξ & ἠχέω)

f. ήσω, p. pass. ἐξήχημαι,

to make to sound forth or abroad; *pass.* to sound forth, be promulgated, 1 Thes. 1.8. L.G.

Ἕξις, εως, ἡ, (ἔχω)

a condition of body or mind, *strictly, as resulting from practice;* habitude, He. 5.14.

Ἐξίστημι, & ἐξιστάω, ῶ, (ἐξ & ἵστημι)

f. ἐκστήσω, a.1. ἐξέστησα, later p. ἐξέστακα,

trans. pr. to put out of its place; to astonish, amaze, Lu. 24.22. Ac. 8.9, 11; *intrans.* a.2. ἐξέστην, & mid. ἐξίσταμαι, to be astonished, Mat. 12.22, et al.; to be beside one's self, Mar. 3.21. 2 Co. 5.13.

Ἐξισχύω, (ἐξ & ἰσχύω)

f. ύσω,

to be fully able, Ep. 3.18. L.G.

Ἔξοδος, ου, ἡ, (ἐξ & ὁδός)

a way out, a going out; a going out, departure, He. 11.22; *met.* a departure from life, decease, death, Lu. 9.31. 2 Pe. 1.15.

Ἐξολοθρεύω, (ἐξ & ὀλοθρεύω)

f. εύσω,

to destroy utterly, exterminate, Ac. 3.23. L.G.

Ἐξομολογέω, ῶ, (ἐξ & ὁμολογέω)

f. ησω

to agree, bind one's self, promise, Lu. 22.6; *mid.* to confess, Mat. 3.6; to profess openly, Phi. 2.11. Re. 3.5; to make open avowal *of benefits;* to praise, celebrate, Mat. 11.25. Lu. 10.21, et al. L.G.

Ἐξόν,

    see Ἔξεστι.

Ἐξορκίζω, (ἐξ & ὁρκίζω)

    f. ίσω,

    to put an oath *to a person,* to adjure, Mat. 26.63: *whence*

Ἐξορκιστής, οῦ, ὁ,

    pr. one who puts an oath; *in N.T.,* an exorcist, one who by various kinds of incantations, &c. pretended to expel demons, Ac. 19.13.

Ἐξορύσσω, (ἐξ & ὀρύσσω)

    f. ξω,

    to dig out or through, force up, Mar. 2.4; to pluck out *the eyes,* Gal. 4.15.

Ἐξουδενόω,

    Mar. 9.12, *equivalent to*

Ἐξουθενέω, ῶ, (ἐξ & οὐθέν, *a later form of* οὐδέν)

    f. ήσω,

    to make light of, set at nought, despise, contemn, treat with contempt and scorn, Lu. 18.9, et al.; to neglect, disregard, 1 Thes. 5.20; ἐξουθενημένος, abject, contemptible, 2 Co. 10.10; *by impl.* to reject with contempt, Ac. 4.11. S.

Ἐξουσία, ας, ἡ (ἔξεστι)

    power, ability, faculty, Mat. 9.8; 10.1, et al.; efficiency, energy, Lu. 4.32, et al.; liberty, license, Jno. 10.18. Ac. 5.4; authority, rule, dominion, jurisdiction, Mat. 8.9; 28.18; *meton. pl.* authorities, potentates, powers, Lu. 12.11. 1 Co. 15.24. Ep. 1.21; right, authority, full power, Mat. 9.6; 21.23; privilege, prerogative, Jno. 1.12; *perhaps,* a veil, 1 Co. 11.10: *whence*

Ἐξουσιάζω,

    f. άσω,

    to have or exercise power or authority over *any one,* Lu. 22.25; to possess independent control over, 1 Co. 7.4, bis; *pass.* to be subject to, under the power or influence of, 1 Co. 6.12. L.G.

Ἐξοχή, ῆς, ἡ, (ἐξέχω, to be prominent)

    pr. prominency, any thing prominent; *in N.T.,* eminence, distinction, Ac. 25.23.

Ἐξυπνίζω,

    f. ίσω,

    to awake, arouse *from sleep,* Jno. 11.11: (L.G.) *from*

Ἔξυπνος, ου, ὁ, ἡ, (ἐξ & ὕπνος)

    awake, aroused *from sleep,* Ac. 16.27. L.G.

Ἔξω, (ἐξ)

    adv. without, 67out of doors, Mat. 12.46, 47; ὁ, ἡ, τὸ ἔξω, outer, external, foreign, Ac. 26.11. 2 Co. 4.16; *met.* not belonging to one's community, Mar. 4.11. 1 Co. 5.12, 13; out, away, *from a place or person,* Mat. 5.13; 13.48; *as a prep.* out of, Mar. 5.10 : *whence*

Ἔξωθεν,

    adv. outwardly, externally, Mat. 23.27, 28. Mar. 7.15; ὁ, ἡ, τὸ ἔξωθεν, outer, external, Mat. 23.25. Lu 11.39; τὸ ἔξωθεν, the exterior, Lu. 11.40; οἱ ἔξωθεν, those who do not belong to the Christian community, 1 Ti. 3.7, et al.

Ἐξωθέω, ῶ, (ἐξ & ὠθέω)

    f. ήσω, & ώσω, a.1. ἐξέωσα, in N.T. ἔξωσα,

to expel, drive out, Ac. 7.45; to propel, urge forward, Ac. 27.39.

Ἐξώτερος, α, ον, (comp. of ἔξω)
    outer, exterior, external, Mat. 8.12; 22.13; 25.30. S.

Ἔοικα
    p., with pr. sig., from absol. εἴκω, to be like, Ja. 1.6, 23.

Ἑορτάζω,
    f. άσω,
    to keep a feast, celebrate a festival, 1 Co. 5.8: *from*

Ἑορτή, ῆς, ἡ
    a solemn feast, public festival, Lu. 2.41; 22.1. Jno. 13.1; *spc. used of* the passover,
    Mat. 26.5; 27.15, et al.

Ἐπαγγελία, ας, ἡ,
    annunciation, 2 Ti. 1.1; a promise, act of promising, Ac. 13.23, 32; 23.21; *meton.* the
    thing promised, promised favour and blessing, Lu. 24.49. Ac. 1.4, et al.: *from*

Ἐπαγγέλλω, (ἐπί & ἀγγέλλω)
    f. ελῶ,
    to declare, announce; *mid.* to promise, undertake, Mar. 14.11. Ro. 4.21, et al.; to
    profess, 1 Ti. 2.10: *whence*

Ἐπάγγελμα, ατος, τό,
    a promise, 2 Pe. 3.13; *meton.* promised favour or blessing, 2 Pe. 1.4.

Ἐπάγω, (ἐπί & ἄγω)
    f. άξω, a.2. ἐπήγαγον
    to bring upon, cause to come upon, 2 Pe. 2.1, 5; *met.* to cause to be imputed or
    attributed to, to bring *guilt* upon, Ac. 5.28.

Ἐπαγωνίζομαι, (ἐπί & ἀγωνίζομαι)
    f. ίσομαι,
    to contend strenuously in defence of, Jude 3. L.G.

Ἐπαθροίζω, (ἐπί & ἀθροίζω, to gather together)
    f. οίσω,
    to collect close upon, or beside; *mid.* to crowd upon, Lu. 11.29.

Ἐπαινέω, ῶ, (ἐπί & αἰνέω)
    f. έσω & έσομαι, a.1. ἐπήνεσα,
    to praise, commend, applaud, Lu. 16.8. Ro. 15.11. 1 Co. 11.2, 17, 22, bis.

Ἔπαινος, ου, ὁ, (ἐπί & αἶνος)
    praise, applause, honour paid, Ro. 2.29. 2 Co. 8.18, et al.; *meton.* ground or reason of
    praise or commendation, Phi. 4.8; *by impl.* favourable regard, reward, Ro. 13.3. 1 Pe.
    2.14. 1 Co. 4.5.

Ἐπαίρω,
    f. αρῶ, a.1. ἐπῆρα, a.1. pass. ἐπήρθην,
    to lift up, raise, elevate; to hoist, Ac. 27.40; τὴν φωνήν, to lift up the voice, to speak in
    a loud voice, Lu 11.27; τὰς χεῖρας, to lift up the hands *in prayer,* Lu. 24.50. 1 Ti. 2.8;
    τοὺς ὀφθαλμούς, to lift up the eyes, to look, Mat. 17.8; τὴν κεφαλήν, to lift up the
    head, to be encouraged, animated, Lu. 21.28; τὴν πτέρναν, to lift up the heel, to
    attack, assault; *or,* to seek one's overthrow or destruction, Jno. 13.18; *pass.* to be
    borne upwards, Ac. 1.9; *met. mid.* to exalt one's self, assume consequence, be elated,
    2 Co. 10.5, et al.

Ἐπαισχύνομαι, (ἐπί & αἰσχύνομαι)
    a.1. ἐπῃσχύνθην, f. ἐπαισχυνθήσομαι,
    to be ashamed of, Mat. 8.38. Lu. 9.26, et al.

Ἐπαιτέω, ῶ, (ἐπί & αἰτέω)

f. ἥσω,
to prefer a suit or request in respect of certain circumstances; to ask alms, beg, Lu. 16.3.

Ἐπακολουθέω, ῶ, (ἐπί & ἀκολουθέω)
f. ἥσω,
to follow upon; to accompany, be attendant, Mar. 16.20; to appear in the sequel, 1 Ti. 5.24; *met.* to follow *one's steps,* to imitate, 1 Pe. 2.21; to follow *a work,* pursue, prosecute, be studious of, devoted to, 1 Ti. 5.10.

Ἐπακούω, (ἐπί & ἀκούω)
f. ούσομαι,
to listen or hearken to; to hear with favour, 2 Co. 6.2.

Ἐπακροάομαι, ῶμαι, (ἐπί & ἀκροάομαι, to hear)
to hear, hearken, listen to, Ac. 16.25.

Ἐπάν, (ἐπεί & ἄν)
conj. whenever, as soon as, Mat. 2.8. Lu. 11.22, 34.

Ἐπάναγκες, (ἐπί & ἀνάγκη)
adv. of necessity, necessarily; τὰ ἐπαναγκες, necessary things, Ac. 15.28.

Ἐπανάγω, (ἐπί & ἀνάγω)
f. ξω, a.2. ἐπανήγαγον,
68to bring up or back; *intrans.* to return, Mat. 21.18; *a nautical term,* to put off from shore, Lu. 5.3, 4.

Ἐπαναμιμνήσκω, (ἐπί & ἀναμιμνήσκω)
f. ἐπαναμνήσω,
to remind, put in remembrance, Ro. 15.15.

Ἐπαναπαύω, (ἐπί & ἀναπαύω)
f. αύσω,
pr. to make to rest upon; *mid.* to rest upon; to abide with, Lu. 10.6; to rely on, confide in, abide by confidingly, Ro. 2.17. L.G.

Ἐπανέρχομαι, (ἐπί & ἀνέρχομαι)
a.2. ἐπανῆλθον,
to come back, return, Lu. 10.35; 19.15.

Ἐπανίστημι, (ἐπί & ἀνίστημι)
to raise up against; *mid.* to rise up against, Mat. 10.21. Mar. 13.12.

Ἐπανόρθωσις, εως, ἡ, (ἐπανορθόω, to set upright again; to set to rights; ἐπί & ἀνορθόω)
correction, reformation, 2 Ti. 3.16.

Ἐπάνω, (ἐπί & ἄνω)
adv. above, over, upon, *of place,* Mat. 2.9; 5.14; over, *of authority,* Lu. 19.17, 19; above, more than, Mar. 14.5, et al. (ἄ)

Ἐπαρκέω, ῶ,(ἐπί & ἀρκέω)
f. έσω,
pr. to ward off; to assist, relieve, succour, 1 Ti. 5.10, 16, bis.

Ἐπαρχία, ας, ἡ, (ἔπαρχος, a prefect, &c.)
a prefecture, province, Ac. 23.34; 25.1. L.G.

Ἔπαυλις, εως, ἡ, (ἐπί & αὐλίζομαι)
pr. a place to pass the night in; a cottage; *in N.T.,* a dwelling, habitation, Ac. 1.20.

Ἐπαύριον, (ἐπί & αὔριον)
tomorrow; ἡ ἐπαύριον, *sc.* ἡμέρα, the next or following day, Mat. 27.62. Mar. 11.12, et al.

Ἐπαυτοφώρῳ, (ἐπί & αὐτόφωρος, fr. αὐτός & φώρ, a thief)
adv. pr. in the very theft; *in N.T.,* in the very act, Jno. 8.4.

Ἐπαφρίζω, (ἐπί & ἀφρίζω)
    f. ίσω,
    to foam out; to pour out like foam, vomit forth, Jude 13.

Ἐπεγείρω, (ἐπί & ἐγείρω)
    f. γερῶ,
    to raise or stir up against, excite or instigate against, Ac. 13.50; 14.2.

Ἐπεί,
    conj. when, after, as soon as, Lu. 7.1; since, because, in as much as, Mat. 18.32; 27.6;
    for, for then, for else, since in that case, Ro. 3.6; 11.6, et al.

Ἐπειδή, (ἐπεί & δή)
    conj. since, because, in as much as, Mat. 21.46. Lu. 11.6. Ac. 13.46, et al.

Ἐπειδήπερ, (ἐπειδή & περ)
    conj. since now, since indeed, considering that, Lu. 1.1.

Ἐπεῖδον,
    a.2. of ἐφοράω, imperat. ἔπιδε,
    to look upon, regard; *in N.T.,* to view with favour, Lu. 1.25. Ac. 4.29.

Ἔπειμι, (ἐπί & εἶμι)
    part. ἐπιών,
    to come upon; to come after; to succeed immediately, Ac. 7.26; 16.11; 20.15; 21.18;
    23.11.

Ἐπείπερ, (ἐπεί & περ)
    conj. since indeed, seeing that, Ro. 3.30.

Ἐπεισαγωγή, ῆς, ἡ, (ἐπί & εἰσάγω)
    a superinduction, a further introduction, *whether by way of addition or substitution,*
    He. 7.19.

Ἔπειτα, (ἐπί & εἶτα)
    adv. thereupon, then, after that, in the next place, afterwards, Mar. 7.5. Lu. 16.7, et al.

Ἐπέκεινα, (i.e. ἐπ᾽ ἐκεῖνα)
    adv. on yonder side, beyond, Ac. 7.43.

Ἐπεκτείνω, (ἐπί & ἐκτείνω)
    f. ενῶ,
    pr. to stretch out further; *in N.T., mid.* to reach out towards, strain for, Phi. 3.14.

Ἐπενδύτης, ου, ὁ,
    the outer or upper tunic, *worn between the inner tunic and the external garments,* Jno.
    21.7: (ῠ) *from*

Ἐπενδύω, (ἐπί & ἐνδύω)
    f. ύσω,
    to put on over or in addition to; *mid.* to put on oneself in addition; to be further
    invested, 2 Co. 5.2, 4.

Ἐπέρχομαι, (ἐπί & ἔρχομαι)
    f. ελεύσομαι, a.2. ἐπῆλθον,
    to come to, Ac. 14.19; to come upon, Lu. 1.35; 21.26. Ac. 1.8. Ja. 5.1; to come upon
    unexpectedly, overtake, Lu. 21.35; to be coming on, to succeed, Ep. 2.7; to occur,
    happen to, Ac. 8.24; 13.40; to come against, attach, Lu. 11.22.

Ἐπερωτάω, ῶ, (ἐπί & ἐρωτάω)
    f. ήσω,
    to interrogate, question, ask, Mat. 12.10; 17.10, et al.; *in N.T.,* to request, require, Mat.
    16.1; *fr. the Heb.* ἐπερ. τὸν Θεόν, to seek after, 69desire an acquaintance with God,
    Ro. 10.20: *whence*

Ἐπερώτημα, ατος, τό,

pr. an interrogation, question; *in N.T.,* profession, pledge, 1 Pe. 3.21.

Ἐπέχω, (ἐπὶ & ἔχω)
 f. ἐφέξω, imperf. ἐπεῖχον, a.2. ἐπέσχον,
 trans. to hold out, present, exhibit, display, Phi. 2.16; *intrans.* to observe, take heed to, attend to, Lu. 14.7. Ac. 3.5. 1 Ti. 4.16; to stay, delay, Ac. 19.22.

Ἐπηρεάζω,
 f. άσω,
 to harass, insult, Mat. 5.44. Lu. 6.28; to traduce, calumniate, 1 Pe. 3.16.

Ἐπί,
 prep., with the gen. upon, on, Mat. 4.6; 9.2; 27.19, et al.; in, *of locality,* Mar. 8.4, et al.; near upon, by, at, Mat. 21.19. Jno. 21.1, et al.; upon, over, *of authority,* Mat. 2.22. Ac. 8.27, et al.; in the presence of, *especially in a judicial sense,* 2 Co. 7.14. Ac. 25.9, et al.; in the case of, in respect of, Jno. 6.2. Gal. 3.16; in the time of, at the time of, Ac. 11.28. Ro.1.10, et al.; ἐπ᾽ ἀληθείας, really, bona fide, Mar. 12.32, et al.; *with the dat.* upon, on Mat. 14.8. Mar. 2.21. Lu. 12.44, et al.; close upon, by, Mat. 24.33. Jno. 4.6, et al.; in the neighbourhood or society of, Ac. 28.14; over, *of authority,* Mat. 24.47, et al.; to, *of addition,* besides, Mat. 25.20. Ep. 6.16. Col. 3.14, et al.; immediately upon, Jno. 4.27; upon, *of the object of an act,* towards, to, Mar. 5.33. Lu. 18.7. Ac. 5.35, et al.; against, *of hostile posture or disposition,* Lu. 12.52, et al.; in dependance upon, Mat. 4.4. Lu. 5.5. Ac. 14.3, et al.; upon the ground of, Mat. 19.9. Lu. 1.59. Phi. 1.3. He. 7.11; 8.6; 9.17, et al.; with a view to, Gal. 5.13. 1 Thes. 4.7, et al.;
 with the accu., upon, *with the idea of previous or present motion,* Mat. 4.5; 14.19, 26, et al.; towards, *of place,* to Mat. 3.13; 22.34, et al.; towards, *of the object of an action,* Lu. 6.35; 9.38, et al.; against, *of hostile movement,* Mat. 10.21, et al.; over, *of authority,* Lu. 1.33, et al.; to the extent of, *both of place and time,* Re. 21.16. Ro. 7.1, et al.; near, by, Mat. 9.9, et al.; about, at, *of time,* Ac. 3.1, et al.; in order to, with a view to, for the purpose of, Mat. 3.7. Lu. 7.44, et al.

Ἐπιβαίνω, (ἐπί & βαίνω)
 f. βήσομαι, p. βίβηκα, a.2. ἐπέβην,
 pr. to step upon; to mount, Mat. 21.5; to go on board, Ac. 21.6; Ac. 21.2; 27.2; to enter, Ac. 20.18; to enter upon, Ac. 25.1.

Ἐπιβάλλω, (ἐπί & βάλλω)
 f. βαλῶ, a.2. ἐπέβαλον
 to cast or throw upon, Mar. 11.7. 1 Co. 7.35; to lay on, apply to, Lu. 9.62; to put on, sew on, Mat. 9.16. Lu. 5.36; τὰς χεῖρας, to lay hands on, offer violence to, sieze, Mat. 26.50, et al. *also,* to lay hand to, undertake, commence, Ac. 12.1; *intrans.* to rush, dash, beat into, Mar. 4.37; to ponder, reflect on, Mar. 14.72; to fall to one's share, pertain to, Lu. 15.12.

Ἐπιβᾰρέω, ῶ, (ἐπί & βαρέω)
 f. ήσω,
 to burden; *met.* to be burdensome, chargeable to, 1 Thes. 2.9. 2 Thes. 3.8; to bear hard upon, overcharge, over-censure, 2 Co. 2.5. L.G.

Ἐπιβιβάζω, (ἐπί & βιβάζω)
 f. άσω,
 to cause to ascend or mount, to set upon, Lu. 10.34; 19.35. Ac. 23.24.

Ἐπιβλέπω, (ἐπί & βλέπω)
 f. ψω,
 to look upon; to regard with partiality, Ja. 2.3; to regard with kindness and favour, compassionate, Lu. 1.48; 9.38.

Ἐπίβλημα, ατος, τό, (ἐπιβάλλω)
that which is put over or upon; *in N.T.,* a patch, Mat. 9.16. Mar. 2.21. Lu. 5.36, bis. L.G.

Ἐπιβοάω, ῶ, (ἐπί & βοάω)
f. ήσω,
to cry out to or against; to vociferate, Ac. 25.24.

Ἐπιβουλή, ῆς, ἡ, (ἐπί & βουλή)
a purpose or design against any one; conspiracy, plot, Ac. 9.24; 20.3, 19, 23.30.

Ἐπιγαμβρεύω, (ἐπί & γαμβρεύω, to marry)
f. εύσω,
to marry *a wife* by the law of affinity, Mat. 22.24. S.

Ἐπίγειος, είου, ὁ, ἡ, τόν, -ον, (ἐπί & γῆ)
pr. on the earth, Phi. 2.10; earthly, terrestial, Jno. 3.12. 1 Co. 15.40. 2 Co. 5.1. Phi. 3.19; earthly, low, grovelling, Ja. 3.15.

Ἐπιγίνομαι, (ἐπί & γίνομαι)
to come on, spring up, *as the wind,* Ac. 28.13.

Ἐπιγῑνώσκω, (ἐπί & γινώσκω)
f. γνώσομαι, a.1. pass. ἐπεγνώσθην,
pr. to make *a thing* a subject of observation; *hence,* to arrive at knowledge 70from preliminaries; to attain to a knowledge of, Mat. 11.27, et al; to ascertain, Lu. 7.37; 23.7, et al.; to perceive, Mar. 2.8; 5.30, et al.; to discern, detect, Mat. 7.16, 20, et al.; to recognise, Mar. 6.33. Lu. 24.16, 31. Ac. 3.10, et al.; to acknowledge, admit, 1 Co. 14.37. 1 Ti. 4.3, et al.; *pass.* to have one's character discerned and acknowledged, 2 Co. 6.9; *fr. the Heb.* to regard with favour and kindness, 1 Co. 16.18: *whence*

Ἐπίγνωσις, εως, ἡ,
the coming at the knowledge *of a thing,* ascertainment, Ro. 3.20; a distinct perception or impression, acknowledgment, Col. 2.2, et al.

Ἐπιγρᾰφή, ῆς, ἡ
an inscription; a legend *of a coin,* Mat. 22.20. Mar. 12.16. Lu. 20.24; a label *of a criminal's name and offence,* Mar. 15.26. Lu. 23.38: *from*

Ἐπιγράφω, (ἐπί & γράφω)
f. ψω,
to imprint a mark on; to inscribe, engrave, write on, Mar. 15.26. Ac. 17.23. Re. 21.12; *met.* to imprint, impress deeply upon, He. 8.10; 10.16. (ᾰ).

Ἐπιδείκνῡμι, v. νύω, & mid. ἐπιδείκνῡμαι, (ἐπί & δείκνυμι)
f. δείξω,
to exhibit, Mat. 16.1. Ac. 9.39; to show, Mat. 22.19. Lu. 17.14; 20.24; 24.40; to point out, Mat. 24.1; to demonstrate, prove, Ac. 18.28. He. 6.17.

Ἐπιδέχομαι, (ἐπί & δέχομαι)
f. δέξομαι,
to admit; to receive kindly, welcome, entertain, 3 Jno. 10; *met.* to admit, approve, assent to, 3 Jn. 9.

Ἐπιδημέω, ῶ, (ἐπί & δῆμος)
f. ήσω,
to dwell among a people; to be at home among one's own people; *and, in N.T.,* to sojourn as a stranger among another people, Ac. 2.10; 17.21.

Ἐπιδιατάσσομαι, (ἐπί & διατάσσω)
f. ξομαι,
to enjoin *any time* additional, superadd an injunction &c. Gal. 3.15. N.T.

Ἐπιδίδωμι, (ἐπί & δίδωμι)

f. δώσω,
to give in addition; *also,* to give to, deliver to, give into one's hands, Mat. 7.9, 10. Lu. 4.17; 24.30, 42, et al.; *intrans., probably a nautical term,* to commit a ship to the wind, let her drive, Ac. 27.15.

Ἐπιδιορθόω, ῶ, (ἐπί & διορθόω)
f. ώσω,
to set further to rights, to carry on an amendment, Tit. 1.5.

Ἐπιδύω, (ἐπί & δύω)
f. δύσω,
of the sun, to set upon, to set during, Ep. 4.26.

Ἐπιείκεια, ας, ἡ,
reasonableness, equity; *in N.T.,* gentleness, mildness, 2 Co. 10.1; lenity, clemency, Ac. 24.4: *from*

Ἐπιεικής, έος, οῦς, ὁ, ἡ, (ἐπί & εἰκός)
pr. suitable; fair, reasonable; gentle, mild, patient, 1 Ti. 3.3. Tit. 3.2. Ja. 3.17. 1 Pe. 2.18; τὸ ἐπιεικές, mildness, gentleness, probity, Phi. 4.5.

Ἐπιζητέω, ῶ, (ἐπὶ & ζητέω)
f. ήσω,
to seek for, make search for, Ac. 12.19; to require, demand, Mat. 12.39; 16.4. Ac. 19.39; to desire, endeavour to obtain, Ro. 11.7. He. 11.14, et al.; to seek with care and anxiety, Mat. 6.32.

Ἐπιθανάτιος, ου, ὁ, ἡ, (ἐπί & θάνατος)
condemned to death, under sentence of death, 1 Co. 4.9. L.G.

Ἐπιθεσις, εως, ἡ, (ἐπιτίθημι)
the act of placing upon, imposition *of hands,* Ac. 8.18, et al.

Ἐπιθυμέω, ῶ, (ἐπί & θυμός)
f. ήσω,
to set the heart upon; to desire, long for, have earnest desire, Mat. 13.17. Lu. 15.16, et al.; to lust after, Mat. 5.28, et al.; *spc.* to covet, Ro. 13.9, et al.: *whence*

Ἐπιθυμητής, οῦ, ὁ,
one who has an ardent desire for *a thing,* 1 Co. 10.6.

Ἐπιθυμία, ας, ἡ,
earnest desire, Lu. 22.15, et al.; irregular or violent desire, cupidity, Mar. 4.19, et al.; *spc.* impure desire, lust, Ro. 1.24, et al.; *met.* the object of desire, what enkindles desire, 1 Jno. 2.16, 17.

Ἐπικαθίζω, (ἐπί & καθίζω)
f. ίσω,
to cause to sit upon, seat upon, Mat. 21.7; *or according to the v.r.* ἐπεκάθισεν, *intrans.* to sit upon.

Ἐπικαλέω, ῶ, (ἐπί & καλέω)
f. έσω, p. pass. ἐπικέκληται, a.1. pass. ἐπεκλήθην,
to call on; to attach or connect a name, Ac. 15.17. Ja. 2.7; to attach an additional name, to surname, Mat. 10.3, et al.; *pass.* to receive an appellation or surname, He. 11.16; *mid.* to call upon, invoke, 2 Co. 1.23, et al.; to appeal to, Ac. 25.11, 12, 21.

Ἐπικάλυμμα, ατος, τό,
71a covering, veil; *met.* a cloak, 1 Pe. 2.16: *from*

Ἐπικαλύπτω, (ἐπί & καλύπτω)
f. ψω,
to cover over; *met.* to pardon, forgive, Ro. 4.7.

Ἐπικατάρᾱτος, ου, ὁ, ἡ, (ἐπί & κατάρατος)

cursed, accursed; obnoxious to the heaviest punishments, Gal. 3.10; infamous, Gal. 3.13; outcast, vile, Jno. 7.49.

Ἐπίκειμαι, (ἐπί & κεῖμαι)
    f. κείσομαι,
    to lie upon, be placed upon, Jno. 11.38; 21.9; to press, urge upon, Lu. 5.1. Ac. 27.20; be urgent, importunate upon, Lu. 23.23; to be imposed upon; be imposed by law, He. 9.10; by necessity, 1 Co. 9.16.

Ἐπικούρειος, ου, ὁ,
    an Epicurean, a follower of the sect of Epicurus, Ac. 17.18.

Ἐπικουριά, ας, ἡ, (ἐπίκουρος, a helper)
    help, assistance, Ac. 26.22.

Ἐπικρίνω, (ἐπί & κρίνω)
    f. ινῶ,
    to decide; to decree, Lu. 23.24. (ῑ).

Ἐπιλαμβάνω, (ἐπί & λαμβάνω)
    f. λήψομαι, & mid. ἐπιλαμβάνομαι,
    to take hold of, Mat. 14.31. Mar. 8.23; to lay hold of, seize, Lu. 23.26. Ac. 16.19, et al.; *met.* to seize on *one's words,* catch *in one's words,* Lu. 20.20, 26; to obtain *as if by seizure,* 1 Ti. 6.12, 19; to assume a portion of, to assume the nature of, He. 2.16; *or,* to succour.

Ἐπιλανθάνομαι, (ἐπί & λανθάνω)
    f. λήσομαι, a.2. ἐπελαθόμην,
    to forget, Mat. 16.5, et al.; to be forgetful, neglectful of, to disregard, Phi. 3.14. He. 6.10, et al.; *p. pass. part.* ἐπιλελησμένος, *in N.T., in a passsive sense,* forgotten, Lu. 12.6.

Ἐπιλέγω, (ἐπί & λέγω)
    f. ξω,
    to call, denominate, Jno. 5.2; *mid.* to select for one's self, choose, Ac. 15.40.

Ἐπιλείπω, (ἐπί & λείπω)
    f. ψω,
    to be insufficient, to run short, to fail, He. 11.32.

Ἐπιλησμονή, ῆς, ἡ, (ἐπιλανθάνομαι)
    forgetfulness, oblivion, Ja. 1.25. S.

Ἐπίλοιπος, ου, ὁ, ἡ, (ἐπιλείπω)
    remaining, still left, 1 Pe. 4.2.

Ἐπίλῠσις, εως, ἡ,
    a loosing, liberation; *met.* interpretation *of what is enigmatical and obsure,* 2 Pe. 1.20: *from*

Ἐπιλύω, (ἐπί & λύω)
    to loose *what has previously been fastened or entangled, as a knot; met.* to solve, to explain *what is enigmatical as a parable,* Mat. 4.34; to settle, put an end to *a matter of debate,* Ac. 19.39.

Ἐπιμαρτυρέω, ῶ, (ἐπί & μαρτυρέω)
    f. ησω,
    to bear testimony to, to testify solemnly, 1 Pe. 5.12.

Ἐπιμέλεια, ας, ἡ, (ἐπιμελής)
    care, attention, Ac. 27.3.

Ἐπιμέλομαι, v. ἐπιμελέομαι, οῦμαι, (ἐπί & μέλομαι)
    f. ἐπιμεληθήσομαι, and later, ἐπιμελήσομαι, a.1. ἐπεμελήθην,
    to take care of, Lu. 10.34, 35. 1 Ti. 3.5.

Ἐπιμελῶς, (ἐπιμελής)
   adv. carefully, diligently, Lu. 15.8.
Ἐπιμένω, (ἐπί & μένω)
   f. νῶ,
   to stay longer, prolong a stay, remain on, Ac. 10.48; 15.34, et al.; to continue, persevere, Jno. 8.7. Ac. 12.16; to adhere to, continue to embrace, Ac. 13.43. Ro. 11.22; to persist in, Ro. 6.1, et al.
Ἐπινεύω, (ἐπί & νεύω)
   f. εύσω,
   to nod to; *met.* to assent to, consent, Ac. 18.20.
Ἐπίνοια, ας, ἡ, (ἐπί & νοῦς)
   cogitation, purpose, device, Ac. 8.22.
Ἐπιορκέω, ῶ, (ἐπί & ὅρκος)
   f. ήσω,
   to forswear one's self, to fail of observing one's oath, Mat. 5.33.
Ἐπίορκος, ου, ὁ, ἡ, (fr. same)
   one who violates his oath, perjured, 1 Ti. 1.10.
Ἐπιοῦσα, ης, ἡ, scil. ἡμέρα
   see ἔπειμι.
Ἐπιούσιος, ίου, ὁ, ἡ,
   supplied with the coming day (ἡ ἐπιοῦσα), daily, *or,* sufficient, Mat. 6.11. Lu. 11.3. N.T.
Ἐπιπίπτω, (ἐπί & πίπτω)
   f. πεσοῦμαι, a.2. ἐπέπεσον,
   to fall upon; to throw one's self upon, Lu. 15.20. Jno. 13.25. Ac. 20.10, 37; to press, urge upon, Mar. 3.10; to light upon, Ro. 15.3; to come over, Ac. 13.11; to come upon, fall upon *mentally or spiritually,* Lu. 1.12. Ac. 8.16; 10.10, 44; 11.15; 19.17.
Ἐπιπλήσσω, v. ττω, (ἐπί & πλήσσω)
   f. ξω,
   72*pr.* to inflict blows upon; *met.* to chide, reprove, 1 Ti. 5.1.
Ἐπιπνίγω, (ἐπί & πνίγω)
   f. ξω,
   pr. to suffocate; *met.* to choke, obstruct the growth of, v.r. Lu. 8.7. N.T.
Ἐπιποθέω, ῶ, (ἐπί & ποθέω)
   f. ήσω,
   to desire besides; *also,* to desire earnestly, long for, 2 Co. 5.2; to have a strong bent, Ja. 4.5; *by impl.* to love, have affection for, 2 Co. 9.14, et al.: *whence*
Ἐπιπόθησις, εως, ἡ,
   earnest desire, strong affection, 2 Co. 7.7, 11.
Ἐπιπόθητος, ου, ὁ, ἡ, τό, -ον,
   earnestly desired, longed for, Phi. 4.1. L.G.
Ἐπιποθία, ας, ἡ,
   earnestly desire, Ro. 15.23. N.T.
Ἐπιπορεύομαι, (ἐπί & πορεύομαι)
   f. εύσομαι,
   to travel to; to come to, Lu. 8.4.
Ἐπιρράπτω, (ἐπί & ῥάπτω)
   f. ψω,
   to sew upon, Mar. 2.21. N.T.
Ἐπιρρίπτω, (ἐπί & ῥίπτω)

f. ψω,

to throw or cast upon, Lu. 19.35; *met.* to devolve upon, commit to, *in confidence,* 1 Pe. 5.7.

Ἐπίσημος, ου, ὁ, ἡ, (ἐπί & σῆμα)

pr. bearing a distinctive mark or device; noted, eminent, Ro. 16.7; notorious, Mat. 27.16.

Ἐπισιτισμός, οῦ, ὁ, (ἐπισιτίζομαι, to provision, fr. ἐπί & σιτίζω, to feed, fr. σῖτος) supply of food, provisions, Lu. 9.12.

Ἐπισκέπτομαι, (ἐπί & σκέπτομαι)

f. ψομαι,

to look at observantly, to inspect; to look out, select, Ac. 6.3; to go to see, visit, Ac. 7.23; 15.36; to visit *for the purpose of comfort and relief,* Mat. 25.36, 43. Ja. 1.27; *from the Heb., of God,* to visit *with gracious interposition,* Lu. 1.68, 78, et al.

Ἐπισκευάζομαι, (ἐπισκευάζω, to put in readiness)

f. άσομαι,

to prepare for a journey, v.r. Ac. 21.15.

Ἐπισκηνόω, ῶ, (ἐπί & σκηνή, a tent)

f. ώσω,

to quarter in or at; *met.* to abide upon, 2 Co. 12.9. L.G.

Ἐπισκιάζω, (ἐπί & σκιάζω, to shade, fr. σκιά)

f. άσω,

to overshadow, Mat. 17.5, et al.; *met.* to shed influence upon, Lu. 1.35.

Ἐπισκοπέω, ῶ, (ἐπί & σκοπέω)

to look at, inspect; *met.* to be circumspect, heedful, He. 12.15; to oversee, to exercise the office of ἐπίσκοπος, 1 Pe. 5.2.

Ἐπισκοπή, ῆς, ἡ,

inspection, oversight, visitation; *of God,* visitation, interposition, *whether in mercy or judgment,* Lu. 19.44. 1 Pe. 2.12; care, the office of an overseer or bishop, 1 Ti. 3.1; *from the Heb.* charge, function, Ac. 1.20. S.

Ἐπίσκοπος, ου, ὁ,

pr. an inspector, overseer; a watcher, guardian, 1 Pe. 2.25; *in N.T.,* an *ecclesiastical* overseer, Ac. 20.28. Phi. 1.1. 1 Ti. 3.2. Tit. 1.7.

Ἐπισπάω, ῶ, (ἐπί & σπάω)

f. άσω,

to draw upon or after; *in N.T., mid.,* to obliterate, circumcision *by artificial extension of the foreskin,* 1 Co. 7.18.

Ἐπίσταμαι, σαι, ται,

to be versed in, to be master of, 1 Ti. 6.4; to be acquainted with, Ac. 18.25; 19.15. Jude 10; to know, Ac. 10.28, et al.; to remember, comprehend, Mar. 14.68.

Ἐπιστάτης, ου, ὁ, (ἐφίσταμαι)

pr. one who stands by; one who is set over; *in N.T., in voc., equivalent to* διδάσκαλε, *or* ῥαββί, Master, Doctor, Lu. 5.5; 8.24, 45, et al. (ă)

Ἐπιστέλλω, (ἐπί & στέλλω)

f. ελῶ,

to send word to; to send injunctions, Ac. 15.20; 21.25; to write to, write a letter, He. 13.22.

Ἐπιστήμων, ονος, ὁ, ἡ, (ἐπίσταμαι)

knowing, discreet, Ja. 3.13.

Ἐπιστηρίζω, (ἐπί & στηρίζω)

f. ίξω,

pr. to cause to rest or lean on, to settle upon; *met.* to confirm, strengthen, establish, Ac. 14.22; 15.32, 41; 18.23.

Ἐπιστολή, ῆς, ἡ, (ἐπιστέλλω)
word sent; an order, command; an epistle, letter, Ac. 9.2; 15.30, et al.

Ἐπιστομίζω, (ἐπί & στόμα)
f. ίσω,
to apply a curb or muzzle; *met.* to put to silence, Tit. 1.11.

Ἐπιστρέφω, (ἐπί & στρέφω)
f. ψω, a.2. pass. ἐπεστράφην,
trans. to turn towards; to turn round; to bring back, convert, Lu. 1.16, 17. Ja. 5.19, 20; *intrans. and mid.,* to turn one's self upon or towards, Ac. 9.40. Re. 1.12; to about, Mat. 9.22. et al.; 73to turn back, return, Mat. 12.44, et al.; *met.* to be converted, Ac. 28.27, et al.: *whence*

Ἐπιστροφή, ῆς, ἡ,
a turning towards, a turning about; *in N.T., met.* conversion, Ac. 15.13.

Ἐπισυνάγω, (ἐπί & συνάγω)
f. ξω,
to gather to *a place;* to gather together, assemble, convene, Mat. 23.37; 24.31, et al.: (L.G.) *whence*

Ἐπισυναγωγή, ῆς, ἡ,
the act of being gathered together or assembled, 2 Thes. 2.1; an assembling together, He. 10.25. S.

Ἐπισυντρέχω, (ἐπί & συντρέχω)
to run together to *a place,* Mar. 9.25. L.G.

Ἐπισύστᾰσις, εως, ἡ, (ἐπισυνίσταμαι)
a gathering, concourse, tumult, Ac. 24.12; a crowding *of calls upon the attention and thoughts,* 2 Co. 11.28.

Ἐπισφᾰλής, έος, οῦς, ὁ, ἡ, τό, -ές, (ἐπί & σφάλλω)
on the verge of falling, unsteady; *met.* insecure, hazardous, dangerous, Ac. 27.9.

Ἐπισχύω, (ἐπί & ἰσχύω)
f. ύσω,
to strengthen; *intrans.* to gather strength; *met.* to be urgent, to press on *a point,* Lu. 23.5.

Ἐπισωρεύω, (ἐπί & σωρεύω, fr. σωρός, a heap)
f. εύσω,
to heap up, accumulate largely; *met.* to procure in abundance, 2 Ti. 4.3. L.G.

Ἐπιτᾱγή, ῆς, ἡ, *a later form for* ἐπίταξις *or* ἐπίταγμα,
injunction, 1 Co. 7.6, 25. 2 Co. 8.8; a decree, Ro. 16.26. 1 Ti. 1.1. Tit. 1.3; authoritativeness, strictness, Tit. 2.15: *from*

Ἐπιτάσσω, (ἐπί & τάσσω)
f. ξω,
to set over or upon; to enjoin, charge, Mar. 1.27; 6.39. Lu. 4.36, et al.

Ἐπιτελέω, ῶ, (ἐπί & τελέω)
f. έσω,
to bring to an end; to finish, complete, perfect, Ro. 15.28. 2 Co. 8.6, 11; to perform, Lu. 13.32; to carry into practice, to realise, 2 Co. 7.1; to discharge, He. 9.6; to execute; He. 8.5; *mid.* to end, make an end, Gal. 3.3; to carry out to completion, Phi. 1.6; *pass.* to be fully undergone, endured, 1 Pe. 5.9.

Ἐπιτήδειος, εία, ειον, (ἐπιτηδές)
fit, suitable, necessary, Ja. 2.16.

Ἐπιτίθημι, (ἐπί & τίθημι)
    f. ἐπιθήσω,
    to put, place, or lay upon, Mat. 9.18. Lu. 4.40, et al.; to impose *a name,* Mar. 3.16, 17; to lade, Ac. 28.3; to inflict, Ac. 16.23. Lu. 10.30. Re. 22.18; *mid.* to set to fall upon, assail, assault, attach, Ac. 18.10.

Ἐπιτῑμάω, ῶ, (ἐπί & τιμάω)
    f. ήσω,
    pr. to set a value upon; to assess a penalty; to allege as a crimination; *hence,* to reprove, chide, censure, rebuke, reprimand, Mat. 19.13. Lu. 23.40, et al.; *in N.T.,* to admonish strongly, enjoin strictly, Mat. 12.16. Lu. 17.3.

Ἐπιτιμία, ας, ἡ, *used in N.T. in the sense of* ἐπιτίμημα or ἐπιτίμησις,
    a punishment, penalty, 2 Co. 2.6.

Ἐπιτρέπω, (ἐπί & τρέπω)
    f. ψω, a.2. pass. ἐπεταράπην, p. ἐπιτέτραμμαι,
    to give over, to leave to the entire trust or management of *any one; hence,* to permit, allow, suffer, Mat. 8.21. Mar. 5.13, et al.: *whence*

Ἐπιτροπή, ῆς, ἡ,
    a trust; a commission, Ac. 26.12.

Ἐπίτροπος, ου, ὁ,
    one to whose charge or control a thing is left; a steward, bailiff, agent, manager, Mat. 20.8; steward or overseer *of the revenue,* treasurer, Lu. 8.3; a guardian *of children,* Gal. 4.2.

Ἐπιτυγχάνω, (ἐπί & τυγχάνω)
    a.2. ἐπίτῠχον,
    to light upon, find; to hit, reach; to acquire, obtain, attain, Ro. 11.7. He. 6.15; 11.33. Ja. 4.2.

Ἐπιφαίνω, (ἐπί & φαίνω)
    f. φανῶ, a.1. ἐπίφηνα, later in the N.T., ἐπέφᾱνα, a.2. pass. ἐπέφᾰνην,
    to make to appear, to display; *pass.* to be manifested, revealed, Tit. 2.11; 3.4; *intrans.* to give light, shine, Lu. 1.79. Ac. 27.20.

Ἐπιφάνεια, ας, ἡ,
    appearance, manifestation, 1 Ti. 6.14. 2 Ti. 1.10, et al.; glorious display, 2 Thes. 2.8: *from*

Ἐπιφᾰνής, έος, οῦς, ὁ, ἡ,
    pr. in full and clear view; splendid, glorious, illustrious, Ac. 2.20.

Ἐπιφαύσκω, (φῶς)
    in N.T. f. αύσω,
    to shine upon, give light to, enlighten, Ep. 5.14.

Ἐπιφέρω, (ἐπί & φέρω)
    f. ἐποίσω, a.2. ἐπένεγκον,
    to bring upon or against, Ac. 25.18. Jude 9; to 74inflict, Ro. 3.5; to bring to, apply to, Ac. 19.12; to bring in addition, add, superadd, Phi. 1.16.

Ἐπιφωνέω, ῶ, (ἐπί & φωνέω)
    f. ήσω,
    to cry aloud, shout, raise a shout in favour or against *any one,* Lu. 23.21. Ac. 12.22; 22.24.

Ἐπιφώσκω, *a varied form of* ἐπιφαύσκω,
    to dawn, Mat. 21.1; *hence, used of the reckoned commencement of the day,* to be near commencing, to draw on, Lu. 23.54.

Ἐπιχειρέω, ῶ, (ἐπί & χείρ)

f. ἤσω,
to put hand to *a thing;* to undertake, attempt, Lu. 1.1. Ac. 9.29; 19.13.
Ἐπιχέω, ῶ, (ἐπί & χέω)
f. εύσω,
to pour upon, Lu. 10.34.
Ἐπιχορηγέω, ῶ, (ἐπί & χορηγέω)
f. ἤσω,
to supply further; to superadd, 2 Pe. 1.5; to supply, furnish, give, 2 Co. 9.10. Gal. 3.5.
2 Pe. 1.11; *pass.* to gather vigour, Col. 2.19.
Ἐπιχορηγία, ας, ἡ,
supply, aid, Ep. 4.16. Phi. 1.19. L.G.
Ἐπιχρίω, (ἐπί & χρίω)
f. ίσω,
to smear upon, to anoint, Jno. 9.6, 11. (ῑ).
Ἐποικοδομέω, ῶ, (ἐπί & οἰκοδομέω)
f. ἤσω,
to build upon; *pass. met.* to be built upon, rest firmly on, Ep. 2.20. Col. 2.7; to build
besides or further; to build up, carry up a building; *met.* to carry up to a higher degree
of faith and spiritual advancement, Ac. 20.32, et al.
Ἐποκέλλω, (ἐπί & ὀκέλλω, idem)
a.1. ἐπώκειλα,
to run *a ship* aground, Ac. 27.41.
Ἐπονομάζω, (ἐπί & ὀνομάζω)
f. άσω,
to attach a name to; *pass.* to be named, to be styled, Ro. 2.17.
Ἐποπτεύω,
f. εύσω,
to look upon, observe, watch; to witness, be an eye-witness of, 1 Pe. 2.12; 3.2: *from*
Ἐπόπτης, ου, ὁ, (ἐπί & ὄψομαι)
a looker on, eye-witness, 2 Pe. 1.16.
Ἔπος, εος, τό, (εἶπον)
a word, that which is expressed by words; ὡς ἔπος εἰπεῖν, so to say, if the expression
may be allowed, He. 7.9.
Ἐπουράνιος, ίου, ὁ, ἡ, (ἐπί & οὐρανός)
heavenly, *in respect of locality,* Ep. 1.20; Phi. 2.10, et al.; τὰ ἐπουράνια, the upper
regions *of the air,* Ep. 6.12; heavenly, *in respect of essence and character,* unearthly,
1 Co. 15.48, 49, et al.; *met.* divine, spiritual, Jno. 3.12, et al.
Ἑπτά, οἱ, αἱ, τά,
seven, Mat. 15.34, 37, et al.; *by Jewish usage for a round number,* Mat. 12.45. Lu.
11.26: *whence*
Ἑπτάκις,
adv. seven times, Mat. 18.21, 22. Lu. 17.4, bis. (ᾱ)
Ἑπτακισχίλιοι, ας, α, (ἑπτάκις & χίλιοι)
seven thousand, Ro. 11.4.
Ἐργάζομαι, (ἔργον)
f. άσομαι, a.1. εἰργασάμην, p. εἴργασμαι,
intrans. to work, labour, Mat. 21.28. Lu. 13.14; to trade, traffic, do business, Mat.
25.16. Re. 18.17; to act, exert one's power, be active, Jno. 5.17; *trans.* to do, perform,
commit, Mat. 26.10. Jno. 6.28; to be engaged in, occupied upon, 1 Co. 9.13. Re.
18.17; to acquire, gain by one's labour, Jno. 6.27, et al.: *whence*

Ἐργᾰσία, ας, ἡ,

    work, labour; *in N.T.*, ἐργασίαν διδόναι, *operam dare,* to endeavour, strive, Lu. 12.58; performance, practice, Ep. 4.19; a trade, business, craft, Ac. 19.25; gain *acquired by labour or trade,* profit, Ac. 16.16, 19; 19.24, 25.

Ἐργάτης, ου, ὁ,

    a workman, labourer, Mat. 9.37, 38; 20.1, 2, 8; *met.* a *spiritual* workman or labourer, 2 Co. 11.13, et al.; an artisan, artificer, Ac. 19.25; a worker, practiser, Lu. 13.27. (ᾰ)

Ἔργον, ου, τό,

    a work, any thing done or to be done; a deed, work, action, Jno. 3.21. Ep. 2.10. 2 Co. 9.8, et al. freq.; duty enjoined, office, charge, business, Mar. 13.34. Jno. 4.34, et al. freq.; a process, course of action, Ja. 1.4; a work, product of an action or process, Ac. 7.41. He. 1.10. et al.

Ἐρεθίζω, (ἐρέθω, idem, ἔρις)

    f. ίσω, a.1. ἠρέθισα,

    to provoke; to irritate, exasperate, Col. 3.21; to incite, stimulate, 2 Co. 9.2.

Ἐρείδω,

    f. είσω, a.1. ἤρεισα,

    to make to lean upon; to fix firmly; *intrans.* to become firmly fixed, stick fast, Ac. 27.41.

Ἐρεύγομαι,

    f. ξομαι,

    75to vomit, disgorge, *met.* to utter, declare openly, Mat. 13.35.

Ἐρευνάω, ῶ,

    f. ήσω.

    to search, trace, investigate, explore, Jno. 5.39; 7.52, et al.

Ἐρημία,

    a solitude, uninhabited region, waste, desert, Mat. 15.33, et al.: *from*

Ἔρημος, ου, ὁ, ἡ, & η, ον,

    lone, desert, waste, uninhabited, Mat. 14.13, 15. Mar. 6.31, 32, 35; lone, abandoned *to ruin,* Mat. 23.38. Lu. 13.35; *met.* lone, unmarried, Gal. 4.27; *as a subs.* a desert, uninhabited region, waste, Mat. 3.1; 24.26. Ac. 7.36, et al.: *whence*

Ἐρημόω, ῶ,

    f. ώσω, p. pass. ἠρήμωμαι, a.1. pass. ἠρημώθην,

    to lay waste, make desolate, bring to ruin, Mat. 12.25. Lu. 11.17. Re. 17.16; 18.16, 19: *whence*

Ἐρήμωσις, εως, ἡ,

    desolation, devastation, Mat. 24.15. Mar. 13.14, et al. L.G.

Ἐρίζω, (ἔρις)

    f. ίσω,

    to quarrel; to wrange; to use the harsh tone of a wrangler or brawler, to grate, Mat. 12.19.

Ἐρῑθεία, ας, ἡ, (ἐριθεύομαι, to serve for hire, to serve a party; ἐρῑθος, a hired labourer)

    the service of a party, party spirit; feud, faction, 2 Co. 12.20; contentious disposition, Ja. 3.14, ; *by impl.* untowardness, disobedience, Ro. 2.8.

Ἔριον, ου, τό, (ἔρος, εἶρος, idem)

    wool, He. 9.19. Re. 1.14.

Ἔρις, ιδος, ἡ,

    altercation, strife, Ro. 13.13; contentious disposition, Ro. 1.29. Phi. 1.15, et al.

Ἐρίφιον, ίου, τό,

    a goat, kid, Mat. 25.33: *dim. from*

Ἔρῐφος, ου, ὁ, ἡ,
> a goat, kid, Mat. 25.32. Lu. 15.29.

Ἑρμηνεία, ας, ἡ,
> interpretation, explanation, 1 Co. 14.26; *meton.* the power or faculty of interpreting, 1 Co. 12.10: *from*

Ἑρμηνεύω, (ἑρμηνεύς, an interpreter)
> f. εύσω,
> to explain, interpret, translate, Jno. 1.39, 43; 9.7. He. 7.2.

Ἑρμῆς, οῦ, ὁ,
> Hermes or Mercury, *son of Jupiter and Maia, the messenger and interpreter of the gods, and the patron of eloquence, learning, &c.,* Ac. 14.12.

Ἑρπετόν, οῦ, τό, (ἕρπω, to creep)
> a creeping animal, a reptile, Ac. 10.12, et al.

Ἐρυθρός, ά, όν,
> red, Ac. 7.36. He. 11.29.

Ἔρχομαι,
> f. ἐλεύσομαι, a.2. ἤλῠθον, by sync. ἦλθον, p. ἐλήλῠθα,
> to come, to go, to pass. *By the combination of this verb with other terms, a variety of meaning result, which, however, is due, not to a change of meaning in the verb, but to the adjuncts.* Ὁ ἐρχόμενος, He who is coming, the expected Messiah, Mat. 11.3. et al.

Ἐρωτάω, ῶ,
> f. ήσω,
> to ask, interrogate, inquire of, Mat. 21.24. Lu. 20.3; *in N.T.,* to ask, request, beg, beseech, Mat. 15.23. Lu. 4.38. Jno. 14.16, et al.

Ἐσθής, ῆτος, ἡ, (ἕννυμι, to clothe)
> a robe, vestment, raiment, Lu. 23.11. Ac. 1.10, et al.: *whence*

Ἔσθησις, εως, ἡ,
> a garment, robe, raiment, Lu. 24.4. L.G.

Ἐσθίω, (ἔδω)
> f. ἔδομαι, & in N.T. φάγομαι, εσια, a.2. ἔφαγον,
> to eat, Mat. 12.1; 15.27; ἐσθίειν καὶ πίνειν, to eat and drink, to eat and drink in the usual manner, follow the common mode of living, Mat. 11.18; *also with the associated notion of supposed security,* Lu. 17.27; to feast, banquet, Mat. 24.49; met. to devour, consume, He. 10.27. Ja. 5.3; *from the Heb.* ἄρτον ἐσθίειν, to eat bread, to take food, take the usual meals, Mat. 15.2, et al.

Ἔσοπτρον, ου, τό, (ὄψομαι)
> a mirror, speculum, Ja. 1.23. 1 Co. 13.12.

Ἑσπέρα, ας, ἡ,
> fem. of ἕσπερος, evening, Lu. 24.29. Ac. 4.3; 28.23.

Ἔσχᾰτος, η, ον,
> farthest; last, latest, Mat. 12.45. Mar. 12.6; lowest, Mat. 19.30; 20.16, et al.: *whence*

Ἐσχάτως,
> adv. extremely; ἐσχάτως ἔχειν, to be in the last extremity, Mar. 5.23.

Ἔσω,
> adv., *for the more usual form* εἴσω, in, within, in the interior of, Mat. 26.58. Jno. 20.26, et al.; ὁ, ἡ, τό ἔσω, inner, interior, internal; *met.* within the pale of community, 761 Co. 5.12; ὁ ἔσω ἄνθρωπος, the inner man, the mind, soul, Ro. 7.22: *whence*

Ἔσωθεν,

adv. from within, from the interior, Mar. 7.21, 23; within, in the internal parts, Mat. 7.15, et al.; ὁ, ἡ, τό ἔσωθεν, interior, internal, Lu. 11.39, 40; ὁ ἔσωθεν ἄνθρωπος, the mind, soul, 2 Co. 4.16.

Ἐσώτερος, α, ον,
    inner, interior, Ac. 16.24. He. 6.19.

Ἑταῖρος, ου, ὁ,
    a companion, associate, fellow, comrade, friend, Mat. 11.16; 20.13; 22.12; 26.50.

Ἑτερόγλωσσος, ου, ὁ, ἡ, (ἕτερος & γλῶσσα)
    one who speaks another or foreign language, 1 Co. 14.21. L.G.

Ἑτεροδιδασμαλέω, ῶ, (ἕτερος & διδασκαλία)
    f. ήσω,
    to teach other or different doctrine, *and spc.* what is foreign to the Christian religion, 1 Ti. 1.3; 6.3. N.T.

Ἑτεροζυγέω, ῶ, (ἕτερος & ζυγός)
    to be unequally yoked or matched, 2 Co. 6.14.

Ἕτερος, α, ον,
    other, another, some other, Mat. 8.21; 12.45; *met.* different, Lu. 9.29, et al.; ὁ ἕτερος, the other *of two,* Mat. 6.24; τῇ ἑτέρᾳ, the next day, Ac. 20.15; 27.3; ὁ ἕτερος, one's neighbour, Ro. 13.8, et al.; foreign, strange, Ac. 2.4. 1 Co. 14.21; illicit, Jude 7: *whence*

Ἑτέρως,
    adv. otherwise, differently, Phi. 3.15.

Ἔτι
    adv. yet, still, Mat. 12.46; still, further, longer, Lu. 16.2; further, besides, in addition, Mat. 18.16; *with a compar.,* yet, still, Phi. 1.9.

Ἑτοιμάζω, (ἕτοιμος)
    f. άσω,
    to make ready, prepare, Mat. 22.4; 26.17, et al.: *whence*

Ἑτοιμασία, ας, ἡ,
    preparation; preparedness, readiness, alacrity, Ep. 6.15.

Ἕτοιμος, η, ον, ὁ, ἡ, also ἑτοῖμος,
    ready, prepared, Mat. 22.4, 8. Mar. 14.15, et al.: *whence*

Ἑτοίμως,
    adv. in readiness, preparedly, Ac. 21.13, et al.

Ἔτος, εος, τό,
    a year, Lu. 2.41; 3.23, et al.

Εὖ
    adv. well, good, happily, rightly, Mar. 14.7. Ac. 15.29; well! well done! Mat. 25.21, 23, et al.

Εὐαγγελίζω,
    f. ίσω,
    to address with good tidings, Re. 10.7; 14.6; *but elsewhere mid.* εὐαγγελίζομαι, to proclaim as good tidings, to announce good tidings of, Lu. 1.19, et al.; *absol.* to announce the good tidings *of the gospel,* Lu. 4.18; 9.6, et al.; *pass.* to be announced as good tidings, Lu. 16.16; to be addressed with good tidings, Mat. 11.5. Lu. 7.22. He. 4.2.

Εὐαγγέλιον, ου, τό, (εὖ & ἄγγελος)
    glad tidings, good or joyful news, Mat. 4.23; 9.35; the gospel, doctrines of the gospel, Mat. 26.13. Mar. 8.35; *meton.* the preaching of, or instruction in the gospel, 1 Co. 4.15; 9.14, et al.

Εὐαγγελιστής, οῦ, ὁ, (εὐαγγελίζω)
>   *pr.* one who announces glad tidings; an evangelist, preacher of the gospel, teacher of the Christian religion, Ac. 21.8. Ep. 4.11. 2 Ti. 4.5. N.T.

Εὐαρεστέω, ῶ,
>   f. ήσω, p. εὐηρέστηκα,
>   to please well, He. 11.5, 6; *pass.* to take pleasure in, be well pleased with, He. 13.6: (L.G.) *from*

Εὐάρεστος, ου, ὁ, ἡ, τό, -ον, (εὖ & ἀρεστός, fr. ἀρέσκω)
>   well pleasing, acceptable, grateful, Ro. 12.1, 2, et al.: *whence*

Εὐαρέστως,
>   *adv.* acceptably, He. 12.28.

Εὐγενής, έος, οῦς, ὁ, ἡ, (εὖ & γένος)
>   well born, of high rank, honourable; Lu. 19.12. 1 Co. 1.26; generous, ingenuous, candid, Ac. 17.11.

Εὐδία, ας, ἡ, (εὖ & Ζεύς, Διός, Jupiter, *lord of the air and heavens)*
>   serenity of the heavens, a cloudless sky, fair or fine weather, Mat. 16.2.

Εὐδοκέω, ῶ, (εὖ & δοκέω)
>   to think well, approve, acquiesce, take delight or pleasure, Mat. 3.17; 17.5. Mar. 1.11. Lu. 3.22; 12.32, et al.: (L.G.) *whence*

Εὐδοκία, ας, ἡ,
>   approbation; good will, favour, Lu. 2.14; good pleasure, purpose, intention, Mat. 11.26. Lu. 10.21; Ep. 1.5, 9. Phi. 2.13; *by impl.* desire, Ro. 10.1.

Εὐεργεσία, ας, ἡ, (εὐεργέτης)
>   well doing; a good deed, benefit conferred, Ac. 4.9; duty, good office, 1 Ti. 6.2.

Εὐεργετέω, ῶ,
>   77f. ήσω,
>   to do good, exercise beneficence, Ac. 10.38: *from*

Εὐεργέτης, ου, ὁ, (εὖ & ἔργον)
>   a well doer; a benefactor, Lu. 22.25.

Εὔθετος, ου, ὁ, ἡ, (εὖ & τίθημι)
>   *pr.* well arranged, rightly disposed; fit, proper, adapted, Lu. 9.62; 14.35; useful, He. 6.7.

Εὐθέως, (εὐθύς)
>   *adv.* immediately, forthwith, instantly, at once, Mat. 8.3; 13.5, et al.;

Εὐθυδρομέω, ῶ, (εὐθύς & δρόμος)
>   f. ήσω,
>   to run on a straight course; to sail on a direct course, Ac. 16.11; 21.1. L.G.

Εὐθῡμέω, ῶ,
>   f. ήσω,
>   to be cheerful, be in good spirits, take courage, Ac. 27.22, 25. Ja. 5.13: *from*

Εὔθῡμος, ου, ὁ, ἡ, (εὖ & θυμός)
>   of good cheer or courage, cheerful, Ac. 27.36: *whence*

Εὐθυμότερον, (pr. neut. comp. of preced.)
>   *adv.* more cheerfully, Ac. 24.10.

Εὐθύμως,
>   *adv.* cheerfully, v.r. Ac. 24.10.

Εὐθύνω,
>   f. υνῶ, a.1 ῦνα,
>   to guide straight; to direct, guide, steer *a ship,* Ja. 3.4; to make straight, Jno. 1.23: *from*

Εὐθύς, εῖα, ύ,
    straight, Mat. 3.3. Mar. 1.3; *met.* right, upright, true, Ac. 8.21, et al.
Εὐθύς,
    adv. straight forwards; directly, immediately, instantly, forthwith, Mat. 3.16; 13.20, 21, et al.
Εὐθύτης, τητος, ἡ,
    rectitude, righteousness, equity, He. 1.8. (ῠ).
Εὐκαιρέω, ῶ, (εὔκαιρος)
    f. ήσω, a.1 ηὐκαίρησα,
    to have convenient time or opportunity, have leisure, Mar. 6.31. 1 Co. 16.12; to be at leisure *for a thing,* give one's self up *to a thing,* Ac. 17.21. L.G.
Εὐκαιρία, ας, ἡ,
    convenient opportunity, favourable occasion, Mat. 26.16. Lu. 22.6: *from*
Εὔκαιρος, ου, ὁ, ἡ, (εὖ & καιρός)
    timely, opportune, seasonable, convenient, Mar. 6.21. He. 4.16: *whence*
Εὐκαίρως,
    adv. opportunely, seasonably, conveniently, Mar. 14.11. 2 Ti. 4.2.
Εὐκοπώτερος, α, ον, (comp. of εὔκοπος, easy, fr. εὖ & κόπος)
    easier, more feasible, Mat. 9.5; 19.24. Mar. 2.9, et al. L.G.
Εὐλάβεια, ας, ἡ,
    the disposition of one who is εὐλαβής, caution, circumspection; *in N.T.,* reverence *to God,* piety, He. 5.7; 12.28.
Εὐλαβέομαι, οῦ,
    f. ήσομαι, a.1. ηὐλαβήθην,
    to be cautious or circumspect; to fear, be afraid or apprehensive, Ac. 23.10; *in N.T., absol.* to reverence *God,* to be influenced by pious awe, He. 11.7: *from*
Εὐλᾰβής, έος, οῦς, ὁ, ἡ, (εὖ & λαμβάνω)
    pr. taking hold of well, *i.e.* warily; *hence,* cautious, circumspect; full of reverence *towards God,* devout, pious, religious, Lu. 2.25. Ac. 2.5; 8.2.
Εὐλογέω, ῶ, (εὖ & λόγος)
    f. ήσω, p. ηκα, a.1. ησα,
    pr. to speak well of; *in N.T.,* to bless, ascribe praise and glorification, Lu. 1.64, et al.; to bless, invoke a blessing upon, Mat. 5.44, et al.; to bless, confer a favour or blessing upon, Ep. 1.3. He. 6.14; *pass.* to be blessed, be an object of favour or blessing, Lu. 1.28, et al.: *whence*
Εὐλογητός, οῦ, ὁ, ἡ,
    worthy of praise or blessing, blessed, Mar. 14.61. Lu. 1.68, et al. S.
Εὐλογία, ας, ἡ,
    pr. good speaking; fair speech, flattery, Ro. 16.18; *in N.T.,* blessing, praise, celebration, 1 Co. 10.16. Re. 5.12, 13; invocation of good, benediction, Ja. 3.10; a favour conferred, gift, benefit, Ro. 15.29. 2 Co. 9.5, 6, et al.
Εὐμετάδοτος, ου, ὁ, ἡ, (εὖ & μεταδίδωμι)
    ready in imparting, liberal, bountiful, 1 Ti. 6.18. L.G.
Εὐνοέω, ῶ, (εὔνοος, εὖ & νόος, νοῦς)
    to have kind thoughts, be well affected or kindly disposed *towards,* Mat. 5.25.
Εὔνοια, ας, ἡ, (fr. same)
    good will, kindliness; heartiness, Ep. 6.7; conjugal duty, 1 Co. 7.3.
Εὐνουχίζω,
    f. ίσω, a.1. εὐνούχισα,

to emasculate, make a eunuch; to impose chaste abstinence on, to bind to a practical emasculation, Mat. 19.12: (L.G.) *from*

Εὐνοῦχος, ου, ὁ, (εὐν, a bed, & ἔχω)
78*pr.* one who has charge of the bedchamber; *hence,* a eunuch, one emasculated, Mat. 19.12; *as eunuchs in the East often rose to places of power and trust, hence,* a minister of court. Ac. 8.27, 34.

Εὐοδόω, (εὖ & ὁδός)
f. ώσω,
to give a prosperous journey; cause to prosper or be successful; *pass.* to have a prosperous journey, to succeed *in a journey,* Ro.1.10; *met.* to be furthered, to prosper, *temporally or spiritually,* 1 Co. 16.2. 3 Jno. 2, *bis.*

Εὐπάρεδρος, ου, ὁ, ἡ, (εὖ & πάρεδρος, one who sits by, an assistant, assessor, fr. παρά & ἕδρα, a seat)
constantly attending; assiduous, devoted to; τὸ εὐπάρεδρον, assiduity, devotedness, v.r. 1 Co. 7.35. L.G.

Εὐπειθής, έος, οῦς, ὁ, ἡ, (εὖ & πείθω)
easily persuaded, pliant, Ja. 3.17.

Εὐπερίστᾰτος, ου, ὁ, ἡ, (εὖ & περιίσταμαι)
easily or constantly environing or besetting, He. 12.1. N.T.

Εὐποιΐα, ας, ἡ, (εὖ & ποιέω)
doing good, beneficence, He. 13.16. L.G.

Εὐπορέομαι, οῦμαι, (εὐπορέω, to supply, fr. εὔπορος, easy, abounding, in easy circumstances)
f. ήσομαι,
to be in prosperous circumstances, enjoy plenty, Ac. 11.29.

Εὐπορία, ας, ἡ, (fr. same)
wealth, abundance, Ac. 19.25.

Εὐπρέπεια, ας, ἡ, (εὐπρεπής, well looking, fr. εὖ & πρέπει)
grace, beauty, Ja. 1.11.

Εὐπρόσδεκτος, ου, ὁ, ἡ, (εὖ & προσδέχομαι)
acceptable, grateful, pleasing, Ro. 15.16, 31. 2 Co. 8.12. 1 Pe. 2.5; *in N.T.,* gracious, 2 Co. 6.2. L.G.

Εὐπρόσεδρος, ου, ὁ, ἡ, (εὖ & πρόσεδρος, an assessor)
contantly attending, assiduous, devoted to, 1 Co. 7.35; *equivalent to* εὐπάρεδρος.

Εὐπροσωπέω, ῶ, (εὐπρόσωπος, of a fair countenance, fr. εὖ & πρόσωπον)
f. ήσω,
to carry or make fair appearance, to be specious, Gal. 6.12. N.T.

Εὑρίσκω,
f. εὑρήσω, p. εὕρηκα, a.2. εὗρον, a.1. pass. εὑρέθην, later a. 1. εὕρησα, and a. mid. εὑράμην,
He. 9.12; to find, to meet with, light upon, Mat. 18.28; 20.6, to find out, to detect, discover, Lu. 23.2, 4, 14; to acquire, obtain, win, gain, Lu. 1.30; 9.12; to find *mentally,* to comprehend, recognise, Ac. 17.27. Ro. 7.21; to find *by experience,* observe, gather, Ro. 7.18; to devise *as feasible,* Lu. 5.19; 19.48.

Εὐροκλύδων, (εὗρος, the east wind, & κλύδων, a wave)
Euroclydon, *the name of a tempestuous wind,* Ac. 27.14. *There are, however, two various readings,* Εὐρυκλύδων (εὐρύς) *and* Εὐρακύλων. Euroaquilo. (ῠ). N.T.

Εὐρύχωρος, ου, ὁ, ἡ, (εὐρύς, broad, & χώρα)
spacious; broad, wide, Mat. 7.13.

Εὐσέβεια, ας, ἡ, (εὐσεβής)

reverential feeling; piety, devotion, godliness, Ac. 3.12. 1 Ti. 2.2; 4.7, 8, et al.; religion, the *Christian* religion, 1 Ti. 3.16.

Εὐσεβέω, ῶ,

   f. ήσω,

   to exercise piety; *towards a deity,* to worship, Ac. 17.23; *towards relatives,* to be dutiful towards, 1 Ti. 5.4: *from*

Εὐσεβής, έον, οῦς, ὁ, ἡ, (εὖ & σέβομαι)

   reverent; pious, devout, religious, Ac. 10.2, 7; 22.12. 2 Pe. 2.9: *whence*

Εὐσεβῶς,

   adv. piously, religiously, 2 Ti. 3.12. Tit. 2.12.

Εὔσημος, ου, ὁ, ἡ, (εὖ & σῆμα)

   pr. well marked, strongly marked; *met.* significant, intelligible, perspicuous, 1 Co. 14.9.

Εὔσπλαγχνος, ου, ὁ, ἡ, (εὖ & σπλάγχνον)

   in N.T., tender-hearted, compassionate, Ep. 4.32. 2 Pe. 3.8.

Εὐσχημόνως, (εὐσχήμων)

   adv. in a becoming manner, with propriety, decently, gracefully, Ro. 13.13. 1 Co. 14.40. 1 Thes. 4.12.

Εὐσχημοσύνη, ης, ἡ,

   comeliness, gracefulness; *artificial* comeliness, ornamental array, embellishment, 1 Co. 12.23: *from*

Εὐσχήμων, ονος, ὁ, ἡ, (εὖ & σχῆμα)

   of good appearance, pleasing to look upon, comely, 1 Co. 12.24; *met.* becoming, decent; τὸ εὔσχημον, decorum, propriety, 1 Co. 7.35; honourable, reputable, of high standing and influence, Mar. 15.43. Ac. 13.50; 17.12.

Εὐτόνως, (εὔτονος, on the stretch, fr. εὖ & τείνω)

   79*adv.* intensely, vehemently, strenuously, Lu. 23.10. Ac. 18.28.

Εὐτραπελία, ας, ἡ, (εὐτράπελος, ready, witty, fr. εὖ & τρέπω, to turn)

   facetiousness, pleasantry; *hence,* buffoonery, ribaldry, Ep. 5.4.

Εὐφημία, ας, ἡ,

   pr. use of words of good omen; *hence,* favourable expression, praise, commendation, 2 Co. 6.8: *from*

Εὔφημος, ου, ὁ, ἡ, (εὖ & φήμη)

   pr. of good omen, auspicious; *hence,* of good report, commendable, laudable, reputable, Phi. 4.8.

Εὐφορέω, ῶ, (εὔφορος, εὖ & φέρω)

   to bear or bring forth well or plentifully, yield abundantly, Lu. 12.16.

Εὐφραίνω, (εὔφρων, εὖ & φρήν)

   f. ανῶ, a.1. εὔφρηνα & εὔφρανα,

   to gladden, 2 Co. 2.2; *pass.* to be glad; exult, rejoice, Lu 12.19. Ac. 2.26; *mid.* to feast in token of joy, keep a day of rejoicing, Lu. 15.23, 24, 29, 32, et al.

Εὐφροσύνη, ης, ἡ, (εὔφρων)

   joy, gladness, rejoicing, Ac. 2.28; 14.17.

Εὐχαριστέω, ῶ, (εὐχάριστος)

   f. ήσω, a.1. ησα,

   to thank, give thanks, Mat. 15.36; 26.27, et al.

Εὐχαριστία, ας, ἡ,

   gratitude, thankfulness, Ac. 24.3; thanks, the act of giving thanks, thanksgiving, 1 Co. 14.16, et al.; conversation marked by the gentle cheefulness of a grateful heart, *as contrasted with the unseemly mirth of* εὐτραπελία, Ep. 5.4: *from*

Εὐχάριστος, ου, ὁ, ἡ, (εὖ & χάρις)
    grateful, pleasing; grateful, mindful of benefits, thankful, Col. 3.15.
Εὐχή, ῆς, ἡ,
    a wish, prayer, Ja. 5.15; a vow, Ac. 21.23.
Εὔχομαι,
    f. ξομαι, a.1. ηὐξάμην,
    to pray, offer prayer, Ac. 26.29. 2 Co. 13.7, 9. Ja. 5.16; to wish, desire, Ac. 27.29. Ro. 9.3. 3 Jno 2.
Εὔχρηστος, ου, ὁ, ἡ, (εὖ & χρηστός)
    highly useful, very profitable, 2 Ti. 2.21; 4.11. Phile. 11.
Εὐψυχέω, ῶ, (εὔψυχος, of good courage, εὖ & ψυχή)
    f. ήσω,
    to be animated, encouraged, in good spirits, Phi. 2.19.
Εὐωδία, ας, ἡ, (εὐώδης, εὖ & ὄδωδα, ὄζω)
    a sweet smell, grateful odour, fragrance, 2 Co. 2.15. Ep. 5.2. Phi. 4.18.
Εὐώνῠμος, ου, ὁ, ἡ, (εὖ & ὄνομα)
    of good name or omen; *used also as an euphemism by the Greeks instead of* ἀριστερός, *which was a word of bad import, as all omens on the left denoted misfortune;* the left, Mat. 20.21, 23; 25.33, 41, et al.
Ἔφᾰγον,
    a. 2. of ἐσθίω.
Ἐφάλλομαι, (ἐπί & ἅλλομαι)
    f. αλοῦμαι,
    to leap or spring upon, assault, Ac. 19.16.
Ἐφάπαξ, (ἐπί & ἅπαξ)
    adv. once for all, Ro. 6.10; at once, 1 Co. 15.6.
Ἐφεσῖνος, η, ον,
    Re. 2.1, and
Ἐφέσιος, ία, ιον,
    Ephesian, of Ἔφεσος, ου, ἡ, Ephesus, *a city of Asia Minor,* Ac. 19.28, 34, 35; 21.29.
Ἐφευρετής, οῦ, ὁ, (ἐφευρίσκα, to come upon, find, discover, fr. ἐπί & εὑρίσκω)
    an inventor, deviser, Ro. 1.30.
Ἐφημερία, ας, ἡ,
    pr. daily course; the daily service of the temple; a course *of priests to which the daily service for a week was allotted in rotation,* Lu. 1.5, 8: (L.G.) *from*
Ἐφήμερος, ου, ὁ, ἡ, (ἐπί & ἡμέρα)
    lasting for a day; daily; sufficient for a day, necessary for every day, Ja. 2.15.
Ἐφικνέομαι, οῦμαι, (ἐπί & ἱκνέομαι, to come)
    f. ίξομαι, a.2 ἐφικόμην,
    to come or reach to, to reach *a certain point or end;* to reach, arrive at, 2 Co. 10.13, 14.
Ἐφίστημι, (ἐπί & ἵστημι)
    f. ἐπιστήσω,
    trans. to place upon, over, close by; *intrans.* p. ἐφέστηκα, part. ἐφεστώς, a.2. ἐπέστην, mid. ἐφίσταμαι, to stand by or near, Lu. 2.38; 4.39; to come suddenly upon, Lu. 2. 9, 24; to come upon, assault, Ac. 6.12; 17.5; to come near, approach, Lu. 10.40; to impend, be instant, be at hand, 1 Thes. 5.3; to be present, Ac. 28.2; to be pressing, urgent, earnest, 2 Ti. 4.2.
Ἐφφαθα, (Aramaean, אתפתח)
    be thou opened, Mar. 7.34.

Ἔχθρα, ας, ἡ,
> enmity, discord, feud, Lu. 23.12. Gal. 5.20; alienation, 80Ep. 2.15, 16; a principle or state of enmity, Ro. 8.7.

Ἐχθρός, ά, όν,
> hated, under disfavour, Ro. 11.28; inimical, hostile, Mat. 13.28. Col. 1.21; *as a subs.* an enemy, adversary, Mat. 5.43, 44; 10.36. Lu. 6.27, 35, et al.

Ἔχιδνα, ης, ἡ, (ἔχις)
> a viper, poisonous serpent, Ac. 28.3; *used also fig. of persons,* Mat. 3.7.

Ἔχω
> f. ἕξω, imperf. εἶχον, a.2. ἔσχον, p. ἔσχηκα,
> to hold, Re. 1.16, et al.; to seize, possess *a person,* Mar. 16.8; to have, possess, Mat. 7.29, et al. freq.; to have, have ready, be furnished with, Mat. 5.23. Jno. 5.36; 6.68, et al.; to have *as a matter of crimination,* Mat. 5.23. Mar. 11.25, et al.; to have *at command,* Mat. 27.65; to have *the power,* be able, Mat. 18.25. Lu. 14.14. Ac. 4.14, et al.; to have *in marriage,* Mat. 14.4. et al.; to have, be affected by, subjected to, Mat. 3.14; 12.10. Mar. 3.10. Jno. 12.48; 15.22, 24; 16.21, 22. Ac. 23.29. 1 Ti. 5.12. He. 7.28. 1 Jno. 1.8; 4.18; χάριν ἔχειν, to feel gratitude, be thankful, 1 Ti. 1.12. 2 Ti. 1.3. Phile. 7; to hold, esteem, regard, Mat. 14.5. Lu. 14.18, 19, et al.; to have or hold *as an object of knowledge, faith, or practice,* Jno. 5.38, 42; 14.21. 1 Jno. 5.12. 2 Jno. 9; *intrans.* with adverbs or adverbial expressions, to be, to fare, Mat. 9.12. Mar. 2.17; 5.23. Lu. 5.31. Jno. 4.52. Ac. 7.1; 12.15; 15.36; 21.13. 2 Co. 10.6; 12.14. 1 Ti. 5.25. 1 Pe. 4.5; τὸ νῦν ἔχον, for the present; *in N.T.,* ἔχειν ἐν γαστρί, to be pregnant, Mat. 1.18, et al.; as also ἔχειν κοίτην, Ro. 9.10; ἔχειν δαιμόνιον, to be possessed, Mat. 11.18, et al.; *of time,* to have continued, to have lived, Jno. 5.5, 6; 8.57; *of space,* to embrace, be distant, Ac. 1.12; *mid. pr.* to hold by, cling to; *hence,* to border upon, be next, Mar. 1.38. Lu. 13.33. Ac. 20.15; 21.26; to tend immediately to, He. 6.9.

Ἕως,
> conj., *of time,* while, as long as, Jno. 9.4; until, Mat. 2.9. Lu. 15.4; *as also in N.T.,* ἕως οὗ, ἕως ὅτου, Mat. 5.18, 26; ἕως ἄρτι, until now, Mat. 11.12; ἕως πότε, until when, how long, Mat. 17.17; ἕως σήμερον, until this day, to this time, 2 Co. 8.15; *as prep., of time,* until, Mat. 24.21; *of place,* unto, even to, Mat. 11.23. Lu. 2.15; ἕως ἄνω, to the brim, Jno. 2.7; ἕως εἰς, even to, as far as, Lu. 24.50; ἕως κάτω, to the bottom; ἕως ὧδε, to this place, Lu. 23.5; *of state,* unto, even to, Mat. 26.38; *of number,* even, so much as, Ro. 3.12, et al. freq.

Z, ζ, *Ζῆτα*

Ζάω, ζῶ, ζῆς, ζῆ,
> f. ζήσω & ζήσομαι, a.1. ἔζησα, p. ἔζηκα,
> to live, to be possessed of vitality, to exercise the functions of life, Mat. 27.63. Ac. 17.28, et al.; τὸ ζῆν, life, He. 2.15; to have means of subsistence, 1 Co. 9.14; to live, to pass existence *in a specific manner,* Lu. 2.36; 15.13, et al.; to be instinct with life and vigour; *hence,* ζῶν, living, *an epithet of God, in a sense peculiar to Himself;* ἐλπὶς ζῶσα, a vigorous and enduring hope, 1 Pe. 1.3; ὕδωρ ζῶν, a perennial flow of water, Jno 4.10; to be cheered and happy, 1 Thes. 3.8; to be exempt from spiritual condemnation, to have fruition of salvation, 1 Jno. 4.9, et.al.

Ζεστός, ή, όν, (ζέω)
> pr. boiled; boiling, boiling hot; *met.* glowing with zeal, fervent, Re. 3.15, 16.

Ζεῦγος, εος, τό,
> a yoke *of animals*; a pair, couple, Lu 2.24; 14.19.

Ζευκτηρία, ας, ἡ,

   (pr. fem. of ζευκτήριος. fr. ζεύγνυμι, to yoke, join) a fastening, bank, Ac. 27.40.

Ζεύς, Διός, ὁ,

   the supreme God of the Greeks, answering to the Jupiter *of the Romans*, Ac. 14.12, 13.

Ζέω,

   f. ζέσω,

   to boil, to be hot; *in N.T., met.* to be fervent, ardent, zealous, Ac. 18.25. Ro. 12.11

Ζηλεύω,

   f. εύσω,

   i. q. ζηλόω, v.r. Re. 3.19: *from*

Ζῆλος, ου, ὁ (ζέω)

   in a good sense generous rivalry; noble aspiration; *in N.T.*, zeal, ardour in behalf of, ardent affection, Jno 2.17. Ro. 10.2; *in a bad sense*, jealousy, envy, malice, Ac. 13.45. Ro. 13.13; indignation, wrath, Ac. 5.17 et. al. *whence*

Ζηλόω, ῶ,

   f. ώσω,

   to have strong affection towards, be ardently devoted to, 2 Co. 11.2; to make a show of affection and devotion towards, Gal. 4.17; to desire earnestly, 81aspire eagerly after, 1 Co. 12.31; 14.1, 39; *absol.* to be fervent, to be zealous, Re. 3.19; to be jealous, envious, spiteful, Ac. 7.9; 17.5 1 Co. 13.4. Ja 4.2; *pass.* to be an object of warm regard and devotion, Gal. 4.18: *whence*

Ζηλωτής, οῦ, ὁ,

   pr. a generous rival, an imitator; *in N.T.*, an aspirant, 1 Co. 14.12. Tit. 2.14; a devoted adherent, a zealot, Ac. 21.20; 22.3. Gal. 1.14.

Ζημία, ας, ἡ

   damage, loss, detriment, Ac. 27.10, 21. Phi. 3.7, 8: *whence*

Ζημιόω, ῶ,

   f. ώσω,

   to visit with loss or harm; *pass.* to suffer loss or detriment, 1 Co. 3.15. 2 Co. 7.9; to lose, to forfeit, Mat. 16.26. Mar. 8.36. Phi. 3.8.

Ζητέω, ῶ,

   f. ήσω,

   to seek, look for, Mat. 18.12. Lu. 2.48, 49; to search after, Mat. 13.45; to be on the watch for Mat. 26.16; to pursue, endeavour to obtain, Ro. 2.7; 1 Pe. 3.11, et al.; to desire, wish, want, Mat. 12.47; to seek, strive for, Mat. 6.33; to endeavour, Mat. 21.46; to require, demand, ask for, Mar. 8.11. Lu. 11.16; 12.48; to inquire or ask questions, question, Jno. 16.19; to deliberate, Mar. 11.18. Lu. 12.29; *in N.T. fr. Heb.* ζητεῖν τὴν ψυχήν, to seek the life *of any one,* to seek to kill, Mat. 2.20: *whence*

Ζήτημα, ατος, τό,

   a question; a subject of debate or controversy, Ac. 15.2; 18.15; 23.29 et al.

Ζήτησις, εως, ἡ

   a seeking; an inquiry, a question; a dispute, debate, discussion, Jno. 3.25. 1 Ti. 1.4; a subject of dispute or controversy, Ac. 25.20, et al.

Ζιζάνιον, ου, τό,

   zizanium, darnel, spurious wheat, *a plant found in Palestine, which resembles wheat both in its stalk and grain, but is worthless and deleterious,* Mat. 13.26, 27, 29, 30, 36, 38, 40. L.G.

Ζόφος, ου, ὁ,

   gloom, thick darkness, 2 Pe. 2.4, 17. Jude 6, 13

Ζυγός, ου, ὁ,

    a collateral form of ζυγόν, (ζεύγνυμι)
    pr. a cross bar or band; a yoke; *met.* a yoke *of bondage,* state of slavery, servile
    condition, 1 Ti. 6.1; service or obligation, Mat. 11.29, 30. Ac. 15.10. Gal 5.1; the
    beam of a balance; *by synecd.* a balance, pair of scales, Re. 6.5.

Ζύμη, ης, ἡ,

    leaven, Mat. 16.12; 13.33 *met.* leaven *of the mind and conduct,* a system of doctrine
    or morals, *used in a bad sense,* Mat. 16.6, 11. 1 Co. 5.6, et al.: *whence*

Ζυμόω, ῶ,

    f. ώσω,
    to leaven, cause to ferment, Mat. 13.33. Lu. 13.21. 1 Co. 5.6. Gal. 5.9.

Ζωγρέω, ῶ,

    f. ήσω, p. ἐζώγρηκα, (ζωός, alive, & ἀγρεύω)
    pr. to take alive, take prisoner in war *instead of killing;* to take captive, enthral, 2 Ti.
    2.26 *also* to catch animals, *as fish; in which sense it is used figuratively,* Lu. 5.10.

Ζωή, ῆς, ἡ, (ζάω)

    life, animated existence, state of being alive, Lu. 16.25. Ac. 17.25; life, manner of life,
    conduct, Ro. 6.4; *in N.T.,* life, deliverance from the proper penalty of sin, *expressed*
    by θάνατος, Jno. 6.51. Ro. 5.18, et al.; life, the final state of the redeemed, Mat. 25.46,
    et al.; the author of life, means of attaining life, Jno. 5.39; 11.25. Col. 3.4.

Ζώνη, ης, ἡ,

    zone, belt, girdle, Mat. 3.4; 10.9, et al.

Ζώννῡμι, and it N.T. ζωννύω,

    f. ζώσω,
    to gird, gird on, put on one's girdle, Jno. 21.18 *bis.*

Ζωογονέω, ῶ, (ζωός & γόνος)

    f. ήσω,
    to bring forth living creatures; *in N.T.,* to preserve alive, save, Lu. 17.33. Ac. 7.19.

Ζῶον, ου, τό,

    a living creature, animal, He. 13.11. 2 Pe. 2.12, et al.

Ζωοποιέω, ῶ, (ζωός & ποιέω)

    f. ήσω,
    pr. to engender living creatures; to impart life, make alive, vivify, Ro. 4.17; 8.11. 1
    Co. 15.36; *in N.T., met.* to impart the life *of salvation,* Jno. 6.63. 2 Co. 3.6, et al.

Η, η, Ἦτα

Ἤ,

    either, or, Mat. 6.24, et al.; *after comparatives, and* ἄλλος, ἕτερος, *expressed or*
    implied, than, Mat. 10.15, 18.8. Ac. 17.21; 24.21; *intensive after* ἀλλά & πρίν, Lu.
    12.51. Mat. 1.18; *it also serves to point an interrogation,* Ro. 3.29, et al.

Ἦ,

    82*a particle occurring in the N.T. only in the combination* ἦ μήν, *introductory to the*
    terms of an oath, He. 6.14.

Ἡγεμονεύω, (ἡγεμών)

    f. εύσω,
    to be a guide, leader, chief; *in N.T.,* to hold the office of a Roman provincial governor,
    Lu. 2.2; 3.1.

Ἡγεμονία, ας, ἡ,

    leadership, sovereignty; *in N.T.,* a reign, Lu. 3.1: *from*

Ἡγεμών, όνος, ὁ,
    a guide; a leader; a chieftain, prince, Mat. 2.6; a Roman provincial governor, *under whatever title,* Mat. 27.2, et al.
Ἡγέομαι, οῦμαι,
    f. ήσομαι,
    to lead the way; to take the lead, Ac. 14.12; to be chief, to preside, govern, rule, Mat. 2.6. Ac. 7.10; ἡγούμενος, a chief officer *in the church,* He. 13.7, 17,24; *also, with* p. ἥγημαι, to think, consider, count, esteem, regard, Ac. 26.2. 2 Co. 9.5, et al.
Ἡδέως, (ἡδύς)
    adv. with pleasure, gladly, willingly, Mar. 6.20; 12.37. 2 Co. 11.19.
Ἤδη,
    adv. before now, now, already, Mat. 3.10; 5.28, et al.; ἤδη ποτέ, at length, Ro. 1.10. Phi. 4.10.
Ἥδιστα,
    adv. (pr. neut. pl. superlat. of ἡδύς) with the greatest pleasure, most gladly, 2 Co. 12.9, 15.
Ἡδονή, ῆς, ἡ, (ἥδος)
    pleasure, gratification, *esp.* sensual pleassure, Lu. 8.14. Tit. 3.3. Ja. 4.3. 2 Pe. 2.13; a passion, Ja. 4.1.
Ἡδύοσμον, ου, τό, (ἡδύς & <u>ὀσμή</u>)
    garden mint, Mat. 23.23. Lu. 11.42.
Ἦθος, εος, τό,
    pr. a place of customary resort, a haunt; *hence,* a settled habit of mind and manners, 1 Co. 15.33.
Ἥκω,
    f. ἥξω, imperf. ἧκον,
    to be come, have arrived, Lu. 15.27, et al.
Ἡλί, (Heb. אלי)
    my God! Mat. 27.46.
Ἡλικία, ας, ἡ, (ἧλιξ)
    a particular period of life; the period fitted for a particular function, prime, He. 11.11; full age, years of discretion, Jno. 9.21, 23; *perhaps,* the whole duration of life, Mat. 6.27. Lu. 12.25; *otherwise,* stature, Lu. 19.3. Ep. 4.13.
Ἡλίκος, η, ον,
    as great as; how great, Col. 2.1. Ja. 3.5. (ῐ).
Ἥλιος, ου, ὁ,
    the sun, Mat. 13.43; 17.2. Mar. 1.32, et al.; *meton.* light of the sun, light, Ac. 13.11.
Ἧλος, ου, ὁ,
    a nail, Jno. 20.25, *bis.*
Ἡμέρα, ας, ἡ,
    day, a day, the interval from sunrise to sunset, *opp. to* ηύξ, Mat. 4.2; 12.40. Lu 2.44; the interval of twenty-four hours, *comprehending day and night,* Mat. 6.34; 15.32; *fr. the Heb.* ἡμέρᾳ καὶ ἡμέρᾳ, day by day, every day, 2 Co. 4.16; ἡμέραν ἐξ ἡμέρας, from day to day, continually, 2 Pe. 2.8; καθ' ἡμέραν, every day, daily, Ac. 17.17. He. 3.13; a point or period of time, Lu. 19.42. Ac. 15.7. Ep. 6.13 et al.; a judgment, trial, 1 Co. 4.3.
Ἡμέτερος, α, ον,
    our, Ac. 2.11; 24.6, et al.
Ἡμιθᾰνής, έος, οῦς, ὁ, ἡ, (ἡμι— & <u>θνήσκω</u>)
    half dead, Lu. 10.30.

Ἥμῑσυς, σεια, συ,
> half, Mar. 6.23. Lu. 19.8. Re. 11.11; 12.14.

Ἡμιώριον, ου, τό, (ἡμι— & ὥρα)
> half an hour, Re. 8.1. L.G.

Ἡνίκα,
> *adv.* when, 2 Co. 3.15, 16. (ῑ)

Ἥπερ, (ἤ & περ)
> *an emphatic form of* ἤ, than, Jno. 12.43.

Ἥπιος, ου, ὁ, ἡ,
> mild, gentle, kinid, 1 Thes. 2.7. 2 Ti. 2.24.

Ἤρεμος, ου, ὁ, ἡ,
> *equivalent to the ordinary form* ἠρεμαῖος, tranquil, quiet, 1 Ti. 2.2. N.T.

Ἡρωδιανοί, ῶν, οἱ,
> Herodians, partisans of Ἡρώδης, Herod Antipas, Mat. 22.16. Mar. 3.6; 12.13.

Ἡσυχάζω, (ἥσυχος)
> f. άσω,
> to be still, at rest; to live peaceably, be quiet, 1 Thes. 4.11; to rest *from labour,* Lu. 23.56; to be silent or quiet, acquiesce, to desist *from discussion* Lu. 14.4. Ac. 11.18; 21.14.

Ἡσυχία, ας, ἡ,
> rest, quiet, tranquillity; a quiet tranquil life, 2 Thes. 3.12; silence, silent attention, Ac. 22.2. 1 Ti. 2.11, 12.

Ἡσύχιος, ου, ὁ, ἡ,
> *equivalent to* ἥσῦχος, quiet, tranquil, peaceful, 1 Ti. 2.2. 1 Pe. 3.4.

Ἤτοι, (ἤ & τοι)
> *conj. in N.T. only in the usage,* ἤτοι— ἤ, whether, *with an elevated tone,* Ro. 6.16.

Ἡττάομαι, ῶμαι,
> 83f. ἡττηθησομαι & ἡττήσομαι, p. ἥττημαι, (ἥττων)
> to be less, inferior to; to fare worse, to be in a less favoured condition, 2 Co. 12.13; *by impl.* to be overcome, vanquished, 2 Pe. 2.19, 20: *whence*

Ἥττημα, ατος, τό,
> an inferiority *to a particular standard;* default, failure, shortcoming, Ro. 11.12 1 Co. 6.7. S.

Ἥττων, *Att. for* ἥσσων, ονος, ὁ, ἡ,
> less, 2 Co. 12.15; worse, 1 Co. 11.17.

Ἠχέω, ῶ, (ἠχή)
> f. ήσω,
> to sound, ring, 1 Co. 13.1; to roar, *as the sea,* Lu. 21.25.

Ἦχος, ου, ὁ,
> *equivalent to* ἠχή, sound, noise, Ac. 2.2. He. 12.19; *met.* report, fame, rumour, Lu. 4.37.

Θ, θ, *Θῆτα*

Θάλασσα, ης, ἡ
> the sea, Mat. 23.15. Mar. 9.42; a sea, Ac. 7.36; an inland sea, lake, Mat. 8.24, et al.

Θάλπω,
> f. ψς,
> to impart warmth; *met.* to cherish, nurse, foster, Ep. 5.29. 1 Thes. 2.7.

Θαμβέω, ῶ,

f. ήσω, a.1. ἐθάμβησα,
to be astonished, amazed, Ac. 9.6; *later, pass.* to be astonished, amazed, awe-struck, Mar. 1.27; 10.24, 32: *from*

Θάμβος, εος, τό,
astonishment, amazement, awe, Lu. 4.36, et al.

Θανάσῐμος, ου, ὁ, ἡ, (θάνατος)
deadly, mortal, fatal, Mar. 16.18.

Θανατηφόρος, ου, ὁ, ἡ, (θάνατος & φέρω)
mortiferous, bringing or causing death, deadly, fatal, Ja. 3.8.

Θάνᾰτος, ου, ὁ (θνήσκω)
death, the extinction of life, *whether naturally,* Lu. 2.26. Mar. 9.1; *or violently,* Mat. 10.21; 15.4; imminent danger of death, 2 Co. 4.11, 12; 11.23; *in N.T.* death, *as opposed to* ζωή *in its spiritual sense,* spiritual condemnation, exclusion from salvation, the penal state of loss of salvation. Jno. 8.51. Ro. 6.16, et al.: *whence*

Θανατόω, ῶ,
f. ώσω, a.1. ἐθανάτωσα,
to put to death, deliver to death, Mat. 10.21; 26.59. Mar. 13.12; *pass.* to be exposed to imminent danger of death, Ro. 3.36; *in N.T., met.* to subdue, mortify, Ro. 8.13; *pass.* to be dead to, to be rid, parted from, *as if by the intervention of death,* Ro. 7.4.

Θάπτω,
f. ψω, τέτᾰφα, a.1. ἔθαχα, a.2. pass ἐτάφην,
to bury, inter, Mat. 8.21, 22; 14.12, et al.

Θαρσέω, ῶ, & new Attic, θαρρέω, ῶ, (θάρσος, θάρρος),
f. ήσω, imperat. θάρσει,
to be of good courage, be of good cheer, Mat. 9.2, et al.; to be confident, hopeful, 2 Co. 7.16, et al.; to be bold, maintain a bold bearing, 2 Co. 10.1, 2.

Θάρσος, εος, τό,
courage, confidence, Ac. 28.15.

Θαῦμα, ατος, τό,
a wonder; wonder, admiration, astonishment, Re. 17.6: *whence*

Θαυμάζω,
f. άσω, p. τεθαύμακα, a.1. ἐθαύμασα,
to admire, regard with adminration, wonder at, Lu. 7.9. Ac. 7.31; to reverence, adore, 2 Thes. 1.10; *absol* to wonder, be filled with wonder, admiration, or astonishment, Mat. 8.10. Lu. 4.22, et al.; *whence*

Θαυμάσιος, α, ον,
wonderful, admirable, marvellous; τὸ θαυμάσιον, a wonder, wonderful work, Mat. 21.13.

Θαθμαστός, ή, όν,
wondrous, glorious, 1 Pe. 2.9. Re. 15.1; marvellous, strange, uncommon, Mat. 21.42. Mar. 12.11.

Θεά, ᾶς, ἡ, (Θεός)
a goddess, Ac. 19.27, 35, 37.

Θεάομαι, ῶμαι,
f. άσομαι, p. τεθέᾱμαι, a.1. pass. ἐθεάθην,
to gaze upon, Mat. 6.1; 23.5. Lu. 7.24; to see, discern with the eyes, Mar. 16.11, 14. Lu. 5.27. Jno. 1.14, 32, 38, et al.; to see, visit, Ro. 15.24.

Θεατρίζομαι,
to be exposed as in a theatre, be made a gazing-stock, object of scorn, He. 10.33 (N.T.) *from*

Θέᾱτρον, ου, τό, (θεάομαι)
  a theatre, a place where public games and spectacles are exhibited, Ac. 19.29, 31; *meton.* a show, gazing-stock, 1 Co. 4.9.

Θεῖον, ου, τό,
  brimstone, sulphur, Lu. 17.29. Re. 9.17.18, et al.

Θεῖος, α, ον, (Θεός)
  divine, pertaining to God, 2 Pe. 1.3, 4; τὸ θεῖον, 84the divine nature, divinity, Ac. 17.29: *whence*

Θειότης, τητος, ἡ,
  divinity, deity, godhead, divine majesty, Ro. 1.20. L.G.

Θειώδης, εος, ους, ὁ, ἡ, (θεῖον)
  of brimstone, sulphurous, Re. 9.17. L.G.

Θέλημα, ατος, τό, (θέλω)
  will, bent, inclination, 1 Co. 16.12. Ep. 2.3. 1 Pe. 4.3; resolve, 1 Co. 7.37; will, purpose, design, 2 Ti. 2.26. 2 Pe. 1.21; will, sovereign pleasure, behest, Mat. 18.14. Lu. 12.47. Ac. 13.22, et al. freq.; ἐν τῷ θελήματι Θεοῦ, Deo permittente, if God please or permit, Ro. 1.10. S.

Θέλησις, εως, ἡ,
  will, pleasure, He. 2.4: (L.G.) *from*

Θέλω,
  see ἐθέλω.

Θεμέλιος, ίου, ὁ, (pr. an adj. fr. θέμα, τίθημι)
  θεμέλιον, τό, a foundation, Lu. 6.48, 49. He. 11.10; *met.* a foundation *laid in elementary instruction,* He. 6.1; a foundation *of a superstructure of faith, doctrine, or hope,* 1 Co. 3.10, 11, 12. Ep. 2.20. 1 Ti. 6.19; a foundation *laid in a commencement of preaching the gospel,* Ro. 15.20: *whence*

Θεμελιόω, ῶ,
  f. ώσω, p. τεθεμελίωκα, a.1. ἐθεμελίωσα,
  to found, lay the foundation of, Mat. 7.25. Lu. 6.48. He. 1.10; *met.* to ground, establish, render firm and unwavering, Ep. 3.17. Col. 1.23. 1 Pe. 5.10.

Θεοδίδακτος, ου, ὁ, ἡ (Θεός & διδακτός)
  taught of God, divinely instructed, 1 Thes. 4.9. N.T.

Θεομᾰχέω, ῶ, (Θεός & μάχομαι)
  f. ήσω,
  to fight or content against God, to seek to counteract the divine will, Ac. 23.9.

Θεομάχος, ου, ὁ,
  fighting against God, in conflict with God, Ac. 5.39. (ᾰ). N.T.

Θεόπνευστος, ου, ὁ, ἡ, (Θεός & πνέω)
  divinely inspired, 2 Ti. 3.16. L.G.

Θεός, οῦ, ὁ & ἡ,
  a deity, Ac. 7.43. 1 Co. 8.5; an idol, Ac. 7.40. **GOD**, the true God, Mat. 3.9, et al. freq.; God, possessed of true godhead, Jno. 1.1. Ro. 9.5; *fr. the Heb. applied to potentates,* Jno. 10.34, 25; ᾧ θεῷ *an intensive term, fr. the Heb.,* exceedingly, Ac. 7.20, &, *perhaps* 2 Co. 10.4.

Θεοσέβεια, ας, ἡ,
  worshipping of God, reverence towards God, piety, 1 Ti. 2.10: *from*

Θεοσεβής, έος, οῦς, ὁ, ἡ, (Θεός & σέβομαι)
  reverencing God, pious, godly, devout, a sincere worshipper of God, Jno. 9.31.

Θεοστῠγής, έος, οῦς, ὁ, ἡ, (Θεός & στυγέω, to hate)
  God-hated; *in N.T.,* a hater and contemner of God, Ro. 1.30.

Θεότης, τητος, ἡ, (Θεός)
    divinity, deity, godhead, Col. 2.9. L.G.
Θεραπεία,
    service, attendance; healing, cure, Lu. 9.11; Re. 22.2; *meton.* those who render
    service, servants, domestics, family, household, Mat. 24.45. Lu. 12.42: *from*
Θεραπεύω,
    f. εύσς, a.1. ἐθεράπευσα,
    to serve, minister to, render service and attendance; to render divine service, worship,
    Ac. 17.25; to heal, cure, Mat. 4.23, 24; 8.16, et al.: *from*
Θεράπων, οντος, ὁ,
    an attendant, a servant; a minister, He. 3.5.
Θερίζω, (θέρος)
    ίσω, a.1. ἐθέρισα,
    to gather in harvest, reap, Mat. 6.26; 25.24, 26; *met.* to reap *the reward of labour,* 1
    Co. 9.11. 2 Co. 9.6; to reap *the harvest of vengeance,* Re. 14.15, 16: *whence*
Θερισμός, οῦ, ὁ,
    harvest, the act of gathering the harvest, reaping, Jno. 4.23, et al.; *met.* the harvest *of*
    the Gospel, Mat. 9.37, 38, Lu. 10.2; a crop; *met.* the crop *of vengeance,* Re. 14.15
Θεριστής, οῦ, ὁ,
    one who gathers in the harvest, a reaper, Mat. 13.30, 39.
Θερμαίνω,
    f. ανῶ,
    to warm; *mid.* to warm one's self, Mar. 14.54, 67. Jno. 18.18, 25. Ja. 2.16: *from*
Θέρμη, ης, ἡ, (θερμός, θέρω)
    heat, warmth, Ac. 28.3.
Θέρος, εος, τό,
    the warm season of the year, summer, Mat. 24.32. Mar. 13.38. Lu. 21.30.
Θεωρέω, ῶ,
    f. ήσω,
    to be a spectator, to gaze on, contemplate; to behold, view *with interest and attention*
    Mat. 27.55; 28.1, et al.; 85to contemplate *mentally,* consider, He. 7.4; *in N.T.,* to see,
    perceive, Mar. 3.11, et al.; to come to a knowledge of, Jno. 6.40 *fr. the Heb.* to
    experience, undergo, Jno. 8.51, et al.:
Θεωρία, ας, ἡ,
    a beholding; a sight, spectacle, Lu. 23.48.
Θήκη, ης, ἡ, (τίθημι)
    a repository, receptacle; a case, sheath, scabbard, Jno. 18.11.
Θηλάζω, (θηλή, a nipple)
    f. άσω, a.1. ἐθήλασα,
    to suckle, give suck, Mat. 24.19. Mar. 13.17. Lu. 21.23; 23.29; to suck, Mat. 21.16.
    Lu. 11.27.
Θῆλυς, θήλεια, θῆλυ,
    female; τὸ θῆλυ, sc. γενός, a female, Mat. 19.4. Mar. 10.6. Ga. 3.28; ἡ θήλεια,
    woman, Ro. 1.26, 27.
Θήρα, ας, ἡ, (θήρ, a wild beast)
    hunting, the chase; *met.* means of capture, a cause of destruction, Ro. 11.9: *whence*
Θηρεύω,
    f. εύσω,
    to hunt, catch; *met.* to seize on, lay hold of, Lu. 11.54.
Θηριομαχέω, ῶ, (θηρίον & μάχομαι)

f. ήσω, a.1. ἐθηριομάχησα,

to fight with wild beasts; *met.* to be exposed to furious hostility, 1 Co. 15.32. L.G.

Θηρίον, ου, τό, (equivalent to θήρ, but pr. a dmin. from it)

a beast, wild animal, Mar. 1.13. Ac. 10.12, et al.; *met.* a brutish man, Tit. 1.12.

Θησαυρίζω,

f. ίσω, a.1. ἐθησαύρισα,

to collect and lay up stores or wealth, treasure up, Mat. 6.19, 20; to heap up, accumulate, Ro. 2.5. 1 Co. 16.2; to reserve, keep in store, 2 Pe. 3.7: *from*

Θησαυρός, οῦ, ὁ,

a treasury, a store, treasure, precious deposit, Mat. 6.19, 20, 21, et al.; a receptacle in which precious articles are kept, a casket, Mat. 2.11; a store house, Mat. 12.35.

Θιγγάνω,

f. θίξομαι, a.2. ἔθιγον,

to touch, Col. 2.21. He. 12.20; to harm, He. 11.28.

Θλίβω,

f. ψω, p. pass. τέθλιμμαι,

to squeeze, press; to press upon, emcumber, throng, crowd, Mar. 3.9; *met.* to distress, afflict, 2 Co. 1.6; 4.8, et al.; *pass.* to be compressed, narrow, Mat. 7.14: (ῑ) *whence*

Θλῖψις, εως, ἡ

pr. pressure, compression; *met.* affliction, distress *of mind,* 2 Co. 2.4; distressing circumstances, trail, affliction, Mat. 24.9, et al. L.G.

Θνήσκω,

f. θανοῦμαι, p. τέθνηκα, a.2. ἔθανον,

to die; *in N.T., only in the p. and plup.,* τέθηνκα, ἐτεθνήκειν, to be dead, Mat. 2.20; Mar. 15.44, et al.: *whence*

Θνητός, ή, όν,

mortal, obnoxious to death, Ro. 6.12; 8.11. 2 Co. 4.11; τὸ θνητόν, mortality, 1 Co. 15.53, 54. 2 Co. 5.4.

Θορυβέω, ῶ,

f. ήσω,

intrans. to make a din, uproar; *trans.* to disturb, throw into commotion, Ac. 17.5; *in N.T., mid.* to manifest agitation of mind, to raise a lament, Mat. 9.23. Mar. 5.39. Ac. 20.10: *from*

Θόρῠβος, ου, ὁ,

an uproar, din; an outward expression of mental agitation, Mar. 5.38; a tumult, commotion, Mat. 26.5, et al.

Θραύω,

f. αύσω, pass. p. part. τεθραυσμένος,

to break, shiver; *met.* shattered, crushed *by cruel oppression,* Lu. 4.18.

Θρέμμα, ατος, τό, (τρέφω)

that which is reared; *pl.* cattle, Jno. 4.12.

Θρηνέω, ῶ,

f. ήσω, a.1. ἐθρήνησα,

to lament, bewail, Mat. 11.17. Lu. 7.32. Jno. 16.20: *from*

Θρῆνος, ου, ὁ, (θρέομαι, to shriek)

wailing, lamentation, Mat. 2.18.

Θρησκεία, ας, ἡ,

religious worship, Col. 2.18; religion, a religious system, Ac. 26.5; religion, piety, Ja. 1.26, 27: *from*

Θρῆσκος, ου, ὁ, ἡ,

occupied with religious observances; *in N.T.,* religious, devout, pious, Ja. 1.26.

Θριαμβεύω, (θρίαμβος, a hymn in hornour of Bacchus; a triumph)

    f. εύσω

    pr. to celebrate a triumph; *trans.* to lead in triumph, celebrate a triumph over, Col. 2.15; *in N.T.* to cause to triumph, 2 Co. 2.14. L.G.

Θρίξ, τρῐχός, ἡ,

    pl. αἱ τρίχες, dat. θριξί, the hair *of the head,* Mat. 5.36; 10.30, et al.; *of an animal,* Mat. 3.4. Mar. 1.6

Θροέω, ῶ, (θρόος, an uproar, fr. θρέομαι)

    to make a clamour to cry aloud; *in N.T., pass.* 86to be disturbed, disquieted, alarmed, terrified, Mat. 24.6. Mar. 13.7. 2 Th. 2.2.

Θρόμβος, ου, ὁ,

    a lump; *espec.* a clot *of blood,* Lu. 22.44.

Θρόνος, ου, ὁ, (θράω, to set)

    a seat, a throne, Mat. 5.34; 19.28. Lu. 1.52; *meton.* power, dominion, Lu. 1.32. He. 1.8; a potentate, Col. 1.16, et al.

Θῠγάτηρ, τέρος, τρός,

    dat. τέρι, τρί, acc. τέρα, voc. θύγατερ, ἡ,

    a daughter, Mat. 9.18; 10.35, 37; *in the vocative, an expression of affection and kindness,* Mat. 9.22; *fr. the Heb.* one of the female posterity *of any one,* Lu. 1.5; *met.* a city, Mat. 21.5. Jno. 12.15; *pl.* female inhabitants, Lu. 23.28: (ἄ) *whence dimin.*

Θυγάτριον, ίου, τό,

    a little daughter, female child, Mar. 5.23; 7.25.

Θύελλα, ης, ἡ, (θύω)

    a tempest, whirlwind, hurricane, He. 12.18.

Θύϊνος, η, ον,

    thyine, of θυΐα, thya, *an aromatic everygreen tree, arbor vitœ, resembling the cedar, and found in Lybia,* Re. 18.12. (ῐ).

Θυμίᾱμα, ατος, τό, (θυμιάω)

    incense, any odoriferous substance burnt in religious worship, Re. 5.8; 8.3, 4; 18.13; *or,* the act of burning incense, Lu. 1.10, 11.

Θυμιᾱτήριον, ίου, τό,

    a censer *for burning incense,* He. 9.4: *from*

Θυμιάω, ῶ, (θύω)

    f. άσω,

    to burn incense, Lu. 1.9.

Θυμομᾰχέω, ῶ, (θυμός & μάχομαι)

    f. ήσω,

    to wage war fiercely; to be warmly hostile to, be enraged against, Ac. 12.20. L.G.

Θῡμός, ου, ὁ, (θύω)

    pr. the soul, mind; *hence,* a strong passion or emotion of the mind; anger, wrath, Lu. 4.28. Ac. 19.28, et al.; *pl.* swellings of anger, 2 Co. 12.20. Ga. 5.20: *whence*

Θυμόω, ῶ,

    f. ώσω,

    to provoke to anger; *pass.* to be angered, enraged, Mat. 2.16.

Θύρα, ας, ἡ,

    a door, gate, Mat. 6.6. Mar. 1.33; an entrance, Mat. 27.60, et al.; *in N.T., met.* an opening, occasion, opportunity, Ac. 14.27. 1 Co. 16.9, et al.; *meton.* a medium or means of entrance, Jno. 10.7, 9: *whence*

Θυρεός, οῦ, ὁ,

a stone or other material employed to close a doorway, *later,* a large oblong shield, Ep. 6.16.

Θυρίς, ίδος, ή

a small opening; a window, Ac. 20.9. 2 Co. 11.33.

Θυρωρός, οῦ, ὁ (θύρα & οὖρος, a keeper)

a door-keeper, porter, Mar. 13.34. Jno. 10.3; 18.16, 17.

Θυσία, ας, ή, (θύω)

sacrifice, act of sacrificing, He. 9.26; the thing sacrificed, a victim, Mat. 9.13; 12.7; the flesh of victims, *eaten by the sacrificers,* 1 Co. 10.18; *in N.T.,* an offering or service *to God,* Phi. 4.18, et al.

Θυσιαστήριον, ίου, τό,

an altar, Mat. 5.23, 24. Lu. 1.11, et al.; *spc.* the altar of burnt offering, Mat. 23.35. Lu. 11.51; *meton.* a class of sacrifices, He. 13.10: (S.) *from*

Θύω,

f. θύσω, p. τεθῦκα, a.1. ἔθῦσα, pass. p. τέθυμαι, a.1. ἐτύθην,

to offer; to kill in sacrifice, sacrefice, immolate, Ac. 14.13, 18, et al.; *in N.T.,* to slaughter *for food,* Mat. 22.4, et al. (-ῦ in θύω, ῠ in ἐτύθην).

Θώραξ, ᾱκος, ὁ,

a breastplate, armour for the body, *consisting of two parts, one covering the breast and the other the back,* Re. 9.9, 17. Ep. 6.14. 1 Th. 5.8.

I, ι, Ἰῶτα

Ἴᾱμα, ατος, το,

healing, cure, 1 Co. 12.9, 28, 30: *from*

Ἰάομαι, ῶμαι,

f. ἀσομαι, a.1. ἰᾱσάμην, p. pass. ἴᾱμαι, a.1. ἰάθην,

to heal, cure, Mat. 8.8. Lu. 9.2; *met.* to heal *spiritually,* restore from a state of sin and condemnation, Mat. 13.15. He. 12.13, et al.: *whence*

Ἴᾱσις, εως, ή,

healing, cure, Lu. 13.32. Ac. 4.22, 30.

Ἴασπις, ιδος, ή,

jasper, *a precious stone of various colours as purple, cerulean, green,* &c. Re. 4.3; 21.11, 18, 19.

Ἰᾱτρος, οῦ, ὁ, (ἰάομαι)

a physician, Mat. 9.12. Mar. 2.17; 5.26, et al.

Ἴδε, or ἰδέ, imperat. of εἶδον, *used as an interj.,*

lo! behold! Jno. 11.36; 16.29; 19.4, 5, et al.

Ἰδέα, ας, ή, (ἰδεῖν)

form; look, aspect, Mat. 28.3.

Ἴδιος, ια, ιον,

87one's own, Mar. 15.20. Jno. 7.18, et al.; due, proper, specially assigned, Ga. 6.9. 1 Ti. 2.6; 6.15. Tit. 1.3; *also used in N.T. as a simple possessive,* Eph. 5.22, et al.; τὰ ἴδια, one's home, household, people, Jno. 1.11; 16.32; 19.27; οἱ ἴδιοι, members of one's household, friends, Jno. 1.11. Ac. 24.23, et al.; ἰδίᾳ, *adverbially,* severally, respectively, 1 Co. 12.11; κατ' ἰδίαν, *adv.* privately, aside, by one's self, alone, Mat. 14.13, 23, et al.; *whence*

Ἰδιώτης, ου, ὁ,

pr. one in private life; one devoid of special learning or gifts, a plain person, Ac. 4.13. 1 Co. 14.16, 23, 24. 2 Co. 11.6.

Ἰδού, *varied in accent from* ἰδοῦ,
    imperat. of εἰδόμην, *a particle serving to call attention,* lo! Mat. 1.23. Lu. 1.38. Ac. 8.36, et al. freq.
Ἰδρώς, ῶτος, ὁ, (ἶδος, sweat)
    sweat, Lu. 22.44.
Ἱερᾱτεία, ας, ἡ,
    priesthood, sacerdotal office, Lu. 1.9.
Ἱεράτευμα, ατος, τό,
    a priesthood; *meton.* a body of priests, 1 Pe. 2.5, 9: (S.) *from*
Ἱερατεύω,
    to officiate as a priest, perform sacred rites, Lu. 1.8: *from*
Ἱερεύς, έως, ὁ, (ἱερός)
    a priest, one who performs sacrificial rites, Mat. 8.4. Lu. 1.5. Jno. 1.19, et al.
Ἱερόθῡτος, ου, ὁ, ἡ, (ἱερός & θύω)
    offered in sacrifice, v.r. 1 Co. 10.28.
Ἱερόν, ου, ὁ (ἱερός)
    a temple, Mat. 4.5. Lu. 4.9. Ac. 19.27, et al.
Ἱεροπρεπής, έος, οῦς, ὁ, ἡ, (ἱερός & πρέπει)
    beseeming what is sacred; becoming holy persons, Tit. 2.3.
Ἱερός, ά, όν,
    hallowed; holy, divine, 2 Ti. 3.15; τὰ ἱερά, sacred rites, 1 Co. 9.13. *bis.*
Ἱεροσολυμίτης, ου, ὁ,
    an inhabitant, of Ἱεροσόλυμα, v. Ἱερουσαλήμ, Jerusalem, Mar. 1.5. Jno. 7.25. (ῑτ).
Ἱεροσῡλέω, ῶ,
    f. ήσω,
    to despoil temples, commit sacrilege, Ro. 2.22: *from*
Ἱερόσῡλος, ου, ὁ, ἡ (ἱερός & συλάω)
    one who despoils temples, commits sacrilege, Ac. 19.37.
Ἱερουργέω, ῶ, ἱερός & ἔργον)
    f. ήσω,
    to officiate as priest, perform sacred rites; *in N.T.,* to minister *in a divine commission,* Ro. 15.16. L.G.
Ἱερωσύνη, ης, ἡ, (ἱερεύς)
    priesthood, sacerdotal office, He. 7.11, 12, 14, 24. (ῡ).
Ἰησοῦς, οῦ, ὁ, (Heb. יֵשׁוּעַ contr. יֵשׁוּ)
    a Saviour, Jesus, Mat. 1.21, 25; 2.1, et al. freq.; Joshua, Ac. 7.45. He. 4.8; Jesus, *a Jewish Christian,* Col. 4.11.
Ἱκᾰνός, ή, όν, (ἵκω, v. ἱκάνω, to arrive at, reach to)
    befitting; sufficient, enough, Lu. 22.38; ἱκανὸν ποιεῖν τινί, to satisfy, gratify, Mar. 15.15; τὸ ἱκανὸν λαμβάνειν, to take security or bail *of any one,* Ac. 17.9; *of persons,* adequate, competent, qualified, 2 Co. 2.16; fit, worthy, Mat. 3.11; 8.8; *of number or quantity,* considerable, large, great, much, *and pl.* many, Mat. 28.12. Mar. 10.46, et al.: *whence*
Ἱκανότης, τητος, ἡ,
    sufficiency, ability, fitness, qualification, 2 Co. 3.5.
Ἱκανόω, ῶ,
    f. ώσω, a.1. ἱκάνωσα,
    to make sufficient or competent, qualify, 2 Co. 3.6. Col. 1.12. L.G.
Ἱκετηρία, ας, ἡ, (fem. of ἱκετήριος, sc. ῥάβδος, fr. ἱκέτης, suppliant)
    pr. an olive branch, *borne by suppliants in their hands;* supplication, He. 5.7.

Ἰκμάς, άδος, ή,
  moisture, Lu. 8.6.
Ἱλᾰρός, ά, όν,
  cheerful, not grudging, 2 Co. 9.7. *whence*
Ἱλαρότης, τητος, ή,
  cheerfulness, Ro. 12.8. L.G.
Ἱλάσκομαι,
  f. ἱλάσομαι, a.1. ἱλάσθην,
  to appease, render propitious; *in N.T.,* to expiate, make an atonement or expiation for,
  He. 2.17; ἱλάσθητι, be gracious, show mercy, pardon, Lu. 18.13: *whence*
Ἱλασμός, οῦ, ὁ,
  propitiation, expiation; one who makes expiation, 1 Jno. 2.2; 4.10.
Ἱλαστήριος, α, ον, (ἱλάσκομαι)
  propitiatory; invested with propitiatory power, Ro. 3.25; *in N.T. & S.,* τὸ ἱλαστήριον,
  the cover of the ark of the covenant, the mercy-seat, He. 9.5.
Ἵλεως, ων, ὁ, ή, (Att. for ἵλαος,)
  propitious, favorable, merciful, clement, He. 8.12; *fr. the Heb.* ἵλεώς σοι (ὁ Θεός),
  88God have mercy on thee, God forbid, far be it from thee, Mat. 16.22.
Ἱμάς, άντος, ὁ,
  a strap or thong of leather, Ac. 22.25; a shoe-latchet, Mar. 1.7. Lu. 3.16. Jno. 1.27.
Ἱματίζω,
  f. ίσω, p. pass. ἱμάτισμαι,
  to clothe; *pass.* to be clothed, Mar. 5.15. Lu. 8.35: (N.T.) *from*
Ἱμάτιον, ίου, τό, (ἕννυμι, εἶμα)
  a garment; the upper garment, mantle, Mat. 5.40; 9.16, 20, 21; *pl.* the mantle and tunic
  together, Mat. 26.65; *pl. genr.* garments, raiment, Mat. 11.8; 24.18, et al.
Ἱματισμός, οῦ, ὁ, (ἱματίζω)
  a garment; raiment, apparel, clothing, Lu. 7.25; 9.29, et al. L.G.
Ἱμείρω & ἱμείρομαι, (ἵμερος, desire)
  to desire earnestly; *by impl.* to have a strong affection for, love fervently, 1 Th. 2.8.
Ἵνα,
  conj. that, in order that, Mat. 19.13. Mar. 1.38. Jno. 1.22; 3.15; 17.1; ἵνα μή, that not,
  lest, Mat. 7.1; *in N.T., equivalent to* ὥστε, so that, so as that, Jno. 9.2, et al.; *also,*
  marking a simple circumstance, the circumstance that, Mat. 10.25. Jno. 4.34; 6.29. 1
  Jno. 4.17; 5.3, et al.
Ἵνατι, (ἵνα & τί)
  adv. why is it that? wherefore? why? Mat. 9.4; 27.46, et al.
Ἰός, οῦ, ὁ,
  a missile, weapon, arrow, dart; venom, poison, Ro. 3.13. Ja. 3.8; rust, ærugo, Ja. 5.3.
Ἰουδαία, ας, ή (Ἰουδαῖος)
  Judea, Mat. 2.1, 5, 22; 3.1, et al.; *meton.* the inhabitants of Judea, Mat. 3.5.
Ἰουδαΐζω, (fr. same)
  f. ίσω,
  to judaise, live like a Jew, follow the manners and customs of the Jews, Ga. 2.14.
Ἰουδαϊκός, ή, όν, (fr. same)
  Jewish, current among the Jews, Tit. 1.14: *whence*
Ἰουδαϊκῶς,
  adv. Jewishly, in the manner of Jews, Ga. 2.14.
Ἰουδαῖος, αία, αῖον,
  Jewish, Mar. 1.5. Jno. 3.22. Ac. 16.1; 24.24.

Ἰουδαῖος, ου, ὁ (Heb. יְדוּהִי)

    pr. one sprung from the tribe of Judah, or a subject of the kingdom of Judah; *in N.T.,* a descendant of Jacob, a Jew, Mat. 28.15. Mar. 1.3, Ac. 19.34. Ro. 2.28, 29, et al.

Ἰουδαϊσμος, ου, ὁ,

    Judaism, the character and condition of a Jew; practice of the Jewish religion, Ga. 1.13, 14.

Ἱππεύς, έως, ὁ (ἵππος)

    a horseman; *pl.* ἵππεις, horsemen, cavalry, Ac. 23.23, 32.

Ἱππικός, ή, όν,

    equestrian; τό ἱππικόν, cavalry, horse, Re. 9.16: *from*

Ἵππος, ου, ὁ

    a horse, Ja. 3.3. Re. 6.2, 4, 5, 8, et al.

Ἴρις, ἴριδος,

    a rainbow, iris, Re. 4.3; 10.1.

Ἰσάγγελος, ου, ὁ, ἡ, (ἴσος & ἄγγελος)

    equal or similar to angels, Lu. 20.36. N.T.

Ἴσᾶσι,

    3 pl. of οἶδα, *usually in N.T.,* οἴδασι, Ac. 26.4.

Ἴσος, η, ον,

    equal, like, Mat. 20.12. Lu. 6.34, et al.; *neut. pl.* ἴσα, *adverbially,* on an equality, Phi. 2.6; *met.* correspondent, consistent, Mar. 14.56, 59: *whence*

Ἰσότης, τητος, ἡ,

    equality, equal proportion, 2 Co. 8.13, 14; fairness, equity, what is equitable, Col. 4.1.

Ἰσότῑμος, ου, ὁ, ἡ, (ἴσος & τιμή)

    of equal price, equally precious or valuable, 2 Pe. 1.1.

Ἰσόψῡχος, ου, ὁ, ἡ, (ἴσος & ψυχή)

    like-minded, of the same mind and spirit, Phil. 2.20.

Ἰσραηλίτης, ου, ὁ,

    an Israelite, a descendant of Ἰσραήλ, Israel or Jacob, Jno. 1.48. Ac. 2.22, et al.

Ἴστημι, and in N.T. ἱστάω, ῶ,

    f. στήσω, a.1. ἔστησα,

    trans. to make to stand, set, place, Mat. 4.5, et al.; to set forth, appoint, Ac. 1.23; to fix, appoint, Ac. 17.31; to establish, confirm, Ro. 10.3. He. 10.9; to set down, impute, Ac. 7.60; to weigh out, pay, Mat. 26.15;

    intrans. p. ἔστηκα, inf. ἑστάναι, part. ἑστώς, plup. εἰστήκειν, a.2. ἔστην, pass. ἴσταμαι, f. σταθήσομαι, a.1. ἑστάθην (ἄ), to stand, Mat. 12.46, et al.; to stand fast, be firm, be permanent, endure, Mat. 12.25. Eph. 6.13, et al.; to be confirmed, proved, Mat. 18.16. 2 Co. 13.1; to stop, Lu. 7.14; 8.44. Ac. 8.38, et al.

Ἱστορέω, ῶ, (ἵστωρ, knowing)

    f. ήσω,

    89to ascertain by inquiry and examination; to inquire of; *in N.T.,* to visit *in order to become acquainted with,* Ga. 1.18.

Ἰσχῡρός, ά, όν,

    strong, mighty, rebust, Mat. 12.29. Lu. 11.21; powerful, mighty, 1 Co. 1.27; 4.10. 1 Jno. 2.14; strong, fortified, Re. 18.18; vehement, Mat. 14.30; energetic, 2 Co. 10.10; sure, firm, He. 6.18, et al.: *from*

Ἰσχύς, ύος, ἡ

    strength, might, power, Re. 18.2. Eph. 1.19; faculty, ability, 1 Pe. 4.11. Mar. 12.30, 33. Lu. 10.27: *whence*

Ἰσχύω,

f. ύσω, a.1. ἴσχῡσα,

to be strong, be well, be in good health, Mat. 9.12; to have power, be able, Mat. 8.28; 26.40; to have power or efficiency, avail, be valid, Ga. 5.6. He. 9.17; to be of service, be serviceable, Mat. 5.13; *meton.* to prevail, Ac. 19.16. Re. 12.8, et al. (ῡ).

Ἴσως, (ἴσος)

adv. equally; perhaps, it may be that, Lu. 20.13.

Ἰταλικός, ή, όν,

Italian, Ac. 10.1.

Ἰχθύδιον, ου, τό,

a small fish, Mat. 15.34. Mar. 8.7: *dimin. of*

Ἰχθύς, ύος, ὁ,

a fish, Mat. 15.36; 17.27. Lu. 5.6, et al.

Ἴχνος, εος, τό (ἵκω)

a footstep, track; *in N.T., pl.* footsteps, line of conduct, Ro. 4.12. 2 Co. 12.18. 1 Pe. 2.21.

Ἰῶτα,

indec. τό, iota; *in N.T., used like Heb.* ‏יוד‎ *the smallest letter in the Hebrew alphabet, as an expression for* the least or minutest part; a jot, Mat. 5.18.

Κ, κ, *Κάππα*

Κἀγώ,

contracted from καὶ εγω, dat. κἀμοί, accus. κἀμέ, καί *retaining, however, its independent force,* Jno. 6.58; 10.15, et al.

Καθά (καθ' ἅ)

adv. lit. according to what; as according as, Mat. 27.10.

Καθαίρεσις, εως, ἡ,

pr. a taking down; a pulling down, overthrow, demolition, 2 Co. 10.4; *met.* a razing *as respects spiritual state, a counter process to religious advancement by apostolic instrumentality,* 2 Co. 10.8; 13.10: *from*

Καθαιρέω, ῶ, (κατά & αἱρέω)

ήσω, & καθελω, καθεῖλον,

to take down, Mat. 15.36, 46. Lu. 23.53. Ac. 13.29; to pull down, demolish, Lu. 12.18; to throw or cast down, degrade, Lu. 1.52; to destroy, put an end to, Ac. 19.27; to overthrow, conquer, Ac. 13.19; to pull down, subvert, 2 Co. 10.5.

Καθαίρω, (καθαρός)

f. αρῶ, p. pass. κεκάθαρμαι,

to cleanse *from filth* to clear *by pruning,* prune, Jno. 15.2; *met.* to cleanse, *from sin,* make expiation, He. 10.2.

Καθάπερ, (καθ' ἅ περ)

adv. even as, just as, Ro. 4.6, et al.

Καθάπτω, (κατά & ἅπτω)

f. ψω,

trans. to fasten or fit to; *in N.T., equivalent to* καθάπτομαι, to fix one's self upon, fasten upon, Ac. 28.3.

Καθαρίζω,

ίσω, & ιῶ, ἐκαθάρισα, *a later equivalent to* καθαίρω,

to cleanse, render pure, Mat. 23.25. Lu. 11.39; to cleanse *from leprosy,* Mat. 8.2, 3; 10.8; *met.* to cleanse *from sin,* purify by an expiatory offering, make expiation for, He.

9.22, 23. 1 Jno. 1.7; to cleanse *from sin,* free from the influence of error and sin, Ac. 15.9. 2 Co. 7.1; to pronounce, ceremonially clean, Ac. 10.15; 11.9, et al.: *whence*

Καθαρισμός, οῦ, ὁ,
ceremonial cleansing, purification, Lu. 2.22. Jno. 2.6; mode of purification, Jno. 2.6; 3.35; cleansing *of lepers,* Mar. 1.44; *met.* expiation, He. 1.3. 2 Pe. 1.9, et al. L.G.

Κάθαρμα, ατος, τό, (καθαίρω)
offscouring, filth; *met.* a mean and abject person, an outcast, 1 Co. 4.13.

Καθαρός, ά, όν,
clean, pure, unsoiled, Mat. 23.26; 27.59; *met.* clean *from guilt,* guiltless, innocent, Ac. 18.6; 20.26; sincere, unfeigned, upright, virtuous, void of evil, Mat. 5.8; Jno. 15.3; clean *ceremonially,* Lu. 11.41: *whence*

Καθαρότης, τητος, ἡ,
cleanness, *ceremonial* purity, He. 9.13.

Καθέδρα, ας, ἡ, (κατά & ἕδρα)
a seat, Mat. 21.12; 23.2. Mar. 11.15.

Καθέζομαι,
f. καθεδοῦμαι,
to seat one's self, sit down, Mat. 26.55. Lu. 2.46, et al.

Καθεῖς, (καθ' εἷς)
90one by one, one after another, 1 Co. 14.31. Ep. 5.33. N.T.

Καθεξῆς, (κατά & ἑξῆς)
adv. in a continual order or series, successively, consecutively, Lu. 1.3. Ac. 11.4; 18.23; ὁ, ἡ, καθεξῆς, succeeding, subsequent, Lu. 8.1. Ac. 3.24. L.G.

Καθεύδω, (κατά & εὕδω, to sleep)
f. ευδήσω,
to sleep, be fast asleep, Mat. 8.24; 9.24, et al.; *met.* to be slothful, careless, secure, Ep. 5.14. 1 Th. 5.6; to sleep *the sleep of death,* 1 Th. 5.10.

Καθηγητής, οῦ, ὁ, (καθηγέομαι, to lead, conduct, fr. κατά & ἡγέομαι)
pr. a guide, leader; *in N.T.,* a teacher, instructor, Mat. 23.8, 10. L.G.

Καθήκω, (κατά & ἥκω)
to reach, extend to; καθήκει, *impers.* it is fitting, meet, Ac. 22.22; τὸ καθῆκον, what is fit, right, duty; τὰ μὴ καθήκοντα, *by litotes for* what is abominable or detestable, Ro. 1.28.

Κάθημαι, (κατά & ἧμαι, to sit)
2 per. κάθησαι & κάθη, imperat. κάθησο & κάθου,
to sit, be sitting, Mat. 9.9; Lu. 10.13; to be seated, 1 Co. 14.30; to dwell, Mat. 4.16. Lu. 1.79; 21.35, et al.

Καθημερινός, ή, όν, (καθ' ἡμέραν, daily)
daily, day by day, Ac. 6.1. L.G.

Καθίζω,
f. ίσω, p. κεκάθικα, a.1. ἐκάθισα,
trans. to cause to sit, place; καθίζομαι, to be seated, sit, Mat. 19.28. Lu. 22.30; to cause to set *as judges,* place, appoint, 1 Co. 6.4;
intrans. to sit, sit down, Mat. 13.48; 26.36; to remain, stay, continue, Lu. 24.49.

Καθίημι, (κατά & ἵημι)
f. καθήσω, a.1. καθῆκα,
to let down, lower, Lu. 5.19. Ac. 9.25; 10.11; 11.5.

Καθίστημι, and in N.T. καθιστάω, ῶ, (κατά & ἵστημι)
f. καταστήσω, a.1. κατέστησα, a.1. pass. κατεστάθην, (ἄ)

to place, set, Ja. 3.6; to set, constitute, appoint, Mat. 24.45, 47. Lu. 12.14; to set down *in a place,* conduct, Ac. 17.15; to make, render, or cause to be, 2 Pe. 1.8; *pass.* to be rendered, Ro. 5.19.

Καθό, (καθ' ὅ)
    as, Ro. 8.26; according as, in proportion as, 2 Co. 8.12. 1 Pe. 4.13.

Καθόλου, (καθ' ὅλου)
    on the whole, in general, altogether; *and with a negative,* not at all, Ac. 4.18.

Καθοπλίζω, (κατά & ὁπλίζω)
    f. ίσω,
    to arm completely, Lu. 11.21.

Καθοράω, ῶ, (κατά & ὁράω)
    pr. to look down upon, *in N.T.,* to mark, percieve, discern, Ro. 1.20.

Καθότι, (καθ' ὅτι)
    according as, in proportion as, Ac. 2.45; 4.35; inasmuch as, Lu. 1.7; 19.9. Ac. 2.24.

Καθώς, (κατά & ὡς)
    as, in the manner that, Mat. 21.6; 26.24; how, in what manner, Ac. 15.14; according as, Mar. 4.33; inasmuch as, Jno. 17.2; *of time,* when, Ac. 7.17. L.G.

Καί,
    conj., and Mat. 2.2, 3, 11; 4.22; καὶ—καὶ, both—and; *as a cumulative particle,* also, too, Mat. 5.39. Jno. 8.19. 1 Co. 11.6, et al.; *emphatic,* even, also, Mat. 10.30. 1 Co. 2.10, et al.; *in N.T., adversative,* but, Mat. 11.19, et al.; *also introductory of the apodosis of a sentence,* Ja. 2.4. Ga. 3.28.

Καίγε, (καί & γε)
    at least, were it only, Lu. 19.42; and even, yea too, Ac. 2.18. L.G.

Καινός, ή, όν,
    new, recently made, Mat. 9.17. Mar. 2.22; new *in species, character, or mode,* Mat. 26.28, 29. Mar. 14.24, 25. Lu. 22.20. Jno. 13.34. 2 Co. 5.17. Ga. 6.15. Eph. 2.15; 4.24. 1 Jno. 2.7. Re. 3.12, et al.; novel, stange, Mar. 1.27. Ac. 17.19; new *to the possessor,* Mar. 1.27; Ac. 17.19; *met.* renovated, better, of higher excellence, 2 Co. 5.17. Re. 5.9, et al.: *whence*

Καινότερος, α, ον,
    pr. comparat. of preced., newer, more recent; *but used for the positive,* new, novel, Ac. 17.21.

Καινότης, τητος, ή,
    newness, Ro. 6.4; 7.6.

Καίπερ, (καί & περ)
    though, although, Phi. 3.4. Re. 17.8, et al.

Καιρός, οῦ, ὁ,
    pr. fitness, proportion, suitableness; a fitting situation, suitable place, 1 Pe. 4.17; a limited period of time marked by a suitableness of circumstances, a fitting season, 1 Co. 4.5. 1 Ti. 2.6; 6.15. Tit. 1.3; opportunity, Ac. 24.25. Ga. 6.10. He. 11.15; 91 a limited period of time distinguished by characteristic circumstances, a signal juncture, a marked season, Mat. 16.3. Lu. 12.56; 21.8. 1 Pe. 1.11, et al.; a destined time, Mat. 8.29; 26.18. Mar. 1.15. Lu. 21.24. 1 Th. 5.1, et al.; a season *in ordinary succession, equivalent to* ὥρα, Mat. 13.30. Ac. 14.17, et al.; *in N.T.,* a limited time, a short season, Lu. 4.13, et al.; *simply,* a point of time, Mat. 11.24. Lu. 13.1, et al.

Καίτοι, (καί & enclit. τοι)
    and yet, though, although, He. 4.3.

Καίτοιγε, (καίτοι & γε)
    although, indeed, Jno. 4.2. Ac. 14.17; 17.27.

Καίω,
f. καύσω, pass. a.1. ἐκαύθην,
to cause to burn, kindle, light, Mat. 5.15; *pass.* to be kindled, burn, flame, Lu. 12.35; *met.* to be kindled *into emotion,* Lu. 24.32; to consume with fire, Jno. 15.6. 1 Co. 13.3.

Κἀκεῖ, (by crasis for καί ἐκεῖ)
and there, Mat. 5.23; 10.11; there also, Mar. 1.38; thither also, Ac. 17.13, et al.

Κἀκεῖθεν, (by crasis for καί ἐκεῖθεν)
and thence, Mar. 10.1. Ac. 7.4; 14.26; 20.15; 21.1; 27.4, 12; 28.15; and then, afterwards, Ac. 13.21.

Κἀκεῖνος, είνη, εῖνο, (by crasis for καί ἐκεῖνος)
and he, she, it; and this, and that, Mat. 15.18; 23.23; he, she, it also; this also, that also, Mat. 20.4.

Κακία, ας, ἡ (κακός)
malice, malignity, Ro. 1.29. Ep. 4.31; wickedness, depravity, Ac. 8.22. 1 Co. 5.8; *in N.T.,* evil, trouble, calamity, Mat. 6.34.

Κακοήθεια, ας, ἡ, (κακός & ἦθος)
disposition for mischief, malignity, Ro. 1.29.

Κακολογέω, ῶ, κακός & λέγω)
f. ησω,
to speak evil of, revile, abuse, assail with reproaches, Mar. 9.39. Ac. 19.9; to address with offensive language, to treat with disrespect, contemn, Mat. 15.4. Mar. 7.10.

Κακοπάθεια, ας, ἡ,
a state of suffering, affliction, trouble; *in N.T.,* enduraance in affliction, Ja. 5.10.

Κακοπᾰθέω, ῶ, (κακός & πάσχω)
f. ήσω,
to suffer evil or afflictions, 2 Ti. 2.9; to be vexed, troubled, dejected, Ja. 5.18; *in N.T.,* to show endurance in trials and afflictions, 2 Ti. 2.3.

Κακοποιέω, ῶ, κακός & ποιέω)
f. ήσω,
to cause evil, injure, do harm, Mar. 3.4. Lu. 6.9; to do evil, commit sin, 1 Pe. 3.17.

Κακοποιός, οῦ, ὁ, ἡ, (fr. same)
an evil-doer, 1 Pe. 2.12, et al.; a malefactor, cirminal, Jno. 18.30.

Κακός, ή, όν,
bad, of a bad quality or disposition, worthless, corrupt, depraved, Mat. 21.41; 24.48. Mar. 7.21; wicked, criminal, morally bad; τὸ κακόν, evil, wickedness, crime, Mat. 27.23. Ac. 23.9 malediction, 1 Pe. 3.10; mischievous, harmful, baneful; τὸ κακόν, evil, mischief, harm, injury, Tit. 1.12; afflictive, τὸ κακόν, evil, misery, affliction, suffering, Lu. 16.25.

Κακοῦργος, ου, ὁ, ἡ, (κακός & ἔργον)
an evil-doer, malefactor, criminal, Lu. 23.32, 33, 39. 2 Ti. 2.9.

Κακουχέω, ῶ, (κακός & ἔχω)
to maltreat, afflict, harass; *pass.* to be afflicted, be oppressed with evils, He. 11.37; 13.3.

Κακόω, ῶ, (κακός)
f. ώσω, a.1. ἐκάκωσα,
to maltreat, cause evil to, oppress, Ac. 7.6, 19; 12.1; 18.10. 1 Pe. 3.13; *in N.T.,* to disaffect, cause to be evil affected, Ac. 14.2.

Κακῶς, (fr. same)

adv. ill, badly; *physically* ill, sick, Mat. 4.24; 8.16, et al.; grievously, vehemently, Mat. 15.22; wretchedly, miserably, Mat. 21.41; wickedly, reproachfully, Ac. 23.5; wrongly, criminally, Jno. 18.23; amiss, Ja. 4.3.

Κάκωσις, εως, ή, <u>κακόω</u>
  ill-treatment, affliction, misery, Ac. 7.34.

Καλάμη, ης, ή,
  the stalk *of grain,* straw, stubble, 1 Co. 3.12. (ă).

Κάλᾰμος, ου, ὁ,
  a reed, a cane, Mat. 11.7; 12.20. Lu. 7.24; a reed *in its various applicances; as,* a wand, a staff, Mat. 27.29, 30, 48. Mar. 15.19, 36; a measuring rod, Re. 11.1; a writer's reed, 3 Jno. 13.

Καλέω, ῶ,
  f. έσω, p. κέκληκα, a.l. ἐκάλεσα, p. pass. κέκλημαι, a.l. pass. ἐκλήθην,
  to call, call to, Jno. 10.3; to call *into one's presence,* send for *a person,* Mat. 2.7; to summon, Mat. 2.15; 25.14, et al.; to invite, Mat. 22.9, et al.; to call *to the performance of a certain thing,* Mat. 9.13. He. 1.8, et al.; 92to call *to a participation in the privileges of the Gospel,* Ro. 8.30; 9.24. 1 Co. 1.9; 7.18, et al.; to call *to an office or dignity,* He. 5.4; to name, style, Mat. 1.21, et al.; *pass.* to be styled, regarded, Mat. 5.9, 19, et al.

Καλλιέλαιος, ου, ὁ, ή, (κάλλος & <u>ἔλαιον</u>)
  pr. adj. productive of good oil; *as subst.* a cultivated olive-tree, Ro. 11.24.

Καλλίων, ονος, ὁ, ή, (comp. of <u>καλός</u>)
  better; neut. κάλλῑον, *as an adv.* full well, Ac. 25.10.

Καλοδιδάσκᾰλος, ου, ὁ, ή, (<u>καλός</u> & <u>διδάσκαλος</u>)
  teachng what is good, a teacher of good, Tit. 2.3. N.T.

Καλοποιέω, ῶ (<u>καλός</u> & <u>ποιέω</u>)
  f. ήσω,
  to do well, do good, 2 Th. 3.13. S.

Καλός, ή, όν,
  pr. beautiful; good, of good quality or disposition; fertile, rich, Mat. 13.8, 23; useful, profitable, Lu. 14.34; καλόν ἐστι, it is profitable; it is well, Mat. 18.8, 9;excellent, choice, select, goodly, Mat. 7.17, 19; καλόν ἐστι, it is pleasant, delightful, Mat. 17.4; just, full *measure,* Lu. 6.38; honourable, distinguished, Ja. 2.7; good, possessing moral excellence, worthy, upright, virtuous, Jno. 10.11, 14. 1 Ti. 4.6; τὸ καλὸν & τὸ καλὸν ἔργον, what is good and right, a good deed, rectitude, virture, Mat. 5.16. Ro. 7.18, 21; right, duty, propriety, Mat. 15.26; benefit, favour, Jno. 10.32, 33, et al.

Κάλυμμα, ατος, τό,
  a covering; a veil, 2 Co. 3.13; *met.* a veil, a blind *to spiritual vision,* 2 Co. 3.14, 15, 16: *from*

Καλύπτω,
  f. ψω, a.1. ἐκάλυψα, p. pass. κεκάλυμμαι,
  to cover, Mat. 8.24. Lu. 8.16; 23.30; to hide, conceal, Mat. 10.26. 2 Co. 4.3; *met.* to cover, throw a veil over, consign to oblivion, Ja. 5.20. 1 Pe. 4.8.

Καλῶς,
  adv. well, rightly, suitably, with propriety, becomingly, 1 Co. 7.37; 14.17. Ga. 4.17; 5.7, et al.; truly, justly, corrrectly, Mar. 12.32. Lu. 20.39. Jno. 4.17, et al.; appositely, Mat. 15.7. Mar. 7.6; becomingly, honourably, Ja. 2.3; well, effectually, Mar. 7.9, 37, et al.; καλῶς εἰπεῖν, to speak well, praise, applaud, Lu. 6.26; καλῶς ἔχειν, to be convalescent, Mar. 16.18; καλῶς ποιεῖν, to do good, confer benefits, Mat. 5.44; 12.12; to do well, act virtuously, Phi. 4.14, et al.

Κἀμέ, (καὶ ἐμέ)
    see κἀγώ.
Κάμηλος, ου, ὁ, ἡ, (Heb. למָג)
    a camel, Mat. 3.4; 23.34, et al.
Κάμῑνος, ου, ἡ,
    a furnace, oven, kiln, Mat. 13.42, 50. Re. 1.15; 9.2.
Καμμύω, (contr. for καταμύω, fr. κατά & μύω)
    f. ύσω, a.1. ἐκάμμῠσα,
    to shut, close *the eyes*, Mat. 13.15. Ac. 28.27.
Κάμνω,
    f. καμοῦμαι, p. κέκμηκα, a.2. ἔκᾰμον,
    pr. to tire with exertion, labour to weariness; to be wearied, tried out, exhausted, He. 12.3. Re. 2.3; to labour *under disease,* be sick, Ja. 5.15.
Κἀμοί, (καὶ ἐμοί)
    see κἀγώ.
Κάμπτω,
    f. ψω, a.1. ἔκαμψα,
    trans. to bend, inflect, *the knee,* Ro. 11.4. Ep. 3.14; *intrans.* to bend, bow, Ro. 14.11. Phi. 2.10.
Κἄν, (by crasis καὶ ἐάν)
    and if, Mar. 16.18; also if, Mat. 21.21; even if, if even, although, Jno. 10.38; if so much as, He. 12.20; *also in N.T., simply equivalent to* καί *as a particle of emphasis, by a pleonasm of* ἄν, at least, at all events, Mar. 6.56. Ac. 5.15. 2 Co. 11.16.
Κανανίτης, ου, ὁ, (Aram. אנק, fr. Heb. אנק, to be zealous)
    Canaanite, i.q. ζηλωτής, zealot, Mat. 10.4. Mar. 3.18; coll. Lu. 6.15, & Ac. 1.13.
Κανών, ονος, ὁ, (κάννα v. κάνη, a cane)
    a measure, rule; *in N.T.,* prescribed range *of action or duty,* 2 Co. 10.13, 15, 16; *met.* rule *of conduct or doctrine,* Ga. 6.16. Phil. 3.16.
Καπηλεύω,
    f. εύσω,
    (*pr.* to be κάπηλος, a retailer, huckster; *and, as these persons had the reputation of increasing their profits by adulteration, hence,) in N.T.,* to corrupt, adulterate, 2 Co. 2.17.
Καπνός, οῦ, ὁ,
    smoke, Ac. 2.19. Re. 8.4, et al.
Καρδία, ας, ἡ, (κέαρ, idem)
    the heart; the heart, *regarded as the seat of feelings, impulse, affection, desire,* Mat. 6.21; 22.37. Phil. 1.7, et al.; the heart, *as the seat of intellect,* Mat. 13.15. Ro. 1.21, et al.; 93the heart, *as the inner and mental frame,* Mat. 5.8. Lu. 16.15. 1 Pe. 3.4, et al.; the conscience, 1 Jno. 3.20, 21; the heart, the inner part, middle, centre, Mat. 12.40, et al.
Καρδιογνώστης, ου, ὁ, (καρδία & γινώσκω)
    heart-knower, searcher of hearts, Ac. 1.24; 15.8. N.T.
Καρπός, οῦ, ὁ,
    fruit, Mat. 3.10; 21.19, 34; *fr. the Heb.* καρπὸς κοιλίας, fruit of the womb, offspring, Lu. 1.42; καρπὸς ὀσφύος, fruit of the loins, offspring, posterity, Ac. 2.30; καρπὸς χειλέων, fruit of the lips, praise, He. 13.15; *met.* conduct, actions, Mat. 3.8; 7.16. Ro. 6.22; benefit, profit, emolument, Ro. 1.13; 6.21; reward, Phi. 4.17, et al.
Καρποφορέω, ῶ, (καρπός & φορέω, fr. φέρω
    f. ήσω, a.1. ἐκαρποφόρησα,

to bear fruit, yield, Mar. 4.28; *met.* to bring forth or exhibit actions or conduct, Mat. 13.23. Ro. 7.5; *mid.* to expand by fruitfulness, to develop itself by success, Col. 1.6.

Καρποφόρος, ου, ὁ, ἡ, (fr. same)
    fruitful, adapted to bring forth fruit, Ac. 14.17.

Καρτερέω, ῶ, (καρτερός, by metath. fr. κράτος)
    f. ήσω, a.1. ἐκαρτέρησα,
    to be stout; to endure patiently, bear up with fortitude, He. 11.27.

Κάρφος, εος, τό, (κάρφω, to shrivel)
    any small dry thing, *as* chaff, stubble, splinter, mote, &c.; Mat. 7.3, 4.5. Lu. 6.41, 42.

Κατά,
    prep., with a genitive, down from, adown, Mat. 8.32; down upon, upon, Mar. 14.3. Ac. 27.14; down into; κατὰ βάθους, profound, deepest, 2 Co. 8.2; down over, throughout *a space,* Lu. 4.14; 23.5; concerning, *in cases of pointed allegation,* 1 Co. 15.15; against, Mat. 12.30, et al.; by, *in oaths, Mat. 26.63, at al.;*
    with an accusative, of place, in the quarter of; about, near, at, Lu. 10.32. Ac. 2.10; throughout, Lu. 8.39; in, Ro. 16.5; among, Ac. 21.21; in the presence of, Lu. 2.31; in the direction of, towards, Ac. 8.26. Phi. 3.14; *of time,* within the range of; during, in the course of, at, about, Ac. 21.1; 27.27; *distributively,* κατ' οἶκον, by houses, from house to house, Ac. 2.46; κατὰ δύο, two and two, 1 Co. 14.27; καθ' ἡμέραν, daily, Mat. 26.55, et al.; *trop.,* according to, conformably to, in proportion to, Mat. 9.29; 25.15; after the fashion or likeness of, He. 5.6; in virtue of, Mat. 19.3; as respects, Ro. 1.3. Ac. 25.14. He. 9.9.

καταβαίνω, (κατά & βαίνω)
    f. βήσομαι, a.2. κατέβην, imperat. κατάβηθι, & κατάβα, p. καταβέβηκα,
    to come or go down, descend, Mat. 8.1; 17.9; to lead down, Ac. 8.26; to come down, fall, Mat. 7.25, 27, et al.; to be let down, Ac. 10.11; 11.5.

Καταβάλλω, (κατά & βάλλω)
    f. βαλῶ,
    to cast down, Re. 12.10; to prostrate, 2 Co. 4.9; *mid.* to lay down, lay *as foundation,* He. 6.1.

Καταβαρέω, ῶ, (κατά & βαρέω)
    f. ήσω,
    pr. to weigh down; *met.* to burden, be burdensome to, 2 Co. 12.16. L.G.

Καταβαρύνω, (κατά & βαρύνω)
    f. υνῶ,
    to weigh down, oppress; *pass.* to be weighted down *by sleep,* by drowsy, v.r. Mar. 14.40.

Κατάβᾰσις, εως, ἡ, (καταβαίνω)
    the act of descending; a way down, descent, Lu. 19.37.

Καταβιβάζω, (κατά & βιβάζω)
    f. άσω,
    to cause to descend, bring or thrust down, Mat. 11.23. Lu. 10.15.

Καταβολή, ῆς, ἡ, (καταβάλλω)
    pr. a casting down; laying the foundation, foundation; beginning, commencement, Mat. 13.35; 25.34, et al.; conception *in the womb,* He. 11.11.

Καταβραβεύω, (κατά & βραβεύω)
    f. εύσω,
    pr. to give an unfavourable decision as respects a prize, to disappoint of the palm; *hence,* to beguile of, cause to miss, Col. 2.18.

Καταγγελεύς, έως, ὁ,

one who announces *any thing,* a proclaimer, publisher, Ac. 17.18: *equivalent to* κατάγγελος. N.T.

Καταγγέλλω, (κατά & ἀγγέλλω)
    f. γελῶ, a.2. κατηγγέλην,
    to announce, proclaim, Ac. 13.38; *in N.T.,* to laud, celebrate, Ro. 1.8. 1 Co. 11.26; to set forth, teach, inculcate, preach, Ac. 4.2; 13.5, et al.

Καταγελάω, ῶ, (κατά & γελάω)
    f. άσω, άσομαι,
    to deride, jeer, Mat. 9.24. Mar. 5.40. Lu. 8.53.

Καταγινώσκω, (κατά & γινώσκω)
    f. γνώσομαι,
    94to determine against, condemn, blame, reprehend, Ga. 2.11. 1 Jno. 3.20, 21.

Κατάγνυμι, v. -ύω, (κατά & ἄγνυμι, to break)
    f. κατάξω, & κατεάξω, a.1. κατέαξα, a.2. pass. κατεάγην (ᾱ), subj. κατεαγῶ,
    to break in pieces, crush, break in two, Mat. 12.20. Jno. 19.31, 32, 33.

Κατάγω, (κατά & ἄγω)
    f. ξω, a.2. κατήγαγον,
    to lead, bring, or conduct down, Ac. 9.30; 22.30; 23.15, 20, 28; to bring *a ship* to land; *pass.* κατάγομαι, a.1. κατήχθην, to come to land, land, touch, Lu. 5.11, et al.

Καταγωνίζομαι, (κατά & ἀγωνίζομαι)
    f. ίσομαι a.1 κατηγωνισάμην,
    to subdue, vanquish, conquer, He. 11.33. L.G.

Καταδέω, (κατά & δέω)
    f. ήσω,
    to bind down; to bandage *a wound,* Lu. 10.34.

Κατάδηλος, ου, ὁ, ἡ, τό, -ον, (κατά & δῆλος)
    quite manifest or evident, He. 7.15.

Καταδικάζω, (κατά & δικάζω)
    f. άσω,
    to give judgement against, condemn, Mat. 12.7, 37. Lu. 6.37. Ja. 5.6.

Καταδίκη, ης, ἡ, (κατά & δίκη)
    condemnation, sentence of condemnation, v.r. Ac. 25.15.

Καταδιώκω, (κατά & διώκω)
    f. ξω,
    to follow hard upon; to track, follow perseveringly, Mar. 1.36.

Καταδουλόω, ῶ (κατά & δουλόω)
    f. ώσω,
    to reduce to absolute servitude, make a slave of, 2 Co. 11.20.

Καταδυναστεύω, (κατά & δυναστεύω, to rule, reign)
    f. εύσω,
    to tyrannise over, oppress, Ac. 10.38. Ja. 2.6.

Κατάθεμα, ατος, τό, (κατατίθημι)
    an execration, curse, *by meton.* what is worthy of execration, i.q. κατανάθεμα, v.r. Re. 22.3: (N.T.) *whence*

Καταθεματίζω,
    f. ίσω,
    to curse, v.r. Mat. 26.74. N.T.

Καταισχύνω, (κατά & αἰσχύνω)
    f. υνῶ,

to shame, put to shame, put to the blush, 1 Co. 1.27; *pass.* to be ashamed, be put to the blush, Lu. 13.17; to dishonour, disgrace, 1 Co. 11.4, 5; *fr. the Heb.* to frustrate, disappoint, Ro. 5.5; 9.33.

Κατακαίω, (κατά & καίω)
    f. καύσω, a.2. pass. κατεκάην,
    to burn up, consume with fire, Mat. 3.12; 13.30, 40, et al.

Κατακαλύπτομαι, (mid of κατακαλύπτω, to veil, fr. κατά & καλύπτω)
    to veil one's self, to be veiled or covered, 1 Co. 11.6, 7.)

Κατακαυχάομαι, ῶμαι,(κατά & καυχάομαι)
    f. ήσομαι,
    to vaunt one's self against, to glory over, to assume superiority over, Ro. 11.18. Ja. 2.13; 3.14. S.

Κατάκειμαι, (κατά & κεῖμαι)
    f. είσομαι,
    to lie, be in a recumbent posture, be laid down, Mar. 1.30; 2.4; to recline *at table,* Mar. 2.15; 14.3, et al.

Κατακλάω, ῶ, (κατά & κλάω)
    f. άσω, a.1. κατέκλᾰσα,
    to break, break in pieces, Mar. 6.41. Lu. 9.16.

Κατακλείω, (κατά & κλείω)
    f. είσω,
    to close, shut fast; to shut up, confine, Lu. 3.20. Ac. 26.10.

Κατακληροδοτέω, ῶ, (κατά, κλῆρος, & δίδωμι
    f. ήσω,
    to divide out by lot, distribute by lot, Ac. 13.19. S.

Κατακληρονομέω, ῶ, (κατά, κλῆρος, & νέμω, to distribute)
    same a preceding, for which it is a v.r.

Κατακλίνω, (ῑ), (κατά & κλίνω)
    f. ινῶ, a.1. κατέκλῑνα, a.1. pass. κατεκλίθην (ῑ),
    to cause to lie down, cause to recline *at table,* Lu. 9.14; *mid.* to lie down, recline, Lu. 14.8; 24.30.

Κατακλύζω, (κατά & κλύζω, to lave, wash)
    f. ύσω, a.1. pass. κατεκλύσθην,
    to inundate, deluge, 2 Pe. 3.6: *whence*

Κατακλυσμός, οῦ, ὁ,
    an inundation, deluge, Mat. 24.38, 39, et al.

Κατακολουθέω, ῶ (κατά & ἀκολουθέω)
    f. ήσω,
    to follow closely or earnestly, Lu. 23.55. Ac. 16.17

Κατακόπτω, (κατά & κόπτω)
    f. ψω,
    to cut or dash in pieces; to mangle, wound, Mar. 5.5.

Κατακρημνίζω, (κατά & κρημνός, a precipice)
    f. ίσω,
    to cast down headlong, precipitate, Lu. 4.29.

Κατάκρῐμα, ατος, τό,
    condemnation, condemnatory sentence, Ro. 5.16, 18; 8.1: (L.G.) *from*

Κατακρίνω, (ῑ), (κατά & κρίνω)
    f. ινῶ, a.1. κατέκρῑνα, p. pass. κατακέκρῐμαι, a.1. pass. κατεκρίθην (ῐ),

95to give judgment against, condemn, Mat. 27.3 Jno. 8.10, 11, et al.; to condemn, to place in a guilty light *by contrast,* Mat. 12.41, 42. Lu. 11.31, 32. He. 11.7: *whence*

Κατάκρῐσις, εως, ἡ,
  condemnation, 2 Co. 3.9; censure, 2 Co. 7.3. S.

Κατακυριεύω, (κατά & κυριεύω)
  f. εύσω,
  to get into one's power; *in N.T.,* to bring under, master, overcome, Ac. 19.16; to domineer over, Mat. 20.25, et al. L.G.

Καταλᾰλέω, ῶ, (κατά & λαλέω)
  f. ήσω,
  to blab out; to speak against, calumniate, Ja. 4.11. 1 Pe. 2.12; 3.16: *whence*

Καταλαλία, ας, ἡ
  evil-speaking, detraction, backbiting, calumny, 2 Co. 12.20. 1 Pe. 2.1. S.

Κατάλᾰλος, ου, ὁ, ἡ,
  slanderous, a detractor, calumniator, Ro. 1.30. N.T.

Καταλαμβάνω, (κατά & λαμβάνω)
  f. λύψομαι, a.2. κατέλᾰβον,
  to lay hold of, grasp; to obtain, attain, Ro. 9.30. 1 Co. 9.24; to seize, take possesssion of, Mar. 9.18; to come suddenly upon, overtake, surprise, Jno. 12.35; to deprehend, detect in the act, seize, Jno. 8.3, 4; *met.* to comprehend, apprehend, Jno. 1.5; *mid.* to understand, perceive, Ac. 4.13; 10.34, et al.

Καταλέγω, (κατά & λέγω)
  f. ξω,
  to select; to reckon in a number, enter in a list or catalogue, enrol. 1 Ti. 5.9.

Κατάλειμμα, ατος, τό,
  a remnant, a small residue, Ro. 9.27: (L.G.)*from*

Καταλείπω, (κατά & λείπω)
  f. ψω, a.2 κατέλῐπον,
  to leave behind; to leave behind *at death,* Mar. 12.19; to relinquish, let remain, Mar. 14.52; to quit, depart from, forsake, Mat. 4.13; 16.4; to neglect, Ac. 6.2; to leave alone, or without assistance, Lu. 10.40; to reserve, Ro. 11.4.

Καταλιθάζω, (κατά & λιθάζω)
  f. άσω,
  to stone, kill by stoning, Lu. 20.6. S.

Καταλλᾰγή, ῆς, ἡ,
  pr. an exchange; reconciliation, restoration to favour, Ro. 5.11; 11.15. 2 Co. 5.18, 19: *from*

Καταλλάσσω, (κατά & ἀλλάσσω)
  f. άξω, a.2. pass. κατηλλάγην (ᾰ),
  to change, exchange; to reconcile; *pass.* to be reconciled, Ro. 5.10. 1 Co. 7.11. 2 Co. 5.18-20.

Κατάλοιπος, ου, ὁ, ἡ, (καταλείπω)
  remaining; οἱ κατάλοιποι, the rest, Ac. 15.17.

Κατάλῠμα, ατος, τό,
  a lodging, inn, khan, Lu. 2.7; a guest-chamber, cœnaculum, Mar. 14.14. Lu. 22.11: (L.G.) *from*

Καταλύω (ῠ), (κατά & λύω)
  f. ύσω, a.1. pass. κατελύθην (ῠ),

to dissolve; to destroy, demolish, overthrow, throw down, Mat. 24.2; 26.61; *met.* to nullify, abrogate, Mat. 5.17. Ac. 5.38, 39, et al.; *intrans.* to unloose *harness, &c.,* to halt, to stop for the night, lodge, Lu. 9.12.

Καταμανθάνω, (κατά & μανθάνω)
    f. μαθήσομαι, a.2. κατέμᾰθον,
    to learn or observe thoroughly; to consider accurately and diligently, contemplate, mark, Mat. 6.28.

Καταμαρτῠρέω, ῶ, (κατά & μαρτυρέω)
    f. ήσω,
    to witness or testify against, Mat. 26.62; 27.13, et al.

Καταμένω, (κατά & μένω)
    f. ενῶ,
    to remain; to abide, dwell, Ac. 1.13.

Καταμόνας, (κατά & μόνος)
    alone, apart, in private, Mar. 4.10. Lu. 9.18.

Κατανάθεμα, ατος, τό, (κατά & ἀνάθεμα)
    a curse, execration; *meton.* one accursed, execrable, Re. 22.3: (N.T.) *whence*

Καταναθεματίζω,
    f. ίσω,
    to curse, Mat. 26.74. N.T.

Κατανᾱλίσκω, (κατά & ἀναλίσκω)
    f. λώσω,
    to consume, *as fire,* He. 12.29.

Καταναρκάω, ῶ,(κατά & ναρκάω, to grow torpid)
    f. ήσω,
    in N.T., to be torpid to the disadvantage of *any one,* to be a dead weight upon; *by impl.* to be troublesome, burdensome to, *in respect of maintenance,* 2 Co. 11.9; 12.13, 14.

Κατανεύω, (κατά & νεύω)
    f. εύσομαι,
    pr. to nod, signify assent by a nod; *genr.* to make signs, beckon, Lu. 5.7.

Κατανοέω, ῶ (κατά & νοέω)
    f. ήσω,
    to perceive, understand, apprehend, 96Lu. 20.23; to observe, mark, contemplate, Lu. 12.24, 27; to discern, descry, Mat. 7.3; to have regard to, make account of, Ro. 4.19.

Καταντάω, ῶ, (κατά & ἀντάω)
    f. ήσω,
    to come to, arrive at, Ac. 16.1; 20.15; *of an epoch,* to come upon, 1 Co. 10.11; *met.* to reach, attain to, Ac. 26.7, et al. L.G.

Κατάνυξις, εως, ἡ,
    in N.T., deep sleep, stupor, dulness, Ro. 11.8. S.

Κατανύσσω, (κατά & νύσσω)
    f. ξω, a.2. pass. κατενύγην,
    to pierce through; to pierce *with compunction and pain of heart,* Ac. 2.37.

Καταξιόω, ῶ (κατά & ἀξιόω)
    f. ώσω,
    to account worthy of, Lu. 20.35; 21.36. Ac. 5.41. 2 Th. 1.5.

Καταπᾰτέω, ῶ, (κατά & πατέω)
    f. ήσω,
    to trample upon, tread down or under feet, Mat. 5.13; 7.6 Lu. 8.5; 12.1; *met.* to treat with contumely, spurn, He. 10.29.

Κατάπαυσις, εως, ή,

pr. the act of giving rest; a state of settled cessation or rest, He. 3.11, 18; 4.3, 11, et al.; a place of rest, place of abode, dwelling, habitation, Ac. 7.49: *from*

Καταπαύω, (κατά & παύω)

f. αύσω,

to cause to cease, restrain, Ac. 14.18; to cause to rest, give rest to, introduce into a permanent settlement, He. 4.8; *intrans.* to rest, desist from, He. 4.4, 10.

Καταπέτασμα, ατος, τό, (καταπετάννυμι, to expand)

a veil, curtain, Mat. 27.51. Mar. 15.38. Lu. 23.45. He. 6.19; 10.20. S.

Καταπίνω, (κατά & πίνω)

f. πίομαι, a.2. κατέπῐον, a.1. pass. κατεπόθην,

to drink, swallow, gulp down, Mat. 23.24; to swallow up, absorb, Re. 12.16. 2 Co. 5.4; to ingulf, submerge, overwhelm, He. 11.29; to swallow greedily, devour, 1 Pe. 5.8; to distroy, annihilate, 1 Co. 15.54. 2 Co. 2.7.

Καταπίπτω, (κατά & πίπτω)

f. πεσοῦμαι, a.2. κατέπεσον, p. πέπτωκα,

to fall down, fall prostrate, Ac. 26.14; 28.6.

Καταπλέω, (κατά & πλέω)

f. εύσομαι, a.1. κατέπλευσα,

to sail towards land, to come to land, Lu. 8.26.

Καταπονέω, ῶ, (κατά & πονέω)

f. ήσω,

to exhaust by labour or suffering; to weary out, 2 Pe. 2.7; to overpower, oppress, Ac. 7.24.

Καταποντίζω, (κατά & ποντίζω, to sink, fr. πόντος)

f. ίσω,

to sink in the sea; *pass.* to sink, Mat. 14.30; to be plunged, submerged, Mat. 18.6

Κατάρα, ας, ή, (κατά & ἀρά)

a cursing, execration, imprecation, Ja. 3.10. *fr. the Heb.* condemnation, doom, Ga. 3.10, 13. 2 Pe. 2.14; *meton.* a doomed one, one on whom condemation falls, Ga. 3.13: (ἄρ)*whence*

Καταράομαι, ῶμαι,

f. άσομαι, a.1. κατηρᾱσάμην, in N.T., p. pass. part. κατηραμένος,

to curse, to wish evil to, imprecate evil upon, Mat. 5.44. Mar. 11.21, et al.; *in N.T., pass.* to be doomed, Mat. 25.41.

Καταργέω, ῶ, (κατά & ἀργός)

f. ήσω, p. κατήργηκα, a.1. κατήργησα, p. pass. κατήργημαι, a.1. pass. κατηργήθην,

to render useless or unproductive, occupy unprofitably, Lu. 13.7; to render powerless, Ro. 6.6; to make empty and unmeaning, Ro. 4.14; to render null, to abrogate, cancel, Ro. 3.3, 31. Eph 2.15, et al.; to bring to an end, 1 Co. 2.6; 13.8; 15.24, 26. 2 Co. 3.7, et al.; to destroy, annihilate, 2 Th. 2.8. He. 2.14; to free from, diserver from, Ro. 7.2, 6. Ga. 5.4.

Καταριθμέω, ῶ, (κατά & ἀριθμέω)

f. ήσω,

to enumerate, number with, count with, Ac. 1.17.

Καταρτίζω, (κατά & ἀρτίζω)

f. ίσω, a.1. κατήρτισα,

to adjust thoroughly; to knit together, unite completely, 1 Co. 1.10; to frame, He. 11.3; to prepare, provide, Mat. 21.16. He. 10.5; to qualify fully, to elevate to a complete standard, Lu. 6.40. He. 13.21. 1 Pe. 5.10; *p. pass.* κατηρτισμένος, fit, ripe,

Ro. 9.22; to repair, refit, Mat. 4.21. Mar. 1.19; to supply, make good, 1 Th. 3.10; to restore *to a forfeited condition,* to reinstate, Ga. 6.1: *whence*

Κατάρτῖσις, εως, ἡ

pr. a complete adjustment; a state of completeness, perfection, 2 Co. 13.9. L.G.

Καταρτισμός, οῦ, ὁ,

completeness of qualification, a perfecting, Ep. 4.12. L.G.

Κατασείω, (κατά & σείω)

f. σείσω,

to shake down or violently; τὴω χεῖρε *or* τῇ χειρί, to wave the hand, beckon; 97to sign silence by waving the hand, Ac. 12.17, et al.

Κατασκάπτω, (κατά & σκάπτω)

f. ψω,

pr. to dig down under, undermine; *by impl.* to overthrow, demolish, raze, Ro. 11.3; τὰ κατεσκαμμένα, ruins, Ac. 15.16.

Κατασκευάζω, (κατά & σκευάζω, fr. σκεῦος)

f. άσω,

to prepare, put in readiness, Mat. 11.10. Mar. 1.2. Lu. 1.17; 7.27; to construct, form, build, He. 3.3, 4; 9.2, 6; 11.7. 1 Pe. 3.20.

Κατασκηνόω, ῶ, (κατά & σκηνόω, fr. σκηνή)

f. ώσω,

to pitch one's tent; *in N.T.,* to rest in *a place,* settle, abide, Ac. 2.26; to haunt, roost, Mat. 13.32. Mar. 4.32. Lu. 13.19: *whence*

Κατασκήνωσις, εως, ἡ,

pr. the pitching a tent; a tent; *in N.T.,* a dwelling-place; a haunt, roost, Mat. 8.20. Lu. 9.58. L.G.

Κατασκιάζω, (κατά & σκιάζω, idem)

f. άσω,

to overshadow, He. 9.5.

Κατασκοπέω, ῶ, (κατά & σκοπέω)

f. κατασκέψομαι, in N.T., a.1. inf. κατασκοπῆσαι,

to view closely and accurately; to spy out, Ga. 2.4.

Κατάσκοπος, οῦ, ὁ,

a scout, spy, He. 11.31.

Κατασοφίζομαι, (κατά & σοφίζω)

f. ίσομαι,

to exercise cleverness to the detriment of *any one,* to outwit; to make a victim of subtlety, to practise on by insidious dealing, Ac. 7.19. L.G.

Καταστέλλω, (κατά & στενός)

f. στελῶ, a.1. κατέστειλα, p. pass. κατέσταλμαι,

to arrange, dispose in regular order; to appease, quiet, pacify, Ac. 19.35, 36.

Κατάστημα, ατος, τό (καθίστημι)

determinate state, condition; personal appearance, mien, deportment, Tit. 2.3. L.G.

Καταστολή, ῆς, ἡ, (καταστέλλω)

pr. an arranging in order; adjustment of dress; *in N.T.,* apparel, dress. 1 Ti. 2.9.

Καταστρέφω, (κατά & στρέφω)

f. ψω,

to invert; to overturn, overthrow, throw down, Mat. 21.12. Mar. 11.15

Καταστρηνιάω, (κατά & στρηνιάω, to be headstrong, wanton, fr. στρηνίσ, v. στρηνός, hard, harsh)

f. άσω,

to be headstrong or wanton towards, 1 Ti. 5.11. N.T.

Καταστροφή, ῆς, ἡ, (καταστρέφω)
an overthrow, destruction, 2 Pe. 2.6; *met.* overthrow *of right principle or faith,* utter detriment, perversion, 2 Ti. 2.14.

Καταστρώννυμι v. νύω, (κατά & στρώννυμι,—νύω)
f. καταστρώσω, a.1. pass. κατεστρώθην,
to strew down, lay flat; *pass.* to be strewn, laid prostrate *in death,* 1 Co. 10.5.

Κατασύρω, (κατά & σύρω)
to drag down; to drag away, Lu. 12.58. (ῡ).

Κατασφάζω, v. σφάττω, (κατά & σφάζω v. σφάττω)
f. σφάξω,
to slaughter, slay, Lu. 19.27.

Κατασφρᾱγίζω, (κατά & σφραγίζω)
f. ίσω, p. pass. κατεσφράγισμαι,
to seal up, Re. 5.1

Κατάσχεσις, εως, ἡ, (κατέχω)
a possession, thing possessed, A. 7.5. S.

Κατατίθημι, (κατά & τίθημι)
f. θήσω, a.1. κατέθηκα,
to lay down, deposit, Mar. 15.46; *mid.* to deposit or lay up for one's self; χάριν, v. χάριτας, to lay up a store of favour for one's self, earn a title to favour *at the hands of a person,* to curry favour with, Ac. 24.27; 25.9.

Κατατομή, ῆς, ἡ, (κατατέμνω, to cut up, fr. κατά & τέμνω)
concision, mutilation, Phi. 3.2.

Κατατοξεύω, (κατά & τοξεύω, to shoot with a bow)
f. εύσω,
to shoot down *with arrows;* to transfix *with an arrow or dart,* to transfix *with an arrow or dart,* He. 12.20.

Κατατρέχω, (κατά & τρέχω)
f. δραμοῦμαι, a.2. ἐδρᾰμον,
to run down, Ac. 21.32.

Καταφέρω, (κατά & φέρω)
f. κατοίσω, a.1. pass. κατηνέχθην,
to bear down; to overpower, *as sleep,* Ac. 20.9; καταφέρειν ψῆφον, to give a vote or verdict, Ac. 26.10.

Καταφεύγω, (κατά & φεύγω)
f. ξομαι, a.2. κατέφῠγον,
to flee to *for refuge,* Ac. 14.6. He. 6.18.

Καταφθείρω, (κατά & φθείρω)
f. φθερῶ, f. pass. καταφθαρήσομαι,)
to destroy, cause to perish, 2 Pe. 2.12; to corrupt, deprave, 2 Ti. 3.8.

Καταφῐλέω, ῶ, (κατά & φιλέω)
98f. ήσω,
to kiss affectionately or with a semblance of affection, to kiss with earnest gesture, Mat. 26.49. Lu. 7.38. Ac. 20.37, et al.

Καταφρονέω, ῶ, (κατά & φρονέω)
f. ήσω,
pr. to think in disparagement of; to contemn, scorn, despise, Mat. 18.10. Ro. 2.4; to slight, Mat. 6.24. Lu. 16.13. 1 Co. 11.22. 1 Ti. 4.12; 6.2. 2 Pe. 2.10; to disregard, He. 12.2: *whence*

Καταφρονητής, οῦ, ὁ,
    a contemner, despiser, scorner, Ac. 13.41. L.G.
Καταχέω, (κατά & χέω)
    f. εύσω,
    to pour down upon, Mat. 26.7. Mar. 14.3
Καταχθόνιος, ίου, ὁ, ἡ, (κατά & χθών, the earth)
    under the earth, subterranean, infernal, Phi. 2.10.
Καταχράομαι, ῶμαι, (κατά & χράομαι)
    f. ήσομαι,
    to use downright; to use up, consume; to make an unrestrained use of, use eagerly, 1
    Co. 7.31; to use to the full, stretch to the utmost, 1 Co. 9.18.
Καταψύχω, (κατά & ψύχω)
    f. ξω,
    to cool, refresh, Lu. 16.24. (ῡ).
Κατείδωλος, ου, ὁ, ἡ, (κατά & εἴδωλον)
    rife with idols, sunk in idolatry, grossly idolatrous, Ac. 17.16. N.T.
Κατέναντι, (κατά & ἔναντι)
    adv. over against, opposite to, Mar. 11.2; 12.41; 13.3; ὁ, ἡ, τὸ κατέναντι, opposite, Lu.
    19.30; before, in the presence of, in the sight, Ro. 4.17. S.
Κατενώπιον, (κατά & ἐνώπιον)
    adv. v. prep. in the presence of, in the sight of, 2 Co. 2.17; 12.19. Ep. 1.4. S.
Κατεξουσιάζω, (κατά & ἐξουσιάζω)
    f. άσω,
    to exercise lordship over, domineer over, Mat. 20.25. Mar. 10.42. N.T.
Κατεργάζομαι, (κατά & ἐργάζομαι)
    f. άσομαι,
    to work out; to effect, produce, bring out as a result, Ro. 4.15; 5.3; 7.13. 2 Co. 4.17;
    7.10. Phi. 2.12. 1 Pe. 4.3. Ja. 1.3; to work, practise, realise in practice, Ro. 1.27; 2.9, et
    al.; to work or mould into fitness, 2 Co. 5.5; to dispatch, subdue, Eph. 6.13.
Κατέρχομαι, (κατά & ἔρχομαι)
    f. ελεύσομαι, a.2. κατῆλθον,
    to come or go down, Lu. 4.31; 9.37; Ac. 8.5; 9.32, et al.; to land at, touch at, Ac.
    18.22; 27.5.
Κατεσθίω, (κατά & ἐσθίω)
    f. καθέδομαι, a.2. κατέφαγον,
    to eat up, devour, Mat. 13.4, et al.; to consume, Re. 11.5; to expend, squander, Lu.
    15.30; met. to make a prey of, plunder, Mat. 23.13. Mar. 12.40. Lu. 20. 47. 2 Co.
    11.20; to vex, injure, Ga. 5.15.
Κατευθύνω, (κατά & εὐθύνω, fr. εὐθύς, straight)
    f. ὺνῶ, a.1. ῦηα,
    to make straight; to direct, guide aright, Lu. 1.79. 1 Th. 3.11. 2 Th. 3.5.
Κατέφαγον,
    a.2. of κατεσθίω.
Κατεφίστημι, (κατά & ἐφίστημι)
    intrans. a.2. κατεπέστην,
    to come upon suddenly, rush upon, assault, Ac. 18.12. N.T.
Κατέχω, (κατά & ἔχω)
    f. καθέξω, & κατασχήσω, imperf. κατεῖχον, a.2. κατέσχον,
    to hold down; to detain, retain, Lu. 4.42. Philem. 13; to hinder, restrain, 2 Th. 2.6, 7;
    to hold downright, hold in a firm grasp, to have in full and secure possession, 1 Co.

7.30. 2 Co. 6.10; to come into full possession of, seize upon, Mat. 21.38; to keep, retain, 1 Th. 5.21; to occupy, Lu. 14.9; *met.* to hold fast *mentally,* retain, Lu. 8.15. 1 Co. 11.2; 15.2; to maintain, He. 3.6, 14; 10.23; *intrans., a nautical term,* to land, touch, Ac. 27.40; *pass.* to be in the grasp of, to be bound by, Ro. 7.6; to be afflicted with, Jno. 5.4.

Κατηγορέω, ῶ, (κατά & ἀγορεύω, to harangue)
f. ήσω,
to speak against, accuse, Mat. 12.10; 27.12. Jno. 5.45, et al.: *whence*

Κατηγορία, ας, ἡ,
an accusation, crimination, Lu. 6.7, et al.

Κατήγορος, ου, ὁ
an accuser, Jno. 8.10. Ac. 23.30, 35; 24.8, et al.

Κατήγωρ, ορος, ὁ
an accuser, v.r. Re. 12.10, *a barbarous form for* κατήγορος.

Κατήφεια, ας, ἡ, (κατηφης, having a downcast look κατά & φάος)
dejection, sorrow, Ja. 4.9.

Κατηχέω, ῶ (κατά & ἠχέω)
f. ήσω,
pr. to sound in the ears, make the ears ring; to instruct orally, 99inform by teaching, Lu. 1.4. 1 Co. 14.19, et al.; *pass.* to be made acquainted with, be informed of, learn by report, Ac. 21.21, 24. L.G.

Κατῖόω, ῶ, (κατά & ιός)
f. ώσω, p. pass. κατίωμαι,
to cover with rust; *pass.* to rust, become rusty or tarnished, Ja. 5.3. L.G.

Κατισχύω, (κατά & ἰσχύω)
f. ύσω,
to overpower, Mat. 16.18; *intrans.* to predominate, get the upper hand, Lu. 23.23. (ῡ).

Κατοικέω, ῶ, (κατά & οἰκέω)
f. ήσω,
trans. to inhabit, Ac. 1.19, et al.; *intrans.* to have an abode, dwell, Lu. 13.4, Ac. 11.29, et al.; to take up or find an abode, Ac. 7.2, et al.; to indwell, Eph. 3.17. Ja. 4.5, et al.: *whence*

Κατοίκησις, εως, ἡ,
an abode, dwelling, habitation, Mar. 5.3.

Κατοικητήριον, ίου, τό,
the same, Ep. 2.22. Re. 18.2.

Κατοικία, ας, ἡ,
habitation, i.q. κατοίκησις, Ac. 17.26. L.G.

Κατοπτρίζω, (κάτοπτρον, a mirror)
f. ίσω,
to show in a mirror; to present a clear and correct image of *a thing; mid.* to have presented in a mirror, to have a clear image presented, *or, perhaps,* to reflect, 2 Co. 3.18. L.G.

Κατόρθωμα, ατος, τό, (κατορθόω, to setup upright, accomplish happily, fr. κατά & ὀρθόω, to make straight)
any thing happily and successfully accomplished; a beneficial and worthy deed, Ac. 24.3. L.G.

Κάτω, (κατά)
adv. & pre. down, downwards. Mat. 4.6. Lu. 4.9; beneath, below, under, Mat. 27.51. Mar. 14.66, et al.; ὁ, ἡ, τὸ, κάτω, what is below, earthly, Jno. 8.23.

Κατώτερος, α, ον, (comparat. fr. κάτω)
    lower, Ep. 4.9.
Κατωτέρω, (compar. of κάτω)
    adv. lower, further down; of time, under, Mat. 2.16.
Καῦμα, ατος, τό, (καίω)
    heat, scorching or burning heat, Re. 7.16; 16.9: whence
Καυματίζω,
    f. ίσω,
    to scrorch, burn, Mat. 13.6. Mar. 4.6. Re. 16.8, 9. L.G.
Καῦσις, εως, ἡ, (καίω)
    burning, being burned, He. 6.8: whence
Καυσόομαι, οῦμαι,
    to be on fire, burn intensely, 2 Pe. 3.10, 12. L.G.
Καύσων, ωνος, ὁ
    fervent scorching heat; the scorching of the sun, Mat. 20.12; hot weather, a hot time,
    Lu. 12.55; the scorching wind of the East, Eurus, Ja. 1.11.
Καυτηριάζω, (καυτήριον, an instrument for branding, fr. καίω)
    f. άσω, p. pass. κεκαυτηρίασμαι,
    to cauterise, brand; pass. met. to be branded with marks of guilt, or, to be seared into
    insensibility, 1 Ti. 4.2.
Καυχάομαι, ῶμαι,
    f. ήσομαι, a.1. ἐκαυχησάμην, p. κεκαύχημαι,
    to glory, boast, Ro. 2.17, 23; ὑπέρ τινος, to boast of a person or thing, undertake a
    laudatory testimony to, 2 Co. 12.5; to rejoice, exult, Ro. 5.2, 3, 11, et al.: whence
Καύχημα, ατος, τό
    a glorying, boasting, 1 Co. 5.6; ground or matter of glorying or boasting, Ro. 4.2; joy,
    exultation, Phi. 1.26; laudatory testimony, 1 Co. 9.15, 16. 2 Co. 9.3, et al.
Καύχησις, εως, ἡ,
    a later equivalent to καυχημα, Ro. 3.27. 2 Co. 7.4, 14; 11.10, et al.
Κέδρος, ου, ἡ,
    a cedar, Jno. 18.1, where κέδρων is a false reading for the proper name Κεδρών.
Κεῖμαι,
    f. κείσομαι,
    to lie, to be laid; to recline, to be lying, to have been laid down, Mat. 28.6. Lu 2.12, el
    al.; to have been laid, placed, set, Mat. 3.10. Lu. 3.9. Jno. 2.6, et al.; to be situated as a
    city, Mat. 5.14. Re. 21.16; to be in store, Lu. 12.19; met. to be specially set, solemnly
    appointed, destined, Lu. 2.34. Phi. 1.17. 1 Th. 3.3; to lie under an influence, to be
    involved in, 1 Jno. 5.19.
Κειρία, ας, ἡ,
    a bandage, swath, roller; in N.T., pl. grave-clothes, Jno. 11.44.
Κείρω,
    f. κερῶ, a.1. mid. ἐκειράμην,
    to cut off the hair, shear, shave, Ac. 8.32; 18.18. 1 Co. 11.6, bis.
Κέλευσμα, ατος, τό,
    a word of command; a mutual cheer; hence, in N.T., a loud shout, an arousing outcry,
    1 Th. 4.16: from
Κελεύω, (κέλω, κέλομαι, idem)
    f. εὐσω, a.1 ἐκέλευσα,
    100to order, command, direct, bid, Mat. 8.18; 14.19, 28, et al.
Κενοδοξία, ας, ἡ

emply conceit, vain glory, Phi. 2.3: *from*

Κενόδοξος, ου, ὁ, ἡ, (κενός & δόξα)
   vain-glorious, desirous of vain glory, Ga. 5.26.

Κενός, ή, όν,
   empty; having nothing, empty-handed, Mar. 12.3; *met.* vain, fruitless, void of effect, Ac. 4.25. 1 Co. 15.10; εἰς κενόν, in vain, to no purpose, 2 Co. 6.1, et al.; hollow, fallacious, false, Ep. 5.6. Col. 2.8; inconsiderate, foolish, Ja. 2.20.

Κενοφωνία, ας, ἡ, (κενός & φωνή)
   vain, empty babbling, vain disputation, fruitless discussion, 1 Ti. 6.20. 2 Ti. 2.16. N.T.

Κενόω, ῶ, (κενός)
   f. ώσω, a.1. ἐκένωσα,
   to empty, evacuate; ἑαυτόν, to divest one's self, of one's prorogatives, abase one's self, Phi. 2.7; to deprive *a thing* of its proper functions, Ro. 4.14. 1 Co. 1.17; to show to be without foundation, falsify, 1 Co. 9.15. 2 Co. 9.3.

Κέντρον, ου, τό, (κεντέω, to prick)
   a sharp point; a sting, Re. 9.10; a prick, stimulus, goad, Ac. 9.5; 26.14. *met., of death,* destructive power, deadly venom, 1 Co. 15.55, 56.

Κεντυρίων, ωνος, ὁ (Lat. *centurio,* fr. *centum,* a hundred)
   in its original signification, a commander of a hundred foot-soldiers, a centurion, Mar. 15.39, 44, 45.

Κενῶς (κενός)
   adv. in vain, to no purpose, unmeaningly, Ja. 4.5. L.G.

Κεραία, ας, ἡ (κέρας)
   pr. a horn-like projection, a point, extremity; *in N.T.,* an apex, or fine point, *as of letters;* the minutest part, a tittle, Mat. 5.18. Lu. 16.17.

Κερᾰμεύς, έως, ὁ, (κέραμος)
   a potter, Mat. 27.7, 10. Ro. 9.21.

Κεραμῐκός, ή, όν, (fr. same)
   made by a potter, earthen, Re. 2.27.

Κεράμιον, ίου, τό, (dimin. of κέραμος)
   an earthenware vessel, a pitcher, jar, Mar. 14.13. Lu. 22.10

Κέρᾰμος, ου, ὁ,
   potter's clay; earthenware; a tile, tiling, Lu. 5.19.

Κεράννῡμι, v. νύω, (κεράω)
   f. κεράσω, a.1. ἐκέρᾰσα, p. pass. κέκρᾱμαι later κεκέρασμαι,
   to mix, mingle, *drink;* to prepare *for drinking,* Re. 14.10; 18.6, *bis.*

Κέρας, ᾰτος, τό,
   a horn, Re. 5.6; 12.3, et al.; a projecting extremity *at the corners of an altar,* Re. 9.13; *fr. the Heb., used symbolically for* strength, power, Lu. 1.69.

Κεράτιον, ίου, τό, (dimin. of κέρας)
   pr. a little horn; *in N.T.,* a pod, the pod of the carob tree, or Ceratonia siliqua *of Linnæus, a common tree in the East and the south of Europe, growing to a considerable size, and producing long slender pods, with a pulp of sweetish taste and several brown shining seeds like beans, sometimes eaten by the poorer people in Syria and Palestine, and commonly used for fattening swine,* Lu. 15.16.

Κερδαίνω,
   f. δανῶ, κερδήσω & ομαι, a.1. ἐκέρδησα,
   to gain *as a matter of profit,* Mat. 25.17, et al.; to win, acquire possession of, Mat. 16.26; to profit in the avoidance of, to avoid, Ac. 27.21; *in N.T.,* Χριστόν, to win

Christ, to become possessed of *the privileges of the gospel,* Ph. 3.8; to win over *from estrangement* Mat. 18.15; to win over *to embrace the gospel,* 1 Co. 9.19, 20, 21, 22. 1 Pe. 3.1; *absol.* to make gain, Ja. 4.13: *from*

Κέρδος, εος, τό,
    gain, profit, Phi. 1.21; 3.7. Tit. 1.11.

Κέρμα, ατος, τό, (κείρω)
    something clipped small; small change, small pieces of money, coin, Jno. 2.15: *whence*

Κερματιστής, οῦ, ὁ,
    a money changer, Jno. 2.14. N.T.

Κεφάλαιον, ου, τό, (κεφαλή)
    a sum total; a sum of money, capital, Ac. 22.28; the crowning or ultimate point *to preliminary matters,* He. 8.1: *whence*

Κεφαλαιόω, ῶ,
    f. ώσω,
    to sum up; *but in N.T., equiv. to* κεφαλίζω, to wound on the head, Mar. 12.4.

Κεφᾰλή, ῆς, ἡ,
    the head, Mat. 5.36; 6.17, et al.; the head, top; κεφαλή γωνίας, the head of the corner, the chief corner stone, Mat. 21.42. Lu. 20.17; *met.* 101the head, superior, chief, principal, one to whom others are subordinate, 1 Co. 11.3. Ep. 1.22, et al.

Κεφαλίς, ίδος, ἡ, (dimin. of κεφαλή)
    in N.T., a roll, volume, division *of a book,* He. 10.7.

Κημόω, ῶ, (κημός, a curb, bridle, muzzle)
    f. ώσω,
    to muzzle, v.r. 1 Co. 9.9.

Κῆνσος, ου, ὁ, (Lat. *census*)
    a census, assessment, enumeration of the people and a valuation of their property; *in N.T.,* tribute, tax, Mat. 17.25; poll-tax, Mat. 22.17, 19. Mar. 12.14.

Κῆπος, ου, ὁ,
    a garden, any place planted with trees and herbs, Lu. 13.19. Jno. 18.1, 26; 19.41.

Κηρουρός, οῦ, ὁ, (κῆπος & οὖρος, a watcher)
    a garden-keeper, gardener, Jno. 20.15.

Κηρίον, ου, τό, (κηρός, beeswax)
    a honeycomb; a comb filled with honey, Lu. 24.42.

Κήρυγμα, ατος, τό, (κηρύσσω)
    proclamation, proclaiming, public annunciation, Mat. 12.41; public inculcation, preaching, 1 Co. 2.4; 15.14; *meton.* what is publicly inculcated, doctrine, &c. Ro. 16.25, et al.

Κήρυξ, ῠκος, ὁ,
    a herald, public messenger; *in N.T.,* a proclaimer, publisher, preacher, 1 Ti. 2.7. 2 Ti. 1.11. 2 Pe. 2.5.

Κηρύσσω,
    f. κηρύξω, a.1. ἐκήρυξα,
    to publish, proclaim, *as a herald,* 1 Co. 9.27; to announce openly and publicly, Mar. 1.4. Lu. 4.18; to noise abroad, Mar. 1.45; 7.36; to announce *as a matter of doctrine,* inculcate, preach, Mat. 24.14. Mar. 1.38; 13.10. Ac. 15.21. Ro. 2.21, et al.

Κῆτος, εος, τό,
    a large fish, sea monster, whale, Mat. 12.40.

Κηφᾶς, ᾶ, ὁ, (Aramæan, אפיכ)
    Cephas, a rock, *rendered into Greek by* Πέτρος, Jno. 1.43. 1 Co. 1.12, et al.

Κιβωτός, οῦ, ἡ,
    a chest, coffer; the ark *of the covenant*, He. 9.4; the ark *of Noah*, Mat. 24.38. Lu. 17.27, et al.
Κιθάρα, ας, ἡ,
    a lyre, 1 Co. 14.7. Re. 5.8; 14.2; 15.2. (ἄ): *whence*
Κιθαρίζω,
    f. ίσω
    to play on a lyre, to harp, 1 Co. 14.7. Re. 14.2.
Κιθαρῳδός, οῦ, ὁ, (κιθάρα & ἀείδω)
    one who plays on a lyre and accompanies it with his voice, a harper. Re. 14.2. 18.22.
Κινάμωμον, v. κιννάμωμον, ου, τό,
    cinnamon, *the aromatic bark of the* Laurus cinnamomum, *which grows in Arabia, Syria, &c.* Re. 18.13.
Κινδυνεύω,
    f. εύσω,
    to be in danger or peril, Lu. 8.23. Ac. 19.27, 40. 1 Co. 15.30: *from*
Κίνδῡνος, ου, ὁ,
    danger, peril, Ro. 8.35. 2 Co. 11.26.
Κῑνέω, ῶ, (κίω, to go)
    f. ήσω, a.1. ἐκίνησα,
    to set a-going; to move, Mat. 23.4; to excite, agitate, Ac. 24.5; 21.30; to remove, Re. 2.5; 6.14; *in N.T.,* κεφαλήν, to shake the head *in derision,* Mat. 27.39. Mar. 15.29; *mid.* to move, possess the faculty of motion, exercise the functions of life, Ac. 17.28: *whence*
Κίνησις, εως, ἡ,
    a moving, motion, Jno. 5.3.
Κιννάμωμον,
    see κινάμωμον.
Κλάδος, ου, ὁ, (κλάω, to break off)
    a bough, branch, shoot, Mat. 13.32; 21.8, et al.; *met.* offspring, progeny, posterity, Ro. 11.16, 21.
Κλαίω,
    f. κλαύσομαι, in N.T. κλαύσω, a.1. ἔκλαυσα,
    intrans. to weep, shed tears, Mat. 26.75. Mar. 5.38, 39. Lu. 19.41; 23.28, et al.; *trans.* to weep for, bewail, Mat. 2.18.
Κλάσις, εως, ἡ, (κλάω)
    a breaking, the act of breaking, Lu. 24.35. Ac. 2.42.
Κλάσμα, ατος, τό, (fr. same)
    a piece broken off, fragment, Mat. 14.20; 15.37. Mar. 6.43. et al.
Κλαυθμός, οῦ, ὁ, (κλαίω)
    weeping, Mat. 2.18; 8.12. et al.
Κλάω,
    f. κλάσω, a.1. ἔκλᾰσα,
    to break off; *in N.T.,* to break *bread,* Mat. 14.19, et al.; *with figurative reference to the violent death of Christ,* 1 Co. 11.24.
Κλείσ, κλειδός, κλειδί, κλεῖδα & κλεῖν, ἡ, pl. κλεῖδες, & κλεῖς,
    a key *used in the N.T. as the symbol of power, authority,* &c. Mat. 16.19. Re. 1.18; 3.7; 9.1; 20.1; *met.* 102means of attaining *knowledge,* Lu. 11.52: *from*
Κλείω,
    f. είσω, a.1. ἔκλεισα, p. pass. κέκλεισμαι, a.1. pass. ἐκλείσθην,

to close, shut, Mat. 6.6; 25.10, et al.; to shut up *a person,* Re. 20.3; *met. of the heavens,* Lu. 4.25. Re. 11.6; κλεῖσαι τὰ σπλάγχνα, to shut up one's bowels, to be hardhearted, void of compassion, 1 Jno. 3.17; κλείειν τὴν βασιλείαν τῶν οὐρανῶν, to endeavour to prevent entrance into the kingdom of heaven, Mat. 23.14.

Κλέμμα, ατος, τό, (κλέπτω)
 theft, Re. 9.21.

Κλέος, τό,
 pr. rumour, report; good report, praise, credit, 1 Pe. 2.20.

Κλέπτης, ου, ὁ,
 a thief, Mat. 6.19, 20; 24.43, et al.; *trop.* a deceiver, imposter, Jno. 10.8: *from*

Κλέπτω,
 f. ψω, & ψομαι, p. κέκλοφα, a.1. ἔκλεψα,
 to steal, Mat. 6.19, 20; 19.18, et al.; to take away stealthily, remove secretly, Mat. 27.64; 28.13.

Κλῆμα, ατος, τό, (κλάω)
 a branch, shoot, twig, *esp. of the vine,* Jno. 15.2, 4, 5, 6.

Κληρονομέω, ῶ, (κληρονόμος)
 f. ήσω, p. κεκληρονόμηκα, a.1. ἐκληρονόμησα,
 pr. to acquire by lot; to inherit, obtain by inheritance; *in N.T.,* to obtain, acquire, receive possession of, Mat. 5.5; 19.29, et al.; *absol.* to be heir, Ga. 4.30: *whence*

Κληρονομία, ας, ἡ,
 an inheritance, patrimony, Mat. 21.38. Mar. 12.7; a possession, portion, property, Ac. 7.5; 20.32, et al.; *in N.T.,* a share, participation *in privileges,* Ac. 20.32. Eph. 1.14, et al.

Κληρονόμος, ου, ὁ, (κλῆρος & νέμομαι)
 an heir, Mat. 21.38. Ga. 4.1, et al.; a possessor, Ro. 4.13. He. 11.7. Ja. 2.5; et al.

Κλῆρος, ου, ὁ,
 a lot, die, a thing used in determining chances, Mat. 27.35. Mar. 15.24, et al.; assignment, investiture, Ac. 1.17, 25; allotment, destination, Col. 1.12; a part, portion, share, Ac. 8.21; 26.18; a constituent portion *of the church,* 1 Pe. 5.3: *whence*

Κληρόω, ῶ,
 f. ώσω,
 to choose by lot; *mid.* κληροῦμαι, a.1. ἐκληρώθην, to obtain by lot or assignment; to obtain a portion, receive a share, Eph. 1.11.

Κλῆσις, εως, ἡ, (καλέω)
 a call, calling, invitation; *in N.T.,* the call or invitation *to the privileges of the Gospel,* Ro. 11.29. Ep. 1.18, et al.; the favour and privilege of the invitation, 2 Th. 1.11. 2 Pe. 1.10; the temporal condition in which the call found a person, 1 Co. 7.20; 1.26.

Κλητός, ή, όν, (fr. same)
 called, invited; *in N.T.,* called *to privileges or functions,* Mat. 20.16; 22.14. Ro. 1.1, 6, 7. 1 Co. 1.1, 2, et al.

Κλίβᾰνος, ου, ὁ, (At. κρίβανος)
 an oven, Mat. 6.30. Lu. 12.28.

Κλίμα, ατος, τό, (κλίνω)
 pr. a slope; a portion of the *ideal* slope *of the earth's surface;* a tract or region *of country,* Ro. 15.23. 2 Co. 11.10. Ga. 1.21.

Κλίνη, ης, ἡ, (fr. same)
 a couch, bed, Mat. 9.2, 6. Mar. 4.21, et al.

Κλῑνίδιον, ίου, τό, (dim. of κλίνη)
 a small couch or bed, Lu. 5.19, 24.

Κλίνω,

f. ινῶ, p. κέκλῐκα, a.1. ἔκλῑνα,

pr. trans. to cause to slope or bend; to bow down, Lu. 24.5. Jno. 19.30; to lay down *to rest*, Mat. 8.20. Lu. 9.58; to put to flight *troops,* He. 11.34; *intrans., of the day,* to decline, Lu. 9.12; 24.29.

Κλῐσία, ας, ἡ, (κλίνω)

pr. a place for reclining; a tent, seat, couch; *in N.T.,* a company of persons reclining *at a meal,* Lu. 9.14.

Κλοπή, ῆς, ἡ, (κλέπτω)

theft, Mat. 15.19. Mar. 7.22.

Κλύδων, ωνος, ὁ, (κλύζω, to dash, surge, like the waves)

a wave, billow, surge, Ja. 1.6: *whence*

Κλυδωνίζομαι,

to be tossed by waves; *met.* to fluctuate *in opinion,* be agitated, tossed to and fro, Ep. 4.14. L.G.

Κνήθω, (κνάω)

f. κνήσω,

to scratch, to tickle, cause titillation; *in N.T., mid., met.* to procure pleasurable excitement for, to indulge an itching, 2 Ti. 4.3.

Κοδράντης, ου, ὁ, (Lat. *quadrans*)

a Roman brass coin, *equivalent to the* fourth part *of an* as, *or* ἀσσάριον, *or to* δύο λεπτα, *and equal too about 103three-fourths of a farthing,* Mat. 5.26. Mar. 12.42. N.T.

Κοιλία, ας, ἡ, (κοῖλος, hollow)

a cavity; the belly, Mat. 15.17. Mar. 7.19; the stomach, Mat. 12.40. Lu. 15.16; the womb, Mat. 19.12. Lu. 1.15, et al.; *fr. the Heb.* the inner self, Jno. 7.38.

Κοιμάω, ῶ

f. ήσω, p. pass. κεκοίμημαι,

to lull to sleep; *pass.* to fall asleep, be asleep, Mat. 28.13. Lu. 22.45; *met.* to die, be dead, Ac. 7.60; 13.36, et al.: *whence*

Κοίμησις, εως, ἡ,

sleep; *meton.* rest, repose, Jno. 11.13.

Κοινός, ή, όν,

common, belonging equally to several, Ac. 2.44; 4.32; *in N.T.,* common, profane, He. 10.29; *ceremonially* unclean, Mar. 7.2. Ac. 10.14, et al.: *whence*

Κοινόω, ῶ,

f. ώσω, p. κεκοίνωκα, a.1. ἐκοίνωσα,

to make common; *in N.T.,* to profane, desecrate, Ac. 21.28; to render *ceremonially* unclean, defile, pollute, Mat. 15.11, 18, 20; to pronounce unclean *ceremonially,* Ac. 10.15; 11.9.

Κοινωνέω, ῶ, (κοινωνός)

f. ήσω, p. κεκοινώνηκα, a.1. ἐκοινώνησα,

to have in common, share, He. 2.14; to be associated in, to become a sharer in, Ro. 15.27. 1 Pe. 4.13; to become implicated in, be a party to, 1 Ti. 5.22. 2 Jno. 11; to associate one's self with *by sympathy and assistance,* to communicate with *in the way of aid and relief,* Ro. 12.13. Ga. 6.6: *whence*

Κοινωνία, ας, ἡ,

fellowship, partnership, Ac. 2.42. 2 Co. 6.14. Ga. 2.9. Phi. 3.10. 1 Jno. 1.3, et al.; participation, communion, 1 Co. 10.16, et al.; aid, relief, He. 13.16, et al.; contribution in aid, Ro. 15.26.

Κοινωνικός, ή, όν,

    social; *in N.T.,* ready to communicate *in kind offices,* liberal, beneficent, 1 Ti. 6.18.

Κοινωνός, οῦ, ὁ, ἡ, (κοινός)

    a fellow-partner, Mat. 23.30. Lu. 5.10. 1 Co. 10.18, 20. 2 Co. 8.23. Phile. 17. He. 10.33; a sharer, partaker, 2 Co. 1.7. 1 Pe. 5.1. 2 Pe. 1.4.

Κοίτη, ης, ἡ, (κεῖμαι)

    a bed, Lu. 11.7; the *conjugal* bed, He. 13.4; *meton.* sexual intercourse, concubitus; *hence,* lewdness, whoredom, chambering, Ro. 13.13; *in N.T.,* conception, Ro. 9.10: *whence*

Κοιτών, ῶνος, ὁ,

    a bed-chamber, Ac. 12.20.

Κόκκῐνος, η, ον, (κόκκος, kernel of the coccus ilicis *of Linnœus, a small insect, found on the leaves of the* quercus cocciferus, *or holm oak, which was used by the ancients, as the cochineal insect now is, for dyeing a beautiful crimson or deep scarlet colour, and supposed by them to be the* berry *of a plant or tree)*

    dyed with coccus, crimson, scarlet, Mat. 27.28. He. 9.19. Re. 17.3, 4; 18.12, 16.

Κόκκος, ου, ὁ,

    a kernel, seed, grain, Mat. 13.31; 17.20, et al.

Κολάζω,

    f. άσομαι & άσω,

    pr. to curtail, to coerce; to chastise, punish, Ac. 4.21. 2 Pe. 2.9.

Κολακεία, ας, ἡ, (κόλαξ, a flatterer)

    flattery, adulation, obsequiousness, 1 Th. 2.5.

Κόλᾰσις, εως, ἡ , (κολάζω)

    chastisement, punishment, Mat. 25.46; painful disquietude, torment, 1 Jno. 4.18.

Κολαφίζω, (κόλαφος, a blow with the fist)

    f. ίσω,

    to beat with the fist, buffet, Mat. 26.67. Mar. 14.65; *met.* to maltreat, treat with contumely and ignominy, 1 Co. 4.11; to punish, 1 Pe. 2.20; to buffet, fret, afflict, 2 Co. 12.7.

Κολλάω, ῶ,

    f. ήσω,

    to glue or weld together; *mid.* to adhere to, Lu. 10.11; *met.* to attach one's self to, unite with, associate with, Lu. 15.15. Ac. 5.13, et al.

Κολλούριον, v. κολλύριον, ου, τό, (dimin. of κολλύρα, a cake)

    collyrium, eye-salve, Re. 3.18.

Κολλυβιστής, οῦ, ὁ, (κόλλυβος, small coin)

    a money-changer, Mat. 21.12. Mar. 11.15. Jno. 2.15.

Κολλύριον,

    see κολλούριον.

Κολοβόω, ῶ, (κολοβός, curtailed, mutilated, fr. κόλος, id.)

    f. ώσω,

    in N.T., of time, to cut short, shorten, Mat. 24.22. Mar. 13.20.

Κόλπος, ου, ὁ,

    the bosom, Lu. 16.22, 23. Jno 1.18; 13.23; the bosom of a garment, Lu. 6.38; a bay, creek, inlet, Ac. 27.39.

Κολυμβάω, ῶ,

    f. ήσω,

    to dive; *in N.T.,* to swim, Ac. 27.43: *whence*

Κολυμβήθρα, ας, ἡ,

104a place where one may swim; a pond, pool, Jno. 5.2, 4, 7; 9.7, 11.

Κολωνία, ας, ἡ, (Lat. *colonia*)
    a Roman colony, Ac. 16.12.

Κομάω, ῶ,
    f. ήσω,
    to have long hair, wear the hair long, 1 Co. 11.14, 15: *from*

Κόμη, ης, ἡ,
    the hair; a head of long hair, 1 Co. 11.15.

Κομίζω, (κομέω, to take care of)
    f. ίσω, & ιῶ, mid. ιοῦμαι, a.1. ἐκόμισα,
    pr. to take into kindly keeping, to provide for; to convey, bring, Lu. 7.37; *mid.* to bring for one's self; to receive, obtain, 2 Co. 5.10. Ep. 6.8, et al.; to receive again, recover, Mat. 25.27. He. 11.19.

Κομψότερον, (comp. of κόμψως, well, smarthly)
    adv. in N.T., in better health, Jno. 4.52.

Κονιάω, ῶ, (κόνις, v. κονία, dust, limedust)
    f. άσω, p. pass. κεκονίᾱμαι,
    to white-wash, *or,* plaster, Mat. 23.27. Ac. 23.3.

Κονιορτός, οῦ, ὁ, (κόνις & ὄρνυμι, to raise)
    dust excited; dust, Mat. 10.14. Lu. 9.5; 10.11. Ac. 13.51; 22.23.

Κοπάζω, (κόπος)
    f. άσω,
    pr. to grow weary, suffer exhaustion; to abate, be stilled, Mat. 14.32. Mar. 4.39; 6.51.

Κοπετός, οῦ, ὁ, (κόπτω)
    pr. a beating of the breast, &c. in token of grief; a wailing, lamentation, Ac. 8.2.

Κοπή, ῆς, ἡ, (κόπτω)
    a stroke, smiting; *in N.T.,* slaughter, He. 7.1.

Κοπιάω, ῶ,
    f. άσω, p. κεκοπίᾱκα, a.1. ἐκοπίᾱσα,
    to be wearied or spent with labour, faint from weariness, Mat. 11.28. Jno. 4.6; *in N.T.,* to labour hard, to toil, Lu. 5.5. Jno. 4.38, et al.: *from*

Κόπος, ου, ὁ, (κόπτω)
    trouble, vexation, uneasiness, Mat. 26.10. Mar. 14.6; labour, wearisome labour, travail, toil, 1 Co. 3.8; 15.58, et al.; *meton.* the fruit or consequences of labour, Jno. 4.38. 2 Co. 10.15.

Κοπρία, ας, ἡ,
    dung, manure, Lu. 13.8; 14.35.

Κόπριον, ου, τό,
    the same, v.r. Lu. 13.8. L.G.

Κόπτω,
    f. ψω,
    to smite, cut; to cut off or down, Mat. 21.8. Mar. 11.8. *mid.* to beat one's self *in mourning,* lament, bewail, Lu. 8.52; 23.27; et al.

Κόραξ, ἄκος, ὁ,
    a raven, crow, Lu. 12.24.

Κοράσιον, ίου, τό, (dim. of κόρη)
    a girl, damsel, maiden, Mat. 9.24, 25, 14.11, et al. (ă).

Κορβᾶν, ὁ, indec. v. κορβανᾶς, ᾶ, ὁ, (Heb. וְבָּרק; Aram. אָנברק, *explained in Greek by* δῶρον)
    corban, a gift, offering, oblation, any thing consecrated to God, Mar. 7.11; *meton.* the sacred treasury, Mat. 27.6.

Κορέννυμι,
f. κορέσω, p. pass. κεκόρεσμαι,
to satiate, satisfy, Ac. 27.38. 1 Co. 4.8.
Κορίνθιος, ία, ιον,
Corinthian; an inhabitant of Κόρινθος, Corinth, Ac. 18.8. 2 Co. 6.11.
Κόρος, ου, ὁ, (Heb. רכ)
a cor, *the largest Jewish measure for things dry, equal to the homer, and about fifteen bushels English, according to Josephus,* (Ant. 1.xv. c.9. s.2.), Lu. 16.7.
Κοσμέω, (κόσμος)
f. ήσω, p. κεκόσμηκα, a.1. ἐκόσμησα,
to arrange, set in order; to adorn, decorate, embellish, Mat. 12.44; 23.29; to prepare, put in readiness, trim, Mat. 25.7; *met.* to honour, dignify, Tit. 2.10.
Κοσμικός, ή, όν, (κόσμος, the world)
pr. belonging to the universe; *in N.T.,* accommodated to the present state of things, adapted to this world, worldly, Tit. 2.12; τὸ κοσμικόν, *as a subst.,* the apparatus *for the service of the tabernacle,* He. 9.1.
Κόσμιος, ία, ιον, v. ου, ὁ, ἡ, (κόσμος)
decorous, well-ordered, 1 Ti. 2.9; 3.2.
Κοσμοκράτωρ, ορος, ὁ, (κόσμος & κρατέω)
pr. monarch of the world; *in N.T.,* a worldly prince, a power paramount in the world *of the unbelieving and ungodly,* Ep. 6.12. (ᾰ). L.G.
Κόσμος, ου, ὁ,
pr. order, regular disposition; ornament, decoration, embellishment, 1 Pe. 3.3; the world, the material universe, Mat. 13.35, et al.; the world, the aggregate of sensitive 105existance, 1 Co. 4.9; the *lower* world, the earth, Mar. 16.15, et al.; the world, the aggregate of mankind, Mat. 5.14, et al.; the world, the public, Jno. 7.4; *in N.T.,* the present order of things, the *secular* world, Jno. 18.36, et al.; the human race *external to the Jewish nation,* the *heathen* world, Ro. 11.12, 15; the world *external to the Christian body,* 1 Jno. 3.1, 13, et al.
Κοῦμι, (Aram. ימוק sec. pers. fem. sing. imperat. of םוק, to arise)
cumi, arise, Mar. 5.41.
Κουστωδία, ας, ἡ, (Lat. *custodia)*
a watch, guard, Mat. 27.65, 66; 28.11.
Κουφίζω, (κοῦφος, light)
f. ίσω,
to lighten, make light or less heavy, Ac. 27.38.
Κόφϊνος, ου, ὁ,
a basket, Mat. 14.20; 16.9. Mar. 6.43, et al.
Κράββατος, ου, ὁ, (Lat. *grabatus)*
a couch *capable of holding one person,* Mar. 2.4, 9, 11, 12, et al. L.G.
Κράζω,
f. κεκράξομαι, a. ἔκραγον, later f. κράξω, a. ἔκραξα, p. κέκραγα
with a pres. signif., to utter a cry, Mat. 14.26, et al.; to exclaim, vociferate, Mat. 9.27. Jno. 1.15, et al.; to cry *for vengeance,* Ja. 5.4; to cry *in supplication,* Ro. 8.15. Ga. 4.6.
Κραιπάλη, ης, ἡ,
debauch, Lu. 21.34. (ᾰ).
Κρᾱνίον, ου, τό, (κάρα)
a skull, Mat. 27.33. Mar. 15.22. Lu. 23.33. Jno. 19.17.
Κράσπεδον, ου, τό,
a margin, border; *in N.T.,* a fringe, tuft, tassel, Mat. 9.20; 14.36; 23.5, et al.

Κραταιός, ά, όν, (κράτος)
strong, mighty, powerful, 1 Pe. 5.6.
Κραταιόω, ῶ, (fr. same)
f. ώσω,
to strengthen, render strong, corroborate, confirm; *pass.* to grow strong, acquire strength, Lu. 1.80; 2.40. Ep. 3.16; to be firm, resolute, 1 Co. 16.13. L.G.
Κρατέω, ῶ, (fr. same)
f. ήσω, p. κεκράτηκα, a.1. ἐκράτησα,
pr. to be strong; to be superior to any one, subdue, vanquish, Ac. 2.24; to get into one's power, lay hold of, seize, apprehend, Mat. 14.3; 18.28; 21.46; to gain, compass, attain, Ac. 27.13; *in N.T.,* to lay hold of, grasp, clasp, Mat. 9.25. Mar. 1.31; 5.41; to retain, to keep under reserve, Mar. 9.10; *met.* to hold fast, observe, Mar. 7.3, 8. 2 Th. 2.15; to hold to, adhere to, Ac. 3.11. Col. 2.19; to restrain, hinder, repress, Lu. 24.16. Re. 7.1; to retain, not to remit *sins,* Jno. 20.23.
Κράτιστος, η, ον, (super. from κρατύς, strongest)
in N.T., κράτιστε, *a term of respect,* most excellent, noble, or illustious, Lu. 1.3. Ac. 23.26; 24.3; 26.25.
Κράτος, εος, τό,
strength, power, might, force, Ac. 19.20. Ep. 1.19; *meton.* a display of might, Lu. 1.51; power, sway, dominion, He. 2.14. 1 Pe. 4.11; 5.11, et al. (ἄ).
Κραυγάζω,
f. άσω, a.1. ἐκραύγασα,
to cry out, exclaim, vociferate, Mat. 12.19; 15.22, et al.: *from*
Κραυγή, ῆς, ἡ, (κράζω)
a cry, outcry, clamour, vociferation, Mat. 25.6. Ac. 23.9. Ep. 4.31. Re. 14.18; a cry *of sorrow,* wailing, lamentation, Re. 21.4; a cry *for help,* earnest supplication, He. 5.7.
Κρέας, ατος, έως, τό, pl. κρέατα, κρέα
flesh, meat, Ro. 14.21. 1 Co. 8.13.
Κρείττων, v. σσων, ονος, ὁ, ἡ, τὸ, -ον, (used as the comp. of ἀγαθός)
better, more useful or profitable, more conducive to good, 1 Co. 7.9, 38; superior, more excellent, of a higher nature, more valuable, He. 1.4; 6.9; 7.7, 19, 22. et al.
Κρεμάννυμι,
f. άσω, a.1. ἐκρέμασα, a.1. pass. ἐκρεμάσθην,
to hang, suspend, Ac. 5.30; 10.39; *pass.* to be hung, suspended, Mat. 18.6. Lu. 23.39; *mid.* κρέμαμαι, to hang, be suspended, Ac. 28.4. Ga. 3.13, et al.; *met.* κρέμαμαι ἐν, to hang upon, to be referable to *as an ultimate principle,* Mat. 22.40.
Κρημνός, οῦ, ὁ, (κρεμάννυμι)
a hanging steep, precipice, a steep bank, Mat. 8.32. Mar. 5.13. Lu. 8.33.
Κρής, ητός, pl. κρῆτες,
a Cretan, an inhabitant of Κρήτη, Ac. 2.11. Tit. 1.12.
Κριθή, ῆς, ἡ,
barley, Re. 6.6: *whence*
Κρίθϊνος, η, ον,
made of barley, Jno. 6.9. 13.
Κρίμα, v. κρῖμα, ατος, τό, (κρίνω)
106judgment; a sentence, award, Mat. 7.2. Lu. 24.20. Ro. 2.2, et al.; an administrative decree, Ro. 11.33; condemnation, Mat. 23.18. Lu. 23.40. Ro. 3.8; 5.16, et al.; administration of judgment, Jno. 9.39. Ac. 24.25, et al.; execution of justice, 1 Pe. 4.17; a lawsuit, 1 Co. 6.7.
Κρίνον, ου, τό,

a lily, Mat. 6.28. Lu. 12.27.

Κρίνω,

f. ῐνῶ, a.1. ἔκρῑνα, p. κέκρῐκα, p. pass. κέκρῐμαι, a.1. pass. ἐκρίθην,

pr. to separate; to make a distinction between; to decide, determine, resolve, Ac. 3.13; 15.19; 27.1, et al.; to deem, Ac. 13.46. Ro. 14.5; to resolve on, decree, Ac. 16.4. Re. 16.5; to form a judgment, to pass judgment on, Jno. 8.15, et al.; to judge *judicially,* try, Jno. 18.31, et al.; to sentence, Jno. 7.51; to condemn, Lu. 19.22. Ac. 13.27; *in N.T.,* to execute sentence upon, to punish, Ac. 7.7, et al.; to administer a government over, Mat. 19.28. Lu. 22.30; *perhaps,* to avenge, He. 10.30; *pass.* to be brought to trail, Ac. 25.1, 20. Ro. 3.4 et al.; *mid.* to go to law, litigate, Mat. 5.40: *whence*

Κρίσις, εως, ἡ,

pr. distinction; discrimination; judgment, decision, sentence, Jno. 7.24; 5.30; judgment, trail, Jno. 12.31. He. 9.27; administration of justice, Jno. 5.22, 27; condemnatory sentence, condemnation, Jno. 12.31; *in N.T., meton.* ground of condemnation, Jno. 3.10; a court of justice, tribunal, Mat. 5.21, 22; *fr. the Heb.* justice, equity, Mat. 23.23. Lu. 11.42. (ῐ).

Κριτήριον, ίου, τό,

pr. a standard or means by which to judge, criterion; a court of justice, tribunal, Ja. 2.6; a cause, controversy, 1 Co. 6.2, 4: *from*

Κρῐτής, οῦ, ὁ, (κρίνω)

a judge, Mat. 5.25; 12.27. Lu. 12.14, et al., *fr. the Heb.* a ruler, prince, Ac. 13.20: *whence*

Κριτικός, ή, όν,

able or quick to discern or judge, He. 4.12.

Κρούω,

f. ούσω,

to knock *at a door,* Mat. 7.7, 8. Lu. 11.9, 10; 13.25, et al.

Κρύπτη, ἡ,

a vault or closet, a cell *for storage,* v.r. Lu. 11.33.

Κρυπτός, ή, όν,

hidden, concealed, secret, clandestine, Mat. 6.4, 6, 18, et al.; τὰ κρυπτά, secrets, Ro. 2.16. 1 Co. 14.25: *from*

Κρύπτω,

f. ψω, a.1. ἔκρυψα, p. pass. κέκρυμμαι, a. 2. pass. ἐκρύβην, (ῠ),

to hide, conceal, Mat. 5.14, et al.; *in N.T.,* to lay up in store, Col. 3.3. Re. 2.17; κεκρυμμένος, concealed, secret, Jno. 19.38.

Κρυσταλλίζω,

f. ίσω,

to be clear, brilliant like crystal, Re. 21.11: (N.T.) *from*

Κρύσταλλος, ου, ὁ, (κρύος, cold)

pr. clear ice; crystal, Re. 4.6; 22.1.

Κρυφαῖος, αία, αῖον, (κρύπτω)

secret, hidden, v.r. Mat. 6.18.

Κρυφή, (fr. same)

adv. in secret, secretly, not openly, Ep. 5.12.

Κτάομαι, ῶμαι,

f. ήσομαι,

to get, procure, provide, Mat. 10.9; to make gain, gain, Lu. 18.12; to purchase, Ac. 8.20; 22.28; to be the cause or occasion of purchasing, Ac. 1.18; to preserve, save, Lu.

21.19; to get under control, to be winning the mastery over, 1 Th. 4.4; p. κέκτημαι, to possess: *whence*

Κτῆμα, ατος, τό,
    a possession, property, & *spc.* real estate, Mat. 19.22. Mar. 10.22. Ac. 2.45; 5.1.

Κτῆνος, εος, τό,
    pr. property, *generally used in the plural* τὰ κτήνη; property *in animals;* a beast of burden, Lu. 10.34. Ac. 23.24; beasts, cattle, 1 Co. 15.39. Re. 18.13.

Κτήτωρ, ορος, ὁ, (κτάομαι)
    a possessor, owner, Ac. 4.34. L.G.

Κτίζω,
    f. ίσω, a.1. ἔκτισα, p. pass. ἔκτισμαι,
    pr. to reduce from a state of disorder and wildness; *in N.T.,* to call into being, to create, Mar. 13.19, et al.; to call into individual existence, to frame, Eph. 2.15; to create *spiritually,* to invest with a *spiritual* frame, Eph. 2.10; 4.25: *whence*

Κτίσις, εως, ἡ,
    pr. a framing, founding; *in N.T.,* creation, the act of creating, Ro. 1.20; creation, the material universe, Mar. 10.6; 13.19. He. 9.11. 2 Pe. 3.4; a created thing, a creature, Ro. 1.25; 8.39. Col. 1.15. He. 4.13; the human race, Mar. 16.15. Ro. 8.19, 20, 21, 22. Col. 1.23; 107a *spiritual* creation, 2 Co. 5.17. Ga. 6.15; an institution, ordinance, 1 Pe. 2.13.

Κτίσμα, ατος, τό,
    pr. a thing founded; *in N.T.,* a created being, creature, 1 Ti. 4.4. Ja. 1.18, et al. L.G.

Κτιστής, οῦ, ὁ, v. κτίστης, ου, ὁ,
    a founder; *in N.T.,* a creator, 1 Pe. 4.19. L.G.

Κυβεία, ας, ἡ, (κυβεύω, to play at dice, fr. κύβος, a cube, die)
    pr. dicing; *met.* sleight, versatile artifice, Eph. 4.14.

Κυβέρνησις, εως, ἡ, (κυβερνάω, to steer, direct)
    government, office of a governor or director; *meton.* a director, 1 Co. 12.28.

Κυβερνήτης, ου, ὁ, (fr. same)
    a pilot, helmsman, Ac. 27.11. Re. 18.17.

Κυκλόθεν,
    adv. around, round about, Re. 4.3, 4, 8; 5.11: *from*

Κύκλος, ου, ὁ,
    a circle; *in N.T.,* κύκλῳ, *adverbially,* round, round about, around, Mar. 3.34; 6.6, 36, et al.: *whence*

Κυκλόω, ῶ,
    f. ώσω, a.1. ἐκύκλωσα,
    to encircle, surround, encompass, come around, Jno. 10.24. Ac. 14.20. *spc.* to besiege, Lu 21.20. He. 11.30. Re. 20.9.

Κύλισμα, ατος, τό,
    pr. a rolling thing; *in N.T.,* a place of rolling or wallowing, wallowing-place, 2 Pe. 2.22: (L.G.) *from*

Κυλίω, (a later form from κυλίνδω)
    f. ίσω, a.1. ἐκύλῑσα,
    to roll; *mid.* to roll one's self, to wallow, Mar. 9.20. (ῑ).

Κυλλός, ή, όν,
    pr. crooked, bent; mained, lame, crippled, Mat. 18.8, et al.

Κῦμα, ατος, τό,
    a wave, surge, billow, Mat. 8.24; 14.24, et al.

Κύμβᾰλον, ου, τό, (κύμβος, a hollow)

a cymbal, 1 Co. 13.1.

Κύμῑνον, ου, τό,

cumin, cuminum sativum *of Linnœus, a plant, a native of Egypt and Syria, whose seeds are of an aromatic, warm, bitterish taste, with a strong but not disagreeable smell, and used by the ancients as a condiment,* Mat. 23.23.

Κυνάριον, ίου, το, (dmin. of κύων)

a little dog; a cur, Mat. 15.26, 27. Mar. 7.27, 28.

Κύπριος, ου, ό,

a Cypriot, an inhabitant of Κύπρος, Cyprus, Ac. 4.36; 11.20; 21.16.

Κύπτω,

f. ψω, a.1. ἔκυψα,

to bend forwards, stoop down, Mar. 1.7. Jno. 8.6, 8.

Κυρηναῖος, ου, ό,

a Cyrenian, an inhabitant of Κυρήνη, Cyrene, Mat. 27.32, et al.

Κυρία, ας, ή, (κύριος)

a lady, 2 Jno. 1, 5.

Κυριακός, ή, όν, (fr. same)

pertaining to the Lord Jesus Christ, the Lord's, 1 Co. 11.20. Re. 1.10. N.T.

Κυριεύω,

f. εύσω, a.1. ἐκυρίευσα,

to be lord over, to be possessed of master over, Ro. 6.9, 14; 7.1; 14.9. 2 Co. 1.24; to exercise sway over, Lu. 22.25: *from*

Κύριος, ίου, ό

a lord, master, Mat. 12.8, et al.; an owner, possessor, Mat. 20.8, et al.; a potentate, sovereign, Ac. 25.26; a power, deity, 1 Co. 8.5; the Lord, Jehovah, Mat. 1.22, et al.; the Lord Jesus Christ, Mat. 24.42. Mar. 16.19. Lu. 10.1. Jno. 4.1. 1 Co. 4.5, et al. freq.; Κύριε, *a term of respect of various force,* Sir, Lord, Mat. 13.27. Ac. 9.6, et al. freq.: *whence*

Κυριότης, τητος, ή,

lordship; constituted authority, Eph. 1.21. 2 Pe. 2.10. Ju. 8; *pl.* authorities, potentates, Col. 1.16. N.T.

Κυρόω, ῶ, (κῦρος, authority, confirmation)

f. ώσω, p. κεκύρωκα,

to confirm, ratify, Ga. 3.15; to assure, 2 Co. 2.8.

Κύων, κυνός, ό, ή,

a dog, Lu. 16.21. 2 Pe. 2.22; *met.* a dog, a religious corrupter, Phi. 3.2; miscreant, Re. 22.15.

Κῶλον, ου, τό,

a member or limb of the body, He. 3.17.

Κωλύω,

f. ύσω, a.1. ἐκώλυσα, a.1. pass. ἐκωλύθην (ῡ),

to hinder, restrain, prevent, Mat. 19.14. Ac. 8.36. Ro. 1.13, et al.

Κώμη, ης, ή,

a village, a country town, Mat. 9.35; 10.11. Lu. 8.1, et al.

Κωμόπολις, εως, ή, (κώμη & πόλις)

a large village, open town, Mar. 1.38. L.G.

Κῶμος, ου, ό,

108*pr.* a festive procession, a merry-making; *in N.T.,* a revel, lascivious feasting, Ro. 13.13. Ga. 5.21. 1 Pe. 4.3.

Κώνωψ, ωπος, ό,

a gnat, culex, *which is found in wine when acescent,* Mat. 23.24.

Κωφός, ή, όν,

    pr. blunt, dull, *as a weapon;* dull of hearing, deprived of hearing, deaf, Mat. 11.5. Mar. 7.32, 37. Lu. 7.22; dumb, mute, Mat. 9.32, 33, et al.; *meton.* making dumb, causing dumbness, Lu. 11.14.

Λ, λ, *Λάμβδα*

Λαγχάνω,

    f. Λήξομαι, p. εΐληχα, p.2. λέλογχα, a.2. ἔλᾰχον,

    to have assigned to one, to obtain, receive, Ac. 1.17. 2 Pe. 1.1; to have fall to one by lot, Lu. 1.9; *absol.* to cast lots, Jno. 19.24

Λάθρα, (λανθάνω)

    adv. secretly, Mat. 1.19; 2.7, et al.

Λαίλαψ, ᾰπος, ἡ

    a squall of wind, a hurricane, Mar. 4.37, et al.

Λακτίζω, (λάξ, with the heel)

    f. ίσω,

    to kick, Ac. 9.5; 26.14.

Λαλέω, ῶ

    f. ήσω, p. λελάληκα, a.1. ἐλάλησα,

    to make vocal utterance; to babble, to talk; *in N.T., absol.,* to exercise the faculty of speech, Mat. 9.33, et al.; to speak, Mat. 10.20, et al.; to hold converse with, to talk with, Mat. 12.46. Mar. 6.50. Re. 1.12, et al.; to discourse, to make an address, Lu. 11.37. Ac. 11.20; 21.39, et al.; to make an announcement, to make a declaration, Lu. 1.55, et al.; to make mention, Jno. 12.41. Ac. 2.31. He. 4.8. 2 Pe. 3.16; *trans.,* to speak, address, preach, Mat. 9.18. Jno. 3.11. Tit. 2.1, et al.; to give utterance to, to utter, Mar. 2.7. Jno. 3.34, et al.; to tell, recount, Mat. 26.13, et al.; to declare, announce, reveal, Lu. 24.25, et al.; to disclose, 2 Co. 12.4.

Λαλιά, ᾶς, ἡ,

    talk; *in N.T.,* matter of discourse, Jno. 4.42; 8.43; language, dialect, Mat. 26.73. Mar. 14.70.

Λαμά v. Λαμμᾶ (Heb. המל)

    for what? why? wherefore? Mat. 27.46. Mar. 15.34.

Λαμβάνω,

    f. λήψομαι, p. εΐληφα, a.2. ἔλᾰβον, a.1. pass. ἐλήφθην,

    to take, take up, take in the hand, Mat. 10.38; 13.31, 33, et al.; to take on one's self, sustain, Mat. 8.17; to take, seize, seize upon, Mat. 5.40; 21.34. Lu. 5.26. 1 Co. 10.13, et al.; to catch, Lu 5.5. 2 Co. 12.16; to assume, put on, Phi. 2.7; to make a rightful or successful assumption of, Jno. 3.27; to conceive, Ac. 28.15; to take *by way of provision,* Mat. 16.5; to get, get together, Mat. 16.9; to receive *as payment,* Mat. 17.24. He. 7.8; to take *to wife,* Mar. 12..19; to admit, give reception to, Jno. 6.21; 2 Jno. 10; *met.* to give *mental* reception to, Jno. 3.11, et al.; to be *simply* recipient of; to receive, Mat. 7.8 Jno. 7.23, 39; 19.30. Ac. 10.43; *in N.T.,* λαμβάνειω πεῖραν, to make encounter of *a matter of difficulty or trail,* He. 11.29, 36; λαμβάνειν ἀρχή, to begin, He. 2.3; λαμβάνειν συμβούλιον, to take counsel, consult, Mat. 12.14; λαμβάνειν λήθην, to forget, 2 Pe. 1.9; λαμβάνειν ὑπόμνησιν, to recollect, recall to mind, 2 Ti. 1.5.; λαμβάνειν περιτομήν, to receive circumcision, be circumcised, Jno. 7.23; λαμβάνειν καταλλαγήν, to be reconciled, Ro. 5.11; λαμβάνειν κρίμα, to receive condemnation or punishment, be punished, Mar. 12.40; *fr. the Heb.* πρόσωπον λαμβάνειν, to accept the person *of any one,* to show partiality towards, Lu. 20.21.

Λαμμᾶ,
    see λαμά.

Λαμπάς, άδος, ἡ, (λάμπω)
    a light, Ac. 20.8; a lamp, Re. 4.5; a *portable* lamp, lantern, or flambeau, Mat. 25.1, 3, 4, 7, 8. Jno. 18.3.

Λαμπρός, ά, όν, (λάμπω)
    bright, resplendent, Re. 22.16; clear, pellucid, Re. 22.1; white, glishtering, Ac. 10.30. Re. 15.6; of a bright colour, gaudy, Lu. 23.11; *by impl.* splendid, magnificent, sumptuous, Ja. 2.2, 3. Re. 18.14: *whence*

Λαμπρότης, τητος, ἡ,
    brightness, splendour, Ac. 26.13.

Λαμπρῶς,
    adv. splendidly; magnificently, sumptuously, Lu. 16.19.

Λάμπω,
    f. ψω & ψομαι, a.1. ἔλαμψα,
    to shine, give light, Mat. 5.15, 16; 17.2. Lu. 17.24, et al.

Λανθάνω,
    f. λήσω, a.2. ἔλᾰθον, p. λέληθα,
    109to be unnoticed; to escape the knowledge or observation of *a person,* Ac. 26.26. 2 Pe. 3. 5, 8; *absol.* to be concealed, escape detection, Mar. 7.24. Lu. 8.47; *with a participle of another verb,* to be unconscious *of an action while the subject or object of it,* He. 13.2.

Λαξευτός, ή, όν, (λᾶς, a stone, & ξέω, to cut, hew)
    cut in stone, hewn out of stone or rock, Lu. 23.53. S.

Λαοδῐκεύς, έως, ὁ,
    a Laodicean, an inhabitant of Λαοδίκεια, Laodicea, Col. 4.16. Re. 3.14.

Λαός, οῦ, ὁ,
    a body of people; a concourse of people, a multitude, Mat. 27.25. Lu. 8.47, et al.; the common people, Mat. 26.5, et al.; a people, nation, Mat. 2.4. Lu. 2.32. Ti. 2.14, et al.; ὁ λαός, the people *of Israel,* Lu. 2.10.

Λάρυγξ, υγγος, ὁ,
    the throat, gullet, Ro. 3.13.

Λάσκω,
    f. λᾱκήσω, a.1. ἐλάκησα,
    pr. to emit a sound, ring; *hence,* to break with a sharp noise; to burst, Ac. 1.18.

Λᾱτομέω, ῶ, (λᾶς, a stone, & τέμνω)
    f. ήσω, p. λελατόμηκα, a.1. ἐλατόμησα,
    to hew stones; to cut out of stone, hew from stone, Mat. 27.60. Mar. 15.46. L.G.

Λατρεία, ας, ἡ,
    service, servitude; religious service, worship, Jno. 16.2. Ro. 9.4; 12.1. He. 9.1, 6: *from*

Λατρεύω, (λάτρις, a servant)
    f. εύσω, a.1. ἐλάτρευσα,
    to be a servant, to serve, Ac. 27.23; to render religious service and homage, worship, Mat. 4.10. Lu. 1.74; *spc.* to offer sacrifices, present offerings, He. 8.5; 9.9.

Λάχᾰνον, ου, τό, (λαχαίνω, to dig)
    a garden herb, vegetable, Mat. 13.32. Lu. 11.42. Ro. 14.2.

Λεγεών, ῶνος, ὁ, (Lat. *legio*)

a *Roman* legion; *in N.T.,* legion *used indefinitely for a great number,* Mat. 26.53. Mar. 5.9, 15. Lu. 8.30.

Λέγω,

f. ξς,

to say, Mat. 1.20, et al. freq.; to speak, make an address or speech, Ac. 26.1; to say *mentally, in thought,* Mat. 3.9. Lu. 3.8; to say *in written language,* Mar. 15.28. Lu. 1.63. Jno. 19.37, et al.; to say, *as distinguished from acting,* Mat. 23.3; to mention, speak of, Mar. 14.71. Lu. 9.31. Jno. 8.27; to tell, declare, narrate, Mat. 21.27. Mar 10.32; to express, He. 5.11; to put forth, propound, Lu. 5.36; 13.6. Jno. 16.29; to mean, to intend to signify, 1 Co. 1.12; 10.29; to say, declare, affirm, maintain, Mat. 3.9; 5.18. Mar. 12.18 Ac. 17.7; 26.22. 1 Co. 1.10, et al.; to enjoin, Ac. 15.24; 21.21. Ro. 2.22; to term designate, call, Mat. 19.17. Mar. 12.37. Lu. 20.37; 23.2. 1 Co. 8.5, et al.; to call *by a name,* Mat. 2.23, et al.; *pass.* to be further named, to be surnamed, Mat. 1.16, et al.; to be explained, interpreted, Jno. 4.25; 20.16, 24; *in N.T.,* σὺ λέγεις, thou sayest, *a form of affirmative answer to a question,* Mat. 27.11. Mar. 15.2. Jno. 18.37.

Λεῖμμα, ατος, τό, (λείπω)

pr. a remnant; *in N.T.,* a small residue, Ro. 11.5.

Λεῖος, εία, εῖον,

smooth, level, plain, Lu. 3.5.

Λείπω,

f. ψω, a.2. ἔλιπον,

trans. to leave, forsake; *pass.* to be left, deserted; *by impl.* to be destitute of, deficient in, Ja. 1.4, 5; 2.15; *intrans.* to fail, be wanting, be deficient, Lu. 18.22, et al.

Λειτουργέω, ῶ, (λειτουργός)

f. ησω, p. λελειτούργηκα,

pr. to perform some public service at one's own expense; *in N.T.,* to officiate *as a priest,* He. 10.11; to minister *in the Christian church,* Ac. 13.2; to minister to, assist, succour, Ro. 15.27.

Λειτουργία, ας, ἡ, (fr. same)

pr. a public service discharged by a citizen at his own expense; *in N.T.,* a *sacred* ministration, Lu. 1.23. Phi. 2.17. He. 8.6; 9.21; a kind office, aid, relief, 2 Co. 9.12. Phi. 2.30.

Λειτουργικός, ή, όν,

ministering; engaged in subordinate service, He. 1.14: (S) *from*

Λειτουργος, οῦ, ἱ (λεῖτος, public, & ἔργον)

pr. a person of property who performed a public duty or service to the state at his own expense; *in N.T.,* a minister or servant, Ro. 13.6, et al.; one who ministers relief, Phi. 2.25.

Λέντιον, ίου, τό, (Lat. *linteum)*

a coarse cloth, *with which servants were girded,* 110a towel, napkin, apron. Jno. 13.4, 5.

Λεπίς, ίδος, ἡ,

a scale, shell, rind, crust, incrustation, Ac. 9.19: *whence*

Λέπρα, ας, ἡ,

the leprosy, Mat. 8.3. Mar. 1.42. Lu. 5.12, 13.

Λεπρός, οῦ, ὁ, (fr. same)

leprous; a leper, Mat. 8.2; 10.8, et al.

Λεπτόν, οῦ, τό, (λεπτός, thin, fine, small)

a mite, *the smallest Jewish coin, equal to half a* κοδράντης, *and consequently to about three-eighths of a farthing,* Mar. 12.42, et al.

Λευΐτης, ου, ὁ,
a Levite, one of the posterity of Λευΐ, Levi, Lu. 10.32. Jno. 1.19. Ac. 4.36: *whence*

Λευϊτικός, ή, όν,
Levitical, pertaining to the Levites, He. 7.11.

Λευκός, ή, όν,
pr. light, bright; white, Mat. 5.36; 17.2, et al.; whitening, growing white, Jno. 4.35.

Λέων, οντος, ὁ,
a lion, He. 11.33. 1 Pe. 5.8, et al.; *met.* a lion, cruel adversary, tyrant, 2 Ti. 4.17; a lion, a hero, deliverer, Re. 5.5.

Λήθη, ης, ἡ (λανθάνω)
forgetfulness, oblivion, 2 Pe. 1.9.

Ληνός, οῦ, ὁ, ἡ,
pr. a tub, trough; a wine-press, *into which grapes were cast and trodden,* Re. 14.19, 20; 19.15; a wine-vat, i.q. ὑπολήνιον, *the lower vat into which the juice of the trodden grapes flowed,* Mat. 21.33.

Λῆρος, ου, ὁ,
idel talk; an empty tale, Lu. 24.11.

Λῃστής, οῦ, ὁ, (λῃΐζομαι, λῃΐς, plunder)
a plunderer, robber, highwayman, Mat. 21.13; 26.55. Mar. 11.17. Lu. 10.30. 2 Co. 11.26, et al.; a bandit, brigand, Mat. 27.38, 44. Mar. 15.27. Jno. 18.40; *trop.* a robber, rapacious imposter, Jno. 10.1, 8.

Λῆψις, εως, ἡ (λαμβάνω)
a taking; receiving, receipt, Phi. 4.15.

Λίαν,
adv. much, greatly, exceedingly, Mat. 2.16; 4.8; 8.28, et al.

Λιβᾰνός, οῦ, ὁ,
arbor thurifera, the tree producing frankincense, *growing in Arabia and Mount Lebanon; in N.T.,* frankincense, *the transparent gum which distils from incisions in the tree,* Mat. 2.11. Re. 18.13: *whence*

Λιβανωτός, οῦ, ὁ, ἡ,
frankincense, *in N.T.,* a censer, Re. 8.3, 5.

Λιβερτῖνος, ου, ὁ (Lat. *libertinus*)
a freed-man, one who having been a slave has obtained his freedom, or whose father was a freedman; *in N.T.,* the λιβερτῖνοι *probably denote Jews who had been carried captive to Rome, and subsequently manumitted,* Ac. 6.9.

Λιθάζω, (λίθος)
f. άσω,
to stone, pelt or kill with stones, Jno. 10.31, 32, 33, et al.

Λίθῐνος, η, ον, (fr. same)
made of stone, Jno. 2.6, et al.

Λιθοβολέω, ῶ, (λίθος & βάλλω)
f. ήσω, a.1. ἐλιθοβόλησα,
to stone, pelt with stones, *in order to kill,* Mat. 21.35; 23.37, et al. L.G.

Λίθος, ου, ὁ,
a stone, Mat. 3.9; 4.3, 6, et al.; *used figuratively, of Christ* Eph. 2.20. 1 Pe. 2.6, et al.; *of believers,* 1 Pe. 2.5; *meton.* a tablet of stone, 2 Co. 3.7; a precious stone, Re. 4.3, et al.

Λιθόστρωτον, ου, τό, (neut. of λιθόστρωτος, paved with stone, λίθος & στρώννυμι) a tessellated pavement, Jno. 19.13.

Λικμάω, ῶ,
f. ήσω
pr. to winnow grain; in N.T., to scatter like chaff, Mat. 21.44. Lu. 20.18.

Λῐμήν, ένος, ὁ
a port, haven, harbour, Ac. 27.8, 12.

Λίμνη, ης, ἡ,
a tract of standing water; a lake, Lu. 5.1, 2, et al.

Λῑμός, οῦ, ὁ,
famine, scarcity of food, want of grain, Mat. 24.7; famine, hunger, famishment, Lu. 15.17. Ro. 8.35, et al.

Λίνον, ου, τό,
flax; by meton. a flaxen wick, Mat. 12.20; linen, Re. 15.6.

Λῐπᾰρός, ά, όν, (λίπος, fat, fatness)
fat; dainty, delicate, sumptuous, Re. 18.14.

Λίτρα, ας, ἡ,
a pound, libra, equivalent to about twelve ounces avoirdupois, Jno. 12.3; 19.39.

Λίψ, Λιβός, ὁ,
pr. the south-west wind; meton. the south-west quarter of the heavens, Ac. 27.12.

Λογία, ας, ἡ, (λέγω, to collect)
111a gathering, collection, 1 Co. 16.1, 2. N.T.

Λογίζομαι, (λόγος)
f. ίσομαι, a.1. ἐλογισάμην, a.1. pass. ἐλογίσθην, f. λογισθήσομαι, p. λελόγισμαι,
pr. to count, calculate; to count, enumerate, Mar. 15.28. Lu. 22.37; to set down as a matter of account, 1 Co. 13.5. 2 Co. 3.5; 12.6; to impute, Ro. 4.3. 2 Co. 5.19. 2 Ti. 4.16, et al.; to account, Ro. 2.26; 8.36; εἰς οὐδὲν λογισθῆναι, to be set at nought, despised, Ac. 19.27; to regard, deem, consider, Ro. 6.11; 14.14. 1 Co. 4.1. 2 Co. 10.2. Phi. 3.13; to infer, conclude, presume, Ro. 2.3; 3.28; 8.18. 2 Co. 10.2, 7, 11. He. 11.19. 1 Pe. 5.12; to think upon, ponder, Phi. 4.8; absol. to reason, Mar. 11.31. 1 Co. 13.11.

Λογικός, ή, όν, (fr. same)
pertaining to speech; pertaining to reason; in N.T., rational, spiritual, pertaining to the mind and soul, Ro. 12.1. 1 Pe. 2.2.

Λόγιον, ίου, τό, (fr. same)
an oracle, a divine communication or revelation, Ac. 7.38. Ro. 3.2, et al.

Λόγιος, ου, ὁ, ἡ, (fr. same)
gifted with learning or eloquence, Ac. 18.24.

Λογισμός, οῦ, ὁ, (λογίζομαι)
pr. a computation, act of computing; a thought, cogitation, Ro. 2.15; a conception, device, 2 Co. 10.5.

Λογομᾰχέω, ῶ, (λόγος & μάχομαι)
f. ήσω,
to contend about words; by impl. to dispute about trivial things, 2 Ti. 2.14: (N.T.)
whence

Λογομαχία, ας, ἡ,
contention or strife about words; by impl. a dispute about trivial things, unprofitable controversy, 1 Ti. 6.4. N.T.

Λόγος, ου, ὁ, (λέγω)
a word, a thing uttered, Mat. 12.32, 37. 1 Co. 14.19; speech, language, talk, Mat. 22.15. Lu. 20.20. 2 Co. 10.10. Ja. 3.2; converse, Lu. 24.14; mere talk, wordy show, 1

Co. 4.19, 20. Col. 2.23. 1 Jno. 3.18; language, mode of discourse, style of speaking, Mat. 5.37. 1 Co. 1.17. 1 Th. 2.5; a saying, a speech, Mar. 7.29. Eph. 4.29; an expression, form of words, formula, Mat. 26.44. Ro. 13.9. Ga. 5.14; a saying, a thing propounded in discourse, Mat. 7.24; 19.11. Jno. 4.37; 6.60. 1 Ti. 1.15, et al.; a message, announcement, 2 Co. 5.19; a *prophetic* announcement, Jno. 12.38; an account, statement, 1 Pe. 3.15; a story, report, Mat. 28.15. Jno. 4.39; 21.23; 2 Th. 2.2; a *written* narrative, a treatise, Ac. 1.1; a set discourse, Ac. 20.7; doctrine, Jno. 8.31, 27. 2 Ti. 2.17; subject-matter, Ac. 15.6; reckoning, account, Mat. 12.36; 18.23; 25.19. Lu. 16.2 Ac. 19.40; 20.24. Ro. 9.28. Phi. 4.15, 17. He. 4.13; a plea, Mat. 5.32. Ac. 19.38; a motive, Ac. 10.29; reason, Ac. 18.14; ὁ λόγος, the word *of God, especially in the gospel,* Mat. 13.21, 22. Mar. 16.20. Lu. 1.2. Ac. 6.4, et al.; ὁ λόγος, the *divine* Word, *or* Logos, Jno. 1.1.

Λόγχη, ης, ἡ,
    pr. the head of a javelin; a spear, lance, Jno. 19.34.
Λοιδορέω, ῶ, (λοίδορος)
    f. ήσω,
    to revile, rail at, Jno. 9.28. Ac. 23.4, et al.
Λιοδορία, ας, ἡ,
    reviling, railing; 1 Ti. 5.14. 1 Pe. 3.9: *from*
Λοίδορος, ου, ὁ, ἡ,
    reviling, railing; *as subst.* a reviler, railer, 1 Co. 5.11; 6.10.
Λοιμός, οῦ, ὁ,
    a pestilence, plague, Mat. 24.7. Lu. 21.11; *met.* a pest, pestilent fellow, Ac. 24.5.
Λοιπός, ή, όν, (λείπω)
    remaining; the rest, remainder, Mat. 22.6, et al.; *as an adv.* τοῦ λοιποῦ, henceforth, Ga. 6.17; τὸ λοιπόν, v. λοιπόν, henceforwards, thenceforwards, Mat. 26.45. 2 Ti. 4.8. Ac. 27.20, et al.; as to the rest, besides, 1 Co. 1.16; finally, Eph. 6.10, et al.; ὅ δὲ λοιπόν, cæterum, but, now, 1 Co. 4.2.
Λουτρόν, οῦ, τό,
    a bath, water for bathing; a bathing, washing, ablution, Ep. 5.26. Tit. 3.5. *from*
Λούω,
    f. σω, a.1. ἔλουσα, p. pass. λέλουμαι,
    pr. to bathe the body, *as distinguished from washing only the extremities,* Jno. 13.10; to bathe, wash, Ac. 9.37; 16.33. He. 10.23. 2 Pe. 2.22; *met.* to cleanse *from sin,* Re. 1.5.
Λυκαονιστί,
    adv. in the dialect of Λυκαονία, Lycaonia, Ac. 14.11.
Λύκος, ου, ὁ,
    a wolf, Mat. 10.16. Lu. 10.3. Jno. 10.12; *met.* a person of wolf-like character, Mat. 7.15. Ac. 20.29.
Λυμαίνομαι, (λύμν, outrage)
    f. οῦμαι,
    112to outrage, violently maltreat; *in N.T.,* to make havock of, Ac. 8.3.
Λυπέω, ῶ,
    f. ήσω, p. λελύπηκα, a.1. ἐλύπησα,
    to occasion grief or sorrow to, to distress, 2 Co. 2.2, 5; 7.8; *pass.* to be grieved, pained, distressed, sorrowful, Mat. 17.23; 19.22, et al.; to aggrieve, cross, vex, Eph. 4.30; *pass.* to feel pained, Ro. 14.15: *from*
Λύπη, ης, ἡ,

pain, distress, Jno. 16.21; grief, sorrow, Jno. 16.6, 20, 22, et al.; *meton.* cause of grief, trouble, affliction, 1 Pe. 2.19.

Λύσις, εως, ἡ, (λύω)
    a loosing; *in N.T.,* a release *from the marriage bond,* a divorce, 1 Co. 7.27.

Λυσιτελέω, ῶ, (λύω, to pay, & τέλος, an impost)
    f. ήσω,
    pr. to compensate for incurred expense; *by impl.* to be advantageous to, to profit, advantage; *impers.* Lu. 17.2.

Λύτρον, ου, τό (λύω, to pay quittance)
    pr. price paid; a ransom, Mat. 20.28. Mar. 10.45: *whence*

Λυτρόω, ῶ
    f. ώσω,
    to release for a ransom; *mid.* to ransom, redeem; deliver, liberate, Lu. 24.21. Tit. 2.14. 1 Pe. 1.18: *whence*

Λύτρωσις, εως, ἡ,
    redemption, He. 9.12; liberation, deliverance, Lu. 1.68; 2.38. L.G.

Λυτρωτής, ου, ὁ,
    a redeemer; a deliverer, Ac. 7.35. S.

Λυχνία, ας, ἡ,
    a candlestick, lampstand, Mat. 5.15, et al.; *met.* a candlestick *as a figure of a Christian church,* Re. 1.12, 13, 20; *of a teacher or prophet,* Re. 11.4: (L.G.) *from*

Λύχνος,
    a light, lamp, candle, &c. Mat. 5.15. Mar. 4.21, et al.; *met.* a lamp, *as a figure of a distinguished teacher,* Jno. 5.35.

Λύω,
    f. ύσω, p. λέλυκα, a.1. ἔλυσα, p. pass. λέλυμαι, a.1. pass. ελύθην, (ὔ),
    to loosen, unbind, unfasten, Mar. 1.7, et al.; to loose, untie, Mat. 21.2. Jno. 11.44; to disengage, 1 Co. 7.27; to set free, set at liberty, deliver, Lu. 13.16; to break, Ac. 27.41. Re. 5.2, 5; to break up, dismiss, Ac. 13.43; to destroy, demolish, Jno. 2.19. Ep. 2.14; *met.* to infringe, Mat. 5.19. Jno. 5.18; 7.23; to make void, nullify, Jno. 10.35; *in N.T.,* to declare to be lawful and allowable, *or,* to admit to privileges, Mat. 16.19, et al.

M, μ, *Mῦ*

Μαγεία, ας, ἡ,
    pr. the system of the magians; magic, Ac. 8.11: *from*

Μαγεύω,
    f. εύσω,
    to be a magian; to use magical arts, practise magic, sorcery, &c. Ac. 8.9: *from*

Μάγος, ου, ὁ, (Pers. *mogh,* Heb. בֹּג *akin to* μέγας, magnus)
    a magus, sage of the magian religion, magian, Mat. 2.1, 7, 16; a magician, sorcerer, Ac. 13.6, 8.

Μαθητεύω,
    f. εύσω, a.1. ἐμαθήτευσα,
    intrans. to be the disciple of, follow as a disciple, Mat. 27.57; *in N.T., trans.* to make a disciple of, to train in discipleship, Mat. 28.19. Ac. 14.21; *pass.* to be trained, disciplined, instructed, Mat. 13.52: (L.G.) *from*

Μαθητής, οῦ, ὁ, (μανθάνω)
    a disciple, Mat. 10.24, 42, et al.: *whence*

Μαθήτρια, ας, ἡ,
   a female disciple, a female Christian, Ac. 9.36.
Μαίνομαι,
   f. μανήσομαι & μανοῦμαι, p. μέμηνα,
   to be disordered in mind, mad, Jno. 10.20, et al.
Μακαρίζω,
   f. ίσω, At. ιῶ,
   to pronounce happy, felicitate, Lu. 1.48. Ja. 5.11: *from*
Μακάριος, ία, ιον, (μάκαρ, idem)
   happy, blessed, Mat. 5.3, 4, 5, 7. Lu. 1.45, et al.
Μακαρισμός, οῦ, ὁ, (μακαρίζω)
   a calling happy, the act of pronouncing happy, felicitation, Ro. 4.6, 9; self-congratulation, Ga. 4.15.
Μάκελλον, ου, τό, (Lat. *macellum*)
   a place where all kinds of provisions are exposed to sale, provision mart, shambles, 1 Co. 10.25.
Μακράν, (acc. fem. of μακρός)
   adv. far, far off, at a distance, far distant, Mat. 8.30. Mar. 12.34, et al.; *met.* οἱ μακράν, remote, foreign, alien, Ep. 2.13, 17.
Μακρόθεν, (fr. same)
   adv. far off, at a distance, from afar, from a distance, Mar. 8.3; 11.13; *preceded by* ἀπό, *in the same sense,* Mat. 26.58.
Μακροθῡμέω, ῶ, (μακρόθυμος, μακρός & θυμός)
   f. ήσω,
   113to be slow towards, be long enduring; to exercise patience, be long suffering, clement, or indulgent, to forbear, Mat. 18.26, 29. 1 Co. 13.4. 1 Th. 5.14. 2 Pe. 3.9; to have patience, endure patiently, wait with patient expectation, He. 6.15. Ja. 5.7, 8; to bear long with entreaties for deliverance and avengement, Lu. 18.7: *whence*
Μακροθυμία, ας, ἡ,
   patience; patient enduring of evil, fortitude, Col. 1.11; slowness of avenging injuries, long suffering, forbearance, clemency, Ro. 2.4; 9.22. 2 Co. 6.6; patient expectation, He. 6.12, et al.
Μακροθύμως,
   adv. patiently, with indulgence, Ac. 26.3.
Μακρός, ά, όν, (μῆκος)
   long; *of space,* far, distant, remote, Lu. 15.13; 19.12; *of time,* of long duration; prolix, Mat. 23.13. Mar. 12.40. Lu. 20.47.
Μακροχρόνιος, ου, ὁ, ἡ, (μακρός & χρόνος)
   of long duration; long-lived, Ep. 6.3. L.G.
Μαλακία, ας, ἡ,
   softness; languor, indisposition, weakness, infirmity of body, Mat. 4.23, et al.; *from*
Μαλᾰκός, ή, όν,
   soft, soft to the touch, delicate, Mat. 11.8. Lu. 7.25; *met.* cinædus, an instrument of unnatural lust, effeminate, 1 Co. 6.9.
Μάλιστα, (superlat. of μάλα, very, much)
   adv. most, most of all, chiefly, especially, Ac. 20.38; 25.26, et al.
Μᾶλλον, (comparat. of μάλα)
   adv. more, to a greater extent, in a higher degree, Mat. 18.13; 27.24. Jno. 5.18. 1 Co. 14.18, et al.; rather, in preference, Mat. 10.6. Eph. 4.28, et al.; *used in a periphrasis for the comparative,* Ac. 20.35, et al.; *as an intensive with a comparative term,* Mat.

6.26. Mar. 7.36. 2 Co. 7.13. Phi. 1.23; μᾶλλον δέ, yea rather, Ro. 8.34. Ga. 4.9. Eph. 5.11.

Μάμμη, & μάμμα, ης, ἡ,
a mother; *later,* a grandmother, 2 Ti. 1.5.

Μαμμωνᾶς, v. Μαμωνᾶς, ᾶ, ὁ, (Aram. ממון)
wealth, riches, Lu. 16.9, 11; *personified, like the Greek* Πλοῦτος, Mammon, Mat. 6.24. Lu. 16.13.

Μανθάνω,
f. μαθήσομαι, a.2. ἔμαθον, p. μεμάθηκα,
to learn, be taught, Mat. 9.13; 11.29; 24.32; to learn *by practice or experience,* acquire a custom or habit, Phi. 4.11. 1 Ti. 5.4, 13; to ascertain, be informed, Ac. 23.27, et al.; to understand, comprehend, Re. 14.3.

Μανία, ας, ἡ, (μαίνομαι)
madness, insanity, Ac. 26.24.

Μάννα, τό, (Heb. מן, Exod. 16.15.)
manna, *the miraculous food of the Israelites while in the desert,* Jno. 6.31, 49, 58, et al.

Μαντεύομαι, (μάντις, a soothsayer, diviner)
f. εύσομαι,
to utter oracles, to divine, Ac. 16.16

Μαραίνω,
f. ανῶ, a.1. pass. ἐμαράνθην,
to quench, cause to decay, fade, or wither; *pass.* to wither, waste away; *met.* to fade away, disappear, perish, Ja. 1.11.

Μαρὰν ἀθά, (Aram. מרן אתא)
i.q. κύριος ἔρχεται, the Lord cometh, or will come *to judgment,* 1 Co. 16.22.

Μαργαρίτης, ου, ὁ, (μάργαρος)
a pearl, Mat. 7.6; 13.45, 46, et al. (ī).

Μάρμᾰρος, ου, ὁ, (μαρμαίρω, to glisten, shine)
a white glistening stone, marble, Re. 18.12.

Μαρτῠρέω, ῶ,
f. ήσω, p. μεμαρτύρηκα, a.1. ἐμαρτύρησα,
trans. to testify, depose, Jno. 3.11, 32. 1 Jno. 1.2. Re. 1.2; 22.20; *absol.* to give evidence, Jno. 18.23; to bear testimony, testify, Lu. 4.22. Jno. 1.7, 8, et al.; to bear testimony *in confirmation,* Ac. 14.3; to declare *distinctly and formally,* Jno. 4.44; *pass.* to be the subject of testimony, to obtain attestation *to character,* Ac. 6.3; 10.22. 1 Ti. 5.10. He. 11.2, 4; *mid., equivalent to* μαρτύρομαι, to make a solemn appeal, Ac. 26.22. 1 Th. 2.12.

Μαρτυρία, ας, ἡ,
judicial evidence, Mar. 14.55, 56, 59. Lu. 22.71; testimony *in general,* Tit. 1.13. 1 Jno. 5.9; testimony, declaration *in a matter of fact or doctrine,* Jno. 1.19; 3.11. Ac. 22.18, et al.; attestation *to character,* Jno. 5.34, 36, et al.; reputation, 1 Ti. 3.7.

Μαρτύριον, ίον, τό,
testimony, evidence, 2 Co. 1.12. Ja. 5.3; testification, Ac. 4.33; *in N.T.,* testimony, mode of solemn declaration or 114testification, Mat. 8.4. Lu. 9.5, et al.; testimony, matter of solemn declaration, 1 Co. 1.6; 2.1. 1 Ti. 2.6; σκηνὴ τοῦ μαρτυρίου, *a title of the Mosaic tabernacle,* Ac. 7.44. Re. 15.5.

Μαρτύρομαι,
to call to witness; *intrans.* to make a solemn affirmation or declaration, asseverate, Ac. 20.26. Ga. 5.3; to make a solemn appearl, Eph. 4.17.

Μάρτυς, υρος, ὁ, ἡ,

a *judicial* witness, deponent, Mat. 18.16. He. 10.28, et al.; *generally,* a witness *to a circumstance,* Lu. 24.48. Ac. 10.41, et al.; *in N.T.,* a witness, a testifier *of a doctrine,* Re. 1.5; 3.14; 11.3; a martyr, Ac. 22.20. Re. 2.13.

Μασσάομαι, *rather* μασάομαι, ῶμαι,

f. ήσομαι,

to chew, masticate; *in N.T.,* to gnaw, Re. 16.10.

Μαστῑγόω, ῶ, (μάστιξ)

f. ώσω, a.1. ἐμαστίγωσα,

to scourge, Mat. 10.17; 20.19, et al.; *met.* to chastise, He. 12.6.

Μάστίζω,

f. ίξω,

to scourge, Ac. 22.25: (poet. & L.G.) *from*

Μάστιξ, ῑγος, ἡ,

a scourge, whip, Ac. 22.24. He. 11.36; *met.* a scourge, pain, disease, Mar. 3.10; 5.29, 34. Lu. 7.21.

Μαστός, οῦ, ὁ, (a collateral form of μαζός)

the breast, pap, Lu. 11.27, et al.

Ματαιολογία, ας, ἡ,

vain talking, idle disputation, 1 Ti. 1.6: (L.G.) *from*

Ματαιολόγος, ου, ὁ, ἡ, (μάταιος & λέγω)

a vain talker, given to vain talking or trivial disputation, Tit. 1.10.

Μάταιος, αία, αιον,

vain, ineffective, bootless, 1 Co. 3.20; groundless, deceptive, fallacious, 1 Co. 15.17; uselesss, fruitless, unprofitable, Tit. 3.9. Ja. 1.26; *fr. the Heb.* erroneous *in principle,* corrupt, perverted, 1 Pe. 1.18; τὰ μάταια, superstition, idolatry, Ac. 14.15: *whence*

Ματαιότης, τητος, ἡ,

vanity, folly, 2 Pe. 2.18; *fr. the Heb., religious* error, Eph. 4.17; false religion, Ro. 8.20. S.

Ματαιόω, ῶ,

f. ώσω,

to make vain; *fr. the Heb., pass.* to fall into religious error, to be perverted, Ro. 1.21. S.

Μάτην,

adv. in vain, fruitlessly, without profit, Mat. 15.9. Mar. 7.7.

Μάχαιρα, ας, ἡ,

a large knife, poniard; a sword, Mat. 26.47, 51, et al.; the sword *of the executioner,* Ac. 12.2. Ro. 8.35. He. 11.37; *hence,* φορεῖν μάχαιραν, to bear the sword, to have the power of life and death, Ro. 13.4; *meton.* war. Mat. 10.34.

Μάχη, ης, ἡ,

a fight, battle; *in N.T.,* contention, strife, dispute, controversy, 2 Co. 7.5. 2 Ti. 2.23, et al.: *from*

Μάχομαι,

f. οῦμαι, v. ἔσομαι,

to fight, to quarrel, Ac. 7.26; to contend, dispute, Jno. 6.52, et al.

Μεγαλαυχέω, ῶ, (μέγας & αὐχέω, to boast)

f. ήσω,

to boast, vaunt; to cause a great stir, Ja. 3.5.

Μεγαλεῖος, εία, εῖον, (μέγας)

magnificent, splendid; τὰ μεγαλεῖα, great things, wonderful works, Lu. 1.49. Ac. 2.11: *whence*

Μεγαλειότης, τητος, ἡ,
    majesty, magnificence, glory, Lu. 9.43. Ac. 19.27. 2 Pe. 1.16. S.

Μεγαλοπρεπής, έος, οῦς, ὁ, Ἡ, (μέγας & πρέπω)
    pr. becoming a great man, magnificent, glorious, most splendid, 2 Pe. 1.17.

Μεγαλύνω, (μέγας)
    f. υνῶ, a.1. ἐμεγάλῦνα,
    to enlarge, amplify, Mat. 23.5; to manifest in an extraordinary degree, Lu. 1.58; to magnify, exalt, extol, Lu. 1.46. Ac. 5.13, et al.

Μεγάλως, (μέγας)
    adv. greatly, very much, vehemently, Phi. 4.10.

Μεγαλωσύνη, ης, ἡ,
    greatness, majesty, He. 1.3; 8.1; *ascribed* majesty, Jude 25: (S.) *from*

Μέγας, μεγάλη, μέγα,
    compar. μείζων, superl. μέγιστος,
    great, large in size, Mat. 27.60. Mar. 4.32, et al.; great, much, numerous, Mar. 5.11. He. 11.26; great, grown up, adult, He. 11.24; great, vehement, intense, Mat. 2.10; 28.8; great, sumptuous, Lu. 5.29; great, important, weighty, of moment, 1 Co. 9.11; 13.13; great, splended, magnificent, Re. 15.3; extraordinary, wonderful, 2 Co. 11.15; great, solemn, Jno. 7.37; 19.31; great *in rank,* noble, Re. 11.18; 13.16; great *in dignity,* distinguished, 115eminent, illustrious, powerful, Mat. 5.19; 18.1, 4, et al.; great, arrogant, boastful, Re. 13.5: *whence*

Μέγεθος, εος, τό,
    greatness, vastness, Eph. 1.19.

Μεγιστᾶνες, ων, οἱ
    great men, lords, chiefs, nobles, princes, Mar. 6.21. Re. 6.15; 18.23. L.G.

Μέγιστος, η, ον,
    greatest; pre-eminent, 2 Pe. 1.4.

Μεθερμηνεύω, (μετά & ἑρμηνεύω)
    f. εύσω,
    to translate, interpret, Mat. 1.23. Mar. 5.41, et al. L.G.

Μέθη, ης, ἡ, (μέθυ)
    strong drink; drunkenness, Lu. 21.34; a debauch in drinking, Ro. 13.13. Ga. 5.21.

Μεθίστημι, later also μεθιστάνω, (ᾰ) (μετά & ἵστημι)
    f. μεταστήσω, a.1. μετέστησα,
    to cause a change of position; to remove, transport, 1 Co. 13.2; to transfer, Col. 1.13; *met.* to cause to change sides; *by impl.* to pervert, mislead, Ac. 19.26; to remove *from office,* dismiss, discard, Lu. 16.4. Ac. 13.22.

Μεθοδεία, ας, ἡ, (μεθοδεύω, to trace, investigate; to handle methodically; to handle cunningly; fr. μέθοδος, μετά & ὁδός)
    artifice, wile, Ep. 4.14; 6.11. N.T.

Μεθόριον, ου, τό, (neut. from μεθόριος, interjacent, μετά & ὅρος)
    confine, border, Mar. 7.24.

Μεθύσκω, (μέθυ, strong drink)
    f. μεθύσω, a.1. pass. ἐμεθύσθην,
    to inebriate, make drunk; *pass.* to be intoxicated, to be drunk, Lu. 12.45. 1 Th. 5.7, et al.; to drink freely, Jno. 2.10.

Μέθῠσος, ου, ὁ, ἡ, (μέθυ)
    drunken; a drunkard, 1 Co. 5.11; 6.10.

Μεθύω, (μέθυ)
 to be intoxicated, be drunk, Mat. 24.49, et al. (ŭ).
Μειζότερος, α, ον,
 greater, 3 Jno. 4: *double comparat. from*
Μείζων, ονος, ὁ, ἡ, τό, -ον,
 greater: *comparat. of* μέγας.
Μέλαν, άνος, τό, (neut. fr. μέλας)
 ink, 2 Co. 3.3. 2 Jno. 12. 3 Jno. 13.
Μέλας, αινα, αν,
 black, Mat. 5.36. Re. 6.5, 12.
Μέλει,
 f. μελήσει, imperf. ἔμελε, imperat. μελέτω,
 impers. verb, there is a care, it concerns, Mat. 22.16. Ac. 18.17. 1 Co. 9.9, et al.:
 whence
Μελετάω, ῶ,
 f. ήσω, a.1. ἐμελέτησα,
 to care for; to bestow careful thought upon, to give painful attention to, be earnest in,
 1 Ti. 4.15; to devise, Ac. 4.25; *absol.* to study beforehand, premeditate, Mar. 13.11.
Μέλι, ἴτος, τό,
 honey, Mat. 3.4. Mar. 1.6. Re. 10.9, 10.
Μελίσσιος, ιου, ὁ, ἡ, τόν, -ον, (μέλισσα, a bee, μέλι)
 of bees, made by bees, Lu. 24.42.
Μέλλω,
 f. ήσω, imperf. ἐμελλον, At. ἤμελλον,
 to be about to, be on the point of, Mat. 2.13. Jno. 4.47; *it serves to express in general*
 a settled futurity, Mat. 11.14. Lu. 9.31. Jno. 11.51, et al.; to intend, Lu. 10.1, et al.;
 particip. μέλλων, ουσα, ον, future *as distinguished from past and present,* Mat. 12.32.
 Lu. 13.9, et al.; to be always, as it were, about to do, to delay, linger, Ac. 22.16.
Μέλος, εος, τό
 a member, limb, any part of the body, Mat. 5.29, 30. Ro. 12.4. 1 Co. 6.15; 12.12, et al.
Μεμβράνα, ης, ἡ, (Lat. *membrana*)
 parchment, vellum, 2 Ti. 4.13.
Μέμφομαι,
 f. ψομαι, a.1. ἐμεμψάμην,
 to find fault with, blame, censure; to intimate dissatisfaction with, He. 8.8; *absol.* to
 find fault, Ro. 9.19.
Μεμψίμοιρος, ου, ὁ, ἡ, (μέμψις, a finding fault, fr. μέμφομαι, & μοῖρα, a portion, lot)
 finding fault or being discontented with one's lot, querulous; a discontented, querulous
 person, a repiner, Jude 16.
Μέν,
 a particle serving to intimate that the term or clause with which it is used, stands
 distinguished from another, usually in the sequal, and then mostly with δέ
 correspondent, Mat. 3.11; 9.37. Ac. 1.1; ὁ μὲν,—ὁ δὲ, this—that, the one—the other,
 Phi. 1.16, 17; one—another, οἱ μὲν—οἱ δὲ, some—others, Mat. 22.5, 6; ὅς μὲν—ὅς
 δὲ, one—another, *pl.* some—others, Mat. 13.8; 21.35; ἄλλος μὲν—ἄλλος δὲ, one—
 another, 1 Co. 15.39; ὧδε μὲν—ἐκεῖ δὲ, here—there, He. 7.8; τοῦτο μὲν—τοῦτο δὲ,
 partly—partly, He. 10.33, et al. freq.
Μενοῦν, v. μὲν οὖν,
 see οὖν.
Μενοῦνγε, (μέν, οὖν, γε)

116a combination of particles serving to take up what has just preceded with either addition or abatedment, like the Latin imo; yea indeed, yea truly, yea rather, Lu. 11.28. Ro. 9.20; 10.18. Phi. 3.8. N.T.

Μέντοι, (μέν & τοι)
    conj. truly, certainly, sure, Ju. 8; nevertheless, however, Jno. 4.27, et al.

Μένω,
    f. μενῶ, p. μεμένηκα, a.1. ἔμεινα,
    to stay, Mat. 26.38. Ac. 27.31; to continue, 1 Co. 7. 11. 2 Ti. 2.13; to dwell, lodge, sojourn, Jno. 1.39. Ac. 9.43, et al.; to remain, Jno. 9.41; to rest, settle, Jno. 1.32, 33; 3.36; to last, endure, Mat. 11.23. Jno. 6.27. 1 Co. 3.14; to survive, 1 Co. 15.6; to be existent, 1 Co. 13.13; to continue unchanged, Ro. 9.11; to be permanent, Jno. 15.16. 2 Co. 3.11. He. 10.34; 13.14. 1 Pe. 1.23; to perservere, be constant, be stedfast, 1 Ti. 2.15. 2 Ti. 3.14; to abide, to be in close and settled union, Jno. 6.56; 14.10; 15.4, et al.; to indwell, Jno. 5.38. 1 Jno. 2.14; *trans.* to wait for, Ac. 20.5, 23.

Μερίζω, (μέρις)
    f. ίσω,
    to divide; to divide out, distribute, Mar. 6.41; to assign, bestow, Ro. 12.3. 1 Co. 7.17. 2 Co. 10.13. He. 7.2; *mid.* to share, Lu. 12.13; *pass.* to be subdivided, to admit distinctions, 1 Co. 1.13; to be servered *by discord,* be at variance, Mat. 12.35, et al.; to differ, 1 Co. 7.34.

Μέριμνα, ης, ἡ, (μερίζειν τὸν νοῦν, dividing the mind)
    care, Mat. 13.22. Lu. 8.14, et al.; anxious interest, 2 Co. 11.28: *whence*

Μεριμνάω, ῶ,
    f. ήσω, a.1. ἐμερίμνησα,
    to be anxious, or solicitous, Phi. 4.6; to expend careful thought, Mat. 6.27; to concern one's self, Mat. 6.25, et al.; to have the thoughts occupied with, 1 Co. 7.32, 33, 34; to feel an interest in, Phi. 2.20.

Μερίς, ίδος, ἡ,
    a part; a division *of a country,* district, region, tract, Ac. 16.12; *met.* share, participation, Ac. 8.21. Col. 1.12; fellowship, consort, connection, 2 Co. 6.15; a part *assigned,* lot, Lu. 10.42.

Μερισμός, οῦ, ὁ, (μερίζω)
    a dividing, act of dividing, He. 4.12; distribution, gifts distributed, He. 2.4.

Μεριστής, οῦ, ὁ, (fr. same)
    a divider; an apportioner, arbitrator, Lu. 12.14. N.T.

Μέρος, εος, τό,
    a part, portion, division, *of a whole,* Lu. 11.36; 15.12. Ac. 5.2. Eph. 4.16, et al.; a piece, fragment, Lu. 24.42. Jno. 19.23; a party, faction, Ac. 23.9; *allotted* portion, lot, destiny, Mat. 24.51. Lu. 12.46; a calling, craft, Ac. 19.27; a *partner's* portion, partnership, fellowship, Jno. 13.8; *pl.* μέρη, a *local* quarter, district, region, Mat. 2.22; 16.13. Ac. 19.1. Eph. 4.9, et al.; side *of a ship,* Jno. 21.6; ἐν μέρει, in respect, on the score, 2 Co. 3.10; 9.3. Col. 2.16. 1 Pe. 4.16; μέρος τι, partly, in some part, 1 Co. 11.18; ἀνὰ μέρος, alternately, one after another, 1 Co. 14.27; ἀπὸ μέρους, partly, in some part or measure, 2 Co. 1.14; ἐκ μέρους, individually, 1 Co. 12.27; partly, imperfectly, 1 Co. 13.9; κατὰ μέρος, particularly, in detail, He. 9.5.

Μεσημβρία, ας, ἡ, (μέσος & ἡμέρα)
    mid-day, noon, Ac. 22.6; *meton.* the south, Ac. 8.26.

Μεσίασ,
    see Μεσσίας.

Μεσῖτεύω,

f. εύσω, a.1. ἐμεσίτευσα,

to perform offfices between two parties; to intervene, interpose, He. 6.17; (L.G.) *from*

Μεσίτης, ου, ὁ, (μέσος)

one that acts between two parties; a mediator, one who interposes to reconcile two adverse parties, 1 Ti. 2.5; an internuncius, one who is the medium of communication between two parties, Ga. 3.19, 20. He. 8.6, et al. (ῑ). L.G.

Μεσονύκτιον, ίου, τό, (μέσος & νύξ)

midnight, Lu. 11.5, et al.

Μέσος, η, ον,

mid, middle, Mat. 25.6. Ac. 26.13; τὸ μέσον, the middle, the midst, Mat. 14.24; ἀνὰ μέσον, in the midst; *fr. the Heb.* in, among, Mat. 13.25; between, 1 Co. 6.5; διὰ μέσου, through the midst of, Lu. 4.30; εἰς τὸ μέσον, into, or in the midst, Mar. 3.3. Lu. 6.8; ἐκ μέσου, from the midst, out of the way, Col. 2.14. 2 Th. 2.7; *fr. the Heb* from, from among, Mat. 13.49; ἐν τῷ μέσῳ, in the midst, Mat. 10.16; in the midst, in public, publicly, Mat. 14.6; ἐν μέσῳ, in the midst of, among, 117Mat. 18.20; κατὰ μέσον τῆς νυκτὸς, about midnight, Ac. 27.27, et al.

Μεσότοιχον, ου, τό, (μέσος & τοῖχος)

a middle wall; a partition wall, a barrier, Ep. 2.14. N.T.

Μεσουράνημα, ατος, τό, (μέσος& οὐρανὸς)

the mid-heaven, mid-air, Re. 8.13, et al. L.G.

Μεσόω, ῶ, (μέσος)

f. ώσω,

to be in the middle or midst; to be advanced midway, Jno. 7.14.

Μεσσίας, ου, ὁ, (Heb. משיח, fr. משח, to anoint)

the Messiah, the Anointed One, i.q. ὁ Χριστός, Jno. 1.42; 4.25.

Μεστός, ή, όν,

full, full of, filled with, Jno. 19.29, et al.; replete, Ro. 1.29; 15.14, et al.: *whence*

Μεστόω, ῶ,

f. ώσω,

to fill; *pass.* to be filled, be full, Ac. 2.13.

Μετά

prep., with a genitive, with, together with, Mat. 16.27; 12.41; 26.55; with, on the same side or party with, in aid of, Mat. 12.30; 20.20; with, by means of, Ac. 13.17; with *of conflict,* Re. 11.7; with, among, Lu. 24.5; with, to, towards, Lu. 1.58, 72; *with an accusative,*after, *of place,* behind, He. 9.3; *of time,* after, Mat. 17.1; 24.29; *followed by an infin. with the neut. article,* after, after that, Mat. 26.32. Lu. 22.20.

Μεταβαίνω, (μετά & βαίνω)

f. βήσομαι, p. μεταβέβηκα, a.2. μετέβην,

to go or pass from one place to another Jno. 5.24; to pass away, be removed, Mat. 17.20; to go away, depart, Mat. 8.34; et al.

Μεταβάλλω, (μετά & βάλλω)

to change; *mid.* to change one's mind, Ac. 28.6.

Μετάγω, (μετά & ἄγω)

f. ξω,

to lead or move from one place to another; to change direction, turn about, Ja. 3.3, 4.

Μεταδίδωμι, (μετά & δίδωμι)

f. δώσω,

to give a part, to share, Lu. 3.11; to impart, bestow, Ro. 1.11; 12.8, et al.

Μετάθεσις, εως, ἡ, (μετατίθημι)

a removal, translation, He. 11.5; a transmutation, change *by the abolition of one thing and the substitution of another,* He. 7.12.

Μεταίρω, (μετά & αἴρω)
f. αρῶ, a.1. μετῆρα,
to remove, transfer; *in N.T., intrans.,* to go away, depart, Mat. 13.53.

Μετακαλέω, ῶ, (μετά & καλέω)
f. έσω,
to call from one place into another; *mid.* to call or send for, invite to come to one's self, Ac. 7.14, et al.

Μετακῑνέω, ῶ, (μετά & κινέω)
f. ήσω,
to move away, remove; *pass. met.* to stir away from, to swerve, Col. 1.23.

Μεταλαμβάνω, (μετά & λαμβάνω)
f. λήψομαι,
to partake of, share in, Ac. 2.46. 2 Ti. 2.6, et al.; to get, obtain, find, Ac. 24.25: *whence*

Μετάληψις, εως, ἡ,
a partaking of, a being partaken of, 1 Ti. 4.3.

Μεταλλάσσω, (μετά & ἀλλάσσω)
f. ξω,
to exchange, change for or into, transmute, Ro. 1.25, 26.

Μεταμέλομαι, (μετά & μέλομαι)
f. ήσομαι, a.1 μετεμελήθην,
to change one's judgment on past points of conduct; to change one's mind and purpose, He. 7.21; to repent, regret, Mat. 21.29, 32; 27.3. 2 Co. 7.8.

Μεταμορφόω, ῶ, (μετά & μορφόω)
f. ώσω,
to change the external form, transfigure; *mid.* to change one's form, be transfigured, Mat. 17.2. Mar. 9.2; to undergo a *spiritual* transformation, Ro. 12.2. 2 Co. 3.18.

Μετανοέω, ῶ, (μετά & νοέω)
f. ήσω,
to undergo a change in frame of mind and feeling, to repent, Lu. 17.3, 4, et al.; to make a change of principle and practice, to reform, Mat. 3.2, et al.: *whence*

Μετάνοια, ας, ἡ,
a change of mode of thought and feeling, repentance, Mat. 3.8. Ac. 20.21. 2 Ti. 2.25, et al.; *practical* reformation, Lu. 15.7, et al.; reversal *of the past,* He. 12.17.

Μεταξύ, (μετά)
adv. between, Mat. 23.35. Lu. 11.51; 16.26. Ac. 15.9, ἐν τῷ μεταξύ, sc. χρόνω, in the mean time, mean while, Jno. 4.31; *in N.T.,* ὁ μεταξύ, following, succeeding, Ac. 13.42.

Μεταπέμπω, (μετά & πέμπω)
f. ψω,
to send after; *mid.* to send after or for *any one,* invite to come to one's self, Ac. 10.5, et al.

Μεταστρέφω, (μετά & στρέφω)
f. ψω, a.2. pass. μεταστράφην,
118to turn about; convert *into something else,* change, Ac. 2.20. Ja. 4.9; *by impl.* to pervert, Ga. 1.7.

Μετασχηματίζω, (μετά & σχηματίζω, to fashion, σχῆμα)
f. ίσω, a.1. μετεσχημάτισα,

to remodel, transfigure, Phi. 3.21; *mid.* to transform one's self, 2 Co. 11.13, 14, 15; to make an *imaginary* transference of *circumstances from the parties really concerned in them to others,* to transfer *in imagination,* 1 Co. 4.6.

Μετατίθημι, (μετά & τίθημι)
> f. θήσω, a.1. μετέθηκα, a.1. pass. μετετέθην,
> to transport, Ac. 7.16; to transfer, He. 7.12; to translate *out of the world,* He. 11.5; *met.* to transfer *to other purposes,* to pervert, Jude 4; *mid.* to transfer one's self, to change over, Ga. 1.6.

Μετέπειτα, (μετά & ἔπειτα)
> *adv.* afterwards, He. 12.17.

Μετέχω, (μετά & ἔχω)
> f. μεθέξω, p. μετέσχηκα, a.2. μετέσχον,
> to share in, partake, 1 Co. 9.10, 12; 10.17, 21, et al.; to be a member of, He. 7.13.

Μετεωρίζω, (μετέωρος, raised from the ground)
> f. ίσω,
> to raise aloft; *met.* to unsettle in mind; *pass.* to be excited with anxiety, be in anxious suspense, Lu. 12.29.

Μετοικεσία, ας, ἡ, (μετοικέω, to change one's abode, μετά & οἰκέω)
> change of abode or country, migration, Mat. 1.11, 12, 17. L.G.

Μετοικίζω, (μετά & οἰκίζω, to fix in habitation)
> f. ίσω,
> to cause to change an abode, cause to emigrate, Ac. 7.4.

Μετοχή, ῆς, ἡ, (μετέχω)
> a sharing, partaking; communion, fellowship, 2 Co. 6.14.

Μέτοχος, ου, ὁ, (fr. same)
> a partaker, He. 3.1, 14; 12.8; an associate, partner, fellow, Lu. 5.7. He. 1.9.

Μετρέω, ῶ, (μέτρον)
> f. ήσω, a.1. ἐμέτρησα,
> to mete, measure, Mat. 7.2. Re. 11.1, 2, et al.; *met.* to estimate, 2 Co. 10.12: *whence*

Μετρητής, οῦ, ὁ,
> *pr.* a measurer; *also,* metretes, *Lat.* metreta, *equivalent to the Attic* ἀμφορεύς, *i.e. three-fourths of the Attic* μέδιμνος, *or Hebrew* ,בת *and therefore equal to about nine gallons,* Jno. 2.6.

Μετριοπᾰθέω, ῶ, (μέτριος & πάθος)
> f. ήσω,
> to moderate one's passions, to be gentle, compassionate, He. 5.2. L.G.

Μετρίως, (μέτριος, μέτρον)
> *adv.* moderately; slightly; οὐ μετρίως, no little, not a little, much, greatly, Ac. 20.12.

Μέτρον, ου, τό,
> measure, Mat. 7.2. Mar. 4.24. Lu. 6.38. Re. 21.17, et al.; measure, standard, Eph. 4.13; extent, compass, 2 Co. 10.13; *allottted* measure, specific portion, Ro. 12.3. Eph. 4.7, 16; ἐκ μέτρου, by measure, with definite limitation, Jno. 3.34.

Μέτωπον, ου, τό, (μετά & ὤψ)
> forehead, front, Re. 7.3; 9.4, et al.

Μέχρι, & μέχρις *before a vowel,*
> *adv. of place,* unto, even to, Ro. 15.19; *of time,* until, till, Mat. 11.23; 13.30, et al.

Μή,
> *a particle of negation,* not; *for the particulars of its usage, especially as distinguished from that of* οὐ, *see the grammars; as a conjunction,* least, that not, Mat. 5.29, 30; 18.10; 24.6. Mar. 13.36; μή, or μήτι, or μήποτε, *prefixed to an interrogative clause is*

a mark of tone, since it expresses an intimation either of the reality of the matters respecting which the question is asked, Mat. 12.23, et al.; *or the contrary,* Jno. 4.12, et al.

Μήγε, (μή & γε)
a strenthened form for μή, Mat. 6.1; 9.17, et al.

Μηδαμῶς, (μηδαμός, i.q. μηδείς)
adv. by no means, Ac. 10.14; 11.8.

Μηδέ,
conj. neither *and repeated,* neither—nor, Mat. 6.25; 7.6; 10.9, 10; not even, not so much as, Mar. 2.2, et al.

Μηδείς, μηδεμίᾰ, μηδέν, (μηδέ & εἷς)
not one, none, no one, Mat. 8.4, et al.

Μηδέποτε, (μηδέ & ποτε)
not at any time, never, 2 Ti. 3.7.

Μηδέπω, (μηδέ & πω)
not yet, not as yet, He. 11.7.

Μηκέτι, (μή & ἔτι)
no more, no longer, Mar. 1.45; 2.2, et al.

Μῆκος, εος, τό,
length, Ep. 3.18. Re. 21.16: *whence*

Μηκύνω,
f. υνῶ,
119to lengthen, prolong; *mid.* to grow up, *as plants,* Mar. 4.27.

Μηλωτή, ῆς, ἡ, (μῆλον, a sheep)
a sheepskin, He. 11.37.

Μήν, μηνός, ὁ,
a month, Lu. 1.24, 26, 36, 53, et al.; *in N.T.,* the new moon, the day of the new moon, Ga. 4.10.

Μήν
a particle occuring in the N.T. only in the combination ἦ μήν. See ἦ.

Μηνύω,
f. ύσω, p. μεμήνυκα, a.1. ἐμήνυσα,
to disclose *what is secret,* Jno. 11.57. Ac. 23.30. 1 Co. 10.28; to declare, indicate, Lu. 20.37.

Μήποτε, (μή & ποτε)
has the same signification and usage as μή; *which see;* He. 9.17. Mat. 4.6. Mat. 13.15; *also,* whether, Lu. 3.15.

Μήπω, (μή & πω)
adv. not yet, not as yet, Ro. 9.11. He. 9.8.

Μήπως, (μή & πως)
conj. lest in any way or means, that in no way, Ac. 27.29. Ro. 11.21. 11 Co. 8.9; 9.27, et al.; whether perhaps, 1 Th. 3.5.

Μηρός, οῦ, ὁ,
the thigh, Re. 19.16.

Μήτε, (μή & τε)
conj. neither, μήτε—μήτε, v. μὴ—μήτε, v. μηδὲ—μήτε, neither—nor, Mat. 5.34, 35, 36. Ac. 23.8. 2 Th. 2.2; *in N.T., also equivalent to* μηδέ, not even, not so much as, Mar. 3.20.

Μήτηρ, τέρος, τρός, ἡ,
a mother, Mat. 1.18; 12.49, 59, et al. freq.; a parent *city,* Ga. 4.26. Re. 17.5.

Μήτι, (μή & τι)
 has the same use as μή in the form εἰ μήτι, Lu. 9.13, et al.; also when prefixed to an interrogative clause, Mat. 7.16. Jno. 4.29. See μή.
Μήτιγε, (μήτι & γε)
 strengthened for μήτι, surely then, much more then, 1 Co. 6.3.
Μήτρα, ας, ἡ, (μήτηρ)
 the womb, Lu. 2.23. Ro. 4.19.
Μητραλοίας, v. -λῴας, ου, ὁ, (μήτι & ἀλοιάω, poet. for ἀλοάω, to smite)
 a striker of his mother, matricide, 1 Ti. 1.9.
Μία,
 see in εἷς.
Μιαίνω,
 f. ανῶ, a.1. ἐμίηνα & ἐμίανα, p. μεμίαγκα, p. pass. μεμίασμαι, a.1. pass. ἐμιάνθην,
 pr. to tinge, dye, stain; to pollute, defile, ceremonially, Jno. 18.28; to corrupt, deprave, Tit. 1.15. He. 12.15. Jude 8: whence
Μίασμα, ατος, τό,
 pollution, moral defilement, 2 Pe. 2.10.
Μιασμός, οῦ, ὁ,
 pollution, defiling, 2 Pe. 2.10. L.G.
Μίγμα, or μῖγμα, ατος, τό,
 a mixture, Jno. 19.39: from
Μίγνυμι & νύω,
 f μίξω, a.1. ἔμιξα, p. pass. μέμιγμαι,
 to mix, mingle, Mat. 27.34. Lu. 13.1. Re. 8.7.
Μῑκρός, ό, όν,
 little, small, in size, quantity, &c. Mat. 13.32; small, little in age, young, not adult, Mar. 15.40; little, short in time, Jno. 7.33; μικρόν, sc. χρόνον, a little while, a short time, Jno. 13.33; μετὰ μικρόν, after a little while, a little while afterwards, Mat. 26.73; little in number, Lu. 12.32; small, little in dignity, low, humble, Mat. 10.42; 11.11; μικρόν, as an adv., little, a little, Mat. 26.39, et al.
Μίλιον, ίου, τό, (Lat. miliarium)
 a Roman mile, which contained mille passuum, 1000 paces, or 8 stadia, i.e. about 1680 English yards, Mat. 5.41. L.G.
Μῑμέομαι, οῦμαι, (μῖμος, an imitator)
 to imitate, follow as an example, strive to resemble, 2 Th. 3.7, 9, He. 13.7. 3 Jno. 11: whence
Μιμητής, οῦ, ὁ,
 an imitator, follower, 1 Co. 4.16. Eph. 5.1, et al.
Μιμνήσκομαι, (mid. of μιμνήσκω, to put in mind, remind)
 a.1. ἐμνήσθην, f. μνησθήσομαι, p. μέμνημαι, with pr. sig.,
 to remember, recollect, call to mind, Mat. 26.75. Lu. 1.54, 72; 16.25; in N.T., in a passive sense, to be called to mind, be borne in mind, Ac. 10.31. Re. 16.19, et al.
Μῑσέω, ῶ (μῖσος, hatred)
 f. ήσω, p. μεμίσηκα, a.1. ἐμίσησα,
 to hate, regard with ill-will, Mat. 5.43, 44; 10.22; to detest, abhor, Jno. 3.20. Ro. 7.15; in N.T., to regard with less affection, love less, esteem less, Mat. 6.24. Lu. 14.26.
Μισθαποδοσία, ας, ἡ,
 pr. the discharge of wages; requital; reward, He. 10.35; 11.26; punishment, He. 2.2: from
Μισθαποδότης, ου, ὁ, (μισθός, ἀποδίδωμι)

a bestower of remuneration, recompenser, rewarder, He. 11.6. N.T.

Μίσθιος, ία, ιον,
120hired; *as subst.* a hired servant, hireling, Lu. 15.17, 19: (L.G.) *from*

Μισθός, οῦ, ὁ
hire, wages, Mat. 20.8. Ja. 5.4, et al.; reward, Mat. 5.12, 46; 6.1, 2, 5, 16, et al.; punishment, 2 Pe. 2.13, et al.: *whence*

Μισθόω, ῶ,
f. ώσω,
to hire out, let out to hire; *mid.* to hire, Mat. 20.1, 7: *whence*

Μίσθωμα, ατος, τό,
hire, rent; *in N.T.,* a hired dwelling, Ac. 28.30.

Μισθωτός, οῦ, τό,
a hireling, Mar. 1.20. Jno. 10.12, 13.

Μνᾶ, ᾶς, ἡ,
Lat. mina; *a weight equiv. to 100 drachmæ; also a sum, equiv. to 100 drachmæ, and the sixtieth part of a talent, worth about four pound sterling.*

Μνεία, ας, ἡ, (μιμνήσκομαι)
remembrance, recollection, Ph. 1.3. 1 Th. 3.6. 2 Ti. 1.3; mention; μείαν ποιείσθαι, to make mention, Ro. 1.9. Eph. 1.16. 1 Th. 1.2. Philem. 4.

Μνῆμα, ατος, τό, (μιμνήσκω)
pr. a memorial, monument; a tomb, sepulchre, Mar. 5.5, et al.

Μνημεῖον, ου, τό, (fr. same)
the same, Mat. 8.28; 23.29, et al.

Μνήμη, ης, ἡ, (fr. same)
remembrance, recollection; mention; μνήμην ποιεῖσθαι, to make mention, 2 Pe. 1.15: *whence*

Μνημονεύω,
f. εύσω, a.1. ἐμνημόνευσα,
to remember, recollect, call to mind, Mat. 16.9. Lu. 17.32. Ac. 20.31, et al.; to be mindful of, to fix the thoughts upon, He. 11.15; to make mention, mention, speak of, He. 11.22.

Μνημόσῠνον, ου, τό, (fr. same)
a record, memorial, Ac. 10.4; *honourable* remembrance, Mat. 26.13. Mar. 14.9.

Μνηστεύω,
f. εύσω, a.1. pass. ἐμνηστεύθην,
to ask in marriage; to betroth; *pass.* to be betrothed, affianced, Mat. 1.18. Lu. 1.27; 2.5.

Μογιλάλος, ου, ὁ, ἡ, (μόγις & λαλέω)
having an impediment in one's speech, speaking with difficulty, a stammerer, Mar. 7.32. (ᾰ). S.

Μόγις, (μόγος, labour, toil)
adv. with difficulty, scarcely, hardly, Lu. 9.39.

Μόδιος, ου, ὁ, (Lat. *modius)*
a modius, *a Roman measure for things dry, containing 16 sextarii, and equivalent to about* a peck; *in N.T.,* a corn measure, Mat. 5.15. Mar. 4.21. Lu. 11.33.

Μοιχᾰλίς, ίδος, ἡ, (equiv. to μοιχάς, fem. of μοιχός)
an adulteress, Ro. 7.3. Ja. 4.4; *by meton.* an adulterous mien, lustful significance, 2 Pe. 2.14; *from the Heb., spiritually* adulterous, faithless, ungodly, Mat. 12.39; 16.4. Mar. 8.38. L.G.

Μοιχάομαι, ῶμαι, (mid. of μοιχάω, to defile a married woman, fr. μοιχός)

f. ἥσομαι,
to commit or be guilty of adultery, Mat. 5.32, et al.

Μοιχεία, ας, ἡ, (μοιχός)
adultery, Mat. 15.19. Mar. 7.21, et al.

Μοιχεύω,
f. εύσω, a.1. ἐμοίχευσα,
trans. to commit adultery with, debauch, Mat. 5.28; absol. and mid. to commit adultery, Mat. 5.27. Jno. 8.4, et al.; to commit spiritual adultery, be guilty of idolatry, Re. 2.22: et al.

Μοιχός, οῦ, ὁ,
an adulterer, Lu. 18.11. 1 Co. 6.9. He. 13.4. Ja. 4.4.

Μόλις, (μόλος, labour)
adv. with difficulty, scarcely, hardly, Ac. 14.18; 27.7, 8, 16. Ro. 5.7. 1 Pe. 4.18.

Μολύνω,
f. υνῶ, a.1. ἐμόλῦνα, p. pass. μεμόλυσμαι, a.1. ἐμολύνθην,
pr. to stain, sully; to defile, contaminate morally, 1 Co. 8.7. Re. 14.4; to soil, Re. 3.4: whence

Μολυσμός, οῦ, ὁ,
pollution, 2 Co. 7.1. L.G.

Μομφή, ῆς, ἡ, (μέμφομαι)
a complaint, cause or ground of complaint, Col. 3.13.

Μονή, ῆς, ἡ, (μένω)
a stay in any place; an abode, dwelling, mansion, Jno. 14.2, 23.

Μονογενής, έος, οῦς, ὁ, ἡ, (μόνος & γένος)
only begotten, only born, Lu. 7.12; 8.42; 9.38. He. 11.17; by impl. most dear, most beloved, Jno. 1.14, 18; 3.16, 18. 1 Jno. 4.9.

Μόνον,
adv. only Mat. 5.47; 8.8; οὐ μόνον—ἀλλὰ καὶ, not only—but also, Mat. 21.21. Jno. 5.18; μὴ μόνον—ἀλλὰ, not only—but, Ph. 2.12, et al.: from

Μόνος, η, ον,
121without accompaniment, alone, Mat. 14.23; 18.15. Lu. 10.40, et al.; singly existent, sole, only, Jno. 17.3, et al.; lone, solitary, Jno. 8.29; 16.32; alone in respect of restriction, only, Mat. 4.4; 12.4, et al.; alone in respect of circumstances, only, Lu. 24.18; not multiplied by reproduction, lone, barren, Jno. 12.24.

Μονόφθαλμος, ου, ὁ, ἡ, (μόνος & ὀφθαλμός)
one-eyed; deprived of an eye, Mat. 18.9. Mar. 9.47.

Μονόω, ῶ, (μόνος)
f. ώσω, p. pass. μεμόνωμαι,
to leave alone; pass. to be left alone, be lone, 1 Ti. 5.5.

Μορφή, ῆς, ἡ,
form, Mar. 16.12. Phi. 2.6, 7: whence

Μορφόω, ῶ,
f. ώσω, a.1. pass. ἐμορφώθην,
to give shape to, mould, fashion, Ga. 4.19: whence

Μόρφωσις, εως, ἡ,
pr. a shaping, moulding; in N.T., external form, appearance, 2 Ti. 3.5; a settled form, prescribed system, Ro. 2.20.

Μοσχοποιέω, ῶ, (μόσχος & ποιέω)
f. ήσω, a.1. ἐμοσχοποίησα,
to form an image of a calf, Ac. 7.41. N.T.

Μόσχος, ου, ὁ, ἡ,
> *pr.* a tender branch, shoot; a young animal; a calf, young bullock, Lu. 15.23, 27, 30. He. 9.12, 19. Re. 4.7.

Μουσικός, ή, όν, (μοῦσα, a muse, song, music)
> *pr.* devoted to the arts of the Muses; a musician; *in N.T., perhaps,* a singer, Re. 18.22.

Μόχθος, ου, ὁ,
> wearisome labour, toil, travail, 2 Co. 11.27. 1 Th. 2.9. 2 Th. 3.8.

Μυελός, οῦ, ὁ,
> marrow, He. 4.12.

Μυέω, ῶ, (μύω, to shut *the mouth*)
> f. ήσω, p. pass. μεμύημαι,
> to initiate, instruct *in the sacred mysteries; in N.T. pass.,* to be disciplined *in a practical lesson,* to learn *a lesson,* Phi. 4.12.

Μῦθος, ου, ὁ,
> a word, speech, a tale; a fable, figment, 1 Ti. 1.4, et al.

Μυκάομαι, ῶμαι,
> to low, bellow, *as a bull; also,* to roar, *as a lion,* Re. 10.33.

Μυκτηρίζω, (μυκτήρ, the nose)
> f. ίσω,
> to contract the nose in contempt and derision, toss up the nose; to mock, deride, Ga. 6.7.

Μυλικός, ή, όν, (μύλη, a mill)
> of a mill, belonging to a mill, Mar. 9.42.

Μύλος, ου, ὁ, (fr. same)
> a mill-stone, Mat. 18.6, et al.: *whence*

Μυλών, ῶνος, ὁ,
> a mill-house, *a place where the grinding of corn was performed,* Mat. 24.41.

Μυριάς, άδος, ἡ, (μυρίος, innumerable)
> a myriad, ten thousand, Ac. 19.19; *indefintely,* a vast multitude, Lu. 12.1. Ac. 21.20, et al.

Μυρίζω, (μύρον)
> f. ίσω,
> to anoint, Mar. 14.8.

Μυρίοι, αι, α, (μυρίος, innumerable)
> *indefinitely,* a great number, 1 Co. 4.15; 14.19; *specifically,* μύριοι, a myriad, ten thousand, Mat. 18.24.

Μύρον, ου, τό,
> *pr.* aromatic juice which distils from trees; ointment, unguent, *usually perfumed,* Mat. 26.7, 12. Mar. 14.3, 4, et al.

Μυστήριον, ίου, τό, (μύστης, an initiated person, μυέω)
> a matter to the knowledge of which initiation is necessary; a secret *which would remain such but for revelation,* Mat. 13.11. Ro. 11.25. Col. 1.26, et al.; a concealed power or principle, 2 Th. 2.7; a hidden meaning *of a symbol,* Re. 1.20; 17.7.

Μυωπάζω, (μύω, to shut, close, & ὤψ)
> f. άσω,
> *pr.* to close the eyes, contract the eyelids, wink; to be nearsighted, dimsighted, purblind, 2 Pe. 1.9.

Μώλωψ, ωπος, ὁ,
> the mark of a blow; a stripe, a wound, 1 Pe. 2.24.

Μωμάομαι, ῶμαι,

f. ἥσομαι, a.1. pass. ἐμωμήθην,

to find fault with, censure, blame, 2 Co. 8.20; *passively,* 2 Co. 6.3: *from*

Μῶμος, ου, ὁ,

blame, ridicule; a disgrace *to society,* a stain, 2 Pe. 2.13.

Μωραίνω, (μωρός)

f. ανῶ, a.1. ἐμώρᾱνα,

to be foolish, play the fool; *in N.T., trans.* to make foolish, convict of folly, 1 Co. 1.20; *pass.* to be convicted of folly, to incur the character of folly, Ro. 1.22; to be rendered insipid, Mat. 5.13. Lu. 14.34.

Μωρία, ας, ἡ, (fr. same)

foolishness, 1 Co. 1.18, 21, 23, et al.

Μωρολογία, ας, ἡ, (μωρός & λόγος)

122foolish talk, Ep. 5.4.

Μωρός, ά, όν,

foolish, Mat. 7.26; 23.17, 19. 2 Ti. 2.23, et al.; *fr. the Heb.* a fool, a wicked, impious man, Mat. 5.22.

N, ν, *Nῦ*

Ναζαρηνός, οῦ, ὁ, v. Ναζωραῖος, ου, ὁ

a Nazarene, an inhabitant of Ναζαρέθ, Nazareth, Mat. 2.23. Jno. 1.47; et al.

Ναί,

a particle, used to strengthen an affirmation, verily, Re. 22.20; *to make an affirmation, or express an assent,* yea, yes, Mat. 5.37. Ac. 5.8, et al.

Ναός, οῦ, ὁ (ναίω, to dwell)

pr. a dwelling; the dwelling *of a deity,* a temple, Mat. 26.61. Ac. 7.48, et al.; *used figuratively of individuals,* Jno. 2.19. 1 Co. 3.16, et al.; *spc.* the cell of a temple; *hence,* the Holy Place *of the Temple of Jerusalem,* Mat. 23.35. Lu. 1.9, et al.; a model of a temple, a shrine, Ac. 19.24.

Νάρδος, ου, ὁ, (Heb. נֵרְדְּ)

spikenard, andropogon nardus *of Linn., a species of aromatic plant with grassy leaves and a fibrous root, of which the best and strongest grows in India; in N.T.,* oil of spikenard, *an oil extracted from the plant, which was highly prized and used as an ointment either pure or mixed with other substances,* Mar. 14.3. Jno. 12.3.

Ναυᾱγέω, ῶ, (ναῦς & ἄγνυμι, to break)

f. ήσω, a.1. ἐναυάγησα,

to make shipwreck, be shipwrecked, 2 Co. 11.25. 1 Ti. 1.19.

Ναύκληρος, ου, ὁ, (ναῦς & κλῆρος)

the master or owner of a ship, Ac. 27.11.

Ναῦς, νεώς, ἡ, (νέω, to swim)

a ship, vessel, Ac. 27.41: *whence*

Ναύτης, ου, ὁ,

a shipman, sailor, seaman, Ac. 27.27, 30. Re. 18.17.

Νεᾱνίας, ου, ὁ, (νεάν, idem, fr. νέος)

a young man, youth, Ac. 20.9; 23.17, 18, 22, *used of* one who is in the prime and vigour of life, Ac. 7.58.

Νεᾱνίσκος, ου, ὁ, (fr. same)

a young man, youth, Mar. 14.51; 16.5, et al.; *used of* one in the prime of life, Mat. 19.20, 22; νεαωίσκοι, soldiers, Mar. 14.51.

Νεκρός, ά, όν, (νέκυς, a dead body)

dead, without life, Mat. 11.5; 22.31; *met.* νεκρός τινι, dead to a thing, no longer devoted to, or under the influence of a thing, Ro. 6.11; *in the sense of* vain, fruitless, powerless, inefficacious, Ja. 2.17, 20, 26; *morally or spiritually* dead, sinful, vicious, impious, Ro. 6.13. Ep. 5.14; obnoxious to death, mortal, Ro. 8.10; *met. and including the idea of* future punishment and misery, Ep. 2.1, 5. Col. 2.13; causing death and misery, fatal, having a destructive power, He. 6.1; 9.14, et al.: *whence*

Νεκρόω, ῶ,

> f. ώσω, a.1. ἐνέκρωσα,
> *pr.* to put to death, kill; *in N.T. met.* to deaden, mortify, Col. 3.5; *pass.* to be rendered impotent, effete, Ro. 4.19. He. 11.12: (L.G.) *whence*

Νέκρωσις, εως, ἡ,

> *pr.* a putting to death; dying, abandonment to death, 2 Co. 4.10; deadness, impotency, Ro. 4.19. L.G.

Νέος, α, ον,

> recent, new fresh, Mat. 9.17. 1 Cor. 5.7. Col. 3.13. He. 12.24; young, youthful, Tit. 2.4, et al.: *whence*

Νεοσσός, οῦ, ὁ,

> the young of birds, a young bird, youngling, chick, Lu. 2.25.

Νεότης, ητος, ἡ (νέος)

> youth, Mat. 19.20. Ac. 26.4, et al.

Νεόφυτος, ου, ὁ, ἡ, (νέος & φύω)

> newly or recently planted; *met.* a neophyte, one newly implanted *into the Cchristian Church,* a new convert, 1 Ti. 3.6. S.

Νεύω,

> f. νεύσω, a.1. ἔνευσα,
> to nod; to intimate by a nod or significant gesture, Jno. 13.24. Ac. 24.10.

Νεφέλη, ης, ἡ,

> a cloud, Mat. 17.5; 24.30; 26.64, et al.

Νέφος, εος, τό,

> a cloud; *trop.* a cloud, a throng *of persons,* He. 12.1.

Νεφρός, οῦ, ὁ,

> a kidney; *pl.* νεφροί, the kidneys, reins; *fr. the Heb. put for* the inmost mind, the most secret thoughts, desires, and affections, Re. 2.23.

Νεωκόρος, ου, ὁ, ἡ, (ναός, At. νεώς & κορέω, to sweep clean)

> *pr.* one who 123sweeps or cleanses a temple; *generally,* one who has the charge of a temple, ædituus; *in N.T.,* a devotee city, *as having specially dedicated a temple to some deity,* Ac. 19.35.

Νεωτερικός, ή, όν,

> juvenile, natural to youth, youthful, 2 Ti. 2.22. (L.G.) *from*

Νεώτερος, α, ον, (campar. of νέος)

> younger, more youthful, Lu. 15.12, 13, et al.

Νή,

> *a particle used in affirmative oaths,* by, 1 Co. 15.31.

Νήθω, (νέω, idem)

> f. νήσω,
> to spin, Mat. 6.28. Lu. 12.27.

Νηπιάζω,

> f. άσω,
> to be childlike, 1 Co. 14.20: *from*

Νήπιος, ίου, ὁ, (νή & ἔπος)

pr. not speaking, infans; an infant, babe, child, Mat. 21.16. 1 Cor. 13.11; one below the age of manhood, a minor, Ga. 4.1; *met.* a babe *in knowledge,* unlearned, simple, Mat. 11.25. Ro. 2.20.

Νησίον, ου, τό,
    a small island, Ac. 27.16: *dimin. of*

Νῆσος, ου, ἡ, (νέω, to swim)
    an island, Ac. 13.6; 27.26, et al.

Νηστεία, ας, ἡ,
    fasting, want of food, 2 Co. 6.5; 11.27; a fast religious abstenence from food, Mat. 17.21. Lu. 2.37, et al.; *spc.* the annual public fast of the Jews, the great day of atonement, *occurring in the month Tisri, corresponding to the new moon of October,* Ac. 27.9: *from*

Νηστεύω,
    f. εύσω, a.1. ἐνήστευσα,
    to fast, Mat. 4.2; 6.16, 17, 18; 9.15, et al.: *from*

Νῆστις, ιος, εως, & ιδος, ὁ, ἡ, (νή & ἐσθίω)
    fasting, Mat. 15.32. Mar. 8.3.

Νηφάλιος, and later νηφαλέος, ίου, ὁ, ἡ.
    sober, temperate, abstinent in respect to wine, &c.; *in N.T. met.,* vigilant, circumspect, 1 Ti. 3.2, 11. Tit. 2.2: *from*

Νήφω,
    f. ψω, a.1. ἔνηψα,
    to be sober, not intoxicated; *in N.T. met.,* to be vigilant, circumspect, 1 Th. 5.6, 8, et al.

Νῑκάω, ῶ,
    f. ήσω, p. νενίκηκα, a.1. ἐνίκησα,
    to conquer, overcome, vanquish, subdue, Lu. 11.22. Jno, 16.33; *absol.* to overcome, prevail, Re. 5.5; to come off superior *in a judicial cause,* Ro. 3.4: *from*

Νίκη, ης, ἡ,
    victory; *meton.* a victorious principle, 1 Jno. 5.4.

Νῑκος, εος, τό (a later equiv. to νίκη)
    victory, Mat. 12.20. 1 Co. 15.54, 55, 57.

Νιπτήρ, ῆρος,
    a basin *for washing some part of the person,* Jno. 13.5: (N.T.) *from*

Νίπτω, (a from of later use for νίζω)
    f. ψω, a.1. ἔνιψα,
    to wash; *spc.* to wash *some part of the person, as distingushed from* λούω, Mat. 6.17. Jno. 13.8, et al.

Νοέω, ῶ, (νόος)
    f. ήσω, a.1. ἐνόησα,
    to percieve, observe; to mark *attentively,* Mat. 24.15. Mar. 13.14. 2 Ti. 2.7; to understand, comprehend, Mat. 15.17, et al.; to conceive, Eph. 3.20: *whence*

Νόημα, ατος, τό,
    the mind, the understanding, intellect, 2 Co. 3.14; 4.4; the heart, soul, affections, feeling, disposition, 2 Co. 11.3; a conception of the mind, thought, purpose, device, 2 Co. 2.11; 10.5.

Νόθος, ου, ὁ, ἡ,
    spurious, bastard, He. 12.8.

Νομή, ῆς, ἡ, (νέμω)
    pasture, pasturage, Jno. 10.9; ἔχειν νομήν, to eat its way, spread corrosion, 2. Ti. 2.17.

Νομίζω, (νόμος)
> f. ίσω, p. νενόμικα, a.1. ἐνόμισα,
> to own as settled and established; to deem, 1 Co. 7.26. 1 Ti. 6.5; to suppose, presume, Mat. 5.17; 20.10. Lu. 2.44, et al.; *pass.* to be usual, customary, Ac. 16.13.

Νομικός, ή, όν, (fr. same)
> pertaining to law; relating to the *Mosaic* law, Tit. 3.9; *as subst.* one skilled in law, a jurist, lawyer, Tit. 3.13; *spc.* an interpreter and teacher of the *Mosaic* law, Mat. 22.35, et al.

Νομίμως, (fr. same)
> *adv.* lawfully, agreeably to law or custom, rightfully, 1 Ti. 1.8. 2 Ti. 2.5.

Νόμισμα, ατος, τό, (νομίζω)
> *pr.* a thing sanctioned by law or custom; lawful money, coin, Mat. 22.19.

Νομοδιδάσκᾰλος, ου, ὁ, (νόμος & διδάσκαλος)
> a teacher and interpreter of the *Mosaic* law, Lu. 5.17, et al. N.T.

Νομοθεσία, ας, ἡ,
> legislation; ἡ νομοθεσια, 124the gift of the *divine* Law, *or,* the *Mosaic* Law *itself,* Ro. 9.4: *from*

Νομοθετέω, ῶ,
> f. ήσω,
> to impose a law, give laws; *in N.T., pass.* to have a law imposed on one's self, receive a law, He. 7.11; to be enacted, constitued, He. 8.6: *from*

Νομοθέτης, ου, ὁ, (νόμος & τίθημι)
> a legislator, lawgiver, Ja. 4.12.

Νόμος, ου, ὁ, (νέμω)
> a law, Ro. 4.15. 1 Ti. 1.9; the *Mosaic* law, Mat. 5.14, et al. freq.; the Old Testament Scripture, Jno. 10.34; a legal tie, Ro. 7.2, 3; a law, a rule, standard, Ro. 3.27; a rule *of life and conduct,* Ga. 6.2. Ja. 1.25.

Νοσέω, ῶ, (νόσος)
> f. ήσω,
> to be sick; *met.* to have a diseased appetite or craving of *a thing,* have an excessive and vicious fondness for *a thing,* to dote, 1 Ti. 6.4: *whence*

Νόσημα, ατος, τό,
> disease, sickness, Jno. 5.4.

Νόσος, ου, ἡ,
> a disease, sickness, distermper, Mat. 4.23, 24; 8.17; 9.35, et al.

Νοσσιά, ᾶς, ἡ, (contr. for νεοσσιά, fr. νεοσσός)
> a brood *of young birds,* Lu. 13.34.

Νοσσίον, ου, τό, (contr. for νεοσσίον, dim. from νεοσσός)
> the young of birds, a chick; *pl.* a brood *of young birds,* Mat. 23.37.

Νοσσός, οῦ, ὁ, (contr. for νεοσσός)
> a young bird, v.r. Lu. 2.24.

Νοσφίζω, (νόσφι, apart, separate)
> f. ίσω,
> to deprive, rob; *mid.* to appropriate; to make secret reservation, Ac. 5.2, 3; to purloin, Tit. 2.10.

Νότος, ου, ὁ,
> the south wind, Lu. 12.55. Ac. 27.13; *meton.* the south, the southern quarter of the heavens, Mat. 12.42. Lu. 11.31; 13.29. Re. 21.13.

Νουθεσία, ας, ἡ,
> warning, admonition, 1 Co. 10.11. Ep. 6.4. Tit. 3.10: *from*

Νουθετέω, ῶ, (νοῦς & τίθημι)
    f. ήσω,
    pr. to put in mind; to admonish, warn, Ac. 20.31. Ro. 15.14, et al.
Νουμηνία, ας, ή, (contr. for νεομηνία, νέος & μήν)
    the new moon, Col. 2.16.
Νουνεχῶς, (νουνεχής, νοῦς & ἔχω)
    adv. understanding, sensibly, discreetly, Mar. 12.34.
Νοῦς, νοῦ, & in N.T. νοός, dat. νοΐ, ὁ, (contr. for νόος)
    the mind, intellect, 1 Co. 14.14, 15, 19; understanding, intelligent faculty, Lu. 24.45; intellect, judgment, Ro. 7.23, 25; opinion, sentiment, Ro. 14.5. 1 Co. 1.10; mind, thought, conception, Ro. 11.34. 1 Co. 2.16. Phi. 4.7; settled state of mind, 2 Th. 2.2; frame of mind, Ro. 1.28; 12.2. Col. 2.18. Eph. 4.23, 1 Ti. 6.5. 2 Ti. 3.8. Tit. 1.15.
Νύμφη, ης, ή,
    a bride, Jno. 3.29. Re. 18.23; 21.2, 9; 22.17; *opposed to* πενθερά, a daughter-in-law, Mat. 10.35. Lu. 12.53: *whence*
Νυμφίος, ου, ὁ,
    a bridegroom, Mat. 9.15; 25.1, 5, 6, 10, et al.
Νυμφών, ῶνος, ὁ,
    a bridal chamber, *in N.T.,* υἱοὶ τοῦ νυμφῶνος, sons of the bridal chamber, the bridegroom's attendant, friends, bridemen, *perhaps the same as the Greek* παρανύμφιοι, Mat. 9.15. Mar. 2.19. Lu. 5.34. L.G.
Νῦν, & νυνί,
    adv. now, at the present time, Mar. 10.30. Lu. 6.21, et al. freq.; just now, Jno. 11.8, et al.; forthwith, Jno. 12.31; καὶ νῦν, even now, as matters stand, Jno. 11.22; now, *expressive of a marked tone of address,* Ac. 7.34; 13.11. Ja. 4.13; 5.1; τό νῦν, the present time, Lu. 1.48, et al.; τανῦν, or τὰ νῦν, now, Ac. 4.29, et al.
Νύξ, νυκτός, ή,
    night, Mat. 2.14; 28.13. Jno. 3.2; *met.* spiritual night, *moral* darkness, Ro. 13.12. 1 Th. 5.5.
Νύσσω, v. ττω,
    f. ξω, a.1. ἔνυξα,
    to prick, pierce, Jno. 19.34.
Νυστάζω, (νεύω)
    f. σω & ξω,
    to nod; to nod in sleep; to sink into a sleep, Mat. 25.5; to slumber *in inactivity,* 2 Pe. 2.3.
Νυχθήμερον, ου, τό, (νύξ & ἡμέρα)
    a day and night, twenty-four hours, 2 Co. 11.25. L.G.
Νωθρός, ά, όν,
    slow, sluggish; untoward, He. 5.11; 6.12.
Νῶτος, ου, ὁ,
    the back *of men or animals,* Ro. 11.10.

Ξ, ξ, *Ξῖ*

Ξενία, ας, ή (ξένος)
    125*pr.* state of being a guest; *then,* the reception of a guest or stranger, hospitality; *in N.T.,* a lodging, Ac. 28.23. Phile. 22.
Ξενίζω (fr. same)
    f. ίσω, a.1. ἐξένισα,

to receive as a guest, entertain, Ac. 10.23; 28.7. He. 13.2; *pass.* to be entertained as a guest, to lodge or reside with, Ac. 10.6, 18, 32; 21.16; to strike with a feeling of strangeness, to surprie; *pass. or mid.* to be struck with surprise, be staggered, be amazed, 1 Pe. 4.4, 12; *intrans.* to be strange; ξενίζοντα, strange matters, novelties, Ac. 17.20.

Ξενοδοχέω, ῶ, (ξενοδόχος, ξένος & δέχομαι)
    f. ήσω,
    to receive and entertain strangers, exercise hospitality, 1 Ti. 5.10.

Ξένος, η, ον,
    adj. strange, foreign; alien, Ep. 2.12, 19; strange, unexpected, surprising, 1 Pe. 4.12; novel, He. 13.9; *subst.* a stranger, Mat. 25.35, et al.; a host, Ro. 16.23.

Ξέστης, ου, ὁ,
    (Lat. *sextus,* v. *sextarius*) a sextarius, *a Roman measure containing about one pint English; in N.T. used for* a small vessel, cup, pot, Mar. 7.4, 8.

Ξηραίνω,
    f. ανῶ, a.1. ἐξήρᾱνα, p. pass. ἐξήραμμαι, a.1. pass. ἐξηαάνθην,
    to dry up, parch, Ja. 1.11; *pass.* to be parched, Mat. 13.6, et al.; to be ripened *as corn,* Re. 14.15; to be withered, to wither, Mar. 11.20; *of parts of the body,* to be withered, Mar. 3.1, 3; to pine, Mar. 9.18: *from*

Ξηρός, ά, όν,
    dry, withered, Lu. 23.31; ἡ ξηρά, sc. γῆ, the dry land, land, Mat. 23.15. He. 11.29; *of parts of the body,* withered, tabid, Mat. 12.10.

Ξύλῐος, ίνη, ίνον,
    wooden, of wood, made of wood, 2 Ti. 2.20. Re. 9.20: *from*

Ξύλον, ου, τό,
    wood, timber, 1 Co. 3.12. Re. 18.12; stocks, Ac. 16.24; a club, Mat. 26.47, 55; a post, cross, gibbet, Ac. 5.30; 10.39; 13.29; a tree, Lu. 23.31. Re. 2.7.

Ξυράω, (ξυρόν, a razor)
    f. ήσω, a.1. ἐξύρησα, p. pass. ἐξύρημαι,
    to cut off the hair, shear, shave, Ac. 21.24. 1 Co. 11.5, 6.

Ο, ο, Ὀ μῑκρόν

Ὁ, ἡ, τό,
    the prepositive article, answering, to a considerable extent, to the English definite article: but, for the principle and facts of its usage, see the Grammars; ὁ μὲν—ὁ δὲ, the one—the other, Ph. 1.16, 17. He. 7.5, 6, 20, 21, 23, 24; *pl.* some—others, Mat. 13.23; 22.5, 6,; ὁ δὲ, but he, Mat. 4.4; 12.48; οἱ δὲ, but others, Mat. 28.17, et al.; *used, in a poetic quotation, for a personal pronoun,* Ac. 17.28.

Ὀγδοήκοντα, οἱ, αἱ, τά,
    indecl., eighty, Lu. 2.37; 16.7: *from*

Ὄγδοος, η, ον, (ὀκτώ)
    the eighth, Lu. 1.59. Ac. 7.8, et al.

Ὄγκος, ου, ὁ,
    pr. bulk, weight; a burden, impediment, He. 12.1.

Ὅδε, ἥδε, τόδε, (ὁ, ἡ, τό & δε)
    demon. pron. this, that, he, she, it, Lu. 10.39; 16.25. Ac. 15.23, et al.

Ὁδεύω, (ὁδός)
    f. εύσω,
    to journey, travel, Lu. 10.33.

Ὁδηγέω, ῶ,
f. ήσω,
to lead, guide, Mat. 15.14. Lu. 6.39. Re. 7.17; *met.* to instruct, teach, Jno. 16.13. Ac. 8.31: *from*

Ὁδηγός, οῦ, ὁ, (ὁδός & ἡγέομαι)
a guide, leader, Ac. 1.16; *met.* an instructor, teacher, Mat. 15.14; 23.16, 24. Ro. 2.19.

Ὁδοιπορέω, ῶ, (ὁδός & πόρος)
to journey, travel, Ac. 10.9: *whence*

Ὁδοιπορία, ας, ἡ,
a journey, journeying, travel, Jno. 4.6. 2 Co. 11.26.

Ὁδός, οῦ, ἡ,
a way, road, Mat. 2.12; 7.13, 14; 8.28; 22.9, 10; means of access, approach, entrance, Jno. 14.6. He. 9.8; direction, quarter, region, Mat. 4.15; 10.5; the act of journeying, a journey, way, course, Mat. 10.10. Mar. 2.23. 1 Th. 3.11, et al.; a journey, *as regards extent,* Ac. 1.12; *met.* a way, *systematic* course *of pursuit,* Lu. 1.79. Ac. 2.28; 16.17; a way, *systematic* course *of action or conduct,* Mat. 21.32. Ro. 11.33. 1 Co. 4.17, et al.; a way, system of doctrine, Ac. 18.26; ἡ ὁδός, the way, the Christian faith, Ac. 19.9, 23; 24.22.

Ὁδούς, ὀδόντος, ὁ,
126a tooth, Mat. 5.38; 8.12, et al.

Ὁδυνάω, ῶ,
to pain *either bodily or mentally; pass.* to be in an agony, be tormented, Lu. 2.48; 16.24, 25; to be distressed, grieved, Ac. 20.38: *from*

Ὁδύνη, ης, ἡ,
pain *of body or mind;* sorry, grief, Ro. 9.2. 1 Ti. 6.10. (ὔ).

Ὁδυρμός, οῦ, ὁ, (ὀδύρομαι, to lament, bewail)
bitter lamentation, wailing, Mat. 2.18; *meton.* sorrow, mourning, 2 Co. 7.7.

Ὄζω,
f. ὀζήσω, & ὀζέσω,
to smell, emit an odour; to have an offensive smell, stink, Jno. 11.39.

Ὅθεν,
adv. whence, Mat. 12.44. Ac. 14.26; from the place where, Mat. 25.24, 26; whence, from which circumstance, 1 Jno. 2.18; wherefore, whereupon, Mat. 14.7.

Ὀθόην, ης, ἡ,
pr. fine linen; a linen cloth; a sheet, Ac. 10.11; 11.5: *whence the dimin.*

Ὀθόνιον, ου, τό,
a linen cloth; *in N.T.,* a swath, bandage *for a corpose,* Lu.24.12. et al.

Οἶδα,
2 p. *from absol.* εἴδω, *with the sense of the present,* plup. ἤδειν, imper. ἴσθι, subj. εἰδῶ, opt. εἰδείην, imf. εἰδέναι, part. εἰδώς, f. εἴσομαι, & εἰδήσω, to know, Mat. 6.8, et al.; to know how, Mat. 7.11, et al.; *fr. Heb.* to regard with favour, 1 Thess. 5.12.

Οἰκεῖος, εία, εῖον, (οἶκος)
belonging to a house, domestic; *pl.* members of a family, immediate kin, 1 Ti. 5.8; members of a *spiritual* family, Eph 2.19; members of a *spiritual* brotherhood, Ga. 6.10.

Οἰκέτης, ου, ὁ,
pr. an inmate of a house; a domestic servant, household slave, Lu. 16.13. Ac. 10.7. Ro. 14.4. 1 Pe. 2.18: *from*

Οἰκέω, ῶ, (οἶκος)

f. ήσω,
to dwell in, inhabit, 1 Ti. 6.16; *intrans.* to dwell, live; to cohabit, 1 Co. 7.12, 13; to be indwelling, indwell, Ro. 7.17, 18, 20; 8.9, 11. 1 Co. 3.16: *whence*

Οἴκημα, ατος, τό,
a dwelling; *used in various conventional senses, and among them,* a prison, Ac. 12.7.

οἰκητήριον,
a habitation, dwelling, abode, Jude 6; *trop.* the abode *of the soul,* the bodily frame, 2 Co. 5.2.

Οἰκία, ας, ἡ, (οἶκος)
a house, dwelling, abode, Mat. 2.11; 7.24, 27, et al.; *trop.* the abode *of the soul,* the body, 2 Co. 5.1; *meton.* a household, family, Mat. 10.13; 12.25; *meton.* goods, property, means, Mat. 23.13. et al.: *whence*

Οἰκιᾰκός, οῦ, ὁ,
belonging to a house; *pl.* the members of a household or family, kindred, Mat. 10.25, 36. L.G.

Οἰκοδεσποτέω, ῶ,
f. ήσω,
pr. to be master of a household; to occupy one's self in the management of a household, 1 Ti. 5.14: (L.G.) *from*

Οἰκοδεσπότης, ου, ὁ, (οἶκος & δεσπότης)
the master or head of a house or family, Mat. 10.25; 13.27, 52, et al. L.G.

Οἰκοδομέω, ῶ, (οἰκοδόμος)
f. ήσω, a.1. ᾠκοδόμησα, p. pass. ᾠκοδόμημαι,
to build a house; to build, Mat. 7.24, et al.; to repair, embellish, and amplify *a building,* Mat. 23.29, et al.; *met.* to contribute to advancement *in religious knowledge,* to edify, 1 Co. 14.4, 17; to advance *a person's spiritual condition,* to edify, 1 Co. 8.1, et al; *pass.*to make *spiritual* advancement, be edified, Ac. 9.31; to advance *in presumption,* be emboldened, 1 Co. 8.10.

Οἰκοδομή, ῆς, ἡ,
pr. the act of building; a building, structure, Mat. 24.1, et al.; *in N.T.,* a *spiritual* structure, *as instanced in the Christian body,* 1 Co. 3.9. Eph. 2.21; *religious* advancement, edification, Ro. 14.19. 1 Co. 14.3, et al. L.G.

Οἰκοδομία, ας, ἡ,
pr. a building of a house; *met. spiritual* advancement, edification, v.r. 1 Ti. 1.4.

Οἰκοδόμος, ου, ὁ, (οἶκος & δέμω)
a builder, architect, v.r. Ac. 4.11.

Οἰκονομέω, ῶ, (οἰκονόμος)
f. ήσω,
to manage a household; to manage the affairs *of any one,* be steward, Lu. 16.2: *whence*

Οἰκονομία, ας, ἡ,
pr. the management of a household; a stewardship, Lu. 16.2, 3, 4; *in N.T.,* an *apostolic* stewardship, a *ministerial* commission *in the publication and 127furtherance of the Gospel,* 1 Co. 9.17. Eph. 1.10; 3.2. Co. 1.25; *or,* on arranged plan, a scheme, Eph. 1.10; a due discharge of a commission, 1 Ti. 1.4.

Οἰκονόμος, ου, ὁ,
the manager of a household; a steward, Lu. 12.42; 16.1, 3, 8. 1 Co. 4.2; a manager, trustee, Ga. 4.2; a *public* steward, treasurer, Ro. 16.23; a *spiritual* steward, the holder of a commission *in the service of the Gospel,* 1 Co. 4.1. Tit. 1.7. 1 Pe. 4.10.

Οἶκος, ου, ὁ,

a house, dwelling, Mat. 9.6, 7. Mar. 2.1, 11; 3.20, et al.; place of abode, seat, site, Mat. 23.38. Lu. 13.35; *met.* a spiritual house or structure, 1 Pet. 2.5; *meton.* a household, family, Lu. 10.5; 11.17; a *spiritual* household 1 Ti. 3.15. He. 3.6; family, lineage, Lu. 1.27, 69; 2.4; *fr. the Heb.* a people, nation, Mat. 10.6; 15.24.

Οἰκουμένη, ης, ἡ, (pr. fem. part. pass of οἰκέω)
scil. γῆ, the habitable earth, world, Mat. 24.14. Ro. 10.18. He. 1.6, et al.; *used, however, with various restriction of meaning, according to the context,* Lu. 2.1. Ac. 17.6, et al.; *meton.* the inhabitants of the earth, the whole human race, mankind, Ac. 17.31; 19.27. Re. 3.10.

Οἰκουργός, οῦ, ὁ, ἡ, (οἶκος & ἔργον)
one who is occupied in domestic affairs, v.r. Tit. 2.5. N.T.

Οἰκουρός, οῦ, ὁ, Ἡ, (οἶκος & οὖρος, a watcher)
pr. a keeper or guard of a house; a home-keeper, stay-at-home, domestic, Tit. 2.5.

Οἰκτείρω, later(οἶκτος, compassion)
f. ήσω,
to compassionate, have compassion on, exercise grace or favour towards, Ro. 9.15: *whence*

Οἰκτιρμός, οῦ, ὁ,
compassion; kindness *in relieving sorrow and want,* Ph. 2.1. Col. 3.12; favour, grace, mercy, Ro. 12.1. 2 Co. 1.3.

Οἰκτίρμων, ονος, ὁ, ἡ,
compassionate, merciful, Lu. 6.36. Ja. 5.11.

Οἰνοπότης, ου, ὁ, ἡ, (οἶνος & πότης, πίνω)
wine-drinking; *in a bad sense,* a wine-bibber, tippler, Mat. 11.19. Lu. 7.34.

Οἶνος, ου, ὁ,
wine, Mat. 9.17. Mar. 2.22, et al.; *meton.* the vine and its clusters, Re. 6.6; *met.* οἶνος, a potion, οἶνος τοῦ θυμοῦ, a furious potion, Re. 14.8, 10; 16.19; 17.2, 18.3.

Οἰνοφλυγία, ας, ἡ, (οἰνόφλυξ, οἶνος & φλύω, to bubble over, overflow)
a debauch with wine, drunkenness, 1 Pe. 4.3.

Οἴομαι, syncop. οἶμαι,
f. οἰήσομαι,
to think, suppose, imagine, presume, Jno. 21.25. Phil. 1.16. Ja. 1.7.

Οἷος, οἵα, οἷον,
rel. pron. correlative to ποῖος, & τοῖος, what, of what kind or sort, as Mat. 24.21. Mar. 9.3, et al.; οὐχ οἷον, not so as, Ro. 9.6.

Οἴσω,
fut. of φέρω; *which see.*

Ὀκνέω, ῶ, (ὄκνος, backwardness, slowness)
f. ήσω, a.1. ὤκνησα,
to be slow, loth; to delay, hesitate, Ac. 9.38: *whence*

Ὀκνηρός, ά, όν,
slow, slothful, indolent, idle, Mat. 25.26. Ro. 12.11; tedious, troublesome, Ph. 3.1.

Ὀκταήμερος, ου, ὁ, ἡ, (ὀκτώ & ἡμέρα)
on the eighth day, Ph. 3.5. N.T.

Ὀκτώ, οἱ, αἱ, τά,
eight, Lu. 2.21; 9.28, et al.

Ὄλεθρος, ου, ὁ, (ὄλλυμι, to destroy)
perdition, destruction, 1 Co. 5.5, et al.

Ὀλίγον (pr. neut. of ὀλίγος)
adv. a little, Mar. 1.19; 6.31, et al.

Ὀλιγόπιστος, ου, ὁ, ἡ, (ὀλίγος & πίστις)
    scant of faith, of little faith, one whose faith is small and weak, Mat. 6.30; 8.26, et al.
    N.T.
Ὀλίγος, η, ον,
    little, small, *in number,* &c.; *pl.* few, Mat. 7.14; 9.37; 20.16. Lu. 13.23; δι' ὀλίγων, sc.
    λόγων, in a few words, briefly, 1 Pe. 5.12; little *in time,* short, brief, Ac. 14.28. Re.
    12.12; πρὸς ὀλίγον, sc. χρόνον, for a short time, for a little while, Ja. 4.14; little,
    small, light, &c. *in magnitude, amount,* &c., Lu. 7.47. Ac. 12.18; 15.2; ἐν ὀλίγῳ,
    concisely, briefly, Ep. 3.3; almost, Ac. 26.28, 29.
Ὀλιγόψῦχος, ου, ὁ, ἡ, (ὀλίγος & ψυχή)
    faint-hearted, desponding, 1 Th. 5.14. L.G.
Ὀλιγωρέω, ῶ, (ὀλίγος & ὥρα, care)
    f. ήσω,
    to neglect, regard slightly, 128make light of, despise, contemn, He. 12.5.
Ὀλίγως, (ὀλίγος)
    adv. a little, scarcely, v.r. 2 Pe. 2.18.
Ὀλοθρευτής, οῦ, ὁ,
    a destroyer, 1 Co. 10.10: (N.T.) *from*
Ὀλοθρεύω, (ὄλεθρος)
    f. εύσω,
    to destroy, cause to perish, He. 11.28. S.
Ὀλοκαύτωμα, ατος, τό, (ὁλοκαυτόω, to offer a whole burnt offering, ὁλόκαυτος, ὅλος &
    καίω)
    a holocaust, whole burnt offering, Mar. 12.33. He. 10.6, 8. S.
Ὀλοκηρία, ας, ἡ,
    perfect soundness, Ac 3.16: (S.) *from*
Ὀλόκληρος, ου, ὁ, ἡ, (ὅλος & κλῆρος)
    whole, having all its parts, sound, perfect, complete in every part; *in N.T.,* the whole,
    1 Th. 5.23; *morally,* perfect, faultless, blameless, Ja. 1.4.
Ὀλολύζω,
    f. ξω, a.1. ὠλόλυξα,
    pr. to cry aloud in invocation; to howl, utter cries of distress, lament, bewail, Ja. 5.1.
Ὅλος, η, ον,
    all, whole, entire, Mar. 1.22; 4.23, 24, et al. freq.
Ὀλοτελής, έος, ὁ, ἡ, (ὅλος & τελος)
    complete; all, the whole, 1 Th. 5.13.
Ὄλυνθος, ου, ὁ,
    an unripe or unseasonable fig, *such as lying under the foliage, do not ripen at the*
    usual season, but hang on the trees during winter, Re. 6.13.
Ὅλως, (ὅλος)
    adv. wholly, altogether; actually, really, re vera, 1 Co. 5.1; 6.7; 15.29; *with a negative,*
    at all, Mat. 5.34.
Ὄμβρος, ου, ὁ, (Lat. *imber*)
    rain, a storm of rain, Lu. 15.54.
Ὀμείρομαι,
    to desire earnestly, have a strong affection for, v.r. 1 Th. 2.8.
Ὀμῑλέω, ῶ, (ὅμιλος)
    f. ήσω,
    to be in company with, associate with; to converse with, talk with, Lu. 24.14, 15. Ac.
    20.11; 24.26.

Ὁμῑλία, ας, ἡ,
    intercourse, communication, converse, 1 Co. 15.33: *from*
Ὅμιλος, ου, ὁ, (ὁμοῦ, & ἴλη, a band)
    a multitude, company, crowd, Re. 18.17.
Ὁρίχλη, ης, ἡ,
    a mist, fog; a cloud, v.r. 2 Pe. 2.17.
Ὅμμα, ατος, τό,
    the eye, Mar. 8.23.
Ὀμνύω, v. ὄμνῡμι,
    f. ὀμοῦμαι, p. ὀμώμοκα, a.1. ὤμοσα,
    to swear, Mat. 5.24, et al.; to promise with an oath, Mar. 6.23. Ac. 2.30; 7.17, et al.
    (ῠ).
Ὁμοθυμᾱδόν, (ὁμοῦ & θυμός)
    adv. with one mind, with one accord, unanimously, Ac. 1.14. Ro. 15.6; together, at
    once, at the same time, Ac. 2.1, 46; 4.24, et al.
Ὁμοιάζω, (ὅμοιος)
    f. άσω,
    to be like, resemble, Mar. 14.70. N.T.
Ὁμοιοπᾰθής, έος, οῦς, ὁ, ἡ, (ὅμοιος & πάθος)
    being affected in the same way *as another,* subject to the same incidents, of like
    infirmities, obnoxious to the same frailties and evils, Ac. 14.14. Ja. 15.17.
Ὅμοιος, οία, οιον, (ὁμός)
    like, similar, resembling, Mat. 11.16; 13.31, 33, 44, 45, 47, 52. Jno. 8.55, et al. freq.;
    like, of similar drift and force, Mat. 22.39. Mar. 12.31: *whence*
Ὁμοιότης, τητος, ἡ
    likeness, similitude, He. 4.15; 7.15.
Ὁμοιόω, ῶ,
    f. ώσω, a.1. ὡμοίωσα,
    to make like, cause to be like or resemble, assimilate; *pass.* to be made like, become
    like, resemble, Mat. 6.8; 13.24; 18.23; to liken, compare, Mat. 7.24, 26; 11.16, et al.;
    whence
Ὁμοίωμα, ατος, τό,
    pr. that which is conformed or assimilated; form, shape, figure, Re. 9.7; likeness,
    resemblance, similitude, Ro. 1.23; 5.14; 6.5; 8.3. Ph. 2.7.
Ὁμοίως, (ὅμοιος)
    adv. likewise, in a similar manner, Mat. 22.26; 27.41. Mar. 4.16, et al.
Ὁμοίωσις, εως, ἡ, (ὁμοιόω)
    pr. assimilation; likeness, resemblance, Ja. 3.9.
Ὁμολογέω, ῶ, (ὁμός, like, & λόγος)
    f. ήσω, a.1. ὡμολόγησα,
    to speak in accordance, adopt the same terms of language; to engage, promise, Mat.
    14.7; to admit, avow frankly, Jno. 1.20. Ac. 24.14; to confess 1 Jno. 1.9; to profess,
    confess, Jno. 9.22; 12.42. Ac. 23.8, et al.; to avouch, declare openly and solemnly,
    Mat. 7.23; *in N.T.,* ὁμολογεῖν ἐν, to accord belief, Mat. 10.32. Lu. 12.8; 129to accord
    approbation, Lu. 12.8; *fr. Heb.* to accord praise, He. 13.15: *whence*
Ὁμολογία, ας, ἡ,
    assent, consent; profession, 2 Co. 9.13. 1 Ti. 6.12, 13. He. 3.1; 4.14; 10.23.
Ὁμολογουμένως, (ὁμολογούμενος, pass. pr. part. of ὁμολογέω)
    adv. confessedly, avowedly, without controversy, 1 Ti. 3.16.
Ὁμότεχνος, ου, ὁ, ἡ, (ὁμός, the same, & τέχνη)

of the same trade or occupation, Ac. 18.3.

Όμοῦ, (ὁμός)
adv. together; in the same place, Jno. 21.2; together, at the same time, Jno. 4.36; 20.4.

Όμόφρων, ονος, ὁ, ἡ, (ὁμός & φρήν)
of like mind, of the same mind, like-minded, 1 Pe. 3.8.

Όμως, (ὁμός)
conj. yet, nevertheless; with μέντοι, but nevertheless, but for all that, Jno. 12.42; in N.T., even, though it be but, 1 Co. 14.7. Ga. 3.15.

Όναρ, τό,
indec., a dream, Mat. 1.20; 2.12, 13, 19, 22; 27.19.

Όνάριον, ίου, τό, (dimin. of ὄνος)
a young ass, an ass's colt, Jno. 12.14.

Όνειδίζω, (ὄνειδος)
f. ίσω, a.1. ὠνείδισα,
to censure, inveigh against, Mat. 11.20. Mar. 16.14; to upbraid, Ja. 1.5; to revile, insult with opprobrious language, Mat. 5.11, et al.: whence

Όνειδισμός, οῦ, ὁ,
censure, 1 Ti. 3.7; reproach, reviling, contumely, Ro. 15.3, et al. L.G.

Όνειδος, εος, τό,
pr. fame, report, character; usually, reproach, disgrace, Lu. 1.25.

Όνίνημι,
f. ὀνήσω,
to help, profit, benefit; mid. ὀνίναμαι, a.2. ὠνήμην & ὠνάμην, opt. ὀναίμην, to receive profit, pleasure, &c.; with a gen. to have joy of, Phile. 20.

Όνικός, ή, όν, (ὄνος)
pertaining to an ass; μύλος ὀνικός, a millstone turned by an ass, a large, or, an upper, millstone, Mat. 18.6. Lu. 17.2. N.T.

Όνομα, ατος, τό,
a name; the proper name of a person, &c., Mat. 1.23, 25; 10.2; 27.32, et al.; a mere name or reputation, Re. 3.1; in N.T., a name as the representation of a person Mat. 6.9. Lu. 6.22; 11.2; the name of the author of a commission, delegated authrioty, or religious profession, Mat. 7.22; 10.22; 12.21; 18.5, 20; 19.29; 21.9; 28.19. Ac. 3.16; 4.7, 12, et al.; εἰς ὄνομα, ἐν ὀνόματι, on the score of being possessor of a certain character, Mat. 10.41, 42. Mar. 9.41: whence

Όνομάζω,
f. άσω,
to name, Lu. 6.14; to style, entitle, Lu. 6.13. 1 Co. 5.11; to make mention of, 1 Co. 5.1. Eph. 5.3; to make known, Ro. 15.20; to pronounce in exorcism, Ac. 19.13; in N.T., to profess, 2 Ti. 2.19.

Όνος, ου, ὁ, ἡ,
an ass, male or female, Mat. 21.2, 5, 7, et al.

Όντως, (ὤν, ὄντος, pres. part. of εἰμί)
really, in truth, truly, Mar. 11.32. Lu. 23.47, et al.

Όξος, εος, τό,
vinegar; a wine of sharp flavour, posca, which was an ordinary beverage, and was often mixed with bitter herbs, &c., and thus given to condemned criminals in order to stupify them, and lessen their suffering, Mat. 27.38, 48. Mar. 15.36. Lu. 23.36. Jno. 19.29, 30: from

Όξύς, εῖα, ύ
sharp, keen, Re. 1.16; 2.12; 14.14, 17, 18; 19.15; swift, nimble, Ro. 3.15.

Ὀπή, ῆς, ἡ
  a hole, vent, opening, Ja. 3.11; a hole, cavern, He. 11.38.
Ὄπισθεν,
  adv. of place, from behind, behind, after, at the back of, Mat. 9.20; 15.23, et al.
Ὀπίσω,
  adv. behind, after, at one's back, Mat. 4.10; Lu. 7.38. Re. 1.10; τὰ ὀπίσω, the things
  which are behind, Phi. 3.14; ὀπίσω & εἰς τὰ ὀμίσω, back, backwards, Mat. 24.18.
  Mar. 13.16. Lu. 9.62.
Ὁπλίζω,
  f. ίσω,
  to arm, equip; mid. to arm one's self, equip one's self, 1 Pe. 4.1: from
Ὅπλον, ου, τό,
  an implement, Ro. 6.13; pl. τὰ ὅπλα, arms, armour, weapons, whether offensive or
  defensive, Jno. 18.3. Ro.. 13.12. 2 Co. 6.7; 10.4.
Ὁποῖος, οία, οἶον,
  what, of what sort or manner, 1 Co. 3.13. Ga. 2.6. 1 Th. 1.9. Ja. 1.24; after τοιοῦτος,
  as, Ac. 26.29.
Ὁπότε,
  130adv. when, Lu. 6.3.
Ὅπου,
  adv. where, in which place, in what place, Mat. 6.19, 20, 21. Re. 2.13; whither, to
  what place, Jno. 8.21; 14.4; ὅπου, ἄν, v. ἐὰν, wherever, in whatever place, Mat. 24.28;
  whithersoever, Mat. 8.19. Ja. 3.4; met. where, in which thing, state, &c., Col. 3.11;
  whereas, 1 Co. 3.3. 2 Pe. 2.11.
Ὀπτάνομαι,
  to be seen, appear, Ac. 1.3.
Ὀπτασία, ας, ἡ, (ὀπτάζω, equiv. to ὁράω)
  a vision, apparition, Lu. 1.22; 24.23. Ac. 26.19. 2 Co. 12.1. L.G.
Ὀπτός, ή, όν, (ὀπτάω, to roast)
  dressed by fire, roasted, broiled, &c. Lu. 24.42.
Ὀπώρα, ας, ἡ,
  autumn; the fruit season; meton. fruits, Re. 18.14.
Ὅπως,
  adv. how, in what way or manner, by what means, Mat. 22.15. Lu. 24.20; conj. that,
  in order that, and ὅπως μή, that not, lest, Mat. 6.2, 4, 5, 16, 18. Ac. 9.2, et al. freq.
Ὅραμα, ατος, τό, (ὁράω)
  a thing seen, sight, appearance, Ac. 7.31; a vision, Mat. 17.9. Ac. 9.10, 12, et al.
Ὅρασις, εως, ἡ, (fr. same)
  seeing, sight; appearance, aspect, Re. 4.3; a vision, Ac. 2.17. Re. 9.17.
Ὁρᾱτός, ή, όν,
  visible, Col. 1.16: from
Ὁράω, ῶ,
  f. ὄψομαι, rarely a.1. ὠψάμην, imperf. ἑώρων, p. ἑώρᾱκα, a.2. εἶδον, a.1. pass. ὤφθην,
  f. ὀφθήσομαι,
  to see, behold, Mat. 2.2, et al. freq.; to look, Jno. 19.37; to visit, Jno. 16.22. He. 13.23;
  to mark, observe, Ac. 8.23. Jas. 2.24; to be admitted to witness, Lu. 17.22. Jno. 3.36.
  Col. 2.18; with θεόν, to be admitted into the more immediate presence of God, Mat.
  5.8. He. 12.14; to attain to a true knowledge of God, 3 Jno. 11; to see to a thing, Mat.
  27.4. Ac. 18.15; ὅρα, see, take care, Mat. 8.4. He. 8.5, et al.; pass. to appear, Lu. 1.11.
  Ac. 2.3, et al.; to reveal one's self, Ac. 26.16; to present one's self, Ac. 7.26.

Ὀργή, ῆς, ἡ,

    pr. mental bent, impulse; anger, indignation, wrath, Ep. 4.31. Col. 3.8; μετ᾽ ὀργῆς, indignantly, Mar. 3.5; vengeance, punishment, Mat. 3.7. Lu. 3.7; 31.23. Ro. 13.4, 5, et al.: *whence*

Ὀργίζω,

    f. ίσω, & ιῶ, a.1. ὠργίσθην,

    to provoke to anger, irritate; *pass.* to be angry, indignant, enraged, Mat. 5.22; 18.34, et al.

Ὀργίλος, η, ον,

    prone to anger, irascible, passionate, Tit. 1.7. (ῐ).

Ὀργυιά, ᾶς, ἡ,

    the space measured by the arms outstretched; a fathom, Ac. 27.28, *bis.: from*

Ὀρέγω,

    f. ξω,

    to extend, stretch out; *mid.* to stretch one's self out, to reach forward to; *met.* to desire earnestly, long after, 1 Ti. 3.1. He. 11.16; *by impl.* to indulge in, be devoted to, 1 Ti. 6.10.

Ὀρεινός, ή, όν, (ὄρος)

    mountainous, hilly, Lu. 1.39, 65.

Ὄρεξις, εως, ἡ, (ὀρέγομαι)

    desire, longing; lust, concupiscence, Ro. 1.27.

Ὀρθοποδέω, ῶ, (ὀρθός, & πούς)

    f. ήσω,

    to walk in a straight course; to be straightforward *in moral conduct,* Ga. 2.14. N.T.

Ὀρθός, ή, όν, (ὄρω)

    erect, upright, Ac. 14.10; plain, level, straight, He. 12.13.

Ὀρθοτομέω, ῶ, (ὀρθός, & τέμνω)

    to cut straight; to direct aright; to set forth truthfully, without perversion or distortion, 2 Ti. 2.15. S.

Ὀρθρίζω, (ὄρθρος)

    f. ίσω,

    to rise early in the morning; to come with the dawn, Lu. 21.38. S.

Ὀρθρινός, ή, όν, (fr. same)

    of or belonging to the morning, morning, Re. 22.16: (*usually* ῐ) *a later form for*

Ὄρθριος, ία, ιον,

    at day-break, earily, Lu. 24.22: *from*

Ὄρθρος, ου, ὁ,

    the dawn; the morning, Jno. 8.2. Ac. 5.21; ὄρθρος βαθύς, the first streak of dawn, the early dawn, Lu. 24.1.

Ὀρθῶς, (ὀρθός)

    straightly; rightly, correctly, Mar. 7.35. Lu. 7.43, et al.

Ὀρίζω, (ὄρος, a bound, limit)

    f. ίσω, pass. a.1. ὡρίσθην, p. ὥρισμαι,

    to set bounds to, to bound; to restrict, He. 4.7; to settle, appoint definitively, Ac. 17.26; 131to fix determinately, Ac. 2.23; to decree, destine, Lu. 22.22. to constitute, appoint, Ac. 10.42; 17.31; to characterise with precision, to set forth distinctively, Ro. 1.4; *absol.* to resolve, Ac. 11.29.

Ὄριον, ου, τό, (fr. same)

    a limit, bound, border of a territory or country; *pl.* τὰ ὅρια, region, territory, district, Mat. 2.16; 4.13; 8.34, et al.

Ὁρκίζω,

    f. ίσω,

    to put to an oath; to obtest, adjure, conjure, Mar. 5.7. Ac. 19.13. 1 Th. 5.27: *from*

Ὅρκος, ου, ὁ,

    an oath, Mat. 14.7, 9; 26.72, et al.; *meton.* that which is solemnly promised, a vow, Mat. 5.33.

Ὁρκωμοσία, ας, ὁ, (ὅρκος & ὄμνυμι)

    the act of taking an oath; an oath, He. 7.20, 21, 28. S.

Ὁρμάω, ῶ,

    f. ήσω, a.1. ὥρμησα,

    pr. trans. to put in motion, incite; *intrans.* to rush, Mat. 8.32. Mar. 5.13. Lu. 8.33, et al.: *from*

Ὁρμή, ῆς, ἡ, (ὅρω, ὄρνυμι, to put in motion)

    impetus, impulse; assault, violent attempt, Ac. 14.5; *met.* impulse *of mind,* purpose will, Ja. 3.4.

Ὅρμημα, ατος, τό, (ὁρμάω)

    violent or impetuous motion; violence, Re. 18.21.

Ὄρνεον, ου, τό,

    a bird, fowl, Re. 18.2; 19.17, 21.

Ὄρνις, ῖθος, ὁ, ἡ,

    a bird, fowl; the *domestic* hen, Mat. 23.37. Lu. 13.34.

Ὁροθεσία, ας, ἡ, (ὅρος, a bound, limit, & τίθημι)

    pr. the act of fixing boundaries; a bound set, certain bound, fixed limit, Ac. 17.26. N.T.

Ὅρος, εος, τό,

    a mountain, hill, Mat. 5.1, 14; 8.1; 17.20, et al.

Ὀρύσσω, v. ττω,

    f. ξω, a.1. ὥρυξα,

    to dig, excavate, Mat. 21.33; 25.18. Mar. 12.1.

Ὀρφᾰνός, ή, όν, v. οῦ, ὁ, ἡ,

    bereaved *of parents,* orphan, Ja. 1.27; bereaved, desolate, Jno. 14.18.

Ὀρχέομαιν, οῦμαι,

    f. ήσομαι, a.1. ὠρχησάμην,

    to dance, Mat. 11.17, et al.

Ὅς, ἥ, ὅ,

    rel. pron. who, which, qui, quæ, quod, Mat. 1.16, 23, 25, et al.; *in N.T., interrog.* ἐφ᾽ ὃ, wherefore, why, Mat. 26.50; *in N.T.,* ὅς μὲν— ὅς δὲ, *for* ὁ μὲν—ὁ δὲ, Mat. 21.35. 2 Co. 2.16, et al.

Ὁσάκις, (ὅσος)

    as often as, 1Co. 1.25, 26. Re. 11.6. (ᾰ.)

Ὅσιος, ία, ιον,

    pr. sanctioned by the supreme law of God and nature; pious, devout, Tit. 1.8; pure, 1 Ti. 2.8; *supremely* holy, Ac. 2.27; 13.35. He. 7.26. Re. 15.4; 16.5; τὰ ὅσια, pledged bounties, mercies, Ac. 13.34: *whence*

Ὁσιότης, τητον, ἡ,

    piety, sacred observance of all duties towards God, holiness, Lu. 1.75. Ep. 5.24.

Ὁσίως,

    adv. piously, holily, 1 Th. 2.10.

Ὀσμή, ῆς, ἡ, (ὄζω)

    smell, odour, fragrant odour, Jno. 12.3. Ep. 5.2; Phil. 4.18; *met.* 2 Co. 2.14, 16.

Ὅσος, η, ον,

    a correlative to τόσος, τοσοῦτος, &c., *as great, as much,* Mar. 7.36. Jno. 6.11. He. 1.4; 8.6; 10.25; ἐφ' ὅσον χρόνον, for how long a time, while, as long as, Ro. 7.1; *so* ἐφ' ὅσον, sc. χρόνον, Mat. 9.15; ὅσον χρόνον, how long, Mar. 2.19; *neut.* ὅσον *repeated,* ὅσον ὅσον, *used to give intensity to other qualifying words,* e.g. μικρόν, the very least, a very, very little while, He. 10.37; ἐφ' ὅσον, in as much as, Mat. 25.40, 45; καθ' ὅσον, by how much, so far as, He. 3.3; *or,* in as much as, as, so, He. 7.20; 9.27; *pl.* ὅσα, so far as, as much as, Re. 1.2; 18.7; how great, how much, how many, what, Mar. 3.8; 5.19, 20; how many soever, as many as, all who, 2 Cor. 1.20. Ph. 3.15. 1 Ti. 6.1; ὅσος ἄν, v. ἐὰν, whosoever, whatsoever, Mat. 7.12; 18.18.

Ὅσπερ, ἥπερ, ὅπερ, (ὅς & περ)

    an emplatic form of the relative, Mar. 15.6.

Ὀστέον, οῦν, έου, οῦ, τό,

    a bone, Mat. 23.27. Lu. 24.39, et al.

Ὅστις, ἥτις, ὅ τι, (ὅς & τις)

    gen. οὗτινος, ἧστινος, οὗτινος, & ὅτου,

    rel. pron. whoever, whatever; whosoever, whatsoever, Mat. 5.39, 41; 13.12; 18.4; *its use in place of the simple relative is also required in various cases, which may be learnt from the grammars;* ἕως ὅτου. sc. χρόνου, until, Lu. 13.8; while, Mat. 5.25.

Ὀστράκϊνος, η, ον, (ὄστρᾰκον, an earthen vessel)

    132earthen, of earthenware, 2 Co. 4.7. 2 Ti. 2.20. L.G.

Ὄσφρησις, εως, ἡ, (ὀσφραίνομαι, to smell)

    smell, the sense of smelling, 1 Co. 12.17.

Ὀσφύς, ύος, ἡ, & pl. αἱ ὀσφύες,

    the loins, Mat. 3.4. Mar. 1.6, et al..

Ὅταν, (ὅτε & ἄν)

    conj. when, whenever, Mat. 5.11; 6.2. Mar. 3.11. Re. 4.9, et al. freq.; *in N.T.,* in case of, on occasion of, Jno. 9.5. 1 Co. 15.27. He. 1.6.

Ὅτε,

    adv. when, at the time that, at what time, Mat. 7.28; 9.25. Lu. 13.35, et al. freq.

Ὅτι, (ὅστις)

    that, Mat. 2.16, 22, 23; 6.5, 16; *often used pleonastically in reciting another's words,* Mat. 9.18. Lu. 19.42. Ac. 5.23; *as a causal particle,* for that, for, because, Mat. 2.18; 5.3, 4, 5; 13.13; because, seeing that, since, Lu. 23.40. Ac. 1.17.

Ὅτου,

    see in ὅστις.

Οὗ, (pr. gen. of ὅς)

    adv. where, in what place, Mat. 2.9; 18.20; whither, to what place, Lu. 10.1; 22.10; 24.28; οὗ ἐὰν, whithersoever, 1 Co. 16.6.

Οὐ,

    before a consonant, οὐκ *before a vowel with a lenis,* & οὐχ *with an aspirate, adv. of negation,* not, no. Mat. 5.37; 12.43; 23.37; *the peculiariteis of its usage, and as distinct from* μή, *may be learnt from the grammars.*

Οὐά, (Lat. *vah*)

    interj. expressive of insult and derision, ah! aha! Mar. 15.29.

Οὐσί, (Lat. *væ*)

    interj. wo! alas! Mat. 11.21; 18.7; 23.13–16, et al.; ἡ οὐαί, *subs.* a woe, calamity, Re. 9.12; 11.14.

Οὐδαμῶς, (οὐδαμός)

    by no means, Mat. 2.6.

Οὐδέ (οὐ & δέ)

    adv. neither, nor, and not, also not, Mat. 5.15; 6.15, 20, 26, 28; *when single,* not even, Mat. 6.29; 8.10.

Οὐδείς, οὐδεμία, οὐδέν, (οὐδέ & εἷς)

    not one, no one, none, nothing, Mat. 5.13; 6.24; 19.17; *met.* οὐδέν, nothing, of no account, naught, Jno. 8.54. Ac. 21.24.

Οὐδέποτε, (οὐδέ & πότε)

    never, Mat. 7.23; 21.16, 42, et al. freq.

Οὐδέπω, (οὐδέ & πω)

    not yet, never yet, never, Lu. 23.53. Jno. 7.39, et al.

Οὐθείς, οὐθέν,

    later forms for οὐδείς, οὐδέν, v.r. 1 Co. 13.2.

Οὐκ,

    see οὐ.

Οὐκέτι, (οὐκ & ἔτι)

    no longer, no more, Mat. 22.46, et al.

Οὐκοῦν,

    then, therefore, Jno. 18.37.

Οὖν,

    a particle expressing either simple sequence or consequence; then, now then, Mat. 13.18. Jno. 19.29. et al.; then, thereupon, Lu. 15.28. Jno. 6.14, et al.; therefore, consequently, Mat. 5.48. Mar. 10.9, et al.; *it also serves to mark the resumption of discourse after an interruption by a parenthesis,* 1 Co. 8.4, et al.

Οὔπω, (οὐ & πω)

    adv. not yet, Mat. 15.17; 16.19; 24.6. Jno. 2.4, et al.

Οὐρά, ᾶς, ἡ,

    a tail, Re. 9.10, 19; 12.4.

Οὐράνιος, ία, ιον, v. ίου, ὁ, ἡ, (οὐρανός)

    heavenly, celestial, Mat. 6.14, 26, 32; 15.13, et al.

Οὐρανόθεν,

    adv. from heaven, Ac. 14.17; 26.13: *from*

Οὐρανός, οῦ, ὁ, & pl. οὐρανοί, ῶν, οἱ,

    heaven, the heavens, the visible heavens and all their phenomena, Mat. 5.18; 16.1; 24.29, et al. freq.; the air, atmosphere, *in which the clouds and tempests gather, the birds fly, &c.* Mat. 6.26; 16.2, 3, et al.; heaven, the peculiar seat and abode of God, of angels, of glorified spirits, &c., Mat. 5.34, 45, 48; 6.1, 9, 10; 12.50. Jno 3.13, 31; 6.32, 38, 41, 42, 50, 51, 58; *in N.T.,* heaven *as a term expressive of the Divine Being, His administration, &c.,* Mat. 19.14; 21.25. Lu. 20.4, 5. Jno 3.27.

Οὖς, ὠτός, τό,

    the ear, Mat. 10.27. Mar. 7.33. Lu. 22.50. Ac. 7.57, et al.

Οὐσία, ας, ἡ, (ὤν, οὖσα, ὄν, part. of εἰμι)

    substance, propery, goods, fortune, Lu. 15.12, 13.

Οὔτε, (οὐ & τε)

    neither, nor, Lu. 20.36; οὔτε—οὔτε v. οὐδὲ—οὔτε, neither—nor, Lu. 20.35; Ga. 1.12; *in N.T., also used singly in the sense of* οὐδέ, not even, Mar. 5.3. Lu. 12.26. 1 Co. 3.2.

Οὗτος, αὕτη, τοῦτο,

    133*demons. pron.* this, this person or thing, Mat. 3.3, 9, 17; 8.9; 19.2; 24.34, et al. freq.; *used by way of contempt,* this fellow, Mat. 13.55; 27.47; αὐτὸ τοῦτο, this very thing, this same thing, 2 Co. 2.3; 7.11; εἰς αὐτὸ τοῦτο, *and elliptically,* αὐτὸ τοῦτο; for this same purpose, on this account, Ep. 6.18, 22. 2 Pe. 1.5; καὶ οὗτος, and moreover,

Lu. 7.12; 16.1; 20.30; καὶ τοῦτο, and that too, 1 Co. 6.6, 8; τοῦτο μὲν—τοῦτο δὲ, partly—partly, He. 10.33.

Οὕτως, & οὕτω *before a consonant*, (<u>οὗτος</u>)
    adv. thus, in this way, Mat. 1.18; 2.5; 5.16, et al. freq.; ὅς μὲν οὕτως, ὅς δὲ οὕτως, one so, and another so, one in one way, and another in another, 1 Co. 7.7, 26, 40; 9.14; so, Mat. 7.12; 12.40; 24.27, 37, et al. freq.; thus, under such circumstances, Ac. 20.11; 27.17; in an ordinary way, Jno. 4.6.

Οὐχ,
    see <u>οὐ</u>.

Οὐχί (<u>οὐ</u>)
    adv. not, Jno. 13.10, 11; *when followed by* ἀλλά, nay, not so, by no means, Lu. 1.60; 12.51; *used also in negative interrogations,* Mat. 5.46, 47; 6.25.

Ὀφειλέτης, ου, ὁ, (<u>ὀφείλω</u>)
    a debtor, one who owes another, Mat. 18.24; *met.* one who is in any way bound, or under obligation to perform any duty, Ro. 1.14; 8.12; 15.27. Ga. 5.3; *in N.T.,* one who fails in duty towards any one, a delinquent, offender, Mat. 6.12; a sinner, Lu. 13.4, cf. v. 2.

Ὀφειλή, ῆς, ἡ, (fr. same)
    a debt, Mat. 18.32; *met.* a duty, due, Ro. 13.7. 1 Co. 7.3.

Ὀφείλημα, ατος, τό,
    a debt; a due, Ro. 4.4; *in N.T.,* a delinquency, offence, fault, sin, Mat. 6.12. cf. v. 14:
    from

Ὀφείλω,
    f. ήσω, a.2. ὤφελον,
    to owe, be indebted, Mat. 18.28, 30, 34; to incur a bond, to be bound to make discharge, Mat. 23.16, 18; to be bound *by what is due or fitting,* Lu. 17.10. Jno. 13.14, et al.; to incur desert, to deserve, Jno. 19.7; to be due or fitting, 1 Co. 7.3, 36; *fr. the Aram.* to be delinqent, Lu. 11.4.

Ὄφελον, (pr. a.2. of <u>ὀφείλω</u>)
    used later and in N.T. as an interj., O that! would that! 1 Co. 4.8. Gal. 5.12, et al.

Ὄφελος, εος, τό, (ὀφέλλω, to further, augment)
    profit, utility, advantage, 1 Co. 15.32, et al.

Ὀφθαλμοδουλεία, ας, ἡ, (<u>ὀφθαλμός</u> & <u>δουλεία</u>)
    eye-service, service rendered only while under inspection, Ep. 6.6. Col. 3.22. N.T.

Ὀφθαλμός, οῦ, ὁ, (<u>ὄψομαι</u>, ὤφθην)
    an eye, Mat. 5.29, 38; 6.23; 7.3–5, et al.; ὀφθαλμὸς πονηρός, an evil eye, an envious eye, envy, Mat. 20.15. Mar. 7.22; *met.* the *intellectual* eye, Mat. 13.15. Mar. 8.18. Jno. 12.40. Ac. 26.18.

Ὄφις, εως, ὁ,
    a serpent, Mat. 7.10; 10.16; an *artificial* serpent, Jno. 3.14; *used of* the devil or Satan, Re. 12.9, 14, 15; 20.2; *met.* a man of serpentine character, Mat. 23.33.

Ὀφρύς, ύος, ἡ,
    a brow, eye-brow; the brow *of a mountain,* edge of a precipice, Lu. 4.29.

Ὀχλέω, ῶ, (<u>ὄχλος</u>)
    f. ήσω,
    pr. to mob; to vex, trouble, Lu. 6.18. Ac. 5.16.

Ὀχλοποιέω, ῶ, (<u>ὄχλος</u> & <u>ποιέω</u>)
    f. ήσω,
    to collect a mob, create a tulmult, Ac. 17.5. N.T.

Ὄχλος, ου, ὁ,

a crowd, a confused multitude of people, Mat. 4.25; 5.1; 7.28; *spc.* the common people, Jno. 7.49; a multitude, great number, Lu. 5.29; 6.17. Ac. 1.15; *by impl.* tumult, uproar, Lu. 22.6. Ac. 24.18.

Ὀχύρωμα, ατος, τό, (ὀχυρόω, to fortify, ὀχυρός, firm, strong)
    a strong-hold; *met.* an *opposing* bulwark *of error or vice,* 2 Co. 10.4. S.

Ὀψάριον, ίου, τό, (dimin. of ὄψον, cooked provision as distinguished from bread; a dainty dish; fish)
    a little fish, Jno. 6.9, 11; 21.9, 10, 13.

Ὀψέ,
    adv. late; *put for* the first watch, at evening, Mar. 11.19; 13.35; ὀψὲ σαββάτων, after the close of the sabbath, Mat. 28.1: *whence*

Ὄψϊμος, ου, ὁ, ἡ,
    late; latter, Ja. 5.7; *poetic and later prose for*

Ὄψιος, ία, ιον,
    late, Mar. 11.11; ἡ ὀψία, sc. ὥρα, evening, *two of which were reckoned by the Hebrews; one from the ninth hour, until sunset,* Mat. 8.16; 14.15, et al.; *and the other, 134from sunset until dark,* Mat. 14.23; 16.2, et al.

Ὄψις, εως, ἡ,
    a sight; the face, visage, countenance, Jno. 11.44. Re. 1.16; external appearance, Jno. 7.24: *from*

Ὄψομαι,
    see ὁράω.

Ὀψώνιον, ίον, τό, (ὄψον, cooked provisions, &c.)
    provisions; a stipend or pay *of soldiers,* Lu. 3.14. 1 Co. 9.7; wages *of any kind,* 2 Co. 11.8; *due* wages, a *stated* recompense, Ro. 6.23. L.G.

Π, π, Πῖ

Παγιδεύω,
    f. εύσω,
    to ensnare, entrap, entangle Mat. 22.15: *from*

Παγίς, ίδος, ἡ, (πήγνυμι)
    a snare, trap, gin, Lu 21.35; *met.* artifice, stratagem, device, wile, 1 Ti. 3.7; 6.9. 2 Ti. 2.26; *met.* source of harm, Ro. 11.9.

Πάγος, ου, ὁ, (fr. same)
    a hill; Ἄρειος πάγος, Areopagus, the hill of Mars *at Athens,* Ac. 17.19, 22.

Πάθημα, ατος, τό, (πάσχω)
    what is suffered; suffering, affliction, Ro. 8.18. 2 Co. 1.5, 6, 7. Ph. 3.10, et al.; emotion, passion, Ro. 7.5. Ga. 5.24.

Παθητός, οῦ, ὁ, ἡ, (fr. same)
    passible, capable of suffering, liable to suffer; *in N.T.,* destined to suffer, Ac. 26.23.

Πάθος, εος, τό, (fr. same)
    suffering; an affection, passion, Ro. 1.26.

Παιδαγωγός, οῦ, ἡ, (παῖς & ἀγωγός, ἄγω)
    a pedagogue, child-tender, *a person, usually a slave or freedman, to whom the boys of a family were committed, whose duty it was to attend them at their play, lead them to and from the public school, and exercise a constant superintendence over their conduct and safety; in N.T.,* an ordinary director or minister *contrasted with an Apostle, as a pedagogue occupies an inferior position to a parent,* 1 Co. 4.15; *a term*

applied to the Mosaic Law as dealing with men as in a state of mere childhood and tutelage, Ga. 3.24, 25.

Παιδάριον, ίου, τό, (dimin. of παῖς)
a little boy, child, a boy, lad, Mat. 11.16. Jno 6.9.

Παιδεία, ας, ἡ, (παιδεύω)
education, training up, nurture of children, Ep. 6.4; instruction, discipline, 2 Ti. 3.16; in N.T., correction, chastisement, He. 12.5, 7, 8, 11.

Παιδευτής, οῦ, ὁ,
a preceptor, instructor, teacher, pr. of boys; genr. Ro. 2.20; a chastiser, He. 12.9: from

Παιδεύω, (παῖς)
f. εύσω, a.1. ἐπαίδευσα,
to educate, instruct children, Ac. 7.22; 22.3; genr. παιδεύομαι, to be taught, learn, 1 Ti. 1.20; to admonish, instruct by admonition, 2 Ti. 2.25. Tit. 2.12; in N.T., to chastise, chasten, 1 Co. 11.32. 2 Co. 6.9. He. 12.6, 7, 10. Re. 3.19; of criminals, to scourge, Lu. 23.16, 22.

Παιδιόθεν,
adv. from childhood, from a child, Mar. 9.21: (N.T.) from

Παιδίον, ου, τό, (dimin. of παῖς)
an infant, babe, Mat. 2.8, et al.; but usually in N.T. as equiv. to παῖς, Mat. 14.21. Mar. 7.28. et al. freq; pl. voc. used by way of endearment, my dear children, 1 Jno. 2.18, et al.; also as a term of familiar address, children, my lads, Jno. 21.5.

Παιδίσκη, ης, ἡ, (fem. dim. of παῖς)
a girl, damsel, maiden; a female slave or servant, Mat. 26.69. Mar. 14.66, 69, et al.

Παίζω,
f. παίξομαι,
to play in the manner of children; to sport, to practise the festive gestures of idolatrous worship, 1 Co. 10.7: from

Παῖς, παιδός, ὁ, ἡ,
a child in relation to parents, of either sex, Jno. 4.51, et al.; a child in respect of age, either male or female, and of all ages from infancy up to manhood, a boy, youth, girl, maiden, Mat. 2.16; 17.18. Lu. 2.43; 8.54; a servant, slave, Mat. 8.6, 8, 13, cf. v.9. Lu. 7.7. cf v.3, 10; an attendant, minister, Mat. 14.2. Lu. 1.69. Ac. 4.25; also Lu. 1.54, or perhaps, a child in respect of fatherly regard.

Παίω,
f. παίσω, p. πέπαικα, a.1. ἔπαισα,
to strike, smite, with the fist, Mat. 26.68. Lu. 22.64; with a sword, Mar. 14.47. Jno. 18.10; to strike as a scorpion, to sting, Re. 9.5.

Πάλαι,
adv. of old, long ago, Mat. 11.21. Lu. 10.13. He. 1.1. Jude 4; οἱ πάλαι, old, former, 2 Pe. 1.9; 135some time since, already, Mar. 15.44: whence

Παλαιός, ά, όν,
old, not new or recent, Mat. 9.16, 17; 13.52. Lu. 5.36, et al.: whence

Παλαιότης, τητος, ἡ,
oldness, antiquatedness, obsoleteness, Ro. 7.6.

Παλαιόω, ῶ, (fr. same)
f. ώσω, p. πεπαλαίωκα,
to make old; pass. to grow old, to become worn or effete, Lu. 12.33. He. 1.11; met. to treat as antiquated, to abrogate, supersede, He. 8.13.

Πάλη, ης, ἡ, (πάλλω, to swing round, sway backward and forward)
wrestling; struggle, contest, Ep. 6.12.

Παλιγγενεσία, ας, ή, (πάλιν & γένεσις)
>a new birth; regeneration, renovation, Mat. 19.28. Tit. 3.5. L.G.

Πάλιν,
>adv. pr. back; again, back again, Jno. 10.17. Ac. 10.16; 11.10, et al.; again by repetition, Mat. 26.43, et al.; again in continuation, further, Mat. 5.33; 13.44, 45, 47; 18.19; again, on the other hand, 1 Jno. 2.8, et al.

Παμπλύθει, (πᾶς & πλῆθος)
>adv. the whole multitude together, all at once, Lu. 23.18.

Πάμπολυς, παμπόλλη, πάμπολυ, (πᾶς & πολύς)
>very many, very great, vast, Mar. 8.1.

Πανδοχεῖον, ου, τό,
>a public inn, place where travellers may lodge, called in the East by the name of menzil, khan, caravanserai, Lu. 10.34: from

Πανδοχεύς, έως, ὁ, (a later form for πανδοκεύς, πᾶς & δέχομαι)
>the keeper of a public inn or caravanserai, a host, Lu. 10.35.

Πανήγῠρις, εως, ή, (πᾶς & ἄγυρις, an assembly)
>pr. an assembly of an entire people; a solemn gathering at a festival; a festive convocation, He. 12.23.

Πανοικί, (πᾶς & οἶκος)
>adv. with one's whole household or family, Ac. 16.34.

Πανοπλία, ας, ή, (πᾶς & ὅπλον)
>panoply, complete armour, a complete suit of armour both offensive and defensive, as the shield, sword, spear, helment, breastplate, &c., Lu. 11.22. Ep. 6.11, 13.

Πανουργία, ας, ή,
>knavery, craft, cunning, Lu. 20.23. 1 Co. 3.19, et al.: from

Πανοῦργος, ου, ὁ, ή, (πᾶς & ἔργον)
>pr. ready to do any thing; hence, crafty, cunning, artful, wily, 2 Co. 12.16.

Πανταχόθεν,
>adv. from all parts, from every quarter, Mar. 1.45: from

Πανταχοῦ, (πᾶς)
>adv. in all places, every where, Mar. 16.20. Lu. 9.6, et al.

Παντελής, έος, ὁ, ή, (πᾶς & τέλος)
>perfect, complete; εἰς τὸ παντελές, adverbially, throughout, through all time, ever, He. 7.25; with a negative, at all, Lu. 13.11.

Πάντη, (πᾶς)
>adv. every where; in every way, in every instance, Ac. 24.3.

Πάντοθεν, (πᾶς & θεν)
>from every place, from all parts, Jno. 18.20; on all sides, on every side, round about, Lu. 19.43. He. 9.4.

Παντοκράτωρ, ορος, ὁ, (πᾶς & κράτος)
>almighty, omnipotent, 2 Co. 6.18. Re. 1.8; 4.8, et al. (ᾰ) L.G.

Πάντοτε, (πᾶς)
>adv. always, at all times, ever, Mat. 26.11. Mar. 14.7. Lu. 15.31; 18.1, et al. L.G.

Πάντως, (πᾶς)
>adv. wholly, altogether; at any rate, by all means, 1 Co. 9.22; by impl. surely, assuredly, certainly, Lu. 4.23. Ac. 18.21; 21.22; 28.4; οὐ πάντως, in nowise, not in the least, Ro. 3.9. 1 Co. 5.10; 16.12.

Παρά

*prep., with a genitive,*from, *indicating source or origin,* Mat. 2.4, 7. Mar. 8.11. Lu. 2.1, et al.; οἱ παρ' αὐτοῦ, his relatives or kinsmen, Mar. 3.21; τὰ παρ' αὐτῆς πάντα, all her substance, property, &c., Mar. 5.26;

with a dative, with, by, nigh to, in among, &c. Matthew 6.1; 19.26; 21.25; 22.25; παρ' ἑαυτῷ, at home, 1 Co. 16.2; in the sight of, in the judgment or estimation of, 1 Co. 3.19. 2 Pe. 2.11; 3.8;

with an accusative, motion by, near to, along, Mat. 4.18; *motion* towards, to, at, Mat. 15.30. Mar. 2.13; *motion terminating in rest,* at, by, near, by the side of, Mar. 4.1, 4. Lu. 5.1; 8.5; 136in deviation from, in violation of, inconsistently with, Ac. 18.13. Ro. 1.26; 11.24; above, more than, Lu. 13.2, 4. Ro. 1.25;

after comparatives, Lu. 3.13. 1 Co. 3.11; except, save, 2 Co. 11.24; beyond, past, He. 11.11; in respect of, on the score of, 1 Co. 12.15, 16.

Παραβαίνω, (παρά & βαίνω)
    f. βήσομαι, a.2. παρέβην,
    pr. to step by the side of; to deviate; *met.* to transgress, violate, Mat. 15.2, 3. 2 Jno. 9; to incur forfeiture, Ac. 1.25.

Παραβάλλω, (παρά & βάλλω)
    f. βαλῶ,
    to cast or throw by the side of; *met.* to compare, Mar. 4.30; *absol. a nautical term,* to bring to, land, Ac. 20.15.

Παράβᾰσις, εως, ἡ, (παραβαίνω)
    a stepping by the side, deviation; a transgression, violation of law, Ro. 2.23; 4.15, et al.

Παραβάτης, ου, ὁ, (fr. same)
    a transgressor, violator of law, Ro. 2.25, 27. Ga. 2.18. Ja. 2.9, 11. (ᾰ.)

Παραβιάζομαι, (παρά & βιάζω)
    f. άσομαι,
    to force; to constrain, press *with urgent entreaties,* Lu. 24.29. Ac. 16.15. L.G.

Παραβολεύομαιν, (παράβολος, risking, venturesome)
    f. εύσομαι,
    to stake or risk one's self, v.r. Ph. 2.30. N.T.

Παραβολή, ῆς, ἡ, (παραβάλλω)
    a place one thing by the side of another; a comparing; a parallel case cited in illustration; a comparison, simile, similitude, Mar. 4.30. He. 11.19; a parable, *a short relation under which something else is figured, or in which that which is fictitious is employed to represent that which is real,* Mat. 13.3, 10, 13, 18, 24, 31, 33, 34, 36, 53; 21.33, 45; 22.1; 24.32, et al.; *in N.T.,* a type, pattern, emblem, He. 9.9; a sentiment, grave and sententious precept, maxim, Lu. 14.7; an obscure and enigmatical saying, any thing expressed in remote and ambiguous terms, Mat. 13.35. Mar. 7.17; a proverb, adage, Lu. 4.23.

Παραβουλεύομαι, (παρά & βουλεύω)
    f. εύσομαι,
    to be reckless, regardless, Ph. 2.30. N.T.

Παραγγελία, ας, ἡ,
    a command, order, charge, Ac. 5.28; direction, precept, 1 Th. 4.2, et al.: *from*

Παραγγέλλω, (παρά & ἀγγέλλω)
    f. ελῶ
    to announce, notify; to command, direct, charge, Mat. 10.5. Mar. 6.8; 8.6. Lu. 9.21, et al.; to charge, obtest, entreat solemnly, 1 Ti. 6.13.

Παραγίνομαι, (παρά & γίνομαι)

f. γενήσομαι, a.2. παρεγενόμην,

to be by the side of; to come approach, arrive, Mat. 2.1; 3.13. Mar. 14.43. Lu. 7.4, et al.; *seq.* ἐπί, to come upon *in order to seize,* Lu. 22.52; to come forth in public, make appearance, Mat. 3.1. He. 9.11.

Παράγω, (παρά & ἄγω)

f. άξω,

to lead beside; *intrans.* to pass along or by, Mat. 20.30. Jno. 9.1; to pass on, Mat. 9.9, 27; *intrans & mid.* to pass away, be in a state of transition, 1 Co. 7.31. 1 Jno. 2.8, 17.

Παραδειγματίζω, (παράδειγμα, an example)

to make an example of; to expose to ignominy and shame, Mat. 1.19. He. 6.6. L.G.

Παράδεισος, ου, ὁ, (of Oriental origin: in Heb. סדרפ)

a park, a forest where wild beasts were kept for hunting; a pleasure park, a garden of trees of various kinds; *used in the LXX. for* the Garden of Eden; *in N.T., the celestial paradise,* Lu. 23.43. 2 Co. 12.4. Re. 2.7.

Παραδέχομαι, (παρά & δέχομαι)

f. ξομαι,

to accept, receive; *met.* to receive, admit, yield assent to, Mar. 4.20. Ac. 16.21; 22.18. 1 Ti. 5.19; *in N.T.,* to receive or embrace with favour, approve, love, He. 12.6.

Παραδιατρῖβή, ῆς, ἡ, (παρά & διατριβή)

useless disputation, 1 Ti. 6.5. N.T.

Παραδίδωμι, (παρά & δίδωμι)

f. δώσω,

to give over, hand over, deliver up, Mat. 4.12; 5.25; 10.4, 17, et al.; to commit, intrust, Mat. 11.27; 25.14, et al.; to commit, commend, Ac. 14.26. 15.40; to yield up, Jno. 19.30. 1 Co. 15.24; to abandon, Ac. 7.42. Eph. 4.19; to expose *to danger,* hazard, Ac. 15.26; to deliver *as a matter of injunction, instruction, &c.,* Mar. 7.13. Lu. 1.2. Ac. 6.14, et al.; *absol.* to render a yield, to be matured, Mar. 4.29.

Παράδοξος, ου, ὁ, ἡ, (παρά & δόξαν, beside expectation)

unexpected, 137strange, wonderful, astonishing, Lu. 5.26.

Παράδοσις, εως, ἡ, (παραδίδωμι)

delivery, handing over, transmission; *in N.T.,* what is transmitted *in the way of teaching,* precept, doctrine, 1 Co. 11.2. 2 Th. 2.15; 3.6; tradition, traditionary law, *handed down from age to age,* Mat. 15.2, 3, 6, et al.

Παραζηλόω, (παρά & ζηλόω)

f. ώσω,

to provoke to jealousy, Ro. 10.19; to excite to emulation, Ro. 11.11, 14; to provoke to indignation, 1 Co. 10.22. S.

Παραθαλάσσιος, ία, ιον, (παρά & θάλασσα)

by the sea-side, situated on the sea-coast, maritime, Mat. 4.13.

Παραθεωρέω, ῶ, (παρά & θεωρέω)

f. ήσω

to look at things placed side by side, *as in comparison,* compare in thus looking; to regard less in comparison, overlook, neglect, Ac. 6.1.

Παραθήκη, ης, ἡ, (παρατίθημι)

a deposit, a thing committed to one's charge, a trust, 2 Ti. 1.12; v.r. 1 Ti. 6.20. 2 Ti. 1.14.

Παραινέω, ῶ, (παρά & αἰνέω)

f. έσω,

to advice, exhort, Ac. 27.9, 22.

Παραιτέομαι, οὔμαι, (παρά & αἰτέω)

f. ήσομαι,
to entreat; to beg off, excuse one's self, Lu. 14.18, 19; to deprecate, entreat against, Ac. 25.11. He. 12.19, to decline receiving, refuse, reject, 1 Ti. 4.7; 5.11. Tit. 3.10. He. 12.25; to decline, avoid, shun, 2 Ti. 2.23.

Παρακαθίζω, (παρά & καθίζω)
f. ίσω,
to set beside; *intrans.* to sit by the side of, sit near, Lu. 10.39.

Παρακαλέω, (παρά & καλέω)
f. έσω,
to call for, invite to come, send for, Ac. 28.20; to call upon, exhort, admonish, persuade, Lu. 3.18. Ac. 2.40; 11.23; to beg, beseech, entreat, implore, Mat. 8.5, 31; 18.29. Mar. 1.40; to animate, encourage, comfort, console, Mat. 2.18; 5.4. 2 Co. 1.4, 6; *pass.* to be cheered, comforted, Lu. 16.25. Ac. 20.12. 2 Co. 7.13, et al.

Παρακαλύπτω, (παρά & καλύπτω)
f. ψω,
to cover over, veil; *met. pass.* to be veiled *from comprehension,* Lu. 9.45.

Παρακαταθήκη, ης, ή, (παρακατίθημι, to lay down by, deposit)
a deposit, a thing committed to one's charge, a trust, 1 Ti. 6.20. 2 Ti. 1.14.

Παράκειμαι, (παρά & κεῖμαι)
to lie near, be adjacent; *met.* to be at hand, be present, Ro. 7.18, 21.

Παράκλησις, εως, ή, (παρακαλέω)
a calling upon, exhortation, incitement, persuasion, Ro. 12.8. 1 Co. 14.3; hortatory instruction, Ac. 13.15; 15.31; entreaty, importunity, earnest supplication, 2 Co. 8.4; solace, consolation, Lu. 2.25. Ro. 15.4, 5. 2 Co. 1.3–7; cheering and supporting influence, Ac. 9.31; joy, gladness, rejoicing, 2 Co. 7.13; cheer, joy, enjoyment, Lu. 6.24.

Παράκλητος, ου, ὁ,
one called or sent for to assist another; an advocate, one who pleads the cause of another, 1 Jno. 2.1; *genr.* one present to render various beneficial service, *and thus* the Paraclete, *whose influence and operation were to compensate for the departure of Christ himself,* Jno. 14.16, 26; 15.26; 16.7.

Παρακοή, ῆς, ή, (παρακούω)
an erroneous or imperfect hearing; disobdience, Ro. 5.10; a deviation from obedience, 2 Co. 10.6. He. 2.2.

Παρακολουθεω, ῶ, (παρά & ἀκολουθέω)
f. ήσω,
to follow or accompany closely; to accompany, attend, characterise, Mar. 16.17; to follow *with the thoughts,* trace, Lu. 1.3; to conform to, 1 Ti. 4.6; 2 Ti. 3.10.

Παρακούω, (παρά & ἀκούω)
f. ούσομαι,
to hear amiss, to fail to listen, neglect to obey, disregard, Mat. 18.17.

Παρακύπτω, (παρά & κύπτω)
f. ψω,
to stoop beside; to stoop down *in order to take a view,* Lu. 24.12. Jno. 20.5, 11; to bestow a close and attentive look, to look intently, to penetrate, Ja. 1.25. 1 Pe. 1.12.

Παραλαμβάνω, (παρά & λαμβάνω)
f. λήψομαι,
pr. to take to one's side, to take, receive to one's self, Mat. 1.20. Jno. 14.3; to take *with one's self,* Mat. 2.13, 14, 20, 21; 4.5, 8; to receive *in charge or possession,* Col. 4.17. He. 12.28; to receive *as a matter of instruction,* Mar. 7.4. 1 Co. 11.23; 15.3; 138to

receive, admit, acknowledge, Jno. 1.11. 1 Co. 15.2. Col. 2.6; *pass.* to be carried off, Mat. 24.40, 41. Lu. 17.34–36.

Παραλέγομαι, (παρά & λέγω)
    to sail by, coast along, Ac. 27.8, 13.

Παράλιος, ιου, ὁ, ἡ, (παρά & ἅλς)
    adjacent to the sea, maritime; ἡ παράλιος, sc. χώρα, the sea-coast, Lu. 6.17.

Παραλλᾰγή, ῆς, ἡ, (παραλλάσσω, to interchange)
    a shifting, mutation, change, Ja. 1.17.

Παραλογίζομαι, (παρά & λογίζομαι)
    f. ίσομαι,
    to misreckon, make a false reckoning; to impose upon, deceive, delude, circumvent, Col. 2.4. Ja. 1.22.

Παραλυτικός, ή, όν,
    paralytic, palsied, Mat. 4.24; 8.6; 9.2, 6, et al.: *from*

Παραλύω, (παρά & λύω)
    f. ύσω,
    to unloose from proper fixity or consistency of substance; to enervate or paralyse *the body or limbs; pass.* to be enervated or enfeebled, He. 12.12; *pass. part.*
    παραλελυμένος, paralytic, Lu. 5.18, 24, et al.

Παραμένω,
    f. μενῶ,
    to stay beside; to continue, stay, abide, 1 Co. 16.6. He. 7.23; *met.* to remain constant in, persevere in, Ja. 1.25.

Παραμυθέομαι, οῦμαι,(παρά & μυθέομαι, to speak, fr. μῦθος)
    f. ήσομαι,
    to exercise a gentle influence by words; to soothe, comfort, console, Jno. 11.19, 31. 1 Th. 5.14; to cheer, exhort, 1 Th. 2.11: *whence*

Παραμυθία, ας, ἡ,
    comfort, encouragement, 1 Co. 14.3.

Παραμύθιον, ίου, τό,
    gentle cheering, encouragement, Ph. 2.1.

Παρανομέω, ῶ, (παρά & νόμος)
    f. ησω,
    to violate or transgress law, Ac. 23.3: *whence*

Παρανομία, ας, ἡ,
    violation of law, transgression, 2 Pe. 2.16.

Παραπικραίνω, (παρά & πικραίνω)
    f. ανῶ, a.1. παρεπίκρᾱνα,
    pr. to incite to bitter feelings; to provoke; *absol.* to act provokingly, be refractory, He. 3.16: (S.) *whence*

Παραπικρασμός, οῦ, ὁ,
    exacerbation, exasperation, provocation; contumacy, rebellion, He. 3.8, 15. S.

Παραπίπτω, (παρά & πίπτω)
    f. πεσοῦμαι, a.2. παρέπεσον,
    pr. to fall by the side of; *met.* to fall off or away from, make defection from, He. 6.6.

Παραπλέω, ῶ, (παρά & πλέω)
    f. εύσομαι,
    to sail by or past *a place,* Ac. 20.16.

Παραπλύσιος, ου, ὁ, ἡ, τό, -ον, (παρά & πλησίος, near)

pr. near alongside; *met.* like, similar; *neut.* παραπλήσιον, *adverbially,* near to, with a near approach to, Ph. 2.27: *whence*

Παραπλησίως,
    adv. like, in the same or like manner, He. 2.14.

Παραπορεύομαι,(παρά & πορεύομαι)
    f. εύσομαι,
    to pass by the side of; to pass along, Mat. 27.39. Mar. 11.20; 15.29, et al.

Παράπτωμα, ατος, τό, (παραπίπτω)
    pr. a stumbling aside, a false step; *in N.T.,* a trespass, fault, offence, transgression, Mat. 6.14, 15; 11.25, 26, Ro. 4.25, et al.; a fall, defalcation *in faith,* Ro. 11.11, 12. L.G.

Παραρρέω, (παρά & ρέω)
    f. ρεύσομαι, a.2. παρερρύην,
    to flow beside; to glide aside from; to fall off *from profession,* decline *from steadfastness,* forefeit faith, He. 2.1.

Παράσημον, ου, τό, (παρά & σῆμα)
    a distinguishing mark; an ensign or device *of a ship,* Ac. 28.11.

Παρασκευάζω, (παρά & σκευάζω)
    f. άσω,
    to prepare, make ready, 2 Co. 9.2, 3; *mid.* to prepare one's self, put one's self in readiness, Ac. 10.10. 1 Co. 14.8.

Παρασκευή, ῆς, ἡ,
    a getting ready, preparation; *in N.T.,* preparation *for a feast,* day of preparation, Mat. 27.62. Mar. 15.42, et al.

Παρατείνω, (παρά & τείνω)
    to extend, stretch out; to prolong, continue, Ac. 20.7.

Παρατηρέω, ῶ, (παρά & τηρέω)
    f. ήσω,
    to watch narrowly, Ac. 9.24; to observe or watch insidiously, Mar. 3.2. Lu. 6.7; 14.1; 20.20, to observe scrupulously, Ga. 4.10; *whence*

Παρατήρησις, εως, ἡ,
    careful watching, intent observation, Lu. 17.20. L.G.

Παρατίθημι, (παρά & τίθημι)
    f. παραθήσω,
    to place by the side of, 139near; to set before, Mar. 6.41; 8.6, 7. Lu. 9.16; *met.* to set or lay before, propound, Mat. 13.24, 31; to inculcate, Ac. 17.3; to deposit, commit to the charge of, intrust, Lu. 12.48; 23.46; to commend, Ac. 14.23.

Παρατυγχάνω, (παρά & τυγχάνω)
    f. τεύξομαι, a.2. παρέτυχον,
    to happen, to chance upon, chance to meet, Ac. 17.17.

Παραυτίκα, (παρά & αὐτίκα)
    adv. instantly, immediately; ὁ, ἡ, τὸ παραυτίκα, momentary, transient, 2 Co. 4.17.

Παραφέρω, (παρά & φέρω)
    f. οίσω, a.2. παρήνεγκον
    to carry past; to cause to pass away, Mar. 14.36. Lu. 22.42; *pass.* to be swept along, v.r. Jude 12; to be led away, misled, seduced, v.r. He. 13.9.

Παραφρονέω, ῶ, (παρά & φρονέω)
    f. ήσω,
    to be beside one's wits; παραφρονῶν, in a foolish style, 2 Co. 11.23: *whence*

Παραφρονία, ας, ἡ,

madness, folly, 2 Pe. 2.16. N.T.

Παραχειμάζω, (παρά & χειμάζω)
to winter, spend the winter, Ac. 27.12; 28.11. 1 Co. 16.6. Tit. 3.12: *whence*

Παραχειμασία, ας, ἡ,
a wintering *in a place,* Ac. 27.12. L.G.

Παραχρῆμα, (παρά & χρῆμα)
adv. forthwith, immediately, Mat. 21.19, 20. Lu. 1.64, et al.

Πάρδᾰλις, εως, ἡ, (equiv. to πάρδος)
a leopard, or panther, Re. 13.2.

Παρεδρεύω, (πάρεδρος, one who sits by, παρά & ἕδρα)
f. εύσω,
to site near; to attend, serve, v.r. 1 Co. 9.13.

Πάρειμι, (παρά & εἰμι)
to be beside; to be present, Lu. 13.1, et al.; to be come, Mat. 26.50. Jno. 7.6; 11.28. Col. 1.6, et al.; to be in possession, He. 13.5. 2 Pe. 1.9, 12; *part.* παρών, οὖσα, όν, present, 1 Co. 5.3; τὸ παρόν, the present time, the present, He. 12.11.

Παρεισάγω, (παρά & εἰσάγω)
f άξω,
to introduce stealthily, 2 Pe. 2.1: *whence*

Παρείσακτος, ου, ὁ, ἡ,
clandestinely introduced, brought in stealthily, Ga. 2.4. N.T.

Παρεισδύω, v. δύνω, (παρά & εἰσδύω)
f. δύσω, a.1. παρεισέδῦσα,
to enter privily, creep in stealthily, steal in, Jude 4.

Παρεισέρχομαι, (παρά & εἰσέρχομαι)
a.2. παρεισῆλθον,
to supervene, Ro. 5.20; to steal in, Ga. 2.4.

Παρεισφέρω, (παρά & εἰσφέρω)
f. οίσω, a.1. παρεισήνεγκα,
to bring in beside; to bring into play, superinduce, exhibit in addition, 2 Pe. 1.5.

Παρεκτός, (παρά & ἐκτός)
adv. without, on the outside; except, Mat. 5.32. Ac. 26.29; τὰ παρεκτός, other matters, 2 Co. 11.28. S.

Παρεμβολή, ῆς, ἡ, (παρεμβάλλω, to interpose or insert; παρά & ἐμβάλλω)
an insertion beside, *later,* a marshalling *of an army;* an array *of battle,* army, He. 11.34; a camp, He. 13.11, 13. Re. 20.9; a standing camp, fortress, citadel, castle, Ac. 21.34, 37; 22.24; 23.10, 16, 32.

Παρενοχλέω, ῶ, (παρά & ἐνοχλέω)
f. ήσω,
to superadd molestation; to trouble, harass, Ac. 15.19.

Παρεπίδημος, ου, ὁ, ἡ, (παρά & ἐπίδημος)
residing in a country not one's own, a sojourner, stranger, He. 11.13. 1 Pe. 1.1; 2.11. L.G.

Παρέρχομαι, (παρά & ἔρχομαι)
f. ελεύσομαι, a.2. παρῆλθον,
to pass beside, pass along, pass by, Mat. 8.28. Mar. 6.48; to pass, elapse, *as time,* Mat. 14.15. Ac. 27.9; to pass away, be removed, Mat. 26.39, 42. Mar. 14.35; *met.* to pass away, disappear, vanish, perish, Mat. 5.18; 24.34, 35; to become vain, be rendered void, Mat. 5.18. Mar. 13.31; to pass by, disregard, neglect, Lu. 11.42; 15.29; to come to the side of, come to, Lu. 12.37; 17.7.

Πάρεσις, εως, ἡ, (παρίημι)
a letting pass; remission, forgiveness, pardon, Ro. 3.25.

Παρέχω, (παρά & ἔχω)
f. ἕξω, a.2. παρέσχον,
to hold beside; to hold out to, offer, present, Lu. 6.29; to confer, render, Lu. 7.4. Ac. 22.2; 28.2. Col. 4.1; to afford, furnish, Ac. 16.16; 17.31; 19.24. 1 Ti. 6.17; to exhibit, Tit. 2.7; to be the cause of, occasion, Mat. 26.10. Mar. 14.6. Lu. 11.7, et al.

Παρηγορία, ας, ἡ, (παρηγορέω, to exhort; to console)
140exhortation; comfort, solace, consolation, Col. 4.11.

Παρθενία, ας, ἡ,
virginity, Lu. 2.36: *from*

Παρθένος, ου, ἡ,
a virgin, maid, Mat. 1.23; 25.1, 7, 11. Ac. 2.9, et al.; *in N.T., also masc., chaste*, Re. 14.4.

Παρίημι, (παρά & ἵημι)
f. παρήσω,
to let pass beside, let fall beside; to relax; *pass. p. part.* παρειμένος, hanging down helplessly, unstrung, feeble, He. 12.12.

Παρίστημι, and later also παριστάνω, (παρά & ἵστημι)
f. παραστήσω,
trans. to place beside; to have in readiness, provide, Ac. 23.24; to present, cause to be present, place a the disposal of, Mat. 26.53. Ac. 9.41; to present *to God,* dedicate, consecrate, devote, Lu. 2.22. Ro. 6.13, 19; to prove, demonstrate, show, Ac. 1.3; 24.13; to commend, recommend, 1 Co. 8.8;
intrans. p. παρέστηκα, part. παρεστώς, plp. παρειστήκειν, a.2. ταρέστην, *and mid.,* to stand by or before, Ac. 27.24. Ro. 14.10; to stand by, to be present, Mar. 14.47, 69, 70; to stand in attendance, attend, Lu. 1.19; 19.24; *of time,* to be present, have come, Mar. 4.29; to stand by *in aid,* to aid, assist, support, Ro. 16.2.

Πάροδος, ου, ἡ, (παρά & ὁδός)
a way by; a passing by; ἐν παρόδῳ, in passing, by the way, 1 Co. 16.1.

Παροικέω, ῶ, (πάροικος)
f. ήσω,
to dwell beside; *later,* to reside in a place as a stranger, sojourn, be a stranger or sojourner, Lu. 24.18. He. 11.9: *whence*

Παροικία, ας, ἡ,
a sojourning, temporary residence in a foreign land, Ac. 13.17. 1 Pe. 1.17. S.

Πάροικος, ου, ὁ, ἡ, (παρά & οἶκος)
a neighbour; *later,* a sojourner, temporary resident, stranger, Ac. 7.6, 29. Ep. 2.19. 1 Pe. 2.11.

Παροιμία, ας, ἡ, (πάροιμος, by the road, trite, παρά & οἶμος)
a by-word, proverb, adage, 2 Pe. 2.22; *in N.T.,* an obscure saying, enigma, Jno. 16.25, 29; a parable, similitude, figurative discourse, Jno. 10.6.

Πάροινος, ου, ὁ, ἡ, (παρά & οἶνος)
pr. pertaining to wine; given to wine, prone to intemperance, drunken: *hence,* quarrelsome, insolent, overbearing, 1 Ti. 3.3. Tit. 1.7.

Παροίχομαι, (παρά & οἴχομαι)
f. οιχήσομαι, p. ᾤχημαι,
to have gone by; *p. part.* παρῳχημένος, bygone, Ac. 14.16.

Παρομοιάζω,
f. άσω,

to be like, to resemble, Mat. 23.27: (N.T.) *from*

Παρόμοιος, οία, οιον, (παρά & ὅμοιος)
    nearly resembling, similar, like, Mar. 7.8, 13.

Παροξύνω, (παρά & ὀξύνω, to sharpen, fr. ὀξύς)
    f. υνῶ,
    to sharpen; *met.* to incite, stir up, Ac. 17.16; to irritate, provoke, 1 Co. 13.5: *whence*

Παροξυσμός, οῦ, ὁ,
    an inciting, incitement, He. 10.24; a sharp fit or anger, sharp contention, angry dispute, Ac. 15.39.

Παροργίζω, (παρά & ὀργίζω)
    f. ίσω,
    to provoke to anger, irritate, exasperate, Ro. 10.19. Ep. 6.4: (S.) *whence*

Παροργισμός, οῦ, ὁ,
    provocation to anger; anger excited, indignation, wrath, Ep. 4.26. S.

Παροτρύνω, (παρά & ὀτρύνω, to excite)
    f. υνῶ,
    to stir up, incite, instigate, Ac. 13.50.

Παρουσία, ας, ἡ, (πάρειμι)
    presence, 2 Co.10.10. Phi. 2.12; a coming, arrival, advent, Ph. 1.26. Mat. 24.3, 27, 37, 39. 1 Co. 15.23, et al.

Παροψίς, ίδος, ἡ, (παρά & ὄψον)
    pr. a dainty side-dish; *meton.* a plate, platter, Mat. 23.25, 26.

Παρρησία, ας, ἡ, (ῥῆσις, a speech)
    freedom in speaking, boldness of speech, Ac. 4.13. 1 Ti. 3.13; παρρησίᾳ, *as an adv.* freely, boldly, Jno. 7.13, 26; *so* μετὰ παρρησίαας, Ac. 2.29, 4.29, 31; license, authority, Philem. 8; confidence, assurance, 2 Co. 7.4. Ep. 3.12. He. 3.6; 10.19; openness, frankness, 2 Co. 3.12; παρρησίᾳ, and ἐν παρρησίᾳ, *adverbially,* openly, plainly, perspicuously, unambiguously, Mar. 8.32. Jno. 10.24; publicly, before all, Jno. 7.4: *whence*

Παρρησιάζομαι,
    f. άσομαι,
    to speak plainly, freely, boldly, and confidently, Ac. 13.46; 14.3, et al.

Πᾶς, πᾶσα, πᾶν, gen. παντός, πάσης, παντός,
    141all; *in the sing.* all, the whole, *usually when the subst. has the article,* Mat. 6.29; 8.32. Ac. 19.26, et al.; every, *only with an anarthrous subst.,* Mat. 3.10; 4.4; et al.; *plu.* all, Mat. 1.17, et al. freq.; πάντα, in all respects, Ac. 20.35. 1 Co. 9.25; 10.33; 11.2; *by a Hebraism, a negative with* πᾶς *is sometimes equivalent to* οὐδείς *or* μηδείς, Mat. 24.22. Lu. 1.37. Ac. 10.14. Ro. 3.20. 1 Co. 1.29. Eph. 4.29, et al.

Πάσχα, τό, indec. (Heb. פסח, Aram. פסחא, fr. פסח, to pass over)
    the passover, the paschal lamb, Mat. 26.17. Mar. 14.12; *met.* used of Christ, the true paschal lamb, 1 Co. 5.7; the feat of the passover, the day on which the paschal lamb was slain and eaten, *the 14th of Nisan,* Mat. 26.18. Mar. 14.1. He. 11.28; *more genr.,* the whole paschal festival, *including the seven days of* the feast of unleavened bread, Mat. 26.2. Lu. 2.41. Jno. 2.13, et al.

Πάσχω,
    f. πείσομαι, a.2. ἔπᾰθον, p. πέπονθα,
    to be affected by *a thing whether good or bad;* to suffer, endure *evil,* Mat. 16.21; 17.12, 15; 27.19; *absol.* to suffer *death,* Lu. 22.15; 24.26, et al.

Πατάσσω,
    f. άξω, a.1. ἐπάταξα,

to strike, beat upon; to smite, wound, Mat. 26.51. Lu. 22.49, 50; *by impl.* to kill, slay, Mat. 26.31. Mar. 14.27. Ac. 7.24; to strike gently, Ac. 12.7; *fr. the Heb.* to smite, inflict evil, afflict with disease, plagues, &c. Ac. 12.23. Re. 11.6; 19.15.

Πατέω, ῶ,(πάτος, a path)
    intrans. to tread, Lu. 10.19; *trans.* to tread *the winepress,* Re. 14.20; 19.15; to trample, Lu. 21.24. Re. 11.2.

Πατήρ, τέρος, τρός, ὁ,
    a father, Mat. 2.22; 4.21, 22; *spc. used of* God, *as the* Father *of man by creation, preservation, &c.,* Mat. 5.16, 45, 48; *and peculiarly as the* Father *of our Lord Jesus Christ,* Mat. 7.21. 2 Co. 1.3; the founder of a race, remote progenitor, forefather, ancestor, Mat. 3.9; 23.30, 32; an elder, senior, father *in age,* 1 Jno. 2.13, 14; a *spiritual* father, 1 Co. 4.15; father, author, cause, source, Jno. 8.44. He. 12.9. Ja. 1.17; *used as an appellation of honour,* Mat. 23.9. Ac. 7.2.

Πατραλῷας, ου, ὁ, (πατήρ & ἀλοάω, v. ἀλοιάω, to smite)
    a striker of his father; a parricide, 1 Ti. 1.9.

Πατριά, ᾶς, ἡ, (πατήρ)
    descent, lineage; a family, tribe, race, Lu. 2.4. Ac. 3.25. Ep. 3.15.

Πατριάρχης, ου, ὁ, (πατριά & ἀρχή)
    a patriarch, head or founder of a family, Ac. 2.29; 7.8, 9. He. 7.4. S.

Πατρικός, ή, όν, (πατήρ)
    from fathers or ancestors, ancestral, paternal, Ga. 1.14.

Πατρίς, ίδος, ἡ, (fr. same)
    one's native place, country, or city, Mat. 13.54, 57. Mar. 6.1, 4. Lu. 4.23, 24. Jno. 4.44.

Πατροπαράδοτος, ου, ὁ, ἡ, (πατήρ & παραδοτός, fr. παραδίδωμι)
    handed down or received by trandition from one's fathers or ancestors, 1 Pe. 1.18. L.G.

Πατρῷος, α, ον, (πατήρ)
    received from one's ancestors, paternal, ancestral, Ac. 22.3; 24.14; 28.17.

Παύω,
    f. παύσω,
    to cause to pause or cease, restrain, prohibit, 1 Pe. 3.10; *mid.* p. πέπαυμαι, to cease, stop, leave off, desist, refrain, Lu. 5.4; 8.24, et al.

Παχύνω, (παχύς, fat, gross)
    f. υνῶ, a.1. pass. ἐπαχύνθην,
    to fatten, make gross; *met. pass.* to be rendered gross, dull, unfeeling, Mat. 13.15. Ac. 28.27.

Πέδη, ης, ἡ, (πέζα, the foot)
    a fetter, Mar. 5.4. Lu. 8.29.

Πεδῖνός, ή, όν, (πεδίον, a plain, πέδον, the ground)
    level, flat, Lu. 6.17.

Πεζεύω, (πέζα, the foot)
    f. εύσω,
    pr. to travel on foot; to travel by land, Ac. 20.13.

Πεζῇ, (pr. dat. fem. of πεζός, ή, όν, pedestrian, fr. πέζα, the foot)
    on foot, *or,* by land, Mat. 14.13. Mar. 6.33.

Πειθαρχέω, ῶ, (πείθομαι & ἀρχή)
    f. ήσω,
    to obey one in authority, Ac. 5.29, 32. Tit. 3.1; *genr.* to obey, follow, or conform to advice, Ac. 27.21.

Πειθός, ή, όη, (πείθω)

persuasive, 1 Co. 2.4. N.T.

Πειθώ, όος, οὖς, ἡ,

Suada, the goddess of persusaion; persuasiveness, v.r. 1 Co. 2.4.

Πείθω,

142f. πείσω, p. πέπεικα, a.l. ἔπεισα, p. pass. πέπεισμαι, a.l. pass. ἐπείσθην, to persuade, seek to persuade, endeavour to convince, Ac. 18.4; 19.8, 26; 28.23; to persuade, influence by persuasion, Mat. 27.20. Ac. 13.43; 16.28; to incite instigate, Ac. 14.29; to appease, render tranquil, to quiet, 1 Jno. 3.19; to strive to conciliate, aspire to the favour of, Ga. 1.10; to pacify, conciliate, win over, Mat. 28.14. Ac. 12.20; *pass. & mid.* to be persuaded of, be confident of, Lu. 20.6. Ro. 8.38.. He. 6.9; to suffer one's self to be persuaded, yield to persuasion, to be induced, Ac. 21.14; to be convinced, to believe, yield belief, Lu. 16.31. Ac. 17.4; to assent, listen to, obey, follow, Ac. 5.36, 37, 40; p.2. πέποιθα, to be assured, by confident, 2 Co. 2.3. Ph. 1.6. He. 13.18; to confide in, trust, reply on, place hope and confidence in, Mat. 27.43. Mar. 10.24. Ro. 2.19.

Πεινάω, (πεῖνα, hunger)

f. άσω, & ήσω, a.l. ἐπείνᾱσα, to hunger, be hungry, Mat. 4.2. Mar. 11.12; to be exposed to hunger, be famished, 1 Co. 4.11. Phi. 4.12; *met.* to hunger after, desire earnestly, long for, Mat. 5.6.

Πεῖρα, ας, ἡ,

a trial, attempt, endeavour; λαμβάνειν πεῖραν, to attempt, He. 11.29; *also,* to experience, He. 11.36: *whence*

Πειράζω,

f. άσω, a.l. ἐπείρᾱσα, p. pass. πεπείρασμαι, a.l. pass. ἐπειράσθην, to make proof or trial of, put to the proof, *whether with good or mischievous intent,* Mat. 16.1; 22.35, et al.; *absol.* to attempt, essay, Ac. 16.7; 24.6; *in N.T.,* to tempt, Mat. 4.1, et al.; to try, subject to trail, 1 Co. 10.13, et al.: *whence*

Πειρασμός, οῦ, ὁ,

a putting to the proof, proof, trial, 1 Pe. 4.12. He. 3.8; *direct* temptation *to sin,* Lu. 4.13; trial, temptation, Mat. 6.13; 26.41; 1 Co. 10.13, et al.; trial, calamity, affliction, Lu. 22.28, et al. S.

Πειράομαι, ῶμαι, (i.q. Act. πειράω, fr. πεῖρα)

f. άσομαι, to try, attempt, assay, endeavour, Ac. 9.26; 26.21.

Πεισμονή, ῆς, ἡ, (πείθω)

a yielding to persuasion, assent, Ga. 5.8. N.T.

Πέλᾰγος, εος, τό,

the deep, the open sea, Mat. 18.6; a sea, *contra distinguished from the sea in general and named from an adjacent country,* Ac. 27.5.

Πελεκίζω, (πέλεκυς, an axe)

f. ίσω, to strike or cut with an axe; to behead, Re. 20.4.

Πέμπτος, η, ον, (πέντε)

fifth, Re. 6.9; 9.1; 16.10; 21.20.

Πέμπω,

f. ψω, a.l. ἔπεμψα, a.l. pass. ἐπέμφθην, to send, to dispatch on any message, embassy, business, &c., Mat. 2.8; 11.2; 14.10; to transmit, Ac. 11.29. Re. 1.11; to dismiss, permit to go, Mar. 5.12; to send in or among, 2 Th. 2.11; to thrust in, or put forth, Re. 14.15, 18.

Πένης, ητος, ὁ, ἡ, (πένομαι, to labour *for one's bread*)
   pr. one who labours for his bread; poor, needy, 2 Co. 9.9.
Πενθερά, ᾶς, ἡ,
   a mother-in-law, Mat. 8.14; 10.35. Mar. 1.30. Lu. 4.38; 12.53: *from*
Πενθερός, οῦ, ὁ,
   a father-in-law, Jno. 18.13.
Πενθέω, ῶ,
   f. ήσω, a.1. ἐπένθησα,
   trans. to lament over, 2 Co. 12.21; *abol.* to lament, be sad, mourn, Mat. 5.4; 9.15.
   Mar. 16.10, et al.; *mid.* to bewail one's self, to feel compunction, 1 Co. 5.2: *from*
Πένθος, εος, τόν,
   mourning, sorrow, sadness, grief, Ja. 4.9, et al.
Πενιχρός, ά, όν, (πένης)
   poor, needy, Lu. 21.2.
Πεντάκις, (πέντε)
   adv. five time, 2 Co. 11.24.
Πεντακισχίλιοι, αι, α, (πέντε & χίλιοι)
   five times one thousand, five thousand, Mat. 14.21; 16.9, et al.
Πεντακόσιοι, ας, α, (πέντε)
   five hundred, Lu. 7.41. 1 Co. 15.6.
Πέντε, οἱ, αἱ, τά,
   indec. five, Mat. 14.17, 19; 16.9, et al.
Πεντεκαιδέκατος, η, ον, (πέντε, καί, & δέκα)
   fifteenth, Lu. 3.1.
Πεντήκοντα, οἱ, αἱ, τά, (πέντε)
   fifty, Mar. 6.40. Lu. 7.41, et al.
Πεντηκοστή, ῆς, ἡ, (fem. of πεντηκοστός, fiftieth)
   Pentecost, *or* the Feast of Weeks; *one of the three great Jewish festivals, so called*
   because it was celebrate on the fiftieth 143*day reckoning from the second day of the*
   feast of unleavened bread, i.e. *from the 16th day of Nisan,* Ac. 2.1; 20.16. 1 Co. 16.8.
Πεποίθησις, εως, ἡ, (πέποιθα, 2. p. of πείθω)
   trust, confidence, reliance, 2 Co. 1.15, et al. S.
Περ,
   enclit. *particle, serving to add force to the word to which it is subjoined.*
Πέρᾶν
   adv. across, beyond, over, on the other side, Mat. 4.15, 25; 19.1. Jno. 6.1, 17; ὁ, ἡ, τὸ,
   πέραν, farther, on the farther side, *and* τὸ πέραν, the farther side, the other side, Mat.
   8.18, 28; 14.22, et al.
Πέρας, ἄτος, τό,
   an extremity, end, Mat. 12.42. Lu. 11.31. Ro. 10.18; an end, conclusion, termination,
   He. 6.16.
Περί,
   prep., with a genitive, pr. of place about, around; about, concerning, respecting, Mat.
   2.8; 11.10; 22.31. Jno 8.18. Ro. 8.3, et al. freq.;
   with an accusative, of place about, around, round about, Mat. 3.4. Mar. 3.34. Lu. 13.8;
   οἱ περί τινα, the companions *of a person,* Lu. 22.49; a person and his companions, Ac.
   13.13; *simply* a person, Jno. 11.19; τὰ περί τινα, the condition, circumstances of *any*
   one, Ph. 2.23; *of time,* about, Mat. 20.3, 5, 6, 9; about, concerning, respecting,
   touching, Lu. 10.40. 1 Ti. 1.19; 6.21. Tit. 2.7, et al.
Περιάγω, (περί & ἄγω)

f. ἄξω,

to lead around, carry about *in one's company,* 1 Co. 9.5; to traverse, Mat. 4.23; 9.35; 23.15. Mar. 6.6; *absol.* to go up and down, Ac. 13.11. (ἄ.)

Περιαιρέω, ῶ, (περί & αἱρέω)

f. ήσω, a.2. περιεῖλον,

to take off, lift off, remove, 2 Co. 3.16; to cast off, Ac. 27.40; *met.* to cut off *hope,* Ac. 27.20; *met.* to take away *sin,* remove *the guilt of sin,* make expiation for *sin,* He. 10.11.

Περιαστράπτω, (περί & ἀστράπτω)

f. ψω,

to lighten around, shine like lightning around, Ac. 9.3; 22.6.

Περιβάλλω, (περί & βάλλω)

f. βαλῶ, a.2. περιέβαλον, p. pass. περιβέβλημαι,

to cast around; to clothe, Mat. 25.36, 38, 43; *mid.* to clothe one's self, to be clothed, Mat. 6.29, 31. Lu. 23.11. Jno. 19.2. Ac. 12.8. Re. 4.4, et al.; to cast around a city, to draw *a line of circumvallation,* Lu. 19.43.

Περιβλέπομαι, (i.q. περιβλέπω, fr. περί & βλέπω)

f. ψομαι,

trans. to look round upon, Mar. 3.5, 34; 11.11. Lu. 6.10; *absol.* to look around, Mar. 5.32; 9.8; 10.23.

Περιβόλαιον, ου, τό, (περιβάλλω)

that which is thrown around *any one,* clothing, covering, vesture; a cloak, mantle, He. 1.12; a covering, a veil, 1 Co. 11.15.

Περιδέω, (περί & δέω)

f. ήσω, p.pass. δέδεμαι,

to bind round about; *pass.* to be bound around, be bound up, Jno. 11.44.

Περιεργάζομαι, (περί, *intensive,* & ἐργάζομαι)

f. άσομαι,

to do a thing with excessive or superfluous care; to be a busy-body, 2 Th. 3.11.

Περίεργος, ου, ὁ, ἡ, (περί & ἔργον)

over careful; officious, a busy-body, 1 Ti. 5.13; *in N.T.,* περίεργα, magic arts, sorcery, Ac. 19.19.

Περιέρχομαι, (περί & ἔρχομαι)

a.2. ἦλθον,

to go about, wander about, rove, Ac. 19.13. He. 11.37; to go about, visit *from house to house,* 1 Ti. 5.13; to take a circuitous course, Ac. 28.13.

Περιέχω, (περί & ἔχω)

f. περιέξω, a.2. περιέσχον,

to encompass, enclose; to embrace, contain *as a writing,* Ac. 23.25; *met.* to encompass, seize on *the mind,* Lu. 5.9; περιέχει, *impers.* it is contained, it is among the contents *of a writing,* 1 Pe. 2.6.

Περιζώννυμι, & νύω, (περί & ζώννυμι)

f. ζέσω, p. pass. περιέζωσμαι,

to bind around *with a girdle,* gird; *in N.T.,* *mid.* to gird one's self *in preparation for bodily motion and exertion,* Lu. 12.37; 17.8, et al.; to wear a girdle, Re. 1.13; 15.6.

Περίθεσις, εως, ἡ, (περιτίθημι)

a putting on, wearing *of dress,* &c. 1 Pe. 3.3. N.T.

Περιΐστημι, (περί & ἵστημι)

f. περιστήσω,

to place around; *intrans.* a.2. περιέστην, p. pass. περιεστώς, to stand around, Jno. 11.42. Ac. 25.7; *mid.* to keep aloof from, avoid, shun, 2 Ti. 2.16. Tit. 3.9.

Περικάθαρμα, ατος, τό, (περικαθαιοω, to cleanse, purify, fr. περί & καθαίρω) 144*pr.* offscouring, filth; *met.* refuse, outcast, 1 Co. 4.13. S.

Περικαλύπτω, (περί & καλύπτω)
f. ψω,
to cover round about, cover over; to cover *the face,* Mar. 14.65; to blindfold, Lu. 22.64; *pass.* to be overlaid, He. 9.4.

Περίκειμαι, (περί & κεῖμαι)
f. κείσομαι,
to lie around, be circumjacent; to environ, He. 12.1; to be hung round, Mar. 9.42. Lu. 17.2; to have around one's self, to wear, Ac. 28.20; to be beset, He. 5.2.

Περικεφαλαία, ας, ἡ, (fem. of περικεφάλαιος, περί & κεφαλή)
a helment, Ep. 6.17. 1 Th. 5.8. L.G.

Περικρᾰτής, έος, ὁ, ἡ, (περί & κρατέω)
overpowering; περικρατὴς γενέσθαι, to become master of, to secure, Ac. 27.16. L.G.

Περικρύπτω, (περί & κρύπτω)
f. ψω,
to conceal by envelopment; to conceal *in retirement,* Lu. 1.24. L.G.

Περικυκλόω, (περί & κυκλόω)
f. ώσω,
to encircle, surround, Lu. 19.43.

Περιλάμπω, (περί & λάμπω)
f. ψω,
to shine around, Lu. 2.9. Ac. 26.13. L.G.

Περιλείπω, (περί & λείπω)
f. ψω,
to leave remaining; *pass.* to remain, survive, 1 Th. 4.15, 17.

Περίλῡπος, ου, ὁ, ἡ, (περί & λύπη)
greatly grieved, exceedingly sorrowful, Mat. 26.38. Mar. 6.26; 14.34, et al.

Περιμένω, (περί & μένω)
f. ενῶ,
to await, wait for, Ac. 1.4.

Πέριξ, (περί)
adv. round about; ὁ, ἡ, τό, περιξ, circumjacent, neighbouring, Ac. 5.16.

Περιοικέω, ῶ,
f. ήσω,
to dwell around, or in the vicinity; to be a neighbour, Lu. 1.65: *from*

Περίοικος, ου, ὁ, ἡ, (περί & οἶκος)
one who dwells in the vicinity, a neighbour, Lu. 1.58.

Περιούσιος, ου, ὁ, ἡ, (περιυσία, abundance, wealth, fr. περίειμι, to superabound)
superabundant; peculiar, special, Tit. 2.14. S.

Περιοχή, ῆς, ἡ, (περιέχω)
a compass, circumference, contents; a section, a portion *of Scripture,* Ac. 8.32.

Περιπᾰτέω, ῶ, (περί & πατέω)
f. ήσω,
to walk, walk about, Mat. 9.5; 11.5; 14.24, 26, 29, et al.; to rove, roam, 1 Pe. 5.8; *with* μετά, to accompany, follow, have intercourse with, Jno. 6.66. Re. 3.4; to have one's locality, frequent, Jno. 7.1; 11.54; *fr. the Heb.* to live *in any particular manner,* follow a course of life or conduct, have one's conversation, behave, Ro. 6.4; 8.1, et al.

Περιπείρω, (περί & πείρω)
  f. περῶ, a.1. περιέπειρα,
  to put on a spit, transfix; *met.* to pierce, wound deeply, 1 Ti. 6.10.
Περπίπτω, (περί & πίπτω)
  f. πεσοῦμαι, a.2. περιέπεσον,
  to fall around or upon, to fall in with, Lu. 10.30; to fall into, light upon, Ac. 27.41; to be involved in, Ja. 1.2.
Περιποιέω, (περί & ποιέω)
  f. ήσω,
  to cause to remain over and above, to reserve, save; *mid.* to acquire gain, earn, 1 Ti. 3.13; to purchase, Ac. 20.28: *whence*
Περιποίησις, εως, ή,
  a laying up, keeping; an acquiring or obtaining, acquisition, 1 Th. 5.9. 2 Th. 2.14; a saving, preservation, He. 10.39; a peculiar possession, specialty, Eph. 1.14. 1 Pe. 2.9.
Περιῤῥήγνυμι, (περί & ῥήγνυμι)
  f. ῥήξω,
  to break or tear all round; to strip off, Ac. 16.22.
Περισπάω, ῶ, (περί & σπάω)
  f. άσω,
  to draw off from around; to wheel about; to distract; *pass.* to be distracted, over-busied, Lu. 10.40.
Περισσεία, ας, ή, (περισσεύω)
  superabundance, Ro. 5.17. 2 Co. 8.2; 10.15. Ja. 1.21. S.
Περίσσευμα, ατος, τό,
  more than enough, residue over and above, Mar. 8.8; abundance, exuberance, Mat. 12.34. Lu. 6.45; superabundance, affluence, 2 Co. 8.13, 14. (L.G.) *from*
Περισσεύω,
  f. εύσω,
  to be over and above, to be superfluous, Mat. 14.20; Mar. 12.44. Lu. 21.4, et al.; to exit in full quantity, to abound, be abundant, Ro. 5.15. 2 Co. 1.5; to increase, be augmented, Ac. 16.5; to be advanced, be rendered more prominent, Ro. 3.7; *of persons,* to be abundantly gifted, richly furnished, abound, Lu. 15.17. Ro. 15.13. 1 Co 14.12. 2 Co. 8.7, et al.; 145to be possessed of a full sufficiency, Phi. 4.12, 18; to abound *in performance,* 1 Co. 15.58; to be a gainer, 1 Co. 8.8; *in N.T., trans.* to cause to be abundant, 2 Co. 4.15; 9.8. Eph. 1.8; to cause to be abundantly furnished, cause to abound, 1 Th. 3.12; *pass.* to be gifted with abundance, Mat. 13.12; 25.29: *from*
Περισσός, ή, όν, (περί)
  over and above, Mat. 5.37; superfluous, 2 Co. 9.1; extraordinary, Mat. 5.47; *compar.* more, greater, Mat. 11.9; 23.14, et al.; excessive, 2 Co. 2.7; *adverbially,* περισσόν, in full abundance, Jno. 10.10; περισσότερον & ἐκ περισσοῦ, exceedingly, vehemently, Mar. 6.51; 7.36. 1 Co. 15.10. Eph. 3.20, et al.; τὸ περισσόν, pre-eminence, advantage, Ro. 3.1: *whence*
Περισσοτέρως,
  adv. more, more abundantly, more earnestly, more vehemently, Mar. 15.14. 2 Co. 7.13, et al.; exceedingly, Ga. 1.14.
Περισσῶς,
  adv. much, abundantly, vehemently, Ac. 26.11; more, more abundantly, Mat. 27.23. Mar. 10.26.
Περιστερά, ᾶς, ή,
  a dove, pigeon, Mat. 3.16; 10.16, et al.

Περιτέμνω, (περί & τέμνω)
　　f. τεμῶ, p. pass. περιτέτμημαι, a.2. περιέτεμον,
　　to cut around; to circumcise, remove the prepuce, Lu. 1.59; 2.21, et al.; *met.* Col. 2.11;
　　mid. to submit to circumcision, Ac. 15.1, et al.
Περιτίθημι, (περί & τίθημι)
　　f. περιθήσω, a.1. περιέθηκα, a.2. περιέθην,
　　to place around, put about or around, Mat. 21.33; 27.28, et al.; *met.* to attach, bestow,
　　1 Co. 12.23.
Περιτομή, ῆς, ἡ, (περιτέμνω)
　　circumcision, the act or custom of circumcision, Jno. 7.22, 23. Ac. 7.8; the state of
　　being circumcised, the being circumcised, Ro. 2.25, 26, 27; 4.10; *meton.* the
　　circumcision, those who are circumcised, Ro. 3.30; 4.9; *met. spiritual* circumcision *of
　　the heart and affections,* Ro. 2.29. Col. 2.11; *meton.* persons *spiritually* circumcised,
　　Phi. 3.3. S.
Περιτρέπω, (περί & τρέπω)
　　f. ψω,
　　to turn about; to bring round *into any state,* Ac. 26.24.
Περιτρέχω, (περί & τρέχω)
　　a.2. περιέδραμον,
　　to run about, run up and down, Mar. 6.55.
Περιφέρω, (περί & φέρω)
　　f. περιοίσω, a. περιήνεγκα & περιήνεγκον,
　　to bear or carry about, Mar. 6.55; 2 Co. 4.10; *pass.* to be borne about hither and
　　thither, to be whirled about, driven to and fro, Ep. 4.14. He. 13.9. Jude 12.
Περιφρονέω, ῶ, (περί & φρήν)
　　f. ήσω,
　　to contemplate, reflect on; to despise, disregard, Tit. 2.15.
Περίχωρος, ὁ, ἡ, (περί & χώρα)
　　circumjacent; ἡ περίχωρος, sc. γῆ, an adjacent or circumjacent region, country round
　　about, Mat. 14.35. Mar. 1.28; *meton.* inhabitants of the region round about, Mat. 3.5.
　　L.G.
Περίψημα, ατος, τό, (περιψάω, to wipe on every side)
　　filth which is wiped off; offscouring; *met.* 1 Co. 4.13. N.T.
Περπερεύομαι, (πέρπερος, braggart)
　　f. εύσομαι,
　　to vaunt one's self, 1 Co. 13.4. L.G.
Πέρῠσι, (πέρας)
　　adv. last year, a year ago, 2 Co. 8.10.
Πετάομαι, ῶμαι,
　　a later form for πέτομαι, Re. 4.7; 14.6; 19.17.
Πετεινόν, οῦ, τό, (neut. of πετεινός, ή, όν, winged, flying fr. πέτομαι)
　　a bird, fowl, Mat. 6.26; 8.20. et al.
Πέτομαι,
　　f. πετήσομαι & πτήσομαι)
　　to fly, Re. 12.14.
Πέτρα, ας, ἡ,
　　a rock, Mat. 7.24, 25, et al.; *met.* Ro. 9.33. 1 Pe. 2.8; crags, clefts, Re 6.15, 16; stony
　　ground, Lu. 8.6, 13.
Πέτρος, ου, ὁ,

a stone; *in N.T., the Greek rendering of the surname Cephas, given to Apostle Simon, and having, therefore, the same sense as* πέτρα, Peter, Mat. 4.18; 8.14, et al.

Πετρώδης, εος, ους, ὁ, ἡ, τό, -ες, (πέτρα, πέτρος)

like rock; stony, rocky, Mat. 13.5, 20. Mar. 4.5, 16.

Πήγᾰνον, ου, τό,

rue, *a plant,* ruta graveolens *of Linn.,* Lu. 11.42.

Πηγή, ῆς, ἡ

a source, spring, fountain, Ja. 3.11, 12; a well, Jno. 4.6; an issue, flux, flow, Mar. 5.29; *met.* Jno 4.14.

Πήγνυμι & πηγνύω

f. ξω, a.1. ἔπηκα,

to fasten; pitch *a tent,* He. 8.2

Πηδάλιον, ίον, τό, (πηδόν, the blade of an oar)

146a rudder, Ac. 27.40. Ja. 3.4.

Πηλίκος, η, ον,

how large, Ga. 6.11; how great *in dignity,* He. 7.4. (ῑ)

Πηλός, οῦ, ὁ,

moist earth, mud, slime, Jno. 9.6, 11. 14.15; clay, potter's clay, Ro. 9.21.

Πήρα, ας, ἡ,

a leather bag or sack *for provisions,* scrip, wallet, Mat. 10.10. Mar. 6.8, et al.

Πῆχυς, εως, ὁ,

pr. cubitus, the forearm; *hence,* a cubit, *a measure of length, equal to the distance from the elbow to the extremity of the little finger, usually considered as equivalent to a foot and a half, or* 17 *inches and a half,* Jno. 21.8. Re. 21.7; *met. of time,* a span, Mat. 6.27. Lu. 12.25.

Πιάζω, (a later form for πιέζω, derived from the Doric)

f. άσω, a.1. ἐπίασα,

to press; *in N.T.,* to take or lay hold of, Ac. 3.7; to take, catch *fish,* &c., Jno. 21.3, 10. Re. 19.20; to take, seize, apprehend, arrest, Jno. 7.30, 32, 44, et al.

Πιέζω,

f. έσω, p. pass. πεπίεσμαι,

to press, to press or squeeze down, make compact by presure, Lu. 6.38.

Πιθανολογία, ας, ἡ, (πιθανός, persuasive, πείθω & λόγος)

persuasive speech, plausible discourse, Col. 2.4.

Πικραίνω, ανῶ, (πικρός)

to embitter, render bitter, Re. 10.9; *pass.* to be embittered, be made bitter, Re. 8.11; 10.10; *met. pass.* to be embittered, to grow angry, harsh, Col. 3.19.

Πικρία, ας, ἡ,

bitterness, Ac. 8.23. He. 12.15; *met.* bitterness *of spirit and language,* harshness, Ro. 3.14. Ep. 4.31: *from*

Πικρός, ή, όν,

bitter, Ja. 3.11; *met.* bitter, harsh, Ja. 3.14: *whence*

Πικρῶς,

adv. bitterly, Mat. 26.75. Lu. 22.62.

Πίμπλημι,

f. πλήσω, a.1. pass. ἐπλήσθην,

to fill, Mat. 27.48, et al.; *pass.* to be filled *mentally,* be under full influence, Lu. 1.15; 4.28, et al.; to be fulfilled, v.r. Lu. 21.22; *of stated time,* to be brought to a close, arrive at its close, Lu. 1.23, 57; 2.6, 21, 22.

Πίμπρημι,

f. πρήσω,
to set on fire, burn, inflame; *in N.T., pass.* to swell from inflammation, Ac. 28.6.

Πινακίδιον, ίου, τό,
a small tablet *for writing,* Lu. 1.63: *dimin. of*

Πίναξ, ἄκος, ὁ,
pr. a board or plant; *in N.T.,* a plate, platter, dish *on which food was served,* Mat. 14.8, 11, et al.

Πίνω,
f. πίομαι, & πιοῦμαι, a.2. ἔπιον, p. πέπωκα,
to drink, Mat. 6.25, 31; 26.27, 29, et al. freq.; *trop. of the earth,* to drink in, imbibe, He. 6.7.

Πιότης, τητος, ἡ, (πίων, fat)
fatness, richness, Ro. 11.17.

Πιπράσκω, (redupl. fr. περάω, to bring from a distance to sell)
p. πέπρᾱκα, pass. p. πέπρᾱμαι, a.1. ἐπράθην,
to sell, Mat. 13.46; 18.25, et al.; *met. with* ὑπό, *pass.* to be sold under, to be a slave to, be devoted to, Ro. 7.14.

Πίπτω,
f. πεσοῦμαι, p. πέπτωκα, a.2. ἔπεσον, & in N.T., a.1. ἔπεσα,
to fall, Mat. 15.27. Lu. 10.18; to fall, fall prostrate, fall down, Mat. 17.6; 18.29. Lu. 17.16; to fall down dead, Lu. 21.24; to fall, fall in ruins, Mat. 7.25, 27. Lu. 11.17; *met.* to fall, come by change, *as a lot,* Ac. 1.26; to fall, to fail, become null and void, fall to the ground, Lu. 16.17; to fall, to come into a worse state, Re. 2.5; to come to ruin, Ro. 11.11. He. 4.11; to fall *into sin,* Ro. 11.22. 1 Co. 10.12; to fall *in judgment,* be condemned and punished, Re. 14.8, to fall *upon,* seize, Re. 11.11; to light *upon,* Re. 7.16; to fall *under,* incur, Ja. 5.12.

Πιστεύω, (πίστις)
f. εὐσω, p. πεπίστευκα,
to believe, give credit to, Mar. 1.15; 16.13. Lu. 24.25; *intrans.* to believe, have a mental persuasion, Mat. 8.13; 9.28. Ja. 2.19; to believe, be of opinion, Ro. 14.2; *in N.T.,* πιστεύειν ἐν, εἰς, ἐπί, to believe in or on, Mat. 18.6; 27.42. Jno. 3.15, 16, 18; *absol.* to believe, be a believer, profess the religion of Jesus, Ac. 2.44; 4.4, 32; 13.48; *trans.* to intrust, commit to the charge or power of, Lu. 16.11. Jno. 2.24; *pass.* to be intrusted with, Ro. 3.2. 1 Co. 9.17.

Πιστικός, ἡ, όν, (πιστός)
genuine, pure, unadulterated *or* (πίνω) — Mar. 14.3. Jon. 12.3. N.T.

Πίστις, εως, ἡ, (πείθομαι)
147faith, belief, firm persusasion, 2 Co. 5.7. He. 11.1; assurance, firm conviction, Ro. 14.23; argument, proof, assurance, Ac. 17.31; good faith, honesty, integrity, Mat. 23.23. Ga. 5.22. Tit. 2.10; faithfulness, truthfulness, Ro. 3.3; *in N.T.,* faith *in God and Christ,* Mat. 8.10. Ac. 3.16, et al. freq.; ἡ πίστις, the *matter of Gospel* faith, Ac. 6.7. Jude 3, et al.

Πιστός, ἡ, όν, (πείθω)
faithful, true, trusty, Mat. 24.45; 25.21, 23. Lu. 12.42. 2 Ti. 2.2; true, veracious, Re. 1.5; 2.13; credible, sure, certain, indubitable, Ac. 13.34. 1 Ti. 1.15; believing, yielding belief and confidence, Jno. 20.27. Ga. 3.9; *spec.* a *Christian* believer, Ac. 10.45; 16.1, 15. 2 Co. 6.15: *whence*

Πιστόω, ῶ,
f. ώσω,
to make trustworthy; *pass.* to be assured, feel sure belief, 2 Ti. 3.14.

Πλανάω, ῶ,

    f. ήσω, a.1 ἐπλάνησα,

    to lead astray, cause to wander; *pass.* to go astray, wander about, stray, Mat. 18.12, 13. 1 Pe. 2.25; *met.* to mislead, deceive, Mat. 24.4, 5, 11, 24; *pass.* to be deceived, err, mistake, Mat. 22.29; to seduce, delude, Jno. 7.12; *pass.* to be seduced or wander from the path of virtue, to sin, transgress, Tit. 3.3. He. 5.2. Ja. 5.19, et al.: *from*

Πλάνη, ης, ἡ,

    a wandering; deceit, deception, delusion, imposture, fraud, Mat. 27.64. 1 Th. 2.3; seduction, deceiving, Ep. 4.14. 2 Th 2.11. 1 Jno. 4.6; error, false opinion, 2 Pe. 3.17; wandering *from the path of truth and virtue,* perverseness, wickedness, sin. Ro. 1.27. Ja. 5.20. 2 Pe. 2.18. Jude 11: *whence*

Πλανήτης, ου, ὁ,

    a rover, roving, a wanderer, wandering; ἀστὴρ πλανήτης, a wandering star. Jude 13.

Πλάνος, η, ον & ος, ον,

    a wanderer, vagabond; *also act.* deceiving, seducing; a deceiver, impostor, Mat. 27.63. 2 Co. 6.8. 1 Ti. 4.1. 2 Jno. 7.

Πλάξ, ακός, ἡ,

    a flat broad surface; a table, tablet, 2 Co. 3.3. He. 9.4.

Πλάσμα, ατος, τό

    a thing formed or fashioned; *spc.* a potter's vessel, Ro. 9.20: *from*

Πλάσσω, v. ττω,

    f. πλάσω, a.1. ἔπλασα, a.1. pass. ἐπλάσθην,

    to form, fashion, mould, Ro. 9.20. 1 Ti. 2.13: *whence*

Πλαστός, ἡ, όν,

    formed, fashioned, moulded; *met.* fabricated, counterfeit, delusive, 2 Pe. 2.3.

Πλατεῖα, ας, ἡ, (pr. fem. of πλατύς)

    a street, broad way, Mat. 6.5; 12.19. Lu. 10.10, et al.

Πλάτος, εος, τό, (fr. same)

    breadth, Ep. 3.18. Re. 20.9; 21.16, bis.

Πλατύνω,

    f. υνῶ, p. pass. πεπλάτυμαι, a.1. pass. ἐπλατύνθην,

    to make broad, widen, enlarge, Mat. 23.5; *pass. met., of the heart, from the Heb.,* to be expanded *with kindly and genial feelings,* 2 Co. 6.11, 13: *from*

Πλατύς, εῖα, ύ,

    broad, wide, Mat. 7.13.

Πλέγμα, ατος, τό, (πλέκω)

    any thing plaited or intertwined; a braid *of hair,* 1 Ti. 2.9.

Πλεῖστος, η, ον,

    most; very great, Mat. 11.20; 21.8; τὸ πλεῖστον, *as an adv.* at most, 1 Co. 14.27: *superlat. of* πολύς.

Πλείων, ονος, ὁ, ἡ, τό, -ον & πλέον, (comp. of πολύς)

    more *in number,* Mat. 21.36; 26.53; more *in quantity,* Mar. 12.43. Lu. 21.3; οἱ πλείονες v. πλείους, the greater part, the majority, Ac. 19.32; 27.12; the more, 1 Co. 9.19. 2 Co. 4.15; *neut.* πλεῖον, *as an adv.* more, Lu. 7.42; ἐπὶ πλεῖον, more, *of time,* longer, further, Ac. 24.4; *of space,* more widely, Ac. 4.17. 2 Ti. 2.16; 3.9; *for the pos.* much, *of time,* longer, Ac. 20.9; more, higher, greater, more excellent, of higher value, Mat. 5.20; 6.25.

Πλέκω,

    f. ξω,

    to interweave, weave, braid, plait, Mar. 15.17. Jno. 19.2.

Πλεονάζω, (πλείων, πλέον)
　　f. άσω, a.1. ἐπλεόνασα,
　　to be more than enough; to have in abundance, superabound, 2 Co. 8.15; to abound,
　　be abundant, to increase, be augmented, Ro. 5.20; 6.1; *in N.T., trans.* to cause to
　　abound or increase, to augment, 1 Th. 3.12.
Πλεονεκτέω, ῶ, (πλείων, πλέον & ἔχω)
　　f. ήσω,
　　to have more *than another;* to take advantage of; to overreach, make gain of, 2 Co.
　　7.2; 12.17, 18; to wrong, 1 Th. 4.6; 148to get the better, or an advantage of, 2 Co.
　　2.11: *whence*
Πλεονέκτης, ου, ὁ,
　　one who has or claims to have more than his share; a covetous, avaricious person, one
　　who defrauds for the sake of gain, 1 Co. 5.10, 11; 6.10. Ep. 5.5.
Πλεονεξία, ας, ἡ,
　　some advantage which one possesses over another; an inordinate desire of riches,
　　covetousness, Lu. 12.15, et al.; grasping, over-reaching, extortion, Ro. 1.29. 1 Th. 2.5,
　　et al.; a gift exacted by importunity and conferred with grudging, 2 Co. 9.5; a scheme
　　of extortion, Mar. 7.22.
Πλευρά, ας,
　　pr. a rib; the side *of the body,* Jno. 19.34; 20.20, 25, 27. Ac. 12.7.
Πλέω,
　　f. πλεύσομαι & πλευσοῦμαι, a.1. ἔπλευσα, p. πέπλευκα,
　　to sail, Lu. 8.23. Ac. 21.3; 27.2, 6, 24.
Πληγή, ῆς, ἡ, (πλήσσω)
　　a blow, stroke, stripe, Lu. 10.30; 12.48; *meton.* a wound, Ac. 16.33. Re. 13.3, 12, 14;
　　fr. the Heb. a plague, affliction, calamity, Re. 9.20; 11.6.
Πλῆθος, εος, τό, (πλήθω)
　　fullness, amplitude, magnitude; a multitude, a great number, Lu. 1.10; 2.13; 5.6; a
　　multitude, a crowd, throng, Mar. 3.7, 8. Lu. 6.17, et al.: *whence*
Πληθύνω,
　　f. υνῶ, a.1. ἐπλήθῡνα, a.1. pass. ἐπληθύνθην,
　　trans. to multiply, cause to increase, augment, 2 Co. 9.10. He. 6.14; *pass.* to be
　　multiplied, increase, be accumulated, Mat. 24.12. Ac. 6.7; 7.17, et al.; *intrans.* to
　　multiply, increase, be augmented, Ac. 6.1.
Πλήθω,
　　see πίμπλημι.
Πλήκτης, ου, ὁ, (πλήσσω)
　　a striker, one apt to strike; a quarrelsome, violent person, 1 Ti. 3.3. Tit. 1.7.
Πλύμμῡρα, ας, ἡ, (πλύμμη, to flow of the sea, πλήθω)
　　the flood-tide; a flood, inundation, Lu. 6.48.
Πλήν, (πλέον)
　　adv. besides, except, Mar. 12.32. Ac. 8.1; 20.23; *as a conj.* but, however,
　　nevertheless, Mat. 18.7. Lu. 19.27. Eph. 5.33, et al.
Πλήρης, εος, ους, ὁ, ἡ, (πλέος)
　　full, filled, Mat. 14.20; 15.37; full of *disease,* Lu. 5.12; *met.* full of, abounding in,
　　wholly occupied with, completely under the influence of, or affected by, Lu. 4.1. Jno.
　　1.14. Ac. 9.36, et al.; full, complete, perfect, Mar. 4.28.
Πληροφορέω, ῶ, (πλήρης & φορέω)
　　f. ήσω, a.1. ἐπληροφόρησα,

to bring full measure, to give in full; to carry out fully, to discharge completely, 2 Ti. 4.5; 4.17; *pass. of things,* to be fully established *as a matter of certainty,* Lu. 1.1; *of persons,* to be fully convinced, assured, Ro. 4.21: *whence*

Πληροφορία, ας, ἡ,
full conviction, firm persuasion, assurance, 1 Th. 1.5. Col. 2.2, et al. N.T.

Πληρόω, ῶ, (πλήρης)
f. ώσω, p. πεπλήρωκα, a.1. ἐπλήρωσα,
to fill, make full, fill up, Mat. 13.48; 23.32. Lu. 3.5; to fill up *a deficiency,* Phi. 4.18, 19; to pervade, Jno. 12.3. Ac. 2.2; to pervade *with an influence,* to influence fully, possess fully, Jno. 16.6. Ac. 2.28; 5.3. Ro. 1.29. Eph. 5.18, et al.; to complete, perfect, Jno. 3.29. Eph. 3.19, et al.; to bring to an end, Lu. 7.1; to perform fully, discharge, Mat. 3.15. Ac. 12.25; 13.25; 14.26. Ro. 13.8.. Col. 4.17; to consummate, Mat. 5.17; to realise, accomplish, fulfil, Lu. 1.20; 9.31. Ac. 3.18; 13.27; *fr. the Heb.* to set forth fully, Ro. 15.19. Col. 1.25; *pass. of time,* to be fulfilled, come to an end, be fully arrived, Mar. 1.15. Lu. 21.24. Jno. 7.8, et al.; *of prophecy,* to receive fulfilment, Mat. 1.22, et al. freq.: *whence*

Πλήρωμα, ατος, τό,
that which fills up; full measure, entire contents, Mar. 8.20. 1 Co. 10.26, 28; complement, full extent, full number, Ga. 4.4. Eph. 1.10; that which fills up a deficiency, a supplement, a patch, Mat. 9.16; fulness, abundance, Jno. 1.16. Ro. 15.29; a fulfilling, perfect performance, Ro. 13.10; complete attainment *of entire belief,* full acceptance, Ro. 11.12; full development, plenitude, Eph. 1.23; 3.19; 4.13. Col. 1.19; 2.9.

Πλησίον, (πέλας, idem)
adv. near, near by, Jno. 4.5; ὁ πλησίον, a neighbour, Mat. 19.19. Ro. 15.2, et al.; a friendly meighbour, Mat. 5.43.

Πλησμονή, ῆς, ἡ, (πίμπλημι)
a filling up; *met.* gratification, satisfaction, Col. 2.23.

Πλήσσω,
149f. ξω, a. pass. ἐπλήγην,
to strike, smite; *fr. the Heb.* to smite, to plague, blast, Re. 8.12.

Πλοιάριον, ου, τό,
a small vessel, boat, Mar. 3.9, et al.: *dimin. of*

Πλοῖον, ου, τό, (πλέω)
a vessel, ship, bark, *whether large or small,* Mat. 4.21, 22. Ac. 21.2, 3, et al.

Πλόος, οῦς, όου, οῦ, and later, πλοῦς, πλοός, ὁ, (fr. same)
sailing, navigation, voyage, Ac. 21.7; 27.9, 10.

Πλούσιος, α, ον, (πλοῦτος)
rich, opulent, wealthy; *and pl.* οἱ πλούσιοι, the rich, Mat. 19.23, 24; 27.57, et al.; *met.* rich, abounding in, distinguished for, Ep. 2.4. Ja. 2.5. Re. 2.9; 3.17; *meton. used of one who is* in a state of glory, dignity, happiness, &c. 2 Co. 8.9: *whence*

Πλουσίως,
adv. richly, largely, abundantly, Col. 3.16, et al.

Πλουτέω, ῶ, (πλοῦτος)
f. ήσω, p. πεπλούτηκα, a.1. ἐπλούτησα,
to be or become rich, Lu. 1.25. 1 Ti. 6.9; *trop.* Lu. 12.21; *met.* to abound in, be abundantly furnished with, 1 Ti. 6.18; to be *spiritually* enriched, 2 Co. 8.9, et al.

Πλουτίζω,
f. ίσω, a.1. ἐπλούτισα,
to make rich, enrich; *met.* to enrich *spiritually,* 1 Co. 1.5. 2 Co. 6.10; 9.11: *from*

Πλοῦτος, ου, ὁ,

riches, wealth, opulence, Mat. 13.22. Lu. 8.14; *in N.T., πλοῦτος τοῦ Θεοῦ,* v. Χριστοῦ, those rich benefits, those abundant blessings which flow from God or Christ, Ep. 3.8. Phi. 4.19; *met.* richness, abundance, copiousness, Ro. 2.4; 11.33. 2 Co. 8.2; *meton.* a *spiritual* enriching, Ro. 11.12.

Πλύνω,

f. υνῶ, a.1. ἔπλῦνα,
to wash *garments,* Re. 7.14.

Πνεῦμα, ατος, τό, (πνέω)

wind, air in motion, Jno 3.8; breath, 2 Th. 2.8; *the substance* spirit, Jno. 3.6; a spirit, spiritual being, Jno. 4.24. Ac. 23.8, 9. He. 1.14; a *bodyless* spirit, spectre, Lu. 24.37; a *foul* spirit, διαμόνιον, Mat. 8.16. Lu. 10.20; spirit, *as a vital principle,* Jno. 6.63. 1 Co. 15.45; the *human* spirit, the soul, Mat. 26.41; 27.50. Ac. 7.59. 1 Co. 7.34. Ja. 2.26; the spirit *as the seat of thought and feeling,* the mind, Mar. 8.12. Ac. 19.21, et al.; spirit, mental frame, 1 Co. 4.21. 1 Pe. 3.4; a *characteristic* spirit, as influential principle, Lu. 9.55. 1 Co. 2.12. 2 Ti. 1.7; a pervading influence, Ro. 11.8; spirit, frame of mind, *as distinguished from outward circumstances and actions,* Mat. 5.3; spirit *as distinguished from outward show and form,* Jno. 4.23; spirit, a spiritual frame, Ro. 8.4. Jude 19; spirit, *latent* spiritual import, spiritual significance, *as distinguished from the mere letter,* Ro. 2.29; 7.6. 2 Co. 3.6, 17; spirit, *as a term from a principle superior to a merely natural or carnal course of things,* Ro. 8.4. Ga. 4.29; a spiritual dispensation, He. 9.14; the Holy Spirit, Mat. 3.16; 12.31. Jno 1.32, 33, et al.; a gift of the Holy Spirit, Jno. 7.39. Ac. 19.2. 1 Co. 14.12, et al.; an operation or influence of the Holy Spirit, 1 Co. 12.3, et al.; a spiritual influence, an inspiration, Mat. 22.43. Lu. 2.27. Eph 1.17; a professedly divine communication, *or,* a professed possessor of a spiritual communication, 1 Co. 12.10. 2 Th. 2.2. 1 Jno. 4.1, 2, 3: *whence*

Πνευματικός, ή, όν,

spiritual, pertaining to the soul, *as distinguished from what concerns the body,* Ro. 15.27. 1 Co. 9.11; spiritual, pertaining to the nature of spirits, 1 Co. 15.44; τὰ πνευματικὰ τῆς πονηρίας, i.q. τὰ πνεύματα τὰ πονηρά, evil spirits, Ep. 6.12; spiritual, pertaining or relating to the influences of the Holy Spirit, *of things,* Ro. 1.11; 7.14, et al.; τὰ πνευματικά, spiritual gifts, 1 Co. 12.1; 14.1; suprior in process to the natural course of things, miraculous, 1 Co. 10.3; *of persons,* gifted with a spiritual frame of mind, spiritually affected, 1 Co. 2.13, 15; endowed with spiritual gifts, inspired, 1 Co.14.37: *whence*

Πνευματικῶς,

adv. spiritually, through spiritual views and affections, 1 Co. 2.14; spiritually, in a spiritual sense, allegorically, Re. 11.8.

Πνέω,

f. πνεύσω, later πνεύσομαι & πνευσοῦμαι, a.1. ἔπνευσα,
to breathe; to blow, *as the wind,* Mat. 7.25, 27; et al.

Πνίγω,

f. ξω, ξομαι, & ξοῦμαι, a.1. ἔπνιξα,
to stifle, suffocate, choke, 150Mat. 5.13; to seize by the throat, Mat. 18.28: (ῑ) *whence*

Πνικτός, ή, όν,

strangled, suffocated; *in N.T.,* τὸ πνικτόν, the flesh of animals killed by strangulation or suffocation, Ac. 15.20, 29; 21.25.

Πνοή, ῆς, ἡ, (πνέω)

breath, respiration, Ac. 17.25; a wind, a blast of wind, breeze, Ac. 2.2.

Ποδήρης, εος, ους, ὁ, ἡ, (ποῦς & ἄρω, to fit)

reaching to the feet; *as subst., sc.* ἐσθής, a long, flowing robe reaching down to the feet, Re. 1.13.

Πόθεν,
adv. whence? whence, *used of place,* &c. Mat. 15.33; *met. of a state of dignity,* Re. 2.5; *used of origin,* Mat. 21.25; *of cause, source, author,* &c. Mat. 13.27, 54, 56. Lu. 1.43; how? in what way?, Mar. 8.4; 12.37.

Ποιέω, ῶ,
f. ήσω, p. πεποίηκα, a.1. ἐποίησα,
to make, form, construct, Mat. 17.4. Mar. 9.5. Jno. 2.15; *of God,* to create, Mat. 19.4. Ac. 4.24; to make, prepare *a feast,* &c. Mat. 22.2. Mar. 6.21; *met.* to make, establish, ratify, *a covenant,* He. 8.9; to make, assume, consider, regard, Mat. 12.33; to make, effect, bring to pass, cause to take place, do, accomplish, Mat. 7.22; 21.21. Mar. 3.8; 6.5; 7.37; *met.* to perfect, accomplish, fulfil, put in execution *a purpose, promise,* &c. Lu. 16.4; 19.48; to cause, make, Mat. 5.32. Jno. 11.37. Ac. 24.12; to make *gain,* gain, acquire, profit, Mat. 25.16. Lu. 19.18; to get procure, Lu. 12.33; to make, to cause to be or become *any thing,* Mat. 21.13; 23.15; to use, treat, Lu. 15.19; to maek, constitute, appoint *to some office,* Mat. 4.19. Mar 3.14; to make, declare to be, 1 Jno. 1.10; 5.10; to do, to perform, execute, practise, act, Mat. 5.46, 47; 6.2, 3; to commit *evil,* Mat. 13.41; 27.23; to be devoted to, follow, practise, Jno. 3.21; 5.29. Ro. 3.12; to do, execute, fulfil, keep, observe, obey, *precepts,* &c. Mat. 1.24; 5.19; 7.21, 24, 26; to bring *evil* upon, inflict, Ac. 9.13; to keep, celebrate *a festival,* Mat. 26.18; to institute the celebration of *a festival,* He. 11.28; ποιεῖν τινα ἔξω, to cause to leave *a place,* i.q. ἔξω ἄγειν, to lead or conduct out, Ac. 5.34; to pass, spend *time,* continue for *a time,* Mat. 20.12. Ac. 15.33; 18.23. Ja. 1.10; to bear, *as trees,* yield, produce, Mar. 3.8, 10; 7.17, 18, 19;
with a substantive or adjective it forms a periphrasis for the verb corresponding to the noun or adjective, e.g. δῆλον ποιεῖν, i.q. δηλοῦν, to make manifest, betray, Mat. 26.73;
ἐκδίκησιν π., i.q. ἐκδικεῖν, to vindicate, avenge, Lu. 18.7, 8;
ἔκθετον π., i.q. ἐκτιθέναι, to expose *infants,* Ac. 7.19;
ἐνέδραν π., i.e. ἐνεδρεύειν, to lie in wait, Ac. 25.3;
ἐξουσίαν, π., i.e. ἐξουσιάζειν, to exercise power or authority, Re. 13.12;
κρίσιν π., i.q. κρίνειν, to judge, act as judge, Jno. 5.27;
λύτπωσιν π., i.q. λυτροῦν, to deliver, set free, Lu. 1.68;
μονὴν π. i.q. μένειν, to remain, dwell, Jno. 14.23;
πόλεμον π., i.q. πολεμεῖν, to make or wage war, fight, Re. 11.7;
συμβούλιον π. i.q. συμβουλεύσθαι, to consult together, deliberate, Mat. 3.6;
συνωμοσίαν π., i.q. συνομνύναι, & συστροφὴν π., i.q. συστρέφεσθαι, to conspire together, form a conspiracy, Ac. 23.12, 13;
φανερὸν π., i.q. φανεροῦν, to make known, betray, Mat. 12.16;
ἀναβολὴν ποιεῖσθαι, i.q. ἀναβάλλεσθαι, to delay, procrastinate, Ac. 25.17;
βέβαιον π., i.q. βεβαιοῦν, to confirm, render firm and sure, 2 Pe. 1.10;
δεήσεις π., i.q. δεῖσθαι, to pray, offer prayer, Lu. 5.33;
ἐκβολὴν π., i.q. ἐκβάλλειν, to cast out, throw overboard, Ac. 27.18;
καθαρισμὸν π., i.e. καθαρίζειν, to cleanse *from sin,* He. 1.3;
κοινωνίαν π., i.q. κοινωνεῖν, to communicate in liberality, bestow alms, Ro. 15.26;
κοπετὸν π., i.q. κόπτεσθαι, to lament, bewail, Ac. 8.2;
λόγον π., to regard, make account of, Ac. 20.24;
μνείαν π., i.q. μνησθῆναι, to call to mind, Ro. 1.9;
μνήμην π., to remember, retain in memory, 2 Pe. 1.15;

πορείαν π., i.q. πορεύεσθαι, to go, journey, travel, Lu. 13.22;

πρόνοιαν π., i.q. προνοεῖσθαι, to take care of, provide for, Ro. 13.14;

σπουδὴν π., i.e. σπουδάζειν, to act with diligence and earnestness, Jude 3: *whence*

Ποίημα, ατος, τό,
    that which is made or done; a work, workmanship, creation, Ro. 1.20; *met.* Ep. 2.10.

Ποίησις, εως, ἡ,
    a making; an acting, doing, performance; observance *of a law,* Ja. 1.25.

Ποιητής, οῦ, ὁ,
    a maker; the maker 151or author of a song or poem, a poet, Ac. 17.28; a doer; a performer *of the enactments of a law,* Ro. 2.13, et al.

Ποικίλος, η, ον,
    of various colours, variegated, chequered; various, diverse, manifold, Mat. 4.24, et al. (ῐ.)

Ποιμαίνω,
    f. ανῶ, a.1. ἐποίμᾱνα,
    to feed, pasture, tend a flock, Lu. 17.7. 1 Co. 9.7; *trop.* to nourish, promote the interest of, Jude 12; *met.* to tend, direct, superintend, Mat. 2.6. Jno. 21.16, et al.; to rule, Re. 2.27: *from*

Ποιμήν, ένος, ὁ,
    one who tends flocks or heards, a shepherd, herdsman, Mat. 9.36; 25.32; *met.* a pastor, superintendent, guardian, Jno. 10.11, 14, 16, et al.

Ποίμνη, ης, ἡ
    a flock *of sheep,* Lu. 2.8. 1 Co. 9.7; *met.* a flock *of disciples,* Mat. 26.31. Jno. 10.16.

Ποίμνιον, ου, τό, (contr. for ποιμένιον, a flock)
    a flock; *met.* a flock *of Christian disciples,* Lu. 12.32. Ac. 20.28, 29. 1 Pe. 5.2, 3.

Ποῖος, οία, οῖον,
    of what kind, sort, or species, Jno. 12.33; 21.19; what? which?, Mat. 19.18; 21.23, 24, 27, et al.

Πολεμέω, ῶ,
    f. ήσω, a.1. ἐπολέμησα,
    to make or wage war, fight, Re. 2.16; 12.7, et al.; to battle, quarrel, Ja. 4.2: *from*

Πόλεμος, ου, ὁ,
    war, Mat. 24.6. Mar. 13.7; battle, engagement, combat, 1 Co. 14.8. He. 11.34; battling, strife, Ja. 4.1, et al.

Πόλις, εως, ἡ,
    a city, an enclosed and walled town, Mat. 10.5, 11; 11.1; *meton.* the inhabitants of a city, Mat. 8.34; 10.15; *with a gen. of person, or a personal pron.,* the city *of any one,* the city *of one's birth or residence,* Mat. 9.1. Lu. 2.4, 11; ἡ πόλις, the city, κατ᾽ ἐξοχήν, Jerusalem, Mat. 21.18; 28.11; *met.* a place of permanent residence, abode, home, He. 11.10, 16; 13.14.

Πολῑτάρχης, ου, ὁ, (πόλις & ἄρχω)
    a ruler or prefect of a city, city magistrate, Ac. 17.6, 8. N.T.

Πολῑτεία, ας, ἡ, (πολιτεύω)
    the state of being a citizen; citizenship, the right or privilege of being a citizen, freedom of a city or state, Ac. 22.28; a commonwealth, community, Eph. 2.12.

Πολίτευμα, ατος, τό,
    the administration of a commonwealth; *in N.T., equivalent to* πολιτεία, a community, commonwealth, Phi. 3.20: *from*

Πολιτεύω,
    f. εύσω,

intrans. to be a citizen; *trans.* to govern a city or state, administer the affairs of a state; *pass.* to be governed; *in N.T.,* to order one's life and conduct, converse, live, *in a certain manner as to habits and principles,* Ac. 23.1. Ph 1.27: *from*

Πολίτης, ου, ὁ, (πόλις)
  a citizen, Lu. 15.15; 19.14. Ac. 21.39. (ῑ.)

Πολλάκις, (πολύς)
  adv. many times, often, frequently, Mat. 17.15. Mar. 5.4; 9.22, et al. (ᾰ.)

Πολλαπλᾰσίων, ονος, ὁ, ἡ, τό, -ον, (a later equivalent to πολλαπλάσιος, fr. πολύς)
  manifold, many times more, Lu. 18.30.

Πολυεύσπλαγχνος, ου, ὁ, ἡ, (πολύς, εὖ, & σπλάγχνον)
  very merciful, very compassionate, v.r. Ja. 5.11. N.T.

Πολυλογία, ας, ἡ, (πολύς & λόγος)
  wordiness, loquacity, Mat. 6.7.

Πολυμερῶς, (πολυμερής, consisting of many parts, πολύς & μέρος)
  adv. in many parts *or* parcels, He. 1.1.

Πολυποίκῑλος, ου, ὁ, ἡ, (πολύς & ποικίλος)
  exceedingly various, multifarious, multiform, manifold; *by impl.* immense, infinite, Ep. 3.10.

Πολύς, πολλή, πολύ, *gen.* πολλοῦ, πολλῆς, πολλοῦ,
  great *in magnitude or quantity,* much, large, Mat. 13.5. Jno. 3.23; 15.8; *pl.* many, Mat. 3.7; *in time,* long, Mat. 25.19. Mar. 6.35. Jno. 5.6; οἱ πολλοί, the many, the mass, Ro. 5.15; 12.5. 1 Co. 10.33; τὸ πολύ, much, 2 Co. 8.15; πολύ, *as an adv.* much, greatly, Mar. 12.27. Lu. 7.47; *of time,* ἐπ᾽ πολύ, a long time, Ac. 28.6; μετ᾽ οὐ πολύ, not long after, Ac. 27.14; *followed by a compar.* much, 2 Co. 8.22; πολλῷ, much, by much, Mat. 6.30. Mar. 10.48; τὰ πολλά, *as an adv.* most frequently, generally, Ro. 15.22; πολλά, *as an adv.* much, greatly, vehemently, Mar. 1.45; 3.12; *of time,* many times, frequently, often Mat. 9.14.

Πολύσπλαγχνος, ου, ὁ, ἡ, (πολύς & σπλάγχνον)
  152very merciful, very compassionate, Ja. 5.11. N.T.

Πολυτελής, έος, οὖς, ὁ, ἡ, (πολύς & τέλος)
  expensive, costly, Mar. 14.3. 1 Ti. 2.9; of great value, very precious, 1 Pe. 3.4.

Πολύτῑμος, ου, ὁ, ἡ, (πολύς & τιμή)
  of great price, costly, precious, Mat. 13.46. Jno. 12.3.

Πολυτρόπως, (πολύτροπος, manifold, various, πολύς & τρόπος)
  adv. in many ways, in various modes, He. 1.1.

Πόμα, ατος, τό, (πέπομαι, p. pass. of πίνω)
  drink, 1 Co. 10.4. He. 9.10.

Πονηρία, ας, ἡ,
  pr. badness, bad condition; *in N.T.,* evil disposition *of mind,* wickedness, mischief, malignity, Mat. 22.18, et al.; *pl.* πονηρίαι, wicked deeds, villainies, Mar. 7.23. Ac. 3.26: *from*

Πονηρός, ά, όν,
  bad, unsound, Mat. 6.23; 7.17, 18; evil, afflictive, Ep. 5.16; 6.13. Re. 16.2; evil, wrongful, malignant, malevolent, Mat. 5.11, 39. Ac. 28.21; evil, wicked, impious, *and* τὸ πονηρόν, evil, wrong, wickedness, Mat. 5.37, 45; 9.4; slothful, inactive, Mat. 25.26. Lu. 19.22; ὁ πονηρός, the evil one, the devil, Mat. 13.19, 38. Jno. 17.15; evil *eye,* i.q. φθονερός, envious, Mat. 20.15. Mar. 7.22; *impl.* covetous, niggardly, Mat. 7.11: *from*

Πόνος, ου, ὁ, (πένομαι)
  labour, travail; pain, misery, anguish, Re. 16.10, 11; 21.4.

Ποντικός, ή, όν,
    belonging to, or an inhabitant of Πόντος, Ac. 18.2.
Πορεία, ας, ἡ,
    a going, progress; a journey, travel, Lu. 13.22; *fr. the Heb.* way or manner of life,
    business, occupation, Ja. 1.11: *from*
Πορεύομαι, (mid. of πορεύω, to convey, transport, fr. πόρος)
    f. εύσομαι, a. ἐπορεύθην,
    to go, pass from one place to another, Mat. 17.27; 18.12; to go away, depart, Mat.
    24.1; 25.41. Jno. 14.2, 3; *trop.* to go away, depart *from life,* to die, Lu. 22.22; to go,
    pass on one's way, journey, travel, Mat. 2.8, 9. Lu 1.39. 2.41; πορεύομαι ὀπίσω, to go
    after, to become a follower or partisan, Lu. 21.8; *or,* to pursue after, be devoted to, 2
    Pe. 2.10; *fr. the Heb.* to go or proceed *in any way or course of life,* live *in any manner,*
    Lu. 1.6; 8.14. Ac. 9.31.
Πορθέω, ῶ, (a collateral from of πέρθω)
    f. ήσω,
    to lay waste, destroy; *impl.* to harass, ravage, Ac. 9.21. Ga. 1.13, 23.
Πορισμός, οῦ, ὁ, (πορίζομαι, to furnish to one's self, acquire, gain, *mid. of* πορίζω, to furnish,
supply)
    a providing, procuring; *meton.* source of gain, 1 Ti. 6.5, 6. L.G.
Πορνεία, ας, ἡ,
    fornication, whoredom, Mat. 15.19. Mar. 7.21. Ac. 15.20, 29; concubinage, Jno. 8.41;
    adultery, Mat. 5.32; 19.9; incest, 1 Co. 5.1; lewdness, uncleanness, *genr.,* Ro. 1.29;
    from the Heb. put symbolically for idolatry, Re. 2.21; 14.8: *from*
Πορνεύω,
    f. εύσω, a.1. ἐπόρνευσα,
    to commit fornication or whoredom, 1 Co. 6.18; 10.8. Re. 2.14, 20; *fr. the Heb.* to
    commit *spiritual* fornication, practise idolatry, Re. 17.2; 18.3, 9: *from*
Πόρνη, ης, ἡ, (περνάω, v. πέρνημαι, to sell)
    a prostitute, a whore, harlot, an unchaste female, Mat. 21.32, 32; *fr. the Heb.* an
    idolatress, Re. 17.1, 5, 15.
Πόρνος, ου, ὁ, (fr. same)
    a catamite; *in N.T.,* a fronicator, impure person, 1 Co. 5.9, 10, 11; 6.9, et al.
Πόρρω, (a later form of πρόσω, fr. πρό)
    adv. forward, in advance, far advanced; far, far off, at a distance, Mat. 15.8. Mar. 7.6:
    whence
Πόρρωθεν,
    adv. from a distance, from afar, He. 11.13; at a distance, far, far off, Lu. 17.12.
Πορρωτέρω, (compar. of πόρρω)
    adv. farther, beyond, Lu. 24.28.
Πορφύρα, ας, ἡ,
    purpura, murex, *a species of shell fish that yielded the purple dye, highly esteemed by*
    the ancients, its tint being a bright crimson, in N.T., a purple garment, robe of purple,
    Lu. 16.19. Re. 17.4; 18.12, et al.: (ῠ) *whence*
Πορφύρεος, οῦς, έα, ᾶ, εον, οῦν,
    purple, crimson, Jno. 19.2, 5, *col.* Mat. 27.28, 31, et al.
Πορφυρόπωλις, εως, ἡ, (fem. of πορφυροπώλης, πορφύρα & πωλέω)
    153a female seller of purple cloths, Ac. 16.14.
Ποσάκις, (πόσος)
    adv. how many times? how often?, Mat. 18.21; 23.37. Lu. 13.34. (ᾰ.)
Πόσις, εως, ἡ, (πίνω)

drinking; drink, beverage, Jno. 6.55. Ro. 14.17. Col. 2.16.

Πόσος, η, ον,

    interrog. to ὅσος *&* τόσος, how great? how much?, Mat. 6.23. Lu. 16.5, 7. 2 Co. 7.11; πόσῳ *adverbially before a comparative,* how much? by how much:, Mat. 7.11; 10.25. He. 10.29; *of time,* how long? Mar. 9.21; *of number, pl.* how many? Mat. 15.34; 16.9, 10, et al.

Ποτᾰμός, οῦ, ὁ,

    a river, stream, Mar. 1.5. Ac. 16.13; *met. and allegor.* Jno. 7.38. Re. 22.1, 2; a flood, winter torrent, *for* χείμαρρος ποταμός, Mat. 7.25, 27.

Ποταμορφόρητος, ου, ὁ, ἡ, (ποταμός, & φορητός, fr. φορέω)

    borne along or carried away by a flood or torrent, Re. 12.15. N.T.

Ποτᾰπός, ής, όν,

    a later form of ποδαπός, of what country;*in N.T., equivalent to* ποίος, what? of what manner? of what kind or sort?, Lu. 1.29; 7.39; *denoting admiration,* what? what kind of? how great? Mat. 8.27. Mar. 13.1, et al.

Πότε,

    interrog. particle, when? at what time?, Mat. 24.3; 25.37, 38, 39, 44; ἕως πότε, till when? how long?, Mat. 17.17, et al.

Ποτέ,

    an enclitic particle of time, once, some time or other, *either past for future;* formerly, Jno. 9.13; at length, Lu. 22.32; at any time, ever, Ep. 5.29. He. 2.1; *intensive after interrogatives,* ever, 1 Co. 9.7. He. 1.5, et al.

Πότερος, α, ον,

    which of the two? whether? ; πότερον, *adverbially,* whether?, Jno. 7.17.

Ποτήριον ίου, τό, (ποτήρ, πότος, πίνω)

    a vessel for drinking, cup, Mat. 10.42; 23.25, 26; *meton.* the contents of a cup, liquor contained in a cup, Lu. 22.20. 1 Co. 10.16; *fr. the Heb.,* the cup or potion *of what God's administration deals out,* Mat. 20.22, 23. Re. 14.10, et al.

Ποτίζω, (fr. same)

    f. ίσω, At. ιῶ, p. πεπότικα, α.1. ἐπότισα,

    to cause to drink, give drink to, Mat. 10.42, et al.; *met.* 1 Co. 3.2. Re. 14.8; to water, irrigate, *met.* 1 Co. 3.6, 7, 8.

Πότος, ου, ὁ, (πίνω)

    a drinking; a drinking together, drinking-bout, compotation, 1 Pe. 4.3.

Που

    an enclitic indefinite particle, somewhere, in a certain place, He. 2.6; 4.4; *with numerals,* thereabout, Ro. 4.19.

Ποῦ

    an interrog. particle, of place, where? in what place?; *direct,* Mat. 2.2. Lu. 8.25. Jno 1.39; *indirect,* Mat. 2.4. Jno 1.40; whither, Jno. 3.8; 7.35; 13.36.

Πούς, ποδός, ἡ

    the foot, Mat. 4.6; 5.35; 7.6; 22.44; 28.9. Lu. 1.79. Ac. 5.9. Ro. 3.15, et al.

Πρᾶγμα, ατος, τό, (πράσσω)

    a thing done, fact, deed, work, transaction, Lu. 1.1. Ja. 3.16; a matter, affair, Mat. 18.19. Ro. 16.2; a matter *of dispute,* 1 Co. 6.1; a thing, *genr.,* He. 10.1; 11.1; τὸ πρᾶγμα, *an euphemism for* profligacy, *perhaps,* 1 Th. 4.6.

Πραγματεία, ας, ἡ,

    an application to a matter of business; *in N.T.,* business, affair, transaction, 2 Ti. 2.4: *from*

Πραγματεύομαι, (πρᾶγμα)

f. ευσομαι,

to be occupied with or employed in any business, do business; to trade, traffic, Lu. 19.13.

Πραιτώριον, ίον, τό, (Lat. prætorium, fr. prætor)

when used in reference to a camp, the tent of the general or commander-in-cheif; hence, in reference to a province, the palace in which the governor of the province resided, Mat. 27.27. Mar. 15.16. Ac. 23.35, et al.; the camp occupied by the prætorian cohorts at Rome, the prætorian camp, or, the Roman emperor's palace, Phi. 1.13.

Πράκτωρ, ορος, ὁ, (πράσσω)

an exactor of dues or penalties; an officer who enforced payment of debts by imprisonment, Lu. 12.58.

Πρᾶξις, εως, ἡ, (fr. same)

operation, business, office, Ro. 12.4; πρᾶξις & πράξεις, actions, mode of acting, ways, deeds, practice, behaviour, Mat. 16.27. Lu. 23.51, et al.

Πρᾶος, εῖα, ον,

154mild; gentle, kind, Mat. 11.29: whence

Πραότης, τητος, ἡ,

meekness, forbearance, 1 Co. 4.21. Ga. 5.23; gentleness, kindness, benevolence, 2 Co. 10.1, et al.

Πρασιά, ᾶς, ἡ,

a small area or bed in a garden; trop. a company of persons disposed in squares; fr. the Heb. πρασιαὶ προσιαί, by areas, by squares, like beds in a garden, Mar. 6.40.

Πράσσω, v. ττω,

f. ξω, p. πέπρᾱχα, a.1. ἔπραξα,

to do, execute, perform, practise, act, transact, and of evil, to commit, Lu. 22.23; 23.15. Jno 3.20. Ac. 26.9, 20, 26, 31, et al.; to fulfil, obey, observe a law, Ro. 2.25; to do to any one, Ac. 16.28; 5.35; to occupy one's self with, be engaged in, busy one's self about, Ac. 19.19. 1 Th. 4.11; to fare, Ac. 15.29. Ep. 6.21; to exact, require, collect tribute, money lent, &c. Lu. 3.13; 19.23.

Πραϋπάθεια, ας, ἡ, (πραΰς & πάθος, fr. πάσχω)

meekness, gentleness of mind, kindness, v.r. 1 Ti. 6.11. L.G.

Πραΰς, εῖα, ύ, έος, οὖς, είας, έος, οὖς, i.q. πρᾶος,

meek, gentle, kind, forgiving, Mat. 5.5; mild, benevolent, humane, Mat. 21.5. 1 Pe. 3.4: whence

Πραΰτης, τητος, ἡ, i.q. πραότης,

meekness, mildness, forbearance, 1 Pe. 3.15; gentleness, kindness, Ja. 1.21; 3.13. S.

Πρέπει,

impers. verb, it becomes, it is fitting, it is proper, it is right, &c., and part. πρέπον, becoming, suitable, decorous, &c. Mat. 3.15. 1 Co. 11.13. Ep. 5.3. 1 Ti. 2.10, et al.

Πρεσβεία, ας, ἡ,

eldership, seniority; an embassy, legation; ambassadors, legates, Lu. 14.32; 19.14: from

Πρεσβεύω, (πρέσβυς, an old man, an ambassador)

f. εύσω,

to be elder; to be an ambassador, perform the duties of an ambassador, 2 Co. 5.20. Ep. 6.20.

Πρεσβυτέριον, ίου, τό,

a body of old men, an assembly of elders; the Jewish Sanhedrin, Lu. 22.66. Ac. 22.5; a body of elders in the Christian church, a presbytery, 1 Ti. 4.14; (N.T.) from

Πρεσβύτερος, τέρα, τέρον, (comp. of πρέσβυς)

elder, senior; older, more advanced in years, Lu. 15.25. Jno. 8.9. Ac. 2.17; an elder *in respect of age,* person advanced in years, 1 Ti. 5.1, 2; *pl. spc.* ancients, ancestors, fathers, Mat. 15.2. He. 11.2; *as an appellation of dignity,* an elder, *local* dignitary, Lu 7.3; an elder, member of the Jewish Sanhedrin, Mat. 16.21; 21.23; 26.3, 47, 57, 59; an elder or presbyter *of the Christian church,* Ac. 11.30; 14.23, et al. freq.

Πρεσβύτης, ου, ὁ (fr. same)

an old man, aged person, Lu. 1.18. Tit. 2.2. Phile. 9: (ῡ) *whence fem.*

Πρεσβῦτις, ιδος, ἡ,

an aged woman, Tit. 2.3.

Πρηνής, ίος, οῦς, ὁ, ἡ,

prone, headforemost; πρηνὴς γενόμενος, falling headlong, Ac. 1.18.

Πρίζω, v. πρίω,

a.1. ἐπρίσθην,

to saw, saw asunder, He. 11.37.

Πρίν

adv. before, *of time,* Mat. 26.34. 75. Mar. 14.72; πρὶν ἤ, sooner than, before, Mat. 1.18. Lu. 2.26, et al.

Πρό,

prep. with a gen., before, *of place,* in front of, in advance of, Mat. 11.10. Lu. 1.76. Ac. 5.23; before, *of time,* Mat. 5.12. Lu. 11.38; *before an infin. with the gen. of the article,* before, before that, Mat. 6.8. Lu. 2.21; before, above, *in preference,* Ja. 5.12. 1 Pe. 4.8.

Προάγω, (πρό & ἄγω)

f. ἄξω,

to lead, bring, or conduct forth, produce, Ac. 12.6; 16.30; 25.26; *intrans.* to go before, to go first, Mat. 2.9; 21.9. Mar. 6.45. 1 Ti. 5.24; *part.* προάγων, ουσα, ον, preceding, previous, antecedent, 1 Ti. 1.18. He. 7.18; *hence, in N.T., trans.* to precede, Mat. 14.22, et al.; to be in advance of, Mat. 21.31. (ἄ.)

Προαιρέομαι, οῦμαι, (πρό & αἱρέω)

f. ἥσομαι,

to prefer, choose; *met.* to purpose, to intend considerately, 2 Co 9.7.

Προαιτιάομαι, ῶμαι, (πρό & αἰτιάομαι, fr. αἰτία)

f. άσομαι,

pr. to charge beforehand; to convict beforehand, Ro. 3.9, *since the charges in the case in question were drawn from Scripture.* N.T.

Προακούω, (πρό & ἀκούω)

155to hear beforehand; a.1. προήκουσα, to have heard of previously, or already, Col. 1.5.

Προαμαρτάνω, (πρό & ἁμαρτάνω)

to sin before; p. προημάρτηκα, to have already sinned, have sinned heretofore, 2 Co. 12.21; 13.2. N.T.

Προαύλιον, ίου, τό, (πρό & αὐλή)

the exterior court *before an edifice,* Mar. 14.68, *col.* Mat. 26.71.

Προβαίνω, (πρό & βαίνω)

f. βήσομαι, a.2. προὔβην, part. προβάς,

to go forward, advance, Mat. 4.21. Mar. 1.19; to advance *in life,* Lu. 1.7, 18; 2.36.

Προβάλλω, (πρό & βάλλω)

f. βαλῶ, a.2. προὔβαλον,

to cast before, project; to put or urge forward, Ac. 19.33; to put forth, *as a tree its blossoms,* &c. Lu. 21.30.

Προβατικός, ή, όν,
>   belonging or pertaining to sheep; ἡ προβατικὴ (πύλη) the sheep-gate, Jno. 5.2: *from*
Πρόβᾰτον, ου, τό,
>   a sheep, Mat. 7.15; 9.36; 10.16; *met.* Mat. 10.6; 15.24, et al.
Προβιβάζω, (πρό & βιβάζω)
>   f. άσω,
>   to cause any one to advance, to lead forward; to advance, push forward, Ac. 19.33;
>   *met.* to incite, instigate, Mat. 14.8.
Προβλέπω, (πρό & βλέπω)
>   f. ψω,
>   to foresee; *mid.* to provide beforehand, He. 11.40. S.
Προγίνομαι, (πρό & γίνομαι)
>   p. προγέγονα,
>   to be or happen before, be previously done or committed; προγεγονώς, bygone,
>   previous, Ro. 3.25.
Προγινώσκω, (πρό & γινώσκω)
>   f. γνώσομαι, a.2. προέγνων, p. pass. προέγνωσμαι,
>   to know beforehand, to be previously acquainted with, Ac. 26.5. 2 Pe. 3.17; to
>   determine on beforehand, to fore-ordain, 1 Pe. 1.20; *in N.T., fr. the Heb.,* to foreknow,
>   to appoint as the subjects of future privileges, Ro. 8.29; 11.2: *whence*
Πρόγνωσις, εως, ἡ,
>   foreknowledge, prescience; *in N.T.,* previous determination, purpose, Ac. 2.23. 1 Pe.
>   1.2.
Πρόγονος, ου, ὁ, (προγίνομαι)
>   born earlier, elder; a progenitor, *pl.* progenitors; parents, 1 Ti. 5.4; forefathers,
>   ancestors, 2 Ti. 1.3.
Προγράφω, (πρό & γράφω)
>   f. ψω, p. pass. προγεγράμμαι, a.2. pass. προεγράφην
>   to write before or aforetime, Ro. 15.4. Ep. 3.3; to make a subject of public notice; to
>   set forth unreservedly and distinctly, Ga. 3.1; to designate clearly, Jude 4.
Πρόδηλος, ου, ὁ, ἡ, τό, -ον, (πρό & δῆλος)
>   previously manifest, before known; plainly manifest, very clear, prominently
>   conspicuous, 1 Ti. 5.24, 25. He. 7.14.
Προδίδωμι, (πρό & δίδωμι)
>   f. δώσω,
>   to give before, precede in giving, Ro. 11.35; to give up, abandon, betray: *whence*
Προδότης, ου, ὁ,
>   a betrayer, traitor, Lu 6.16. Ac. 7.52. 2 Ti. 3.4.
Πρόδρομος, ου, ὁ, ἡ, (δραμεῖν)
>   a precursor, forerunner, one who advances to explore and prepare the way, He. 6.20.
Προεῖδον,
>   part. προϊδών, 2. aor. of προοράω: *which see.*
Προεῖπα,
>   1. aor. & προεῖπον, 2. aor., of προλέγω: *which see.*
Προείρηκα,
>   perf. of προλέγω.
Προελπίζω, (πρό & ἐλπίζω)
>   f. ίσω,
>   to repose hope and confidence *in a person or thing* beforehand, Ep. 1.12.
Προενάρχομαι, (πρό & ἐνάρχομαι)

f. ξομαι,
to begin before *a particular time,* 2 Co. 8.6, 10. N.T.

Προεπαγγέλλομαι, (πρό & ἐπαγγέλλομαι)
a. 1. προεπηγγειλάμην,
to promise beforehand, or aforetime, Ro. 1.2. L.G.

Προέρχομαι, (πρό & ἔρχομαι)
f. ελεύσομαι, a.2. προῆλθον
to go forwards, advance, proceed, Mat. 26.39. Mar. 14.35. Ac. 12.10; to precede, go before *any one,* Lu. 22.47; to precede *in time,* be a forerunner or precursor, Lu. 1.17; to outgo, outstrip in going, Mar. 6.33; to travel in advance of *any one,* precede, Ac. 20.5, 13. 2 Co. 9.5.

Προετοιμάζω, (πρό & ἑτοιμάζω)
f. άσω,
to prepare beforehand; *in N.T.,* to appoint beforehand, Ro. 9.23. Ep. 2.10.

Προευαγγελίζομαι,
f. ίσομαι,
to announce joyful tidings beforehand, Ga. 3.8. L.G.

Προέχω, (πρό & ἔχω)
156f. ξω,
to have or hold before; *intrans. & mid.* to excel, surpass, have advantage or preeminence, Ro. 3.9.

Προηγέομαι, οῦμαι, (πρό & ἡγέομαι)
f. ήσομαι,
to go before, precede, lead onward; *met.* to endeavour to take the lead of, vie with, *or,* to give precedence to, to prefer, Ro. 12.10.

Πρόθεσις, εως, ἡ, (προτίθημι)
a setting forth or before; οἱ ἄρτοι τῆς προθέσεως, & ἡ πρόθεσις τῶν ἄρτων, the shewbread, *the twelve loaves of bread, corresponding to the twelve tribes, which were set on in two rows upon the golden table in the sanctuary,* Mat. 12.4. Mar. 2.26. Lu. 6.4. He 9.2; predetermination, purpose, Ac 11.23; 27.13. Ro. 8.28. 2 Ti 3.10, et al.

Προθεσμία, ας, ἡ, (pr. fem. of προθέσμιος, before appointed, πρό & θεσμός)
sc. ἡμέρα,
a time before appointed, set or appointed time, Ga. 4.2.

Προθυμία, ας, ἡ,
promptness, readiness, alacrity of mind, willingness, Ac. 17.11. 2 Co. 8.11, 12, 19; 9.2: *from*

Πρόθῡμος, ου, ὁ, ἡ, (πρό & θυμός)
ready in mind, prepared, prompt, willing, Mat. 26.41. Mar. 14.38; τὸ πρόθυμον, i.q. ἡ προθυμία, readiness, alacrity of mind, Ro. 1.15: *whence*

Προθύμως,
adv. promptly, with alacrity, readily, willingly, cheerfully, 1 Pe. 5.2.

Προΐστημι, (πρό & ἵστημι)
f. προστήσω,
to set before; *met.* to set over, appoint with authority; *intrans.* a.2. προύστην, p. προέστηκα, part. πρεοστώς, *and mid.* προΐσταμαι, to preside, govern, superintend, Ro. 12.8. 1 Th. 5.12. 1 Ti. 3.4, 5, 12; 5.17; *mid.* to undertake resolutely, to practise diligently, to maintain the practice of, Tit. 3.8, 14.

Προκαλέομαι, οῦμαι, (προκαλέω, to call forth, invite to stand forth, fr. πρό & καλέω)
f. έσομαι,

to call out, challenge to fight; to provoke, irritate with feelings of ungenerous rivalry, Ga. 5.26.

Προκαταγγέλλω, (πρό & καταγγέλλω)

    f. γελῶ,

    to declare or announce beforehand, foretel, predict, Ac. 3.18, 24; 7.52. 2 Co. 9.5. L.G.

Προκαταρτίζω, (πρό & καταρτίζω)

    to make ready, prepare, or complete beforehand, 2 Co. 9.5.

Πρόκειμαι, (πρό & κεῖμαι)

    f. είσομαι,

    to lie or be placed before; *met.* to be proposed or set before *as a duty, example, reward, &c.* He. 6.18; 12.1, 2. Jude 7; to be at hand, be present, 2 Co. 8.12.

Προκηρύσσω, (πρό & κηρύσσω)

    f. ξω,

    to announce publicly; *in N.T.,* to announce before, Ac. 3.20; 13.24.

Προκοπή, ῆς, ἡ

    advance upon a way; *met.* progress, advancement, furtherance, Phi. 1.12. 1 Ti. 4.15;

    from

Προκόπτω, (πρό & κόπτω)

    f. ψω,

    pr. to cut *a passage* forward; to advance, make progress; to advance *as time,* to be far spent, Ro. 13.12; *met.* to advance *in wisdom, age, or stature,* Lu. 2.52; *seq.* ἐν, to make progress or proficiency in Ga. 1.4; *with* ἐπὶ πλεῖον, to proceed or advance further, 2 Ti. 2.16; 3.9; *with* ἐπὶ τὸ χεῖρον, to grow worse and worse, 2 Ti. 3.13.

Πρόκρῐμα, ατος, τό, (προκρίνω, to prejudge, prefer)

    previous judgment, prejudice, prepossession, *or,* preference, partiality, 1 Ti. 5.21. N.T.

Πρόκῠρόω, ῶ, (πρό & κυρόω)

    f. ώσω,

    to sanction and establish previously, ratify and confirm before, Ga. 3.17. N.T.

Προλαμβάνω, (πρό & λαμβάνω)

    f. λήψομαι, a.2. προὔλᾰβον,

    to take before *another,* 1 Co. 11.21; *trop.* to anticipate, do beforehand, Mar. 14.8; to take by surprise; *pass.* to be taken unexpectedly, be overtaken, be taken by surprise, Ga. 6.1.

Προλέγω, (πρό & λέγω)

    f. ξω, a.1. προεῖπα, a.2. προεῖπον, p. προείρηκα,

    to tell beforehand, to foretel, Mat. 24.25. Ac. 1.16. Ro. 9.29. 2 Co. 13.2. Ga. 5.21. 1 Th. 3.4, et al.

Προμαρτύρομαι, (πρό & μαρτύρομαι)

    pr. to witness or testify beforehand; to declare beforehand, predict, 1 Pe. 1.11. N.T.

Προμελετάω, ῶ, (πρό & μελετάω)

    f. ήσω,

    to practise beforehand; to premeditate, Lu. 21.14.

Προμεριμνάω, ῶ (πρό & μεριμνάω)

    157f. ήσω,

    to be anxious or solicitous beforehand, to ponder beforehand, Mar. 13.11. N.T.

Προνοέω, ῶ, (πρό & νοέω)

    f. ήσω,

to perceive beforehand, foresee; to provide for, 1 Ti. 5.8; *mid.* to provide for one's self; *by impl.* to apply one's self to *a thing,* practise, strive to exhibit, Ro. 12.17. 2 Co. 8.21.

Πρόνοια, ας, ἡ,

forethought; providence, provident care, Ac. 24.3; provision, Ro. 13.14.

Προοράω, ῶ, (πρό & ὁράω)

f. προόψομαι, p. προεώρᾱκα, a.2. προεῖδον,

to foresee, Ac. 2.31. Ga. 3.8; to see before, Ac. 21.29; *in N.T.,* to have vividly present to the mind, to be mindful of, Ac. 2.25.

Προορίζω, (πρό & ὁρίζω)

f. ίσω,

to limit or mark out beforehand; to design definitively beforehand, ordain beforehand, predestine, Ac. 4.28. Ro. 8.29, 30, et al.

Προπάσχω, (πρό & πάσχω)

a.2. προέπαθον,

to experience previously; *of ill treatment,* 1 Th. 2.2.

Προπέμπω, (πρό & πέμπω)

f. ψω,

to send on before; to accompany or attend out of respect, escort, accompany for a certain distance on setting out on a journey, Ac. 15.3; 20.38; 21.5, et al.; to furnish with things necessary for a journey, Tit. 3.13. 3 Jno. 6.

Προπετής, έος, οὖς, ὁ, ἡ, τό, -ές, (πρό & πίπτω)

falling forward; *met.* precipitate, rash, Ac. 19.36. 2 Ti. 3.4.

Προπορεύομαι, (πρό & πορεύομαι)

f. εύσομαι,

to precede, go before, Ac. 7.40. Lu. 1.76.

Πρός,

prep., with a genitive, from; met. for the benefit of, Ac. 27.34; *with a dative,* near, by, at, by the side of, in the vicinity of, Mar. 5.11. Lu. 19.37; *with an accusative, used of the place to which any thing tends,* to, unto, towards, Mat. 2.12; 3.5, 13; at, close upon, Mat. 3.10. Mar. 5.22; near to, in the vicinity of, Mar. 6.45; *after verbs of speaking, praying, answering to a charge,* &c., to, Mat. 3.15; 27.14; *of place where,* with, in among, by, at, &c., Mat. 26.55. Mar. 11.4. Lu. 1.80; *of time,* for, during, Lu. 8.13. 1 Co. 7.5; near, towards, Lu. 24.29; *of the end, object, purpose for which an action is exerted, or to which any quality,* &c. *has reference,* to, Jno. 4.35. Ac. 3.10; 27.12; *before an infi.* with τό, in order to, that, in order that, Mat. 6.1; 13.30; 26.12; so as to, so that, Mat. 5.28; *of the relation which any action, state, quality,* &c. *bears to any person or thing,* in relation to, of, concerning, in respect to, with reference to, Mat. 19.8; Lu 12.41; 18.1; 20.19; as it respects, as it concerns, with relation to, Mat. 27.4. Jno. 21.22, 23; according to, in conformity with, Lu. 12.47. 2 Co. 5.10; in comparison with, Ro. 8.18; in attention to Eph. 3.4; *of the actions, dispositions,* &c. *exhibited with respect to any one, whether friendly,* towards, Ga. 6.10. Ep. 6.9; *or unfriendly,* with, against, Lu. 23.12. Ac. 23.30; *after verbs signifying to converse, dispute, make a covenant,* &c., with, Lu. 24.14. Ac. 2.7; 3.25.

Προσάββατον, ου, τό, (πρό & σάββατον)

the day before the sabbath, sabbath-eve, Mar. 15.42. S.

Προσαγορεύω, πρός & ἀγορευω, to speak)

f. εύσω,

to speak to, accost, to name, denominate; to nominate, declare, He. 5.10.

Προσάγω, (πρός & ἄγω)

f. ξω, a.2. προσήγαγον,
to lead or conduct to, bring, Lu. 9.41. Ac. 16.20; to conduct to the presence of, *met.* 1 Pe. 3.18; *intrans.* to approach, Ac. 27.27: (ᾰ) *whence*

Προσαγωγή, ῆς, ἡ
approach; to access, admission *to the presence of any one,* Ro. 5.2. Ep. 2.18.

Προσαιτέω, ῶ,(πρός & αἰτέω)
f. ήσω,
to ask for in addition; to ask earnestly, beg; to beg *alms,* Mar. 10.46. Lu. 18.35. Jno. 9.8: *whence*

Προσαίτης, ου, ὁ,
a beggar, mendicant, v.r. Jno. 9.8. N.T.

Προσαναβαίνω, (πρός & ἀναβαίνω)
f. βήσομαι, a.2. έβην
to go up further, Lu. 14.10.

Προσανᾱλίσκω, (πρός & ἀναλίσκω)
f. λώσω,
to consume besides; to expend *on a definite object,* Lu. 8.43.

Προσαναπληρόω, ῶ, (πρός & ἀναπληρόω)
f. ώσω,
158to fill up by addition or to supply *deficiencies,* 2 Co. 9.12; 11.9.

Προσανατίθημι, (πρός & ἀνατίθημι)
to lay upon over and above; *mid.* to put one's self in free communication with, to confer with, Ga. 1.16; to confer upon, to propound as a matter of consideration, Ga. 2.6.

Προσαπειλέω, ῶ,(πρός & ἀπειλέω)
f. ήσω,
to threaten in addition, utter additional threats, Ac. 4.21.

Προσδαπανάω, ῶ, (πρός & δαπανάω)
f. ήσω,
to spend besides, expend over and above, Lu. 10.35. L.G.

Προσδέομαι, (πρός & δέομαι)
f. δεήσομαι,
to want besides or in addition, Ac. 17.25.

Προσδέχομαι, (πρός & δέχομαι)
f. δέξομαι,
to receive, accept; to receive, admit, grant access to, Lu. 15.2; to receive, admit, accept, *and with* οὐ, to reject, He. 11.35; to submit to, He. 10.34; to receive kindly, *as a guest,* entertain, Ro. 16.2; to receive, admit, *as a hope,* Ac. 24.15; to look or wait for, expect, await, Mar. 15.43. Lu. 2.25, et al.

Προσδοκάω, ῶ,
f. ήσω,
to look for, be expectant of, Mat. 11.3. Lu. 7.19, 20. Ac. 3.5. 2 Pe. 3.12, 13, 14; to expect, Ac. 28.6; to wait for, Lu. 1.21; 8.40. Ac. 10.24; 27.33; *absol.* to think, anticipate, Mat. 24.50. Lu. 12.46: *whence*

Προσδοκία, ας, ἡ,
a looking for, expectation, anticipation, Lu. 21.26; *meton.* expectation, what is expected or anticipated, Ac. 12.11.

Προσδραμών,
a.2. part. of προστρέχω: *which see.*

Προσεάω, ῶ, (πρός & ἐάω)

f. άσω,
to permit an approach, Ac. 27.7. N.T.

Προσεγγίζω, (πρός & ἐγγίζω)
f. ίσω,
to approach, come near, Mar. 2.4. L.G.

Προσεδρεύω, (πρός & ἕδρα)
f. εύσω,
to sit near; *met.* to wait or attend upon, have charge of, 1 Co. 9.13.

Προσεργάζομαι, (πρός & ἐργάζομαι)
f. άσομαι,
pr. to work in addition; to gain in addition *in trade,* Lu. 19.16.

Προσέυχομαι, (πρός & ἔρχομαι)
f. ελεύσομαι, a.2. προσῆλθον, p. προσελήλυθα,
to come or go to *any one,* approach, Mat. 4.3, 11; 5.1; 8.19, 25, et al. freq.; *trop.* to come, or go to, approach, draw near, *spiritually,* He. 7.25; 11.16; 4.16. 1 Pe. 2.4; *met.* to assent to, accede to, concur in, 1 Ti. 6.3.

Προσευχή, ῆς, ἡ,
prayer, Mat. 17.21; 21.13, 22. Lu. 6.12. Ac. 1.14, et al.; *meton.* a place where prayer is offered, an oratory, *perhaps,* Ac. 16.13, 16. S.

Προσεύχομαι,
f. εύξομαι, imperf. προσηυχόμην, a.1. προσηυξάμην,
to pray, offer prayer, Mat. 5.44; 6.5, 6, et al.

Προσέχω, (πρός & ἔχω)
f. ξω,
to have in addition; to hold to, bring near; *absol.* to apply the mind to *a thing,* to give heed to, attend to, observe, consider, Ac. 5.35. He. 2.1. 2 Pe. 1.19; to take care of, provide for, Ac. 20.28; *when followed by* ἀπό, μή, v. μήποτε, to beware of, take heed of, guard against, Mat. 6.1; 7.15; to assent to, yield credence to, follow, adhere or be attached to, Ac. 8.6, 10, 11; 16.14; to give one's self up to, be addicted to, engage in, be occupied with, 1 Ti. 1.4; 3.8, et al.

Προσηλόω, ῶ, (πρός & ἧλος)
f. ώσω,
to nail to, affix with nails, Col. 2.14.

Προσήλῠτος, ου, ὁ, ἡ, (προσέρχομαι)
pr. a new comer, a stranger; *in N.T.,* a proselyte, convert from paganism to Judaism, Mat. 23.15. Ac. 2.10; 6.5; 13.43. S.

Πρόσκαιρος, ου, ὁ, ἡ, τό, -ον, (πρός & καιρός)
opportune; *in N.T.,* continuing for a limited time, temporary, transient, Mat. 13.21. Mar. 4.17. 2 Co. 4.18. He. 11.25. L.G.

Προσκαλέομαι, οῦμαι, (mid. of προσκαλέω, to call to, summon, invite, fr. πρός & καλέω)
f. έσομαι, p. προσκέκλημαι,
to call to one's self, summon, Mat. 10.1; 15.10, 32; 18.2, et al.; to invite, Ac. 2.39; to call *to the performance of a thing,* appoint, Ac. 13.2; 16.10.

Προσκαρτερέω, ῶ, (πρός & καρτερέω)
f. ήσω,
to persist in adherence to *a thing;* to be intently engaged in; attend constantly to, Ac. 1.14; 2.42. Ro. 13.6, et al.; to remain 159constantly in *a place,* Ac. 2.46; to constantly attend upon, continue near to, be at hand, Mar. 3.9. Ac. 8.13; 10.7: *whence*

Προσκαρτέρησις, εως, ἡ
perseverance, unremitting continuance in *a thing,* Ep. 6.18. N.T.

Προσκεφάλαιον, ου, τό, (πρός & κεφαλή)
  pr. a cushion for the head, pillow; *also,* a boat-cushion, Mar. 4.38.
Προσκληρόω, ῶ, (πρός & κληρόω)
  f. ώσω,
  pr. to assign by lot; *in N.T., mid.* a.1. προσεκληρώθην, to adjoin one's self to,
  associate with, follow as a disciple, Ac. 17.4.
Προσκλίνω, (πρός & κλίνω)
  f. ινῶ,
  pr. to make to lean upon or against *a thing; met., mid.* προσεκλίθην, to join one's self
  to, follow as an adherent, v.r. Ac. 5.36: *whence*
Πρόσκλῐσις, εως, ή,
  pr. a leaning upon or towards *a thing; met.* a leaning towards *any one,* inclination *of
  mind* towards, partiality, 1 Ti. 5.21. L.G.
Προσκολλάω, ῶ, (πρός & κολλάω)
  f. ήσω,
  pr. to glue to; *in N.T., mid.,* a.1. προσεκολλήθη f. προσκολληθήσομαι, to join one's
  self to *any one,* follow as an adherent, Ac. 5.36; to cleave closely to, Mat. 19.5. Mar.
  10.7. Ep. 5.31.
Πρόσκομμα, ατος, τό, (προσκόπτω)
  a stumbling, Ro. 9.32, 33. 1 Pe. 2.8; *met.* a stumbling-block, an occasion of sinning,
  means of inducing to sin, Ro. 14.13. 1 Co. 8.9; *met. a moral* stumbling, a shock *to the
  moral or religious sense,* a *moral* embarrassment, Ro. 14.20. L.G.
Προσκοπή, ῆς, ή,
  pr. a stumbling; offence, *in N.T.,* an offence, shock, ground of exception, 2 Co. 6.3:
  from
Προσκόπτω, (πρός & κόπτω)
  f. ψω,
  to dash against, to beat upon, Mat. 7.27; to strike *the foot* against, Mat. 4.6. Lu. 4.11;
  to stumble, Jno 11.9, 10; *met.* to stumble at, to take offence at, Ro. 9.32; 14.21, 1 Pe.
  2.8.
Προσκυλίω, v. προσκυλίνδω, (πρός & κυλίω)
  f. ίσω,
  to roll to or against, Mat. 27.60. Mar. 15.46. (ῐ.)
Προσκυνέω, ῶ, (πρός & κυνέω, to kiss)
  f. ήσομαι, & ήσω, a.1. προσεκύνησα,
  to do reverence or homage by kissing the hand; *in N.T.,* to do reverence or homage by
  prostration, Mat. 2.2, 8, 11; 20.20. Lu. 4.7; 24.52; to pay *divine* homage, worship,
  adore, Mat. 4.10. Jno. 4.20, 21. He. 1.6, et al.; to bow one's self in adoration, He.
  11.21: *whence*
Προσκυνητής, οῦ, ό,
  a worshipper, Jno. 4.23. N.T.
Προσλᾰλέω, ῶ, (πρός & λαλέω)
  f. ήσω,
  to speak to, converse with, Ac. 13.43; 28.20. L.G.
Προσλαμβάνω, (πρός & λαμβάνω)
  to take besides; *mid.* προσλαμβάνομαι, f. λήψομαι, to take to one's self, assume, take
  as a companion or associate, Ac. 17.5; 18.26; to take, *as food,* Ac. 27.33, 34, 36; to
  receive kindly or hospitably, admit to one's society and friendship, treat with
  kindness, Ac. 28.2. Ro. 14.1, 3; 15.7. Phile. 12, 17; to take or draw to one's self *as a
  preliminary to an address of admonition,* Mat. 16.22. Mar. 8.32: *whence*

Πρόσληψις, εως, ἡ
    an assuming; a receiving, reception, Ro. 11.15.
Προσμένω, (πρός & μένω)
    f. ενῶ,
    to continue, remain, stay *in a place,* 1 Ti. 1.3; to remain or continue with *any one,* Mat. 15.32. Mar. 8.2. Ac. 18.18; to adhere to, Ac. 11.23; *met.* to remain constant in, persevere in, Ac. 13.43. 1 Ti. 5.5.
Προσορμίζω, (πρός & ὁρμίζω, fr. ὅρμος, a station for ships)
    f. ίσω,
    to bring a ship to its station or to land; *mid.* to come to the land, Mar. 6.53.
Προσοφείλω, (πρός & ὀφείλω)
    f. ήσω,
    to owe besides, or in addition, Phile. 19.
Προσοχθίζω, (πρός & ὀχθίζω, to be vexed, offended)
    f. ίσω,
    to be vexed or angry at, He. 3.10. S.
Πρόσπεινος, ου, ὁ, ἡ, (πρός & πεῖνα)
    very hungry, Ac. 10.10. N.T.
Προσπήγνυμι, (πρός & πήγνυμι)
    f. πήξω,
    to fix to, affix to, Ac. 2.23.
Προσπίπτω, (πρός & πίπτω)
    f. πεσοῦμαι, a.2. έπεσον,
    to fall or impinge upon or against *a thing;* to fall down to *any one,* Mar. 3.11; 7.25, et al.; to rush violently upon, beat against, Mat. 7.25.
Προσποιέω, ῶ, (πρός & ποιέω)
    160f. ήσω,
    to add or attach; *mid.* to attach to one's self; to claim or arrogate to one's self; to assume the appearance of, make a show of, pretend, Lu. 24.28.
Προσπορεύομαι, (πρός & πορεύομαι)
    f. εύσομαι,
    to go or come to *any one,* Mar. 10.35. L.G.
Προσρήγνυμι, (πρός & ῥήγνυμι)
    f. ήξω,
    to break or burst upon, dash against, Lu. 6.48. N.T.
Προστάτις, ιδος, ἡ, (fem. of προστάτης, one who stands in front or before; a leader; a protector, champion, patron, fr. προΐστημι)
    a patroness, protectress, Ro. 16.2. (ᾰ.)
Προστάσσω, v. ττω, (πρός & τάσσω)
    f. ξω,
    pr. to place or station at or against; to enjoin, command, direct, Mat. 1.24; 8.4; 21.6. Mar. 1.44, et al.; to assign, constitute, appoint, Ac. 17.26.
Προστίθημι, (πρός & τίθημι)
    f. θήσω, a.1. pass. προσετέθην,
    to put to or near; to lay with or by the side of, Ac. 13.36; to add, superadd, adjoin, Mat. 6.27, 33. Lu. 3.20. Ac. 2.41, et al.; *fr. the Heb.* προστίθεμαι, *before an infinitive, and the part.* προσθείς *before a finite verb, denote* continuation *or* repetition, Lu. 19.11; 20.11, 12. Ac. 12.3.
Προστρέχω, (πρός & τρέχω)
    a.2. προσέδραμον,

to run to, *or* up, Mar. 9.15; 10.17. Ac. 8.30.

Προσφάγιον, ου, τό, (πρός & φαγεῖν)

what is eaten besides; *hence, genr.* victuals, food, Jno. 21.5. N.T.

Πρόσφᾰτος, ου, ὁ, ἡ, (πρός & πέφαμαι)

pr. recently killed; *hence, genr.* recent, new, newly or lately made, He. 10.20: *whence*

Προσφάτως,

adv. newly, recently, lately, Ac. 18.2.

Προσφέρω, (πρός & φέρω)

f. προσοίσω, a.1. προσήνεγκα, a.2. προσήνεγκον,

to bear or bring to, Mat. 4.24; 25.20; to bring to or before *magistrates,* Lu. 12.11; 23.14; to bring near to, apply to, Jno. 19.29; to offer, tender, proffer, *as money,* Ac. 8.18; to offer, present, *as gifts, oblations,* &c., Mat. 2.11; 5.23. He. 5.7; to offer *in sacrifice,* Mar. 1.44. Lu. 5.14; to offer up *any one as a sacrifice to God,* He. 9.25, 28, 11.17, et al.; *mid.* to bear one's self towards, behave or conduct one's self towards, to deal with, treat, *any one,* He. 12.7.

Προσφῐλής, έος, οὺς, ὁ, ἡ, (πρός & φίλος)

friendly, amiable, grateful, acceptable, Phi. 4.8.

Προσφορά, ας, ἡ, (προσφέρω)

pr. a bringing to; *in N.T.,* an offering, an act of offering up or sacrificing, He. 10.10; *trop.* Ro. 15.16; an offering, oblation, a thing offered, Ep. 5.2. He. 10.5, 8; a sacrifice, victim offered, Ac. 21.26; 24.17.

Προσφωνέω, ῶ, (πρός & φωνέω)

f. ήσω,

to speak to, address, Mat. 11.16. Lu. 7.32; 13.12, et al.; to address, harangue, Ac. 22.2; to call *to one's self,* Lu. 6.13.

Πρόσχῠσις, εως, ἡ, (προσχέω, to pour out upon, besprinkle, fr. πρός & χέω)

an effusion, sprinkling, He. 11.28. L.G.

Προσψαύω, (πρός & ψαύω, to touch)

f. αύσω,

to touch upon, to touch lightly, Lu. 11.46.

Προσωποληπτέω, ῶ,

f. ήσω,

to accept or respect the person *of any one,* to pay regard to external appearance, condition, circumstances, &c., to show partiality to, Ja. 2.9: (N.T.) *from*

Προσωπολήπτης, ου, ὁ, ἡ, (πρόσωπον & λαμβάνω)

a respecter of persons, Ac. 10.34. N.T.

Προσωποληψία, ας, ἡ, (πρόσωποληπτέω)

respect of persons, partiality, Ro. 2.11, et al. N.T.

Πρόσωπον, ου, τό, (πρός & ὤψ)

the face, countenance, visage, Mat. 6.16, 17; 17.2, 6, *according to later usage,* a person, individual, 2 Co. 1.11; *hence,* personal presence, 1 Th. 2.17; *fr. the Heb.* πρόσωπον πρὸς πρόσωπον, face to face, clearly, perfectly, 1 Co. 13.12; face, surface, external form, figure, appearance, Mat. 16.3. Lu. 12.56; external circumstances, or condition *of any one,* Mat. 22.16. Mar. 12.14; πρόσωπον λαμβάνειν, to have respect to the external circumstances *of any one,* Lu. 20.21. Ga. 2.6; ἐν προσώπῳ, in the person, in the name, or by the authority, 2 Co. 2.10; ἀπὸ προσώπου, from the presence of, from, Ac. 3.19, 161from before, Ac. 7.45; εἰς πρόσωπον, in the presence of, before, 2 Co. 8.24; κατὰ πρόσωπον, in the presence of, before, Ac. 3.13; openly, Ga. 2.11; κατὰ πρόσωπον ἔχειν, to have before one's face, to have *any one* present, Ac. 25.16; ἀπὸ προσώπου, from Re. 12.14; πρὸ προσώπου, before, Ac. 13.24.

Προτάσσω, v. ττω, (πρό & τάσσω)
    f. ξω,
    to place or arrange in front; to assign beforehand, foreordain, Ac. 17.26.
Προτείνω, (πρό & τείνω)
    f. ενῶ,
    to extend before; to stretch out, Ac. 22.25.
Πρότερον,
    adv. before, first, Jno. 7.51. 2 Co. 1.15; ὁ, ἡ, πρότερον, former, He. 10.32, et al.: *pr.*
    neut. of
Πρότερος, α, ον, (comp. of πρό)
    former, prior, Ep. 4.22; τὸ πρότερον, *as an adv.* before, formerly, Jno. 6.62, et al.
Προτίθημι, (πρό & τίθημι)
    f. προθήσω,
    to place before; to set forth, propose publicly, Ro. 3.2; προτίθεμαι, to purpose,
    determine, design beforehand, Ro. 1.13. Ep. 1.9.
Προτρέπω, (πρό & τρέπω)
    f. ψω,
    to turn forwards; to impel; to excite, urge, exhort, Ac. 18.27.
Προτρέχω, (πρό & τρέχω)
    a.2. προὔδραμον,
    to run before, or in advance, Lu. 19.4. Jno. 20.4.
Προϋπάρχω, (πρό & ὑπάρχω)
    f. ξω, imperf. προϋπῆρχον,
    to be before, or formerly, Lu. 23.12. Ac. 8.9.
Πρόφᾶσις, εως, ἡ, (πρό & φαίνω)
    pr. that which appears in front, that which is put forward to hide the true state of
    things; a fair show or pretext, Ac. 27.30; a specious cloke, Mat. 23.13. 1 Th. 2.5; an
    excuse, Jno. 15.22.
Προφέρω, (πρό & φέρω)
    f. προοίσω,
    to bring before, present; to bring forth or out, produce, Lu. 6.45, *bis.*
Προφητεία, ας, ἡ,
    prophecy, a prediction of future events, Mat. 13.14. 2 Pe. 1.20, 21; prophecy, a gifted
    faculty of setting forth and enforcing revealed truth, 1 Co. 12.10; 13.2, et al.;
    prophecy, matter of divine teaching set forth by special gift, 1 Ti. 1.18: *from*
Προφητεύω,
    f. εύσω, a.1. προεφήτευσα,
    to exercise the function of a προφήτης; to prophesy, to foretel the future, Mat. 11.13;
    to divine, Mat. 26.68. Mar. 14.65. Lu. 22.64; to prophesy, to set forth matter of divine
    teaching by special faculty, 1 Co. 13.9; 14.1, et al.: *from*
Προφήτης, ου, ὁ, (πρό & φημί)
    pr. a spokesman for *another; spc.* a spokesman or interpreter *for a deity;* a prophet,
    seer, Tit 1.12; *in N.T.,* a prophet, a divinely commissioned and inspired person, Mat.
    14.5. Lu. 7.16, 39. Jno. 9.17, et al.; a prophet *in the Christian Church,* a person gifted
    for the exposition of divine truth, 1 Co. 12.28, 29, et al.; a prophet, a foreteller of the
    future, Mat. 1.22, et al. freq.; οἱ προφῆται, the prophetic scriptures of the Old
    Testament, Lu. 16.29, et al.: *whence*
Προφητικός, ή, όν,
    prophetic, uttered by prophets, Ro. 16.26. 2 Pe. 1.19. L.G.
Προφῆτις, ιδος, ἡ,

a prophetess, a divinely gifted female teacher, Lu. 2.36. Re. 2.20.

Προφθάνω, (πρό & φθάνω)
    f. άσω, & ήσομαι, a.1. προέφθᾰσα,
    to outstrip, anticipate; to anticipate *any one in doing or saying a thing,* be beforehand with, Mat. 17.25.

Προχειρίζομαι, (πρό & χείρ)
    f. ίσομαι,
    to take into the hand, to make ready for use or action; to constitute, destine, Ac. 22.14; 26.16.

Προχειροτονέω, ῶ,(πρό & χειροτονέω)
    f. ήσω,
    pr. to elect before; to fore-appoint, Ac. 10.41.

Πρύμνα, ης, ἡ, (πρυμνός, last, hindmost)
    the hinder part of a vessel, stern, Mar. 4.38, et al.

Πρωΐ,
    adv. in the morning, early, Mat. 16.3; 20.1. Mar. 15.1. Ac. 28.23, et al.; the morning watch, *which ushers in the dawn,* Mar. 13.35; *whence*

Πρωΐα, ας, ἡ, (pr. fem. of πρώϊος, α, ov, in the morning, early)
    sc. ὥρα,
    morning, the morning hour, Mat. 21.18; 27.1. Jno. 18.28; 21.4.

Πρώϊμος, η, ov,
    early, Ja. 5.7.

Πρωϊνός, ή, όν, (a later form of πρώϊος)
    belonging to the morning, morning, Re. 2.28; 22.16.

Πρῷρα, ας, ἡ, (πρό)
    the forepart of a vessel, prow, Ac. 27.30, 41.

Πρωτεύω (πρῶτος)
    162f. εύσω
    to be first, to hold the first rank or highest dignity, have the preeminence, be chief, Col. 1.18.

Πρωτοκαθεδρία, ας, ἡ, (πρῶτος & καθέδρα)
    the first or uppermost seat, the most honourable seat, Mat. 23.6. Mar. 12.39. Lu. 11.43; 20.46. N.T.

Πρωτοκλισία, ας, ἡ, (πρῶτος & κλισία)
    the first place of reclining *at table,* the most honourable place at table, Mat. 23.6. Mar. 12.39. Lu. 14.7, 8; 20.46. N.T.

Πρῶτον,
    adv. first *in time,* in the first place, Mar. 4.28; 16.9; τὸ πρῶτον, at the first, formerly, Jno. 12.16; 19.39; first *in dignity, importance, &c.,* before all things, Mat. 6.33. Lu. 12.1: *pr. neut. of*

Πρῶτος, η, ov, (superl. of πρό, as if contr. from πρότατος)
    first *in time, order, &c.* Mat. 10.2; 26.17; first *in dignity, importance, &c.,* chief, principal, most important, Mar. 6.21. Lu. 19.47. Ac. 13.50; 16.12; *as an equivalent to the compar.* πρότερος, prior, Jno. 1.15, 30; 15.18; Mat. 27.64; *adverbially,* first, Jno. 1.42; 5.4; 8.7.

Πρωτοστάτης, ου, ὁ, (πρῶτος & ἵστημι)
    pr. one stationed in the first rank *of an army;* a leader; a chief, ringleader, Ac. 24.5. (ᾰ.)

Πρωτοτόκια, ων, τά,
    the rights of primogeniture, birthright, He. 12.16: (S.) *from*

Πρωτότοκος, ου, ὁ, ἡ, τό, -ον, (πρῶτος & τίκτω)
    firstborn, Mat. 1.25. Lu. 2.7. He. 11.28; *in N.T.*, prior in generation, Col. 1.15; a
    firstborn *head of a spiritual family,* Ro. 8.29. He. 1.6; firstborn, *as possessed of the*
    peculiar privilege of spiritual generation, He. 12.23.
Πταίω,
    f. αίσω, a.1. ἔπταισα,
    to cause to stumble; *intrans.* to stumble, stagger, fall; to make a false step; *met.* to err,
    offend, transgress, Ro. 11.11. Ja. 2.10; 3.2, *bis; met.* to fail *of an object,* 2 Pe. 1.10.
Πτέρνα, ης, ἡ,
    the heel, Jno. 13.18.
Πτερύγιον, ου, τό,
    a little wing; the extremity, the extreme point *of a thing;* a pinnacle, or apex *of a*
    building, Mat. 4.5. Lu. 4.9: *dimin. of*
Πτέρυξ, υγος, ἡ, (πτερόν)
    a wing pinion, Mat. 23.37. Lu. 13.34, et al.
Πτηνόν, οῦ, τό, (pr. neut. of πτηνός, ή, όν, winged, fr. πέτομαι, to fly)
    a bird, fowl, 1 Co. 15.39.
Πτοέω, ῶ,
    f. ήσω, a.1. pass. ἐπτοήθην,
    to terrify, affright; *pass.* to be terrified, be in consternation, Lu. 21.9; 24.37: *whence*
Πτόησις, εως, ἡ,
    consternation, dismay, 1 Pe. 3.6.
Πτύον, ου, τό, (πτύω)
    a fan, winnowing-shovel, Mat. 3.12. Lu. 3.17.
Πτύρω,
    to scare, terrify; *pass.* to be terrified, be in consternation, Phi. 1.28.
Πτύσμα, ατος, τό, (πτύω)
    spittle, saliva, Jno. 9.6.
Πτύσσω,
    f. ξω, a.1. ἔπτυξα,
    to fold; to roll up *a scroll,* Lu. 4.20.
Πτύω
    f. ύσω, a.1. ἔπτῦσα,
    to spit, spit out, Mar. 7.33; 8.23. Jno. 9.6.
Πτῶμα, ατος, τό, (πίπτω)
    a fall; a dead body, carcase, corpse, Mat. 24.28. Mar. 6.29. Re. 11.8, 9.
Πτῶσις, εως, ἡ, (fr. same)
    a fall, crash, ruin, Mat. 7.27; *met.* downfall, ruin, Lu. 2.34.
Πτωχεία, ας, ἡ,
    begging; beggary; poverty, 2 Co. 8.2, 9. Re. 2.9: *from*
Πτωχεύω,
    f. εύσω,
    to be a beggar; to be or become poor, be in poverty, 2 Co. 8.9: *from*
Πτωχός, ή, όν,
    reduced to beggary, mendicant; poor, indigent, Mat. 19.21; 26.9, 11, et al.; *met.*
    spiritually poor, Re. 3.17; *by impl.* a person of low condition, Mat. 11.5. Lu. 4.18;
    7.22; *met.* beggarly, sorry, Ga. 4.9; *met.* lowly, Mat. 5.3. Lu. 6.20.
Πυγμή, ῆς, ἡ, (πύξ)
    the fist; πυγμῇ, together with the fore-arm, *or,* with care, carefully, Mar. 7.3.
Πύθων, ωνος, ὁ

Python, *the name of the mythological serpent slain by Apollo, thence named the Pythian; later, equivalent to* ἐγγαστρίμαντις, a soothsaying ventriloquist; πνεῦμα πύθωνος, i.q. δαιμόνιον, μαντικόν, a soothsaying demon, Ac. 16.16.

Πυκνός, ή, όν,
    dense, thick, frequent, 1 Ti. 5.23; πυκνά, *as an adverb,* 163frequently, often, Lu. 5.33; *so the compar.* πυκνότερον, very frequently, Ac. 24.26.

Πυκτεύω, (πύκτης, a boxer, fr. πύξ)
    to box, fight as a pugilist, 1 Co. 9.26.

Πύλη, ης, ἡ,
    a gate, Mat. 7.13, 14. Lu. 7.12. Ac. 12.10, et al.; τύλαι ᾅδου, the gates of hades, the nether world and its powers, the powers of destruction, dissolution, Mat. 16.18: *whence*

Πυλών, ῶνος, ὁ,
    a gateway, vestibule, Mat. 26.71. Lu. 16.20; a gate, Ac. 14.13. Re. 21.12, 13, 15, 21, 25, et al. L.G.

Πυνθάνομαι,
    f. πεύσομαι, a.2. ἐπυθόμην,
    to ask, inquire, Mat. 2.4. Lu. 15.26, et al.; to investigate, examine *judicially,* Ac. 23.20; to ascertain by inquiry, understand, Ac. 23.34.

Πῦρ, πυρός, τό,
    fire, Mat. 3.10; 7.19; 13.40, et al. freq.; πυρός, *used by Hebraism with the force of an adjective,* fiery, fierce, He. 10.27; fire *used figuratively to express various circumstances of severe trial,* Lu. 12.49. 1 Co. 3.13. Jude 23: *whence*

Πυρά, ᾶς, ἡ,
    a fire, heap of combustibles, Ac. 28.2, 3.

Πύργος, ου, ὁ,
    a tower, Mat. 21.33. Mar. 12.1. Lu. 13.4; *genr.* a castle, palace, Lu. 14.28.

Πυρέσσω, v. ττω,
    f. ξω,
    to be feverish, be sick of a fever, Mat. 8.14. Mar. 1.30: *from*

Πυρετός, οῦ, ὁ, (πῦρ)
    scorching and noxious heat; a fever, Mat. 8.15. Mar. 1.31, et al.

Πύρινος, η, ον, (fr. same)
    pr. of fire, fiery, burning; shining, glittering, Re. 9.17.

Πυρόω, ῶ, (fr. same)
    f. ώσω,
    to set on fire, burn; *pass.* to be kindled, be on fire, burn, flame, Ep. 6.16. 2 Pe. 3.12. Re. 1.15; *met. of anger,* to be inflamed, incensed, provoked, 2 Co. 11.29; *of lust,* to be inflamed, burn, 1 Co. 7.9; to be tried with fire, *as metals,* Re. 3.18.

Πυρράζω,
    f. άσω,
    to be fiery red, Mat. 16.2, 3: (N.T.) *from*

Πυρρός, ά, όν, (πῦρ)
    of the colour of fire, fiery-red, Re. 6.4; 12.3.

Πύρωσις, εως, ἡ, (πυρόω)
    a burning, conflagration, Re. 18.9, 18; *met.* a fiery test *of trying circumstances,* 1 Pe. 4.12.

Πω,
    an enclitic particle, yet: *see in* μήπω, μηδέπω, οὔπω, οὐδέπω, πώποτε.

Πωλέω, ῶ,

f. ἥσω,

to sell, Mat. 10.29; 13.44, et al.

Πῶλος, ου, ὁ, ἡ,

a youngling; a foal or colt, Mat. 21.2, 5, 7. Mar. 11.2, et al.

Πώποτε, (πω & πότε)

adv. ever yet, ever, at any time, Lu. 19.30. Jno. 1.18, et al.

Πωρόω, ῶ, (πῶρος, a stony concreation)

f. ώσω,

to petrify; to harden; in N.T., to harden *the feelings,* Jno. 12.40; *pass.* to become callous, unimpressible, Mar. 6.52; 8.17. Ro. 11.7. 2 Co. 3.14: *whence*

Πώρωσις, εως, ἡ,

a hardening; *met.* hardness of heart, callousness, insensibility, Mar. 3.5. Ro. 11.25. Ep. 4.18.

Πως,

an enclitic particle, in any way, by any means: *see* εἴπως, μήπως.

Πῶς,

adv. how? in what manner? by what means? Mat. 7.4; 22.12. Jno. 6.52; *used in interrogations which imply a negative,* Mat. 12.26, 29, 34; 22.45; 23.33. Ac. 8.31; *put concisely for* how is it that? how does it come to pass that? Mat. 16.11; 22.43. Mar. 4.40. Jno. 7.15; *with an indirect interrogation,* how, in what manner, Mat. 6.28; 10.19. Mar. 11.18; *put for* τί, what? Lu. 10.26; *put for* ὡς, *as a particle of exclamation,* how, how much, how greatly, Mar. 10.23, 24.

P, ρ, Ῥῶ

Ῥαββί, ὁ indec. (later Heb. רבי fr. רב, which was deemed less honourable)

Rabbi, my master, teacher, doctor, Mat. 23.7, 8; 26.25, 49, et al.

Ῥαββονί, v. Ῥαββουνί (later Heb. רבון, Aram. with suffix, רבוני)

Rabboni, my master, *the highest title of honour in the Jewish schools,* Mar. 10.51. Jno. 20.16.

Ῥαβδίζω,

f. ίσω, a.1. ἐῤῥάβδισα, a.1. pass. ἐῤῥαβδίσθην,

164to beat with rods, Ac. 16.22. 2 Co. 11.25: *from*

Ῥάβδος, ου, ἡ,

a rod, wand, He. 9.4. Re. 11.1; a rod *of correction,* 1 Co. 4.21; a staff, Mat. 10.10. He. 11.21; a sceptre, He. 1.8. Re. 2.27.

Ῥαβδοῦχος, ου, ὁ, (ῥάβδος & ἔχω)

the bearer of a wand *of office;* a lictor, serjeant, *a public servant who bore a bundle of rods before the magistrates as insignia of their office, and carried into execution the sentences they pronounced,* Ac. 16.35, 38.

Ῥᾳδιούργημα, ατος, τό, (ῥᾳδιουργέω, to do easily, to act recklessly; ῥάδιος, easy, & ἔργον)

pr. any thing done lightly, levity; reckless conduct, crime, Ac. 18.14. L.G.

Ῥᾳδιουργία, ας, ἡ, (fr. same)

facility of doing *any thing;* levity in doing; recklessness, profligacy, wickedness, Ac. 13.10.

Ῥακά,

an Aramaean term of bitter contempt, worthless fellow, Mat. 5.22.

Ῥάκος, εος, τό, (ῥάσσω, ῥήσσω)

a torn garment; a shred or strip of cloth, Mat. 9.16. Mar. 2.21.

Ῥαντίζω, (ῥαίνω, idem)

f. ίσω, a.1. ἐρράντισα, p. pass. ἐρράντισμαι,
    to sprinkle, besprinkle, He. 9.13, 19, 21; *met. and by impl.* to cleanse by sprinkling,
    purify, free from pollution, He. 10.22: (L.G.) *whence*

Ῥαντισμός, οῦ, ὁ,
    a sprinkling; *met.* a cleansing, purification, lustration. He. 12.24. 1 Pe. 1.2. S.

Ῥαπίζω, (ῥαπίς, a rod)
    f. ίσω, a.1. ἐρράπισα,
    to beat with rods; to strike with the palm of the hand, cuff, slap, Mat. 5.39; 26.67:
    whence

Ῥάπισμα, ατος, τό,
    a blow with the palm of the hand, cuff, slap, Mar. 14.65. Jno. 18.22; 19.3. L.G.

Ῥαφίς, ίδος, ἡ, (ῥάπτω, to sew, sew together)
    a needle, Mat. 19.24. Mar. 10.25. Lu. 18.25.

Ῥέδα, v. ῥέδη, ης, ἡ, (Lat., rheda)
    a carriage with four wheels *for travelling,* chariot, Re. 18.13.

Ῥεμφάν, v. Ῥεφάν,
    the name of an idol, Ac. 7.43. *The original passage, Amos* 5.26, *has* ;ןויכ*the Sept.*
    Ῥαιφάν, *the Egyptian name for the planet Saturn.*

Ῥέω,
    f. ῥεύσομαι, a.1. ἔρρευσα,
    to flow, Jno. 7.38.

Ῥηθείς,
    part. of ἐρρήθην, a.1. pass. used in connexion with λέγω, φημί, and εἰπεῖν.

Ῥῆγμα, ατος, τό,
    a rent; a crash, ruin, Lu. 6.49: *from*

Ῥήγνυμι, v. ῥήσσω,
    f. ξω, a.1. ἔρρηξα,
    to rend, shatter; to break or burst in pieces, Mat. 9.17. Mar. 2.22. Lu. 5.37, et al.; to
    rend, lacerate, Mat. 7.6; to cast or dash *upon the ground,* convulse, Mar. 9.18. Lu.
    9.42; *absol.* to break forth *into exclamation,* Ga. 4.27.

Ῥῆμα, ατος, τό, (ἐρῶ)
    that which is spoken; declaration, saying, speech, word, Mat. 12.36; 26.75. Mar. 9.32;
    14.72; a command, mandate, direction, Lu. 3.2; 5.5; a promise, Lu. 1.38; 2.29; a
    prediction, prophecy, 2 Pe. 3.2; a doctrine *of God or Christ,* Jno. 3.34; 5.47; 6.63, 68.
    Ac. 5.20; an accusation, charge, crimination, Mat. 5.11; 27.14; *fr. the Heb.* a thing,
    Mat. 4.4. Lu. 4.4; a matter, affair, transaction, business, Mat. 18.16. Lu. 1.65. 2 Co.
    13.1, et al.

Ῥήσσω,
    see ῥήγνυμι.

Ῥήτωρ, ορος, ὁ, (ἐρῶ)
    an orator, advocate, Ac. 24.1.

Ῥητῶς, (ῥητός, ἐρῶ)
    in express words, expressly, 1 Ti. 4.1. L.G.

Ῥίζα, ης, ἡ,
    a root *of a tree,* Mat. 3.10; 13.6; *met.* ἔχειν ῥίζαν, v. ἔχειν ῥίζαν ἐν ἑαυτῷ, to be rooted
    in faith, Mat. 13.21. Mar. 4.17. Lu. 8.13; *met.* cause, source, origin, 1 Ti. 6.10. He.
    12.15; *by synecd,* the trunk, stock *of a tree, met.* Ro. 11.16, 17, 18; *met.* offspring,
    progeny, a descendant, Ro. 15.12. Re. 5.5; 22.16: *whence*

Ῥιζόω, ῶ,
    f. ώσω,

to root, cause to take root; *pass. part. perf.* ἐρἑιζωμένος, firmly rooted, strengthened with roots; *met.* firm, constant, firmly fixed, Ep. 3.18. Col. 2.7.

Ῥιπή, ῆς, ἡ (ῥίπτω)

    pr. a rapid sweep, jerk; a wink, twinkling *of the eye,* 1 Co. 15.52.

Ῥιπίζω, (ῥιπίς, a fan or bellows, fr. ῥίπτω)

    f. ίσω,

    to fan, blow, ventilate; 165to toss, agitate, e.g. *the ocean by the wind,* Ja. 1.6.

Ῥιπτέω, ῷ,

    to toss repeatedly, toss up *with violent gesture,* Ac. 22.23: *freq. from*

Ῥίπτω

    f. ψω, a.1. ἔῤῥιψα, p. pass. ἔῤῥιμμαι,

    to hurl, throw, cast; to throw or cast down, Mat. 27.5. Lu. 4.35; 17.2; to throw or cast *out,* Ac. 27.19, 29; to lay down, set down, Mat. 15.30; *pass.* to be dispersed, scattered, Mat. 9.36.

Ῥοιζηδόν, (ῥοῖζος, a whizzing, a rushing noise)

    adv. with a noise, with a crash, &c., 2 Pe. 3.10. L.G.

Ῥομφαία, ας, ἡ,

    pr. a *Thracian* broad-sword; a sword, Re. 1.16; 2.12; *by meton,* war, Re. 6.8; *met.* a thrill of anguish, Lu. 2.35.

Ῥύμη, ης, ἡ (ῥύω)

    pr. a rush or sweep *of a body in motion;* a street, Ac. 9.11; 12.10; a narrow street, lane, alley, *as distinguished from* πλατεῖα, Mat. 6.2. Lu. 14.21.

Ῥύομαι,

    f. ῥύσομαι, a.1. ἐῤῥυσάμην,

    to drag *out of danger,* to rescue, save, Mat. 6.13; 27.43; *later also pass.,* a.1. ἐῤῥύσθην, to be rescued, delivered, Lu. 1.74. Ro. 15.31. 2 Th. 3.2. 2 Ti. 4.17.

Ῥυπαρεύομαι, (ῥυπαρός)

    to be filthy, squalid; *met.* to be polluted, v.r. Re. 22.11. N.T.

Ῥυπαρία, ας, ἡ,

    filth; *met. moral* filthiness, uncleanness, pollution, Ja. 1.21: *from*

Ῥυπᾰρός, ά, όν,

    filthy, squalid, sordid, dirty, Ja. 2.2; *met.* defiled, polluted, v.r. Re. 22.11: *from*

Ῥύπος, ου, ὁ,

    filth, squalor, 1 Pe. 3.21: *whence*

Ῥυπόω, ῶ

    f. ώσω,

    to be filthy; *met.* to be *morally* polluted, Re. 22.11, *bis.*

Ῥύσις, εως, ἡ, (ῥέω)

    a flowing; a *morbid* flux, Mar. 5.25. Lu. 8.43, 44.

Ῥυτίς, ίδος, ἡ, (ῥύω)

    a wrinkle; *met.* a *disfiguring* wrinkle, flaw, blemish, Ep. 5.27.

Ῥωμαϊκός, ή, όν,

    Roman, Latin, Lu. 23.38: *from*

Ῥωμαῖος, ου, ὁ, (Ῥώμν, Rome)

    a Roman, Roman citizen, Jno. 11.48. Ac. 2.10; 16.21, et al.: *whence*

Ῥωμαϊστί,

    adv. in the Roman language, in Latin, Jno. 19.20.

Ῥώννυμι, v. νύω,

    f. ῥώσω,

to strengthen, render firm; *pass. perf.* ἔρρωμαι, to be well, enjoy firm health; *imperative* ἔρρωσο, ἔρρωσθε, *at the end of letters, like the Lat.* vale, farewell, Ac. 15.29; 23.30.

Σ, σ, Σίγμα

Σαβαχθανί, (Aram. ינתקבש, fr. קבש, to leave, forsake)
    sabacthani, thou hast forsaken me; *interrogatively,* hast thou forsaken me? Mat. 27.46. Mar. 15.34.
Σαβαώθ, (Heb. תואבצ, pl. of אבצ)
    hosts, armies, Ro. 9.29. Ja. 5.4.
Σαββατισμός, οῦ, ὁ, (σαββατίζω, i.q. Heb. תבש, *whence it is formed,* to cease or rest from labour, *and thus* keep sabbath)
    pr. a keeping of a sabbath; a state of rest, a sabbath-state, He. 4.9.
Σάββᾰτον, ου, τό, (Heb. תבש)
    pr. cessation from labour, rest; the Jewish sabbath, *both in the sing. and pl.,* Mat. 12.2, 5, 8; 28.1. Lu. 4.16; a week, *sing. and pl.,* Mat. 28.1. Mar. 16.9, et al.; *pl.* sabbaths, or times of sacred rest, Col. 2.16.
Σαγήνη, ης, ἡ, (σαγή, fr. σάττω, to load)
    a large net, drag, Mat. 13.47. L.G.
Σαδδουκαῖος, ου, ὁ,
    a Sadducee, one belonging to the sect of the Sadducees, *which, according to the Talmudists, was founded by one* ,codaS קודצ, *about three centuries before the Christian era: they were directly opposed in sentiments to the Pharisees,* Mat. 3.7; 16.1, 6, 11, 12; 22.23, 34, et al.
Σαίνω,
    f. σανῶ, a.1. ἔσηνα & ἔσᾱνα,
    pr. to wag *the tail;* to fawn, flatter, cajole; *pass.* to be cajoled; to be wrought upon, to be perturbed, 1 Th. 3.3.
Σάκκος, ου, ὁ, (Heb. קש)
    sackcloth, *a species of very coarse black cloth made of hair,* Re. 6.12; *a mourning garment of* sackcloth, Mat. 11.21. Lu. 10.13. Re. 11.3.
Σαλεύω,
    f. εύσω, a.1. ἐσάλευσα,
    166to make to rock, to shake, Mat. 11.7; 24.29. Lu. 6.48. Ac. 4.31, et al.; to shake down or together, Lu. 6.38; *met.* to stir up, excite *the people,* Ac. 17.13; to agitate, disturb *mentally,* Ac. 2.25. 2 Th. 2.2; *pass. impl.* to totter, be ready to fall, be near to ruin, *met.* He. 12.27: *from*
Σάλος, ου, ὁ,
    agitation, tossing, rolling, *spc. of the sea,* Lu. 21.25.
Σάλπιγξ, ιγγος, ἡ,
    a trumpet, Mat. 24.31. 1 Th. 4.16, et al.: *from*
Σαλπίζω,
    f. ίγξω, & later, ίσω, a.1. ἐσάλπιγξα & ἐσάλπισα,
    to sound a trumpet, Re. 8.6, 7, 8, 10, 12, 13, et al.: *whence*
Σαλπιστής, οῦ, ὁ,
    a trumpeter, Re. 18.22. L.G.
Σαμαρείτης, ου, ὁ,
    a Samaritan, an inhabitant of the city or region of Σαμάρεια, Samaria, *applied by the Jews as a term of reproach and contempt,* Mat. 10.5. Jno. 4.9; 8.48, et al.: *whence*

Σαμαρεῖτις, ιδος,
    a Samaritan woman, Jno. 4.9, *bis*.
Σανδάλιον, ου, τό, (pr. dimin. of σάνδαλον)
    a sandal, *a sole of wood or hide, covering the bottom of the foot, and bound on with leather thongs,* Mar. 6.9. Ac. 12.8.
Σανίς, ίδος, ἡ,
    a board, plank, Ac. 27.44.
Σαπρός, ά, όν, (σήπω)
    pr. rotten, putrid; *hence,* bad, of a bad quality, Mat. 7.17, 18; 12.33. Lu. 6.43; refuse, Mat. 13.48; *met.* corrupt, depraved, vicious, foul, impure, Ep. 4.29.
Σάπφειρος, ου, ἡ, (Heb. ריפס)
    a sapphire, *a precious stone of a blue colour in various shades, next in hardness and value to the diamond,* Re. 21.19.
Σαργάνη, ης, ἡ,
    twisted or plaited work; a network of cords like a basket, basket of ropes, &c. 2 Co. 11.33. (ἄ)
Σαρδίνος, ου, ὁ,
    a sardine, *a precious stone of a blood-red colour,* Re. 4.3.
Σάρδιον, τό,
    but in the common text of Re. 21.20. σάρδιος, a carnelian.
Σαρδόνυξ, υχος, ἡ (σάρδιον & ὄνυξ)
    sardonyx, *a gem exhibiting the colour of the carnelian and the white of the chalcedony intermingled in alternate layers,* Re. 21.20.
Σαρκικός, ή, όν, (σάρξ)
    freshly; pertaining to the body, corporeal, physical, Ro. 15.27. 1 Co. 9.11; carnal, pertaining to the flesh, 1 Pe. 2.11; carnal, subject to the propensity of the flesh, Ro. 7.14; carnal, low in spiritual knowledge and frame, 1 Co. 3.1, 3; carnal, human *as opposed to divine,* 2 Co. 1.12; 10.4; carnal, earthly, He. 7.16. L.G.
Σάρκῐνος, η, ον,
    of flesh, fleshy, 2 Co. 3.3: *from*
Σάρξ, σαρκός, ἡ,
    flesh, Lu. 24.39. Jno. 3.6, et al.; the *human* body, 2 Co. 7.5; flesh, human nature, human frame, Jno. 1.13, 14. 1 Jno. 4.2, et al.; kindred, Ro. 11.14; consanguinity, lineage, Ro. 1.3; 9.3, et al.; flesh, humanity, human beings, Mat. 24.22. Lu. 3.6. Jno. 17.2, et al.; the circumstances of the body, material circumstances, 1 Co. 5.5; 7.28. Philem. 16, et al.; flesh, mere humanity, human fashion, 1 Co. 1.26. 2 Co. 1.17; flesh *as the seat of passion and frailty,* Ro. 8.1, 3, 5, et al.; carnality, Ga. 5.24. 1 Pe. 4.1; materiality, *as opposed to the spiritual,* Ga. 3.3. Col. 2.18, 23. He. 9.10.
Σαρόω, ῶ, (i.q. σαίρω)
    f. ώσω, p. pass. σεσάρωμαι,
    to sweep, cleanse with a broom, Mat. 12.44. Lu. 11.25; 15.8.
Σατανᾶς, ᾶ, ὁ, & *once,* 2 Co. 12.7, Σατᾶν, ὁ, indec. (Heb. ןטש)
    an adversary, opponent, enemy, *perhaps,* Mat. 16.23. Mar. 8.33. Lu. 4.8; *elsewhere,* Satan, the devil, Mat. 4.10. Mar. 1.13, et al.
Σάτον, ου, τό, (Heb. האס, Chald. אתא)
    a satum or seah, *a Hebrew measure for things dry, containing, as Josephus testifies, (Ant. 1.ix.c.4.§5) an Italian modius and a half, or 24 sextarii, and therefore equivalent to one peck and a half English,* Mat. 13.33. Lu. 13.21. N.T.
Σαυτοῦ, ῆς, οῦ,
    contr. from σεαυτοῦ.

Σβέννυμι,
> f. σβέσω, a.1. ἔσβεσα,
> to extinguish, quench, Mat. 12.20; 25.8. Mar. 9.44, 46, 48, et al.; *met.* to quench, damp, hinder, thwart, 1 Th. 5.19.

Σεαυτοῦ, ῆς, οῦ,
> *reflexive pron.,*167 of thyself, *and dat.* σεαυτῷ, ῇ, ῷ, to thyself, &c. Mat. 4.6; 8.4; 19.19. et al.

Σεβάζομαι, (σέβος)
> f. άσομαι, a.1. ἐσεβάσθην,
> to feel dread of *a thing;* to venerate, adore, worship, Ro. 1.25: *whence*

Σέβασμα, ατος, τό,
> an object of religious veneration and worship, Ac. 17.23. 2 Th. 2.4. L.G.

Σεβαστός, ή, όν,
> *pr.* venerable, august; ὁ Σεβαστός, i.q. *Lat.* Augustus, Ac. 25.21, 25; Augustan, *or,* Sebastan, *named from the city Sebaste,* Ac. 27.1.

Σέβομαι,
> to stand in awe; to venerate, reverence, worship, adore, Mat. 15.9. Ac. 19.27; et al.; *part.* σεβόμενος, η, ον, worshipping, devout, pious, *a term applied to proselytes to Judaism,* Ac. 13.43, et al.

Σειρά, ᾶς, ἡ,
> a cord, rope, bank; *in N.T.,* a chain, 2 Pe. 2.4.

Σεισμός, οῦ, ὁ,
> *pr.* a shaking, agitation, concussion; an earthquake, Mat. 24.7; 27.54, et al.; a tempest, Mat. 8.24: *from*

Σείω,
> f. σείσω, a.1. ἔσεισα,
> to shake, agitate, He. 12.26. Re. 6.13; *pass.* to quake, Mat. 27.51; 28.4; *met.* to put in commotion, agitate, Mat. 21.10.

Σελήνη, ης, ἡ,
> the moon, Mat. 24.29. Mar. 13.24, et al.: *whence*

Σεληνιάζομαι,
> f. άσομαι,
> to be lunatic, Mat. 4.24; 17.15. L.G.

Σεμίδᾱλις, εως, ἡ,
> the finest flour, R. 18.13.

Σεμνός, ή, όν, (σέβομαι)
> august, venerable; honourable, reputable, Phi. 4.8; grave, serious, dignified, 1 Ti. 3.8, 11. Tit. 2.2: *whence*

Σεμνότης, τητος, ἡ,
> *pr.* majesty; gravity, dignity, dignified seriousness, 2. Ti. 2.2; 3.4.

Σημαίνω, (σῆμα, a sign, mark)
> f. ανῶ, a.1. ἐσήμηνα & ἐσήμᾱνα,
> to indicate by a sign, to signal; to indicate, intimate, Jno. 12.33; to make known, communicate, Ac. 11.28. Re. 1.1; to specify, Ac. 25.27.

Σημεῖον, ου, τό (fr. same)
> a sign, a mark, token, *by which any thing is known or distinguished,* Mat. 16.3; 24.3. 2 Th. 3.17; a token, pledge, assurance, Lu. 2.12; a proof, evidence, convincing token, Mat. 12.38; 16.1. Jno. 2.18; *in N.T.,* a sign, wonder, remarkable event, wonderful appearance, extraordinary phenomenon, 1 Co. 14.22. Re. 12.1, 3; 15.1; a portent,

prodigy, Mat. 24.30. Ac. 2.19; a wonderful work, miraculous operation, miracle, Mat. 24.24. Mar. 16.17, 20; *meton.* a sign, a signal character, Lu. 2.34: *whence*

Σημειόω, ῶ,
    f. ώσω,
    to mark, inscribe marks upon; *mid.* to mark for one's self, note, 2 Th. 3.14.
Σήμερον,
    adv. to-day, this day, Mat. 6.11, 30; 16.3; 21.28; now, at present, He. 13.8. 2 Co. 31.15; ἡ σήμερον, sc. ἡμέρα, *sometimes expresed,* this day, the present day, Ac. 20.26; ἕως ν. ἄχρι τῆς σήμερον, until this day, until our times, Mat. 11.23; 27.8, et al. freq.
Σήπω,
    to cause to putrify, make rotten; *mid.* σήπομαι, p. 2. σέσηπα, to putrify, rot, be corrupted or rotten, Ja. 5.2.
Σηρικός, ή, όν, (σήρ, a silkworm)
    silk, of silk, silken; τὸ σηρικόν, silken stuff, silk, Re. 18.12. L.G.
Σής, σεός & σητός, ὁ,
    a moth, Mat. 6.19, 20. Lu. 12.33.
Σητόβρωτος, ου, ὁ, ἡ, τό, -ον, (σής & βιβρώσκω)
    moth-eaten, Ja. 5.2. S.
Σθενόω, ῶ, (σθένος, strength)
    f. ώσω, a.1. ἐσθένωσα,
    to strengthen, impart strength, 1 Pe. 5.10. N.T.
Σιαγών, όνος, ἡ,
    the jaw-bone; *in N.T.,* the cheek, Mat. 5.39. Lu. 6.29.
Σιγάω, ῶ,
    f. ήσω, p. pass. σεσίγημαι,
    to be silent, keep silence, Lu. 9.36; 20.26, et al.; *trans.* to keep in silence, not to reveal, to conceal; *pass.* to be concealed, not to be revealed, Ro. 16.25: *from*
Σιγή, ῆς, ἡ,
    silence, Ac. 21.40. Re. 8.1.
Σιδήρεος, οῦς, εα, ᾶ, εον, οῦν,
    made of iron, Ac. 12.10. Re. 2.27; 9.9; 12.5; 19.15: *from*
Σίδηρος, ου, ὁ,
    iron, Re. 18.12.
Σιδώνιος, ου, ὁ,
    a Sidonian, an inhabitant of Σιδών, Sidon, Ac. 12.20.
Σικάριος, ου, ὁ, (Lat. sicarius, fr. *sica,* a dagger, poniard)
    168an assassin, bandit, robber, Ac. 21.38.
Σίκερα, τό, indec.(Heb. רכש)
    strong or inebriating drink, Lu. 1.15. S.
Σιμικίνθιον, ου, τό, (Lat. *semicinctium,* fr. *semi,* half, & *cingo,* to grid)
    an apron, Ac. 19.12.
Σίναπι, εως, τό,
    mustard; *in N.T.,* probably the shrub Khardal (*Salvadora Persica,* L.), *the fruit of which possesses the pungency of mustard,* Mat. 13.31; 17.20, et al.
Σινδών, όνος, ἡ,
    sindon, *pr.* fine Indian cloth; fine linen; *in N.T.,* a linen garment, an upper garment or wrapper of fine linen, *worn in summer by night, and used to envelope dead bodies,* Mat. 27.59. Mar. 14.51, 52; 15.46. Lu. 23.53.
Σινιάζω, (σινίον, a sieve)

f. άσω,
to sift; *met.* to sift *by trials and temptation,* Lu. 22.31. L.G.
Σιτευτός, ή, όν, (σιτεύω, to feed or fatten, σῖτος)
fed, fatted, Lu. 15.23, 27, 30.
Σιτίον, ου, τό, (σῖτος)
provision of corn, food, v.r. Ac. 7.12.
Σιτιστός, ή, όν, (σιτίζω, to fatten, fr. σῖτος)
fatted, a fatling, Mat. 22.4.
Σιτομέτριον, ου, τό, (σῖτος & μετρέω)
a certain measure of grain *distributed for food at set times to the slaves of a family,* a
ration, Lu. 12.42. L.G.
Σῖτος, ου, ό,
corn, grain, wheat, Mat. 3.12; 13.25, 29, 30. Mar. 4.28, et. al.; *pl.* σῖτα, bread, food,
Ac. 7.12.
Σιωπάω, ῶ,
f. ήσω, a.1. ἐσιώπησα,
to be silent, keep silence, hold one's peace, Mat. 20.31; 26.63, et al.; σιωπῶν, silent,
dumb, Lu. 1.20; *met.* to be silent, still, hushed, calm, *as the sea,* Mar. 4.39.
Σκανδαλίζω,
f. ίσω, a.1. ἐσκανδάλισα, a.1. pass. ἐσκανδαλίσθην,
pr. to cause to stumble; *met.* to offend, vex, Mat. 17.27; to offend, shock, excite
feelings of repugnance, Jno. 6.61. 1 Co. 8.13; *pass.* to be offended, shocked, pained,
Mat. 15.12. Ro. 14.21. 2 Co. 11.29; σκανδαλίζεσθαι ἔν τινι, to be affected with
scruples or repugnance towards any one *as respects his claims or pretensions,* Mat.
11.6; 13.57, et al.; *met.*to cause to stumble *morally,* to cause to falter, or err, Mat.
5.29; 18.6, et al.; *pass.* to falter, fall away, Mat. 13.21, et al.: (S.) *from*
Σκάνδᾰλον, ου, τό, (a later equivalent to σκανδάληθρον)
pr. a trap-spring; *also genr.* a stumbling-block, any thing against which one stumbles,
an impediment; *met.* a cause of ruin, destruction, misery, &c. R. 9.33; 11.9; a cause or
occasion of sinning, Mat. 18.7, *ter.* Lu. 17.1; scandal, offence, cause of indignation, 1
Co. 1.23. Ga. 5.11.
Σκάπτω,
f. σκάψω, a.1. ἔσκαψα,
to dig, excavate, Lu. 6.48; 13.8; 16.3: *whence*
Σκάφη, ης, ή,
pr. any thing excavated or hollowed; a boat, skiff, Ac. 27.16, 30, 32.
Σκέλος, εος, τό, pl. τὰ σκέλη,
the leg, Jno. 19.31, 32, 33.
Σκέπασμα, ατος, τό, (σκεπάζω, to cover)
covering; clothing, raiment, 1 Ti. 6.8.
Σκευή, ῆς, ή,
apparatus; tackle, Ac. 27.19: *from*
Σκεῦος, εος, τό,
a vessel, utensil *for containing any thing,* Mar. 11.16. Lu. 8.16. Ro. 9.21; any utensil,
instrument; σκεύη, household stuff, furniture, goods, &c. Mat. 12.29. Mar. 3.27, et al.;
the mast of a ship, *or,* the sail, Ac. 27.17; *met.* an instrument, means, organ, minister,
Ac. 9.15; σκεύη ὀργῆς & σκεύη ἐλέους, vessels of wrath, *or* of mercy, persons visited
by punishment, *or* the divine favour, Ro. 9.22, 23; the vessel or frame *of the human
individual,* 1 Th. 4.4. 1 Pe. 3.7.
Σκηνή, ῆς, ή,

a tent, tabernacle; *genr.* any temporary dwelling; a tent, booth, Mat. 17.4. He. 11.9; the tabernacle *of the covenant,* He. 8.5; 9.1, 21; 13.10; *allegor.* the *celestial or true* tabernacle, He. 8.2; 9.11; a division or compartment of the tabernacle, He. 9.2, 3, 6; a small portable tent or shrine, Ac. 7.43; *trop.* a family, lineage, race, Ac. 15.16; a mansion, habitation, abode, dwelling, Lu. 16.9; Re. 13.6.

Σκηνοπηγία, ας, ἡ, (σκῆνος & πήγνυμι)

pr. a pitching of tents or booths; *hence,* the feast of tabernacles or booths, *instituted in memory of the 40 years' wandering of the Israelites in the desert,* 169 *and as a season of gratitude for the ingathering of harvest, celebrated during eight days, commencing on the 15th of Tisri,* Jno. 7.2.

Σκηνοποιός, οῦ, ὁ, (σκηνή & ποιέω)

a tent-maker, Ac. 18.3. N.T.

Σκῆνος, εος, τό, (equivalent to σκηνή)

a tent, tabernacle; *met.* the *corporeal* tabernacle, 2 Co. 5.1, 4: *whence*

Σκηνόω, ῶ,

f. ώσω, a.1. ἐσκήνωσα,

to pitch tent, encamp; to tabernacle, dwell in a tent; to dwell, have one's abode, Jno. 1.14. Re. 7.15; 12.12; 13.6; 21.3: *whence*

Σκήνωμα, ατος, τό,

a habitation, abode, dwelling, Ac. 7.46; the *corporeal* tabernacle *of the soul,* 2 Pe. 1.13, 14.

Σκιά, ᾶς, ἡ,

a shade, shadow, Mar. 4.32. Ac. 5.15; *met.* a shadow, a shadowing forth, adumbration, *in distinction from* ἡ εἰκών, *the perfect image or delineation,* & τὸ σῶμα, *the reality,* Col. 2.17. He. 8.5; 10.1; gloom; σκιὰ θανάτου, death-shade, the thickest darkness, Mat. 4.16. Lu. 1.79.

Σκιρτάω, ῶ,

f. ήσω, a.1. ἐσκίρτησα,

to leap, Lu. 1.41, 44; to leap, skip, bound *for joy,* Lu. 6.23.

Σκληροκαρδία, ας, ἡ, (σκληρός, & καρδία)

hardness of heart, obduracy, obstinacy, perverseness, Mat. 19.8. Mar. 10.5; 16.14. S.

Σκληρός, ά, όν,

dry, hard; *met.* harsh, severe, stern, Mat. 25.24; vehement, violent, fierce, Ja. 3.4; grievous, painful, Ac. 9.5; 26.14; grating *to the mind,* repulsive, offensive, Jno. 6.60; stubborn, contumacious, Jude 15: *whence*

Σκληρότης, τητος, ἡ,

hardness; *met.* σκληρότης τῆς καρδίας, hardness of heart, obduracy, obstinacy, perverseness, Ro. 2.5.

Σκληροτράχηλος, ου, ὁ, ἡ, (σκληρός & τράχηλος)

stiff-necked, obstinate, refractory, Ac. 7.51. S.

Σκληρύνω,

f. υνῶ, a.1. ἐσκλήρυνα,

to harden; *met.* to harden *morally,* to make stubborn, He. 3.8, 15; 4.7; *as a negation of* ἐλεεῖν, to leave to stubbornness and contumacy, Ro. 9.38; *mid. & pass.* to put on a stubborn frame, become obdurate, Ac. 19.9. He. 3.13.

Σκολιός, ά, όν,

crooked, tortuous, Lu. 3.5; *met.* perverse, wicked, Ac. 2.40. Phi. 2.15; crooked, peevish, morose, 1 Pe. 2.18.

Σκόλοψ, οπος, ὁ

any thing pointed, *met.* a thorn, a plague, 2 Co. 12.7.

Σκοπέω, ῶ,
    f. ήσω,
    to view attentively, watch, reconnoitre; to see, observe, take care, beware, Lu. 1.35.
    Ga. 6.1; to regard, have respect to, 2 Co. 4.18. Phi. 2.4; to mark, note, Ro. 16.17. Ph.
    3.17: *from*
Σκοπός, οῦ, ὁ, (σκέπτομαι)
    a watcher; *also,* a distant object on which the eye is kept fixed; a mark, goal, Ph. 3.14.
Σκορπίζω,
    f. ίσω, a.1. ἐσκόρπισα,
    to disperse, scatter, Jno. 10.12; 16.32; to dissipate, waste, Mat. 12.30. Lu. 11.23; to
    scatter abroad *one's gifts,* give liberally, 2 Co. 9.9.
Σκορπίος, ου, ὁ,
    a scorpion, scorpio. Afer *of Linn., a large insect, sometimes several inches in length,*
    shaped somewhat like a crab, and furnished with a tail terminating in a sting, whence
    it emits a dangerous poison, Lu. 10.19; 11.12, et al.
Σκοτεινός, ή, όν, (σκότος)
    dark, darkling, Mat. 6.23. Lu. 11.34, 36.
Σκοτία, ας, ἡ, (fr. same)
    darkness, Jno. 6.17; 20.1; privacy, Mat. 10.27. Lu. 12.3; *met. moral or spiritual*
    darkness, Jno. 1.5, *bis.;* 8.12; 12.38, 46, et al.
Σκοτίζω,
    f. ίσω,
    to darken, shroud in darkness; *pass.* to be darkened, obscured, Mat. 24.29. Lu. 23.45;
    met. to be shrouded in *moral* darkness, to be benighted, Ro. 1.21, et al.: (L.G.) *from*
Σκότος, ου, ὁ
    darkness, He. 12.18.
Σκότος, εος, τό, *but* ου, ὁ,
    He. 12.18, *according to ordinary Greek usage,* darkness, Mat. 27.45. Ac. 2.20; gloom
    of punishment and misery, Mat. 8.12. 2 Pe. 2.17; *met. moral or spritual* darkness,
    Mat. 4.16. Jno. 3.19. Ep. 5.11; *meton.* men in a state of *moral* darkness, Ep. 5.8; 6.12:
    whence
Σκοτόω, ῶ,
    f. ώσω,
    to darken, shroud in darkness, Re. 16.10.
Σκύβᾰλον, ου, τό,
    170offal, dung, sweepings, refuse, Phi. 3.8.
Σκυθρωπός, οῦ, ὁ, ἡ, & ἡ, όν (σκυθρός, stern, gloomy, & ὤψ)
    of a stern, morose, sour, gloomy, or dejected countenance, Mat. 6.16. Lu. 24.17.
Σκύλλω,
    f. υλῶ, p. pass. ἔσκυλμαι,
    to flay, lacerate; *met.* to vex, trouble, annoy, Mar. 5.35. Lu. 7.6; 8.49; *pass. met.,*
    ἐσκυλμένοι, jaded, in sorry plight, v.r. Mat. 9.36: *whence*
Σλῦλον, ου, τό, (σκύλλω)
    spoils stripped of an enemy; σκῦλα, spoil, plunder, booty, Lu. 11.22.
Σκωληκόβρωτος, (σκώληξ, & βιβρώσκω)
    eaten of worms, consumed by worms, Ac. 12.23.
Σκώληξ, ηκος, ὁ,
    a worm; *met.* gnawing anguish, Mar. 9.44, 46, 48.
Σμαράγδῐνος, ίνη, ινον,
    of smaragdus or emerald, Re. 4.3: (N.T.) *from*

Σμάραγδος, ου, ὁ, & ἡ,

smaragdus, the emerald, *a gem of a pure green colour; but under this name the ancients probably comprised all stones of a fine green colour,* Re. 21.19.

Σμύρνα, ης, ἡ, (Heb. רום)

myrrh, *an aromatic bitter resin, or gum, issuing by incision, and sometimes spontaneously, from the truck and larger branches of a small thorny tree growing in Egypt, Arabia, and Abyssinia, much used by the ancients in unguents,* Mat. 2.11. Jno. 19.39.

Σμυρναῖος, ου, ὁ

a Smyrneans, an inhabitant of Σμύρνα, Smyrna, Re. 1.11; 2.8.

Σμυρνίζω, (σμύρνα)

f. ίσω,

to mingle or impregnate with myrrh, Mar. 15.23. N.T.

Σορός, οῦ, ἡ,

a coffer; an urn for receiving the ashes of the dead; a coffin; *in N.T.,* a bier. Lu. 7.14.

Σός, σή, σόν, (σύ)

thine, Mat. 7.3, 22, et al.; οἱ σοί, thy kindred, friends, &c. Mar. 5.19; τὸ σόν & τὰ σά, what is thine, thy property, goods, &c. Mat. 20.14; 25.25. Lu. 6.30.

Σουδάριον, ου, τό, (Lat. *sudarium*)

a handkerchief, napkin, &c. Lu. 19.20. Jno. 11.44, et al.

Σοφία, ας, ἡ, (σοφός)

wisdom *in general,* knowledge, Mat. 12.42. Lu. 2.40, 52; 11.31. Ac. 7.10; ability, Lu. 21.15. Ac. 6.3, 10; *practical* wisdom, prudence, Col. 4.5, learning, science, Mat. 13.54. Mar. 6.2. Ac. 7.22; *scientific* skill, 1 Co. 1.17; 2.1; *professed* wisdom, *human* philosophy, 1 Co. 1.19, 20, 22; 2.4, 5, 6, et al.; *superior* knowledge and enlightenment, Col. 2.23; *in N.T., Divine* wisdom, Ro. 11.33. Eph. 3.10. Col. 2.3; *revealed* wisdom, Mat. 11.19. Lu. 11.49. 1 Co. 1.24, 30; 2.7; *Christian* enlightenment, 1 Co. 12.8. Eph. 1.8, 17. Col. 1.9, 28; 3.16. Ja. 1.5; 3.13.

Σοφίζω,

f. ίσω, a.1. ἐσόφισα,

to make wise, enlighten, 2 Ti. 3.15; *mid.* to invent skilfully, devise artfully, *pass.* 2 Pe. 1.16: *from*

Σοφός, ή, όν,

wise *generally,* 1 Co. 1.25; shrewd, sagacious, clever, Ro. 16.19. 1 Co. 3.10; 6.5; learned, intelligent, Mat. 11.25. Ro. 1.14, 22. 1 Co. 1.19, 20, 26, 27; 3.18; *in N.T., divinely* instructed, Mat. 23.34; furnished with *Christian* wisdom, *spiritually* enlightened, Ja. 3.13; all-wise, Ro. 16.27. 1 Ti. 1.17. Jude 25.

Σπαράσσω, v. ττω, (σπάω)

f. ξω, a.1. ἐσπάραξα,

pr. to tear, lacerate; *by impl.* to agitate greatly, convulse, distort by convulsion, Mar. 1.26; 9.20, 26. Lu. 9.39.

Σπαργανόω, ῶ, (σπάργανον, a bandage; swadding-cloth)

f. ώσω,

to swathe, wrap in swaddling-cloths, Lu. 2.7, 12.

Σπαταλάω, ῶ, (σπατάλη, riot, luxury)

f. ήσω,

to live luxuriously, voluptuously, wantonly, 1 Ti. 5.6. Ja. 5.5. L.G.

Σπάω, ῶ,

f. άσω, p. ἔσπακα, a.1. mid. ἐσπασάμην,

to draw, pull; to draw a *sword,* Mar. 14.47. Ac. 16.27.

Σπεῖρα, ας, ἡ,

    any thing twisted or wreathed, a cord, coil, band, &c.; a band of soldiers, company, troop; *used for a Roman* maniple, *or,* cohort, Mat. 27.27. Ac. 10.1; the *temple* guard, Jno. 18.3, 12.

Σπείρω,

    f. σπερῶ, a.1. ἔσπειρα, p.2. ἔσπορα, a. pass. ἐσπάρην,

    to sow *seed,* Mat. 6.26; 13.3, 4, 18, 24, 25, 27, 31, 37, 39; *in N.T., used with variety of metaphors.* 171Mat. 13.19; 25.24. 1 Co. 9.11. 2 Co. 9.6. Ga. 6.7, et al.

Σπεκουλάτωρ, ορος, ὁ, (Lat. *speculator*)

    a sentinel, life-guardman, *a kind of soldiers who formed the body-guard of princes, &c., one of whose duties was to put criminals to death,* Mar. 6.27.

Σπένδω,

    f. σπείσω,

    to pour out a libation or drink offering; *in N.T., mid.* to make a libation of one's self *by expending energy and life in the service of the gospel,* Phi. 2.17; *pass.* to be in the act of being sacrificed *in the cause of the gospel,* 2 Ti. 4.6.

Σπέρμα, ατος, τό, (σπείρω)

    seed, Mat. 13.24, 27, 37, 38; semen virile, He. 11.11; offspring, progeny, posterity, Mat. 22.24, 25. Jno. 7.42; a seed *of future generations,* Ro. 9.29; *in N.T., met.* a seed or principle *of spiritual life,* 1 Jno. 3.9.

Σπερμολόγος, ου, ὁ, (σπέρμα & λέγω, to pick)

    pr. seed-picking; one who picks up and retails scraps of information; a babbler, Ac. 17.18.

Σπεύδω,

    f. σπεύσω, a.1. ἔσπευσα,

    trans. to urge on, impel, quicken; to quicken *in idea,* to be eager for the arrival of, 2 Pe. 3.12; *intrans.* to hasten, make haste, Ac. 20.16; 22.18; *the part. has the force of an adverb,* quickly, hastily, Lu. 2.16; 19.5, 6.

Σπήλαιον, ου, τό, (σπέος)

    a cave, cavern, den, Mat. 21.13. et al.

Σπιλάς, άδος, ἡ,

    a sharply cleft portion of rock; *in N.T.,* a flaw, stigma, Jude 12.

Σπῖλος, & σπίλος, ὁ,

    a spot, stain, blot; a *moral blot,* Eph. 5.27. 2 Pe. 2.13; (L.G.) *whence*

Σπιλόω, ῶ,

    f. ώσω,

    to spot, soil; to contaminate, defile, Ja. 3.6. Jude 23. L.G.

Σπλαγχνίζομαι,

    f. ίσομαι, a.1. ἐσπλαγχνίσθην,

    to be moved with pity or compassion, Mat. 9.36; 14.14; 20.34. Lu. 7.13, et al.; to compassionate, Mat. 18.27: (N.T.) *from*

Σπλάγχνον, ου, τό,

    but usually, and in N.T. only in pl. τὰ σπλάγχνα, ων, the chief intestines, viscera; the entrails, bowels, Ac. 1.18; *met.* the heart, the affections of the heart, the tender affections, Lu. 1.78. 2 Co. 6.12. Phi. 1.8, et al.; *meton.* a cherished one, dear as one's self, Phile. 12.

Σπόγγος, ου, ὁ,

    a sponge, Mat. 27.48. Mar. 15.36. Jno. 19.29.

Σποδός, οῦ, ἡ,

    ashes, Mat. 11.21, et al.

Σπορά, ᾶς, ἡ, (σπείρω)
   a sowing; seed sown; *met. generative* seed, generation, 1 Pe. 1.23.
Σπόρϊμος, ου, ὁ, ἡ, (fr. same)
   sown, fit to be sown; *in N.T.,* τὰ σπόριμα, fields which are sown, fields of grain, corn
   fields, Mat. 12.1. Mar. 2.23. Lu. 6.1.
Σπόρος, ου, ὁ, (fr. same)
   a sowing; *in N.T.,* seed, that which is sown, Mar. 4.26, 27. Lu. 8.5, 11; *met.* the seed
   sown *in almsgiving,* 2 Co. 9.10.
Σπουδάζω, (σπουδή)
   f. άσω, & άσομαι, p. ἐσπούδακα, a.1. ἐσπούδασα,
   to hasten; to be in earnest about, be bent upon, Ga. 2.10; to endeavour earnestly,
   strive, Ep. 4.3, et al.
Σπουδαῖος, α, ον, (fr. same)
   earnest, eager, forward, 2 Co. 8.17, 22; *compart. neut.* σπουδαιοτέρον, *as an adv.*
   earnestly, sedulously, 2 Ti. 1.17: *whence*
Σπουδαίως,
   adv. earnestly, eagerly, diligently, Lu. 7.4. Tit. 3.13; *compar.* σπουδαιοτέρως, more
   earnestly, Phi. 2.28.
Σπουδή ἧς, ἡ, (σπεύδω)
   haste; μετὰ σπουδῆς, with haste, hastily, quickly, Mar. 6.25. Lu. 1.39; earnestness,
   earnest application, diligence, Ro. 12.8, 11. 2 Co. 7.11, 12, et al.
Σπυρίς, ίδος, ἡ,
   a basket, handbasket *for provisions,* Mat. 15.37; 16.10. Mar. 8.8, 20. Ac. 9.25.
Στάδιον, ου, τό, pl. στάδια & στάδιοι,
   pr. a fixed standard of measure; a stadium, *the eighth part of a Roman mile, and
   nearly equal to a furlong, containing 201.45 yards,* Lu. 24.13, et al.; a race-course, a
   race, 1 Co. 9.24.
Στάμνος, ου, ὁ, ἡ,
   a wine jar; a pot, jar, urn, vase, He. 9.4.
Στάσις, εως, ἡ, (ἵστημι)
   a setting; a standing; an *effective* position, an *unimpaired* standing or dignity, He. 9.8;
   a gathered party, a group; 172*hence,* a tumultuous assemblage, popular outbreak, Mar.
   15.7. Ac. 19.40, et al.; seditious movement, Ac. 24.5; discord, dispute, dissension, Ac.
   15.2; 23.7, 10.
Στατήρ, ῆρος, ὁ, (ἵστημι, to weigh)
   pr. a weight; a stater, *an Attic silver coin, equal in value to the Jewish shekel, or to 4
   Attic or 2 Alexandrian drachms, and equivalent to about 3s. in our money,* Mat.
   17.27.
Σταυρός, οῦ, ὁ,
   a stake; a cross, Mat. 27.32, 40, 42. Phi. 2.8; *by impl.* the punishment of the cross,
   crucifixion, Ep. 2.16. He. 12.2; *meton.* the crucifixion *of Christ in respect of its
   import,* the doctrine of the cross, 1 Co. 1.17, 18. ga. 5.11; 6.12, 14; *met. in the phrases*
   αἴρειν, v. βαστάζειν, v. λαμβάνειν τὸν σταυρὸν αὐτοῦ, to take up, or bear one's cross,
   to be ready to encounter any extremity, Mat. 10.38; 16.24, et al.: *whence*
Σταυρόω, ῶ,
   f. ώσω, a.1. ἐσταύρωσα, p. pass. ἐσταύρωμαι,
   to fix stakes; *later,* to crucify, affix to the cross, Mat. 20.19; 23.34; *met.* to crucify, to
   mortify, to deaden, to make a sacrifice of, Ga. 5.24; *pass.* to be cut off *from a thing,
   as by a violent death,* to become dead to, Ga. 6.14.
Σταφϋλή, ῆς, ἡ,

a cluster or bunch of grapes, Mat. 7.16. Lu. 6.44. Re. 14.18.

Στάχυς, υος, ὁ,
    an ear of corn, Mat. 12.1. Mar. 2.23; 4.28. Lu. 6.1.

Στέγη, ῆς, ἡ,
    a roof, flat roof *of a house,* Mat. 8.8. Mar. 2.4. Lu. 7.6: *from*

Στέγω,
    f. ξω,
    to cover; to hold off, to hold in; *hence,* to hold out against, to endure patiently, 1 Co. 9.12; 13.7; *absol.* to contain one's self, 1 Th. 3.1, 5.

Στεῖρος, α, ον,
    sterile; barren, not bearing children, Lu. 1.7, 36; 23.29. Ga. 4.27.

Στέλλω,
    f. στελῶ, p. ἔσταλκα, a.1. ἔστειλα,
    pr. to place in set order, to arrange; to equip; to dispatch; to stow; to contract; *mid.* to contract one's self, to shrink; to withdraw from, avoid, shun, 2 Co. 8.20. 2 Th. 3.6.

Στέμμα, ατος, τό, (στέφω, to encircle)
    a crown; a fillet, wreath, Ac. 14.13.

Στεναγμός, οῦ, ὁ
    a sighing, groaning, groan, Ac. 7.34; *an inward* sighing, aspiration, Ro. 8.26: *from*

Στενάζω,
    f. άξω, a.1. ἐστέναξα,
    to groan, sigh, Ro. 8.23. 2 Co. 5.2, 4. He. 13.17; to sigh *inwardly,* Mar. 7.34; to give vent to querulous or censorious feelings, Ja. 5.9.

Στενός, ή, όν,
    narrow, strait, Mat. 7.13, 14. Lu. 13.24.

Στενοχωρέω, ῶ, (στενός & χώρα)
    f. ήσω,
    to crowd together into a narrow place, straiten; *pass. met.* to be in straits, to be cooped up, to be crampled *from action,* 2 Co. 4.8; to be cramped *in feelinig,* 2 Co. 6.12: *whence*

Στενοχωρία, ας, ἡ,
    pr. narrowness of place, a narrow place; *met.* straits, distress, anguish, Ro. 2.9; 8.35. 2 Co. 6.4; 12.10.

Στερεός, ά, όν,
    stiff, hard; *of food,* solid, *as opposed to what is liquid and light,* He. 5.12; firm, stedfast, 2 Ti. 2.19. 1 Pe. 5.9: *whence*

Στερεόω, ῶ,
    f. ώσω, a.1. ἐστερέωσα,
    to render firm; to strengthen, Ac. 3.7, 16; to settle, Ac. 16.5: *whence*

Στερέωμα, ατος, τό,
    pr. what is solid and firm; *met.* firmness, stedfastness, constancy, Col. 2.5.

Στέφανος, ου, ὁ, (στέφω, to encircle)
    that which forms an encirclement; a crown, Mat. 27.39. Re. 4.4, 10; a chaplet, wreath, *conferred on a victor in the public games,* 1 Co. 9.25; *met.* a crown, reward, prize, 2 Ti. 4.8. Ja. 1.12; a crown, ornament, honour, glory, Phi. 4.1, et al.: *whence*

Στεφανόω, ῶ,
    f. ώσω, a.1. ἐστεφάνωσα,
    to encompass; to crown; to crown *as victor in the games,* 2 Ti. 2.5; *met.* to crown, adorn, decorate, He. 2.7, 9.

Στῆθος, εος, τό, & pl. τὰ στήθη,

the breast, Lu. 18.13; 23.48. Jno. 13.25, et al.

Στήκω, *a late equivalent to* ἕστηκα,
    to stand, Mar. 11.25; *met.* to stand *when under judgment,* to be approved, Ro. 14.4;
    173to stand firm, be constant, persevere, 1 Co. 16.13, et al.

Στηριγμός, οῦ, ὁ,
    pr. a fixing, settling; a state of firmness, fixedness; *met.* firmness *of belief,* settled
    frame *of mind,* 2 Pe. 3.17: *from*

Στηρίζω, (ἵστημι)
    f. ίξω, a.1. ἐστήριξα,
    to set fast; to set *in a certain position or direction,* Lu. 9.51; *met.* to render *mentally*
    stedfast, to settle, confirm, Lu. 22.32. Ro. 1.11, et al.; *p. pass.* ἐστήριγμαι, to stand
    immoveable, Lu. 16.26; *met.* to be *mentally* settled, 2 Pe. 1.12.

Στίγμα, ατος, τό, (στίζω, to prick; to burn in marks, brand)
    a mark, brand, Ga. 6.17.

Στιγμή, ῆς, ἡ, (fr. same)
    pr. a point; *met.* a point *of time,* moment, instant, Lu. 4.5.

Στίλβω,
    f. στίλψω,
    to shine, glisten, Mar. 9.3.

Στοά, ᾶς, ἡ, (ἵστημι)
    a colonnade, piazza, cloister, covered walk supported by columns, Jno. 5.2; 10.23. Ac.
    3.11; 5.12.

Στοιβάς, άδος, ἡ, (στείβω, to tread)
    a stuffing of leaves, boughs, *in N.T.,*c.; *meton.* a bough, branch, Mar. 11.8. N.T.

Στοιχεῖον, ου, τό, (dimin. of στοῖχος, a row, a straight rod or rule, fr. στείχω, to go in a
straight line)
    an element; an element *of the natural universe,* 2 Pe. 3.10, 12; an element or rudiment
    of any intellectual or religious system, Ga. 4.3, 9. Col. 2.8, 20. He. 5.12.

Στοιχέω, ῶ, (fr. same)
    f. ήσω,
    pr. to advance in a line; *met.* to frame one's conduct *by a certain rule,* Act. 21.24. Ro.
    4.12. Ga. 5.25; 6.16. Phi. 3.16.

Στολή, ῆς, ἡ, (στέλλω, to arrange, to equip)
    equipment; dress; a long garment, flowing robe, *worn by priests, kings, and persons
    of distinction,* Mat. 12.38; 16.5. et al.

Στόμα, ατος, τό,
    the mouth, Mat. 12.34; 15.11, 17, 18; 21.16, et al.; speech, words, Mat. 18.16. 2 Co.
    13.1; command of speech, facility of language, Lu. 21.15; *fr. Heb.* ἀνοίγειν τὸ στόμα,
    to make utterance, to speak, Mat. 5.2; 13.35, et al.; *also, used of the earth,* to rend,
    yawn, Re. 12.16; στόμα πρὸς στόμα λαλεῖν, to speak mouth to mouth, face to face, 2
    Jno. 12. 3 Jno. 14; the edge of point *of a weapon,* Lu. 21.24. He. 11.34.

Στόμαχος, ου, ὁ, (στόμα)
    pr. the gullet *leading to the stomach; hence, later,* the stomach *itself,* 1 Ti. 5.23.

Στρατεία, ας, ἡ, (στρατεύω)
    a military expedition, campaign; *and genr.* military service, warfare; *met.* the
    Christian warfare, 2 Co. 10.4. 1 Ti. 1.18.

Στράτευμα, ατος, τό,
    an army, Mat. 22.7, et al.; an armed force, corps, Ac. 23.10, 27; troops, guards, Lu.
    23.11: *from*

Στρατεύω, (στρατός, an army)

f. εύσω, & mid. στρατεύομαι,
to perform military duty, serve as a soldier, Lu. 3.14. 1 Co. 9.7. 2 Ti. 2.4; to battle, Ja. 4.1. 1 Pe. 2.11; to be *spiritually* militant, 2 Co. 10.3. 1 Ti. 1.18.

Στρατηγός, οῦ, ὁ, (στρατός & ἄγω)
a leader or commander of an army, general; a *Roman* prætor, provincial magistrate, Ac. 16.20, 22, 35, 36, 38; στρατηγὸς τοῦ ἱεροῦ, the captain or prefect of the temple, *the chief of the Levites who kept guard in and around the temple,* Lu. 22.4, 52. Ac. 4.1; 5.24, 26.

Στρατιά, ᾶς, ἡ, (στρατός)
an army, host; *fr. Heb.* στρατιὰ οὐράνιος, v. τοῦ οὐρανοῦ, the heavenly host, the host of heaven, the hosts of angels, Lu. 2.13; the stars, &c., Ac. 7.42: *whence*

Στρατιώτης, ου, ὁ
a soldier, Mat. 8.9; 27.27, et al.; *met.* a soldier *of Christ,* 2 Ti. 2.3.

Στρατολογέω, ῶ, (στρατός & λέγω)
f. ήσω,
to collect or levy an army, enlist troops, 2 Ti. 2.4. L.G.

Στρατοπεδάρχης, ου, ὁ, (στρατόπεδον & ἄρχω)
a commandant of a camp; a legionary tribune; *perhaps* the prefect of the prætorian camp, Ac. 28.16. L.G.

Στρατόπεδον, (στρατός & πέδον)
pr. the site of an encampment; an encampment; *meton.* an army, Lu. 21.20.

Στρεβλόω, ῶ, (στρεβλή, a windlass, a wrench, instrument of torture, rack)
f. ώσω,174
pr. to distort *the limbs* on a rack; *met.* to wrench, distort, pervert, 2 Pe. 3.16.

Στρέφω,
f. ψω, a.1. ἔστρεψα, a.2. pass. ἐστράφην,
to twist; to turn, Mat. 5.39; to make a change *of substance,* to change, Re. 11.6; *absol.* to change or turn *one's course of dealing,* Ac. 7.42; *mid.* to turn one's self about, Mat. 16.23. Lu. 7.9, et al.; to turn back, Ac. 7.39; to change one's direction, to turn *elsewhere,* Ac. 13.46; to change one's course of principle and conduct, to be converted, Mat. 18.3.

Στρηνιάω, ῶ,
f. άσω,
to be wanton, to revel, riot, Re. 18.7, 9: *from*

Στρῆνος, εος, τό, (στρηνής, strong, hard)
headstrong pride; wantonness, luxury, voluptuousness, Re. 18.3.

Στρουθίον, ίου, τό, (dimin. of στρουθός)
any small bird, *spc.* a sparrow, Mat. 10.29, 31. Lu. 12.6, 7.

Στρώννυμι, v. στρωννύω, (by metath. for στορέννυμι)
f. στρώσω, a.1. ἔστρωσα, p. pass. ἔστρωμαι,
to spread, to strew, Mat. 21.8. Mar. 11.8; to spread *a couch,* Ac. 9.34; *used of a supper chamber, pass.* to have the couches spread, to be prepared, furnished, Mar. 14.15. Lu. 22.12.

Στυγητός, ή, όν, & ος, ον, (στυγέω, to hate)
hateful, odious, detested, Tit. 3.3.

Στυγνάζω, (στυγνός, gloomy)
f. άσω, a.1. ἐστύγνασα,
to put on a gloomy and downcast look, Mar. 10.22; *of the sky,* to lower, Mat. 16.3. S.

Στῦλος, ου, ὁ,

a pillar, column, Re. 10.1; *used of persons of authority, influence, &c.,* a support or pillar *of the church,* Ga. 2.9. Re. 3.12; a support *of true doctine,* 1 Ti. 3.15.

Στωϊκός, ή, όν,

stoic, belonging to the sect of the Stoics, *founded by Zeno, and deriving their name frm the portico, στοά, where he tought,* Ac. 17.18.

Σύ,

gen. σοῦ, dat. σοί, acc. σέ, & enclit. σου, σοι, σε, pl. ὑμεῖς. *pron. 2 pers.* thou, Mat. 1.20; 2.6, et al. freq.

Συγγένεια, ας, ή,

kindred; kinsfolk, kinsmen, relatives, Lu. 1.61. Ac. 7.3, 14: *from*

Συγγενής, έος, οὓς, ὁ, ή, (σύν & γένος)

kindred, akin; *as a subs.* a kinsman or kinswoman, relative, Mar. 6.4. Lu. 1.36, 58, et al.; one *nationally akin,* a fellow-countryman, Ro. 9.3.

Συγγνώμη, ης, ή, (συγγινώσκω, to agree in judgment with)

pardon; concession, leave, permission, 1 Co. 7.6.

Συγκάθημαι, (σύν & κάθημαι)

to sit company with, Ma. 14.54. Ac. 26.30.

Συγκαθίζω, (σύν & καθίζω)

f. ίσω,

trans. to cause to sit with, seat in company with, Ep. 2.6; *intrans.* to sit in company with; to sit down together, Ac. 22.55.

Συγκακοπαθέω, ῶ, (σύν & κακοπαθέω)

f. ήσω,

to suffer evils along with *any one;* to be enduringly adherent, 2 Ti. 1.8. N.T.

Συγκακουχέομαι, οῦμαι, (σύν & κακουχέω)

to encounter adversity along with *any one,* He. 11.25. N.T.

Συγκαλέω, ῶ, (σύν & καλέω)

f. έσω,

to call togetther, convoke, Mar. 15.16; *mid.* to call around one's self, Lu. 9.1, et al.

Συγκαλύπτω, (σύν & καλύπτω)

f. ψω, p. pass. συγκεκάλυμμαι,

to cover altogether, to cover up; *met.* to conceal, Lu. 12.2.

Συγκάμπω, (σύν & κάμπω)

f. ψω,

to bend or bow together; to bow down *the back of any one afflictively,* Ro. 11.10.

Συγκαταβαίνω, (σύν & καταβαίνω)

f. βήσομαι,

to go down with *any one,* Ac. 25.5.

Συγκατάθεσις, εως, ή,

assent; *in N.T.,* accord, alliance, 2 Co. 6.16: (L.G.) *from*

Συγκατατίθημι, (σύν & κατατίθημι)

to set down together with; *mid.* to assent, accord, Lu. 23.51.

Συγκαταψηφίζω, (σύν & καταψηφίζω, ψῆφος)

ίσω,

to count, number with, Ac. 1.26. N.T.

Συγκεράννυμι, v. νύω, (σύν & κεράννυμι)

f. κεράσω, συνεκέρᾰσα, p. κέκρᾱμαι,

to mix with, mingle together, commingle; to blend, 1 Co. 12.24. *pass.* to be attempered, combined. He. 4.2.

Συγκῑνέω, ῶ, (σύν & κινέω)

f. ήσω,175
to move together, commove, put in commotion; to excite, Ac. 6.12.

Συγκλείω, (σύν & κλείω)
f. είσω,
to shut up together, to hem in; to enclose, Lu. 5.6; *met.* to band *under a sweeping sentence,* Ro. 11.32. Ga. 3.22; *pass.* to be banded *under a bar of disability,* Ga. 3.23.

Συγκληρονόμος, ου, ὁ, ἡ, (σύν & κληρονόμος)
pr. a coheir, Ro. 8.17; a fellow participant, Ep. 3.6. He. 11.9. 1 Pe. 3.7. N.T.

Συγκοινωνέω, ῶ,
f. ήσω,
to be a joint partaker, participate with *a person; in N.T.,* to mix one's self up *in a thing,* to involve one's self, be an accomplice in, Ep. 5.11. Re. 18.4; to sympathise actively in, to relieve, Phi. 4.14: *from*

Συγκοινωνός, οῦ, ὁ, ἡ, (σύν & κοινωνός)
one who partakes jointly; a coparticipant, copartner, Ro. 11.17. 1 Co. 9.23. Phi. 1.7. Re. 1.9. N.T.

Συγκομίζω, (σύν & κομίζω)
f. ίσω,
to bring together, collect; to prepare for burial, take charge of the funeral *of any one,* bury, Ac. 8.2.

Συγκρίνω, (σύν & κρίνω)
f. ινῶ,
to combine, compound; to compare, to estimate by comparing with *something else, or,* to match, 2 Co. 10.12, *bis;* to explain, illustrate, *or,* to suit, 1 Co. 2.13.

Συγκύπτω, (σύν & κύπτω)
f. ψω,
to bend or bow together; to be bowed together, bent double, Lu. 13.11.

Συγκυρία, ας, ἡ, (συγκυρέω, to happen together, σύν & κυρέω, to happen)
concurrence, coincidence, change, accident; κατὰ συγκυρίαν, by change, accidentally, Lu. 10.31.

Συγχαίρω, (σύν & χαίρω)
a.2. συνεχάρνη,
to rejoice with *any one,* sympathise in joy, Lu. 15.6, 9. Phi. 2.17, 18; *met.* 1 Co. 12.26; to sympathise in the advancement of, 1 Co. 13.6.

Συγχέω, & later, ύνω, (σύν & χέω)
imperf. συνέχεον & συνέχυνον, pass. p. συγκέχυμαι, a.1. συνεχύθην,
to pour together, mingle by pouring together; *hence,* to confound, perplex, amaze, Ac. 2.6; to confound *in dispute,* Ac. 9.22; to throw into confusion, fill with uproar, Ac. 19.33; 21.27, 31.

Συγχράομαι, ῶμαι, (σύν & χράομαι)
f. ήσομαι,
to use at the same time with another, use in common; to have social intercourse with, associate with. Jno. 4.9. L.G.

Συγχύνω,
see συγχέω.

Σύγχυσις, εως, ἡ, (συγχέω)
pr. a pouring together; *hence,* confusion, commotion, tumult, uproar, Ac. 19.29.

Συζάω, ῶ, (σύν & ζάω)
f. ήσω,

to live with; to continue in life with *any one,* 2 Co. 7.3; to coexist in life with *another,* Ro. 6.8. 2 Ti. 2.11.

Συζεύγνυμι, (σύν & ζεύγνυμι, to yoke)
    f. ζεύξω, a.1. συνέζευξα,
    to yoke together; *trop.* to conjoin, join together, unite, Mat. 19.6. Mar. 10.9.

Συζητέω, ῶ, (σύν & ζητέω)
    f. ήσω,
    to seek, ask, or inquire with *another;* to deliberate, debate, Mar. 1.27; 9.10; to hold discourse with, argue, reason, Mar. 8.11; 12.28. Ac. 6.9; to question, dispute, cavil, Mar. 9.14, 16, et al.: *whence*

Συζήτησις, εως, ή,
    mutual discussion, debate, disputation, Ac. 15.2, 7; 28.29. L.G.

Συζητητής, οῦ, ὁ,
    a disputation, controversial reasoner, sophist, 1 Co. 1.20. N.T.

Σύζῦγος, ου, ὁ, ή, (συζεύγνυμι)
    a yoke-fellow; an associate, fellow-labourer, coadjutor, Phi. 4.3.

Συζωοποιέω, ῶ, (σύν & ζωοποιέω)
    f. ήσω,
    to quicken together with *another;* to make a sharer in the quickening *of another,* Ep. 2.5. Col. 2.13. N.T.

Συκάμῖνος, ου, ή, & ὁ,
    a sycamine-tree, i.q. συκομοραία, q.v., Lu. 17.6.

Συκῆ, ῆς, ή, *contr. for* συκέα,
    a fig-tree, ficus carica *of Linn.,* Mat. 21.19, et al.

Συκομοραία, v. συκομορέα, ας, ή, (σῦκον & μόρον, a mulberry)
    equivalent to συκόμορος, the fig-mulberry, ficus sycamorus *of Linn., a tree whose leaves resemble those of the mulberry and its fruit that of the fig-tree,* Lu. 19.4. N.T.

Σῦκον, ου, τό,
    a fig, Mat. 7.16, et al.

Συκοφαντέω, ῶ, (συκοφάντης, *pr., among the Athenians,* an informer against those who exported figs contrary to law, σῦκον, φαίνω)
    f. ήσω,176
    to inform against; to accuse falsely; *by impl.* to wrong by false accusations or insidious arts; to extort money by false information, Lu. 3.14; 19.8.

Συλαγωγέω, ῶ, (σύλη, v. σῦλον, & ἄγω)
    f. ήσω,
    to carry off as a prey or booty; *met.* to make victims of imposture, Col. 2.8. L.G.

Συλάω, ῶ, (σύλη v. σῦλον, the right of seizing the goods of a merchant in payment)
    f. ήσω, a.1. ἐσύλησα,
    to strip, rob; to rob, encroach on, 2 Co. 11.8.

Συλλαλέω, ῶ, (σύν & λαλέω)
    f. ήσω,
    to talk, converse, or confer with, Mat. 17.3. Mar. 9.4, et al. L.G.

Συλλαμβάνω, (σύν & λαμβάνω)
    f. λήψομαι, a.2. συνέλαβον, p. συνείληφα, a.1. pass. συνελήφθην,
    to catch up; to seize, apprehend, Mat. 26.55. Ac. 1.16, et al.; to catch, *as prey,* Lu. 5.9; to conceive, become pregnant, Lu. 1.24, 31, 36; 2.21; *met.* Ja. 1.15; *mid.* to help, aid, assist, Lu. 5.7. Phi. 4.3.

Συλλέγω, (σύν & λέγω)
    f. ξω,

to collect, gather, Mat. 7.16; 13.28, et al.

Συλλογίζομαι, (σύν & λογίζομαι)
f. ίσομαι,
to reckon up together; to consider, deliberate, reason, Lu. 20.5.

Συλλυπέομαι, οῦμαι, (σύν & λυπέομαι)
to be grieved together with; to be grieved, Mar. 3.5.

Συμβαίνω, (σύν & βαίνω)
f. βήσομαι, a.2. συνέβην,
to stand with the feet near together; to step or come together; to happen, befall, fall out, Mar. 10.32, et al.

Συμβάλλω, (σύν & βάλλω)
f. βαλῶ
pr. to throw together; absol. to meet and join, Ac. 20.14; to meet in war, to encounter, engage with, Lu. 14.31; to encounter in discourse or dispute, Ac. 17.18; to consult together, Ac. 4.15; mid. to contribute, be of service to, to aid, Ac. 18.27; συμβάλλειν ἐν τῇ καρδίᾳ, to revolve in mind, ponder upon, Lu. 2.19.

Συμβασιλεύω, (σύν & βασιλεύω)
f. εύσω,
to reign with; met. to enjoy honour and felicity with, 1 Co. 4.8. 2 Ti. 2.12. L.G.

Συμβιβάζω, (σύν & βιβάζω)
f. άσω,
pr. to cause to come together; to unite, knit together, Ep. 4.16. Col. 2.2, 19; to infer, conclude, Ac. 16.10; by impl. to prove, demonstrate, Ac. 9.22; in N.T., to teach, instruct, 1 Co. 2.16.

Συμβουλεύω, (σύν & βουλεύω)
f. εύσω,
to counsel, advise, exhort, Jno. 18.14. Re. 3.18; mid. to consult together, plot, Mat. 26.4. et al.

Συμβούλιον, ίου, τό,
counsel, consultation, mutual consultation, Mat. 12.14; 22.15, et al.; a council, counsellors, Ac. 25.12: (N.T.) from

Σύμβουλος, ου, ὁ, (σύν & Βουλή)
a counsellor; one who shares one's counsel, Ro. 11.34.

Συμμαθητής, οῦ, ὁ, (σύν & μαθητής)
a fellow-disciple, Jno. 11.16.

Συμμαρτῠρέω, ῶ, (σύν & μαρτυρέω)
f. ήσω,
to testify or bear witness together with another, add testimony, Ro. 2.15; 8.16; 9.1.

Συμμερίζομαι, (σύν & μερίζω)
f. ίσομαι,
to divide with another so as to receive a part to one's self, share with, partake with, 1 Co. 9.13. N.T.

Συμμέτοχος, ου, ὁ, ἡ, (σύν & μέτοχος)
a partaker with any one, a joint partaker, Ep. 3.6; 5.7. L.G.

Συμμορφίζω, (σύν & μορφίζω)
equivalent to συμμορφόω: which see: v.r. Phi. 3.10.

Σύμμορφος, ου, ὁ, ἡ, (σύν & μορφή)
of like form, assimilated, conformed, Ro. 8.29. Phi. 3.21. N.T.

Συμμορφόω, ῶ, (σύν & μορφόω)
to conform to, Phi. 3.10. N.T.

Συμπαθέω, ῶ,
    f. ήσω,
    to sympathise with, He. 4.15; to compassionate, He. 10.34: *from*
Συμπᾰθής, έος, οῦς, ὁ, ἡ, (σύν & πάθος, πάσχω)
    sympathising, compassionate, 1 Pe. 3.8.
Συμπαραγίνομαι, (σύν & παραγίνομαι)
    a.2. συμπαρεγενόμην,
    to be present together with; to come together, convene, Lu. 23.48; to stand by or support *one judicially,* adesse, 2 Ti. 4.16.
Συμπαρακαλέω, ῶ, (σύν & παρακαλέω)
    f. ήσω,177
    to invite, exhort *along with others;* to animate *in company with others; pass.* to share in mutual encouragement, Ro. 1.12.
Συμπαραλαμβάνω, (σύν & παραλαμβάνω)
    a.2. συμπαρέλαβον,
    to take along with, take as a companion, Ac. 12.25; 15.37, 38. Ga. 2.1.
Συμπαραμένω, (σύν & παραμένω)
    f. μενῶ,
    to remain or conntinue with or among, Phi. 1.25.
Συμπάρειμι, (σύν & πάρειμι)
    to be present with *any one,* Ac. 25.24.
Συμπάσχω, (σύν & πάσχω)
    f. πείσομαι,
    to suffer with, sympathise, 1 Co. 12.26; to suffer as *another,* endure corresponding suffferings, Ro. 8.17.
Συμπέμπω, (σύν & πέμπω)
    f. ψω,
    to send with *any one,* 2 Co. 8.18, 22.
Συμπεριλαμβάνω, (σύν & περιλαμβάνω)
    f. λήψομαιν,
    to enbrace together; to embrace, Ac. 20.10.
Συμπίνω, (σύν & πίνω)
    f. πίομαι, & πιοῦμαι, a.2. συνέπῐον,
    to drink with *any one,* Ac. 10.41. (ῐ)
Συμπίπτω, (σύν & πίπτω)
    a.2. συνέπεσον,
    to fall together; to fall in runis, v.r. Lu. 6.49.
Συμπληρόω, ῶ, (σύν & πληρόω)
    f. ώσω,
    to fill, fill up, fill full, Lu. 8.23; *pass., of time,* to be completed, have fully come, Lu. 9.51. Ac. 2.1.
Συμπνίγω, (σύν & πνίγω)
    f. ιξοῦμαι,
    to throttle, choke; *trop.* to choke *the growth or increase of seed or plants,* Mat. 13.22. Mar. 4.7, 19. Lu. 8.14; to press upon, crowd, throng, Lu. 8.42. (ῐ)
Συμπολίτης, ου, ὁ, (σύν & πολίτης)
    a fellow-citizen, *met.* Ep. 2.19. (ῐ)
Συμπορεύομαι, (σύν & πορεύομαι)
    f. εύσομαι,
    to go with, accompany, Lu. 7.11; 14.25; 24.15; to come together, assemble, Mar. 10.1.

Συμπόσιον, ίου, τό, (συμπίνω)
    a drinking togethers; a feast, banquet; a festive company; *in N.T., pl.* συμπόσια, mess-parties, Mar. 6.39.

Συμπρεσβύτερος, ου, ὁ, (σύν & πρεσβύτερος)
    a fellow-elder, fellow-presbyter, 1 Pe. 5.1. N.T.

Συμφέρω, (σύν & φέρω)
    f. συνοίσω, a.1. συνήνεγκα, a.2. συνήνεγκον,
    to bring together, collect, Ac. 19.19; *absol.* to conduce to, to be for the benefit of *any one,* be profitable, advantageous, expedient, 1 Co. 6.12. 2 Co. 8.10; *particip. neut.* τὸ συμφέρον, good, benefit, profit, advantage, Ac. 20.20. 1 Co. 7.35; *impers.* συμφέρει, it is profitable, advantageous, expedient, Mat. 5.29, 30; 19.10. et al.

Σύμφημι, (σύν & φημί)
    pr. to affirm with; to assent, Ro. 7.16.

Συμφυλέτης, ου, ὁ, (σύν & φυλή)
    pr. one of the same tribe; a fellow-citizen, fellow-countryman, 1 Th. 2.14.

Σύμφῡτος, ου, ὁ, ἡ, (σύν & φύω)
    pr. planted together, grown together; *in N.T., met.* grown together, closely entwined or united with, Ro. 6.5.

Συμφύω, (fr. same)
    f. φύσω, pass. a.2. συνεφύην,
    to make to grow together; *pass.* to grow or spring up with, Lu. 8.7.

Συμφωνέω, ῶ, (σύμφωνος)
    f. ήσω,
    to sound together, to be in unison, be in accord; *trop.* to agree with, accord with *in purport,* Ac. 15.15; to harmonise with, be congruous, suit with, Lu. 5.36; to agree with, make an agreement, Mat. 18.19; 20.2, 13. Ac. 5.9: *whence*

Συμφώνησις, εως, ἡ,
    unison, accord; agreement, concord, 2 Co. 6.15. N.T.

Συμφωνία, ας, ἡ,
    symphony, harmony of sounds; concert of instruments, music, Lu. 15.25.

Σύμφωνος, ου, ὁ, ἡ, (σύν & φωνή)
    agreeing in sound; *met.* accordant, harmonious, agreeing, *and neut.* τὸ σύμφωνον, accord, agreement, 1 Co. 7.5.

Συμψηφίζω, (σύν & ψηφίζω, ψῆφος)
    f. ίσω,
    to calculate together, compute, reckon up, Ac. 19.19.

Σύμψῡχος, ου, ὁ, ἡ, (σύν & ψυχή)
    united in mind, at unity, Phi. 2.2. N.T.

Σύν,
    prep. governing a dat., with, together with, Mat. 25.27; 26.35; 27.38; attendant on, 1 Co. 15.10; besides, Lu. 24.21; with, with the assistance of, 1 Co. 5.4; with, in the same manner as, Ga. 3.9; εἶναι σύν τινι, 178to be with any one, to be in company with, accompany, Lu. 2.13; 8.38; to be on the side of, be a partisan of any one, Ac. 4.13; 14.4; οἱ σύν τινι, those with any one, the companions of any one, Mar. 2.26. Ac. 22.9; the colleagues, associates of any one, Ac. 5.17, 21.

Συνάγω, (σύν & ἄγω)
    f. άξω, a.2. συνήγᾰγον, p. pass. συνῆγμαι, a.1. pass. συνήχθην, f. pass. συναχθήσομαι, to bring together, collect, gather, *as grain, fruits,* &c., Mat. 3.12; 6.26; 13.30, 47; to collect *an assembly,* convoke; *pass.* to convene, come together, meet, Mat. 2.4; 13.2;

18.20; 22.10; *in N.T.,* to receive with kindness and hospitality, to entertain, Mat. 25.35, 38, 43, et al.: (ᾰ) *whence*

Συναγωγή, ῆς, ἡ,
a collecting, gathering; a *Christian* assembly or congregation, Ja. 2.2; the congregation *of a synagogue,* Ac. 9.2, et al.; a synagogue, *place of Jewish worship,* Lu. 7.5, et al.

Συναγωνίζομαι, (σύν & ἀγωνίζομαι)
f. ίσομαι,
to combat in company with *any one;* to exert one's strength with, to be earnest in aiding, Ro. 15.30.

Συναθλέω, ῶ, (σύν & ἀθλέω)
f. ήσω,
pr. to contend on the side of *any one; in N.T.,* to co-operate vigorously with *a person,* Phi. 4.3; to make effort in the cause of, in support of *a thing,* Phi. 1.27. L.G.

Συναθροίζω, (σύν & ἀθροίζω, to gather, ἀθρόος)
f. οίσω,
to gather; to bring together, convoke, Ac. 19.25; *pass.* to come together, convene, Lu. 24.33. Ac. 12.12.

Συναίρω, (σύν & αἴρω)
f. αρῶ,
to take up *a thing* with *any one; in N.T.,* συναίρειν λόγον, to adjust accounts, reckon *in order to payment,* Mat. 18.23, 24; 25.19.

Συναιχμάλωτος, ου, ὁ, ἡ, (σύν & αἰχμάλωτος)
a fellow-captive, Ro. 16.7. Col. 4.10. Phile. 23. N.T.

Συνακολουθέω, ῶ, (σύν & ἀκολουθέω)
f. ήσω,
to follow in company with, accompany, Mar. 5.37. Lu. 23.49.

Συναλίζω, (σύν & ἁλίζω to collect)
f. ίσω,
to cause to come together, collect, assemble, congregate; *mid.* to convene to one's self, Ac. 1.4.

Συναναβαίνω, (σύν & ἀναβαίνω)
f. βήσομαι, a.2. συνανέβην,
to go up, ascend with *any one,* Mar. 15.41. Ac. 13.31.

Συνανάκειμαι, (σύν & ἀνάκειμαι)
f. είσομαιν
to recline with *any one at table,* Mat. 9.10; 14.9, et al. N.T.

Συναναμίγνυμι, (σύν & ἀναμίγνυμι, to mix, mingle)
to mix together with, commingle; *mid. met.* to mingle one's self with, to associate with, have familiar intercourse with, 1 Co. 5.9, 11. 2 Th. 3.14. L.G.

Συναναπαύομαι, (σύν & ἀναπαύομαι)
f. αύσομαι,
to experience refreshment in company with *any one,* Ro. 15.32. L.G.

Συναντάω, ῶ,(σύν & ἀντάω, αντί)
f. ήσω,
to meet with, fall in with, encounter; to meet, Lu. 9.37; 22.10. Ac. 10.25. He. 7.1, 10; to occur, happen to, befall, Ac. 20.22: *whence*

Συνάντησις, εως, ἡ,
a meeting, Mat. 8.34.

Συναντιλαμβάνομαι, (σύν & ἀντιλαμβάνομαι)

f. λήψομαι,

pr. to take hold of with *any one;* to support, help, aid, Lu. 10.40. Ro. 8.26. L.G.

Συναπάγω, (σύν & ἀπάγω)

f. άξω,

to lead or conduct away with; to seduce; *pass.* to be led away, carried astray, Ga. 2.13. 2 Pe. 3.17; *mid.* to conform one's self willingly to *certain circumstance,* Ro. 12.16.

Συναποθνήσκω, (σύν & ἀποθνήσκω)

a.2. συναπέθανον,

to die together with *any one,* Mar. 14.31. 2 Co. 7.3; *met.* to die with, *in respect of a spiritual likeness,* 2 Ti. 2.11.

Συναπόλλυμι, (σύν & ἀπόλλυμι)

a.2. mid. συναπωλόμην

to destroy together with *others; mid.* to perish or be destroyed with *others,* He. 11.31.

Συναποστέλλω, (σύν & ἀποστέλλω)

f. στελῶ,

to send forth together with *any one,* 2 Co. 12.18.

Συναρμολογέω, ῶ, (σύν & ἁρμολογέω, fr. ἁρμός, a joint, & λόγος)

f. ήσω,

to join together fitly, fit or frame together, compact, Ep. 2.21. N.T.

Συναρπάζω, (σύν & ἁρπάλω)

f. άσω,179

to snatch up, clutch, to seize and carry off suddenly, Ac. 6.12; to seize with force and violence, Lu. 8.29; *pass. of a ship,* to be caught and swept on *by the wind,* Ac. 27.15.

Συναυξάνομαι, (σύν & αὐξάνω)

f. ήσομαι,

to grow together *in company,* Mat. 13.30.

Σύνδεσμος, ου, ὁ,

that which binds together; a ligature, Col. 2.19; a band *of union,* Eph. 4.3. Col. 3.14; a bundle, *or,* bond, Ac. 8.23: *from*

Συνδέω, (σύν & δέω)

f. δήσω,

to bind together; *in N.T., pass.* to be in bonds together with, He. 13.3.

Συνδοξάζω, (σύν & δοξάζω)

f. άσω,

in N.T., to glorify together with, to exalt to a state of dignity and happiness in company with, to make to partake in the glorification *of another,* Ro. 8.17.

Σύνδουλος, ου, ὁ, (σύν & δοῦλος)

a fellow-slave, fellow-servant, Mat. 24.49, et al.; a fellow-minister *of Christ,* Col. 1.7, et al.

Συνδρομή, ῆς, ἡ, (σύν & ἔδραμον)

a running together, concourse, Ac. 21.30.

Συνεγείρω, (σύν & ἐγείρω)

f. γερῶ,

to raise up with *any one;* to raise up with *Christ by spiritual resemblance of His resurrection,* Ep. 2.6. Co. 2.12; 3.1. L.G.

Συνέδριον, ίου, τό, (σύν & ἔδρα)

pr. a sitting together, assembley, &c.; *in N.T.,* the Sanhedrin, *the supreme council of the Jewish nation,* Mat. 5.22; 26.59; *meton.* the Sanhedrin *as including the members and place of meeting,* Lu. 22.66. Ac. 4.15, et al.; *genr.* a *judicial* council, tribunal, Mat. 10.17. Mar. 13.9.

Συνείδησις, εως, ἡ, (συνειδέναι)
consciousness, He. 10.2; a present idea, persisting notion, impression of reality, 1 Co. 8.7. 1 Pe. 2.19; conscience, *as an inward moral impression of one's actions and principles,* Jno. 8.9. Ac. 23.1; 24.16. Ro. 9.1. 2 Co. 1.12, et al.; conscience, *as the inward faculty of moral judgement,* Ro. 2.15; 13.5. 1 Co. 8.7, 10, 12; 10.25, 27, 28, 29. 2 Co. 4.2; 5.11, et al.; conscience, *as the inward moral and spiritual frame,* Tit. 1.15, He. 9.14.
Συνεῖδον,
a. 2. συνοράω, part. συνιδών,
to see under one range of view; to take a deliberate glance *of a state of matters,* Ac. 12.12; 14.6.
Συνειδώς,
see σύνοιδα.
Σύνειμι, (σύν & εἰμί)
f. ἔσομαι,
to be with, be in company with, Lu. 9.18. Ac. 22.11.
Σύνειμι, (σύν & εἶμι)
part. συνιών,
to come together, assemble, Lu. 8.4.
Συνεισέρχομαι, (σύν & εἰσέρχομαι)
a.2. συνεισῆλθον,
to enter with *any one,* Jno. 18.15; to embark with, Jno. 6.22.
Συνέκδημος, ου, ὁ, ἡ, (σύν & ἔκδημος, a traveller to foreign countries)
one who accompanies *another* to foreign countries, fellow-traveller, Ac. 19.29. 2 Co. 8.19. L.G.
Συνεκλεκτός, ή, όν, (σύν & ἐκλεκτός)
chosen along with *others;* elected *to Gospel privileges* along with, 1 Pe. 5.13. N.T.
Συνελαύνω, (σύν & ἐλαύνω)
f. ελάσω, a.1. συνήλἄσα,
pr. to drive together; to urge to meet; *in N.T.,* to urge *to union,* Ac. 7.26.
Συνεπιμαρτυρέω, ῶ, (σύν & ἐπιμαρτυρέω)
f. ήσω,
to join in according attestation; to support by attestation, to confirm, sanction, He. 2.4.
Συνεπιτίθεμαι, (σύν & ἐπιτίθημι)
to set upon along with, assail at the same time; to unite in impreaching, v.r. Ac. 24.9.
Συνέπομαι, (σύν & ἕπομαι, to follow)
imperf. συνειπόμην,
to follow with, attend, accompany, Ac. 20.4.
Συνεργέω, ῶ,
f. ήσω,
to work together with, to co-operate, &c., 1 Co. 16.16. 2 Co. 6.1; to assist, afford aid to, Mar. 16.20; to be a motive principle, Ja. 2.22; *absol.* to conspire actively *to a result,* Ro. 8.28: *from*
Συνεργός, οῦ, ὁ, ἡ, (σύν & ἔργον)
a fellow-labourer, associate, coadjutor, Ro. 16.3, 9, 21. 2 Co. 1.24, et al.
Συνέρχομαι, (σύν & ἔρχομαι)
a.2. συνῆλθον,
to come together; to assemble, Mar. 3.20; 6.33; 14.53; to cohabit *matrimonially,* Mat. 1.13. 1 Co. 7.5; to go or come with *any one,* to accompany, Lu. 23.55. Ac. 9.39; 180to company with, associate with, Ac. 1.21, et al.

Συνεσθίω, (σύν & ἐσθίω)
    a.2. συνέφαγον,
    to eat with, 1 Co. 5.11; *by impl.* to associate with, live on familiar terms with, Lu. 15.2. Ga. 2.12.
Σύνεσις, εως, ἡ, (συνίημι)
    pr. a sending together, a junction, *as of streams; met.* understanding, intelligence, discernment, sagaciousness, Lu. 2.47. 1 Co. 1.19, et al.; *meton.* the understanding, intellect, mind, Mar. 12.33.
Συνετός, ή, όν, (fr. same)
    intelligent, discerning, sagacious, wise, prudent, Mat. 11.25. Lu. 20.21, et al.
Συνευδοκέω, ῶ, (σύν & εὐδοκέω)
    f. ήσω,
    to approve with *another;* to accord with in principle, Ro. 1.32; to stamp approval, Lu. 11.48. Ac. 8.1; 22.20; to be willing, agreeable, 1 Co. 7.12, 13.
Συνευωχέομαι, οῦμαι, (σύν & εὐωχέομαι, to feast, banquent)
    f. ήσομαι,
    to feast together with, 2 Pe. 2.13. Ju. 12.
Συνέφαγον,
    a. 2. of συνεσθίω: *which see.*
Συνεφίστημι, (σύν & ἐφίστημι)
    to set together upon; *intrans.* a.2. συνεπέστην, to assail together, Ac. 16.22.
Συνέχω, (σύν & ἔχω)
    f. ἕξω,
    pr. to hold together; to confine, shut up close; τὰ ὦτα, to stop the ears, Ac. 7.57; to confine, straiten, *as a besieged city,* Lu. 19.43; to hold, hold fast, have the custody of *any one,* Lu. 22.63; to hem in, urge, press upon Lu. 8.45; to exercise a constraining influence on, 2 Co. 5.14; *pass.* to be seized with, be affected with, *as fear, disease, &c.,* Mat. 4.24. Lu. 4.38, et al.; to be in a state of *mental* constriction, to be hard pressed *by urgency of circumstances,* Lu. 12.50. Ac. 18.5. Phi. 1.23.
Συνήδομαι, (σύν & ἥδομαι, to be pleased, delighted)
    f. ησθήσομαι,
    to be pleased along with *others;* to congratulate; to delight in, approve cordially, Ro. 7.22.
Συνήθεια, ας, ἡ, (συνηθής, accustomed, familiar, customary, fr. σύν & ἦθος)
    intercourse; use, custom; an established custom, practice, Jno. 18.39. 1 Co. 11.16.
Συνηλικιώτης, ου, ὁ, (σύν & ἡλικιώτης, idem, fr. ἡλικία)
    one of the same age, an equal in age, Ga. 1.14. L.G.
Συνθάπτω, (σύν & θάπτω)
    f. ψω, a.2. pass. συνετάφην,
    to bury with; *pass. in N.T.,* to be buried with *Christ symbolically,* Ro. 6.4. Col. 2.12.
Συνθλάω, ῶ, (σύν & θλάω, to break)
    f. άσω, f. pass. συνθλασθήσομαι,
    to crush together; to break in pieces, shatter, Mat. 21.44. Lu. 20.18.
Συνθλίβω, (σύν & θλίβω)
    f. ψω,
    to press together; to press upon, crowd, throng, Mar. 5.24, 31. (ῑ)
Συνθρύπτω, (σύν & θρύπτω)
    f. ψω,
    to crush to pieces; *met.* to break *the heart of any one,* to make to quail, Ac. 21.13. N.T.

Συνίημι, (σύν & ἵημι, to send)
f. συνήσω, & ἥσομαι, a.1. συνηκα, a.2. subj. συνῶ, and in N.T., pr. 3 pl. συνιοῦσι, part. συνιῶν & συνιών,
pr. to send together; met. to understand, comprehend thoroughly, Mat. 13.51. Lu. 2.50; 18.34; 24.45; to perceive clearly, Mat. 16.12; 17.13. Ac. 7.25. Ro. 15.21. Eph. 5.17; *absol.* to be well judging, sensible, 2 Co. 10.12; to be *spiritually* intelligent, Mat. 13.13, 14, 15. Ac. 28.26, 27, et al.; to be *religiously* wise, Ro. 3.11.
Συνίστημι, and, later, συνιστάω, & συνιστάνω, (σύν & ἵστημι)
f. στήσω,
to place together; to recommend to favourable attention, Ro. 16.1. 2 Co. 3.1; 10.18, et al.; to place in a striking point of view, to evince, Ro. 3.5; 5.8. Ga. 2.18; *intrans.,* p. συνέστηκα, part. συνεστώς, to stand beside, Lu. 9.32; to have been permanently framed, Col. 1.17; to possess consistence, 2 Pe. 3.5.
Συνοδεύω, (σύν & ὁδεύω)
f. εύσω,
to journey or travel with, accompany on a journey, Ac. 9.7. L.G.
Συνοδία, ας, ἡ, (σύν & ὁδός)
pr. a journeying together; *meton.* a company of fellow-travellers, caravan, Lu. 2.44. L.G.
Σύνοιδα,
a perf. with the sense of a present, part. συνειδώς, to share in the knowledge *of a thing;* to be privy to, Ac. 5.2; 181to be conscious; οὐδεν σύνοιδα, to have a clear conscience, 1 Co. 4.4.
Συνοικέω, ῶ, (σύν & οἰκέω)
f. ήσω,
to dwell with; to live or cohabit with, 1 Pe. 3.7.
Συνοικοδομέω, ῶ, (σύν & οἰκοδομέω)
to build in company with *any one; pass.* to be built in along with, form a constituent part of a structure, Ep. 2.22. L.G.
Συνομιλέω, ῶ, (σύν & ὁμιλέω)
f. ήσω,
pr. to be in company with; to talk or converse with, Ac. 10.27. N.T.
Συνομορέω, ῶ, (σύν & ὁμορέω, to border upon, fr. ὁμός & ὅρος)
f. ήσω,
to be contiguous, adjoin, Ac. 18.7. N.T.
Συνοχή, ῆς, ἡ, (συνέχω)
pr. a being held together; compression; *in N.T., met.* distress of mind, anxiety, Lu. 21.25. 2 Co. 2.4.
Συντάσσω, v. ττω, (σύν & τάσσω)
f. ξω,
pr. to arrange or place in order together; *in N.T.,* to order, charge, direct, Mat. 26.19; 27.10.
Συντέλεια, ας, ἡ,
a complete combination; a completion, consummation, end, Mat. 13.39, 40, 49; 24.3; 28.20. He. 9.26: *from*
Συντελέω, ῶ, (σύν & τελέω)
f. έσω,
pr. to bring to an end altogether; to finish, end, Mat. 7.28; to consummate, Ro. 9.28; to ratify *a covenant,* He. 8.8; *pass.* to be terminated, Lu. 4.2. Ac. 21.27; to be fully realised, Mar. 13.4.

Συντέμνω, (σύν & τέμνω)

f. τεμῶ, p. τέτμηκα, p. pass. τέτμημαι,

pr. to cut short, contract by cutting off; *met.* to execute speedily, *or fr. the Heb.,* to determine, decide, decree, Ro. 9.28.

Συντηρέω, ῶ, (σύν & τηρέω)

f. ήσω,

to keep safe and sound, Mat. 9.17. Lu. 5.38; to observe strictly, *or,* to secure from hard, protect, Mar. 6.20; to preserve in memory, keep carefully in mind, Lu. 2.19. L.G.

Συντίθημι, (σύν & τίθημι)

to place together; *mid.,* a.2. συνεθέμην, p. συντέθειμαι, to agree together, come to a mutual understanding, Jno. 9.22. Ac. 23.20; to bargain, to pledge one's self, Lu. 22.5; to second a *statement,* Ac. 24.9.

Συντόμως, (συντέμνω)

adv. concisely, briefly, Ac. 24.4.

Συντρέχω, (σύν & τρέχω)

a.2. συνέδρᾰμον,

to run together, flock together, Mar. 6.33. Ac. 3.11; to run in company with *other, met.* 1 Pe. 4.4.

Συντρίβω, (σύν & τρίβω)

f. ψω, p. pass. συντέτριμμαι, f. pass. συντρῖβήσομαι,

to rub together; to shiver, Mar. 14.3. Re. 2.27; to break, break in pieces, Mar. 5.4. Jno. 19.36; to break down, crush, bruise, Mat. 12.20; *met.* to break the power of *any one,* deprive of strength, debilitate, Lu. 9.39. Ro. 16.20; *pass.* to be broken *in heart,* be contrite, Lu. 4.18: (ῑ) *whence*

Σύντριμμα, ατος, τό,

a breaking, bruising; *in N.T.,* destruction, ruin, Ro. 3.16.

Σύντροφος, ου, ὁ, (συντρέφω, to nurse, bring up together, σύν & τρέφω)

nursed with *another;* one brought up or educated with *another,* Ac. 13.1.

Συντυγχάνω, (σύν & τυγχάνω)

a.2. συνέτῠχον,

to meet or fall in with; *in N.T.,* to get to, approach, Lu. 8.19.

Συνυποκρίνομαι, (σύν & ὑποκρίνομαι)

a.1. συνυπεκρίθην,

to dissemble, feign with, or in the same manner as *another,* Ga. 2.13. L.G.

Συνυπουργέω, ῶ, (σύν & ὑπουργέω, to render service, fr. ὑπό & ἔργον)

f. ήσω,

to aid along with *another,* help together, 2 Co. 1.11. L.G.

Συνωδίνω, (σύν & ὠδίνω, to be in birth-pangs)

f. ινῶ,

pr. to travail at the same time with; *trop.* to be altogether in throes, Ro. 8.22. (ῑ)

Συνωμοσία, ας, ἡ, (συνόμνυμι, to swear together, fr. σύν & ὄμνυμι)

a banding by oath; a combination, conspiracy, Ac. 23.13.

Σύρος, ου, ὁ,

a Syrian, Lu. 4.27.

Συροφοινίκισσα, v. Συροφοινίσσα, ης, ἡ,

a Syrophenician woman, *Phenicia being included in Syria,* Mar. 7.26.

Σύρτις, εως, ἡ

a shoal, sand-bank a place dangerous on account of 182shoals, *two of which were particularly famous on the northern coast of Africa, one lying near Carthage, and the other,* the syrtis major, *lying between Cyrene and Leptis, which is probably referred to in* Ac. 27.17: *from*

Σύρω,

to draw, drag, Jno. 21.8. Re. 12.4; to force away, hale *before magistrates,* &c. Ac. 8.3; 14.19; 17.6. (ῡ)

Συσπαράσσω, v. ττω, (σύν & σπαράσσω)

f. ξω,

to tear to pieces; to convulse altogether, Lu. 9.42. N.T.

Σύσσημον, ου, τό, (σύν & σῆμα)

a concerted signal, Mar. 14.44.

Σύσσωμος, ου, ὁ, ἡ, τό, -ον, (σύν & σῶμα)

united in same body; *met. pl.* joint members *in a spiritual body,* Ep. 3.6. N.T.

Συστασιάστης, ου, ὁ, (συστασιάζω, to join in a sedition with (fr. σύν & στάσις)

an accomplice in sedition, associate in insurrection, Mar. 15.7. L.G.

Συστατικός, ή, όν, (συνίστημι)

commendatory, recommendatory, 2 Co. 3.1, *bis.* L.G.

Συσταυρόω, ῶ, (σύν & σταυρόω)

f. ώσω, p. pass. συνεσταύρωμαι, a.1. συνεσταυρώθην,

to crucify with *another,* Mat. 27.44. Mar. 15.32. Jno. 19.32; *pass. met.* to be crucified with *another in a spiritual resemblance,* Ro. 6.6. Ga. 2.20. N.T.

Συστέλλω, (σύν & στέλλω)

f. ελῶ, a.1. συνέστειλα, p. pass. συνέσταλμαι,

to draw together, contract, straiten; to enwrap; *hence,* i.q. περιστέλλω, to lay out, prepare for burial, Ac. 5.6; *pass.* to be shortened, *or,* to be environed with trials, 1 Co. 7.29.

Συστενάζω, (σύν & στενάζω)

f. ξω,

to groan altogether, Ro. 8.22.

Συστοιχέω, ῶ, (σύν & στοιχέω)

f. ήσω,

pr. to be in the same row with; *met.* to correspond to, Ga. 4.25.

Συστρατιώτης, ου, ὁ, (σύν & στρατιώτης)

a fellow-soldier; *met.* a fellow-soldier, co-militant, *in the service of Christ,* Phi. 2.25. Phile. 2.

Συστρέφω, (σύν & στρέφω)

f. ψω,

to turn or roll together; to collect, gather, Ac. 28.3: *whence*

Συστροφή, ῆς, ἡ,

a gathering, concourse, tumultuous assembly, Ac. 19.40; a combination, conspiracy Ac. 23.12, col. v.13.

Συσχηματιζω, (σύν & σχηματίζω, to form, fr. σχῆμα)

to fashion in accordance with; *mid.* to conform or assimilate one's self to, *met.* Ro. 12.2. 1 Pe. 1.14.

Σφαγή, ῆς, ἡ, (σφάζω)

slaughter, Ac. 8.32. Ro. 8.36. Ja. 5.5.

Σφάγιον, ου, τό,

a victim *slaughtered in sacrifice,* Ac. 7.42: *from*

Σφάζω, v. Att. σφάττω,

f. ξω, a.1. ἔσφαξα, a.2. pass. ἐσφάγην, p. pass. ἔσφαγμαι,

to slaughter, kill, slay; *pr. used of animals killed in sacrifice,* &c., Re. 5.6, 9, 12; 13.8; *of persons,* &c., 1 Jno. 3.12. Re. 6.4, 9; 18.24; to wound mortally, Re. 13.3.

Σφόδρα, (pr. neut. pl. of σφοδρός, vehement, violent, strong)
    adv. much, greatly, exceedingly, Mat. 2.10; 17.6, et al.

Σφοδρῶς, (fr. same)
    adv. exceedingly, vehemently, Ac. 27.18.

Σφραγίζω,
    f. ίσω, a.1. ἐσφράγισα, p. pass. ἐσφράγισμαι, a.1. pass. ἐσφραγίσθην,
    to seal, stamp with a seal, Mat. 27.66; to seal up, to close up, conceal, Re. 10.4; 22.10; to set a mark upon, distinguish by a mark Re. 7.3, 8; to seal, to mark distinctively *as invested with a certain character,* Jno. 6.24; *mid.* to set one's own mark upon, seal as one's own, to impress with a mark of acceptance, 2 Co. 1.22; to obtain a quittance of, to deliver over safely to *any one,* Ro. 15.28; *absol.* to set to one's seal, to make a solemn declaration, Jno. 3.33: *from*

Σφρᾱγίς, ῖδος, ἡ,
    a seal, a signet ring, Re. 7.2; an inscription on a seal, motto, 2 Ti. 2.19; a seal, the impression of a seal, Re. 5.1, et al.; a seal, a distinctive mark, Re. 9.4; a seal, a token, proof, 1 Co. 9.2; a token *of guarantee,* Ro. 4.11.

Σφυρόν, οῦ, τό,
    the ankle; *pl.* τὰ σφυρά, the ankle bones, malleoli, Ac. 3.7.

Σχεδόν, (ἔχω, σχεῖν)
    adv. pr. near *of place; hence,* nearly, almost, Ac. 13.44; 19.26. He. 9.22.

Σχῆμα, ατος, τό, (fr. same)
    183 fashion form; fashion, external show, 1 Co. 7.31; guise, appearance, Phi. 2.8.

Σχίζω,
    f. ίσω, a.1. ἔσχισα, a.1. pass. ἐσχίσθη,
    to split, Mat. 27.51; to rend, tear asunder, Mat. 27.51. Lu. 5.36, et al.; *mid.* to open or unfold *with a chasm,* Mar. 1.10; *pass. met.* to be divided *into parties or factions,* Ac. 14.4; 23.7: *whence*

Σχισμα, ατος, τό,
    a rent, Mat. 9.16. Mar. 2.21; *met.* a division *into parties,* schism, Jno. 7.43; 9.16, et al.

Σχοινίον, ου, τό, (σχοῖνος, a rush)
    pr. a cord made of rushes; *genr.* a rope, cord, Jno. 2.15. Acc. 27.32.

Σχολάζω,
    f. άσω,
    to be unemployed, to be at leisure; to be at leisure *for a thing,* to devote one's self entirely *to a thing,* 1 Co. 7.5; to be unoccupied, empty, Mat. 12.44: *from*

Σχολή, ῆς, ἡ,
    freedom from occupation; *later,* ease, leisure; a school, Ac. 19.9.

Σώζω,
    f. σώσω, p. σέσωκα, a.1. ἔσωσα, a.1. pass. ἐσώθην, p. pass. σέσωσμαι,
    to save, rescue; to preserve safe and unharmed, Mat. 8.25; 10.22; 24.22; 27.40, 42, 49. 1 Ti. 2.15; σώζειν εἰς, to bring safely to, 2 Ti. 4.18; to cure, heal, restore to health, Mat. 9.21, 22. Mar. 5.23, 28, 34; 6.56, et al.; to save, preserve *from being lost,* Mat. 16.25. Mar. 3.4; 8.35; σώζειν ἀπό, to deliver from, set free from, Mat. 1.21. Jno. 12.27. Ac. 2.40; *in N.T.,* to rescue *from unbelief,* convert, Ro. 11.14. 1 Co. 1.21; 7.16; to bring within the pale of Christian privilege, Tit. 3.5. 1 Pe. 3.21; to save *from final ruin,* 1 Ti. 1.15; *pass.* to be brought within the Gospel pale, Ac. 2.47. Eph. 2.5, 8; to be in the way of salvation, 1 Co. 15.2. 2 Co. 2.15.

Σῶμα, ατος, τό,

the body *of an animal;* a *living* body, Mat. 5.29, 30; 6.22, 23, 25. Ja. 3.3; a person, individual, 1 Co. 6.16; a *dead* body, corpse, carcass, Mat. 14.12; 27.52, 58. He. 13.11; the *human* body *considered as the seat and occasion of moral imperfection, as inducing to sin through its appetites and passions,* Ro. 7.24; 8.13; *genr.* a body, a material substance, 1 Co. 15.37, 38, 40; the substance, reality, *as opp. to* ἡ σκιά, Col. 2.17; *in N.T., met.* the *aggregate* body *of believers,* the body *of the church,* Ro. 12.5. Col. 1.18, et al.: *whence*

Σωματικός, ή, όν,
    bodily, of or belonging to the body, 1 Ti. 4.8; corporeal, material, Lu. 3.22: *whence*
Σωματικῶς,
    adv. bodily, in a bodily frame, Col. 2.9.
Σωρεύω, (σωρός, a heap)
    to heap or pile up, Ro. 12.20; *met. pass.* to be laden *with sins,* 2 Ti. 3.6.
Σωτήρ, ῆρος, ὁ, (σώζω)
    a saviour, preserver, deliverer, Lu. 1.47; 2.11. Ac. 5.31, et al.: *whence*
Σωτηρία, ας, ἡ,
    a saving, preservation, Ac. 27.34. He. 11.7; deliverance, Lu. 1.69, 71. Ac. 7.25; salvation, *spiritual and eternal,* Lu. 1.77; 19.9. Ac. 4.12. Re. 7.10; a being placed in a condition of salvation *by an embracing of the Gospel,* Ro. 10.1, 10. 2 Ti. 3.15; means or opportunity of salvation, Ac. 13.26. Ro. 11.11. He. 2.3, et al.; ἡ σωτηρία, the *promised* deliverance *by the Messiah,* Jno. 4.22.
Σωτήριος, ου, ὁ, ἡ, (σωτήρ)
    imparting salvation, saving, Tit. 2.11; *neut.* τὸ σωτήριον, *equivalent to* σωτηρία, Lu. 2.30; 3.6. Ac. 28.28. Eph. 6.17.
Σωφρονέω, ῶ, (σώφρων)
    f. ήσω, a.1. ἐσωφρόνησα,
    to be of a sound mind, be in one's right mind, be sane, Mar. 5.15; to be calm, 2 Co. 5.13; to be sober-minded, sedate, staid, Tit. 2.6. 1 Pe. 4.7; to be of a modest, humble mind, Ro. 12.3.
Σωφρονίζω, (fr. same)
    f. ίσω,
    pr. to render *any one* σώφρων, to restore to a right mind; to make sober minded, to steady *by exhortation and guidance,* Tit. 2.4: *whence*
Σωφρονισμός, οῦ, ὁ,
    a rendering sound-minded; calm vigour of mind, Tit. 1.7.
Σωφρόνως, (σώφρων)
    adv. in the manner of a person in his right mind; soberly, staidly, temperately, 2 Ti. 2.12.
Σωφροσύνη, ης, ἡ,
    sanity, soundness of mind, a sane mind, Ac. 26.25; *female* modesty, 1 Ti. 2.9, 15: *from*
Σώφρων, ονος, ὁ, ἡ, (σῶς, sound & φρήν)
    184of a sound mind, sane; staid, temperate, discreet, 1 Ti. 3.2. Tit. 1.8; 2.2; modest, chaste, Tit. 2.5.

Τ, τ, Ταῦ

Ταβέρνη, ης, ἡ, (Lat. *taberna*)
    a tavern, inn; Τρεῖς Ταβέρναι, the Three Taverns, *the name of a small place on the Apprian road, according to Antoninus, 33 Roman miles from Rome,* Ac. 28.15.

Ταβιθά, ή, (Aram. אתיבט)
i.q. Δορκάς, an antelope, Ac. 9.36, 40.

Τάγμα, ατος, τό, (τάσσω)
pr. any thing placed in order; in N.T., order of succession, 1 Co. 15.23.

Τακτός, ή, όν, (fr. same)
pr. arranged; fixed, appointed, set, Ac. 12.21.

Ταλαιπωρέω, ῶ, (ταλαίπωρος)
f. ήσω, p τεταλαιπώρηκα,
to endure severe labour and hardship; to be harassed; to suffer compunction, Ja. 4.9.

Ταλαιπωρία, ας, ή,
toil, difficulty, hardship; calamity, misery, distress, Ro. 3.16. Ja. 5.1: from

Ταλαίπωρος, ου, ό, ή,
pr. enduring severe effort and hardship; hence, wretched, miserable, afflicted, Ro. 7.24. Re. 3.17.

Ταλαντιαῖος, αία, αῖον,
of a talent weight, weighing a talent, Re. 16.21: from

Τάλαντον, ου, τό, (ταλάω, to sustain)
the scale of a balance; a talent, which as a weight was among the Jews equivalent to 3000 shekels, i.e. as usually estimated, 114lbs. 15dwts. Troy, while the Attic talent, on the usual estimate, was only equal to 56lbs. 11oz. troy; and as a denomination of money, it was equal among the former to 342£. 3s. 9d., or if reckoned of gold, 5,475£., and among the latter to 198£. 15s., or 225£., or 243£. 15s. sterling, according to various estimates, Mat. 18.24; 25.15, 16, 20, 24, 25, 28.

Ταλιθά, (Aram. אתילט)
talitha, i.q. κοράσιον, a damsel, maiden, Mar. 5.41.

Ταμεῖον, ου, τό, equivalent to ταμιεῖον, (ταμιεύω, to be ταμίας, manager, storekeeper)
a storehouse, granary, barn, Lu. 12.24; a chamber, closet, place of retirement and privacy, Mat. 6.6; 24.26. Lu. 12.3.

Τανῦν,
i.e. τά νῦν, q.v.

Τάξις, εως, ή, (τάσσω)
order, regular disposition, arrangement; order, series, succession, Lu. 1.8; an order, distinctive class, as of priests, He. 5.6; 7.11; order, good order, 1 Co. 14.40; orderliness, well regulated conduct, Col. 2.5.

Ταπεινός, ή, όν,
low in situation, of condition, humble, poor, mean, depressed, Lu. 1.52. 2 Co. 7.6. Ja. 1.9; met. of the mind, humble, lowly, modest, Mat. 11.29. Ro. 12.16, et al.

Ταπεινοφροσύνη, ης, ή,
lowliness or humility of mind and deportment, modesty, Ac. 20.19. Ep. 4.2. Phi. 2.3, et al.: (N.T.) from

Ταπεινόφρων, (ταπεινός & φρήν)
humble-minded, v.r., 1 Pe. 3.8. L.G.

Ταπεινόω, ῶ, (ταπεινός)
f. ώσω, a.1. ἐταπείνωσα,
to bring low, depress, level, Lu. 3.5; met. to humble, abase, Phi. 2.8; mid. to descend to, or live in, a humble condition, 2 Co. 11.7; Phi. 4.12; to humble, depress the pride of any one, Mat. 18.4; mid. to humble one's self, exhibit humility and contrition, Ja. 4.10; to humble with respect to hopes and expectations, to depress with disappointment, 2 Co. 12.21: whence

Ταπείνωσις, εως, ή,

depression; meanness, low estate, abject condition, Lu. 1.48. Ac. 8.33. Phi. 3.21. Ja. 1.10.

Ταράσσω, v. ττω,

    f. ξω, a.1. ἐτάραξα, p. pass. τετάραγμαι, a.1. pass. ἐταράχθην,

    to agitate, trouble, *as water,* Jno. 5.4, 7; *met.* to agitate, trouble *the mind; with fear,* to terrify, put in consternation, Mat. 2.3; 14.26; *with grief,* &c., to disquiet, affect with grief, anxiety, &c., Jno. 12.27; 13.21; *with doubt,* &c., to unsettle, perplex, Ac. 15.24. Ga. 1.7, et al.; *whence*

Ταρᾰχή, ῆς, ἡ,

    agitation, troubling, *of water,* Jno. 5.4; *met.* commotion, tumult, Mat. 13.8.

Τάρᾰχος, ου, ὁ

    agitation, commotion; 185perturbation, consternation, terror, Ac. 12.18; excitement, tumult, public contention, Ac. 19.23.

Ταρσεύς, έως, ὁ,

    of, or a native of Τάρσος, Tarsus, *the metropolis of Cilicia,* Ac. 9.11; 21.39.

Ταρταρόω, ῶ, (Τάρταρος, Tartarus, *which in the mythology of the ancients was that part of Hades where the wicked were confined and tormented*)

    to cast or thrust down to Tartarus or Gehenna, 2 Pe. 2.4. N.T.

Τάσσω, v. ττω,

    f. ξω, a.1. ἔταξα, p. pass. τέταγμαι,

    to arrange; to set, appoint, *in a certain station,* Lu. 7.8. Ro. 13.1; to set, devote, *to a pursuit,* 1 Co. 16.15; to dispose, frame, *for an object,* Ac. 13.48; to arrange, appoint, *place or time,* Mat. 28.16. Ac. 28.23; to allot, assign, Ac. 22.10; to settle, decide. Ac. 15.2.

Ταῦρος, ου, ὁ,

    a bull, beeve, Mat. 22.4, et al.

Ταὐτά,

    by crasis for τὰ αὐτά, the same things, 1 Th. 2.14; κατὰ ταὐτά, after the same manner, thus, so Lu. 6.23, 26; 17.30.

Ταφή, ῆς, ἡ, (θάπτω)

    burial, the act of burying, sepulture, Mat. 27.7.

Τάφος, ου, ὁ, (fr. same)

    a sepulchre, Mat. 23.27, 29; 27.61, 64, 66; 28.1; *met.* Ro. 3.13.

Τάχα, (ταχύς)

    adv. pr. quickly, soon; perhaps, possibly, Ro. 5.7. Phile. 15.

Ταχέως, (fr. same)

    adv. quickly, speedily; soon, shortly, 1 Co. 4.19. Ga. 1.6; hastily, Lu. 14.21; 16.6, et al.; with inconsiderate haste, 1 Ti. 5.22.

Ταχῑνός, ή, όν, (fr. same)

    swift, speedy, 2 Pe. 2.1; near at hand, impending, 2 Pe. 1.14.

Τάχιον, (pr. neut. of ταχίων, camparat. of ταχύς)

    adv. more swiftly, more quickly, more speedily, Jno. 20.4. He. 13.19; quickly, speedily, Jno. 13.27, et al.

Τάχιστα, (pr. neut. of the superlat. of ταχύς)

    adv. most quickly, most speedily, very quickly; ὡς τάχιστα, as soon as possible, Ac. 17.15.

Τάχος, εος, τό, (ταχύς)

    swiftness, speed, quickness, celerity; ἐν τάχει, with speed, quickly, speedily; soon, shortly, Lu. 18.8. Ac. 25.4; hastily, immediately, Ac. 12.7, et al.

Ταχύ,

adv. quickly, speedily, hastily, Mat. 28.7, 8; soon, shortly, immediately, Mat. 5.25; suddenly, Re. 2.5, 16; 3.11, et al.; easily, readily, Mar. 9.39; *pr. neut. of*

Ταχύς, εῖα, ύ,
swift, fleet, quick; *met.* ready, prompt, Ja. 1.19.

Τε,
a combinatory enclitic particle serving either as a lightly appending link, Ac. 1.15; and, Ac. 2.3; *or as an inclusive prefix,* Lu. 12.45; both, Lu. 24.20. Ac. 26.16, et al.

Τεῖχος, εος, τό,
a wall *of a city,* Ac. 9.25, et al.

Τεκμήριον, ίου, τό, (τέκμαρ, a fixed mark)
a sign, indubitable token, clear proof, Ac. 1.3.

Τεκνίον, ου, τό, (dimin. of τέκνον)
a little child; τεκνία, *an endearing compellation,* my dear children, Jno. 13.33. Ga. 4.19. 1 Jno 2.1, et al.

Τεκνογονέω, ῶ, (τέκνον & γίγνομαι)
f. ήσω,
to bear children; to rear a family, 1 Ti. 5.14; (L.G.) *whence*

Τεκνογονία, ας, ή,
the bearing of children, the rearing of a family, 1 Ti. 2.15. N.T.

Τέκνον, ου, τό, (τίκτω)
a child, a son or daughter, Mat. 2.18. Lu. 1.7, et al.; *pl.* descendants, posterity, Mat. 3.9. Ac. 2.39; child, son, *as a term of endearment,* Mat. 9.2. Mar. 2.5; 10.24; *pl.* children, inhabitants, people, *of a city,* Mat. 23.37. Lu. 19.44; *fr. the Heb., met.* a child or son *in virtue of discipleship,* 1 Co. 4.17. 1 Ti. 1.2. 2 Ti. 1.2. Tit. 1.4. Phile. 10. 3 Jno. 4; a child *in virtue of gracious acceptance,* Jno. 1.12; 11.52. Ro. 8.16, 21. 1 Jno. 3.1; a child *in virtue of spiritual conformity,* Jno. 8.39. Phi. 2.15. 1 Jno. 3.10; a child of, one characterised by, *some condition or quality,* Mat. 11.19. Eph. 2.3; 5.8. 1 Pe. 1.14. 2 Pe. 2.14.

Τεκνοτροφέω, ῶ, (τέκνον & τρέφω)
f. ήσω,
to rear a family, 1 Ti. 5.10.

Τέκτων, ονος, ὁ,
an artizan; *and spc.* one who works in wood, a carpenter, Mat. 13.55. Mar. 6.3.

Τέλειος, εία, ειου, (τέλος)
brought to completion; fully accomplished, 186fully developed, Ja. 1.4; fully realised, thorough, 1 Jno. 4.18; complete, entire, *as opposed to what is partial and limited,* 1 Co.. 13.10; full grown, of ripe age, 1 Co. 14.20. Eph. 4.13. He. 5.14; fully accomplished *in Christian enlightenment,* 1 Co. 2.6. Phi. 3.15. Col. 1.28; perfect *in some point of character,* without shortcoming *in respect of a certain standard,* Mat. 5.48; 19.21. Col. 4.12. Ja. 1.4; 3.2; perfect, consummate, Ro. 12.2. Ja. 1.17, 25; *comp.* of higher excellence and efficiency, He. 9.11: *whence*

Τελειότης, τητος, ή,
completeness, perfectness, Col. 3.14; ripeness *of knowledge or practice,* He. 6.1. L.G.

Τελειόω, ῶ,
f. ώσω, p. τετελείωκα, a.1. ἐτελείωσα,
to execute fully, discharge, Jno. 4.34; 5.36; 17.4; to reach the end of, run through, finish, Lu. 2.43. Ac. 20.24; to consummate, place in a condition of finality, He. 7.19; to perfect *a person,* advance *a person* to final completeness *of character,* He. 2.10; 5.9; 7.28; to perfect *a person,* advance *a person* to a completeness *of its kink, which needs no further provision* He. 9.9; 10.1, 14; *pass.* to receive fulfilment, Jno. 19.28; to

be brought to the goal, to reach the end of one's course, Lu. 13.32. Phi. 3.12. He. 11.40; 12.23; to be fully developed, 2 Co. 12.9. Ja. 2.22. 1 Jno. 2.5 4.12, 17; to be completely organised, to be closely embodied, Jno. 17.23.

Τελείως,
    adv. perfectly, 1 Pe. 1.13.

Τελείωσις, εως, ἡ,
    a completing; a fulfilment, accomplishment *of predictions, promises,* &c. Lu. 1.45; finality *of function,* completeness *of operation and effect,* He. 7.11.

Τελειωτής, οῦ, ὁ,
    a finisher, one who completes and perfects *a thing;* one who brings through to final attainment, He. 12.2; cf ch. 2.10.

Τελεσφορέω, ῶ, (τελεσφόρος, fr. <u>τέλος</u> & <u>φέρω</u>)
    f. ήσω,
    to bring to maturity, *as fruits,* &c.; *met.* Lu. 8.14.

Τελευτάω, ῶ,
    f. ήσω, p. τετελεύτηκα, a.1. ἐτελεύτησα,
    to end, finish, complete; *absol.* to end *one's life,* to die, Mat. 2.19; 15.4; 22.25, et al.: *from*

Τελευτή, ῆς, ἡ,
    a finishing, end, *hence,* end *of life,* death, decease, Mat. 2.15: *from*

Τελέω, ῶ,
    f. έσω, p. τετέλεκα, a.1. ἐτέλεσα,
    to finish, complete, conclude, *an operation,* Mat. 11.1; 13.53; 19.1, et al.; to finish *a circuit,* Mat. 10.23; to fulfil, to carry out into full operation, Ro. 2.27; Ga. 5.16. Ja. 2.8; to pay *dues,* Mat. 17.24, et al.; *pass.* to be fulfilled, realised, Lu. 12.50; 18.31, et al; *of time,* to be ended, Re. 15.8; 20.3, 5, 7: *from*

Τέλος, εος, τό,
    an end attained, consummation; an end, closing act, Mat. 24.6, 14. 1 Co. 15.24, et al.; full performance, perfect discharge, Ro. 10.4; fulfilment, realisation, Lu. 22.37; final dealing, *developed* issue, Ja. 5.11; issue, final stage, 1 Co. 10.11; issue, result, Mat. 26.58. Ro. 6.21, 22. 1 Pe. 1.9; *anti-typical* issue, 2 Co. 3.13; *practical* issue, 1 Ti. 1.5; ultimate destiny, Phi. 3.19. He. 6.8. 1 Pe. 4.17; an impost, due, Mat. 17.25. Ro. 13.7; εἰς τέλος, to the full, 1 Th. 2.16; εἰς τέλος, continually, Lu. 18.5; εἰς τέλος, μέχρι, ἄχρι τέλους, throughout, Mat. 10.22. Mar. 13.13. Jno. 13.1. He. 3.6, 14; 6.11. Re. 2.26.

Τελώνης, ου, ὁ, (<u>τέλος</u> & <u>ὠνέομαι</u>)
    one who farms the public revenues; *in N.T.,* a publican, collector of imposts, tax-gatherer, Mat. 5.46; 9.10, 11; 10.3, et al.: *whence*

Τελώνιον, ίου, τό,
    a custom-house, toll-house; collector's office, Mat. 9.9. Mar. 2.14. Lu. 5.27.

Τέρας, ἄτος, τό,
    a prodigy, portent, Ac. 2.19; a signal act, wonder, miracle, Jno. 4.48. Ac. 2.43, et al.

Τεσσαράκοντα, οἱ, αἱ, τά, (<u>τέσσαρες</u>)
    forty, Mat. 4.2, et al.

Τεσσαρακονταετής, έος, οὗς, ὁ, ἡ, (preced. & <u>ἔτος</u>)
    of forty years, Ac. 7.23; 13.18.

Τέσσᾰρες, At. τέτταρες, ων, οἱ, αἱ, neut. τέσσαρα, At. τέτταρα, ων,
    four, Mat. 24.31. Mar. 2.3, et al.

Τεσσαρεσκαιδέκατος, η, ον, (<u>τέσσαρες</u>, <u>καί</u>, & <u>δέκατος</u>)
    the fourteenth, Ac. 27.27, 33.

Τεταρταῖος, αία, αῖον,

on the forth day, Jno. 11.39: *from*

Τέταρτυς, η, ον, (τέσσαρες)
187fourth, Mat. 14.25, et al.

Τετράγωνος, ου, ό, ή, (τέσσαρες & γωνία
four-angled, quadrangular, square, Re. 21.16.

Τετράδιον, ίου, τό, (dimin. of τετράς)
a set of four, quaternion; a detachment of four *men,* Ac. 12.4. L.G.

Τετρακισχίλιοι, αι, α, (τετράκις, four times & χίλιοι)
four thousand, Mat. 15.38, et al.

Τετρακόσιοι, αι, α,
four hundred, Ac. 5.36, et al.

Τετράμηνος, ου, ό, ή, τό, -ον, (τέσσαρες & μήν)
of four months, four months in duration, Jno. 4.35.

Τετραπλόος, οῦς, όη, ῆ, όον, οῦν,(τετράς)
quadruple, fourfold, Lu. 19,8.

Τετράπους, οδος, ό, ή, τό, -ουν, (τέσσαρες& πούς)
four-footed; *pl.* τὰ τετράποδα, sc. ζῶα, quadrupeds, Ac. 10.12; 11.6. Ro. 1.23.

Τετραρχέω, ῶ,
f. ήσω,
to be tetrarch, rule as tetrarch, Lu. 3.11, *ter.*: (L.G.) *from*

Τετράρχης, ου, ό, (τετράς & ἄρχω)
a tetrarch; *pr. one of a sovereign body of four; in N.T., according to later usage, a provincial sovereign under the Roman emperor,* Mat. 14.1. Lu. 3.19; 9.7. Ac. 13.1.

Τεφρόω, ῶ, (τέφρά, ashes)
f. ώσω,
to reduce to ashes, to consume, destroy, 2 Pe. 2.6.

Τέχνη, ης, ή,
art, skill, Ac. 17.29; an art, trade, craft, Ac. 18.3. R. 18.22: *whence*

Τεχνίτης, ου, ό,
an artisan, artificer, workman, mechanic, Ac. 19.24, 38. Re. 18.22; an architect, builder, He. 11.10. (ῑ).

Τήκω
f. ξω,
to dissolve, render liquid; *pass.* to be liquefied, melt, 2 Pe. 3.12.

Τηλαυγῶς, (τηλαυγής, widely resplendent, fr. τῆλε, afar, & αὐγή)
clearly, plainly, distinctly, Mar. 8.25.

Τηλικοῦτος, αύτη, οῦτο, (τηλίκος, so great)
so great, 2 Co. 1.10. He. 2.3. Ja. 3.4. Re. 16.18.

Τηρέω, ῶ, (τηρός)
f. ήσω, p. τετήρηκα, a.1. ἐτήρησα,
to keep watch upon, guard, Mat. 27.26, 54; 28.4. Ac. 12.6; to watch over *protectively,* guard, 1 Jno. 5.18. Re. 16.15; to mark attentively, to heed, Re. 1.3; to observe *practically,* keep strictly, Mat. 19.17; 23.3; 28.20. Mar. 7.9. Jno. 8.51, et al.; to perserve, shield, Jno. 17.15; to store up, reserve, Jno. 2.10; 12.7. 1 Pe. 1.4. 2 Pe. 2.4, 9, 17, et al.; to keep in custoday, Ac. 12.5; 16.23, et al.; to maintain, Eph. 4.3. 2 Ti. 4.7; to keep *in a condition,* Jno. 17.11, 12. 1 Co. 7.37. 2 Co. 11.9. 1 Ti. 5.22. Ja. 1.27: *whence*

Τήρησις, εως, ή,
a keeping, custody; *meton.* a place of custody, prison, ward, Ac. 4.3; *met. practical* observance, strict performance, 1 Co. 7.19.

Τίθημι
f. θήσω, a.1. ἔθηκα, p τέθεικα, a.2. ἔθην, a.2. mid. ἐθέμην, pass. a.1. ἐτέθην, p. τέθειμαι, plu. p. ἐτεθείμην,
to place, set, lay, Mat. 5.15. Mar. 6.56. Lu. 6.48. et al.; to produce *at table,* Jno. 2.10; to deposit, lay, Mat. 27.60. Lu. 23.53, Ac. 3.2; to day down, Lu. 19.21, 22. Jno. 10.11, 15, 17, 18. 1 Jno. 3.16, et al.; to lay aside, put off, Jno. 13.4; to allocate, assign, Mat. 24.51. Lu. 12.46; to set, constitute, appoint, Jno. 15.16. Ac. 13.47. He. 1.2; to render, make, Mat. 22.44. Ro. 4.17. 1 Co. 9.18; *mid.* to put *in custody,* Mat. 14.3. Ac. 4.3; to reserve, Ac. 1.7; to commit *as a matter of change,* 2 Co. 5.19; to set, *with design, in a certain arrangement or position,* Ac. 20.28. 1 Co. 12.18, 28. 1 Th. 5.9. 1 Ti. 1.12; *pass.* 1 Ti. 2.7. 2 Ti. 1.11. 1 Pe. 2.8; τιθέναι τὰ γόνατα, to kneel down, Mar. 15.19. Lu. 22.41. Ac. 7.60; 9.40; 20.36; 21.5; τίθεσθαι ἐν τῇ καρδίᾳ, to lay to heart, ponder, Lu. 1.66; *also,* εἰς τὰς καρδίας, Lu. 21.14; τίθεσθαι ἐν τῇ καρδίᾳ, to design, resolve, Ac. 5.4; *also,* ἐν πνεύματι, Ac. 19.21; *also,* βουλήν, Ac. 27.12; τίθεσθαι εἰς τὰ ὦτα, to give attentive audience to, to listen to retentively, Lu. 9.44.

Τίκτω,
f. τέξω, & τέξομαι, a.2. ἔτεκον, p. τέτοκα, a.1. pass. ἐτέχθην,
to bear, bring forth *children,* Mat. 1.21, 23, et al.; *trop.* to bear, produce, *as the earth,* yield, He. 6.7; *met.* to give birth to, Ja. 1.15.

Τίλλω,
f. τιλῶ,
188to pull, pluck off, Mat. 21.1. Mar. 2.23. Lu. 6.1.

Τῑμάω, ῶ,
f. ήσω, a.1. ἐτίμησα,
to estimate in respect of worth; to hold in estimation, respect, honour, reverence, Mat. 15.4, 5, 8; 19.19. Mar. 7.10, et al.; to honour *with reverent service,* Jno. 5.23, *quater;* 8.49; to treat with honour, manifest consideration towards, Ac. 28.10; to treat graciouosly, visit with marks of favour, Jno. 12.26; *mid.* to price, Mat. 27.9: *from*

Τῑμή, ῆς, ἡ, (τίω)
a pricing, estimate of worth; price, value, Mat. 27.9; price *paid,* Mat. 27.6; *meton.* a thing of price, *and collectively,* precious things, Re. 21.24, 26; preciousness, 1 Pe. 2.7; *substantial* value, *real* worth, Col. 2.23; careful regard, honour, state of honour, dignity, Ro. 9.21. He. 5.4; honour *conferred,* observance, veneration, Ro. 2.7, 10; 12.10; mark of favour and consideration, Ac. 28.10: *whence*

Τίμιος, α, ον
precious, costly, of great price, 1 Co. 3.12. Re. 18.12; precious, dear, valuable, Ac. 20.24. 1 Pe. 1.7, 19; honoured, esteemed, respected, Ac. 5.34. He. 13.4: *whence*

Τιμιότης, τητος, ἡ
preciousness, costliness; *meton.* precious things, valuable merchandise, Re. 18.19. N.T.

Τιμωρέω, ῶ, (τιμωρός, an aider, an avenger, fr. τιμή & αἴρω)
f. ήσω, a.1. pass. ἐτιμωρήθην,
to succour, to avenge, *any one; in N.T.,* to punish, Ac. 22.5; 26.11: *whence*

Τιμωρία, ας, ἡ,
punishment, He. 10.29.

Τίνω,
f. τίσω,
to pay; to pay *a penalty,* incur *punishment,* 2 Th. 1.9.

Τις, ὁ, ἡ, τό, -τι, gen. τινός,

indefinite pron., a certain one, some one, Mat. 12.47, et al.; *pl.* some, certain, several, Lu. 8.2. Ac. 9.19. 2 Pe. 3.16, et al.; one, a person, Mat. 12.29. Lu. 14.8. Jno. 6.50, et al.; *combined with the name of an individual,* one, Mar. 15.21, et al.; as it were, in a manner, a kind of, He. 10.27. Ja. 1.18; any *whatever,* Mat. 8.28. Lu. 11.36. Ro. 8.39, et al.; τις, somebody *of consequence,* Ac. 5.36; τι, something *of consequence,* Ga. 2.6; 6.3; τι, any thing *at all,* any thing *worth account,* 1 Co. 3.7; 10.19; τι, at all, Phi. 3.15. Phile. 18.

Τίς, τί, τίνος,
    interrogative pron. strictly of direct inquiry, who? what! Mat. 3.7; 5.13; 19.27; *equivalent to* πότερος, whether? which *of two things?* Mat. 9.5. Phi. 1.22: *neut.* τί, why? wherefore? Mat. 8.26; 9.11, 14; τί ὅτι, why is it that? Mar. 2.16. Jno. 14.22; *neut.* τί, what? *as an emphatic interrogative,* Ac. 26.8; τί, how very! v.r. Mat. 7.14; *in indirect question,* Mat. 10.11; 12.3, et al.

Τίτλος, ου, ὁ, (Lat. *titulus*)
    an inscribed scroll, superscription, Jno. 19.19, 20.

Τοιγαροῦν, (τοι, γάρ & οὖν)
    a doubly strengthened form of the particle τοι, well then, so then, wherefore, 1 Th. 4.8. He. 12.1.

Τοίνυν,
    a strengthening of the particle τοι, *by the enclitic* νυν, well then, therefore now, therefore, Lu. 20.25. 1 Co. 9.26, et al.

Τοιόσδε, τοιάδε, τοιόνδε,
    a more pointedly demonstrative form of τοῖος, such as this; such as follows, 2 Pe. 1.17.

Τοιοῦτος, τοιαύτη, τοιοῦτο & τοιοῦτον,
    a lengthened and more demonstrative form of τοῖος, such, such like, of this kind or sort, Mat. 18.5; 19.14; such, so great, Mat. 9.8. Mar. 6.2; ὁ τοιοῦτος, such a fellow, Ac. 22.22; *also,* the one alluded to, 1 Co. 1.5. 2 Co. 2.6, 7; 12.2, 3, 5.

Τοῖχος, ου, ὁ,
    a wall *of a building, as distinct from a city wall or fortification* (τεῖχος), Ac. 23.3.

Τόκος, ου, ὁ, (τίκτω)
    a brining forth; offspring; *met.* produce *of money lent,* interest, usury, Mat. 25.27. Lu. 19.23.

Τολμάω, ῶ,
    f. ήσω, a.1. ἐτόλμησα,
    to assume resolution *to do a thing,* Mar. 15.43. Ro. 5.7. Phi. 1.14; to dare, Ac. 5.13; 7.32; to presume, Mat. 22.46. Mar. 12.34. Lu 20.40. Jno 21.12. Ro. 15.18. 2 Co. 10.12. Ju. 9; to have the face, 1 Co. 6.1; *absol.* to assume a bold bearing, 2 Co. 10.2; 11.21.

Τολμηρότερος, α, ον, (compar. of τολμηρός, bold, fr. τολμάω)
    bolder 189*neut.* τολμηρότερον, *as an adv.* more boldly, with more confidence, more freely, Ro. 15.15.

Τολμητής, οῦ, ὁ, (τολμάω)
    one who is bold; *in a bad sense,* a presumptuous, audacious person, 2 Pe. 2.10.

Τομώτερος, α, ον, (compar. of τομος, cutting, sharp, keen, fr. τέμνω, to cut)
    keener, sharper, He. 4.10.

Τόξον, ου, τό,
    a bow, Re. 6.2.

Τοπάζιον, ου τό,
    a topaz, *a gem of a yellowish colour, different from the modern topaz,* Re. 21.20. L.G.

Τόπος, ου, ὁ,

a place, locality, Mat. 12.43. Lu. 6.17, et al.; a *limited* spot or ground, Mat. 24.15; 27.33. Jno. 4.20. Ac. 6.13, et al.; a *precise* spot or situation, Mat. 28.6. Mar. 16.6. Lu. 14.9, et al.; a *dwelling* place, abode, mansion, dwelling, seat, Jno. 14.2, 3. Ac. 4.31. a place *of ordinary deposit,* Mat. 26.52; a place, passage *in a book,* Lu. 4.17; place *occupied,* room, space, Lu. 2.7; 14.9, 22; place, opportunity, Ac. 25.16. He. 12.17; place, condition, position, 1 Co. 14.16.

Τοσοῦτος, τοσαύτη, τοσοῦτο & τοσοῦτον,

a lengthened and more demonstrative form of τόσος, so great, so much, Mat. 8.10; 15.33; so long, *of time,* Jno. 14.9; *pl.* so many, Mat. 15.33, et al.

Τότε,

adv. *of time,* then, at that time, Mat. 2.17; 3.5; 11.20; then, thereupon, Mat. 12.29; 13.26; 25.31; ἀπὸ τότε, from that time, Mat. 4.17; 16.21; ὁ τότε, which then was, 2 Pe. 3.6.

Τοὐναντίον, (by crasis for τὸ ἐναντίον)

that which is opposite; *as an adv.* on the contrary, on the other hand, 2 Co. 2.7. Ga. 2.7. 1 Pe. 3.9.

Τοὔνομα, (by crasis for τὸ ὄνομα)

the name; *in the acc.* by name, Mat. 27.57.

Τουτέστι, (by crasis for τοῦτ᾽ ἔστι)

that is, which signifies, which implies, Ac. 1.19; 19.4, et al.

Τράγος, ου, ὁ,

a he-goat, He. 9.12, 13, 19; 10.4.

Τράπεζα, ης, ἡ, (τετράς, four, & πέζα, a foot)

a table, an eating-table, Mat. 15.27. Mar. 7.28. He. 9.2; *by impl.* a meal, feast, Ro. 11.9. 1 Co. 10.21; a table or counter *of a money-changer,* Mat. 21.12; a bank, Lu. 19.23; *by impl., pl.* money matters, Ac. 6.2: *whence*

Τραπεζίτης, ου, ὁ,

a money-charger, broker, banker, *who exchanges or loans money for a premium,* Mat. 25.27. (ῑ.)

Τραῦμα, ατος, τό, (τιτρώσκω)

a wound, Lu. 10.34: *whence*

Τραυματίζω,

f. ίσω, a.1. ἐτραυμάτισα,

to wound, Lu. 20.12. Ac. 19.16.

Τραχηλίζω,

f. ίσω, p. pass. τετραχήλισμαι,

pr. to gripe the neck; to bend the neck back *so as to make bare or expose the throat, as in slaughtering animals,* &c.; *met.* to lay bare *the view,* He. 4.13: *from*

Τράχηλος, ου, ὁ,

the neck, Mat. 18.6, et al.; ἐπιθεῖναι ζυγὸν ἐπὶ τὸν τράχηλον, to put a yoke upon the neck *of any one, met.* to bind to a burdensome observance, Ac. 15.10; ὑποτιθέναι τὸν τράχηλον, to lay down one's neck *under the axe of the executioner,* to imperil one's life, Ro. 16.4.

Τρᾱχύς, εῖα, ύ,

rough, rugged, uneven, Lu. 3.5; εἰς τραχεῖς τόπους, on a rocky shore, Ac. 27.29.

Τρεῖς, οἱ, αἱ, τά, τρία,

three, Mat. 12.40, et al.

Τρέμω, (τρέω, idem)

to tremble, be agitated from fear, Mar. 5.33. Lu. 8.47. Ac. 9.6; *by impl.* to fear, be afraid, 2 Pe. 2.10.

Τρέφω,
> f. θρέψω, a.1. ἔθρεψα, p. pass. τέθραμμαι,
> to thicken; to nourish; to feed, support, cherish, provide for, Mat. 6.26; 25.37, et al.; to bring up, rear, educate, Lu. 4.16; to gorge, to pamper, Ja. 5.5.

Τρέχω,
> f. θρέξομαι, & δραμοῦμαι, a.2. ἔδραμον,
> to run, Mat. 27.48; 28.8, et al.; to run *a race,* 1 Co. 9.24; *met.* 1 Co. 9.24, 26. He. 12.1; *in N.T.,* to run *a certain course of conduct,* Ga. 5.7; to run *a course of exertion,* Ro. 9.16. Ga. 2.2. Phi. 2.16; to run, to progress freely, to advance rapidly, 2 Th. 3.1.

Τριάκοντα, οἱ, αἱ, τά, (τρεῖς)
> thirdy, Mat. 13.8, 23, et al.

Τριακόσιοι, αι, α, (τρεῖς)
> three hundred, Mar. 14.5. Jno. 12.5.

Τρίβολος, ου, ὁ, (τρεῖς & βέλος)
> *pr.* 190three-pronged; *as subst.* a caltrop; *a plant,* land-caltrop, a thorn, Mat. 7.16. He. 6.8.

Τρίβος, ου, ἡ, (τρίβω, to run, wear)
> a beaten track; a road, highway, Mat. 3.3. Mar. 1.3. Lu. 3.4.

Τριετία, ας, ἡ, (τρεῖς & ἔτος)
> the space of three years, Ac. 20.31.

Τρίζω,
> f. ίσω,
> a creak, to utter a creaking, stridulous, grating sound; to gnash, grind *the teeth,* Mar. 9.18.

Τρίμηνον, ου, τό, (τρεῖς & μήν)
> the space of three months, He. 11.23.

Τρίς, (τρεῖς)
> *adv.* three times, thrice, Mat. 26.34, 75, et al.; ἐπὶ τρίς, to the extent of thrice, as many as three times, Ac. 10.16; 11.10.

Τρίστεγον, ου, τό, (neut. of τρίστεγος, having three stories, fr. τρεῖς & στέγη)
> the third floor, third story, Ac. 20.9. L.G.

Τρισχίλιοι, αι, α, (τρεῖς & χίλιοι)
> three thousand, Ac. 2.41.

Τρίτος, η, ον, (τρεῖς)
> third, Mat. 20.3; 27.64; ἐκ τρίτου, the third time, for the third time, Mat. 26.44; τὸ τρίτον, sc. μέρος, the third part, Re. 8.7, 12; τρίτον & τὸ τρίτον, *as an adv.,* the third time, for the third time, Mar. 14.41. Lu. 20.12, et al.

Τρίχϊνος, η, ον, (θρίξ, τριχός)
> of hair, made of hair, Re. 6.12.

Τρόμος, ου, ὁ, (τρέμω)
> *pr.* a trembling, quaking; trembling *from fear,* fear, terror, agitation of mind, Mar. 16.8; anxious diffidence, 1 Co. 2.3; reverence, veneration, awe, 2 Co. 7.15. Ep. 6.5. Phi. 2.12.

Τροπή, ῆς, ἡ, (τρέμω)
> a turning round; a turning back, change, mutation, Ja. 1.17.

Τρόπος, ου, ὁ, (fr. same)
> a turn; mode, manner, way, Jude 7; ὅν τρόπον, & καθ᾽ ὅν τρόπον, in which manner, as, even as, Mat. 23.37. Ac. 15.11, et al.; κατὰ μηδένα τρόπον, in no way, by no

means, 2 Th. 2.3; ἐν παντὶ τρόπῳ, & παντὶ τρόπῳ, in every way, by every means, Phi. 1.18. 2 Th. 3.16; turn *of mind or action,* habit, disposition, He. 13.5.

Τροποφορέω, ῶ, (τρόπος & φορέω)

    f. ἥσω, a.1. ἐτροποφόρησα,

    bear with the disposition, manners, and conduct of *any one,* Ac. 13.18. L.G.

Τροφή, ῆς, ἡ, (τρέφω)

    nutriment, nourishment, food, Mat. 3.4, et al.; provision, victual, Mat. 24.45; sustenance, maintenance, Mat. 10.10; *met.* nutriment *of the mind,* He. 5.12, 14.

Τροφός, οῦ, ἡ, (fr. same)

    a nurse, 1 Th. 2.7.

Τροφοφορέω, ῶ, (τροφός & φορέω

    f. ἥσω,

    to sustain, provide for, cherish, v.r. Ac. 13.18. S.

Τροχιά, ᾶς, ἡ,

    a wheel-track; a track, way, path, *met.* He. 12.13: *from*

Τροχός, οῦ, ὁ, (τρέχω)

    pr. a runner; any thing orbicular, a wheel; drift, course, *with which signification the word is usually written* τρόχος, Ja. 3.6.

Τρύβλιον, ίου, τό,

    a bowl, dish, Mat. 26.23. Mar. 14.20.

Τρυγάω, ῶ, (τρύγη, ripe fruits)

    f. ἥσω, a.1. ἐτρύγησα,

    to harvest, gather, *fruits, and spec. grapes,* Lu. 6.44. Re. 14.18, 19.

Τρυγών, όνος, ἡ, (τρύζω, to murmer)

    a turtle-dove, Lu. 2.24.

Τρυμαλιά, ᾶς, ἡ, (τρύμη, fr. τρύω, to rub, wear)

    a hole, performation; eye *of a needle,* Mar. 10.25. Lu. 18.25.

Τρύπημα, ατος, τό, (τρυπάω, τρύπη, a hole, fr. τρύω)

    a hole; eye *of a needle,* Mat. 19.24.

Τρυφάω, ῶ,

    f. ἥσω, a.1. ἐτρύφησα,

    to live delicately and luxuriously, Ja. 5.5: *from*

Τρυφή, ῆς, ἡ, (θρύπτω, to break small, to enfeeble, enervate)

    delicate living, luxury, Lu. 7.25. 2 Pe. 2.13.

Τρώγω,

    f. τρώξομαι, a.2. ἔτρᾰγον,

    pr. to crunch; to eat, Mat. 24.38; *fr. the Heb.* ἄρτον τρώγειν, to take food, partake of a meal, Jno. 13.18.

Τυγχάνω,

    f. τεύξομαι, p. τετύχηκα & τέτευχα, a.2. ἔτυχον,

    to hit *an object;* to attain to, to obtain, acquire, enjoy, Lu. 20.35. Ac. 24.3, et al.; *intrans.* to happen, fall out, change; *part.* τυχών, οῦσα, όν, common, ordinary, Ac. 19.11; 28.2; *neut.* τυχόν, *as an adv.,* it may be, perchance, perhaps, 1 Co. 16.6; εἰ τύχοι, if it so 191happen, as the case may be, 1 Co. 14.10; 15.37; to be *in a certain condition,* Lu. 10.30.

Τυμπανίζω, (τύμπανον, a drum)

    f. ίσω, a.1. pass. ἐτυμπανίσθην,

    pr. to beat a drum; to drum upon; *in N.T.,* to bastinade, beat to death with rods and clubs, He. 11.35.

Τύπος, ου, ὁ,

pr. a blow; an impress; a print, mark, *of a wound inflicted,* Jno. 20.25; a delineation; an image, statue, Ac. 7.43; a formula, scheme, Ro. 6.17; form, purport, Ac. 23.25; a figure, counterpart, 1 Co. 10.6; an *anticipative* figure, type, Ro. 5.14. 1 Co. 10.11; a model, pattern, Ac. 7.44. He. 8.5; a *moral* pattern, Phi. 3.17. 1 Th. 1.7. 2 Th. 3.9. 1 Ti. 4.12. 1 Pe. 5.3.

Τύπτω,
>f. ψω, a.1. ἔτυψα,
>to beat, strike, smite, Mat. 24.49; 27.30, et al.; to beat *the breast, as expressive of grief, or strong emotion,* Lu. 18.13; 23.48; *in N.T., met.* to wound or shock *the conscience of any one,* 1 Co. 8.12; *fr. the Heb.* to smite *with evil,* punish, Ac. 23.3.

Τυρβάζω, (τύρβη, tumult)
>f. άσω,
>to stir up, render turbid; to throw into a state of perturbation, disquiet; *mid.* to trouble one's self, be troubled, be disquieted, Lu. 10.41.

Τύριος, ου, ὁ, ἡ,
>a Tyrian, an inhabitant of Τύρος, Tyre, Ac. 12.20.

Τυφλός, ή, όν,
>blind, Mat. 9.27, 28; 11.5; 12.22; *met. mentally* blind, Mat. 15.14; 23.16, et al.: *whence*

Τυφλόω, ῶ,
>f. ώσω, p. τετύφλωκα,
>to blind, render blind; *met.* Jno. 12.40. 1 Jno. 2.11. 2 Co. 4.4.

Τυφόω, ῶ, (τῦφος, smoke, fr. τύφω)
>f. ώσω, p. pass. τετύφωμαι,
>to besmoke; *met.* to possess with the fumes *of conceit; pass.* to be demented with conceit, puffed up, 1 Ti. 3.6; 6.4. 2 Ti. 3.4.

Τύφω,
>f. θύψω,
>to raise a smoke; *pass.* to emit smoke, smoke, smoulder, Mat. 12.20.

Τυφωνικός, ή, όν, (τυφῶν, typhon, a hurricane)
>stormy tempestuous, Ac. 27.14.

Τυχόν,
>*see* τυγχάνω.

Υ, υ, *Y ψῑλόν*

Ὑακίνθινος, η, ον,
>hyacinthine, resembling the hyacinth in colour, Re. 9.17: *from*

Ὑάκινθος, ου, ἡ,
>a hyacinth, *a gem resembling the colour of the* hyacinth flower, Re. 21.20.

Ὑάλῐνος, η, ον,
>made of glass; glassy, translucent, Re. 4.6: *from*

Ὕᾰλος, ου, ἡ,
>a transparent stone, crystal, *also,* glass, Re. 21.18, 21.

Ὑβρίζω,
>f. ίσω, a.1. ὕβρισα,
>to run riot; *trans.* to outrage, Mat. 22.6. Lu. 11.45, et al.: *from*

Ὕβρις, εως, ἡ,
>violent wantonness, insolence; contumelious treatment, outrage, 2 Co. 12.10; damage *by sea,* Ac. 27.10.

Ὑβριστής, οῦ, ὁ, (ὑβρίζω)
    an overbearing, wantonly violent person, Ro. 1.30. 1 Ti. 1.13.
Ὑγιαίνω,
    f. ανῶ,
    to be hale, sound, in health, Lu. 5.31; 7.10; to be safe and sound, Lu. 15.27; *met.* to be
    healthful or sound *in faith, doctrine,* &c., Tit. 1.13; 2.2; *part.* ὑγιαίνων, ουσα, ον,
    sound, pure, uncorrupted, 1 Ti. 1.10, et al.: *from*
Ὑγιής, έος, οὺς, ὁ, ἡ, τό, -ές,
    hale, sound, in health, Mat. 12.13; 15.31, et al.; *met. of doctrine,* sound, pure,
    wholesome, Tit. 2.8.
Ὑγρός, ά, όν, (ὕω, to wet)
    pr. wet, moist, humid; *used of a tree,* full of sap, fresh, green, Lu. 23.31.
Ὑδρία, ας, ἡ, (ὕδωρ)
    a water-pot, pitcher, Jno. 2.6, 7; a bucket, pail, Jno. 4.28.
Ὑδροποτέω, ῶ, (ὑδροπότης, ὕδωρ & πίνω)
    to be a water-drinker, 1 Ti. 5.23.
Ὑδρωπικός, ή, όν, (ὕδρωψ, the dropsy, fr. ὕδωρ)
    dropsical, Lu. 14.2.
Ὕδωρ, ὕδατος, τό,
    water, Mat. 3.11, 16; 14.28, 29; 17.15. Jno. 5.3, 4, 7; the watery fluid *of the
    pericardium,* Jno. 19.34; ὕδωρ ζῶν, living water, fresh flowing water, Jno. 4.11; *met.
    of spiritual refreshment,* Jno. 4.10; 7.38.
Ὑετός, οῦ, ὁ, (ὕω, to rain)
    rain, Ac. 14.17, et al.
Υἱοθεσία, ας, ἡ, (υἱός & τίθημι)
    192adoption, a placing in the condition of a son, Ro. 8.15, 23; 9.4. Ga. 4.5. Ep. 1.5.
    N.T.
Υἱός, οί, ὁ,
    a son, Mat. 1.21, 25; 7.9; 13.55, et al. freq.; a *legitimate* son, He. 12.8; a son
    artificially constituted, Ac. 7.21. He. 11.24; a descendant, Mat. 1.1, 20; Mar. 12.35, et
    al.: *in N.T.,* the young *of an animal,* Mat. 21.5; *a spiritual* son *in respect of conversion
    or discipleship,* 1 Pe. 5.13; *fr. Heb.* a disciple, *perhaps* Mat. 12.27; a son *as implying
    connexion in respect of membership, service, resemblance, manifestation, destiny,*
    &c., Mat. 8.12; 9.15; 13.38; 23.15. Mar. 2.19; 3.17. Lu. 5.34; 16.8; 20.34, 36.
    Jno 17.12. Ac. 2.25; 4.36; 13.10. Eph. 2.2; 5.6. Col. 3.6. 1 Th. 5.5. 2 Th. 2.3; υἱὸς
    θεοῦ, κ.τ.λ., son of God *in respect of divinity,* Mat. 4.3, 6, 14.33. Ro. 1.4, et al.; *also,
    in respect of privilege and character,* Mat. 5.9, 45. Lu. 6.35. Ro. 8.14, 19; 9.26. Ga.
    3.26; ὁ υἱὸς τοῦ θεοῦ, κ.τ.λ., *a title of the Messiah,* Mat. 26.63. Mar. 3.11; 14.61. Jno.
    1.34, 50; 20.31, et al.; υἱὸς ἀνθρώπου, a son of man, a man, Mar. 3.28. Eph. 3.5. He.
    22.6; ὁ υἱὸς τοῦ ἀνθρώπου, *a title of the Messiah,* Mat. 8.20, et al. freq.; *as also* ὁ υἱὸς
    Δαβίδ, Mat. 12.23, et al.
Ὕλη, ης, ἡ,
    wood, a forest; *in N.T.,* firewood, a mass of fuel, Ja. 3.5.
Ὑμέτερος, α, ον, *possess. pron.* (ὑμεῖς)
    your, yours, Lu. 6.20. Jno. 7.6; 15.20, et al.
Ὑμνέω, ῶ,
    f. ήσω, a.1. ὕμνησα,
    to hymn, praise, celebrate or worship with hymns, Ac. 16.25. He. 2.12; *absol.* to sing
    a hymn, Mat. 26.30. Mar. 14.26: *from*
Ὕμνος, ου, ὁ,

a song; a hymn, song of praise *to God,* Ep. 5.19. Col. 3.16.

Ὑπάγω, (ὑπό & ἄγω)

f. ξω,

to lead or bring under; to lead or bring from under; to draw on or away; *in N.T.,* *intrans.* to go away, depart. Mat. 8.4, 13; 9.6; ὕπαγε ὀπίσω μου, get behind me! away! begone! Mat. 4.10; 16.23; to go, Mat. 5.41. Lu. 12.58, et al.; to depart *life,* Mat. 26.24.

Ὑπακοή, ῆς, ἡ,

a hearkening to obedience, Ro. 5.19; 6.16. 1 Pe. 1.14; submissiveness, Ro. 16.19. 2 Co. 7.15; submission, Ro. 1.5; 15.18; 16.26. 2 Co. 10.5. He. 5.8. 1 Pe. 1.2, 22; compliance, Philem. 21: (S.) *from*

Ὑπακούω, (ὑπό & ἀκούω)

f. ούσομαι,

to give ear, hearken; to listen, Ac. 12.13; to obey, Mat. 8.27. Mar. 1.27, et al.; *in N.T.,* to render submissive acceptance, Ac. 6.7. Ro. 6.17. 2 Th. 1.8. He. 5.9; *absol.* to be submissive, Phi. 2.12.

Ὕπανδρος, ου, ἡ (ὑπό & & ἀνήρ)

bound to a man, married, Ro. 7.2. L.G.

Ὑπαντάω, ῶ, (ὑπό & & ἀντάω)

f. ήσω,

to meet, Mat. 8.28. Lu. 8.27. Jno. 11.20, 30; 12.18: *whence*

Ὑπάντησις, εως, ἡ,

a meeting, act of meeting, Jno. 12.13. L.G.

Ὕπαρξις, εως, ἡ,

goods, possessed, substance, property, Ac. 2.45. He. 10.34: (L.G.) *from*

Ὑπάρχω, (ὑπό & & ἄρχω)

f. ξω,

to begin; to come into existence; to exist; to be subsist, Ac. 19.40; 28.18; to be in possession, to belong, Ac. 3.6; 4.37; *part. neut. pl.* τὰ ὑπάρχοντα, goods, possessions, property, Mat. 19.21. Lu. 8.3; to be, Lu. 7.25; 8.41, et al.

Ὑπείκω, (ὑπό & & εἴκω)

to yield, give way; *absol.* to be submissive, He. 13.17.

Ὑπεναντίος, ία, ίον, (ὑπό & & ἐναντίος)

over against; contrary, adverse; ὁ ὑπεναντίος, an opponent, adversary, He. 10.27; untoward, inimical, Col. 2.14.

Ὑπέρ,

prep. with a genitive, above, over; *met.* in behalf of, Mat. 5.44. Mar. 9.40. Jno. 17.19, et al.; instead of *beneficially,* Philem. 13; in maintenance of, Ro. 15.8; for the furtherance of, Jno. 11.4. 2 Co. 1.6, 8, et al.; for the fulfilment of, Phi. 2.13; *equivalent to* περί, about, concerning, *with the further signification of interest or concern in the subject,* Ac. 5.41. Ro. 9.27. 2 Co. 5.12; 8.23. 2 Th. 2.1, et al.; *with an acc.,* over, beyond; *met.* beyond, more than, Mat. 10.37. 2 Co. 1.8, et al., *used after comparative terms,* Lu. 16.8. 1932 Co. 12.13. He. 4.12; *in N.T. as an adv.,* in a higher degree, in fuller measure, 2 Co. 11.23.

Ὑπεραίρω, (ὑπέρ & αἴρω)

to raise or lift up above or over; *mid.* to lift up one's self; *met.* to be over-elated, 2 Co. 12.7; to bear one's self arrogantly, to rear a haughty front, 2 Th. 2.4.

Ὑπέρακμος, ου, ὁ, ἡ, (ὑπέρ & ἀκμή, a point, prime)

past the bloom of life, 1 Co. 7.36. N.T.

Ὑπεράνω, (ὑπέρ & ἄνω)

adv. above, over, far above; *of place,* Ep. 4.10. He. 9.5; *of rank, dignity,* &c. Ep. 1.21. L.G. (ā)

Ὑπεραυξάνω, (ὑπέρ & αὐξάνω)
    f. ξήσω,
    to increase exceedingly, 2 Th. 1.3.

Ὑπερβαίνω, (ὑπέρ & βαίνω)
    f. βήσομαι,
    to overstep; to wrong, aggrieve, 1 Th. 4.6.

Ὑπερβαλλόντως,
    adv. exceedingly, above measure, 2 Co. 11.23: *from*

Ὑπερβάλλω, (ὑπέρ & βάλλω)
    f. βαλῶ,
    pr. to cast or throw over or beyond, to overshoot; *met.* to surpass, excel; *part.* ὑπερβάλλων, ουσα, ον, surpassing, 2 Co. 3.10; 9.14, et al.: *whence*

Ὑπερβολή, ῆς, ἡ,
    pr. a throwing beyond, an overshooting; extraordinary amount or character, transcendency, 2 Co. 12.7; 4.7; καθ' ὑπερβολήν, *adverbially,* exceedingly, extremely, Ro. 7.13. 2 Co. 1.8, et al.

Ὑπερεῖδον,
    a.2. of ὑπεροράω,
    to look over or above *a thing; met.* to overlook, disregard; to bear with, Ac. 17.30.

Ὑπερέκεινα, (ὑπέρ ἐκεῖνα)
    adv. beyond, 2 Co. 10.16. N.T.

Ὑπερεκπερισσοῦ, (ὑπέρ, ἐκ, περισσοῦ)
    in over-abundance; beyond all measure, superabundantly, Ep. 3.20. 1 Th. 3.10; 5.13. S.

Ὑπερεκτείνω, (ὑπέρ & ἐκτείνω)
    to over-extend, over-stretch, 2 Co. 10.14. L.G.

Ὑπερεκχύνω, (ὑπέρ & ἐκχύνω)
    to pour out above measure or in excess; *pass.* to run over, overflow, Lu. 6.38. L.G.

Ὑπερεντυγχάνω, (ὑπέρ & ἐντυγχάνω)
    to intercede for, Ro. 8.26. N.T.

Ὑπερέχω, (ὑπέρ & ἔχω)
    f. ξω,
    to hold above; *intrans.* to stand out above, to overtop; *met.* to surpass, excel, Phi. 2.3; 4.7; τὸ ὑπερέχον, excellence, preeminence, Phi. 3.8; to be higher, superior, Ro. 13.1. 1 Pe. 2.13.

Ὑπερηφανία, ας, ἡ,
    hughtiness, arrogance, Mar. 7.22: *from*

Ὑπερήφᾰνος, ου, ὁ, ἡ, (ὑπέρ & φαίνω)
    pr. conspicuous above, supereminent; *met.* assuming, haughty, arrogant, Lu. 1.51. Ro. 1.30. 2 Ti. 3.2. Ja. 4.6. 1 Pe. 5.5.

Ὑπερλίαν, (ὑπέρ & λίαν)
    in the highest degree, preeminently, especially, superlatively, 2 Co. 11.5; 12.11. N.T.

Ὑπερνικάω, ῶ, (ὑπέρ & νικάω)
    f. ήσω,
    to overpower in victory; to be abundantly victorious, prevail mightily, Ro. 8.37. L.G.

Ὑπέρογκος, ου, ὁ, ἡ, (ὑπέρ & ὄγκος)
    pr. over-swollen, overgrown; *of language,* swelling, pompous, boastful, 2 Pe. 2.18. Jude 16.

Ὑπεροχή, ῆς, ἡ (ὑπερέχω)

prominence; *met.* excellence, rare quality, 1 Co. 2.1; eminent station, authority, 1 Ti. 2.2.

Ὑπερπερισσεύω, (ὑπέρ & περισσεύω)

f. εύσω,

to superabound; to abound still more, Ro. 5.20; *mid.* to be abundantly fulled, overflow, 2 Co. 7.4. N.T.

Ὑπερπερισσῶς, (ὑπέρ & περισσῶς)

adv. superabundantly, most vehemently, above all measure, Mar. 7.37. N.T.

Ὑπερπλεονάζω, (ὑπέρ & πλεονάζω)

f. άσω,

to superabound, be in exceeding abundance, over-exceed, 1 Ti. 1.14. N.T.

Ὑπερυψόω, ῶ, (ὑπέρ & ὑψόω)

f. ώσω,

to exalt supremely, Phi. 2.9. S.

Ὑπερφρονέω, (ὑπέρ & φρονέω)

f. ήσω,

to overween, have lofty thoughts, be elated, Ro. 12.3.

Ὑπερῷον, ου, τό, (pr. neut. of ὑπερῷος, upper, fr. ὑπέρ)

the upper part of a house, upper room, or chamber, Ac. 1.13; 9.37, 39; 20.8.

Ὑπέχω, (ὑπό & ἔχω)

f. ὑφέξω,

194*pr.* to hold under; to render, undergo, suffer. Jude 7.

Ὑπήκοος, οῦ, ὁ, ἡ, (ὑπακούω)

giving ear; obedient, submissive, Ac. 7.39. 2 Co. 2.9. Ph. 2.8.

Ὑπηρετέω, ῶ,

f. ήσω, a.1. ὑπηρέτησα,

to subserve, Ac. 13.36; to relieve, supply, Ac. 20.34; to render kind offices, Ac. 24.23: *from*

Ὑπηρέτης, ου, ὁ, (ὑπό & ἐρέτης, a rower)

pr. an under-rower, a rower, one of a ship's crew; a minister, attendant, servant; an attendant *on a magistrate,* a lictor, apparitor, officer, Mat. 5.25; an attendant or officer *of the Sanhedrin,* Mat. 26.58; an attendant, or servant *of a synagogue,* Lu. 4.20; a minister, attendant, assistant *in any work,* Lu. 1.2. Jno. 18.36, et al.

Ὕπνος, ου, ὁ,

sleep, Mat. 1.24, et al.; *met. spiritual* sleep, *religious* slumber, Ro. 13.11.

Ὑπό,

prep., with a genitive, pr. under: *hence used to express influence, causation, agency;* by, Mat. 1.22, et al. freq.; by the agency of, at the hands of, 2 Co. 11.24. He. 12.3; *with an accusative,* under, *with the idea of motion associated,* Mat. 5.15, et al.; under, Jno. 1.49. 1 Co. 10.1; under *subjection to,* Ro. 6.14. 1 Ti. 6.1, et al.; *of time,* at about, Ac. 5.21.

Ὑποβάλλω, (ὑπό & βάλλω)

f. βαλῶ, a.2. ὑπέβαλον,

to cast under; *met.* to suggest, instigate; to suborn, Ac. 6.11.

Ὑπογραμμός, οῦ, ὁ, (ὑπογράφω)

pr. a copy to write after; *met.* an example for imitation, pattern, 1 Pe. 2.21. L.G.

Ὑπόδειγμα, ατος, τό,

a token, intimation; an example, *proposed for imitation or admonition,* Jno. 13.15. He. 4.11. Ja. 5.10. 2 Pe. 2.6; a copy, He. 8.5; 9.23: *from*

Ὑποδείκνυμι, (ὑπό & δείκνυμι)
  to indicate, Ac. 20.35; to intimate, suggest, Mat. 3.7. Lu. 3.7; 6.47; 12.5. Ac. 9.16.
Ὑποδέχομαι, (ὑπό & δέχομαι)
  f. ξομαι, p. ὑπεδέδεγμαι,
  to give reception to; to receive as a guest, entertain, Lu. 10.38; 19.6. Ac. 17.7. Ja. 2.25.
Ὑποδέω, ῶ (ὑπό & δέω)
  f. ήσω, p. pass. ὑποδέδεμαι,
  to bind under; *mid.* to bind under one's self, put on one's own feet, Ac. 12.8; to shoe, Ep. 6.15; *pass.* to be shod, Mar. 6.9: *whence*
Ὑπόδημα, ατος, τό,
  any thing bound under; a sandal, Mat. 3.11; 10.10, et al.
Ὑπόδῐκος, ου, ὁ, ἡ, (ὑπό & δίκη)
  under a legal process; *also,* under a judicial sentence; under verdict *to an opposed party in a suit,* liable to penalty, convict, Ro. 3.19.
Ὑποζύγιον, ίου, τό, (pr. neut. of ὑποζύγιος), under a yoke, fr. ὑπό & ζυγόν)
  an animal subject to the yoke, a beast of draught or burden; *in N.T., spc.* an ass, Mat. 21.5. 2 Pe. 2.16.
Ὑποζώννυμι, (ὑπό & ζώννυμι)
  f. ζώσω,
  to gird under, *of persons;* to undergird *a ship with cables, chains,* &c. Ac. 27.17.
Ὑποκάτω, (ὑπό & κάτω)
  adv. under, beneath, underneath, Mar. 6.11; 7.28, et al.; *met.* He. 2.8. (ἄ)
Ὑποκρίνομαι, (ὑπό & κρίνω)
  f. οῦμαι,
  to answer, respond; to act a part *upon the stage; hence,* to assume a counterfeit character; to pretend, feign, Lu. 20.20: *whence*
Ὑπόκρῐσις, εως, ἡ,
  a response, answer; histrionic personification, acting; hypocrisy, simulation, Mat. 23.28. Mar. 12.15, et al.
Ὑποκρῐτής, οῦ, ὁ,
  the giver of an answer or response; a stage-player, actor; *in N.T.,* a *moral or religious* counterfeit, a hypocrite, Mat. 6.2, 5.16; 7.5, et al.
Ὑπολαμβάνω, (ὑπό & λαμβάνω)
  f. λήψομαι, a.2. ὑπέλαβον,
  to take up, *by placing one's self underneath what is taken up;* to catch away, withdraw, Ac. 1.9; to take up *discourse by continuation; hence,* to answer, Lu. 10.30; to take up *a notion,* to think, suppose, Lu. 7.43. Ac. 2.15.
Ὑπολείπω, (ὑπό & λείπω)
  f. ψω,
  to leave remaining, leave behind; *pass.* to be left surviving, Ro. 11.3.
Ὑπολήνιον, ου, τό, (ὑπό & ληνός)
  a vat, *placed under the press,* ληνός, *to receive the juice,* Mar. 12.1. S.
Ὑπολιμπάνω, (ὑπό & λιμπάνω, to leave)
  195*equivalent to* ὑπολείπω, to leave behind, 1 Pe. 2.21.
Ὑπομένω, (ὑπό & μένω)
  f. νῶ,
  intrans. to remain or stay behind, *when others have departed,* Lu. 2.43; *trans.* to bear up under, endure, suffer patiently, 1 Co. 13.7. He. 10.32; *absol.* to continue firm, hold out, remain constant, persevere, Mat. 10.22; 24.13, et al.

Ὑπομιμνήσκω, (ὑπό & μιμνήσκω)
 f. ὑπομνήσω,
 to put in mind, remind, Jno. 14.26. Tit. 3.1. 2 Pe. 1.12. Jude 5; to suggest recollection of, remind *others* of, 2 Ti. 2.14. 3 Jno. 10; *mid.* ὑπομιμνήσκομαι, a.1. ὑπεμνήσθην, to call to mind, recollect, remember, Lu. 22.61: *whence*
Ὑπόμνησις, εως, ἡ,
 a putting in mind, act of reminding, 2 Pe. 1.13; 3.1; remembrance, recollection, 2 Ti. 1.5.
Ὑπομονή, ῆς, ἡ, (ὑπομένω)
 patient endurance, 2 Co. 12.12. Col. 1.11. et al.; patient awaiting, Lu. 21.19; a patient frame of mind, patience, Ro. 5.3, 4; 15.4, 5. Ja. 1.3, et al.; perseverance, Ro. 2.7; ἐν ὑπομονῇ & δι' ὑπομονῆς, constantly, perseveringly, Lu. 8.15. Ro. 8.25. He. 12.1; an enduring *of affliction*, &c., the act of suffering, undergoing, &c., 2 Co. 1.6; 6.4.
Ὑπονοέω, ῶ, (ὑπό & νοέω)
 f. ήσω,
 to suspect; to suppose, deem, Ac. 13.25; 25.18; 27.27: *whence*
Ὑπόνοια, ας, ἡ,
 suspicion, surmise, 1 Ti. 6.4.
Ὑποπλέω, (ὑπό & πλέω)
 f. εύσομαι,
 to sail under; to sail under *the lee, or,* to the south of, *an island,* &c., Ac. 27.4, 7. L.G.
Ὑποπνέω, (ὑπό & πνέω)
 f. εύσω,
 to blow gently, *as the wind,* Ac. 27.13. N.T.
Ὑποπόδιον, ίου, τό, (ὑπό & πούς)
 a footstool, Mat. 5.35. Ja. 2.3, et al. L.G.
Ὑπόστᾰσις, εως, ἡ (ὑφίσταμαι, to stand under, ὑπό & ἵστημι)
 pr. a being set under; a substructure, basis, bottom; subsistence, essence, He. 1.3; an assumption *of a character,* 2 Co. 11.17; a pledged assumption, vouching, 2 Co. 9.4; a professed engagement, profession, He. 3.14; an assured impression, a realising, He. 11.1.
Ὑποστέλλω, (ὑπό & στέλλω)
 f. στελῶ, a.1. ὑπέστειλα,
 pr. to let down, to stow away; to draw back, withdraw, Ga. 2.12; *mid.* to shrink back, quail, recoil, He. 10.38; to keep back, suppress, conceal, Ac. 20.20, 27: *whence*
Ὑποστολή, ῆς, ἡ,
 a shrinking back, He. 10.39. L.G.
Ὑποστρέφω, (ὑπό & στρέφω)
 f. ψω,
 to turn back, return, Mar. 14.40. Lu. 1.56; 2.39, 43, 45, et al.
Ὑποστρώννυμι, v. ννύω, (ὑπό & στρώννυμι)
 f. στρώσω,
 to strow under, spread underneath, Lu. 19.36.
Ὑποτᾰγή, ῆς, ἡ,
 subordination, 1 Ti. 3.4; submissiveness, 2 Co. 9.13. Ga. 2.5. 1 Ti. 2.11: (N.T.) *from*
Ὑποτάσσω, v. ττω, (ὑπό & τάσσω)
 f. ξω,
 to place or arrange under; to subordinate, 1 Co. 15.27; to bring under influence, Ro. 8.20; *pass.* to be subordinated, 1 Co. 14.32, et al.; to be brought under a state of

influence, Ro. 8.20; *mid.* to submit one's self, render obedience, be submissive, Lu. 2.51; 10.17, et al.

Ὑποτίθημι, (ὑπό & τίθημι)

f. ὑποθήσω,

to place under; to lay down *the neck beneath the sword of the executioner,* to set on imminent risk, Ro. 16.4; *mid.* to suggest, recommend to attention, 1 Ti. 4.6.

Ὑποτρέχω, (ὑπό & τρέχω)

a.2. ὑπέδρᾰμον,

to run under; *as a nautical term,* to sail under *the lee of,* Ac. 27.16.

Ὑποτύπωσις, εως, ἡ, (ὑποτυπόω, to sketch, fr. ὑπό & τυπόω)

a sketch, delineation; form, formula, 2 Ti. 1.13; a pattern, example, 1 Ti. 1.16.

Ὑποφέρω, (ὑπό & φέρω)

a.1. ὑπήνεγκα, a.2. ὑπήνεγκον,

to bear under; to bear up under, support, sustain, 1 Co. 10.13; to endure patiently, 1 Pe. 2.19; to undergo, 2 Ti. 3.11.

Ὑποχωρέω, ῶ, (ὑπό & χωρέω)

f. ήσω,

to withdraw, retire, Lu. 5.16; 9.10.

Ὑπωπιάζω, (ὑπώπιον, the part of the face below the eyes, fr. ὑπό & ὤψ)

pr. to strike one upon the 196parts beneath the eye; to beat black and blue; *hence,* to discipline by hardship, coerce, 1 Co. 9.27; *met.* to weary *by continual importunities,* pester, Lu. 18.5.

Ὗς, ὑός, ὁ, ἡ,

a hog, swine, boar or sow, 2 Pe. 2.22.

Ὕσσωπος, ου, ὁ, ἡ, (Heb. בזוא)

hyssop, hyssopus officinalis *of Linn., a low shrubby plant growing in the south of Europe and the East;* a bunch of hyssop, He. 9.19; a hyssop stalk, Jno. 19.29. L. G.

Ὑστερέω, ῶ, (ὕστερος)

f. ήσω, p. ὑστέρηκα, a.1. ὑστέρησα,

to be behind *in place or time,* to be in the rear; to fall short of, be inferior to, 2 Co. 11.5; 12.11; to fail of, fail to attain, He. 4.1; to be in want of, lack, Lu. 22.35; to be wanting, Mar. 10.21; *absol.* to be defective, in default, Mat. 19.20. 1 Co. 12.24; to run short, Jno. 2.3; *mid.* to come short of *a privilege or standard,* to miss, Ro. 3.23; *absol.* to come short, below standard, 1 Co. 1.7; to come short *of sufficiency,* to be in need, want, Lu. 15.14. 2 Co. 11.8. Phi. 4.12. He. 11.37; to be a loser, suffer detriment, 1 Co. 8.8; *in N.T.,* ὑστερεῖν ἀπό, to be backwards with respect to, to slight, He. 12.15: *whence*

Ὑστέρημα, ατος, τό,

a shortcoming, defect; *personal* shortcoming, 1 Co. 16.17. Phi. 2.30. Col. 1.24. 1 Th. 3.10; want, need, poverty, penury, Lu. 21.4. 2 Co. 8.13, 14, et al. S.

Ὑστέρησις, εως, ἡ,

want, need, Mar. 12.44. Phi. 4.11. N.T.

Ὕστερον

adv. after, afterwards, Mat. 4.2; 22.27, et al.: *pr. neut. of*

Ὕστερος, α, ον,

posterior *in place or time;* subsequent, 1 Ti. 4.1.

Ὑφαντός, ή, όν, (ὑφαίνω, to weave)

woven, Jno. 19.23.

Ὑψηλός, ή, όν, (ὕψος)

high, lofty, elevated, Mat. 4.8; 17.1; et al. τὰ ὑψηλά, the highest *heaven,* He. 1.3; upraised, Ac. 13.17; *met.* highly esteemed, Lu. 16.15; φρονεῖν τὰ ὑψηλά, to have lofty thoughts, be proud, overween, Ro. 12.16.

Ὑψηλοφρονέω, ῶ, (ὑψηλός & φρονέω)
    f. ήσω,
    to have lofy thoughts, be proud, overweening, haughty, Ro. 11.20. 1 Ti. 6.17. N.T.

Ὕψιστος, η, ον,
    highest, loftiest, most elevated; τὰ ὕψιστα, *fr. the Heb.* the highest heaven, Mat. 21.9. Mar. 11.10; *met.* ὁ ὕψιστος, the Most High, Mar. 5.7, et al.; *superlat. formed from*

Ὕψος, εος, τό,
    height, Ep. 3.18. Re. 21.16; *met.* exaltation, dignity, eminence, Ja. 1.9; *fr. the Heb.* the highest heaven, Lu. 1.78; 24.49. Ep. 4.8: *whence*

Ὑψόω, ῶ
    f. ώσω, a.1. ὕψωσα,
    to raise aloft, lift up, Jno. 3.14; 8.28; *met.* to elevate *in condition,* uplift, exalt, Mat. 11.23; 23.12. Lu. 1.52: *whence*

Ὕψωμα, ατος, τό,
    height, Ro. 8.39; a towering *of self-conceit,* presumption, 2 Co. 10.5. L.G.

Φ, φ, *Φῖ*

Φάγομαι,
    see ἐσθίω.

Φάγος, ου, ὁ,
    a glutton, Mat. 11.19. Lu. 7.34. N.T.

Φαιλόνης, v. φελόνης, ου, ἁ (by metath. for φαινόλης, *Lat.* penula)
    a thick cloak *for travelling, with a hood,* 2 Ti. 4.13.

Φαίνω,
    f. φανῶ, p. πέφαγκα, a.2. pass ἐφάνην,
    to cause to appear, bring to light; *absol.* to shine, Jno. 1.5; 5.35. 2 Pe. 1.19. 1 Jno. 2.8. Re. 1.16; 8.12; 21.23; *mid. or pass.* to be seen, appear, be visible, Mat. 1.20; 2.7, 13, 19; 6.5, 16, 18; τὰ φαινόμενα, things visible, things obvious to the senses, He. 11.3; φαίνομαι, to appear, seem, be in appearance, Mat. 23.27. Lu. 24.11; to appear *in thought,* seem *in idea,* be a notion, Mar. 14.64. et al.:*whence*

Φανερός, ά, όν,
    apparent, conspicuous, manifest, clear, known, well-known, Mar. 4.22; 6.14. Ga. 5.10, et al.; ἐν φανερῷ, openly, Mat. 6.4, 6; *also,* in outward guise, externally, Ro. 2.28: *whence*

Φανερόω, ῶ,
    f. ώσω, a.1. ἐφανέρωσα, p. pass. πεφανέρωμα,
    to make manifest, bring to light, disclose, show forth, make known, Mar. 4.22; 16.12, 14. Jno. 1.31, et al.

Φανερῶς,
    197*adv.* manifestly; clearly, plainly, distinctly, Ac. 10.3; openly, publicly, Mar. 1.45. Jno. 7.10.

Φανέρωσις, εως, ἡ, (φανερόω)
    an evidencing, clear display, 2 Co. 4.2; an *outward* evidencing *of a latent principle, active* exhibition, 1 Co. 12.7. N.T.

Φᾶνός, οῦ, ὁ, (φαίνω)
    a torch, lantern, light, Jno. 18.3.

Φαντάζω, (φαίνω)

    f. άσω,

    to render visible, cause to appear; *pass.* to appear, be seen; τὸ φανταζόμενον, the sight, spectacle, He. 12.21: *whence*

Φαντασία, ας, ἡ,

    pr. a rendering visible; a display; pomp, parade, Ac. 25.23.

Φάντασμα, ατος, τό, (φαντάζω)

    a phantom, spectre, Mat. 14.26. Mar. 6.49

Φάραγξ, αγγος, ἡ,

    a cleft, ravine, dell, Lu. 3.5.

Φαρισαῖος, ου, ὁ,

    a Pharisee, a follower of the sect of the Pharisees, *a numerous and powerful sect of the Jews, distinguished for their ceremonial observances, and apparent sanctity of life, and for being rigid interpreters of the Mosaic law; but who not unfrequently violated its spirit by their tranditional interpretations and precepts, to which they ascribed nearly an equal authority with the O.T. Scriptures,* Mat. 5.31, 20; 12.2; 23.14, et al.

Φαρμακεία, ας, ἡ (φάρμακον, a drug)

    employment of drugs *for any purpose;* sorcery, magic, enchantment, Ga. 5.20. Re. 9.21; 18.23.

Φαρμἄκεύς, έως, ὁ, (fr. same)

    pr. one who deals in drugs; an enchanter, magician, sorcerer, Ac. 21.8.

Φαρμἄκός, οῦ, ὁ,

    a sorcerer, Re. 21.8; 22.15.

Φάσις, εως, ἡ, (φημί)

    report, information, Ac. 21.31.

Φάσκω, *equivalent to* φημί,

    imperf. ἔφασκον,

    to assert, affirm, Ac. 24.9; 25.19. Ro. 1.22. Re. 2.2.

Φάτνη, ης, ἡ,

    a manger, crib, Lu. 2.7, 12, 16; 13.15.

Φαῦλος, η, ον,

    sorry, vile, refuse; evil, wicked, Jno. 3.20; 5.29. Tit. 2.8. Ja. 3.16.

Φέγγος, εος, τό,

    light, splendour, Mat. 24.29. Mar. 13.24. Lu. 11.33.

Φείδομαι,

    f. φείσομαι

    to spare, be thrifty of; to spare, be tender of, Ro. 8.32; to spare, *in respect of hard dealing,* Ac. 20.29. Ro. 11.21. 1 Co. 7.28. 2 Co. 1.23; 13.2. 2 Pe. 2.4, 5; *absol.* to forbear, abstain, 2 Co. 12.6: *whence*

Φειδομένως,

    adv. sparingly, parsimoniously, 2 Co. 9.6, *bis.* L.G.

Φελόνης,

    see φαιλόνης.

Φέρω,

    f. οἴσω, a.1. ἤνεγκα, a.2. ἤνεγκον, a.1. pass. ἠνέχθην,

    to bear, carry, Mar. 2.3, et al.; to bring, Mat. 14.11, 18, et al.; to conduct, Mat. 17.17. Jno. 21.18, et al.; to bear, endure, Ro. 9.22. He. 12.20; 13.13; to uphold, maintain, conserve, He. 1.3; to bear, bring forth, produce, Mar. 4.8. Jno. 12.24; 15.2, et al.; to bring forward, advance, allege, Jno. 18.29. Ac. 25.7. 2 Pe. 2.11; to offer, ascribe, Re.

21.24, 26; *absol, used of a gate,* to lead, Ac. 12.10; *pass.* to be brought *within reach,* offered, 1 Pe. 1.13; to be brought in, to enter, He. 9.16; to be under a moving influence, to be moved, be instinct, 2 Pe. 1.21; *mid.* to rush, sweep, Ac. 2.2; to proceed, come forth, have utterance, 2 Pe. 1.17, 18, 21; to proceed, make progress, He. 6.1; *used of a ship,* to drive *before the wind,* Ac. 27.15, 17.

Φεύγω,
    f. ξομαι, a.2. ἔφῠγον,
    absol. to flee, take to flight, Mat. 2.13; 8.33, et al.; to shrink, stand fearfully aloof, 1 Co. 10.14; to make escape, Mat. 23.33; *trans.* to shun, 1 Co. 6.18. 1 Ti. 6.11. 2 Ti. 2.22; to escape, He. 11.34.

Φήμη, ης, ἡ,
    pr. a celestial or oracular utterance; an utterance; fame, rumour, report, Mat. 9.26. Lu. 4.14: *from*

Φημί (φάω)
    f. φήσω, imperf. ἔφην
    to utter, tell forth; to say, speak, Mat. 8.8; 14.8; 26.34, 61; to say, allege, affirm, Ro. 3.8, et al.

Φθάνω,
    f. ήσομαι, & άσω, a.1. ἔφθασο, a.2. ἔφθην,
    to be beforehand with; to outstrip, precede, 1 Th. 4.15; *absol.* to advance, make progress, 2 Co. 10.14. Phi. 3.16; to come up *with,* come *upon,* be close at hand, Mat. 12.28. 1 Th. 2.16; 198to attain an *object of pursuit,* Ro. 9.31.

Φθαρτός, ή, όν, (φθείρω)
    corruptible, perishable, Ro. 1.23. 1 Co. 9.25, et al.

Φθέγγομαι,
    f. γξομαι, a.1. ἐφθεγξάμην,
    to emit a sound; to speak, Ac. 4.18. 2 Pe. 2.16, 18.

Φθείρω, (φθέω, idem)
    f. φθερῶ, p. ἔφθαρκα, a.1. ἔφθειρα, a. pass. ἐφθάρην,
    to spoil, ruin, 1 Co. 3.17. 2 Co. 7.2; to corrupt, *morally* deprave, 1 Co. 15.33. 2 Co. 11.3, et al.

Φθινοπωρῐνός, ή, όν, (φθινόπωρον, the latter part of autumn, fr. φθίνω, to wane, & ὀπώρα) autumnal, sere, bare, Ju. 12.

Φθόγγος, ου, ὁ, (φθέγγομαι)
    a *vocal* sound, Ro. 10.18. 1 Co. 14.7.

Φθονέω, ῶ,
    f. ήσω, a.1. ἐφθόνησα,
    to envy, Ga. 5.26: *from*

Φθόνος, ου, ὁ,
    to envy, jealousy, spite, Mat. 27.18. Mar. 15.10, et al.

Φθορά, ᾶς, ἡ, (φθείρω)
    corruption, decay, ruin; corruptibility, mortality, Ro. 8.21. 1 Co. 15.42; *meton.* corruptible, perishable substance, 1 Co. 15.50; killing, slaughter, 2 Pe. 2.12; *spiritual* ruin, Ga. 6.8. Col. 2.22; *met. moral* corruption, depravity, 2 Pe. 1.4; 2.12, 19.

Φιάλη, ης, ἡ,
    a bowl, shallow cup, patera, Re. 5.8; 15.7; 16.1-4, et al. (ᾰ).

Φιλάγᾰθος, ου, ὁ, ἡ, (φίλος & ἀγαθός)
    a lover of goodness, *or,* of the good, a fosterer of virtue, Tit. 1.8.

Φιλαδελφία, ας, ἡ,

brotherly love; *in N.T.,* love of the *Christian* brotherhood, Ro. 12.10. 1 Th. 4.9, et al.: (L.G.) *from*

Φιλάδελφος, ου, ὁ, ἡ, (φίλος & ἀδελφός)
brother-loving; *in N.T.,* loving the members of the *Christian* brotherhood, 1 Pe. 3.8.

Φίλανδρος, ου, ἡ, (φίλος & ἀνήρ)
husbank-loving, conjugal, Tit. 2.4.

Φιλανθρωπία, ας, ἡ, (φιλάνθρωπος, loving mankind, humane, fr. φίλος & ἄνθρωπος)
philanthropy, love of mankind, Tit. 3.4; benevolence, humanity, Ac. 28.2.

Φιλανθρώπως, (fr. same)
adv. humanely, benevolently, kindly, Ac. 27.3.

Φιλαργυριά, ας, ἡ,
love of money, conventousness, 1 Ti. 6.10: *from*

Φιλάργῠρος, ου, ὁ, ἡ, (φίλος & ἄργυρος)
money-loving, conventous, Lu. 16.14.

Φίλαυτος, ου, ὁ, ἡ, (φίλος & αὐτός)
self-loving; selfish, 2 Ti. 3.2.

Φιλέω, ῶ,
f. ήσω, a.1. ἐφίλησα,
pr. to manifest some act or token of kindness or affection; to kiss, Mat. 26.48. Mar. 14.44. Lu. 22.47; to love, regard with affection, have affection for, Mat. 10.37. Jno. 5.20; to like, be fond of, delight in *a thing,* Mat. 23.6. Re. 22.15; to cherish inordinately, set store by, Jno. 12.25; *followed by an infin.,* to be wont, Mat. 6.5.

Φίλη, ης, ἡ, (φίλος)
a female friend, Lu. 15.9.

Φιλήδονος, ου, ὁ, ἡ, (φίλος & ἡδονή)
pleasure-loving; a lover of pleasure, 2 Ti. 3.4.

Φίλημα, ατος, τό, (φιλέω)
a kiss, Lu. 7.45; 22.48. Ro. 16.16, et al.

Φιλία, ας, ἡ, (φίλος)
affection, fondness, love, Ja. 4.4.

Φιλιππήσιος, ου, ὁ,
Philippian, citizen of Φίλιπποι, Philippi, Ph. 4.15.

Φιλόθεος, ου, ὁ, ἡ, (φίλος & θεός)
God-loving, pious; a lover of God, 2 Ti. 3.4.

Φιλονεικία, ας, ἡ,
a love of contention; rivalry, contention, Lu. 22.24: *from*

Φιλόνεικος, ου, ὁ, ἡ, (φίλος & νεῖκος, contention)
fond of contention; contentious, disputatious, 1 Co. 11.16.

Φιλοξενία, ας, ἡ,
kindness to strangers, hospitality, Ro. 12.13. He. 12.2: *from*

Φιλόξενος, ου, ὁ, ἡ, (φίλος & ξένος)
kind to strangers, hospitable, 1 Ti. 3.2. Tit. 1.8. 1 Pe. 4.9.

Φιλοπρωτεύω, (φίλος & πρωτεύω)
to love or desire to be first or chief, affect preeminence, 3 Jno. 9. N.T.

Φίλος, ου, ὁ,
loved, dear; *as subst.* a friend, Lu. 7.6; 11.5, 6, 8, et al.; a congenial associate, Mat. 11.19. Lu. 7.34. Ja. 4.4; 199*used as a word of courteous compellation,* Lu. 14.10

Φιλοσοφία, ας, ἡ
pr. a love of science; *systematic* philosophy; *in N.T.,* the philosophy *of the Jewish gnosis,* Col. 2.8: *from*

Φιλόσοφος, ου, ὁ, (φίλος & σοφίας)
  pr. a lover of science; a *systematic* philosopher, Ac. 17.18.
Φιλόστοργος, ου, ὁ, ἡ, (φίλος & στοργή, natural affection)
  tenderly affectionate, Ro. 12.10.
Φιλότεκνος, ου, ὁ, ἡ, (φίλος & τέκνον)
  loving one's children, duly parental, Tit. 2.4.
Φιλοτιμέομαι, οῦμαι, (φιλότιμος, studious of honour or distinction, fr. φίλος & τιμή)
  f. ήσομαι,
  pr. to be ambitious of honour; *by impl.* to exert one's self *to accomplish a thing,* use one's utmost efforts, endeavour earnestly, Ro. 15.20. 2 Co. 5.9. 1 Th. 4.11.
Φιλοφρόνως,
  adv. with kindly feeling or manner, courteously, Ac. 28.7: *from*
Φιλόφρων, ονος, ὁ, ἡ, (φίλος & φρήν)
  kindly-minded, benign, courteous, 1 Pe. 3.8.
Φῑμόω, ῶ, (φιμός, a muzzle)
  f. ώσω, a.1. ἐφίμωσα, p. pass. πεφίμωμαι, a.1. ἐφιμώθην,
  to muzzle, 1 Co. 9.9. 1 Ti. 5.18; *met. & by impl.* to silence, put to silence; *pass.* to be silent, speechless, Mat. 22.12, 34. Mar. 1.25, et al.; *trop. pass.* to be hushed, *as winds and waves,* Mar. 4.39.
Φλογίζω,
  f. ίσω,
  to set a flame, kindle, inflame, Ja. 3.6, *bis.: from*
Φλόξ, φλογός, ἡ, (φλέγω, to burn, blaze)
  a flame, Lu. 16.24. Ac. 7.30, et al.
Φλυᾱρέω, ῶ
  f. ήσω,
  to talk folly; *in N.T., trans.* to prate about or against *any one,* 3 Jno. 10: *from*
Φλύᾱρος, ου, ὁ, ἡ, (φλύω, to boil over, bubble; *met.* to babble)
  a prater, tattler, 1 Ti. 5.13.
Φοβερός, ά, όν,
  fearful; terrible, He. 10.27, 31; 12.21: *from*
Φοβέω, ῶ (φόβος)
  f. ήσω,
  to terrify, frighten; *mid.* a.1. ἐφοβήθην, f. φοβνθήσομαι, to fear, dread, Mat. 10.26; 14.5, et. al.; to fear reverentially, to reverence, Mar. 6.20. Lu. 1.50. Ac. 10.2. Eph. 5.33. Re. 11.18, et al.; to be afraid *to do a thing,* Mat. 2.22. Mar. 9.32, et al.; to be reluctant, to scruple, Mat. 1.20; to fear, be apprehensive, Ac. 27.17. 2 Co. 11.3; 12.20; to be fearfully anxious, He. 4.1. *absol.* to be fearful, afraid, alarmed, Mat. 14.27; 17.6, 7. Mar. 16.8, et al.; to be fearfully impressed, Ro. 11.20: *whence*
Φόβητρον, ου, τό,
  something which inspires terror; terrific prodigy or portent, Lu. 21.11.
Φόβος, ου, ὁ, (φέβομαι, to be affrighted, to flee)
  fear, terror, affright, Mat. 14.26. Lu. 1.12; astonishment, amazement, Mat. 28.8. Mar. 4.41; trembling solicitude, 1 Co. 2.3. 2 Co. 7.15; *meton.* a terror, an object or cause of terror, Ro. 13.3; reverential fear, awe, Ac. 9.31. Ro. 3.18; respect, deference, Ro. 13.7. 1 Pe. 2.18.
Φοίνιξ, ῑκος, ὁ,
  the palm-tree, the date-palm, phœnix dactylifera *of Linn.,* Jno. 12.13. Re. 7.9.
Φονεύς, έως, ὁ, (φόνος)
  a homicide, murderer, Mat. 22.7. Ac. 3.14, et al.

Φονεύω,
f. εύσω, a.1. ἐφόνευσα,
to put to death, kill, slay, Mat. 23.31, 35, et al.; *absol.* to commit murder, Mat. 5.21, et al.: *from*
Φόνος, ου, ὁ,
a killing, slaughter, murder, Mat. 15.19. Mar. 7.21; 15.7, et al.
Φορέω, ῶ,
f. ήσω & έσω, a.1. ἐφόρεσα,
to bear; to wear, Mat. 11.8. 1 Co. 15.49, et al.
Φόρον, ου, τό, (Lat. *forum*)
a forum, market-place; Φόρον Ἀππίου Forum Appii, *the name of a small town on the Appian way, according to Antoninus, 43 Roman miles from Rome, or about 40 English miles,* Ac. 28.15.
Φόρος, ου, ὁ (φέρω)
tribute, tax, *strictly such as is laid on dependent and subject people,* Lu. 20.22; 23.2. Ro. 13.6, 7.
Φορτίζω, (φόρτος, a load, φέρω)
f. ίσω, p. pass. πεφόρτισμαι,
to load, lade, burden; *met.* Mat. 11.28. Lu. 11.46.
Φορτίον, ου, τό,
a load, burden, 200*as of a ship,* freight, cargo, v.r. Ac. 27.10; *met.* a burden *of imposed precepts, &c.,* Mat. 11.30; 23.4. Lu. 11.46, *bis; of faults, sins,* &c., Ga. 6.5: *from*
Φόρτος, ου, ὁ, (φέρω)
a load, burden; freight, cargo, Ac. 27.10.
Φραγέλλιον, ίου, τό, (Lat. *flagellum*)
a whip, scourge, Jno. 2.15: (N.T.) *whence*
Φραγελλόω, ῶ,
f. ώσω,
to scourge, Mat. 27.26. Mar. 15.15. N.T.
Φραγμός, οῦ, ὁ, (φράσσω)
a fence, hedge; a hedgeside path, Mat. 21.33. Mar. 12.1. Lu. 14.23; *met.* a parting fence, Ep. 2.14.
Φράζω,
f. άσω, a.1. ἔφρασα,
pr. to propound in distinct terms, to tell; *in N.T.,* to explain, interpret, expound, Mat. 13.36; 15.15.
Φράσσω, v. ττω,
f. ξω, a.1. ἔφραξα,
to fence in; *by impl.* to obstruct, stop, close up, He. 11.33; *met.* to silence, put to silence, Ro. 3.19; 2 Co. 11.10.
Φρέαρ, φρέατος, τό,
a well, cistern, Lu. 14.5. Jno. 4.11, 12; a pit, Re. 9.1, 2.
Φρεναπατάω, ῶ, (φρήν & ἀπατάω)
f. ήσω,
to deceive the mind; to deceive, impose on, Ga. 6.3: (N.T.) *whence*
Φρεναπάτης, ου, ὁ,
a deceiver, seducer, Tit. 1.10. (ἄ) N.T.
Φρήν, ενός, ἡ,
pr. the diaphragm, midriff; the mind, intellect, 1 Co. 14.20, *bis.*

Φρίσσω, v. ττω,
    f. ξω, p. πέφρῖκα, a.1. ἔφριξα,
    to be ruffled, to bristle; to shudder *from fear,* Ja. 2.19.
Φρονέω, ῶ, (φρήν)
    f. ήσω, a.1. ἐφρόνηασ,
    to think, to mind; to be of opinion, Ac. 28.22. Phi. 1.7; to take thought, be considerate,
    Phi. 4.10; to entertain sentiments or inclinationns *of a specific kind,* to be minded, Ro.
    12.16; 15.5. 1 Co. 13.11. 2 Co. 13.11. Ga. 5.10. Phi. 2.2, 3.16; 4.2; to be in a *certain*
    frame of mind, Ro. 12.3. Phi. 2.5; to ween, entertain conceit, 1 Co. 4.6; to heed, pay
    regard to, Ro. 16.4; to incline to, be set upon, mind, Mat. 16.23. Mar. 8.33. Ro. 8.5.
    Phi. 3.15, 19. Col. 3.2.: *whence*
Φρόνημα, ατος, τό,
    frame of thought, will, mind, Ro. 8.6, 7, 27.
Φρόνησις, εως, ἡ,
    a thoughtful frame, sense, rightmindedness, Lu. 1.17; intelligence, Ep. 1.8.
Φρόνῐμος, η, ον,
    considerate, thoughtful, prudent, discreet, Mat. 7.24; 10.16; 24.45, et al.; sagacious,
    wise, Ro. 11.25; 12.16. 1 Co. 4.10; 10.15. 2 Co. 11.19: *whence*
Φρονίμως,
    adv. considerately, providently, Lu. 16.8.
Φροντίζω, (φροντίς, throught, care, fr. φρονέω)
    f. ίσω, p. πεφρόντικα, a.1. ἐφρόντισα,
    to be considerate, be careful, Tit. 3.8.
Φρουρέω, ῶ, (φρουρός, a watcher, guard)
    f. ήσω,
    to keep watch; *trans.* to guard, watch, *with a military guard,* 2 Co. 11.32; to keep *in a*
    condition of restraint, Ga. 3.23; to keep *in a state of settlement or security,* Phi. 4.7. 1
    Pe. 1.5.
Φρυάσσω,
    f. ξω, a.1. ἐφρύαξα, *in classical usage* φρυάσσομαι,
    pr. to snort, neigh, stamp, &c. *as a high-spirited horse; hence,* to be noicy, fierce,
    insolent, and tumultuous, to rage, tumultuate, Ac. 4.25. S.
Φρύγᾰνον, ου, τό, (φρύγω, v. φρύσσω, to parch)
    a dry twig, branch, &c., faggot, Ac. 28.3.
Φυγή, ῆς, ἡ, (φεύγω)
    a fleeing, flight, Mat. 24.20. Mar. 13.18.
Φυλᾰκή, ῆς, ἡ, (φυλάσσω)
    a keeping watch, ward, guard, Lu. 2.8; a place of watch, haunt, Re. 18.2; a watch,
    guard, body of guards, Ac. 12.10; ward, custody, imprisonment, 2 Co. 6.5; 11.23. He.
    11.36; durance, 1 Pe. 3.19; a place of custody, prison, Mat. 14.10; 25.39, 44; a watch
    or division *of the night, which in the time of our Saviour was divided into four*
    watches of three hours each, called ἐψώ, μεσονύκτιον, ἀλεκτοροφωνιά, & πρωΐα, v.
    προΐ, Mat. 14.25; 24.43. Mar. 6.48. Lu. 12.38, *bis: whence*
Φυλακίζω,
    f. ίσω,
    to deliver into custody, put in prison, imprison, Ac. 22.19. S.
Φυλακτήριον, ίου, τό, (φυλάσσω)
    the station of a guard or watch; a preservation, safeguard; *hence,* a phylactery or
    amulet, *worn about the person; from which circumstances the word is used in the N.T.*

as a term for the Jewish Tephillian or prayer-fillets, which took their rise from the injunction, 201Deut. 6.8; 11.18. Mat. 23.5.

Φύλαξ, ἄκος, ὁ

a watchman, guard, sentinel, Ac. 5.23; 12.6, 19: *from*

Φυλάσσω, v. ττω,

f. ξω, a.1. ἐφύλαξα,

to be on watch, keep *watch,* Lu. 2.8; to have in keeping, Ac. 22.20; to have in custody, Ac. 28.16; to keep *under restraint,* confine, Lu. 8.29. Ac. 12.4; 23.35; to guard, defend, Lu. 11.21; to keep safe, preserve, Jno. 12.25; 17.12. 2 Th. 3.3. 2 Pe. 2.5. Jude 24; to keep *in abstinence,* debar, Ac. 21.25. 1 Jno. 5.21; to observe *a matter of injunction or duty,* Mat. 19.20. Mar. 10.20. Lu. 11.28; 18.21. Ac. 7.53; 16.4; 21.24, et al.; *mid.* to be on one's guard, beware, Lu. 12.15. 2 Ti. 4.15, 2 Pe. 3.17.

Φυλή, ῆς, ἡ, (φύω)

a tribe, Mat. 19.28; 24.30. Lu. 2.36; a people, nation, Re. 1.7; 5.9, et al.

Φύλλον, ου, τό,

a leaf, Mat. 21.19, et al.

Φύραμα, ατος, τό, (φυράω, to mix, mingle by kneading, &c.)

that which is mingled and reduced to a uniform consistence by kneading, beating, treading, &c.; a mass *of potter's clay,* Ro. 9.21; *of dough,* 1 Co. 5.6. Ga. 5.9; *met.* Ro. 11.16. 1 Co. 5.7.

Φυσικός, ή, όν, (φύσις)

natural, agreeable to nature, Ro. 1.26, 27; following the instinct of nature, *as animals,* 2 Pe. 2.12: *whence*

Φυσικῶς,

adv. naturally, by natural instinct, Jude 10.

Φῡσιόω, ῶ,

f. ώσω, p. pass. πεφυσίωμαι,

used in N.T. as an equivalent to φυσάω, to inflate, puff up; *met.* to inflate *with pride and vanity,* 1 Co. 8.1; *pass.* to be inflated *with pride,* to be proud, vain, arrogant, 1 Co. 4.6, 19; 5.2; 8.1; 13.4, et al.

Φύσις, εως, ἡ, (φύω)

essence, Ga. 4.8; native condition, birth, Ro. 2.27; 11.21, 24. Ga. 2.15. Eph. 2.3; native species, kind, Ja. 3.7; nature, natural frame, 2 Pe. 1.4; nature, native instinct, Ro. 2.14; 1 Co. 11.14; nature, prescribed course of nature, Ro. 1.26.

Φυσίωσις, εως, ἡ, (φυσιόω)

pr. inflation; *met.* elation of mind, pride, 2 Co. 12.20. N.T.

Φυτεία, ας, ἡ,

plantation, the act of planting; a plant, *met.* Mat. 15.13: *from*

Φυτεύω, (φυτόν, a plant, fr. φύω)

f. εύσω, a.1. ἐφύτευσα,

to plant, set Mat. 21.33. Lu. 13.6, et al.; *met.* Mat. 15.13; to plant *the Gospel,* 1 Co. 3.6-8.

Φύω,

f. φύσω, p. πέφῡκα, a.2. pass. ἐφύην,

to generate, produce; *pass.* to be generated, produced; *of plants,* to germinate, sprout, Lu. 8.6; *intrans.* to germinate, spring or grow up, He. 12.15.

Φωλεός, οῦ, ὁ,

a den, lair, burrow, Mat. 8.20. Lu. 9.58.

Φωνέω, ῶ,

f. ήσω, a.1. ἐφώνησα,

to sound, utter a sound; *of the cock,* to crow, Mat. 26.34, 74, 75; to call, or cry out, exclaim, Lu. 8.8, 54; 16.24; 23.46; to call to, Mat. 27.47. Mar. 3.31, et al.; to call, entitle, Jno. 13.13; to call, summon, Mat. 20.32, et al.; to invite *to a feast,* Lu. 14.12: *from*

Φωνή, ῆς, ἡ,
    a sound, Mat. 24.31. Jno. 3.8. Re. 4.5; 8.5; a cry, Mat. 2.18; an *articulate* sound, voice, Mat. 3.3, 17; 17.5; 27.46, 50; voice, speech, discourse, Jno. 10.16, 27. Ac. 7.31; 12.22; 13.27. He. 3.7, 15; tone *of address,* Ga. 4.20; language, tongue, dialect, 1 Co. 14.10.

Φῶς, φωτός, τό, (contr. for φάος)
    light, Mat. 17.2. 2 Co. 4.6; daylight, broad day, Mat. 10.27. Lu. 12.3; radiance, blaze of light, Mat. 4.16. Ac. 9.3; 12.7, et al.; an instrument or means of light, a light, Mat. 6.23. Ac. 16.29; a fire, Mar. 14.54. Lu. 22.56; *fr. Heb.,* the light *of God's presence,* 2 Co. 11.14. 1 Ti. 6.16; *met.* the light *of divine truth, spiritual* illumination, Lu. 16.8. Jno. 3.19. Ro. 13.12. Eph. 5.8. 1 Pe. 2.9. 1 Jno. 1.7; 2.8, 9, 10, et al.; a source or dispenser of *spiritual* light, Mat. 5.14. Jno. 1.4, 5, 7, 8, 9; 8.12; 9.5, et al.; *pure* radiance, *perfect* brightness, 1 Jno. 1.5: *whence*

Φωστήρ, ῆρος, ὁ,
    a cause of light, illuminator; a light, luminary, Phil. 2.15; 202radiance, *or,* luminary, Re. 21.11.

Φωσφόρος, ου, ὁ, ἡ, (φῶς & φέρω)
    light-bringing; sc. ἀστήρ, Lucifer, the morning star, *met.* 2 Pe. 1.19.

Φωτεινός, ή, όν, (φῶς)
    radiant, lustrous, Mat. 17.5; enlightened, illuminated, Mat. 6.22. Lu. 11.34, 36, *bis.*

Φωτίζω, (fr. same)
    f. ίσω, a.1. ἐφώτισα,
    to light, give light to, illuminate, shine upon, Lu. 11.36. Re. 18.1; *met.* to enlighten *spiritually,* Jno. 1.9. Ep. 1.18; 3.9; He. 6.4; 10.32; to reveal, to bring to light, make known, 1 Co. 4.5. 2 Ti. 1.10: *whence*

Φωτισμός, οῦ, ὁ,
    illumination; a shining forth, effulgence, 2 Co. 4.4, 6. S.

Χ, χ, *Χῖ*

Χαίρω,
    f. χαιρήσω, & , later, χαρήσομαι, a.2. ἐχάρην,
    to rejoice, be glad, be joyful, be full of joy, Mat. 2.10; 5.12; 18.13. Mar. 14.11. Ro. 12.12. 2 Co. 2.3; *imperat.* χαῖρε, χαίρετε, *a term of salutation,* hail, Mat. 26.49; λέγω χαίρειν, to greet, 2 Jno. 10.11; *infin.* χαίρειν, *an epistolary formula,* health, Ac. 15.23.

Χάλαζα, ας, ἡ,
    hail, Re. 8.7; 11.19; 16.21, *bis: from*

Χαλάω, ῶ,
    f. άσω, a.1. ἐχάλᾰσα,
    to slacken; to let down, lower, Mar. 2.4. Lu. 5.4, et al.

Χαλεπός, ή, όν,
    hard, rugged; furious, ferocious, Mat. 8.28; trying, 2 Ti. 3.1.

Χαλῑναγωγέω, ῶ, (χαλινός & ἄγω)
    f. ήσω,
    pr. to guide with a bridle; *met.* to bridle, control, sway, Ja. 1.26; 3.2. L.G.

Χαλῑνός, οῦ, ὁ,

a bridle, bit, curb, Ja. 3.3.

Χάλκεος, έα & έη, εον, contr. οῦς, ῆ, οῦν, (χαλκός)
     brazen, Re. 9.20.

Χαλκευς, έως, ὁ, (fr. same)
     pr. a coppersmith; *hence genr.* a worker in metals, smith, 2 Ti. 4.14.

Χαλκηδών, όνος, ὁ,
     chalcedony, *the name of a gem, generally of a whitish, blush or grey colour,
     susceptible of a high and beautiful polish, and of which there are serveral varieties,
     as the onyx, modern carnelian,* &c. Re. 21.19.

Χαλκίον, ου, τό, (χαλκός)
     a vessel, copper, brazen utensil, Mar. 7.4.

Χαλκολίβανον, ου, ὁ,
     orichalcum, fine bronze, *a factitious metal of which there were several varieties, the
     white being of the highest repute or,* deep-tinted frankinsense, Re. 1.15; 2.18. N.T.

Χαλκός, οῦ, ὁ,
     copper, *also,* bronze, Re. 18.12; a brazen musical instrument, 1 Co. 13.1; copper
     money, Mat. 10.9; money *in general,* Mar. 6.8; 12.41.

Χαλκοῦς,
     see Χάλκεος

Χαμαί,
     adv. on the ground, to the earth, Jno. 9.6; 18.6.

Χαναναῖος, αία, αῖον,
     Canaanitish, Mat. 15.22.

Χαρά, ᾶς, ἡ (χαίρω)
     joy, gladness, rejoicing, Mat. 2.10; 13.20, 44; 28.8, et al.; *meton.* joy, cause of joy,
     occasion of rejoicing, Lu. 2.10. Phi. 4.1. 1 Th. 2.19, 20; bliss, Mat. 25.21, 23.

Χάραγμα, ατος, τό, (χαράσσω, to notch, engrave)
     an imprinted mark, Re. 13.16, et al.; sculpture, Ac. 17.29.

Χαρακτήρ, ῆρος, ὁ, (fr. same)
     a graver, graving tool; an engraven or impressed device; an impress, exact expression,
     He. 1.3.

Χάραξ, ακος, ὁ, ἡ, (fr. same)
     a stake, a pale; a *military* palisade, rampart, *formed from the earth thrown out of the
     ditch and stuck with sharp stakes or palisades,* Lu. 19.43.

Χαρίζομαι, (χάρις)
     f. ίσομαι, a.1. ἐχαρισάμην, pass. f. χαρισθήσομαι, a.1. ἐχαρίσθην,
     to gratify; to bestow *in kindness,* grant *as a free favour,* Lu. 7.21. Ro. 8.32; to grant
     the deliverance of *a person in favour to the desire of others,* Ac. 3.14; 27.24. Philem.
     22; to sacrifice *a person to the demands of enemies,* Ac. 25.11; to remit, forgive, Lu.
     7.42. 2 Co. 2.7, 10.

Χάριν,
     used as a particle governing the genitive case, 203on account of, Lu. 7.47. Eph. 3.1,
     14. 1 Jno. 3.12; for the sake of, in order to, Ga. 3.19. Tit. 1.5, 11. Jude 16; on the score
     of, 1 Ti. 5.14: *pr. the accus. of*

Χάρις, ιτος, ἡ, (χαίρω)
     pleasing show, charm; beauty, gracefulness; a pleasing circumstance, matter of
     approval, 1 Pe. 2.19, 20; kindly bearing, graciousness, Lu. 4.22; a beneficial
     opportunity, benefit, 2 Co. 1.15. Eph. 4.29; a charitable act, generous gift, 1 Co. 16.3.
     2 Co. 8.4, 6, et al.; an act of favour, Ac. 25.3; favour, acceptance, Lu. 1.30, 52. Ac.
     2.47; 7.10, 46; free favour, free gift, grace, Jno. 1.14, 16, 17; Ro. 4.4, 16; 11.5, 6. Eph.

2.5, 8. 1 Pe. 3.7; free favour *specially manifested by God towards man in the Gospel scheme,* grace, Ac. 15.11. Ro. 3.24; 5.15, 17, 20, 21; 6.1. 2 Co. 4.15, et al.; a gracious provision, gracious scheme, grace, Ro. 6.14, 15. He. 2.9; 12.28; 13.9; gracious dealing *from God,* grace, Ac. 14.26; 15.40. Ro. 1.7. 1 Co. 1.4; 15.10. Ga. 1.15, et al.; a commission graciously devolved *by God upon a human agent,* Ro. 1.5; 12.3; 15.15. 1 Co. 3.10. 2 Co. 1.12. Ga. 2.9. Eph. 3.8; grace, graciously bestowed *divine* endowment or influence, Lu. 2.40. Ac. 4.33; 11.23. Ro. 12.6. 2 Co. 12.9, et al.; grace, a graciously vouchsafed *spiritual* position, Ac. 11.43. Ro. 5.2. Ga. 5.4. 2 Pe. 3.18; an emotion correspondent to what is pleasing or kindly; sense of obligation, Lu. 17.9; a grateful frame of mind, 1 Co. 10.30; thanks, Lu. 6.32, 33, 34. Ro. 6.17. 1 Co. 15.57, et al.; χάριν v. χάριτας καταθέσθαι, to oblige, gratify, Ac. 24.27; 25.9

Χάρισμα, ατος, τό, (χαρίζομαι)
 a free favour, free gift, Ro. 5.15, 16; 6.23. 2 Co. 1.11, et al.; benefit, Ro. 1.11; *a divinely conferred* endowment, 1 Co. 12.4, 9, 28, 30, 31, et al. N.T.

Χαριτόω, ῶ, (χάρις)
 f. ώσω, p. pass. κεχαρίτωμαι,
 to favour, visit with favour, to make an object of favour, to gift; *pass.* to be visited with free favour, be an object of gracious vistation, Lu. 1.28. L.G.

Χάρτης, ου, ὁ,
 paper, 2 Jno. 12.

Χάσμα, ατες, τό, (χαινω, to gape, yawn)
 a chasm, gulf, Lu. 16.26.

Χεῖλος, εος, τό,
 a lip, & *pl.* τὰ χείλη, the lips, Mat. 15.8. Ro. 3.13, et al.; *trop.* χεῖλος τῆς θαλάσσης, the sea-shore, He. 11.12; *meton.* language, dialect, 1 Co. 14.21.

Χειμάζω, (χεῖμα)
 f. άσω,
 to excite a tempest, toss with a tempest; *pass.* to be storm-tossed, Ac. 27.18.

Χείμαρρος, ου, ὁ, (χεῖμα & ῥέω)
 winter-flowing; *as subst.* a stream which flows in winter, *but is dry in summer;* a brook, Jno. 18.1.

Χειμών, ῶνος, ὁ, (χεῖμα)
 stormy weather, Mat. 16.3; a storm, tempest, Ac. 27.20; winter, Mat. 24.20, et al.

Χείρ, χειρός, ἡ,
 a hand, Mat. 3.12; 4.6; 8.15, et al. freq.; *fr. the Heb.* χεὶρ Κυρίου, a *special* operation of God, Ac. 11.21; 13.3; ἐν χειρί, by agency, Ac. 7.35. Ga. 3.19.

Χειραγωγέω, ῶ,
 f. ήσω,
 to lead by the hand, Ac. 9.8; 22.11; (L.G.) *from*

Χειραγωγός, οῦ, ὁ, (χείρ & ἀγωγός, a leader)
 one who leads another by the hand, Ac. 13.11.

Χειρόγραφον, ου, τό, (χείρ & γράφω)
 handwriting; a written form, literal instrument *as distinguished from a spiritual dispensation,* Col. 2.14.

Χειροποίητος, ου, ὁ, ἡ, (χείρ & ποιητός, made, fr. ποιέω)
 made by hand, artificial, material, Mar. 14.58. Ac. 7.48, et al.

Χειροτονέω, ῶ, (χείρ & τείνω)
 f. ήσω,
 to stretch out the hand; to constitute by voting; to appoint, constitute, Ac. 14.23. 2 Co. 8.19.

Χείρων, ονος, ὁ, ἡ, (irregular comparat. of κακός)
    worse, Mat. 9.16. 1 Ti. 5.8; more severe, Jno. 5.14. He. 10.29.

Χερουβίμ, (Heb. מיבורכ)
    cherubim, *the emblematic figures, representing cherubim, on the ark,* He. 9.5.

Χήρα, ας, ἡ, (pr. fem. of χῆρος, bereft)
    a widow, Mat. 23.14. Lu. 4.26, et al.

Χθές,
    adv. yesterday, Jno. 4.52. Ac. 7.28. He. 13.8.

Χῑλίαρχος, ου, ὁ, (χιλίοι & ἄρχω)
    204*pr.* a chiliarch, commander of a thousand men; *hence genr.* a commander, military
    chief, Mar. 6.21. Re. 6.15; 19.18; *spc. a legionary* tribune, Ac. 21.31, 32, 33, 37, et
    al.; the prefect *of the temple,* Jno. 18.12.

Χιλιάς, άδος, ἡ,
    the number one thousand, a thousand, Lu. 14.31. Ac. 4.4. et al.: *from*

Χίλιοι, αι, α,
    a thousand, 2 Pe. 3.8. Re. 11.3, et al.

Χιτών, ῶνος, ὁ,
    a tunic, vest, *the inner garment which fitted close to the body, having armholes, and*
    sometimes sleeves, and reaching below the knees, Mat. 5.40; 10.10; *pl.* χιτῶνες,
    clothes, garments *in general,* Mar. 14.63.

Χιών, όνος, ἡ,
    snow, Mat. 28.3. Mar. 9.3. Re. 1.14.

Χλαμύς, ύδος, ἡ,
    chlamys, *a species of* cloak; *a Roman military commander's cloak,* paludamentum,
    Mat. 27.28, 31.

Χλευάζω, (χλεύη, jest)
    f. άσω, a.1. ἐχλεύασα,
    to jeer, scoff, Ac. 2.13; 17.32.

Χλιᾰρός, ά, όν, (χλίω, to become warm)
    warm, tepid; lukewarm, Re. 3.16.

Χλωρός, ά, όν, (χλόη, the first tender shoot of vegetation)
    pale green; green, verdant, Mar. 6.39. Re. 8.7; 9.4; pale, sallow, Re. 6.8.

Χξς΄
    six hundred and sixty-six, *the number denoted by these letters, viz.* χ΄ = 600, ξ΄ = 60,
    ς΄ = 6, Re. 13.18.

Χοϊκός, ή, όν, (χόος, a heap of earth)
    of earth, earthy, 1 Co. 15.47, 48, 49. N.T.

Χοῖνιξ, ῑκος, ἡ,
    a chœnix, *an Attic measure for things dry, being the 48th part of a medimnus,*
    consequently equal to the 8th part of the Roman modius, & nearly equivalent to about
    one quart, being considered a sufficient daily allowance for the sustenance of one
    man, Re. 6.6, *bis*

Χοῖρος, ου, ὁ, ἡ,
    pr. a young swine; a swine, hog or sow, Mat. 8.30, 31, 32, et al.

Χολάω, ῶ, (χολή, *considered as the seat or cause of anger and of melancholy*))
    pr. to be melancholy; *used later as an equivalent to* χολοῦμαι, to be angry, incensed,
    Jno. 7.23.

Χολή, ῆς, ἡ,

the bile, gall; *in N.T.,* a bitter ingredient, *as* wormwood, Mat. 27.34; χολὴ πικρίας, intense bitterness, *met.* thorough disaffection *to divine truth,* utter estrangement, Ac. 8.23.

Χόος, χοῦς, gen. χοός, dat. χοΐ, acc. χοῦν, (χέω)
    earth dug out and heaped up; loose earth, dirt, dust, Mar. 6.11. Re. 18.19.

Χορηγέω, ῶ (χορός & ἡγέομαι)
    to lead a chorus; *at Athens* to defray the cost of a chorus; *hence,* to supply funds; to supply, furnish, 2 Co. 9.10. 1 Pe. 4.11.

Χορός, οῦ, ὁ,
    dancing *with music,* Lu. 15.25.

Χορτάζω, (χόρτος)
    f. άσω, a.1. ἐχόρτασα,
    pr. to feed or fill with grass, herbage, &c., to fatten; *used of animals of prey,* to satiate, gorge, Re. 19.21; *of persons,* to satisfy with food, Mat. 14.20; 15.33, 37; *met.* to satisfy *the desire of any one,* Mat. 5.6, et al.: *whence*

Χόρτασμα, ατος, τό,
    pasture, provender *for cattle;* food, provision, sustenance, *for men,* Ac. 7.11. L.G.

Χόρτος, ου, ὁ,
    an inclosure; pasture ground; fodder *for beasts; in N.T.,* herbage, verdure, Mat. 6.30; 14.19, et al.; a plant *of corn,* Mat. 13.26. Mar. 4.28.

Χοῦς,
    see, χόος.

Χράομαι, ῶμαι,
    f. χρήσομαι,
    to use, to make use of, employ, Ac. 27.17. 1 Co. 7.31, et al.; to avail one's self of, 1 Co. 7.21; 9.12, 15; to use, to treat, behave towards, Ac. 27.3. 2 Co. 13.10: *whence*

Χρεία, ας, ἡ,
    use; need, necessity, requisiteness, Ep. 4.29. He. 7.11; *personal* need, an *individual* want, Ac. 20.34. Ro. 12.13. Phi. 2.25, 4.16, 19; χρείαν ἔχω, to need, require, want, Mat. 6.8; 14.16. Mar. 2.25. Jno 2.25; ἐστὶ χρεία, there is need, Lu. 10.42; τὰ πρὸς χρείαν, necessary things, Ac. 28.10, et al.; a necessary business affair, Ac. 6.3.

Χρεωφειλέτης, ου, ὁ (χρέος, a debt, & ὀφειλέτης)
    205one who owes a debt, a debtor, Lu. 7.41; 16.5. L.G.

Χρή,
    imperson. verb, there is need or occasion, it is necessary, it is requisite; it behoves, it becometh, it is proper, Ja. 3.10.

Χρήζω, (χρεία)
    to need, want, desire, Mat. 6.32. Lu. 11.8; 12.30. Ro. 16.2. 2 Co. 3.1.

Χρῆμα, ατος, τό, (χράομαι)
    anything useful, or needful; *plur.* wealth, riches, Mar. 10.23, 24. Lu. 18.24; money, Ac. 8.18, 20; 24.26; *sing.* price, Ac. 4.37: *whence*

Χρηματίζω,
    f. ίσω, a.1. ἐχρημάτισα,
    to have dealings, transact business; to negotiate; to give answer on deliberation; *in N.T., pass.* to be divinely instructed, receive a revelation or warning from God, Mat. 2.12, 22. Lu. 2.26. Ac. 10.22. He. 8.5; 11.7; 12.25; *intrans.* to receive an appellation, be styled, Ac. 11.26. Ro. 7.3: *whence*

Χρηματισμός, οῦ, ὁ,
    in N.T., a response from God, a divine communication, oracle, Ro. 11.4.

Χρήσῐμος, η, ον, v. ὁ, ἡ, τὸ, -ον,

useful, profitable, 2 Ti. 2.14; *from*

Χρῆσις, εως, ἡ,
 use, employment; manner of using, Ro. 1.26, 27.
Χρηστεύομαι, (χρηστός)
 f. εύσομαι,
 to be gentle, benign, kind, 1 Co. 13.4. N.T.
Χρηστολογία, ας, ἡ, (χρηστός & λόγος)
 blan address, fair speaking, Ro. 16.18. N.T.
Χρηστός, ή, όν, (χράομαι)
 useful, profitable; good, agreeable, Lu. 5.39; easy, *as a yoke,* Mat. 11.30; gentle,
 benign, kind, obliging, gracious, Lu. 6.35. Ep. 4.32. Ro. 2.4. 1 Pe. 2.3; good, *in
 character, disposition,* &c., virtuous, 1 Co. 15.33: *whence*
Χρηστότης, τητος, ἡ
 pr. utility; goodness, kindness, gentleness, Ro. 2.4; 11.22, et al.; kindness *shown,*
 beneficense, Ep. 2.7; goodness, virtue, Ro. 3.12.
Χρήσω,
 fut. of κίχρημι, a.1. ἔχρησα,
 to lend, Lu. 11.5.
Χρῖσμα, ατος, τό (χρίω)
 pr. any thing which is applied by smearing; ointment, unguent; *in N.T.,* an anointing,
 unction, *in the reception of spiritual privileges,* 1 Jno. 2.20, 27, *bis.*
Χριστιανός, οῦ, ὁ,
 a Christian, follower of Christ, Ac. 11.26; 26.28. 1 Pe. 4.16: *from*
Χριστός, οῦ, ὁ,
 pr. anointed; ὁ Χριστός, the Christ, The Anointed One, i.q. Μεσσίας, the Messiah,
 Mat. 1.16, 17. Jno. 1.20, 25, 42, et al. freq.; *meton.* Christ, the word or doctrine of
 Christ, 2 Co. 1.19, 21. Ep. 4.20; Christ, a *truly* Christian frame *of doctrine and
 affection,* Ro. 8.10. Ga. 4.19; Christ, the Church of Christ, 1 Co. 12.12; Christ, the
 distinctive privileges of the Gospel of Christ, Ga. 3.27. Ph. 3.8. He. 3.14: *from*
Χρίω,
 f. ίσω, a.1. ἔχρῖσα,
 to anoint; *in N.T.,* to anoint, *by way of instituting to a dignity, function, or privilege,*
 Lu. 4.18. Ac. 4.27; 10.38. 2 Co. 1.21. He. 1.9
Χρονίζω,
 f. ίσω, At. ιῶ, a.1. ἐχρόνισα,
 to while, spend time; to linger, delay, be long, Mat. 24.48; 25.5. Lu. 1.21; 12.45. He.
 10.37: *from*
Χρόνος, ου, ὁ,
 time, *whether in respect of duration or a definite point of its lapse,* Mat. 2.7; 29.19, et
 al. freq.; an epoch, era, *marked* duration, Ac. 1.7. 1 Th. 5.1.
Χρονοτρῐβέω, ῶ, (χρόνος & τρίβω)
 to spend time, while away time, linger, delay, Ac. 20.16.
Χρύσεος, η, ον, contr. οῦς, ῆ, οὺν, (χρυσός)
 golden, of gold, 2 Ti. 2.20. He. 9.4, et al.
Χρυσίον, ίου, τό, (dim. fr. χρυσός)
 gold, He. 9.4. 1 Pe. 1.7. Re. 21.18, 21; *spc.* gold when coined or manufactured; golden
 ornaments, 1 Pe. 3.3; gold coin, money, Ac. 3.6; 20.33. 1 Pe. 1.18.
Χρυσοδακτύλιος, ου, ὁ, ἡ, (χρυσός & δακτύλιος)
 having rings of gold on the fingers, Ja. 2.2. N.T.
Χρυσόλῐθος, ου, ἡ, (χρυσός & λίθος)

chrysolite, *a name applied by the ancients to all gems of a gold colour, spc. the modern topaz,* Re. 21.20.

Χρυσόπρᾰσος, ου, ὁ, (χρυσός & πράσον, a leek)
    a chrysoprase, 206*a species of gem of a golden green colour like that of a leek,* Re. 21.20.

Χρῡσός, οῦ, ὁ
    gold, Mat. 2.11; 23.16, 17; *meton.* gold ornaments, 1 Ti. 2.9; coin, money, Mat. 10.9, et al.

Χρυσοῦς,
    see χρύσεος.

Χρυσόω, ῶ, (χρυσός)
    f. ώσω, p. pass. κεχρύσωμαι,
    to gild, overlay with gold, adorn or deck with gold, Re. 17.4; 18.16.

Χρώς, χρωτός, ὁ,
    the skin; the body, Ac. 19.12.

Χωλός, ή, όν,
    crippled in the feet, limping, halting, lame, Mat. 11.5; 15.30, 31, et al.; *met.* limping, weak, *spiritually,* He. 12.13; maimed, deprived of a foot, *for* ἀναπηρός, Mar. 9.45.

Χώρα, ας, ἡ,
    space, room; a country, region, tract, province, Mar. 5.10. Lu. 2.8; a district, territory, environs, Mat. 8.28; *meton.* the inhabitants of a country, region, &c., Mar. 1.5. Ac. 12.20; the country, *as opposed to the city or town,* Lu. 21.21; a field, farm, Lu. 12.16. Jno. 4.35.

Χωρέω, ῶ, (fr. same)
    f. ήσω, a.1. ἐχώρησα,
    to make room *either by motion or capacity;* to move, pass, Mat. 15.17; to proceed, go on, 2 Pe. 3.9; to progress, make way, Jno. 8.37; *trans.* to hold *as contents,* contain, afford room for, Mar. 2.2. Jno. 2.6; 21.25; *met.* to give *mental* admittance to, to yield accordance, Mat. 19.11, 12; to admit *to approbation and esteem,* to regard cordially, 2 Co. 7.2.

Χωρίζω, (χωρίς)
    f. ίσω, a.1. ἐχώρισα,
    to sunder, sever, disunite, Mat. 19.6. Ro. 8.35, 39;
    mid. a.1. ἐχωρίσθην, p. κεχώρισμαι,
    to dissociate one's self, to part, 1 Co. 7.10, 11, 15; to withdraw, depart, Ac. 1.4; 18.1, 2. Philem. 15; to be aloof, Re. 7.26.

Χορίον, ου, τό, (pr. dim. fr. χῶρος)
    a place, spot, Mat. 26.36. Mar. 14.32; a field, farm, estate, domain, Jno. 4.5. Ac. 1.18, et al.

Χωρίς,
    adv. apart, Jno. 20.7; apart from, parted from, Jno. 15.5. Ja. 2.18, 20, 26; alien from, Eph. 2.12; apart from, on a distinct footing from 1 Co. 11.11; apart from, distinct from, without the intervention of, Ro. 3.21, 28; 4.6; apart from *the company of,* independently of, 1 Co. 4.8. He. 11.40; without *the presence of,* He. 9.28; without *the agency of,* Jno. 1.3. Ro. 10.14; without *the employment of,* Mat. 13.34. Mar. 4.34. He. 7.20, 21; 9.7, 18, 22; without, Lu. 6.49. Phi. 2.14. 1 Ti. 2.8; 5.21. Philem. 14. He. 10.28; 11.6; 12.8, 14; clear from, He. 7.7; irrespectively of, Ro. 7.8, 9; without reckoning, besides, Mat. 14.21; 15.38. 2 Co. 11.28; with the exception of, He. 4.15.

Χῶρος, ου, ὁ,

Corus, or Caurus, the north-west wind; *meton.* the north-west *quarter of the heavens,* Ac. 27.12.

Ψ, ψ, Ψῖ

Ψάλλω, (ψάω, to touch)
  f. ψαλῶ, a.1. ἔψηλα,
    to move by a touch, to twitch; to touch, strike *the strings or chords of an instrument; absol.* to play on a stringed instument; to sing to music; *in N.T.,* to sing praises, Ro. 15.9. 1 Co. 14.15. Ep. 5.19. Ja. 5.13. *whence*
Ψαλμός, οῦ, ὁ,
    impulse, touch, *of the chords of a stringed instrument; in N.T.,* a sacred song, psalm, 1 Co. 14.26. Ep. 5.19, et al.
Ψευδαδελφός, οῦ, ὁ, (ψευδής & ἀδελφός)
    a false brother, a pretended Christian, 2 Co. 11.26. Ga. 2.4. N.T.
Ψευδαπόστολος, ου, ὁ, (ψευδής & ἀπόστολος)
    a false apostel, pretended minister of Christ, 2 Co. 11.13. N.T.
Ψευδής, έος, οῦς, ὁ, ἡ (ψεύδομαι)
    false, lying, Ac. 6.13. Re. 2.2 *in N.T., pl.* maintainers of *religious* falsehood, corrupters of the truth *of God,* Re. 21.8
Ψευδοδάσκᾰλος, (ψευδής & διδάσκαλος)
    a false teacher, one who in culcates false doctrines, 2 Pe. 2.1. N.T.
Ψευδολόγος, ου, ὁ, ἡ, (ψευδής & λέγω)
    false-speaking, 1 Ti. 4.2.
Ψευδομάρτυρ, ὕρος, ὁ, (ψευδής & μάρτυρ)
    207a false witness, Mat. 26.60, *bis.* 1 Co. 15.15: *whence*
Ψευδομαρτῠρέω, ῶ,
  f. ήσω,
    to bear false witness, give false testimony, Mat. 19.18. Mar. 14.56, 57, et al.: *whence*
Ψευδομαρτυρία, ας, ἡ,
    false witness, false testimony, Mat. 15.19; 26.59.
Ψευδοπροφήτης, ου, ὁ (ψευδής & προφήτης)
    a false prophet, one who falsely claims to speak by divine inspiration, *whether as a foreteller of future events, or a teacher of doctrines,* Mat. 7.15; 24.24, et al.
Ψεῦδος, εος, τό, (ψεύδομαι)
    falsehood, Jno. 8.44. Ep. 4.25. 2 Th. 2.9, 11. 1 Jno. 2.27 *in N.T., religious* falsehood, perversion *of religious truth,* false religion, Ro. 1.25; the practices of false religion, Re. 21.27; 22.15.
Ψευδόχριστος, ου, ὁ, (ψευδής & χριστός)
    a false Christ, pretended Messiah, Mat. 24.24. Mar. 13.22. N.T.
Ψεύδω,
  f. ψεύσω,
    to deceive; *mid.* to speak falsely or deceitfully, utter falsehood, lie, Mat. 5.11. Ro. 9.1, et al.; *trans.* to deceive, or attempt to deceive, by a lie. Ac. 5.3.
Ψευδώνῠμος, ου, ὁ, ἡ, (ψευδής & ὄνομα)
    falsely named, falsely called, 1 Ti. 6.20.
Ψεῦσμα, ατος, τό, (ψεύδω)
    a falsehood, lie; *in N.T.,* delinquency, Ro. 3.7.
Ψευστής, οῦ, ὁ, (fr. same)
    one who utters a falsehood, a liar, Jno. 8.44, 55, et al.; *in N.T.,* a delinquent, Ro. 3.4.

Ψηλαφάω, ῶ, (ψάλλω, ψάω)
    f. ήσω, a.1. ἐψηλάφησα,
    to feel, handle, Lu. 24.39; to feel or grope for or after, *as persons in the dark,* Ac. 17.27.
Ψηφίζω,
    f. ίσω,
    to reckon by means of pebbles, compute by counters; *hence genr.* to compute, reckon, calculate, Lu. 14.28. Re. 13.18: *from*
Ψῆφος, ου, ή,
    a small stone, pebble; a pebble *variously employed, especially in a ballot; hence* a vote, suffrage, Ac. 26.10; a pebble or stone, *probably given as a token,* Re. 2.17.
Ψιθυρισμος, οῦ, ὁ, (ψιθυρίζω, to whisper)
    a whispering; a *calumnious* whispering, detraction, 2 Co. 12.20. L.G.
Ψιθυριστής, οῦ, ὁ, (fr. same)
    a whisperer; a *calumnious* whisperer, detractor, Ro. 1.30.
Ψῐχίον, ίον, τό, (dimin. of ψίξ, a fragment, morsel)
    a small morsel, crumb, bit, Mat. 15.27. Mar. 7.28. Lu. 16.21. N.T.
Ψυχή, ῆς, ἡ, (ψύχω)
    breath; the principle of animal life; the life, Mat. 2.20; 6.25. Mar. 3.4. Lu. 21.19. Jno. 10.11, et al.; an animate being, 1 Co. 15.45; *a human* individual, soul, Ac. 2.41; 3.23; 7.14; 27.37. Ro. 13.1. 1 Pe. 3.20; the *immaterial* soul, Mat. 10.28. 1 Pe. 1.9; 2.11, 25; 4.19, et al,; the soul *as a seat of religious and moral sentiment,* Mat. 11.29. Ac. 14.2, 22; 15.24. Eph. 6.6, et al.; the soul *as a seat of feeling,* Mat. 12.18; 26.38, et.al.; the soul, the *inner* self, Lu. 12.19: *whence*
Ψυχικός, ή, όν,
    pertaining to the life or the soul; *in N.T.,* animal *as distinguished from spriritual subsistence,* 1 Co. 15.44, 46; occupied with mere animal things, animal, sensual, 1 Co. 2.14. Ja. 3.15. Jude 19.
Ψῦχος, εος, τό, (ψύχω)
    cold, Jno. 18.18. Ac. 28.2. 2 Co. 11.27: *whence*
Ψυχρός, ά, όν,
    cool, cold, Mat. 10.42; *met.* Re. 3.15, 16.
Ψύχω,
    f. ξω, pass. a.2. ἐψύγην, f.2. ψυγήσομαι,
    to breathe; to cool; *pass.* to be cooled; *met. of affection,* Mat. 24.12.
Ψωμίζω, (ψωμός)
    f. ίσω,
    pr. to feed by morsels; *hence genr.* to feed, supply with food, Ro. 12.20; to bestow in supplying food, 1 Co. 13.3.
Ψωμιον, ου, τό, (dimin. of ψωμός, a bit, morsel, fr. ψάω, to break into bits)
    a bit, morsel, mouthful, Jno. 13.26.
Ψώχω, (ψάω)
    f. ξω,
    to rub in pieces, *as the ears of grain,* Lu. 6.1.

Ω, ω, Ὦ μέγα

Ω, ω,
    208Omega, *the last letter of the Greek alphabet; hence met.* τὸ Ω, the last, Re. 1.8, 11; 21.6; 22.13.

Ὦ,

    interj. O! Mat. 15.28; 17.17, et al.

Ὧδε *adv.* (ὅδε)

    thus; here, in this place, Mat. 12.6, 41; ὧδε ἤ ὧδε, here or there, Mat. 24.23; τὰ ὧδε, the state of things here, Col. 4.9; *met.* herein, in this thing, Re. 13.10, 18; hither, to this place, Mat. 8.29; 14.18, et al.

Ὠιδή, ῆς, ἡ (contr. for ἀοιδή, fr. ἀείδω)

    an ode, song, hymn, Ep. 5.19. Col. 3.16. Re. 5.9; 14.3; 15.3.

Ὠδίς, ῖνος, ἡ & in N.T., ὠδίν, (ὀδύνη)

    the throe *of a woman in travail,* a birth-pang, 1 Th. 5.3; *pl. met.* birth-throes, preliminary troubles *to the development of a catastrophe,* Mat. 24.8 Mar. 13.9; *fr. the Heb.* a stringent band, a snare, noose, Ac. 2.24: *whence*

Ὠδίνω,

    f. ἰνῶ,

    to be in travail, Ga. 4.27. Re. 12.2; *met.* to travail with, to make effort to bring to *spiritual* birth, Ga. 4.19. (ῑ.)

Ὦμος, ου, ὁ,

    the shoulder, Mat. 23.4. Lu. 15.5.

Ὠνέομαι, οῦμαι,

    f. ἠσομαι, a.1. ὠνησάμην,

    to buy, purchase, Ac. 7.16.

Ὠόν, οῦ, τό,

    an egg, Lu. 11.12.

Ὥρα, ας, ἡ,

    a limited portion of time *marked out by part of a settled routine or train of circumstance;* a season of the year; time of day, Mat. 14.15. Mar. 6.35; 11.11 an hour, Mat. 20.3. Jno. 11.9, et al.; *in N.T.* an *eventful* season, 1 Jno. 2.18, *bis.* Re. 3.10; 14.7; due time, Jno. 16.21 Ro. 13.11; a *destined* period, hour, Mat. 26.24. Mar. 14.35. Jno. 2.4; 7.30, et al.; a short period, Mat. 26.40. Jno 5.35. 2 Co 7.8. Ga. 2.5. 1 Th. 2.17. Philem. 15; a point of time, time, Mat. 8.13; 24.42. Lu. 2.38, et al.: *whence*

Ὡραῖος, α, ον,

    timely, seasonable; in prime, blooming; *in N.T.,* beautiful, Mat. 23.27. Ac. 3.2, 10. Ro. 10.15.

Ὠρύομαι,

    f. ύσομαι,

    to howl; to roar, *as a lion,* 1 Pe. 5.8.

Ὥς, (ὅς)

    adv. as, *correlatively,* Mar. 4.26. Jno. 7.46. Ro. 5.15, et al.; as, like as, Mat. 10.16. Eph. 5.8, et al.; according as, Ga. 6.10, et al.; as, as it were, Re. 8.8, et al.; as, Lu. 16.1. Ac. 3.12, et al.; *before numerals,* about, Mar. 5.13, et al.; *conj.,* that, Ac. 10.28, et al.; how, Ro. 11.2, et al.; when, Mat. 28.9. Phi. 2.23; *as an exclamatory particle,* how, Ro. 10.15; *equivalent to* ὥστε, accordingly, He. 3.11; *also,* on condition that, provided that, Ac. 26.24; ὡς εἰπεῖν, so to speak, He. 7.9

Ὡσαννά, (Heb. אנ־העישוה)

    hosanna! save now, succour now, Mat. 21.9, 15, et al.

Ὡσαύτως, (ὡς & αὕτως, αὐτός)

    adv. just so, in just the same way or manner, likewise, Mat. 20.5; 21.30, et al.

Ὡσεί, *adv.* (ὡς & εἰ)

    as if; as it were, as, like, Mat. 3.16; 9.36, et al.; *with terms of number or quantity,* about, Mat. 14.21. Lu 1.56; 22.41, 59.

Ὥσπερ, (ὡς & περ)
　adv. just as, as, like as, Mat. 6.2; 24.38. 1 Th. 5.3, et al.
Ὡσπερεί, adv. (ὥσπερ & εἰ)
　just as it; as it were, 1 Co. 15.8.
Ὥστε, (ὡς & τε)
　conj. so that, so as that, so as to, Mat. 8.24. Mar. 2.12. Ac. 14.1. Ga. 2.13; as an
　illative particle, therefore, consequently, Mat. 12.12; 23.31, et al.; in N.T. as a
　particle of design, in order that, in order to, Lu. 9.52.
Ὠτίον, ου, τό, (dimin. of οὖς)
　in N.T. simply equivalent to οὖς, an ear, Mat. 26.51. Mar. 14.47. Lu. 22.51, Jno.
　18.10, 26.
Ὠφέλεια, ας, ἡ,
　help; profit, gain, advantage, benefit, Ro. 3.1. Jude 16: from
Ὠφελέω, ῶ, (ὄφελος)
　f. ήσω, a.1. ὠφέλησα,
　to help, profit, benefit, Mat. 27.24. Mar. 7.11. Ro. 2.25. et al.; whence
Ὠφέλιμος, ου, ὁ, ἡ, τό, -ον,
　profitable, useful, beneficial, serviceable, 1 Ti. 4.8, bis. 2 Ti. 3.16, Tit. 3.8.

SUPPLEMENT

SUPPLEMENT

**Containing Additional Words and Form To Be Found In
One Or Another Of The Greek Texts In Current Use,
Especially Those Of Lachmann, Tischendorf,
Tregelles, Westcott and Hort, and
The Revisers of 1881.**

A, α, Ἄλφα

Ἀγαλλιάομαι,
　see Ἀγαλλιάω.
Ἀγγέλλω,
　f. ῶ, a.1. ἤγγειλα,209
　Jn. 4.51 (where many texts read ἀπήγγειλα); (ἄγγελος) to announce, Jn. 20.18.
Ἄγγος, εος, τό
　see ἀγγεῖον.
Ἀηδία, ας, ἡ
　(ἀηδής, ἀ & ἧδος, pleasure, delight) unpleasantness, annoyance; dislike, hatred, Lu.
　23.12 (some MSS.)
Ἀθροίζω,
　p. pass. part. ἠθροισμένος, (ἀθρόος, in crowds, masses) to collect together, assemble;
　pass. to be assembled, convene, Lu. 24.33.

Ἀκατάπαστος, ον,

    so some editors in 2 Pe. 2.14. Possibly fr. πατέομαι, p. pass. πέπασμαι, to taste, eat; whence ἀκατάπαστος insatiable. In prof. writ. κατάπαστος signifies besprinkled, soiled; fr. καταπάσσω. N.T.

Ἄλα, τό,

    read by Tdf. in Mat. 5.13; Mar. 9.30; Lu. 14.34; see ἅλας. N.T.

Ἁλεεύς, ὁ,

    read by Tdf., West.-Hort for ἁλιεύς.

Ἀλλαχοῦ, (ἄλλος)

    adv. of place, elsewhere, in another place, Mar. 1.38.

Ἄλφα, τό, (see A)

    indecl., Alpha, Re. 1.8; 21.6; 22.13.

Ἀμφιάζω, (ἀμφί)

    f. άσω,

    to put on, clothe, Lu. 12.28. L.G. See ἀμφιέννυμι.

Ἀμφιέζω,

    collat. form of ἀμφιάζω.

Ἀνακυλίω (ἀνά & κυλίω)

    to roll up; roll back, Mar. 16.4. L.G.

Ἀναλόω,

    see ἀναλίσκω.

Ἀναμέρος,

    see ἀνά.

Ἀνάμεσον,

    see ἀνά.

Ἀνάπειρος,

    a false spelling in some MSS. for ἀνάπηρος. See Lu. 14.13, 21. S.

Ἀναπηδάω,

    a.1. part. ἀναπηδήσας,

    (ἀνά & πηδάω) to leap up, spring up, start up, Mar. 10.50.

Ἀνατίθημι,

    act. of ἀνατίθεμαι.

Ἀνέλεος, ον, (ἀ priv. & ἔλεος)

    without mercy, merciless, Ja. 2.13. N.T. See ἀνίλεως.

Ἀπασπάζομαι,

    a.1. ἀπησπασάμην, (ἀπό & ἀσπάζομαι)

    to salute on leaving, bid farewell, take leave of, Ac. 21.6. L.G.

Ἀποδεκατεύω,

    for ἀποδεκατόω, Lu. 18.12.

Ἀποκατιστάνω,

    variant form of ἀποκαθιστάνω; see ἀποκαθίστημι.

Ἀραβών,

    collat. form of ἀῤῥαβών, which see.

Ἄραγε, (ἄρα & γέ)

    210surely then, so then (Lat. iteque, ergo), Mat. 7.20; 17.26. Ac. 11.18.

Ἆράγε,

    like ἆρα but more pointed, Ac. 8.30.

Ἄραφος,

    collat. form of ἄῤῥαφος, which see.

Ἀρήν, ἀρνός, ὁ,

a sheep, a lamb, acc. pl. ἄρνας, Lu. 10.3

Ἀσαίνω,
   1 Th. 3.3 in some edd. See σαίνω. N.T.
Ἀτιμάω,
   a.1. ἠτίμησα, (ἀ & τιμάω)
   to deprive of honor, to treat lightly, to treat with contempt or contumely, Mar. 12.4.
   See Soph. Lex.
Αὔξω
   see αὐξάνω.
Αὐτόφωρος, ον, (αὐτός & φώρ, a thief)
   caught in the act of theft; *then univ.*, cought in the act of any other crime, Jn. 8.4.
Αὐχέω,
   imperf. ηὔχουν,
   to lift up the neck; to boast, Ja. 3.5.
Ἀφεῖδον,
   a variant spelling of ἀπεῖδον, which see.
Ἀφελπίζω,
   a variant spelling of ἀπελπίζω, which see.
Ἀφυστερέω,
   f. ῶ, (ἀπό & ὑστερέω)
   to be behindhand, come too late; to cause to fail, take away from, withdraw, defaud,
   Ja. 5.4. L.G.

B, β, *Βῆτα*

Βαθέως,
   adv. deeply; ὄρθρου Βαθέως, *deep in the morning*, at early down, Lu. 24.1 L.G.
Βασιλικός, ή, όν,
   of or belonging to a king, kingly, royal, regal; *of a man*, the officer or minister of a
   prince, a courtier, Jn. 4.46, 49; subject to a king, Ac. 12.20; befitting a king, royal, Ac.
   12.21; *met* principal, chief, Ja. 2.4.
Βιβλιδάριον, ου, τό, (fr βιβλίδιον)
   a little book, Re. 10.8
Βοανεργές
   (Heb. בְּנֵי רֶגֶשׁ) Boanerges (sons of thunder), Mar. 3.17. N.T.

Γ, γ, *Γάμμα*

Γαββαθᾶ, ἡ
   indecl. (Aram. גַּבְּתָא) Gabbatha, Jn. 19.13. N.T.
Γαμίσκω,
   act. of γαμίσκομαι, Mat. 24.38. Lchm.

Δ, δ, *Δέλτα*

Δανίζω,
   collat. form of δανείζω, which see.
Δανιστής
   collat. form of δανειστής, which see.
Δεκα-έξ

sixteen, Re. 13.18. S.
Δεκα-οκτώ
eighteen, Lu. 13.4. S.
Δεξιοβόλος, ου, ὁ (δεξιός & βάλλω)
throwing with the right hand, a slinger, an archer, Ac. 23.23. N.T.
Δηλαυγῶς, (δῆλος & αὐγή)
adv., radiantly, in full light, Mar. 8.25.
Διά-γε
see διά, the γέ expresses that which is least is indicated, at least because, yet because,
Lu. 11.8; 18.5.
Διακαθαίρω
a.1. διεκάθαρα,
to cleanse thoroughly, Lu. 3.17.
Διαλιμπάνω,
imperf. διελίμπανον,
to intermit, cease, Ac. 8.24. S. Apocr.
Διαπορεύω,
act. of διαπορεύομαι.
Διεξέρχομαι
f. διεξελεύσομαι a.2. διεξῆλθον, (διά ἐξ, ἔρχομαι)
to go out through something, Ac. 28.3.
Διερμηνεία, ας, ἡ,
interpretation, of obscure utterances, 1 Co. 12.10. Lchm. N.T.
Δικάζω,
f. άσω, a.1. pass. ἐδικάσθην,
to judge, pass judgement, Lu. 6.37, Treg. mrg.
Δισμυριάς, άδος, ἡ,
twice ten thousand, two myriads, Re. 9.16. Lchm. Tdf.
Δράμω,
see τρέχω
Δυσεντέριον, ου, τό, = δυσεντερία
Ac. 28.8. L.G.
Δύσις, εως, ἡ (δύω)
a sinking, setting, esp. of the heavenly bodies; the west, the quater in which the sun
sets, Mar. 16, Shorter Conclusion.
Δωροφορία, ας, ἡ, (δωροφόρος, bringing gifts)
the offering of a gift or gifts, Ro. 15.31. N.T.

Ε, ε, Ἔ ψῑλόν

Ἑβδομηκονταέξ,
seventy-six, Ac. 27.37.211
Ἑβδομηκονταπέντε,
seventy-five, Ac. 7.14.
Ἔγγιστα,
adv., (neut. pl. sup. of ἐγγύς) nearest, next Mar. 6.36.)
Ἐγκακέω,
f. ῶ, a.1. ἐνεκάκησα,
to be weary in anything; to lose courage, flag, faint, Lu 18.1. 2 Co. 4.1, 16. Gal 6.9.
Eph. 3.13 2 Th. 3.13. L.G.

Ἐγκαυχάομαι,
>   to glory in, 2 Th. 1.4. L.G.

Εἴγε,
>   if indeed, seeing that. See γέ.

Εἰδέα, ας, ἡ,
>   poetic form for ἰδέα, Mat. 28.3.

Εἴδω,
>   whence a.2. εἶδον, p. οἶδα, which see.

Εἴρω
>   a rare pres. whence the f. ἐρῶ. See εἶπον.

Εἴτε,
>   conj., gen. repeated, εἴτε...εἴτε (Lat. sive...sive) whether...or,
>   Ro. 12.6-8. 1 Co. 3.22; 8.5; 10.31; 12.13, 26; 13.8; 15.11. 2 Co.. 1.6; 5.9, 10, 13; 8.23.
>   Eph 6.8. Phi 1.18, 20, 27. Col. 1.16, 20. 1 Th 5.10. 2 Th. 2.15. 1 Pe 2.13, 14;
>   whether...or (Lat. utrum...an) indirect interrog. sense, 2 Co. 12.2, 3; used once, if 1
>   Co. 14.27.

Εἴτεν,
>   rare form of εἶτα, (which see), Mar. 4.28.

Ἐκβαίνω,
>   f. βήσομαι a.2. ἐξέβην
>   to go out, He. 11.13.

Ἐκζήτησις, εως, ἡ (ἐκζητέω, to seek out)
>   an investigating; a subject of subtle inquiry and displute, 1 Ti. 1.4 N.T.

Ἐκθαυμάζω,
>   f. σω, imperf. ἐξεθαύμαζον, (ἐκ & θαυμάζω)
>   to wonder or marvel greatly, Mar. 12.17 L.G.

Ἐκκοπή, ῆς, ἡ,
>   see ἐγκοπή.

Ἐκκρέμομαι,
>   see ἐκκρέμαμαι.

Ἐκνεύω (ἐκ & νεύω, to incline in any direction)
>   f. σω, a.1. ἐξένευσα
>   to bend to one side; to take one's self away, withdraw, Jn. 5.13.

Ἐκσώζω, (ἐκ & σώζω, to save)
>   f. σω, a.1. ἐξέσωσα,
>   to save from, either to keep or to rescue from danger, Ac. 27.39.

Ἔκτρομος,
>   adj., trembling exceedingly, exceedingly terrified, He. 12.25. N.T.

Ἐκύκλευσαν,
>   for ἐκύκλωσαν, fr. κυκλόω.

Ἐλεάω,
>   see ἐλεέω, Ro. 9.16. Jud. 22, 23.

Ἐλεινός,
>   see ἐλεεινός.

Ἕλιγμα, ατος, τό, (ἑλίσσω, to turn about, to roll)
>   a roll, Jn. 19.39.

Ἐλλογάω,
>   see ἐλλογέω. N.T.

Ἐμμέσῳ = ἐν μέσῳ,
>   see μέσος. N.T.

Ἐμπιπράω,

    for ἐμπίπρημι, to burn, set on fire; to be inflamed, swollen, Ac. 28.6

Ἐμπρήθω, (ἐν & πρήθω, to swell out by blowing)

    f. σω, a.1. ἐνέπρησα,

    to burn, destroy by fire, Mat. 22.7.

Ἐνγράφω,

    see ἐγγράφω.

Ἐνδώμησις,

    see ἐνδόμησις. L.G.

Ἐνέγκω,

    a.1 ἤνεγκα, a.2. ἤνεγκον, see φέρω.

Ἐνενήκοντα,

    see ἐννενήκοντα.

Ἐνεός,

    see ἐννεός.

Ἐνεστώς,

    see ἐνίστημι.

Ἐνκ-,

    see ἐγκ- or ἐκκ-.

Ἐνμένω,

    see ἐμμένω.

Ἐνόντα, τά,

    see ἔνειμι.

Ἐνορκίζω,

    to adjure, put under oath, solemnly entreat, 1 Th. 5.27. L.G.

Ἐνπ-,

    see ἐμπ-

Ἐξέλω,

    (whence f. ἐλῶ L.G. a.2 εἷλον), see ἐξαιρέω.

Ἐξεραυνάω,

    see ἐξερευνάω.

Ἐξέφνης,

    see ἐξαίφνης.

Ἐξουδενέω,

    see ἐξουδενόω. S.

Ἐξουθενόω,

    see ἐξουθενέω.

Ἐπάρατος, ον, (ἐπαράομαι, to call down curses upon)

    accursed, Jn. 7.49

Ἐπάρχειος, ον,

    belong to an ἔπαρχος, or prefect, ἡ ἐπάρχειος, sc. ἐξουσία, Ac. 25.1. L.G.

Ἐπεισέρχομαι, (ἐπί, εἰς, & ἔρχομαι)

    f. -ελεύσομαι, 212

    to come in besides or to those who are already within, to enter afterwards; to come in upon, enter against, Lu. 21.35.

Ἐπικέλλω, (ἐπί & κέλλω, to drive on)

    a.1. ἐπέκειλα,

    to run a ship ashore, to bring to land, Ac. 27.41.

Ἐπικεφάλαιον, ου, τό,

    head money, poll-tax, Mar. 12.14.

Ἐπιλείχω, (ἐπί & λείχω, to lick up)
    imperf. ἐπέλειχον,
    to lick the surface of, lick over, Lu. 16.21. N.T.
Ἐπισπείρω, (ἐπί & σπείρω, to sow)
    f. σπερῶ, a.1. ἐπέσπειρα,
    to sow above *or* besides, Mat. 13.25.
Ἐπίστασις, εως, ἡ, (ἐφίστημι)
    an advancing, approach, incursion, on-set, press, Ac. 24.12. 2 Co. 11.28.
Ἐπιτοαυτό,
    Ac. 1.15; 2.1 see αὐτός.
Ἐπιτροπεύω,
    to be ἐπίτροπος *or* procurator, Lu. 3.1.
Ἐραυνάω,
    collat form of ἐρευνάω, which see.
Ἑρμηνευτής, οῦ, ὁ, (ἑρμηνεύω, to expound)
    an interpreter, 1 Co. 14.28.
Ἐρῶ,
    see εἴρω above.
Ἔσθω,
    poet. for ἐσθίω, Mar. 1.6. Lu. 7.33, 34; 10.7; 22.30.
Ἑσπερινός, η, ον,
    belonging to the evening, Lu. 12.38.
Εὖγε,
    used in commendation, well done! Lu. 19.17.
Εὐρακύλων,
    see Εὐροκλύδων.
Ἐφεῖδον,
    see ἐπεῖδον.
Ἔφιδε,
    see ἐπεῖδον.
Ἐφνίδιος,
    see αἰφνίδιος.
Ἐχθέσ
    a longer form of χθές, which see.

Z, ζ, *Ζῆτα*

Ζβέννυμι,
    see σβέννυμι.

H, η, *Ἦτα*

Ἡμεῖς,
    see ἐγώ.
Ἡσσάομαι,
    see ἡττάομαι.
Ἧσσων,
    see ἥττων.

Θ, θ, *Θῆτα*

Θαρρέω,
    see θαρσέω.
Θεολόγος, ου, ὁ, (Θεός & λέγω)
    one who speaks (treats) of the gods and divine things, versed in sacred science, Re. (in
    the heading of Text. Rec.).
Θορυβάζω, (θόρυβος, din, tumult)
    to trouble, disturb, Lu. 10.41. N.T.

Ι, ι, Ἰῶτα

Ἴσμεν and ἴστε,
    1 pl. ind., and 2 pl. ind. or impv., of οἶδα, which see.

Κ, κ, Κάππα

Καθημέραν, καθ' ἡμέραν,
    see ἡμέρα.
Καθολικός, ή, όν,
    general, universal, Ja., Pe., Jn., in the heading or titles.
Καθώσπερ,
    just as, exactly as, 2 Co. 3.18. He. 5.4.
Καλοὶ Λιμένες, (καλός & λιμήν, harbor, haven)
    Fair Havens, a bay of Crete, near the city Lasaea; so called because offering good
    anchorage. Ac. 27.8.
Κάμιλος, ου, ὁ,
    a cable, Mat. 19.24; Lu. 18.25. N.T.
Καταγράφω,
    to draw, delineate, Jn. 8.6.
Καταυγάζω,
    to beam down upon; to shine forth, shine brightly, 2 Co. 4.4. L.G.
Καταφάγω
    see κατεσθίω.
Κατευλογέω,
    to call down blessings on, Mar. 10.16. L.G.
Κατ' ἰδίαν,
    see ἴδιος.
Κατοικίζω,
    a.1. κατῴκισα,
    to cause to dwell, to send or bring into an abode, to give a dwelling to, Ja. 4.5.
Καυσόω,
    act. of καυσόομαι. N.T.
Καυστηριάζω,
    see καυτηριάζω. L.G.
Κερέα,
    see κεραία.
Κεφαλιόω,
    Mar. 12.4. N.T. see κεφαλαιόω.
Κίχρημι,
    to lend, Lu. 11.5.
Κλῖμα

see κλίμα213

Κλινάριον, ου, τό, (dim. of κλινή)
    a small bed, a couch, Ac. 5.15. (On accent see W. gram., p. 50.)

Κοσμίως, (fr. κόσμιος)
    adv., decently 1 Ti. 2.9.

Κρέμαμαι,
    see κρεμάννυμι

Κρεπάλη,
    see κραιπάλη

Κρυπτή,
    see κρύπτη L.G.

Κυκλεύω,
    a.1. ἐκύκλευσα,
    to go round, to encircle, encompass, surround, Jn. 10.24. Re. 20.9.

Κύκλῳ,
    (dat. fr. κύκλος) in a circle, around, round about, on all sides, Mar. 3.34; 6.6, 36. Lu. 9.12. Ro. 15.19. Re. 4.6; 5.11.

Κυλισμός, οῦ, ὁ, (κυλίω)
    a rolling, wallowinig, 2 Pe. 2.22. N.T.

Λ, λ, *Λάμβδα*

Λάκω, & λακέω,
    see λάσκω.

Λεμά,
    see λαμά.

Λευκαίνω,
    a.1. ἐλεύκανα,
    to whiten, make white, Mar. 9.3. Re. 7.14.

Λευκοβύσσινον, (= Βύσσινον λευκόν)
    Re. 19.14. See βύσσινος.

Λημά,
    see λαμά.

Λιμά,
    see λαμά.

M, μ, *Μῦ*

Μαγία,
    see μαγεία.

Μαζός, οῦ, ὁ,
    the breast, Re. 1.13.

Μάρτυρ,
    see μάρτυς.

Μασθός, (Dor. for μαστός)
    See μαστός.

Μετατρέπω,
    f. ψς,
    to turn about; *met.* to transmute, Ja. 4.9.

Μηθέν,

see μηδείς.
Μὴ οὐκ, (οὐκ belonging to the verb, μή being interrogative)
    Ro. 10.18, 19. 1 Co. 9.4, 5; 11.22.
Μήπου, v. μή που,
    that nowhere, least anywhere, Ac. 27.29
Μήτις
    v. μή τις, *prohibitive*, let no one, 1 Co. 16.11. 2 Th. 2.3; *interrogative*, (Lat. num quis)
    hath any one, Jn. 4.33; 7.48. 2 Co. 12.17.
Μητρόπολις, εως, ἡ (μήτηρ & πόλις)
    a metropolis, chief city, 1 Ti. 6.22.
Μνάομαι,
    see μιμνήσκομαι.
Μογγιλάλος, (fr. μόγγος v. μογγός & λάλος)
    speaking with a harsh or thick voice, Mar. 7.32.
Μύλινος, η, ον,
    made of mill-stones; equivalent to μυλικός, Re. 18.21. L.G.

N, ν, Νῦ

Νεομηνία,
    see νουμηνία.

Ξ, ξ, Ξῖ

Ξύν,
    older form of σύν, appearing in composition in 1 Pe. 4.12.

Ο, ο, Ὄ μῑκρόν

Ὁδοποιέω, ῶ,
    to make a road, to level, make passable, smooth, open, a way, Mar. 2.23.
Οἰκειακός, ή, όν,
    see οἰκιακός.
Οἰκέτεια, ας, ἡ, (οἰκέω, to dwell in)
    household, i.e. body of servants, Mat. 24.45.
Οἰοσδηποτοῦν,
    of what kind . . . so-ever, Ja. 5.4.
Ὀλεθφεύω,
    He. 11.28; see ὀλοθρεύω.
Ὀλέθριος, ον,
    destructive, deadly, 2 Th. 1.9.
Ὀλιγοπιστία, ας, ἡ, (ὀλίγος & πίστις)
    littleness of faith, of little faith, Mat. 17.20. N.T.
Ὀμόω,
    see ὀμνύω.
Ὀπτάνω,
    see ὀπτάνομαι. S.
Ὄπτω,
    whence f. ὄψομαι. See ὁράω.
Ὀρινός,

see ὀρεινός.
Ὀρινιξ,
see ὄρνις.
Ὅσγε, (ὅς & γέ, even)
the very one who, precisely he who, Ro. 8.32.
Ὅ,τε, ἥ,τε, τό,τε, (ὁ, ἡ, τό & τε, which see)
214Lu. 2.16; 15.2; 23.12. Jn 2.15; 4.42; 6.18. Ac. 1.13; 2.33; 4.14; 5.24; 7.26; 8.38; 13.1, 2, 44; 14.11, 13; 15.39; 16.11, 13; 17.4, 10, 14; 18.5; 19.12; 21.25; 26.23, 30; 27.1, 3, 5; 28.2. Ro. 1.20, 26; 7.7. Eph. 1.10. He. 2.11; 9.1, 2.
Ὅτι,
Interrog., (ὅ,τι v. ὅ τι) for τί equivalent to διὰ τί, Mar. 2.16, 9.11, 28. L.G.
Οὐ μή,
in no wise, not at all, by no means (see Goodwin's Moods and Tenses, App. II.), Mat. 5.18, 20, 26; 10.23, 42; 13.14; 15.5 16.22, 28; 18.3; 23.39; 24.2, 21, 34, 35; 25.9; 26.29, 35. Mar. 9.1, 41; 10.15; 13.2, 19, 30, 31; 14.25, 31; 16.18 Lu. 1.15; 6.37; 9.27; 10.19; 12.59; 13.35; 18.7, 17, 30; 21.18, 32, 33; 22.16, 18, 34, 67, 68. Jn. 4.14, 48; 6.35, 37; 8.12, 51, 52; 10.5, 28; 11.26, 56; 13.8, 38; 18.11; 20.25. Ac. 13.41; 28.26. Ro. 4.8. 1 Co. 8.13. Gal. 4.30; 5.16. 1 Th. 4.15; 5.3. He. 8.11, 12; 10.17; 13.5. 1 Pe. 2.6. 2 Pe 1.10. Re. 2.11; 3.3, 5, 12; 9.6; 15.4; 18.7, 14, 21, 22, 23; 21.25, 27.
Ὀχετός, οῦ, ὁ, (ὀχέω, to uphold, carry)
a watering-pipe, duct; the intestinal canal, Mar. 7.19.

Π, π, Πῖ

Παλινγεννεσία,
see παλιγγενεσία.
Πανδοκεύς,
see πανδοχεύς.
Πανδοκίον,
see πανδοχεῖον.
Πανπληθεί,
see παμπληθεί.
Πανταχῆ v. πανταχῇ
adv., everywhere, Ac. 21.28.
Παρακαθέζομαι,
to sit down beside, seat one's self, Lu. 10.39.
Παρεμβάλλω,
f. βαλῶ,
to cast by the side of or besides, to insert, to interpose, to bring back into line; to assign to soldiers a place, to draw up in line, to encamp; to cast up (a bank) about (a city), Lu. 19.43.
Πατρολῷας,
see πατραλῷας.
Πεζός, ή, όν,
on foot; by land, Mat. 14.13.
Πειράω,
act of πειράομαι.
Περαιτέρω,
adv., further, beyond, besides, Ac. 19.39.
Περιάπτω,

to bind around, to put around; to kindle a fire around, Lu. 22.55.

Περιβλέπω,
 act of περιβλέπομαι.

Περιδρέμω,
 see περιτρέχω.

Περικαθίζω,
 to sit around, be seated around, Lu. 22.55.

Περιρραίνω,
 to sprinkle around, besprinkle, Re. 19.13.

Πετεινός, ή, όν,
 flying, winged, Mat. 6.28; 8.20; 13.4, 32. Mar. 4.4, 32. Lu. 8.5; 9.58; 12.24; 13.19. Ac. 10.12; 11.6. Ro. 1.23. Ja. 3.7.

Πιθός,
 see πειθός.

Πιμπράω, (for the more commond πίμπρημι)
 to blow, burn; to cause to swell, become tumid, Ac. 28.6.

Πινακίς, ίδος, ή,
 Lu. 1.63, see πινακίδιον.

Πλάνης, ητος, ό,
 see πλανήτης.

Πλέω,
 see πίμπλημι.

Πόνος, ου, ό, (πένομαι, to toil, work)
 to labor, toil; great trouble, intense desire, Col. 4.13; pain, Re. 16.10, 11; 21.4.

Πρέπω,
 see, πρέπει.

Προαιρέω,
 act. of προαιρέομαι.

Προβάτιον, ου, τό,
 a little sheep, Jn. 21.16, 17.

Προεπαγγέλλω,
 act. of προεπαγγέλλομαι. N.T.

Προθέσμιος, α, ον, (πρό & θεσμός, fixed, appointed)
 set beforehand, prearranged, Gal. 4.2.

Πρόϊμος,
 see πρώϊμος.

Προπάτωρ, ορος, ό, (πατήρ)
 a forefather, founder of a family or nation, Ro. 4.1.

Προσανέχω,
 to hold up besides; to rise up so as to approach, rise up towards, Ac. 27.27. L.G.

Προσδρέμω,
 see προστρέχω.

Πρόσκλησις, εως, ή,
 215a judicial summons; an invitation, 1 Ti. 5.21.

Προσπαίω,
 a.1. προσέπαισα,
 to beat against, strike upon, Mat. 7.25.

Πρώϊος, (πρωΐ)
 Mat. 21.18; 27.1. Jn. 18.28.

Πρώτως, (πρῶτος)

adv., first, Ac. 11.26.

Ρ, ρ, *Ῥῶ*

Ῥαίνω,
 see ῥαντίζω.
Ῥαχά,
 see ῥακά.
Ῥοπή, ῆς, ἡ, (ῥέπω, to sink)
 inclination downwards, 1 Co. 15.52.
Ῥυπαίνω, (ῥύπος, filth)
 to make filthy; defile, dishonor, Re. 22.11.

Σ, σ, *Σίγμα*

Σαρδιόνυξ,
 Re. 21.20. N.T. see σαρδόνυξ.
Σειρός, οῦ, ὁ,
 a pit, an underground granary, 2 Pe. 2.4.
Σιρικός,
 see σηρικός.
Σιρός,
 see σειρός.
Στάμνος, ου, ὁ, (ἵστημι)
 an earthen jar *into which wine was drawn off for keeping, also used for other purposes*
 (S. for Heb. צנצנת Ex. 16.30), He. 9.4.
Στασιαστής, οῦ, ὁ, (στασιάζω, to rebel, revolt)
 the author of *or* participant in an insurrrection, Mar. 15.7. L.G.
Στιβάς, άδος, ἡ, (στείβω, to tread on)
 a spread *or* layer of leaves, rushes, straw, etc., serving for a bed; *that which is used in*
 this way, a branch full of leaves, soft foliage, Mar. 11.8
Στρατοπέδαρχος, ου, ὁ,
 Ac. 28.16. N.T. στρατοπεδάρχης.
Συγγενίς, ίδος, ἡ,
 a kinswoman, Lu. 1.36. L.G.
Συλλυπέω,
 act of συλλυπέομαι.
Συμφάγω,
 συνεσθίω.
Συμμιμητής, οῦ, ὁ (σύν & μιμέομαι, to mimic, imitate)
 an imitator with others, Phi. 3.17. N.T.
Σύμφορος, ον,
 fit, suitable, useful; τὸ συμφορον, advantage, profit, 1 Co. 7.35; 10.33.
Συναλλάσσω,
 to reconcile, Ac. 7.26.
Συναυξάνω,
 act. of συναυξάνομαι.
Συνβ-,
 see συμβ-.
Συνγ-,

see συγγ-.
Συνεπιτίθημι,
      act of συνεπιτίθεμαι.
Συνζ-,
      see συζ-.
Συνιέω,
      see συνίημι.
Συνκατανεύω,
      to consent to, agree with, Ac. 18.27.
Συνκ-,
      see αυγκ-.
Συνλ-,
      see συλλ-.
Συνμ-,
      see συμμ-.
Συνπ-,
      see συμπ-.
Συνσ-,
      see συσ- & συσσ-.
Συνστ-,
      see συστ-.
Συνφ-,
      see συμφ-.
Συνχ-,
      see συγχ-.
Συνψ-,
      see συμψ-.
Σφυδρόν, οῦ, τό,
      Ac. 3.7. N.T. See σφυρόν.
Σφυρίς,
      Mat. 16.9. Mar. 8.8 See σπυρίς.

Τ, τ, *Ταῦ*

Τάχειον,
      see τάχιον.
Τεσσαρακονταδύο,
      forty-two, Re. 11.2; 13.5. N.T.
Τεσσαρακοντατέσσαρες, ων,
      forty-four, Re. 21.17. N.T.
Τεσσερ-
      see τεσσαρ-.
Τετρα-
      for τεσσαρα-.
Τετρααρχέω,
      for τετραρχέω.
Τετραάρχης,
      for τετράρχης.
Τεύχω,
      see τυγχάνω.

Τιθέω
    L.G. See τίθημι.
Τοίγε,
    Jn 4.2 Ac. 14.17; 17.27. He. 4.3; see καίτοιγε.
Τρῆμα, ατος, τό,
    a perforation, hole, Mat. 19.24. Lu. 18.25.
Τριχός,
    216see θρίξ.
Τυπικῶς, (τύπος, an impress, counterpart,)
    adv., by way of example (prefiguratively), 1 Co. 10.11. N.T.

Υ, υ, Υ ψῑλόν

Ὑμεῖς,
    see σύ.
Ὑπερ-εγώ,
    2 Co. 11.23; see ὑπέρ.
Ὑπερεκπερισσῶς,
    adv., beyond measure, 1 Th. 5.13. N.T.
Ὑποζύγιος, α, ον,
    under the yoke; see ὑποζύγιον.
Ὑπόλειμμα v. ὑπόλιμμα, τος, τό,
    a remnant, Ro. 9.27.
Ὑποπιάζω, (L.G. for ὑποπιέζω)
    to keep down, keep in subjection, 1 Co. 9.27; see ὑπωπιάζω.
Ὑφαίνω,
    f. ὑφανῶ, to weave, Lu. 12.27.

Φ, φ, Φῖ

Φάγω,
    act. of φάγομαι, see ἐσθίω.
Φάρμακον, ου, τό,
    a drug, an enchantment, Re. 9.21.
Φημίζω,
    to spread a report, to disseminate by report, Mat. 28.15.
Φοινίκισσα,
    see Συροφοινίκισσα.

Χ, χ, Χῖ

Χράω,
    see κίχρημι above.
Χρίσμα,
    see χρῖσμα; see Win. Gram. p. 50.

Ψ, ψ, Ψῖ

Ψεύδομαι,

see ψεύδω.

Ψευδομάρτυς,

see ψευδομάρτυρ.

Ω, ω, Ἰ Ω μέγα

Ὠτάριον, ου, τό, (dim. of οὖς)

the ear, Mar. 14.47. Jn. 18.10.

Footnotes:

[1]*Both the Authorized and the Revised Versions of Heb. ix. 15-16 give countenance to the assumption that our Saviour made his last will and testament, and by his death gave it validity. But in that case would not his resurrection three days later, have rendered it null and void? The subject under discussion in Hebrews ix. is not *two testaments* or *wills*, but *two covenants* or *agreements*; and the death referred to seems to be not the death of a "testator," or mediator but the death of the *sacrifice* which was offered after the custom of ancient times when a solemn covenant was made, and whose blood sprinkled on the ground and over the covenanting parties, sealed the covenant, which was of no force until the sacrifice was slain. The first covenant was sealed with the blood of calves and goats; the second covenant with the blood of the Son of God. Heb. ix. 15-26; xiii. 20; Exod. xxiv. 4-8; Gen. xv. 8-18; Mark xiv. 24. He was not only the mediator of the new covenant, but also the sacrifice which sealed it, all types combining in Him. For an extended discussion of this subject, consulting Macknight on The Epistles, and Granville Penn's Notes on *The New Covenant*. Heb. ix. 15-16.

Postface

Printed in Great Britain
by Amazon.co.uk, Ltd.,
Marston Gate.